The Seven Great Monarchies of The Ancient Eastern World by George Rawlinson

Volume II (of VII) The Second Monarchy: Assyria

George Rawlinson was born on 23rd November 1812 at Chadlington, Oxfordshire. He was the younger brother to the eminent Assyriologist, Sir Henry Rawlinson.

Rawlinson took his degree at Trinity College, Oxford in 1838. Here he also enjoyed playing cricket and was considered to have been a rare talent at the sport. In 1840 he was elected to a fellowship at Exeter College, Oxford. After being ordained in 1841 he became, from 1842 to 1846, a tutor there as well.

In 1846 Rawlinson married Louisa, the daughter of Sir RA Chermside.

His progress continued to be rapid and varied in acknowledgement of his undoubted talents. In 1859 he was made a Bampton lecturer, and was Camden Professor of Ancient History from 1861 to 1889.

By 1872 Rawlinson was appointed canon of Canterbury, and after 1888 he was rector of All Hallows, Lombard Street.

In 1873, he was made proctor in Convocation for the Chapter of Canterbury.

As a scholar he produced, either on his own or in collaboration, several works which are greatly thought of even to this day. His translation of the History of Herodotus (in collaboration with Sir Henry Rawlinson and Sir John Gardiner Wilkinson), 1858–60; The Five Great Monarchies of the Ancient Eastern World, 1862–67; which was later expanded to include The Sixth Great Oriental Monarchy (Parthian), 1873; and The Seventh Great Oriental Monarchy (Sassanian), 1875. Among his other works were Manual of Ancient History, 1869; Historical Illustrations of the Old Testament, 1871; The Origin of Nations, 1877; History of Ancient Egypt, 1881; Egypt and Babylon, 1885; History of Phoenicia, 1889; Parthia, 1893; Memoir of Major-General Sir HC Rawlinson, 1898.

His lectures to an audience at Oxford University on the topic of the accuracy of the Bible in 1859 were published as the apologetic work The Historical Evidences of the Truth of the Scripture Records Stated Anew in later years.

Despite this somewhat prodigious output and alongside his other clerical and family duties he contributed to the Speaker's Commentary, the Pulpit Commentary, Smith's Dictionary of the Bible, and various similar publications.

George Rawlinson died on 7th October, 1902 in Canterbury.

Index of Contents
CHAPTER I - DESCRIPTION OF THE COUNTRY
CHAPTER II - CLIMATE AND PRODUCTIONS
CHAPTER III - THE PEOPLE
CHAPTER IV - THE CAPITAL
CHAPTER V - LANGUAGE AND WRITING.
CHAPTER VI - ARCHITECTURE AND OTHER ARTS
CHAPTER VII - MANNERS AND CUSTOMS

CHAPTER VIII - RELIGION
CHAPTER IX - CHRONOLOGY AND HISTORY

Index of Illustrations
Map
PLATE 22
49. Signet of Kurri-galzu. King of Babylon (drawn by the author from an impression in the possession of Sir H. Rawlinson)
50. The Khabour, from near Arban, looking north (after Layard)
PLATE 23
51. Koukab (ditto)
52. Lake of Khatouniyeh (ditto)
53. Colossal lion, near Seruj (after Chesney)
PLATE 24
54. Plan of the ruins of Nimrud (Calah) (reduced by the Author from Captain Jones's survey)
55. Great wound of Nimrud or Calah (after Layard)
PLATE 25
56. Hand-swipe, Koyunjik (ditto)
57. Assyrian lion, from Nimrud (ditto)
58. Ibex, or wild goat, from Nimrud (ditto)
PLATE 26
59. Wild ass (after Ker Porter)
60. Leopard, from Nimrud (after Layard)
61. Wild ass, from Koyunjik (from an unpublished drawing by Mr. Boutcher in the British Museum)
PLATE 27
62. Gazelle, from Nimrud (after Layard)
63. Stag and hind, from Koyunjik (from an unpublished drawing by Mr. Boutcher in the British Museum)
64. Fallow deer, from Koyunjik (after Layard)
PLATE 28
65. Hare and eagles, from Nimrud (ditto)
66. Hare, from Khorsabad (after Botta)
67. Chase of wild ox, from Nimrud (after Layard)
68. Vulture, from Nimrud (ditto)
69. Vulture feeding on corpse, Koyunjik (ditto)
PLATE 29
70. Ostrich, from a cylinder (after Cullimore)
71. Ostrich, from Nimrud (after Layard)
72. Partridges, from Khorsabad (after Botta)
73. Unknown birds, Khorsabad (ditto)
PLATE 30
74. Assyrian garden and fish-pond, Koyunjik (after Layard)
75. Bactrian or two-humped camel, from Nimrud (ditto)
76. Mesopotamian sheep (ditto)
77. Loading a camel, Koyunjik (ditto)
78. Head of an Assyrian horse, Koyunjik (ditto)
PLATE 31
79. Assyrian horse, from Nimrud (ditto)
80. Mule ridden by two women, Koyunjik (after Layard
PLATE 32

81. Loaded mule, Koyunjik (ditto)
82. Cart drawn by mules, Koyunjik (ditto)
83. Dog modelled in clay, from the palace of
Asshur-bani-pal, Koyunjik, (drawn by the Author from the original in the British Museum)
PLATE 33
84. Dog in relief, on a clay tablet (after Layard)
85. Assyrian cluck, Nimrud (ditto)
86. Assyrians, Nimrud (ditto)
PLATE 34
87. Mesopotamian captives, from an Egyptian monument (Wilkinson)
88. Limbs of Assyrians, from the sculptures (after Layard)
PLATE 35
89. Capture of a city, Nimrud (ditto)
90. Captives of Sargon, Khorsabad (after Botta)
PLATE 36
91. Captive women in a cart, Nimrud (Layard)
92. Ruins of Nineveh (reduced by the Author from Captain Jones's survey)
PLATE 37
93. Khosr-Su and mound of Nebbi-Yunus (after Layard)
94. Gate in the north wall, Nineveh (ditto)
PLATE 38
95. Outer defences of Nineveh, in their present condition (ditto)
PLATE 39
96. Assyrian cylinder (after Birch)
97. Assyrian seals (after Layard)
PLATE 40
98. Assyrian clay tablets (ditto)
99. Black obelisk, from Nimrud (after Birch)
There are several pages here which we have reproduced as fascimilies of the original as they contain many symbols and uses of original languages which are not easily transcribed
Partial Page 171/172/173/174/175/176/177/178
Map of Assyria
PLATE 41
100. Terrace-wall at Khorsabad (after Botta)
101. Pavement-slab, from the Northern Palace.
Koyunjik (Fergusson)
PLATE 42
102. Mound of Khorsabad (ditto)
103. Plan of the Palace of Sargon, Khorsabad (ditto)
PLATE 43
104. Hall of Esar-haddon's Palace, Nimrud (ditto)
106. Remains of Propyheum, or outer gateway, Khorsabad (Layard)
107. King and attendants, Khorsabad (after Botta)
PLATE 44
105. Plan of the Palace of Sargon, Khorsabad (ditto)
PLATE 45
108. Plan of palace gateway (ditto)
109. King punishing prisoners, Khorsabad (ditto)
111. Sargon in his war-chariot, Khorsabad (after Botta)
112. Cornice of temple, Khorsabad (Fergusson)
PLATE 46

110. North-West Court of Sargon's Palace at Khorsabad, restored (after Fergusson)
PLATE 47
113. Armenian louvre ((after Botta)
114. Armenian buildings. from Koyunjik (Layard)
116. Assyrian castle on Nimrud obelisk (drawn by the Author from the original in the British Museum)
PLATE 48
115. Interior of an Assyrian palace, restored (ditto)
PLATE 49
117. Assyrian altar, from a bas-relief, Khorsabad (after Botta)
118. Assyrian temple, Khorsabad (ditto)
119. Assyrian temple, from Lord Aberdeen's black stone (after Fergusson)
120. Assyrian temple, Nimrud (drawn by the Author from the original in the British Museum)
121. Assyrian temple, North Palace, Koyunjik (ditto)
PLATE 50
123. Basement portion of an Assyrian temple,
North Palace. Koyunjik (drawn by the Author from the original in the British Museum)
PLATE 51
122. Circular pillar-base, Koyunjik (after Layard)
124. Porch of the Cathedral, Trent (from an original sketch made by the Author)
PLATE 52
125. Tower of a temple, Koyunjik (after Layard)
126. Tower of ditto, restored (by the Author)
127. Tower of great temple at Nimrud (after Layard)
PLATE 53
PLATE 54
128. Basement of temple-tower, Nimrud, north and west sides (ditto)
129. Ground-plan of Nimrud Tower (ditto)
130. Ground-plans of temples, Nimrud (ditto)
PLATE 55
131. Entrance to smaller temple. Nimrud(ditto)
PLATE 56
132. Assyrian village. Koyunjik (ditto)
133. Village near Aleppo (ditto)
PLATE 57
134. Assyrian hattlemented wall (ditto)
135. Masonry and section of platform wall. Khorsabad (after Botta)
136. Masonry of town-wall. Khorsabad (ditto)
PLATE 58
137. Masonry of tower or moat, Khorsabad (ditto)
139. Arched drain, South-East Palace, Nimrud (ditto)
PLATE 59
138. Arched drain, North-West Palace, Nimrud (after Layard)
140. False arch (Greek)
PLATE 60
141. Assyrian patterns, Nimrud (Layard)
142. Ditto (ditto)
PLATE 61
143. Bases and capitals of pillars (chiefly drawn by the Author from bas-reliefs in the British Museum)
PLATE 62

144. Ornamental doorway, North Palace, Koyunjik (from an unpublished drawing'by Mr. Boutcher in the British Museum)
145. Water transport of stone for building, Koyunjik (after Layard)
PLATE 63
146. Assyrian statue from Kileh-Sherghat (ditto)
147. Statue of Sardanapalus I., from Nimrud (ditto)
148. Clay statuettes of the god Nebo (after Botta)
PLATE 64
149. Clay statuette of the Fish-God (drawn by the Author from the original in the British Museum)
150. Clay statuette from Khorsabad (after Botto)
151. Lion hunt, from Nimrud (after Layard)
PLATE 65
152. Assyrian seizing a wild bull, Nimrud (ditto)
153. Hawk-headed figure and sphinx, Nimrud (ditto)
154. Death of a wild bull, Nimrud(ditto)
PLATE 66
155. King killing a lion, Nimrud (ditto)
156. Trees from Nimrud (ditto)
157. Trees from Koyunjik (ditto)
PLATE 67
158. Groom and horses, Khorsabad (ditto)
159., 160. Assyrian oxen, Koyunjik (ditto)
PLATE 68
161. Assyrian goat and sheep, Koyunjik (ditto)
162. Vine trained on a fir, from the North Palace, Koyunjik (drawn by the Author from a bas-relief in the British Museum)
PLATE 69
163. Lilies, from the North Palace, Koyunjik (ditto)
164. Death of two wild asses, from the North Palace, Koyunjik (from an unpublished drawing by Mr. Boutcher in the British Museum)
165. Lion about to spring, from the North Palace, Koyunjik (ditto)
PLATE 70
166. Wounded wild ass seized by hounds, from the North Palace, Koyunjik
167. Wounded lion about to fall,from the North Palace, Koyunjik (from an unpublished drawing by Mr. Boutcher, in the British Museum)
PLATE 71
168. Wounded lion biting a chariot-wheel, from the North Palace, Koyunjik
PLATE 72
169. King shooting a lion on the spring, from the North Palace, Koyunjik (ditto)
PLATE 73
170. Lion-hunt in a river. from the North Palace, Koyunjik (ditto)
PLATE 74
171. Bronze lion, from Nimrud (after Layard)
172. Fragments of bronze ornaments of the throne, from Nimrud (ditto)
173. Bronze casting, from the throne, Nimrud (ditto)
PLATE 75
174. Feet of tripods in bronze and iron (ditto)
175. Bronze bull's head, from thethrone (ditto)
176. Bronze head, part of throne, showing bitumen inside (ditto)
177. End of a sword-sheath, from the N. W. Palace, Nimrud (ditto)
178. Stool or chair, Khorsabad (after Botta)

PLATE 76
179. Engraved scarab in centre of cup, from the N. W. Palace, Nimrud (Layard)
180. Egyptian head-dresses on bronze dishes, from Nimrud (ditto)
181. Ear-rings from Nimrud and Khorsabad (ditto)
182. Bronze cubes inlaid with gold, original size (ditto)
183. Egyptian scarab (from Wilkinson)

PLATE 77
184. Fragment of ivory panel, from Nimrod (after Layard)
185. Fragment of a lion in ivory, Nimrud (ditto)
187. Fragment of a stag in ivory, Nimrud (ditto)
188. Royal attendant, Nimrud (ditto)

PLATE 78
186. Figures and cartouche with hieroglyphics, on an ivory panel, from the N.W. Palace, Nimrud (ditto)

PLATE 79
189. Arcade work, on enamelled brick, Nimrud (ditto)
190. Human figure, on enamelled brick, from Nimrud (ditto)
191. Ram's head, on enamelled brick, from Nimrud (ditto)
193. Impression of ancient Assyrian cylinder, in serpentine (ditto)

PLATE 80
192. King and attendants, on enamelled brick, from Nimrud (ditto)
197. Assyrian vases. amphorae, etc. (after Birch)

PLATE 81
194. Assyrian seals (ditto)
195. Assyrian cylinder, with Fish-God (ditto)
196. Royal cylinder of Sennacherib (ditto)
198. Funereal Urn from Khorsabad (after Botta)
200. Lustral ewer, from a bas relief, Khorsabad (after Botta)
201. Wine vase, from a bas-relief, Khorsabad (ditto)

PLATE 82
199. Nestorian and Arab workmen, with jar discovered at Nimrud (Layard)
202. Assyrian clay-lamp, (after Layard and Birch)

PLATE 83
203. Amphora, with twisted arrns, Ninirud (Birch)
201. Assyrian glass bottles and bowl (after Layard)
205. Glass vase, bearing the name of Sargon, from Nimrud (ditto)
206. Fragments of hollow tubes, in glass, from Koyunjik (ditto)

PLATE 84
207. Ordinary Assyrian tables, from the bas-reliefs (by the Author)
208, 209. Assyrian tables, from bas-reliefs, Koymrjik (ditto)
210. Table, ornamented with rain's heads, Koyunjik (after Layard)
211. Ornamented table, Khorsabad (ditto)
212. Three-legged table, Koyunjik (ditto)
213. Sennacherib on his throne. Koyunjilc(ditto)

PLATE 85
214. Arm-chair or throne, Khorsahad (after Botta)
215. Assyrian ornamented seat, Khorsabad (ditto)
216. Assyrian couch, from a bas-relief. Koyunjik (by the Author)
217. Assyrian footstools, Koynnjik (ditto)
218. Stands for jars (Layyard)

PLATE 86

219. Royal embroidered dresses, Nimrud (ditto)
220. Embroidery on a royal dress, Nimrud (ditto)
PLATE 87
221. Circular breast ornament on a royal robe, Nimrud (ditto)
PLATE 88
222. Assyrians moving a human-headed bull, partly restored from a bas-relief at Koyunjik (ditto)
225. Part of a bas-relief, showing a pulley and a warrior cutting a bucket from the rope (ditto)
PLATE 89
223. Laborer employed in drawing a colossal bull, Koyunjik (ditto)
224. Attachment of rope to sledge, on which the bull was placed for transport, Koyunjik (ditto)
226. Assyrian war-chariot, Koyunjik from the original in the British Museum)
PLATE 90
227. Chariot-wheel of the early period, Nimrud (from the original in the British Museum)
228. Chariot-wheel of the middle period, Koyunjik (ditto)
229. Chariot-wheel of the latest period, Koyunjik (ditto)
230. Ornamented ends of chariot poles, Nimrud and Koyunjik ditto
PLATE 91
231. End of pole, with cross-bar, Khorsabad (after Botta
232. End of pole, with curved yoke, Koyunjik (after Layard)
233. End of pole, with elaborate cross-bar or yoke, Khorsabad (after Botta)
234. Assyrian chariot containing four warriors, Koyunjik (after Boutcher)
PLATE 92
235. Assyrian war-chariot of the early period, Nimrud (from the original in the British Museum)
236. Assyrian war-chariot of the later period, Koyunjik (ditto)
237. Assyrian chariot of the transition period, Koyunjik (after Boutcher)
PLATE 93
238. Assyrian chariot of the early period, Nimrud (from the original in the British Museum)
239. Chariot-horse protected by clothing, Koyunjik (ditto)
240. Head of a chariot-horse, showing collar with bells attached, Koyunjik(after Boutcher)
PLATE 94
241. Bronze bit, Nimrud (from the original in the British Museum)
242. Bits of chariot-horses, from the sculptures, Nimrud and Koyunjik (ditto)
243. Driving-whips of Assyrian charioteers, from the sculptures (ditto)
244. Mode of tying horses' tails, Koyunjik (ditto)
PLATE 95
245. Mounted spearmen of the time of Sargon, Khorsabad (after Botta)
246. Greave or laced boot of a horseman, Khorsabad (ditto)
248. Horse archer of the latest period, Koyunjik (from the original in the British Museum)
PLATE 96
247. Cavalry soldiers of the time of Sennacherib, Koyunjik (after Layard)
249. Ordinary sandal of the first period, Nimrud (ditto)
250. Convex shield of the first period, Nimrud (after Layard)
251. Foot spearmen of the first period, with wicker shield, Nimrud (from the original in the British Museum)
252. Foot archer with attendant, first period, Nimrud (ditto)
253. Foot archer of the lightest equipment, time of Sargon, Khorsabad (after Botta)
PLATE 97
254. Foot archer of the intermediate equipment, with attendant, time of Sargon, Khorsabad (after Botta)
255. Foot archer of the heavy equipment, with attendant, time of Sargon, Khorsabad (ditto)
256. Foot spearman of the time of Sargon, Khorsabad (ditto)

257. Shield and greave of a spearman, Khorsabad (ditto)
PLATE 98
258. Spear, with weight at the lower end, Khorsabad (ditto)
259. Sling, Koyunjik (from the original in the British Museum)
260. Foot archer of the heavy equipment, with attendant, time of Sennacherib, Koyunjik (ditto)
261. Foot archers of the second class, time of Sennacherib, Koyunjik (ditto)
262. Belts and head-dress of a foot archer of the third class, time of Sennacherib, Koyunjik (after Boutcher)
PLATE 99
263. Mode of carrying the quiver, time of Sennacherib, Koyunjik (from the original in the British Museum)
264. Foot archers of the lightest equipment, time of Sennacherib, Koyunjik
266. Wicker shields, time of Sennacherib, Koyunjik (from the originals in the British Museum)
PLATE 100
267. Metal shield of the latest period, Koyunjik (ditto)
268. Slinger, time of Asshur-bani-pal, Koyunjik (after Boutcher)
269. Pointed helmet, with curtain of scales, Nimrud (after Layard)
270. Iron helmet, from Koyunjik, now in the British Museum (by the Author)
271. Assyrian crested helmets, from the bas-reliefs, Khorsabad and Koyunjik (from the originals in the British Museum)
PLATE 101
272. Scale, Egyptian (after Sir G. Wilkinson)
273. Arrangement of scales in Assyrian scale-armour of the second period, Khorsabad (after Botta)
274. Sleeve of a coat of mail-scale-armor of the first period, Nimrud (from the original in the British Museum)
275. Assyrian gerrha, or large wicker shields (ditto)
276. Soldier undermining a wall, sheltered by gerrhon, Koyunjik (ditto)
PLATE 102
277. Round shields or targes, patterned, Khorsabad (after Botta)
278. Convex shields with teeth, Nimrud (from the originals in the British Museum)
279. Egyptian convex shield, worn on back (after Sir G. Wilkinson)
280. Assyrian ditto, Koyunjik (from the original in the British Museum
PLATE 103
281. Assyrian convex shield, resembling the Greek, Koyunjik (ditto)
282. Quiver, with arrows and javelin, Nimrud (ditto)
283. Ornamented end of bow, Khorsabad (after Botta)
284. Stringing the bow, Koyunjik (from the original in the British Museum)
PLATE 104
285. Assyrian curved bow (ditto)
286. Assyrian angular bow, Khorsabad (after Botta)
287. Mode of carrying the bow in a bow-case, Koyunjik (from the original in the British Museum)
288. Peculiar mode of carrying the quiver, Koyunjik (ditto)
289. Quiver, with rich ornamentation, Nimrud (after Layard)
290. Quivers of the ordinary character, Koyunjik (from the originals in the British Museum)
PLATE 105
291. Quiver with projecting rod, Khorsabad (after Botta)
292. Assyrian covered quivers, Koyunjik (from the originals in the British Museum)
293. Bronze arrow-heads, Nimrud and Koyunjik (ditto)
294. Flint arrow-brad; Nimrud (ditto)
295. Assyrian arrow (ditto)
PLATE 106

296. Mode of drawing the bow, Koyunjik (after Boutcher)
297. Guard worn by an archer, Koyunjik (ditto)
298. Bronze spear-head, Nimrud (from the original in the British Museum)
299. Spear-heads (from the Sculptures)
300. Ornamented ends of spear-shafts, Nimrud (after Layard)
PLATE 107
301. Ornamented handle of short sword, Khorsabad (after Botta)
302. Sheathed sword, Koyunjik (after Boutcher)
303. Ornamented handle of longer sword, Nimrud (from the original in the British Museum?
304. Assyrian curved sword, Khorsabad (after Botta)
308. Scythian battle-axe (after Tester)
309. Ornamented handles of daggers, Nimrud (after Layard)
310. Handle of dagger, with chain, Nimrud (ditto)
PLATE 108
305. Head of royal mace, Khorsabad (ditto)
306. Maces, from the Sculptures
307. Assyrian battle-axes, Koyunjik (from the originals in the British Museum)
311. Sheaths of daggers, Nimrud
312. Assyrian standard, Khorsabad (after Botta)
313. Soldier swimming a river, Koyunjik (after Layard)
PLATE 109
314. Royal tent, Koyunjik (from the original in the British Museum)
315. Ordinary tent, Koyunjik (after Boutcher)
316. Interior of tent, Koyunjik (ditto)
317. King walking in a mountainous country, chariot following, supported by men, Koyunjik (from an obelisk in the British Museum, after Boutcher)
318. Fortified place belonging to an enemy of the Assyrians, Nimrud (after Layard)
PLATE 110
319. Gateway of castle, Koyunjik (after Boutcher)
320. Battering-rams, Khorsabad and Koyunjik (partly after Botta)
322. Crowbar, and mining the wall, Koyunjik (ditto)
PLATE 111
321. Assyrian balistce, Nimrud (after Layard)
324. Soldiers destroying date-palms, Koyunjik (after Layard)
325. Soldier carrying off spoil from a temple, Khorsabad (after Botta)
326. Scribes taking account of the spoil, Khorsabad (ditto)
327. Mace-bearer, with attendant, executing a prisoner, Koyunjtk (from the original in the British Museum)
PLATE 112
323. Implement used in the destruction of cities, Khorsabad (after Botta)
328. Swordsman decapitating a prisoner, Koyunjik (ditto)
329. Female captives, with children, Koyunjik (after Layard)
330. Chasuble or outer garment of the king (chiefly after Botta)
331. King in his robes, Khorsabad (after Botta)
PLATE 113
332. Tiaras of the later and earlier Periods, Koyunjik and Nimrud (Layard and Boutcher)
333. Fillet worn by the king, Nimrud (after Layard)
334. Royal sandals, times of Sargon and Asshur-izir-pal (from the originals in the British Museum)
335. Royal shoe, time of Sennacherib, Koyunjik (ditto)
336. Royal necklace, Nimrud (ditto)
337. Royal collar, Nimrud (ditto)

PLATE 114
338. Royal armlets, Khorsabad (after Botta)
339. Royal bracelets, Khorsabad and Koyunjik (after Botta and Boutcher)
340. Royal ear-rings, Nimrud (from the originals in the British Museum)
341. Early king in his war-costume, Nimrud (ditto)
PLATE 115
342. King, queen, and attendants, Koyunjik (ditto)
343. Enlarged figure of the queen, Koyunjik (ditto)
345. Heads of eunuchs, Nimrud (ditto)
PLATE 116
344. Royal parasols, Nimrud and Koyunjik (ditto)
316. The chief eunuch, Nimrud (ditto)
347. Head-dress of the vizier, Khorsabad (after Botta)
PLATE 117
348. Costumes of the vizier, times of Sennacherib and Asshur-izir-pal, Nimrud and Koyunjik (from the originals in the British Museum)
PLATE 118
349. Tribute-bearers presented by the chief eunuch, Nimrud obelisk (ditto)
350. Fans or fly-flappers, Nimrud and Koyunjik
351. King killing a lion, Nimrud (after Layard)
352. King, with attendants, spearing a lion, Koyunjik (after Boutcher)
PLATE 119
353. King, with attendant, stabbing a lion, Koyunjik (ditto)
354. Lion let out of trap, Koyunjik (ditto)
PLATE 120
355. Hound held in leash, Koyunjik (from the original in the British Museum)
356. Wounded lioness, Koyunjik (ditto)
351. Fight of lion and bull, Nimrud (after Layard)
358. King hunting the wild bull, Nimrud (ditto)
359. King pouring libation over four dead lions,
Koyunjik (from the original in the British Museum)
PLATE 121
360. Hound chasing a wild ass colt, Koyunjik (after Boutcher)
361. Dead wild ass, Koyunjik (ditto)
362. Hounds pulling down a wild ass, Koyunjik (ditto)
563. Wild ass taken with a rope, Koyunjik (from the original in the British Museum)
PLATE 122
364. Hound chasing a doe, Koyunjik (after Boutcher)
365. Hunted stag taking the water, Koyunjik (ditto)
PLATE 123
366. Net spread to take deer, Koyunjik (from the original in the British Museum)
367. Portion of net showing the arrangement of the meshes and the pegs, Koyunjik (ditto)
368. Hunted ibex, flying at full speed. Koyunjik (after Boutcher)
369. Ibex transfixed with arrow-falling (ditto)
PLATE 124
370. Sportsman carrying a, gazelle, Khorsabad (from the original in the British Museum)
371. Sportsman shooting, Khorsabad (after Bntta)
372. Greyhound and hare, Niunrud (from a bronze bowl in the British Museum)
373. Nets, pegs, and balls of string, Koyunjik (after Boutcher)
PLATE 125
374. Man fishing, Nimrud (after Layard)

375. Man fishing, Koyunjik (ditto)
PLATE 126
376. Man fishing, seated on skin, Koyunjik (from the original in the British Museum)
377. Bear standing, Nimrud (from a bronze bowl in the British Museum)
378. Ancient Assyrian harp and harper, Nimrud (from the originals in the British Museum)
330. Triangular lyre, Koyunjik (ditto)
PLATE 127
379. Later Assyrian harps and harpers, Koyunjik (ditto)
381. Lyre with ten strings, Khorsabad (after Botta)
PLATE 128
382. Lyres with five and seven strings, Koyunjik (from the originals in the British Museurn)
383. Guitar or tamboura, Koyunjik (ditto)
384. Player on the double pipe. Koyunjik (ditto)
PLATE 129
385. Tambourine player and other musicians, Koyunjik (ditto)
387. Assyrian tubbuls, or drums, Koyunjik (from the originals in the British Museum)
PLATE 130
386. Eunuch playing on the cymbals, Koyunjik (after Boutcher)
388. Musician playing the dulcimer, Koyunjik (ditto)
389. Roman trumpet (Column of Trajan)
390. Assyrian ditto, Koyunjik (after Layard)
391. Portion of an Assyrian trumpet (from the original in the British Museum)
PLATE 131
392. Captives playing on lyres, Koyunjik (ditto)
PLATE 132
333. Lyre on a Hebrew coin (ditto)
394. Baud of twenty-six musicians, Koyunjik (ditto)
PLATE 133
395. Time-keepers, Koyunjik (after Boutcher)
396. Assyrian coracle, Nimrud (from the original in the British Museum)
397. Common oar, time of Sennacherib, Koyunjik (ditto)
398. Steering oar, time of Asshur-izir-pal, Nimrud (ditto)
399. Early long boat, Nimrud (ditto)
400. Later long boat, Khorsabad (after Botta)
401. Phoenician bireme, Koyunjik (after Layard)
402. Oar kept in place by pegs, Koyunjik (from the original in the British Museum)
PLATE 134
403. Chart of the district about Nimrud, showing the course of the ancient canal and conduit (after the survey of Captain Jones)
404. Assyrian drill-plough (from Lori Aberdeen's black stone, after Fergusson.
405. Modern Turkish plough (after Sir C. Fellows)
406. Modern Arab plough (after C. Niebuhr)
PLATE 135
407. Ornamental belt or girdle, Koyunjik (from the original in the British Museum)
408. Ornamental cross-belt, Khorsabad (after Botta)
409. Armlets of Assyrian grandees, Khorsabad (ditto)
410. Head-dresses of various officials, Koyunjik (from the originals in the British Musemn)
411. Curious mode of arranging the hair, Koyunjik (from the originals in the British Museum)
412. Female seated (from an ivory in the British Museum)
PLATE 136
413. Females gathering grapes (from some ivory fragments in the British Museum)

414. Necklace of flat glass beads (from the original in the British Museum)
415. Metal mirror (ditto)
PLATE 137
416. Combs in iron and lapis lazuli (from the original in the British Museum)
417. Assyrian joints of meat (from the Sculptures)
418. Killing the sheep, Koyunjik (after Boutcher)
419. Cooking meat in caldron, Koyunjik (after Layard)
420. Frying, Nimrud (from the original in the British Museum)
421. Assyrian fruits (from the Monuments)
PLATE 138
422. Drinking scene, Khorsabad (after Botta)
423. Ornamental wine-cup, Khorsabad (ditto)
424. Attendant bringing flowers to a banquet, Koyunjik (after Layard)
425. Socket of hinge, Nimrud (ditto)
PLATE 143
448. Evil genii contending, Koyunjik (after Boutcher)
450. Triangular altar, Khorsabad (after Botta)
451. Portable altar in an Assyrian camp, with priests offering, Khorsabad (ditto)
PLATE 144
449. Sacrificial scene, from an obelisk found at Nimrud (ditto)
452. Worshipper bringing an offering, from a cylinder (after Lajard)
453. Figure of Tiglath-Pileser I. (from an original drawing by Mr. John Taylor)
454. Plan of the palace of Asshur-izir-pal (after Fergusson)
455. Stele of Asshur-izir-pal with an altar in front, Nimrud (from the original in the British Museum)
PLATE 146
456. Israelites bringing tribute to Shalmaneser II., Nimrud (ditto)
457. Assyrian sphinx, time of Asshur-bani-pal (after Layard)
458. Scythian soldiers, from a vase found in a Scythian tomb

CHAPTER I

DESCRIPTION OF THE COUNTRY

"Greek phrase[—]"—HEROD. i. 192.

The site of the second—or great Assyrian-monarchy was the upper portion of the Mesopotamian valley. The cities which successively formed its capitals lay, all of them, upon the middle Tigris; and the heart of the country was a district on either side that river, enclosed within the thirty-fifth and thirty-seventh parallels. By degrees these limits were enlarged; and the term Assyria came to be used, in a loose and vague way, of a vast and ill-defined tract extending on all sides from this central region. Herodotus considered the whole of Babylonia to be a mere district of Assyria. Pliny reckoned to it all Mesopotamia. Strabo gave it, besides these regions, a great portion of Mount Zagros (the modern Kurdistan), and all Syria as far as Cilicia, Judaea, and Phoenicia.

If, leaving the conventional, which is thus vague and unsatisfactory, we seek to find certain natural limits which we may regard as the proper boundaries of the country, in two directions we seem to perceive an almost unmistakable line of demarcation. On the east the high mountain-chain of Zagros. penetrable only in one or two places, forms a barrier of the most marked character, and is beyond a doubt the natural limit for which we are looking. On the south a less striking, but not less clearly defined, line—formed by the abutment of the upper and slightly elevated plain on the alluvium of the lower valley—separates Assyria from Babylonia, which is best regarded as a distinct country. In the two remaining directions, there is more doubt as to the most proper limit. Northwards,we may either view Mount Masius as the natural boundary, or the course of the Tigris from Diarbekr to Til, or even perhaps the Armenian mountain-chain north of this portion of the Tigris, from whence that river receives its early tributaries. Westward, we might confine Assyria to the country watered by the affluents of the Tigris, or extend it so as to in elude the Khabour and its tributaries, or finally venture to carry it across the whole of Mesopotamia, and make it be bounded by the Euphrates. On the whole it is thought that in both the doubted cases the wider limits are historically the truer ones. Assyrian remains cover the entire country between the Tigris and the Khabour, and are frequent on both banks of the latter stream, giving unmistakable indications of a long occupation of that region by the great Mesopotamian people. The inscriptions show that even a wider tract was in process of time absorbed by the conquerors; and if we are to draw a line between the country actually taken into Assyria, and that which was merely conquered and held in subjection, we can select no better boundary than the Euphrates westward, and northward the snowy mountain-chain known to the ancients as Mons Niphates.

If Assyria be allowed the extent which is here assigned to her, she will be a country, not only very much larger than Chaldaea or Babylonia, but positively of considerable dimensions. Reaching on the north to the thirty-eighth and on the south to the thirty-fourth parallel, she had a length diagonally from Diarbekr to the alluvium of 350 miles, and a breadth between the Euphrates and Mount Zagros varying from about 300 to 170 miles. Her area was probably not less than 75,000 square miles, which is more than double that of Portugal, and not much below that of Great Britain. She would thus from her mere size be calculated to play an important (part) in history; and the more so, as during the period of her greatness scarcely any nation with which she came in contact possessed nearly so extensive a territory.

Within the limits here assigned to Assyria, the face of the country is tolerably varied. Possessing, on the whole, perhaps, a predominant character of flatness, the territory still includes some important ranges of hills, while on the two sides it abuts upon lofty mountain-chains. Towards the north and east it is provided by nature with an ample supply of water, rills everywhere flowing from the Armenian and Kurdish ranges, which soon collect into rapid and abundant rivers. The central, southern, and western regions are, however, less bountifully supplied; for though the Euphrates washes the whole western and south-western frontier, it spreads fertility only along its banks; and though Mount Masius sends down upon the Mesopotamian plain a considerable number of streams, they form in the space of 200 miles between Balls and Mosul but two rivers, leaving thus large tracts to languish for want of the precious fluid. The vicinity of the Arabian and Syrian deserts is likewise felt in these regions, which, left to themselves, tend to acquire the desert character, and have occasionally been regarded as actual parts of Arabia.

The chief natural division of the country is that made by the Tigris, which, having a course nearly from north to south, between Til and Samarah, separates Assyria into a western and an eastern district. Of these two, the eastern or that upon the left bank of the Tigris, although considerably the smaller, has always been the more important region. Comparatively narrow at first, it broadens as the course of the river is descended, till it attains about the thirty-fifth parallel a width of 130 or 140 miles. It consists chiefly of a series of rich and productive plains, lying along the courses of the various tributaries which flow from Mount Zagros into the Tigris, and often of a semi-alluvial character. These plains are not, however, continuous. Detached ranges of hills, with a general direction parallel to the Zagros chain, intersect the flat rich country, separating the plains from one another, and supplying small streams and brooks in addition to the various rivers, which, rising within or beyond the great mountain barriers, traverse the plains on their way to the Tigris. The hills themselves—known now as the Jebel Maklub, the Ain-es-sufra, the Karachok, etc.—are for the most part bare and sterile. In form they are hogbacked, and viewed from a distance have a smooth and even outline but on a nearer approach they are found to be rocky and rugged. Their limestone sides are furrowed by innumerable ravines, and have a dry and parched appearance, being even in spring generally naked and without vegetation. The sterility is most marked on the western flank, which faces the hot rays of the afternoon sun; the eastern slope is occasionally robed with a scanty covering of dwarf oak or stunted brushwood. In the fat soil of the plains the rivers commonly run deep and concealed from view, unless in the spring and the early summer, when through the rains and the melting of the snows in the mountains they are greatly swollen, and run bank full, or even overflow the level country.

The most important of these rivers are the following:—the Kurnib or Eastern Khabour, which joins the Tigris in lat. 37° 12'; the Greater Zab (Zab Ala), which washes the ruins of Nimrud, and enters the main stream almost exactly in lat. 30°; the Lesser Zab (Zab Asfal), which effects its junction about lat. 35° 15'; the Adhem, which is received a little below Samarah, about lat. 34°; and the Diyaleh, which now joins below Baghdad, but from which branches have sometimes entered the Tigris a very little below the mouth of the Adhem. Of these streams the most northern, the Khabour, runs chiefly in an untraversed country—the district between Julamerik and the Tigris. It rises a little west of Julamerik in one of the highest mountain districts of Kurdistan, and runs with a general south-westerly course to its junction with another large branch, which reaches it from the district immediately west of Amadiyeh; it then flows due west, or a little north of west, to Zakko, and, bending to the north after passing that place, flows once more in a south-westerly direction until it reaches the Tigris. The direct distance from its source to its embouchure is about 80 miles; but that distance is more than doubled by its windings. It is a stream of considerable size, broad and rapid; at many seasons not fordable at all, and always forded with difficulty.

The Greater Zab is the most important of all the tributaries of the Tigris. It rises near Konia, in the district of Karasu, about lat. 32° 20', long. 44° 30', a little west of the watershed which divides the basins of Lakes Van and Urymiyeh. Its general course for the first 150 miles is S.S.W., after which for 25 or 30 miles it runs almost due south through the country of the Tiyari. Near Amadiyeh it makes a sudden turn, and flows S.E. or S.S.E. to its junction with the Rowandiz branch whence, finally, it resumes its old direction, and runs south-west past the Nimrud ruins into the Tigris. Its entire course, exclusive of small windings, is above 350 miles, and of these nearly 100 are across the plain country, which it enters soon after receiving the Rowandiz stream. Like the Khabour, it is fordable at certain places and during the summer season; but even then the water reaches above the bellies of horses. It is 20 yards wide a little above its junction with the main steam. On account of its strength and rapidity the Arabs sometimes call it the "Mad River."

The Lesser Zab has its principal source near Legwin, about twenty miles south of Lake Urumiyeh, in lat. 36° 40', long. 46° 25'. The source is to the east of the great Zagros chain; and it might have been supposed that the waters would necessarily flow northward or eastward, towards Lake Urumiyeh, or towards the Caspian. But the Legwin river, called even at its source the Zei or Zab, flows from the first westward, as if determined to pierce the mountain barrier. Failing, however, to find an opening where it meets the range, the Little Zab turns south and even south-east along its base, till about 25 or 30 miles from its source it suddenly resumes its original direction, enters the mountains in lat. 36° 20', and forces its way through the numerous parallel ranges, flowing generally to the S.S.W., till it debouches upon the plain near Arbela, after which it runs S.W. and S.W. by S. to the Tigris. Its course among the mountains is from 80 to 90 miles, exclusive of small windings; and it runs more than 100 miles through the plain. Its ordinary width, just above its confluence with the Tigris, is 25 feet.

The Diyaleh, which lies mostly within the limits that have been here assigned to Assyria, is formed by the confluence of two principal streams, known respectively as the Holwan, and the Shirwan, river. Of these, the Shirwan seems to be the main branch. This stream rises from the most eastern and highest of the Zagros ranges, in lat. 34° 45', long. 47° 40' nearly. It flows at first west, and then north-west, parallel to the chain, but on entering the plain of Shahrizur, where tributaries join it from the north-east and the north-west, the Shirwan changes its course and begins to run south of west, a direction, which, it pursues till it enters the low country, about lat. 35° 5', near Semiram. Thence to the Tigris it has a course which in direct distance is 150 miles, and 200 if we include only main windings. The whole course cannot be less than 380 miles, which is about the length of the Great

Zab river. The width attained before the confluence with the Tigris is 60 yards, or three times the width of the Greater, and seven times that of the Lesser Zab.

PLATE XXII

On the opposite side of the Tigris, the traveller comes upon a region far less favored by nature than that of which we have been lately speaking. Western Assyria has but a scanty supply of water; and unless the labor of man is skilfully applied to compensate this natural deficiency, the greater part of the region tends to be, for ten months out of the twelve, a desert. The general character of the country is level, but not alluvial. A line of mountains, rocky and precipitous, but of no great elevation, stretches across the northern part of the region, running nearly due east and west, and extending from the Euphrates at Rum-kaleh to Til and Chelek upon the Tigris. Below this, a vast slightly undulating plain extends from the northern mountains to the Babylonian alluvium, only interrupted about midway by a range of low limestone hills called the Sinjar, which leaving the Tigris near Mosul runs nearly from east to west across central Mesopotamia, and strikes the Euphrates half-way between Rakkeh and Kerkesiyeh, nearly in long. 40°.

The northern mountain region, called by Strabo "Mons Masius," and by the Arabs the Karajah Dagh towards the west, and towards the east the Jebel Tur, is on the whole a tolerably fertile country. It contains a good deal of rocky land; but has abundant springs, and in many parts is well wooded. Towards the west it is rather hilly than mountainous; but towards the east it rises considerably, and the cone above Mardin is both lofty and striking. The waters flowing from the range consist, on the north, of a small number of brooks, which after a short course fall into the Tigris; on the south, of more numerous and more copious streams, which gradually unite, and eventually form two rather important rivers. These rivers are the Belik, known anciently as the Bileeha, and the Western Khabour, called Habor in Scripture, and by the classical writers Aborrhas or Chaboras. [PLATE XXII., Fig. 1.]

The Belik rises among the hills east of Orfa, about long. 39°, lat. 37° 10'. Its course is at first somewhat east of south; but it soon sweeps round, and, passing by the city of Harran—the Haran of Scripture and the classical Carrh—proceeds nearly due south to its junction, a few miles below Rakkah, with the Euphrates. It is a small stream throughout its whole course, which may be reckoned at 100 or 120 miles.

The Khabour is a much more considerable river. It collects the waters which flow southward from at least two-thirds of the Mons Masius, and has, besides, an important source, which the Arabs regard as the true "head of the spring," derived apparently from a spur of the Sinjar range. This stream, which rises about lat. 36° 40', long. 40°, flows a little south of east to its junction near Koukab with the Jerujer or river Nisi-his, which comes down from Mons Masius with a course not much west of south. Both of these branches are formed by the union of a number of streams. Neither of them is fordable for some distance above their junction; and below it, they constitute a river of such magnitude as to be navigable for a considerable distance by steamers. The course of the Khabour below Koukab is tortuous; but its general direction is S.S.W. The entire length of the stream is certainly not less than 200 miles.

The country between the "Mons Masius" and the Sinjar range is an undulating plain, from 60 to 70 miles in width, almost as devoid of geographical features as the alluvium of Babylonia. From a height the whole appears to be a dead level: but the traveller finds, on descending, that the surface, like that of the American prairies and the Roman Campagna, really rises and falls in a manner which offers a decided contrast to the alluvial flats nearer the sea. Great portions of the tract are very deficient in water. Only small streams descend from the Sinjar range, and these are soon absorbed by the thirsty soil; so that except in the immediate vicinity of the hills north and south, and along the courses of the Khabour, the Belik, and their affluents, there is little natural fertility, and cultivation is difficult. The soil too is often gypsiferous, and its salt and nitrous exudations destroy vegetation; while at the same time the streams and springs are from the same cause for the most part brackish and unpalatable. Volcanic action probably did not cease in the region very much, if at all, before the historical period. Fragments of basalt in many places strew the plain; and near the confluence of the two chief branches of the Khabour, not only are old craters of volcanoes distinctly visible, but a cone still rises from the centre of one, precisely like the cones in the craters of Etna and Vesuvius, composed entirely of loose lava, scorim, and ashes, and rising to the height of 300 feet. The name of this remarkable hill, which is Koukab, is even thought to imply that the volcano may have been active within the time to which the traditions of the country extend. [PLATE XXII., Fig. 2.]

Sheets of water are so rare in this region that the small lake of Khatouniyeh seems to deserve especial description. This lake is situated near the point where the Sinjar changes its character, and from a high rocky range subsides into low broken hills. It is of oblong shape, with its greater axis pointing nearly due east and west, in length about four miles, and in its greatest breadth somewhat less than three. [PLATE XXIII., Fig. 1] The banks are low and parts marshy, more especially on the side towards the Khabour, which is not more than ten miles distant. In the middle of the lake is a hilly peninsula, joined to the mainland by a narrow causeway, and beyond it a small island covered with trees. The lake abounds with fish and waterfowl; and its water, though brackish, is regarded as remarkably wholesome both for man and beast.

PLATE XXIII

The Sinjar range, which divides Western Assyria into two plains, a northern and a southern, is a solitary limestone ridge, rising up abruptly from the flat country, which it commands to a vast distance on both sides. The limestone of which it is composed is white, soft, and fossiliferous; it detaches itself in enormous flakes from the mountain-sides, which are sometimes broken into a succession of gigantic steps, while occasionally they present the columnar appearance of basalt. The flanks of the Sinjar are seamed with innumerable ravines, and from these small brooks issue, which are soon dispersed by irrigation, or absorbed in the thirsty plains. The sides of the mountain are capable of being cultivated by means of terraces, and produce fair crops of corn and excellent fruit; the top is often wooded with fruit trees or forest-trees. Geographically, the Sinjar may be regarded as the continuation of that range of hills which shuts in the Tigris on the west, from Tekrit nearly to Mosul, and then leaving the river strikes across the plain in a direction almost from east to west as far as the town of Sinjar. Here the mountains change their course and bend to the south-west, till having passed the little lake described above, they somewhat suddenly subside, sinking from a high ridge into low undulating hills, which pass to the south of the lake, and then disappear in the plain altogether. According to some, the Sinjar here terminates; but perhaps it is best to regard it as rising again in the Abd-el-aziz hills, which, intervening between the Khabour and the Euphrates, run in the same south-west direction from Arban to Zelabi. If this be accepted as the true course of the Sinjar, we must view it as throwing out two important spurs. One of these is near its eastern extremity, and runs to the south-east, dividing the plain of Zerga from the great central level. Like the main chain, it is of limestone; and, though low, has several remarkable peaks which serve as landmarks from a vast distance. The Arabs call it Kebritiyeh, or "the Sulphur range," from a sulphurous spring which rises at its foot. The other spur is thrown out near the western extremity, and runs towards the north-west, parallel to the course of the upper Khabour, which rises from its flank at Ras-el-Ain. The name of Abd-el-aziz is applied to this spur, as well as to the continuation of the Sinjar between Arban and Halebi. It is broken into innumerable valleys and ravines, abounding with wild animals, and is scantily wooded with dwarf oak. Streams of water abound in it.

South of the Sinjar range, the country resumes the same level appearance which characterizes it between the Sinjar and the Mons Masius. A low limestone ridge skirts the Tigris valley from Mosul to Tekrit, and near the Euphrates the country is sometimes slightly hilly; but generally the eye travels over a vast slightly undulating level, unbroken by eminences, and supporting but a scanty vegetation. The description of Xenophon a little exaggerates the flatness, but is otherwise faithful enough:—"In these parts the country was a plain throughout, as smooth as the sea, and full of wormwood; if any other shrub or reed grew there, it had a sweet aromatic smell; but there was not a tree in the whole region." Water is still more scarce than in the plains north of the Sinjar. The brooks descending from that range are so weak that they generally lose themselves in the plain before they have run many miles. In one case only do they seem sufficiently strong to form a river. The Tharthar, which flows by the ruins of El Hadhr, is at that place a considerable stream, not indeed very wide but so deep that horses have to swim across it. Its course above El Hadhr has not been traced; but the most probable conjecture seems to be that it is a continuation of the Sinjar river, which rises about the middle of the range, in long. 41° 50′, and flows south-east through the desert. The Tharthar appears at one time to have reached the Tigris near Tekrit, but it now ends in a marsh or lake to the south-west of that city.

The political geography of Assyria need not occupy much of our attention. There is no native evidence that in the time of the great monarchy the country was formally divided into districts, to which any particular names were attached, or which were regarded as politically separate from one another; nor do such divisions appear in the classical writers until the time of the later geographers, Strabo, Dionysius, and Ptolemy. If it were not that mention is made in the Old Testament of certain districts within the region which has been here termed Assyria, we should have no proof that in the early times any divisions at all had been recognized. The names, however, of Padan-Aram, Aram-Naharaim, Gozan, Halah, and (perhaps) Huzzab, designate in Scripture particular portions of the Assyrian territory; and as these portions appear to correspond in some degree with the divisions of the classical geographers, we are led to suspect that these writers may in many, if not in most cases, have followed ancient and native traditions or authorities. The principal divisions of the classical geographers will therefore be noticed briefly, so far at least as they are intelligible.

According to Strabo, the district within which Nineveh stood was called Aturia, which seems to be the word Assyria slightly corrupted, as we know that it habitually was by the Persians. The neighboring plain country he divides into four regions—Dolomene, Calachene, Chazene, and Adiabene. Of Dolomene, which Strabo mentions but in one place, and which is wholly omitted by other authors, no account can be given. Calachene, which is perhaps the Calacine of Ptolemy, must be the tract about Calah (Nimrud), or the country immediately north of the Upper Zab river. Chazene, like Dolomene, is a term which cannot be explained. Adiabene, on the contrary, is a well-known geographical expression. It is the country of the Zab or Diab rivers, and either includes the whole of Eastern Assyria between the mountains and the Tigris, or more strictly is applied to the region between the Upper and Lower Zab, which consists of two large plains separated from each other by the Karachok hills. In this way Arbelitis, the plain between the Karachok and Zagros, would fall within Adiabene, but it is sometimes made a distinct region, in which case Adiabene must be restricted to the flat between the two Zabs, the Tigris, and the harachok. Chalonitis and Apolloniatis, which Strabo seems to place between these northern plains and Susiana, must be regarded as dividing between them the country south of the Lesser Zab, Apolloniatis (so called from its Greek capital, Apollonia) lying along the Tigris, and Chalonitis along the mountains from the pass of Derbend to Gilan. Chalonitis seems to have taken its name from a capital city called Chala, which lay on the great route connecting Babylon with the southern Ecbatana, and in later times was known as Holwan. Below Apolloniatis, and (like that district) skirting the Tigris, was Sittacene, (so named from its capital, Sittace which is commonly reckoned to Assyria, but seems more properly regarded as Susianian territory.) Such are the chief divisions of Assyria east of the Tigris.

West of the Tigris, the name Mesopotamia is commonly used, like the Aram-Naharaim of the Hebrews, for the whole country between the two great rivers. Here are again several districts, of which little is known, as Acabene, Tigene, and Ancobaritis. Towards the north, along the flanks of Mons Masius from Nisibis to the Euphrates, Strabo seems to place the Mygdonians, and to regard the country as Mygdonia. Below Mygdonia, towards the west, he puts Anthemusia, which he extends as far as the Khabour river. The region south of the Khabour and the Sinjar he seems to regard as inhabited entirely by Arabs. Ptolemy has, in lieu of the Mygdonia of Strabo, a district which he calls Gauzanitis; and this name is on good grounds identified with the Gozan of Scripture, the true original probably of the "Mygdonia" of the Greeks. Gozan appears to represent the whole of the upper country from which the longer affluents of the Khabour spring; while Halah, which is coupled with it in Scripture, and which Ptolemy calls Chalcitis, and makes border on Gauzanitis, may designate the tract upon the main stream, as it comes down from Ras-el-Ain. The region about the upper sources of the Belik has no special designation in Strabo, but in Scripture it seems to be called Padan-Aram, a name which has been explained as "the flat Syria," or "the country stretching out from the foot of the hills." In the later Roman times it was known as Osrhoene; but this name was scarcely in use before the time of the Antonines.

The true heart of Assyria was the country close along the Tigris, from lat. 35° to 36° 30'. Within these limits were the four great cities, marked by the mounds at Khorsabad, Mosul, Nimrud, and Kileh-Sherghat, besides a multitude of places of inferior consequence. It has been generally supposed that the left bank of the river was more properly Assyria than the right; and the idea is so far correct, as that the left bank was in truth of primary value and importance, whence it naturally happened that three out of the four capitals were built on that side of the stream. Still the very fact that one early capital was on the right bank is enough to show that both shores of the stream were alike occupied by the race from the first; and this conclusion is abundantly confirmed by other indications throughout the region. Assyrian ruins, the remains of considerable towns, strew the whole country between the Tigris and Khabour, both north and south of the Sinjar range. On the banks of the Lower Khabour are the remains of a royal palace, besides many other traces of the tract through which it runs having been permanently occupied by the Assyrian people. Mounds, probably Assyrian, are known to exist along the course of the Khabour's great western affluent; and even near Seruj, in the country between Harlan and the Euphrates some evidence has been found not only of conquest but of occupation. Remains are perhaps more frequent on the opposite side of the Tigris; at any rate they are more striking and more important. Bavian, Khorsabad, Shereef-Khan, Neb-bi-Yunus, Koyunjik, and Nimrud, which have furnished by far the most valuable and interesting of the Assyrian monuments, all lie east of the Tigris; while on the west two places only have yielded relics worthy to be compared with these, Arban and Kileh-Sherghat.

It is curious that in Assyria, as in early Chaldaea, there is a special pre-eminence of four cities. An indication of this might seem to be contained in Genesis, where Asshur is said to have "builded Nineveh," and the city Rehoboth, and Calah, and Resen; but on the whole it is more probable that we have here a mistranslation (which is corrected for us in the margin), and that three cities only are ascribed by Moses to the great patriarch. In the flourishing period of the empire, however, we actually find four capitals, of which the native names seem to have been Ninua, Calah, Asshur, and Bit-Sargina, or Dur-Sargina (the city of Sargon)—all places of first-rate consequence. Besides these principal cities, which were the sole seats of government, Assyria contained a vast number of large towns, few of which it is possible to name, but so numerous that they cover the whole face of the country with their ruins. Amomig; them were Tarbisa, Arbil, Arapkha, and Khazeh, in the tract between the Tigris and Mount Zagros; Haran, Tel-Apni, Razappa (Rezeph), and Amida, towards the north-west frontier; Nazibina (Nisibis), on the eastern branch of the Khabour; Sirki (Circesium), at the confluence of the Khabour with the Euphrates; Anat, on the Euphrates, some way below this junction; Tabiti, Magarisi, Sidikan, Katni, Beth-Khalupi,etc., in the district south of the Sinjar, between the lower course of the Khabour and the Tigris. Here, again, as in the case of Chaldaea, it is impossible at present to locate with accuracy all the cities. We must once more confine ourselves to the most important, mind seek to determine, either absolutely or with a certain vagueness, their several positions.

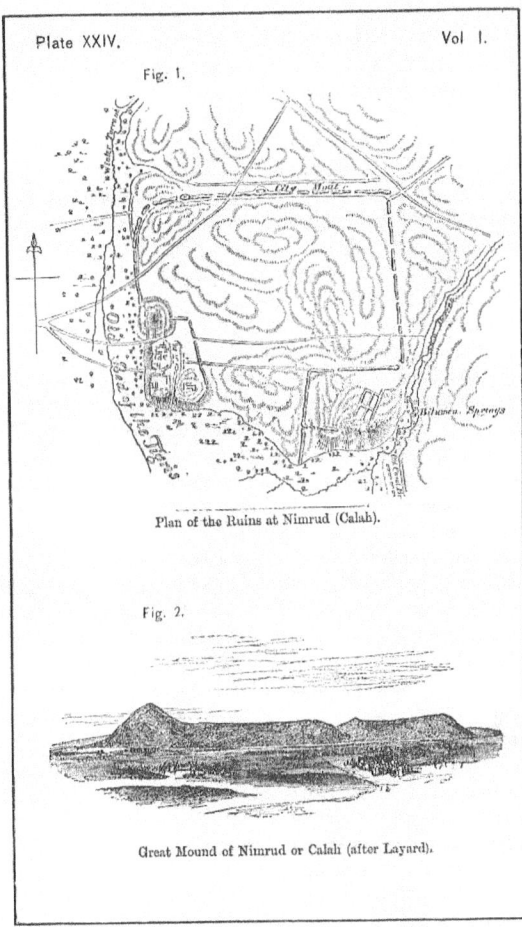

It admits of no reasonable doubt that the ruins opposite Mosul are those of Nineveh. The name of Nineveh is read on the bricks; and a uniform tradition, reaching from the Arab conquest to comparatively recent times, attaches to the mounds themselves the same title. They are the most extensive ruins in Assyria; and their geographical position suits perfectly all the notices of the geographers and historians with respect to the great Assyrian capital. As a subsequent chapter will be devoted to a description of this famous city, it is enough in this place to observe that it was situated on the left or east bank of the Tigris, in lat. 36° 21′, at the point where a considerable brook, the Khosr-su, falls into the main stream. On its west flank flowed the broad and rapid Tigris, the "arrow-stream," as we may translate the word; while north, east, and south, expanded the vast undulating plain which intervenes between the river and the Zagros mountain-range. Mid-way in this plain, at the distance of from 15 to 18 miles from the city, stood boldly up the Jabel Maklub and Ain Sufra hills, calcareous ridges rising nearly 2000 feet above the level of the Tigris, and forming by far the most prominent objects in the natural landscape. Inside the Ain Sufra, and parallel to it, ran the small stream of the Gomel, or Ghazir, like a ditch skirting a wall, an additional defence in that quarter. On the south-east and south, distant about fifteen miles, was the strong and impetuous current of the Upper Zab, completing the natural defences of the position which was excellently chosen to be the site of a great capital.

South of Nineveh, at the distance of about twenty miles by the direct route and thirty by the course of the Tigris, stood the second city of the empire, Calah, the site of which is marked by the extensive ruins at Nimrud. [PLATE XXIV., Fig. 1.] Broadly, this place may be said to have been built at the confluence of the Tigris with the Upper Zab; but in strictness it was on the Tigris only, the Zab flowing five or six miles further to the south, and entering the Tigris at least nine miles below the Nimrud ruins. These ruins at present occupy an area somewhat short of a thousand English acres, which is little more than one-half of the area of the ruins of Nineveh; but it is thought that the place was in ancient times considerably larger, and that the united action of the Tigris and some winter streams has swept away no small portion of the ruins. They form at present an irregular quadrangle, the sides of which face the four cardinal points. On the north and east the rampart may still be distinctly traced. It was flanked with towers along its whole course, and pierced at uncertain intervals by gates, but was nowhere of very great strength or dimensions. On the south side it must have been especially weak, for there it has disappeared altogether. Here, however, it seems probable that the Tigris and the Shor Derreh stream, to which the present obliteration of the wall may be ascribed, formed in ancient times a sufficient protection. Towards the west, it seems to be certain that the Tigris (which is now a mile off) anciently flowed close to the city. On this side, directly facing the river, and extending along it a distance of 600 yards, or more than a third of a mile, was the royal quarter, or portion of the city occupied by the palaces of the kings. It consisted of a raised platform, forty feet above the level of the plain, composed in some parts of rubbish, in others of regular layers of sun-dried bricks, and cased on every side with solid stone masonry, containing an area of sixty English acres, and in shape almost a regular rectangle, 560 yards long, and from 350 to 450 broad. The platform was protected at its edges by a parapet, and is thought to have been ascended in various places by wide staircases, or inclined ways, leading up from the plain. The greater part of its area is occupied by the remains of palaces constructed by various native kings, of which a more particular account will be given in the chapter on the architecture and other arts of the Assyrians. It contains also the ruins of two small temples, and abuts at its north-western angle on the most singular structure which has as yet been discovered among the remains of the Assyrian cities. This is the famous tower or pyramid which looms so conspicuously over the Assyrian plams, and which has always attracted the special notice of the traveller. [PLATE XXIV., Fig. 2.] An exact description of this remarkable edifice will be given hereafter.

It appears from the inscriptions on its bricks to have been commenced by one of the early kings, and completed by another. Its internal structure has led to the supposition that it was designed to be a place of burial for one or other of these monarchs. Another conjecture is, that it was a watch-tower; but this seems very unlikely, since no trace of any mode by which it could be ascended has been discovered.

Forty miles below Calah, on the opposite bank of the Tigris, was a third great city, the native name of which appears to have been Asshur. This place is represented by the ruins at Kileh-Sherghat, which are scarcely inferior in extent to those at Nimrud or Calah. It will not be necessary to describe minutely this site, as in general character it closely resembles the other ruins of Assyria. Long lines of low mounds mark the position of the old walls, and show that the shape of the city was quadrangular. The chief object is a large square mound or platform, two miles and a half in circumference, and in places a hundred feet above the level of the plain, composed in part of sun-dried bricks, in part of natural eminences, and exhibiting occasionally remains of a casing of hewn stone, which may once have encircled the whole structure. About midway on the north side of the platform, and close upon its edge, is a high cone or pyramid. The rest of the platform is covered with the remains of walls and with heaps of rubbish, but does not show much trace of important buildings. This city has been supposed to represent the Biblical Resen; but the description of that place as lying "between Nineveh and Calah" seems to render the identification worse than uncertain.

The ruins at Kileh-Sherghat are the last of any extent towards the south, possessing a decidedly Assyrian character. To complete our survey, therefore of the chief Assyrian towns, we must return northwards, and, passing Nineveh, direct our attention to the magnificent ruins on the small stream of the Khosrsu, which have made the Arab village of Khorsabad one of the best known names in Oriental topography. About nine miles from the north-east angle of the wall of Nineveh, in a direction a very little east of north, stands the ruin known as Khorsabad, from a small village which formerly occupied its summit—the scene of the labors of M. Botta, who was the first to disentomb from among the mounds of Mesopotamia the relics of an Assyrian palace. The enclosure at Khorsabad is nearly square in shape, each side being about 2000 yards long. No part of it is very lofty, but the walls are on every side well marked. Their angles point towards the cardinal points, or nearly so; and the walls themselves consequently face the north-east, the north-west, the south-west, and the south-east. Towards the middle of the north-west wall, and projecting considerably beyond it, was a raised platform of the usual character; and here stood the great palace, which is thought to have been open to the plain, and on that side quite undefended.

Four miles only from Khorsabad, in a direction a little west of north, are the ruins of a smaller Assyrian city, whose native name appears to have been Tarbisa, situated not far from the modern village of Sherif-khan. Here was a palace, built by Esarhaddon for one of his sons, as well as several temples and other edifices. In the opposite direction at the distance of about twenty miles, is Keremles, an Assyrian ruin, whose name cannot yet be rendered phonetically. West of this site, and about half-way between the ruins of Nineveh and Nimrud or Calah, is Selamiyah, a village of some size, the walls of which are thought to be of Assyrian construction. We may conjecture that this place was the Resen, or Dase, of Holy Scripture, which is said to have been a large city, interposed between Nineveh and Calah. In the same latitude, but considerably further to the east, was the famous city of Arabil or Arbil, known to the Greeks as Arbela, and to this day retaining its ancient appellation. These were the principal towns, whose positions can be fixed, belonging to Assyria Proper, or the tract in the immediate vicinity of Nineveh.

Besides these places, the inscriptions mention a large number of cities which we cannot definitely connect with any particular site. Such are Zaban and Zadu, beyond the Lower Zab, probably somewhere in the vicinity of Kerkuk; Kurban, Tidu (?), Napulu, Kapa, in Adiabene; Arapkha and Khaparkhu, the former of which names recalls the Arrapachitis of Ptolemy, in the district about Arbela; Hurakha, Sallat (?), Dur-Tila, Dariga, Lupdu, and many others, concerning whose situations it is not even possible to make any reasonable conjecture. The whole country between the Tigris and the mountains was evidently studded thickly with towns, as it is at the present day with ruins; but until a minute and searching examination of the entire region has taken place, it is idle to attempt an assignment to particular localities of these comparatively obscure names.

In Western Assyria, or the tract on the right bank of the Tigris, while there is reason to believe that population was as dense, and that cities were as numerous, as on the opposite side of the river, even fewer sites can be determinately fixed, owing to the early decay of population in those parts, which seem to have fallen into their present desert condition shortly after the destruction of the Assyrian empire by the conquering Medes. Besides Asshur, which is fixed to the ruins at Kileh-Sherghat, we can only locate with certainty some half-dozen places. These are Nazibina, which is the modern Nisibin, the Nisibis of the Greeks; Amidi, which is Amida or Diarbekr; Haran, which retains its name unchanged; Sirki, which is the Greek Circesium, now Kerkesiyeh; Anat, now Anah, on an island in the Euphrates; and Sidikan, now Arban, on the Lower Khabour. The other known towns of this region, whose exact position is more or less uncertain, are the following:—Tavnusir, which is perhaps Dunisir, near Mardin; Guzana, or Gozan, in the vicinity of Nisibin; Razappa, or Rezeph, probably not far from Harran; Tel Apni, about Orfah or Ras-el-Ain; Tabiti and Magarisi, on the Jerujer, or river of Nisibin; Katni and Beth-Khalupi, on the Lower Khabour; Tsupri and Nakarabani, on the Euphrates, between its junction with the Khabour and Allah; and Khuzirina, in the mountains near the source of the Tigris. Besides these, the inscriptions contain a mention of some scores of towns wholly obscure, concerning which we cannot even determine whether they lay west or east of the Tigris.

Such are the chief geographical features of Assyria. It remains to notice briefly the countries by which it was bordered. To the east lay the mountain region of Zagros, inhabited principally, during the earlier times of the Empire, by the Zimri, and afterwards occupied by the Medes, and known as a portion of Media. This region is one of great strength, and at the same time of much productiveness and fertility. Composed of a large number of parallel ridges. Zagros contains, besides rocky and snow-clad summits, a multitude of fertile valleys, watered by the great affluents of the Tigris or their tributaries, and capable of producing rich crops with very little cultivation. The sides of the hills are in most parts clothed with forests of walnut, oak, ash, plane, and sycamore, while mulberries, olives, and other fruit-trees abound; in many places the pasturage is excellent; and thus, notwithstanding its mountainous character, the tract will bear a large population. Its defensive strength is immense, equalling that of Switzerland before military roads were constructed across the High Alps. The few passes by which it can be traversed seem, according to the graphic phraseology of the ancients, to be carried up ladders; they surmount six or seven successive ridges, often reaching the elevation of 10,000 feet, and are only open during seven months of the year. Nature appears to have intended Zagros as a seven fold wall for the protection of the fertile Mesopotamian lowland from the marauding tribes inhabiting the bare plateau of Iran.

North of Assyria lays a country very similar to the Zagros region. Armenia, like Kurdistan, consists, for the most part of a number of parallel mountain ranges, with deep valleys between them, watered by great rivers or their affluents. Its highest peaks, like those of Zagros, ascend considerably above the snow-line. It has the same abundance of wood, especially in the more northern parts; and though its valleys are scarcely so fertile, or its products so abundant and varied, it is still a country where a numerous population may find subsistence. The most striking contrast which it offers to the Zagros region is in the direction of its mountain ranges. The Zagros ridges run from north-west to south-east, like the principal mountains of Italy, Greece, Arabia, Hindustan, and Cochin China; those of

Armenia have a course from a little north of east to a little south of west, like the Spanish Sierras, the Swiss and Tyrolese Alps, the Southern Carpathians, the Greater Balkan, the Cilician Taurus, the Cyprian Olympus, and the Thian Chan. Thus the axes of the two chains are nearly at right angles to one another, the triangular basin of Van occurring at the point of contact, and softening the abruptness of the transition. Again, whereas the Zagros mountains present their gradual slope to the Mesopotamian lowland, and rise in higher and higher ridges as they recede from the mountains of Armenia ascend at once to their full heignt from the level of the Tigris, and the ridges then gradually decline towards the Euxine. It follows from this last contrast, that, while Zagros invites the inhabitants of the Mesopotamian plain to penetrate its recesses, which are at first readily accessible, and only grow wild and savage towards the interior, the Armenian mountains repel by presenting their greatest difficulties and most barren aspect at once, seeming, with their rocky sides and snow-clad summits, to form an almost insurmountable obstacle to an invading host. Assyrian history bears traces of this difference; for while the mountain region to the east is gradually subdued and occupied by the people of the plain, that on the north continues to the last in a state of hostility and semi-independence.

West of Assyria (according to the extent which has here been given to it), the border countries were, towards the south, Arabia, and towards the north, Syria. A desert region, similar to that which bounds Chaldaea in this direction, extends along the Euphrates as far north as the 36th parallel, approaching commonly within a very short distance of the river. This has been at all times the country of the wandering Arabs. It is traversed in places by rocky ridges of a low elevation, and intercepted by occasional wadys, but otherwise it is a continuous gravelly or sandy plain, incapable of sustaining a settled population. Between the desert and the river intervenes commonly a narrow strip of fertile territory, which in Assyrian times was held by the Tsukhi or Shuhites, and the Aramaeans or Syrians. North of the 36th parallel, the general elevation of the country west of the Euphrates rises. There is an alternation of bare undulating hills and dry plains, producing wormwood and other aromatic plants. Permanent rivers are found, which either terminate in salt lakes or run into the Euphrates. In places the land is tolerably fertile, and produces good crops of grain, besides mulberries, pears, figs, pomegranates, olives, vines, and pistachio-nuts. Here dwelt, in the time of the Assyrian Empire, the Khatti, or Hittites, whose chief city, Carchemish, appears to have occupied the site of Hierapolis, now Bambuk. In a military point of view, the tract is very much less strong than either Armenia or Kurdistan, and presents but slight difficulties to invading armies.

The tract south of Assyria was Chaldaea, of which a description has been given in an earlier portion of this volume. Naturally it was at once the weakest of the border countries, and the one possessing the greatest attractions to a conqueror. Nature had indeed left it wholly without defence; and though art was probably soon called in to remedy this defect, yet it could not but continue the most open to attack of the various regions by which Assyria was surrounded. Syria was defended by the Euphrates—at all times a strong barrier; Arabia, not only by this great stream, but by her arid sands and burning climate; Armenia and Kurdistan had the protection of their lofty mountain ranges. Chaldaea was naturally without either land or water barrier; and the mounds and dykes whereby she strove to supply her wants were at the best poor substitutes for Nature's bulwarks. Here again geographical features will be found to have had an important bearing on the course of history, the close connection of the two countries, in almost every age, resulting from their physical conformation.

CHAPTER II

CLIMATE AND PRODUCTIONS

"Assyria, celebritate et magnitudine, et multiformi feracitate ditissima."—AMM. MARC. xxiii

In describing the climate and productions of Assyria, it will be necessary to divide it into regions, since the country is so large, and the physical geography so varied, that a single description would necessarily be both incomplete and untrue. Eastern Assyria has a climate of its own, the result of its position at the foot of Zagros. In Western Assyria we may distinguish three climates, that of the upper or mountainous country extending from Bir to Til and Jezireh, that of the middle region on either side of the Sinjar range, and that of the lower region immediately bordering on Babylonia. The climatic differences depend in part on latitude; but probably in a greater degree on differences of elevation, distance or vicinity of mountains, and the like.

Eastern Assyria, from its vicinity to the high and snow-clad range of Zagros, has a climate at once cooler and moister than Assyria west of the Tigris. The summer heats are tempered by breezes from the adjacent mountains, and, though trying to the constitution of an European, are far less oppressive than the torrid blasts which prevail on the other side of the river. A good deal of rain falls in the winter, and even in the spring; while, after the rains are past, there is frequently an abundant dew, which supports vegetation and helps to give coolness to the air. The winters are moderately severe.

In the most southern part of Assyria, from lat. 34° to 35° 30′, the climate scarcely differs from that of Babylonia, which has been already described. The same burning summers, and the same chilly but not really cold winters, prevail in both districts; and the time and character of the rainy season is alike in each. The summers are perhaps a little less hot, and the winters a little colder than in the more southern and alluvial region; but the difference is inconsiderable, and has never been accurately measured.

In the central part of Western Assyria, on either side of the Sinjar range, the climate is decidedly cooler than in the region adjoining Babylonia. In summer, though the heat is great, especially from noon to sunset, yet the nights are rarely oppressive, and the mornings enjoyable. The spring-time in this region is absolutely delicious; the autumn is pleasant; and the winter, though cold and accompanied by a good deal of rain and snow, is rarely prolonged and never intensely rigorous. Storms of thunder and lightning are frequent, especially in spring, and they are often of extraordinary violence: hail-stones fall of the size of pigeon's eggs; the lightning is incessant; and the wind rages with fury. The force of the tempest is, however, soon exhausted; in a few hours' time it has passed away, and the sky is once more cloudless: a delightful calm and freshness pervade the air, producing mingled sensations of pleasure and repose.

The mountain tract, which terminates Western Assyria to the north, has a climate very much more rigorous than the central region. The elevation of this district is considerable, and the near vicinity of the great mountain country of Armenia, with its eternal snows and winters during half the year, tends greatly to lower the temperature, which in the winter descends to eight or ten degrees below zero. Much snow then falls, which usually lies for some weeks; the spring is wet and stormy, but the summer and the autumn are fine; and in the western portion of the region about Harran and Orfah, the summer heat is great. The climate is here an "extreme" one, to use on expression of Humboldt's—the range of the thermometer being even greater than it is in Chaldaea, reaching nearly (or perhaps occasionally exceeding) 120 degrees.

Such is the present climate of Assyria, west and east of the Tigris. There is no reason to believe that it was very different in ancient times. If irrigation was then more common and cultivation more widely extended, the temperature would no doubt have been somewhat lower and the air more moist. But neither on physical nor on historical grounds Can it be argued that the difference thus produced was; more than slight. The chief causes of the remarkable heat of Mesopotamnia—so much exceeding that of many countries under the same parallels of latitude—are its near vicinity to the Arabian and Syrian deserts, and its want of trees, those great refrigerators. While the first of these causes would be wholly untouched by cultivation, the second would be affected in but a small degree. The only tree which is known to have been anciently cultivated in Mesopotamia is the date-palm; and as this ceases to bear fruit about lat. 35°, its greater cultivation could have prevailed only in a very small portion of the country, and so would have affected the general climate but little. Historically, too, we find, among the earliest notices which have any climatic bearing, indications that the temperature and the consequent condition of the country were anciently very nearly what they now are. Xenophon speaks of the barrenness of the tract between the Khabour and Babylonia, and the entire absence of forage, in as strong terms as could be used at the present day. Arrian, following his excellent authorities, notes that Alexander, after crossing the Euphrates, kept close to the hills, "because the heat there was not so scorching as it was lower down," and because he could then procure green food for his horses. The animals too which Xenophon found in the country are either such as now inhabit it, or where not such, they are the denizens of hotter rather than colder climates and countries.

The fertility of Assyria is a favorite theme with the ancient writers. Owing to the indefiniteness of their geographical terminology, it is however uncertain, in many cases, whether the praise which they bestow upon Assyria is really intended for the country here called by that name, or whether it does not rather apply to the alluvial tract, already described, which is more properly termed Chaldaea or Babylonia. Naturally Babylonia is very much more fertile than the greater part of Assyria, which being elevated above the courses of the rivers, and possessing a saline and gypsiferous soil, tends, in the absence of a sufficient water supply, to become a bare and arid desert. Trees are scanty in both regions except along the river courses; but in Assyria, even grass fails after the first burst of spring; and the plains, which for a few weeks have been carpeted with the tenderest verdure and thickly strewn with the brightest and loveliest flowers, become, as the summer advances, yellow, parched, and almost herbless. Few things are more remarkable than the striking difference between the appearance of the same tract in Assyria at different seasons of the year. What at one time is a garden, glowing with brilliant hues and heavy with luxuriant pasture, on which the most numerous flocks can scarcely make any sensible impression, at another is an absolute waste, frightful and oppressive from its sterilityr.

If we seek the cause of this curious contrast, we shall find it in the productive qualities of the soil, wherever there is sufficient moisture to allow of their displaying themselves, combined with the fact, already noticed, that the actual supply of water is deficient. Speaking generally, we may say with truth, as was said by Herodotus more than two thousand years ago—that "but little rain falls in Assyria," and, if water is to be supplied in adequate quantity to the thirsty soil, it must be derived from the rivers. In most parts of Assyria there are occasional rains during the winter, and, in ordinary years, frequent showers in early spring. The dependence of the present inhabitants both for pasture and for grain is on these. There is scarcely any irrigation; and though the soil is so productive that wherever the land is cultivated, good crops are commonly obtained by means of the spring rains, while elsewhere nature at once spontaneously robes herself in verdure of the richest kind, yet no sooner does summer arrive than barrenness is spread over the scene; the crops ripen and are gathered in; "the grass withereth, the flower fadeth;" the delicate herbage of the plains shrinks back and disappears; all around turns to a uniform dull straw-color; nothing continues to live but what is coarse, dry, and sapless; and so the land, which was lately an Eden, becomes a desert.

Far different would be the aspect of the region were a due use made of that abundant water supply—actually most lavish in the summer time, owing to the melting of the snows which nature has provided in the two great Mesopotamian rivers and their tributaries. So rapid is the fall of the two main streams in their upper course, that by channels derived from them, with the help perhaps of dams thrown across them at certain intervals, the water might be led to almost any part of the intervening country, and a supply kept up during the whole year. Or, even without works of this magnitude, by hydraulic machines of a very simple construction, the life-giving fluid might be raised from the great streams and their affluents in sufficient quantity to maintain a broad belt on either side of the river-courses in perpetual verdure.

PLATE XXV

Anciently, we know that recourse was had to both of these systems. In the tract between the Tigris and the Upper Zab, which is the only part of Assyria that has been minutely examined, are distinct remains of at least one Assyrian canal, wherein much ingenuity and hydraulic skill is exhibited, the work being carried through the more elevated ground by tunnelling, and the canal led for eight miles contrary to the natural course of every stream in the district. Sluices and dams, cut sometimes in the solid rock, regulated the supply of the fluid at different seasons, and enabled the natives to make the most economical application of the great fertilizer. The use of the hand-swipe was also certainly known, since it is mentioned by Herodotus, and even represented upon the sculptures. [PLATE XXV., Fig. 1.] Very probably other more elaborate machines were likewise employed, unless the general prevalency of canals superseded their necessity. It is certain that over wide districts, now dependent for productive power wholly on the spring rains, and consequently quite incapable of sustaining a settled population, there must have been maintained in Assyrian times some effective water-system, whereby regions that at present with difficulty furnish a few months' subsistence to the wandering Arab tribes, were enabled to supply to scores of populous cities sufficient food for their consumption.

We have not much account of the products of Assyria Proper in early times. Its dates were of small repute, being greatly inferior to those of Babylon. It grew a few olives in places, and some spicy shrubs, which cannot be identified with any certainty. Its cereal crops were good, and may perhaps be regarded as included in the commendations bestowed by Herodotus and Strabo on the grain of the Mesopotamian region. The country was particularly deficient in trees, large tracts growing nothing but wormwood and similar low shrubs, while others were absolutely without either tree or bush. The only products of Assyria which acquired such note as to be called by its name were its silk and its citron trees. The silk, according to Pliny, was the produce of a large kind of silkworm not found elsewhere. The citron trees obtained a very great celebrity. Not only were they admired for their perpetual fruitage, and their delicious odor; but it was believed that the fruit which they bore was an unfailing remedy against poisons. Numerous attempts were made to naturalize the tree in other countries; but up to the time when Pliny wrote, every such attempt had failed, and the citron was still confined to Assyria, Persia and Media.

It is not to be imagined that the vegetable products of Assyria were confined within the narrow compass which the ancient notices might seem to indicate. Those notices are casual, and it is evident that they are incomplete: nor will a just notion be obtained of the real character of the region, unless we take into account such of the present products as may be reasonably supposed to be indigenous. Now setting aside a few plants of special importance to man, the cultivation of which may have been introduced, such as tobacco, rice, Indian corn, and cotton, we may fairly say that Assyria has no exotics, and that the trees, shrubs, and vegetables now found within her limits are the same in all probability as grew there anciently. In order to complete our survey, we may therefore proceed to inquire what are the chief vegetable products of the region at the present time.

In the south the date-palm grows well as far as Anah on the Euphrates and Tekrit on the Tigris. Above that latitude it languishes, and ceases to give fruit altogether about the junction of the Khabour with the one stream and the Lesser Zab with the other. The unproductive tree, however, which the Assyrians used for building purposes, will grow and attain a considerable size to the very edge of the mountains. Of other timber trees the principal are the sycamore and the Oriental plane, which are common in the north the oak, which abounds about Mardin (where it yields gall-nuts and the rare product manna), and which is also found in the Sinjar and Abd-el-Aziz ranges; the silver poplar, which often fringes the banks of the streams; the sumac, which is found on the Upper Euphrates; and the walnut, which grows in the Jebel Tur, and is not uncommon between the foot of Zagros and the outlying ranges of hills. Of fruit-trees the most important are the orange, lemon, pomegranate, apricot, olive, vine, fig, mulberry, and pistachio-nut. The pistachio-nut grows wild in the northern mountains, especially between Orfah and Diarbekr. The fig is cultivated with much care in the Sinjar. The vine is also grown in that region, but bears better on the skirts of the hills above Orfah and Mardin. Pomegranates flourish in various parts of the country. Oranges and lemons belong to its more southern parts, where it verges on Babylonia. The olive clothes the flanks of Zagros in places. Besides these rarer fruits, Assyria has chestnuts, pears, apples, plums, cherries, wild and cultivated, qinces, apricots, melons and filberts.

The commonest shrubs are a kind of wormwood—the apsinthium of Xenophon—which grows over much of the plain extending south of the Khabour—and the tamarisk. Green myrtles, and oleanders with their rosy blossoms, clothe the banks of some of the smaller streams between the Tigris and Mount Zagros; and a shrub of frequent occurrence is the liquorice plant. Of edible vegetables there is great abundance. Truffles and capers grow wild; while peas, beans, onions, spinach, cucumbers, and lentils are cultivated successfully. The carob (Ceratonia Siliqua) must also be mentioned as among the rarer products of this region.

It was noticed above that manna is gathered in Assyria from the dwarf oak. It is abundant in Zagros, and is found also in the woods about Mardin, and again between Orfah and Diarbekr. According to Mr. Rich, it is not confined to the dwarf oak, or even to trees and shrubs, but is deposited also on sand, rocks, and stone. It is most plentiful in wet seasons, and especially after fogs; in dry seasons it fails almost totally. The natives collect it in spring and autumn. The best and purest is that taken from the ground; but by far the greater quantity is obtained from the trees, by placing cloths under them and shaking the branches. The natives use it as food both in its natural state and manufactured into a kind of paste. It soon corrupts; and in order to fit it for exportation, or even for the storeroom of the native housewife, it has to undergo the process of boiling. When thus prepared, it is a gentle purgative; but, in its natural state and when fresh, it may be eaten in large quantities without any unpleasant consequences.

Assyria is far better supplied with minerals than Babylonia. Stone of a good quality, either limestone, sandstone, or conglomerate, is always at hand; while a tolerable clay is also to be found in most plices. If a more durable material is required, basaltic rock may be obtained from the Mons Masius—a substance almost as hard as granite. On the left bank of the Tigris a soft gray alabaster abounds which is easily cut into slabs, and forms an excellent material for the sculptor. The neighboring mountains of Kurdistan contain marbles of many different qualities; and these could be procured without much difficulty by means of the rivers. From the same quarter it was easy to obtain the most useful metals. Iron, copper, and lead are found in great abundance in the Tiyari Mountains within a short distance of Nineveh, where they crop out upon the surface, so that they cannot fail to be noticed. Lead and copper are also obtainable from the neighborhood of Diarbekr. The Kurdish Mountains may have supplied other metals. They still produce silver and antimony; and it is possible that they may anciently have furnished gold and tin. As their mineral riches have never been explored by scientific persons, it is very probable that they may contain many other metals besides those which they are at present known to yield.

Among the mineral products of Assyria, bitumen, naphtha, petroleum, sulphur, alum, and salt have also to be reckoned. The bitumen pits of Kerkuk, in the country between the Lesser Zab and the Adhem, are scarcely less celebrated than those of Hit; and there are some abundant springs of the same character close to Nimrud, in the bed of the Shor Derrell torrent. The Assyrian palaces furnish sufficient evidence that the springs were productive in old times; for the employment of bitumen as a cement, though not so frequent as in Babylonia, is yet occasionally found in them. With the bitumen are always procured both naphtha and petroleum; while at Kerkuk there is an abundance of sulphur also. Salt is obtained from springs in the Kerkuk country; and is also formed in certain small lakes lying between the Sinjar and Babylonia. Alum is plentiful in the hills about Kifri.

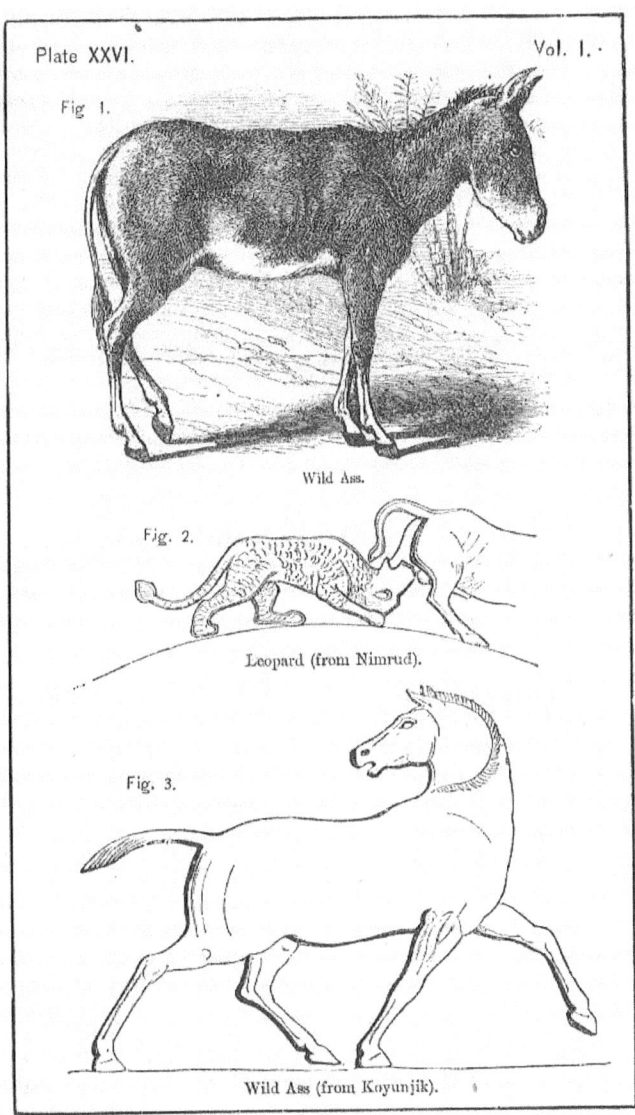

PLATE XXVI

The most remarkable wild animals of Assyria are the following: the lion, the leopard, the lynx, the wild-cat, the hyaena, the wild ass, the bear, the deer, the gazelle, the ibex, the wild sheep, the wild boar, the jackal, the wolf, the fox, the beaver, the jerboa, the porcupine, the badger, and the hare. The Assyrian lion is of the maneless kind, and in general habits resembles the lion of Babylonia. The animal is comparatively rare in the eastern districts, being seldom found on the banks of the Tigris above Baghdad, and never above Kileh-Sherghat. On the Euphrates it has been seen as high as Bir; and it is frequent on the banks of the Khabour, and in the Sinjar. It has occasionally that remarkable peculiarity—so commonly represented on the sculptures—a short horny claw at the extremity of the tail in the middle of the ordinary tuft of hair. The ibex or wild goat—also a favorite subject with the Assyrian sculptors—is frequent in Kurdistan, and moreover abounds on the highest ridges of the Abd-el-Aziz and the Sinjar, where it is approached with difficulty by the hunter. The gazelle, wild boar, wolf, jackal, fox, badger, porcupine, and hare are common in the plains, and confined to no particular locality. The jerboa is abundant near the Khabour. Beau's and deer are found on the skirts of the Kurdish hills. The leopard, hyaena, lynx, and beaver are comparatively rare. The last named animal, very uncommon in Southern Asia, was at one time found in large numbers on the Khabour; but in consequence of the value set upon its musk bag, it has been hunted almost to extermination, and is now very seldom seen. The Khabour beavers are said to be a different species from the American. Their tail is not large and broad, but sharp and pointed; nor do they build houses, or construct dams across the stream, but live in the banks, making themselves large chambers above the ordinary level of the floods, which are entered by holes beneath the water-line.

The rarest of all the animals which are still found in Assyria is the wild ass (Equus hemionous). Till the present generation of travellers, it was believed to have disappeared altogether from the region, and to have "retired into the steppes of Mongolia and the deserts of Persia. But a better acquaintance with the country between the rivers has shown that wild asses, though uncommon, still inhabit the tract where, they were seen by Xenophon." [PLATE XXVI., Fig. 1.] They are delicately made, in color varying from a grayish-white in winter to a bright bay, approaching to pink, in the summer-time; they are said to be remarkably swift. It is impossible to take them when full grown; but the Arabs often capture the foals, and bring them up with milk in their tents. They then become very playful and docile; but it is found difficult to keep them alive; and they have never, apparently, been domesticated. The Arabs usually kill them and eat their flesh.

It is probable that all these animals, and some others, inhabited Assyria during the time of the Empire. Lions of two kinds, with and without manes, abound in the sculptures, the former, which do not now exist in Assyria, being the more common. [PLATE XXV., Fig. 2.] They are represented with a skill and a truth which shows the Assyrian sculptor to have been familiar not only with their forms and proportions, but with their natural mode of life, their haunts, and habits. The leopard is far less often depicted, but appears sometimes in the ornamentation of utensils, and is frequently mentioned in the inscriptions. The wild ass is a favorite subject with the sculptors of the late Empire, and is represented with great spirit, though not with complete accuracy. [PLATE XXVI., Fig. 1.] The ears are too short, the head is too fine, the legs are not fine enough, and the form altogether approaches too nearly to the type of the horse. The deer, the gazelle, and the ibex all occur frequently; and though the forms are to some extent conventional, they are not wanting in spirit. [PLATE XXVII.] Deer are apparently of two kinds. That which is most commonly found appears to represent the gray deer, which is the only species existing at present within the confines of Assyria. The other sort is more delicate in shape, and spotted, seeming to represent the fallow deer, which is not now known in Syria or the adjacent countries. It sometimes appears wild, lying among the reeds; sometimes tame, in the arms of a priest or of a winged figure. There is no representation in the sculptures of the wild boar; but a wild sow and pigs are given in one bas-relief, sufficiently indicating the Assyrian acquaintance with this animal. Hares are often depicted, and with much truth; generally they are carried in the hands of men, but sometimes they are being devoured by vultures or eagles. [PLATE XXVIII Figs. 1, 2.] No representations have been found of bears, wild cats, hyaenas, wolves, jackals, wild sheep, foxes, beavers, jerbdas, porcupines, or badgers.

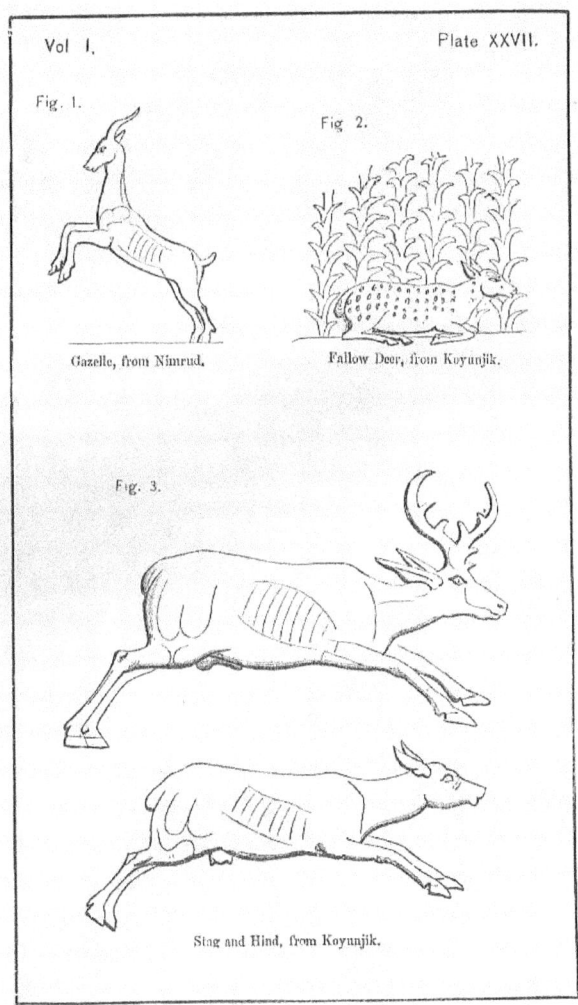

PLATE XXVII

There is reason to believe that two other animals, which have now altogether disappeared from the country, inhabited at least some parts of Assyria during its flourishing period. One of these is the wild bull-often represented on the bas-reliefs as a beast of chase, and perhaps mentioned as such in the inscriptions. This animal, which is sometimes depicted as en-gaged in a contest with the lion, must have been of vast strength and boldness. It is often hunted by the king, and appears to have been considered nearly as noble an object of pursuit as the lion. We may presume, from the practice in the adjoining country, Palestine, 96 that the flesh was eaten as food.

PLATE XXVIII

The other animal, once indigenous, but which has now disappeared, was called by the Assyrians the mithin, and is thought to have been the tiger. Tigers are not now found nearer to Assyria than the country south of the Caspian, Ghilan, and Mazanderan; but as there is no conceivable reason why they should not inhabit Mesopotamia, and as the mithin is constantly joined with the lion, as if it were a beast of the same kind, and of nearly equal strength and courage, we may fairly conjecture that the tiger is the animal intended. If this seem too bold a theory, we must regard the mithin as the larger leopard, an animal of considerable strength and ferocity, which, as well as the hunting leopard, is still found in the country. [PLATE XXVI., Fig. 2.]

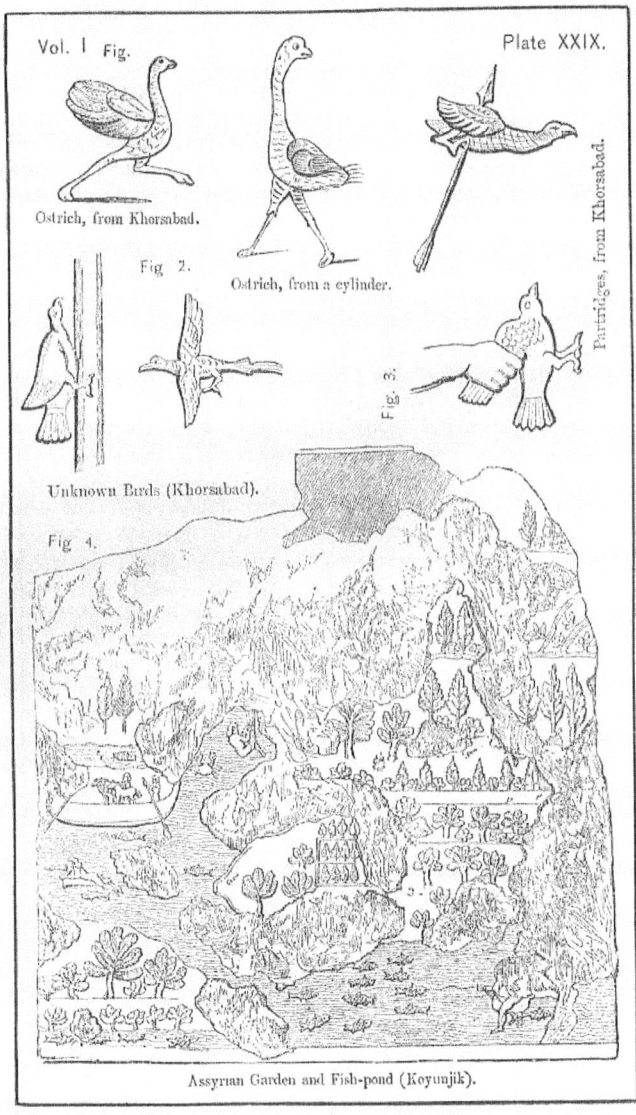

PLATE XXIX

The birds at present frequenting Assyria are chiefly the following: the bustard (which is of two kinds—the great and the middle-sized), the egret, the crane, the stork, the pelican, the flamingo, the red partridge, the black partridge or francolin, the parrot, the Seleucian thrush (Turdus Seleucus), the vulture, the falcon or hunting hawk, the owl, the wild swan, the bramin goose, the ordinary wild goose, the wild duck, the teal, the tern, the sand-grouse, the turtle dove, the nightingale, the jay, the plover, and the snipe. There is also a large kite or eagle, called "agab," or "the butcher," by the Arabs, which is greatly dreaded by fowlers, as it will attack and kill the falcon no less than other birds.

We have little information as to which of these birds frequented the country in ancient times. The Assyrian artists are not happy in their delineation of the feathered tribe; and though several forms of birds are represented upon the sculptures of Sargon and elsewhere, there are but three which any writer has ventured to identify—the vulture, the ostrich, and the partridge. The vulture is commonly represented flying in the air, in attendance upon the march and the battle—sometimes devouring, as he flies, the entrails of one of Assyria's enemies. Occasionally he appears upon the battle-field, perched upon the bodies of the slain, and pecking at their eyes or their vitals. [PLATE XXVIII., Fig. 4.] The ostrich, which we know from Xenophon to have been a former inhabitant of the country on the left bank of the Euphrates, but which has now retreated into the wilds of Arabia, occurs frequently upon cylinders, dresses, and utensils; sometimes stalking along apparently unconcerned; sometimes hastening at full speed, as if pursued by the hunter, and, agreeably to the description of Xenophon, using its wing for a sail. [PLATE XXIX., Figs. 1, 2.] The partridge is still more common than either of these. He is evidently sought as food. We find him carried in the hand of sportsmen returning from the chase, or see him flying above their heads as they beat the coverts, or finally observe him pierced by a successful shot, and in the act of falling a prey to his pursuers. [PLATE XXIX., Fig. 3.]

The other birds represented upon the sculptures, though occasionally possessing some marked peculiarities of form or habit, have not yet been identified with any known species. [PLATE XXIX., Fig. 2.] They are commonly represented as haunting the fir-woods, and often as perched upon the trees. One appears, in a sculpture of Sargon's, in the act of climbing the stein of a tree, like the nut-hatch or the woodpecker. Another has a tail like a pheasant, but in other respects cannot be said to resemble that bird. The artist does not appear to aim at truth in these delineations, and it probably would be a waste of ingenuity to conjecture which species of bird he intended.

We have no direct evidence that bustards inhabited Mesopotamia in Assyrian times; but as they have certainly been abundant in that region front the time of Xenophon to our own, there can be little doubt that they existed in some parts of Assyria during the Empire. Considering their size, their peculiar appearance, and the delicacy of their flesh, it is remarkable that the Assyrian remains furnish no trace of them. Perhaps, as they are extremely shy, they may have been comparatively rare in the country when the population was numerous, and when the greater portion of the tract between the rivers was brought under cultivation.

The fish most plentiful in Assyria are the same as in Babylonia, namely, barbel and carp. They abound not only in the Tigris and Euphrates, but also in the lake of Khutaniyeh, and often grow to a great size. Trout are found in the streams which run down from Zagros; and there may be many other sorts which have not yet been observed. The sculptures represent all the waters, whether river, pond, or marsh, as full of fish; but the forms are for the most part too conventional to admit of identification. [PLATE XXIX., Fig. 3.]

The domestic animals now found in Assyria are camels, horses, asses, mules, sheep, goats, oxen, cows, and dogs. The camels are of three colors—white, yellow, and dark brown or black. They are probably all of the same species, though commonly distinguished into camels proper, and delouls or dromedaries, the latter differing from the others as the English race-horse from the cart-horse. The Bactrian or two-humped camel, though known to the ancient Assyrians, is not now found in the country. [PLATE XXX., Fig. 1.] The horses are numerous, and of the best Arab blood. Small in stature, but of exquisite symmetry and wonderful powers of endurance, they are highly prized throughout the East, and constitute the chief wealth of the wandering tribes who occupy the greater portion of Mesopotamia. The sheep and goats are also of good breeds, and produce wool of an excellent quality. [PLATE XXX., Fig. 2.] The cows and oxen cannot be commended. The dogs kept are chiefly greyhounds, which are used to course the hare and the gazelle.

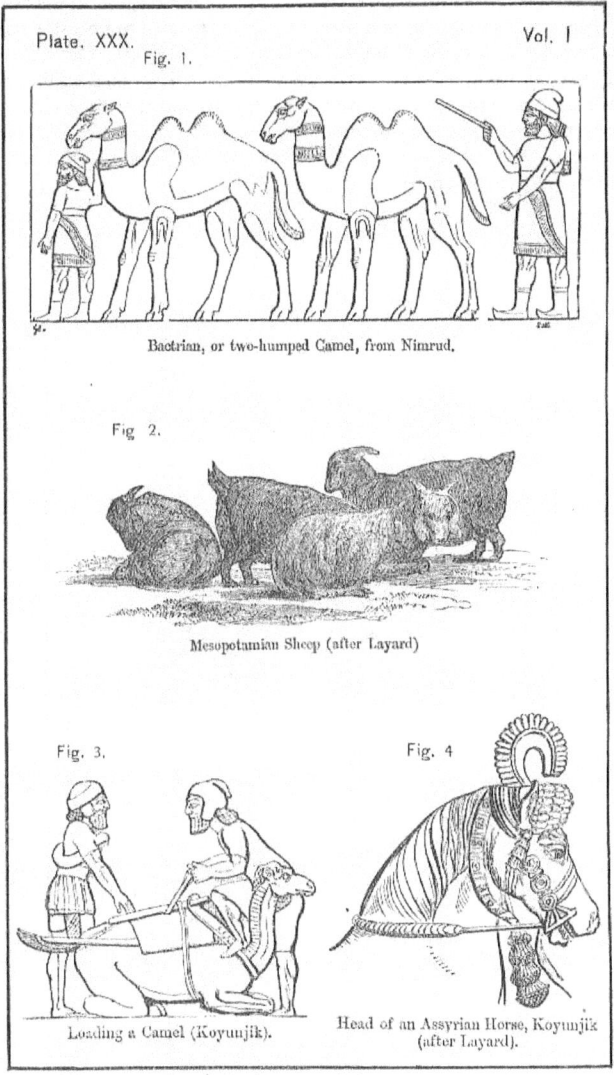

It is probable that in ancient times the animals domesticated by the Assyrians were not very different from these. The camel appears upon the monuments both as a beast of burden and also as ridden in war, but only by the enemies of the Assyrians. [PLATE XXX., Fig. 3.] The horse is used both for draught and for riding, but seems never degraded to ignoble purposes. His breed is good, though he is not so finely or delicately made as the modern Arab. The head is small and well shaped, the nostrils large and high, the neck arched, but somewhat thick, the body compact, the loins strong, the legs moderately slender and sinewy. [PLATE XXX., Fig. 4.] [PLATE XXXI., Fig. 1.] The ass is not found; but the mule appears, sometimes ridden by women, sometimes used as a beast of burden, sometimes employed in drawing a cart. [PLATE XXXI., Fig. 2] [PLATE XXXII., Figs. 1, 2.] Cows, oxen, sheep, and goats are frequent; but they are foreign rather tham Assyrian, since they occur only among the spoil taken from conquered countries. The dog is frequent on the later sculptures; and has been found modelled in clay, and also represented in relief on a clay tablet. [PLATE XXXII., Fig. 3.] [PLATE XXXIII., Fig. 1.] Their character is that of a large mastiff or hound, and there is abundant evidence that they were employed in hunting.

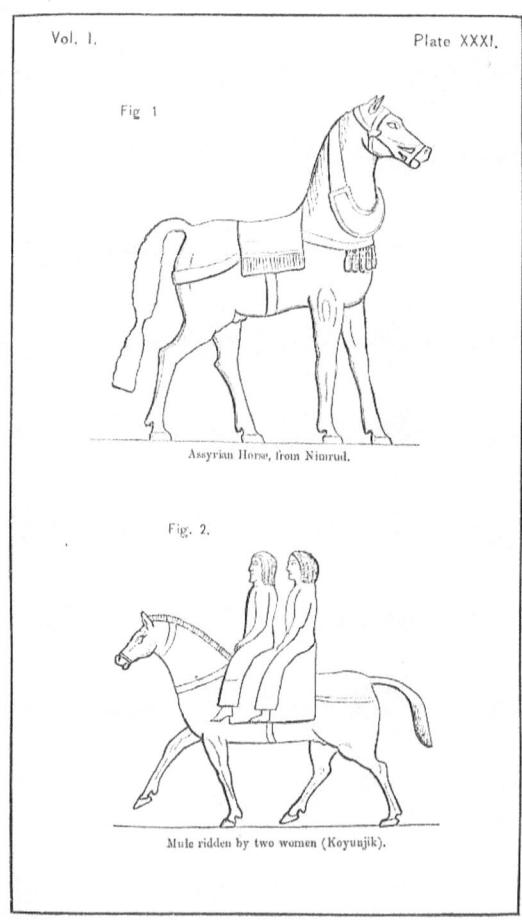

PLATE XXXI

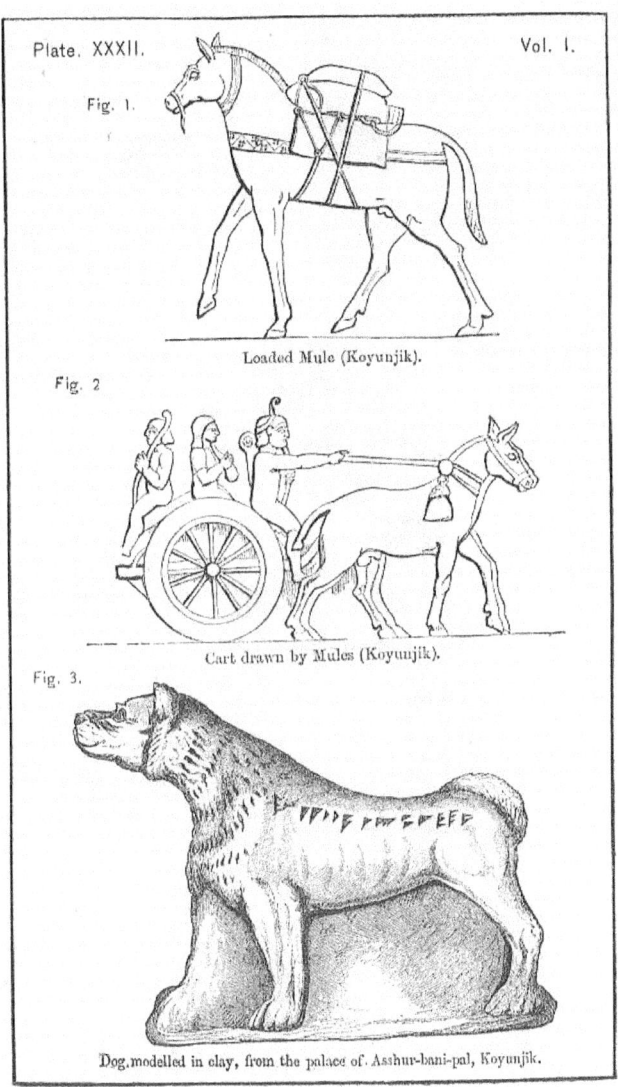

PLATE XXXII

If the Assyrians domesticated any bird, it would seem to have been the duck. Models of the duck are common, and seem generally to have been used for weights. [PLATE XXXIII., Fig. 2.] The bird is ordinarily represented with its head turned upon its back, the attitude of the domestic duck when asleep. The Assyrians seem to have had artificial ponds or stews, which are always represented as full of fish, but the forms are conventional, as has been already observed. Considering the size to which the carp and barbel actually grow at the present day, the ancient representations are smaller than might have been expected.

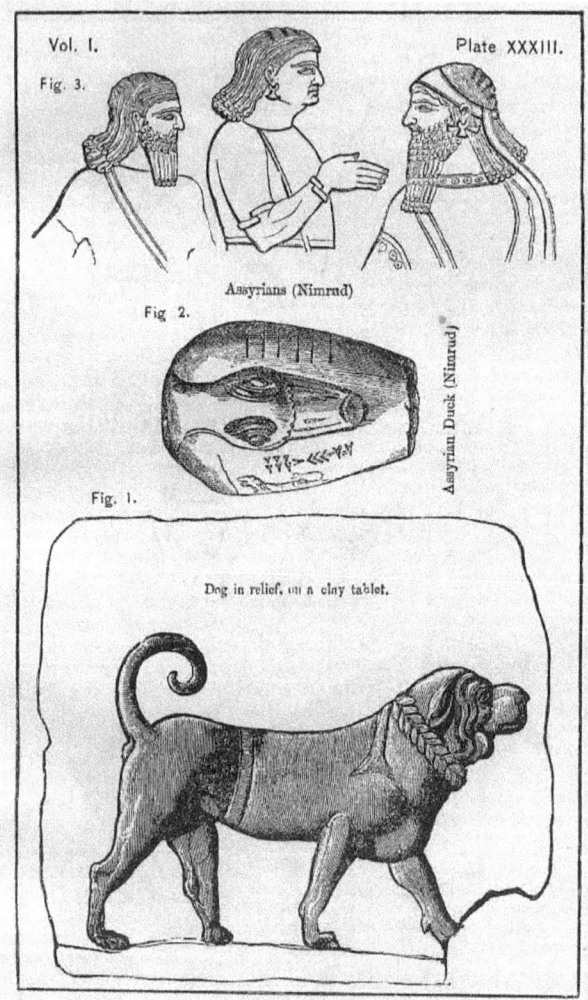

PLATE XXXIII

CHAPTER III

THE PEOPLE

"The Assyrian was a cedar in Lebanon, fair of branches, and with a shadowing shroud, and of high stature; and his top was among the thick boughs. . . . Nor was any tree in the garden of God like unto him in his beauty."—EZEK. xxxi. 3 and 8.

The ethnic character of the ancient Assyrians, like that of the Chaldaeans, was in former times a matter of controversy. When nothing was known of the original language of the people beyond the names of certain kings, princes, and generals, believed to have belonged to the race, it was difficult to arrive at any determinate conclusion on the subject. The ingenuity of etymologists displayed itself in suggesting derivations for the words in question, which were sometimes absurd, sometimes plausible, but never more than very doubtful conjectures. No sound historical critic could be content to base a positive view on any such unstable foundation, and nothing remained but to decide the controversy on other than linguistic considerations.

Various grounds existed on which it was felt that a conclusion could be drawn. The Scriptural genealogies connected Asshur with Aran, Pier, and Joktan, the allowed progenitors of the Armaeians or Syrians, the Israelites or Hebrews, and the northern or Joktanian Arabs. The languages, physical type, and moral characteristics of these races were well known: they all belonged evidently to a single family the family known to ethnologists as the Semitic. Again, the manners and customs, especially the religious customs, of the Assyrians connected then plainly with the Syrians and Phoenicians, with whose practices they were closely allied. Further it was observed that the modern Chaldaeans of Kurdistan, who regard themselves as descendants of the ancient inhabitants of the neighboring Assyria, still speak a Semitic dialect. These three distinct and convergent lines of testimony were sufficient to justify historians in the conclusion, which they commonly drew, that the ancient Assyrians belonged to the Semitic family, and were more or less closely connected with the Syrians, the (later) Babylonians, the Phoenicians, the Israelites, and the Arabs of the northern portion of the peninsula.

Recent linguistic discoveries have entirely confirmed the conclusion thus, arrived at. We now possess in the engraved slabs, the clay tablets, the cylinders, and the bricks, exhumed from the ruins of the great Assyrian cities, copious documentary evidence of the character of the Assyrian language, and (so far as language is a proof) of the ethnic character of the race. It appears to be doubted by none who have examined the evidence, that the language of these records is Semitic. However imperfect the acquaintance which our best Oriental archaeologists have as yet obtained with this ancient and difficult form of speech, its connection with the Syriac, the later Babylonian, the Hebrew, and the Arabic does not seem to admit of a doubt.

Another curious confirmation of the ordinary belief is to be found in the physical characteristics of the people, as revealed to us by the sculptures. Few persons in any way familiar with these works of art can have failed to remark the striking resemblance to the Jewish physiognomy which is presented by the sculptured effigies of the Assyrians. The forehead straight but not high, the full brow, the eye large and almond-shaped, the aquiline nose, a little coarse at the end, and unduly depressed, the strong, firm mouth, with lips somewhat over thick, the well-formed chin—best seen in the representation of eunuchs—the abundant hair and ample beard, both colored as black—all these recall the chief peculiarities of the Jew more especially as he appears in southern countries. [PLATE XXXIII., Fig. 3.] They are less like the traits of the Arab, though to them also they bear a considerable resemblance. Chateaubriand's description of the Bedouin—"la tete ovale, le front haut et argue, le nez aquilia, les yeux grandes et coupe en amandes, le regard humide et singulierement doux" would serve in many respects equally well for a description of the physiognomy of the Assyrians, as they appear upon the monuments. The traits, in fact, are for the most part common to the Semitic race generally, and not distinctive of any particular subdivision of it. They are seen now alike in the Arab, the Jew, and the Chalaedeans of Kurdistan, while anciently they not only characterized the Assyrians, but probably belonged also to the Phoenicians, the Syrians, and other minor Semetic races. It is evident, even from the mannered and conventional sculptures of Egypt, that the physiognomy was regarded as characteristic of the western Asiatic races. Three captives on the monuments of Amenophis III., represented as belonging to the Patana (people of Bashan?), the Asuru (Assyrians), and the Karukamishi (people of Carchemish), present to us the sane style of face, only slightly modified by Egyptian ideas. [PLATE. XXXIV., Fig. 1.]

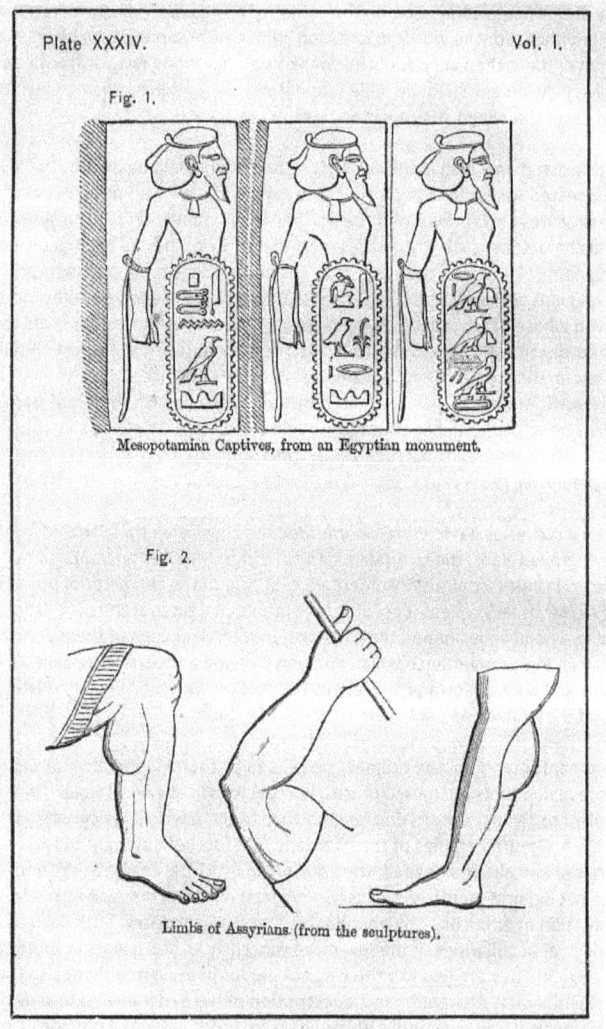

PLATE XXXIV

White in face the Assyrians appear thus to have borne a most close resemblance to the Jews, in shape and make they are perhaps more nearly represented by their descendants, the Chaldaeans of Kurdistan. While the Oriental Jew has a spare form and a weak muscular development, the Assyrian, like the modern Chaldaean, is robust, broad-shouldered, and large-limbed. Nowhere have we a race represented to us monumentally of a stronger or more muscular type than the ancient Assyrian. The great brawny limbs are too large for beauty; but they indicate a physical power which we may well believe to have belonged to this nation—the Romans of Asia—the resolute and sturdy people which succeeded in imposing its yoke upon all its neighbors. [PLATE XXXIV., Fig, 2.]

If from physical we proceed to mental characteristics, we seem again to have in the Jewish character the best and closest analogy to the Assyrian. In the first place, there is observable in each a strong and marked prominency of the religious principle. Inscriptions of Assyrian kings begin and end, almost without exception, with praises, invocations, and prayers to the principal objects of their adoration. All the monarch's successes, all his conquests and victories, and even his good fortune in the chase, are ascribed continually to the protection and favor of guardian deities. Wherever he goes, he takes care to "set up the emblems of Asshur," or of "the great gods;" and forces the vanquished to do them homage. The choicest of the spoil is dedicated as a thank-offering in the temples. The temples themselves are adorned, repaired, beautified, enlarged, increased in manner, by almost, every monarch. The kings worship them in person, and offer sacrifices. They embellish their palaces, not only with representations of their own victories and hunting expeditions, but also with religious figures—the emblems of some of the principal deities, and with scenes in which are portrayed acts of adoration. Their signets, and indeed those of the Assyrians generally, have a religious character. In every way religion seems to hold a marked and prominent place in the thoughts of the people, who fight more for the honor of their gods than even of their king, and aim at extending their belief as much as their dominion.

Again, combined with this prominency of the religious principle, is a sensuousness—such as we observe in Judaism continually struggling against a higher and purer element—but which in this less favored branch of the Semitic family reigns uncontrolled, and gives to its religion a gross, material, and even voluptuous character. The ideal and the spiritual find little favor with this practical people, which, not content with symbols, must have gods of wood and stone whereto to pray, and which in its complicated mythological system, its priestly hierarchy, its gorgeous ceremonial, and finally in its lascivious ceremonies, is a counterpart to that Egypt, from which the Jew was privileged to make his escape.

The Assyrians are characterized in Scripture as "a fierce people." Their victories seem to have been owing to their combining individual bravery and hardihood with a skill and proficiency in the arts of war not possessed by their more uncivilized neighbors. This bravery and hardihood were kept up, partly (like that of the Romans) by their perpetual wars, partly by the training afforded to their manly qualities by the pursuit and destruction of wild animals. The lion—the king of beasts— abounded in their country, together with many other dangerous and ferocious animals. Unlike the ordinary Asiatic, who trembles before the great beasts of prey and avoids a collision by flight if possible, the ancient Assyrian sought out the strongest and fiercest of the animals, provoked them to the encounter, and engaged with them in hand-to-hand combats. The spirit of Nimrod, the "mighty hunter before the Lord," not only animated his own people, but spread on from them to their northern neighbors; and, as far as we can judge by the monuments, prevailed even more in Assyria than in Chaldaea itself. The favorite objects of chase with the Assyrians seem to have been the lion and the wild bull, both beasts of vast strength and courage, which could not be attacked without great danger to the bold assailant.

No doubt the courage of the Assyrians was tinged with ferocity. The nation was "a mighty and strong one, which, as a tempest of hail and a destroying storm, as a flood of mighty waters overflowing, cast down to the earth with the hand." Its capital might well deserve to be called "a bloody city," or "a city of bloods." Few conquering races have been tender-hearted, or much inclined to spare; and undoubtedly carnage, ruin, and desolation followed upon the track of an Assyrian army, and raised feelings of fear and hatred among their adversaries. But we have no reason to believe that the nation was especially bloodthirsty or unfeeling. The mutilation of the slain—not by way of insult, but in proof of their slayer's prowess was indeed practised among them; but otherwise there is little indication of any barbarous, much less of any really cruel, usages. The Assyrian listens to the enemy who asks for quarter; he prefers making prisoners to slaying; he is very terrible in the battle and the assault, but afterwards he forgives, and spares. Of course in some cases he makes exceptions. When a town has rebelled and been subdued, he impales some of the most guilty [PLATE XXXV., Fig. 1]; and in two or three instances prisoners are represented as led before the king by a rope fastened to a ring which passes through the under lip, while now and then one appears in the act of being flayed with it knife [PLATE XXXV., Fig. 2.] But, generally, captives are either released, or else transferred, without unnecessary suffering, from their own country to some other portion of the empire. There seems even to be something of real tenderness in the treatment of captured women, who are never manacled, and are often allowed to ride on mules, or in carts. [PLATE XXXVI., Fig. 1.]

PLATE XXXV

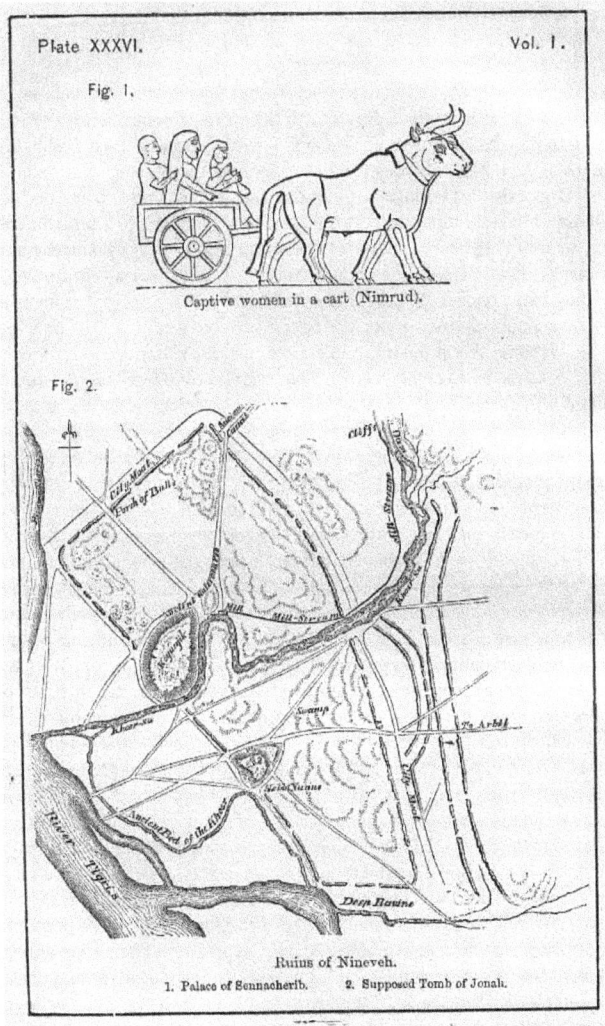

PLATE XXXVI

The worst feature in the character of the Assyrians was their treachery. "Woe to thee that spoilest, though thou wast not spoiled, and dealest treacherously, though they dealt not treacherously with thee!" is the denunciation of the evangelical prophet. And in the same spirit the author of "The Burthen of Nineveh" declares that city to be "full of lies and robbery"—or, more correctly, full of lying and violence. Falsehood and treachery are commonly regarded as the vices of the weak, who are driven to defend themselves against superior strength by the weapon of cunning; but they are perhaps quite as often employed by the strong as furnishing short cuts to success, and even where the moral standard is low, as being in themselves creditable. It certainly was not necessity which made the Assyrians covenant-breakers; it seems to have been in part the wantonness of power—because they "despised the cities and regarded no man;" perhaps it was in part also their imperfect moral perception, which may have failed to draw the proper distinction between craft and cleverness.

Another unpleasant feature in the Assyrian character—but one at which we can feel no surprise—was their pride. This is the quality which draws forth the sternest denunciations of Scripture, and is expressly declared to have called down the Divine judgments upon the race. Isaiah, Ezekiel, and Zephaniah alike dwell upon it. It pervades the inscriptions. Without being so rampant or offensive as the pride of some Orientals—as, for instance, the Chinese, it is of a marked and decided color: the Assyrian feels himself infinitely superior to all the nations with whom he is brought into contact; he alone enjoys the favor of the gods; he alone is either truly wise or truly valiant; the armies of his enemies are driven like chaff before him; he sweeps them away, like heaps of stubble; either they fear to fight, or they are at once defeated; he carries his victorious arms just as far as it pleases him, and never under any circumstances admits that he has suffered a reverse. The only merit that he allows to foreigners is some skill in the mechanical and mimetic arts, and his acknowledgment of this is tacit rather than express, being chiefly known from the recorded fact that he employs foreign artists to ornament his edifices.

According to the notions which the Greeks derived from Ctesias, and passed on to the Romans, and through them to the moderns generally, the greatest defect in the Assyrian character—the besetting sin of their leading men—was luxuriousness of living and sensuality. From Ninyas to Sardanapalus—from the commencement to the close of the Empire—a line of voluptuaries, according to Ctesias and his followers, held possession of the throne; and the principle was established from the first, that happiness consisted in freedom from all cares or troubles, and unchecked indulgence in every species of sensual pleasure. This account, intrinsically suspicious, is now directly contradicted by the authentic records which we possess of the warlike character and manly pursuits of so many of the kings. It probably, however, contains a germ of truth. In a flourishing kingdom like Assyria, luxury must have gradually advanced; and when the empire fell under the combined attack of its two most powerful neighbors, no doubt it had lost much of its pristine vigor. The monuments lend some support to the view that luxury was among the causes which produced the fall of Assyria; although it may be questioned whether, even to the last, the predominant spirit was not warlike and manly, or even fierce and violent. Among the many denunciations of Assyria in Scripture, there is only one which can even be thought to point to luxury as a cause of her downfall; and that is a passage of very doubtful interpretation. In general it is her violence, her treachery, and her pride that are denounced. When Nineveh repented in the time of Jonah, it was by each man "turning from his evil way and from the violence which was in their hands." When Nahum announces the final destruction, it is on "the bloody city, full of lies and robbery." In the emblematic language of prophecy, the lion is taken as the fittest among animals to symbolize Assyria, even at this late period of her history. She is still "the lion that did tear in pieces enough for his whelps, and strangled for his lioness, and filled his holes with prey, and his dens with ravin." The favorite national emblem, if it may be so called, is accepted as the true type of the people; and blood, ravin, and robbery are their characteristics in the mind of the Hebrew prophet.

In mental power the Assyrians certainly deserve to be considered as among the foremost of the Asiatic races. They had not perhaps so much originality as the Chaldaeans, from whom they appear to have derived the greater part of their civilization; but in many respects it is clear that they surpassed their instructors, and introduced improvements which gave a greatly increased value and almost a new character to arts previously discovered. The genius of the people will best be seen from the accounts hereafter to be given of their language, their arts, and their system of government. If it must be allowed that these have all a certain smack of rudeness and primitive simplicity, still they are advances upon aught that had previously existed—not only in Mesopotamia—but in the world. Fully to appreciate the Assyrians, we should compare them with the much-lauded Egyptians, who in all important points are very decidedly their inferiors. The spirit and progressive character of their art offers the strongest contrast to the stiff, lifeless, and unchanging conventionalism of the dwellers on the Nile. Their language and alphabet are confessedly in advance of the Egyptian. Their religion is more earnest and less degraded. In courage and military genius their superiority is very striking; for the Egyptians are essentially an unwarlike people. The one point of advantage to which Egypt may fairly lay claim is the grandeur and durability of her architecture. The Assyrian palaces, magnificent, as they undoubtedly were, must yield the palm to the vast structures of Egyptian Thebes. No nation, not even Rome, has equalled Egypt in the size and solemn grandeur of its buildings. But, except in this one respect, the great African kingdom must be regarded as inferior to her Asiatic rival—which was indeed "a cedar in Lebanon, exalted above all the trees of the field—fair in greatness and in the length of his branches—so that all the trees that were in the garden of God envied him, and not one was like unto him in his beauty."

CHAPTER IV

THE CAPITAL

"Fuit et Ninus, imposita Tigri, ad solis occasum spectans, quondam clarissima."—PLIN. H. N. vi. 13.

The site of the great capital of Assyria had generally been regarded as fixed with sufficient certainty to the tract immediately opposite Mosul, alike by local tradition and by the statements of ancient writers, when the discovery by modern travellers of architectural remains of great magnificence at some considerable distance from this position, threw a doubt upon the generally received belief, and made the true situation of the ancient Nineveh once more a matter of controversy. When the noble sculptures and vast palaces of Nimrud were first uncovered, it was natural to suppose that they marked the real site; for it seemed unlikely that any mere provincial city should have been adorned by a long series of monarchs with buildings at once on so grand a scale and so richly ornamented. A passage of Strabo, and another of Ptolemy, were thought to lend confirmation to this theory, which placed the Assyrian capital nearly at the junction of the Upper Zab with the Tigris; and for awhile the old opinion was displaced, and the name of Nineveh was attached very generally in this country to the ruins at Nimrud.

Shortly afterwards a rival claimant started up in the regions further to the north. Excavations carried on at the village of Khorsabad showed that a magnificent palace and a considerable town had existed in Assyrian times at that site. In spite of the obvious objection that the Khorsabad ruins lay at the distance of fifteen miles from the Tigris, which according to every writer of weight anciently washed the walls of Nineveh, it was assumed by the excavator that the discovery of the capital had been reserved for himself, and the splendid work representing the Khorsabad bas-reliefs and inscriptions, which was published in France under the title of "Monument de Ninive," caused the reception of M. Botta's theory in many parts of the Continent.

After awhile an attempt was made to reconcile the rival claims by a theory, the grandeur of which gained it acceptance, despite its improbability. It was suggested that the various ruins, which had hitherto disputed the name, were in fact all included within the circuit of the ancient Nineveh; which was described as a rectangle, or oblong square, eighteen miles long and twelve broad. The remains of Khorsabad, Koyunjik, Nimrud, and Keremles marked the four corners of this vast quadrangle, which contained an area of 216 square miles—about ten times that of London! In confirmation of this view was urged, first, the description in Diodorus, derived probably from Ctesias, which corresponded (it was said) both with the proportions and with the actual distances; and next, the statements contained in the book of Jonah, which (it was argued) implied a city of some such dimensions. The parallel of Babylon, according to the description given by Herodotus, might fairly have been cited as a further argument; since it might have seemed reasonable to suppose that there was no great difference of size between the chief cities of the two kindred empires.

Attractive, however, as this theory is from its grandeur, and harmonious as it must be allowed to be with the reports of the Greeks, we have nevertheless to reject it on two grounds, the one historical and the other topographical. The ruins of Khorsabad, Keremles, Nimrud, and Koyunjik bear on their bricks distinct local titles; and these titles are found attaching to distinct cities in the historical inscriptions. Nimrud, as already observed, is Calah; and Khorsabad is Dur-Sargina, or "the city of Sargon." Keremles has also its own appellation Dur-* * *, "the city of the God [—]." Now the Assyrian writers do not consider these places to be parts of Nineveh, but speak of them as distinct and separate cities. Calah for a long time is the capital, while Nineveh is mentioned as a provincial town. Dur-Sargina is built by Sargon, not at Nineveh, but "near to Nineveh." Scripture, it must be remembered, similarly distinguishes Calah as a place separate from Nineveh, and so far from it that there was room for "a great city" between them. And the geographers, while they give the name of Aturia or Assyria Proper to the country about the one town, call the region which surrounds the other by a distinct name, Calachene. Again, when the country is closely examined, it is found, not only that there are no signs of any continuous town over the space included within the four sites of Nimrud, Keremles. Khorsabad, and Koyunjik, nor any remains of walls or ditches connecting them, but that the four sites themselves are as carefully fortified on what, by the theory we are examining, would be the inside of the city as in other directions. It perhaps need scarcely be added, unless to meet the argument drawn from Diodorus, that the four sites in question are not so placed as to form the "oblong square" of his description, but mark the angles of a rhombus very munch slanted from the perpendicular.

The argument derived from the book of Jonah deserves more attention than that which rests upon the authority of Diodorus and Ctesias. Unlike Ctesias, Jonah saw Nineveh while it still stood; and though the writer of the prophetical book may not have been Jonah himself, he probably lived not very many years later. Thus his evidence is that of a contemporary, though (it may be) not that of an eye-witness; and, even apart from the inspiration which guided his pen, he is entitled to be heard with the utmost respect. Now the statements of this writer, which have a bearing on the size of Nineveh, are two. He tells us, in one place, that it was "an exceeding great city, of three days' journey;" in another, that "in it were more than 120,000 persons who could not discern between their right hand and their left." These passages are clearly intended to describe a city of a size unusual at the time; but both of them are to such an extent vague and indistinct, that it is impossible to draw front either separately, or even from the two combined, an exact definite notion. "A city of three days' journey" may be one which it requires three days to traverse from end to end, or one which is three days' journey in circumference, or, lastly, one which cannot be thoroughly visited and explored by a prophet commissioned to warn the inhabitants of a coming danger in less than three days' time. Persons not able to distinguish their right hand from their left may (if taken literally) mean children, and 120,000 such persons may therefore indicate a total population of 600,000; or, the phrase may perhaps with greater probability be understood of moral ignorance, and the intention would in that case be to designate by it all the inhabitants. If Nineveh was in Jonah's time a city containing a population of 120,000, it would sufficiently deserve the title of "an exceeding great city;" and the prophet might well be occupied for three days in traversing its squares and streets. We shall find hereafter that the ruins opposite Mosul have an extent more than equal to the accommodation of this number of persons.

The weight of the argument from the supposed parallel ease of Babylon must depend on the degree of confidence which can be reposed in the statement made by Herodotus, and on the opinion which is ultimately formed with regard to the real size of that capital. It would be improper to anticipate here the conclusions which may be arrived at hereafter concerning the real dimensions of "Babylon the Great;" but it may be observed that grave doubts are entertained in many quarters as to the ancient statements on the subject, and that the ruins do not cover much more than one twenty-fifth of the space which Herodotus assigns to the city.

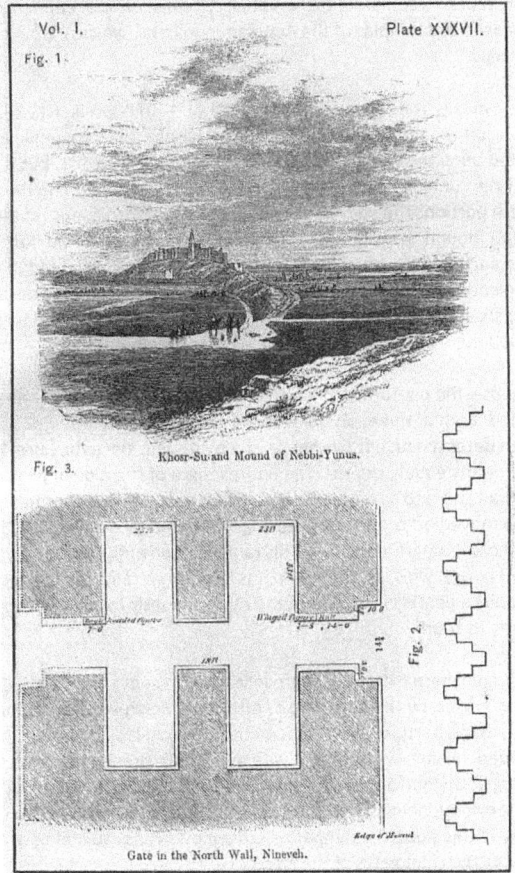

PLATE XXXVII

We may, therefore, without much hesitation, set aside the theory which would ascribe to the ancient Nineveh dimensions nine or ten times greater than those of London, and proceed to a description of the group of ruins believed by the best judges to mark the true site.

The ruins opposite Mosul consist of two principal Mounds, known respectively as Nebbi-Yunus and Koyunjik. [PLATE XXXVI., Fig. 2.] The Koyunjik mound, which lies to the north-west of the other, at the distance of 900 yards, or a little more than half a mile, is very much the more considerable of the two. Its shape is an irregular oval, elongated to a point towards the north-east, in the line of its greater axis. The surface is nearly flat; the sides slope at a steep angle, and are furrowed with numerous ravines, worn in the soft material by the rains of some thirty centuries. The greatest height of the mound above the plum is towards the south-eastern extremity, where it overhangs the small stream of the Khosr; the elevation in this part being about ninety-five feet. The area covered by the mound is estimated at a hundred acres, and the entire mass is said to contain 14,500,000 tons of earth. The labor of a man would scarcely excavate and place in position more than 120 tons of earth in a year; it would require, therefore, the united exertions of 10,000 men for twelve years, or 20,000 men for six years, to complete the structure. On this artificial eminence were raised in ancient times the palaces and temples of the Assyrian monarchs, which are now imbedded in the debris of their own ruins.

The mound of Nebbi-Ymus is at its base nearly triangular: [PLATE XXXVII., Fig. 1.] It covers an area of about forty acres. It is loftier, and its sides are more precipitous, than Koyunjik, especially on the west, where it abutted upon the wall of the city. The surface is mostly flat, but is divided about the middle by a deep ravine, running nearly from north to south, and separating the mound into an eastern and a western portion. The so-called tomb of Jonah is conspicuous on the north edge of the western portion of the mound, and about it are grouped the cottages of the Kurds and Turcomans to whom the site of the ancient Nineveh belongs. The eastern portion of the mound forms a burial-ground, to which the bodies of Mahometans are brought from considerable distances. The mass of earth is calculated at six and a half millions of tons; so that its erection would have given full employment to 10,000 men for the space of five years and a half.

These two vast mounds—the platforms on which palaces and temples were raised—are both in the same line, and abutted, both of them, on the western wall of the city. Their position in that wall is thought to have been determined, not by chance, but by design; since they break the western face of the city into three nearly equal portions. The entire length of this side of Nineveh was 13,600 feet, or somewhat more than two and a half miles. Anciently it seems to have immediately overhung the Tigris, which has now moved off to the west, leaving a plain nearly a mile in width between its eastern edge and the old rampart of the city. This rampart followed, apparently, the natural course of the river-bank; and hence, while on the whole it is tolerably straight, in the most southern of the three portions it exhibits a gentle curve, where the river evidently made a sweep, altering its course from south-east nearly to south.

The western wall at its northern extremity approaches the present course of the Tigris, and is here joined, exactly at right angles, by the northern, or rather the north-western, rampart, which runs in a perfectly straight line to the north-eastern angle of the city, and is said to measure exactly 7000 feet. This wall is again divided, like the western, but with even more preciseness, into three equal portions. Commencing at the north-eastern angle, one-third of it is carried along comparatively high ground, after which for the remaining two-thirds of its course it falls by a gentle decline towards the Tigris. Exactly midway in this slope the rampart is broken by a road, adjoining which is a remarkable mound, covering one of the chief gates of the city.

At its other extremity the western wall forms a very obtuse angle with the southern, which impends over a deep ravine formed by it winter torrent, and runs in a straight line for about 1000 yards, when it meets the eastern wall, with which it forms a slightly acute angle.

It remains to describe the eastern wall, which is the longest and the least regular of the four. Tins barrier skirts the edge of a ridge of conglomerate rock, which here rises somewhat above the level of the plain, and presents a slightly convex sweep to the north east. At first it runs nearly parallel to the western, and at right angles to the northern wall; but, after pursuing this course for about three quarters of a mile, it is forced by the natural convexity of the ridge to retire a little, and curving gently inwards it takes a direction much more southerly than at first, thus drawing continually nearer to the western wall, whose course is almost exactly south-east. The entire length of this wall is 16,000 feet, or above three miles. It is divided into two portions, whereof the southern is somewhat the longer, by the stream of the Khosr-Su; which coming from the north west, finds its way through the ruins of the city, and then runs on across the low plain to the Tigris.

The enceinte of Nineveh forms thus an irregular trapezium, or a "triangle with its apex abruptly cut off to the south." The breadth, even in the broadest part—that towards the north—is very disproportionate to the length, standing to it as four to nine, or as 1 to 2.25. The town is thus of an oblong shape, and so far Diodorus truly described it; though his dimensions greatly exceed the truth. The circuit of the walls is somewhat less than eight miles, instead of being more than fifty and the area which they include is 1100 English acres, instead of being 112,000!

It is reckoned that in a populous Oriental town we may compute the inhabitants at nearly, if not quite, a hundred per acre. This allows a considerable space for streets, open squares, and gardens, since it assigns but one individual to every space of fifty square yards. According to such a mode of reckoning, the population of ancient Nineveh, within the enceinte here described, may be estimated at 175,000 souls. No city of Western Asia is at the present day so populous.

In the above description of the ramparts surrounding Nineveh, no account has been given of their width or height. According to Diodorus, the wall wherewith Ninus surrounded his capital was 100 feet high, and so broad that three chariots might drive side by side along the top. Xenophon, who passed close to the ruins on his retreat with the Ten Thousand, calls the height 150 feet, and the width 50 feet. The actual greatest height at present seems to be 46 feet; but the debris at the foot of the walls are so great, and the crumbled character of the walls themselves is so evident, that the chief modern explorer inclines to regard the computation of Diodorus as probably no exaggeration of the truth. The width of the walls, in their crumbled condition, is from 100 to 200 feet.

The mode in which the walls were constructed seems to have been the following. Up to a certain height—fifty feet, according to Xenophon—they were composed of neatly-hewn blocks of a fossiliferous limestone, smoothed and polished on the outside. Above this, the material used was sun-dried brick. The stone masonry was certainly ornamented along its top by a continuous series of battlements or gradines in the same material [PLATE XXXVII., Fig. 2] and it is not unlikely that a similar ornamentation crowned the upper brick structure. The wall was pierced at irregular intervals by gates, above which rose lofty towers; while towers, probably of lesser elevation, occurred also in the portions of the wall intervening between one gate and another. A gate in the north-western rampart has been cleared by means of excavation, the form and construction of which will best appear from the annexed ground-plan. [PLATE XXXVII., Fig. 3.] It seems to have consisted of three gateways, whereof the inner and outer were ornamented with colossal human-headed bulls and other figures, while the central one was merely panelled with slabs of alabaster. Between the gateways were two large chambers, 70 feet long by 23 feet wide, which were thus capable of containing a considerable body of soldiers. The chambers and gateways are supposed to have been arched over, like the castles' gates on the bas-reliefs. The gates themselves have wholly disappeared: but the debris which filled both the chambers and the passages contained so much charcoal that it is thought they must have been made, not of bronze, like the gates of Babylon, but of wood. The ground within the gate-way was paved with large slabs of limestone, still bearing the marks of chariot wheels.

The castellated rampart which thus surrounded and guarded Nineveh did not constitute by any means its sole defence. Outside the stone basement wall lay on every side a water barrier, consisting on the west and south of natural river courses; on the north and east, of artificial channels into which water was conducted from the Khosr-su. The northern and eastern walls were skirted along their whole length by a broad and deep moat, into which the Khosr-su was made to flow by occupying its natural bed with a strong dam carried across it in the line of the eastern wall, and at the point where the stream now enters the enclosure. On meeting this obstruction, of which there are still some remains, the waters divided, and while part flowed to the south-east, and reached the Tigris by the ravine immediately to the south of the city, which is a natural water-course, part turned at an acute angle to the north-west, and, washing the remainder of the eastern and the whole of the northern wall, gained the Tigris at the north-west angle of the city, where a second dam kept it at a sufficient height. Moreover, on the eastern face, which appears to have been regarded as the weakest, a series of outworks were erected for the further defence of the city. North of the Khosr, between the city wall and that river, which there runs parallel to the wall and forms a sort of second or outermost moat, there are traces of a detached fort of considerable size, which must have strengthened the defences in that quarter. South and south-east of the Khosr, the works are still more elaborate. In the first place, from a point where the Khosr leaves the hills and debouches upon comparatively low ground, a deep ditch, 200 feet broad, was carried through compact silicious conglomerate for upwards of two miles, till it joined the ravine which formed the natural protection of the city upon the south. On either side of this ditch, which could be readily supplied with water from the Khosr at its northern extremity, was built a broad and lofty wall; the eastern one, which forms the outermost of the defences, rises even now a hundred feet above the bottom of the ditch on which it adjoins. Further, between this outer barrier and the city moat wall interposed a species of demilune, guarded by a double wall and a broad ditch and connected (as is thought) by a covered way with Neneveh itself. Thus the city was protected on this, its most vulnerable side, towards the centre by five walls and three broad and deep moats; towards the north, by a wall, a moat, the Khosr, and a strong outpost; towards the south by two moats and three lines of rampart. The breadth of the whole fortification on this side is 2200 feet, or not far from half a mile. [PLATE XXXVIII.]

Outer defences of Nineveh, in their present condition.

PLATE XXXVIII

Such was the site, and such were the defences, of the capital of Assyria. Of its internal arrangements but little can be said at present, since no general examination of the space within the ramparts has been as yet made, and no ancient account of the interior has come down to us. We can only see that the side of the city which was most fashionable was the western, which immediately overhung the Tigris; since here were the palaces of the kings, and here seem also to have been the dwellings of the richer citizens; at least, it is on this side in the space intervening between Koyunjik and the northern rampart, that the only very evident remains of edifices—besides the great Mounds of Koyunjik and Nebbi-Yunus—are found. The river was no doubt the main attraction; but perhaps the western side was also considered the most secure, as lying furthest frown the quarter whence alone the inhabitants expected to be attacked, namely, the east. It is impossible at present to give any account of the character of the houses or the the direction of the streets. Perhaps the time may not be far distant when more systematic and continuous efforts will be made by the enterprise of Europe to obtain full knowledge of all the remains which still lie buried at this interesting site. No such discoveries are indeed to be expected as those which have recently startled the world but patient explorers would still be sure of an ample reward, were they to glean, after Layard in the field from which he swept so magnificent a harvest.

CHAPTER V

LANGUAGE AND WRITING

There has never been much difference of opinion among the learned with regard to the language spoken by the Assyrians. As the Biblical genealogy connected Asshur with Eber and Aram, while the Greeks plainly regarded the Syrians, Assyrians, and Babylonians as a single race, it was always supposed that the people thus associated must have possessed a tongue allied, more or less closely, to the Hebrew, the Syriac, and the Chaldee. These tongues were known to be dialectic varieties of a single form of speech the Semitic; and it was consequently the general belief, before any Assyrian inscriptions had been disinterred, that the Assyrian language was of this type, either a sister tongue to the three above mentioned, or else identical with some one of them. The only difficulty in the way of this theory was the supposed Medo-Persic or Arian character of a certain number of Assyrian royal names; but this difficulty was thought to be sufficiently met by a suggestion that the ruling tribe might have been of Median descent, and have maintained its own national appellatives, while the mass of the population belonged to a different race. Recent discoveries have shown that this last suggestion was needless, as the difficulty which it was intended to meet does not exist. The Assyrian names which either history or the monuments have handed down to us are Semitic, and not Arian. It is only among the fabulous accounts of the Assyrian Empire put forth by Ctesias that Arian names, such as Xerxes, Arius, Armamithres, Mithraus, etc., are to be found.

Together with the true names of the Assyrian kings, the mounds of Mesopotamia have yielded up a mass of documents in the Assyrian language, from which it is possible that we may one day acquire as full a knowledge of its structure and vocabulary as we possess at present of Greek or Latin. These documents have confirmed the previous belief that the tongue is Semitic. They consist, in the first place, of long inscriptions upon the slabs of stone with which the walls of palaces were panelled, sometimes occupying the stone to the exclusion of any sculpture, sometimes carried across the dress of figures, always carefully cut, and generally in good preservation. Next in importance to these memorials are the hollow cylinders, or, more strictly speaking, hexagonal or octagonal prisms, made in extremely fine and thin terra cotta, which the Assyrian kings used to deposit at the corners of temples, inscribed with an account of their chief acts and with numerous religious invocations. [PLATE XXXIX., Fig. 1.] These cylinders vary from a foot and a half to three feet in height, and are covered closely with a small writing, which it often requires a good magnifying glass to decipher. A cylinder of Tiglath-Pileser I. (about B.C. 1180) contains thirty lines in a space of six inches, or five lines to an inch, which is nearly as close as the type of the present volume. This degree of closeness is exceeded on a cylinder of Asshur-bani-pal's (about B.C. 660), where the lines are six to the inch, or as near together as the type of the Edinburgh Review. If the complexity of the Assyrian characters be taken into account, and if it be remembered that the whole inscription was in every ease impressed by the hand, this minuteness must be allowed to be very surprising. It is not favorable to legibility; and the patience of cuneiform scholars has been severely tried by a mode of writing which sacrifices everything to the desire of crowding the greatest possible quantity of words into the smallest possible space. In one respect, however, facility of reading is consulted, for the inscriptions on the cylinders are not carried on in continuous lines round all the sides, but are written in columns, each column occupying a side. The lines are thus tolerably short; and the whole of a sentence is brought before the eye at once.

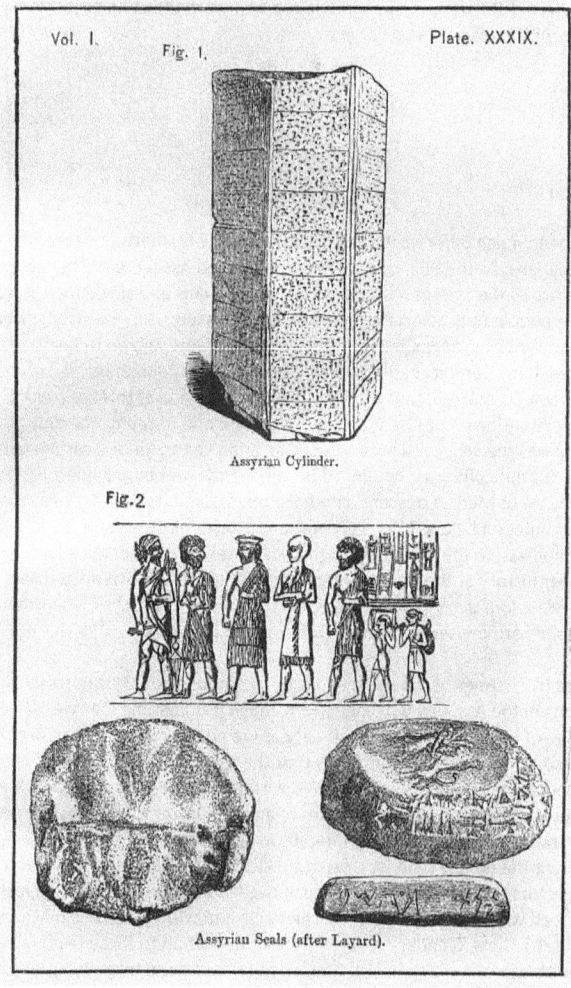

Besides slabs and cylinders, the written memorials of Assyria comprise inscribed bulls and lions, stone obelisks, clay tablets, bricks, and engraved seals. Tin seals generally resemble those of the Chaldaeans, which have been already described: but are somewhat more elaborate, and more varied in their character. [PLATE XXXIX., Fig. 2.] They do not very often exhibit any writing; but occasionally they are inscribed with the name of their owner, while in a few instances they show an inscription of some length. The clay tablets are both numerous and curious. They are of various sizes, ranging from nine inches long by six and a half wide, to an inch and a half long by an inch wide, or even less. [PLATE XL., Fig. 2.]

PLATE XL

Sometimes they are entirely covered with writing; while sometimes they exhibit on a portion of their surface the impressions of seals, mythological emblems, and the like. Some thousands of them have been recovered; and they are found to be of the most varied character. Many are historical, still more mythological; some are linguistic, some geographic, some again astronomical. It is anticipated that, when they are deciphered, we shall obtain a complete eneyclopaedia of Assyrian science, and shall be able by this means to trace a large portion of the knowledge of the Greeks to an Oriental source. Here is a mine still very little worked, from which patient and cautious investigators may one day extract the most valuable literary treasures. The stone obelisks are but few, and are mostly in a fragmentary condition. One alone is perfect—the obelisk in black basalt, discovered by Mr. Layard at Nimrud, which has now for many years been in the British Museum. [PLATE XL., Fig. 1.] This monument is sculptured on each of its four sides, in part with writing and in part with bas-reliefs. It is about seven feet high, and two feet broad at the base, tapering gently towards the summit, which is crowned with three low steps, or gradines. The inscription, which occupies the upper and lower portion of each side, and is also carried along the spaces between the bas-reliefs, consists of 210 clearly cut lines, and is one of the most important documents that has come down to us. It gives an account of various victories gained by the monarch who set it up, and of the tribute brought him by several princes. The inscribed lions and bulls are numerous. They commonly guard the portals of palaces, and are raised in a bold relief on alabaster slabs. The writing does not often trench upon the sculpture, but covers all those portions of the slabs which are not occupied by the animal. It is usually a full account of some particular campaign, which was thus specially commemorated, giving in detail what is far more briefly expressed in the obelisk and slab inscriptions.

This review of the various kinds of documents which have been discovered in the ancient cities of Assyria, seems to show that two materials were principally in use among the people for literary purposes, namely, stone and moist clay. The monarchs used the former most commonly, though sometimes they condescended for some special object to the coarser and more fragile material. Private persons in their business transactions, literary and scientific men in their compositions, employed the latter, on which it was possible to write rapidly with a triangular instrument, and which was no doubt far cheaper than the slabs of fine stone, which were preferred for the royal inscriptions. The clay documents, when wanted for instruction or as evidence, were carefully baked; and thus it is that they have come down to us, despite their fragility, often in as legible a condition, with the letters as clear and sharp, as any legend on marble, stone, or metal that we possess belonging to Greek or even to Roman times. The best clay, skilfully baked, is a material quite as enduring as either stone or metal, resisting many influences better than either of those materials.

It may still be asked, did not the Assyrians use other materials also? Did they not write with ink of some kind on paper, or leather, or parchment? It is certain that the Egyptians had invented a kind of thick paper many centuries before the Assyrian power arose; and it is further certain that the later Assyrian kings had a good deal of intercourse with Egypt. Under such circumstances, can we suppose that they did not import paper from that country? Again, the Persians, we are told, used parchment for their public records. Are not the Assyrians a much more ingenious people, likely to have done the same, at any rate to some extent? There is no direct evidence by which these questions can be determinately answered. No document on any of the materials suggested has been found. No ancient author states that the Assyrians or the Babylonians used them. Had it not been for one piece of indirect evidence, it would have seemed nearly certain that they were not employed by the Mesopotamian races. In some of the royal palaces, however, small humps of fine clay have been found, bearing the impressions of seals, and exhibiting traces of the string by which they were attached to documents, while the documents themselves, being of a different material, have perished. It seems probable that in these instances some substance like paper or parchment was used; and thus we are led to the conclusion that, while clay was the most common, and stone an ordinary writing material among the Assyrians, some third substance, probably Egyptian paper, was also known, and was used occasionally, though somewhat rarely, for public documents.

We may now proceed to consider the style and nature of the Assyrian writing. Derived evidently from the Chaldæan, it is far less archaic in type, presenting no pictorial representations of objects, and but a few characters where the pictorial representations can be traced. It is in no case wholly rectilinear; and indeed preserves a straight line only in a very few characters, as in

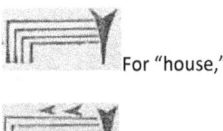 For "house,"

For "gate,"

For "temple, altar,"

And

 For "fish,"

All which are in later inscriptions superseded by simpler forms.

The wedge may thus be said to be almost the sole element of the writing—the wedge, however, under a great variety of forms—sometimes greatly elongated, as thus

Sometimes contracted to a triangle

Sometimes broadened out

Sometimes doubled in such a way as to form an arrowhead

And placed in every direction—horizontal, perpendicular, and diagonal.

The number of characters is very great. Sir H. Rawlinson, in the year 1851, published a list of 216, or, including variants, 366 characters, as occurring in the inscriptions known to him. M. Oppei t, in 1858, gave 318 forms as those "most in use." Of course it is at once evident that this alphabet cannot represent elementary sounds. The Assyrian characters do, in fact, correspond, not to letters, according to our notion of letters, but to syllables. These syllables are either mere vowel sounds, such as we represent by our vowels and diphthongs, or such sounds accompanied by one or two consonants.

The vowels are not very numerous. The Assyrians recognize three only as fundamental—a, i, and u. Besides these they have the diphthongs ai, nearly equivalent to e, and au, nearly equivalent to o. The vowels i and u have also the powers, respectively, of y and v.

> The consonant sounds recognized in the language are sixteen in number. They are the labial, guttural, and dental *tenues*, p, k, t; the labial, guttural, and dental *mediæ*, b, g, d; the guttural and dental aspirates kh (= Heb. ח) and th (= Greek θ); the liquids l, m,[19] n, r; and the sibilants, s, sh (= Heb. שׁ), ts (= Heb. צ), and z. The system here is nearly that of the Hebrews, from which it differs only by the absence of the simple aspirate ה,[2] of the guttural ע, and of the aspirated פ (ph). It has no sound which the Hebrew has not.

From these sounds, combined with the simple vowels, comes the Assyrian syllabarium, to which, and not to the consonants themselves, the characters were assigned. In the first place, each consonant being capable of two combinations with each simple vowel, could give birth naturally to six simple syllables, each of which would be in the Assyrian system represented by a character. Six characters, for instance, entirely different from one another, represented pa, pi, pu, ap, ip, up; six others, ka, ki, ke, ak, ik, uk; six others again, ta, ti, tu, at, it, ut.

If this rule were carried out in every case, the sixteen consonant sounds would, it is evident, produce ninety-six characters. The actual number, however, formed in this way, is only seventy-five. Since these are seven of the consonants which only combine with the vowels in one way. Thus we have ba, bi, bu, but not ab, ib, ub; ga, qi, gu, but not ay, iq,ug; and so on. The sounds regarded as capable of only one combination are the mediae, b, q, d; the aspirates kh, tj; and the sibilants ts and z.

Such is the first and simplest syllabarium: but the Assyrian system does not stop here. It proceeds to combine with each simple vowel sound two consonants, one preceding the vowel and the other following it. If this plan were followed out to the utmost possible extent, the result would be an addition to the syllabarium of seven hundred and sixty-eight sounds, each having its proper character, which would raise the number of characters to between eight and nine hundred! Fortunately for the student, phonetic laws and other causes have intervened to check this extreme luxuriance; and the combinations of this kind which are known to exist, instead of amounting to the full limit of seven hundred and sixty-eight, are under one hundred and fifty. The known Assyrian alphabet is, however, in this way raised from eighty, or, including variants, one hundred, to between two hundred and forty and two hundred and fifty characters.

Finally, there are a certain number of characters which have been called "ideographs," or "monograms." Most of the gods, and various cities and countries, are represented by a group of wedges, which is thought not to have a real phonetic force, but to be a conventional sign for an idea, much as the Arabic numerals, 1, 2, 3. etc., are non-phonetic signs representing the ideas, one, two, three, etc. The known characters of this description are between twenty and thirty.

The known Assyrian characters are thus brought up nearly to three hundred! There still remain a considerable number which are either wholly unknown, or of which the meaning is known, while the phonetic value cannot at present be determined. M. Oppert's Catalogue contains fourteen of the former and fifty-nine of the latter class.

It has already been observed that the monumental evidence accords with the traditional belief in regard to the character of the Assyrian language, which is unmistakably Semitic. Not only does the vocabulary present constant analogies to other Semitic dialects, but the phonetic laws and the grammatical forms are equally of this type. At the same time the language has peculiarities of its own, which separate it from its kindred tongues, and constitute it a distinct form of Semitic speech, not a mere variety of any known form. It is neither Hebrew, nor Arabic, nor Phoenician, nor Chaldee, nor Syriac, but a sister tongue to these, having some analogies with all of them, and others, more or fewer, with each. On the whole, its closest relationship seems to be with the Hebrew, and its greatest divergence from the Aramaic or Syriac, with which it was yet, locally, in immediate connection.

To attempt anything like a full illustration of these statements in the present place would be manifestly unfitting. It would be to quit the province of the historian and archeologist, in order to enter upon that of the comparative philologer or the grammarian. At the same time a certain amount of illustration seems necessary, in order to show that the statements above made are not mere theories, but have a substantial basis.

The Semitic character of the vocabulary will probably be felt to be sufficiently established by the following lists:

NOUNS SUBSTANTIVE.

Abu, "a father." Compare Heb. א, אבי; Arabic *abou*.
Ummu, "a mother." Comp. Heb. אם, and Arabic *um*.
Akhu, "a brother." Comp. Heb. אח, אחי.
Pal or *bal*, "a son." Comp. Syriac *bar*, and perhaps Heb. בן.
Ilu, "God." Comp. Heb. אל, אלוה; Arabic *Allah*.
Sarru, "a king." Comp. Heb. שר.
Malik, "a prince." Comp. Heb. מלך, and Arabic *malik*.
Bilu, "a lord." Comp. Heb. בצל.
Nisu, "a man." Comp. Heb. אנוש, "a mortal," and Chald. נשים, "women."
Dayan, "a judge." Comp. Heb. דין, from דין, *judicare*.
Sumu, "a name." Comp. Heb. שם.
Sami, "heaven." Comp. Heb. שמים, "the heavens."
Irtsit, "the earth." Comp. Heb. ארץ.
Shamas, "the sun." Comp. Heb. שמש.
Tsin, "the moon." Comp. Syriac *sin*.
Marrat, or *varrat*, "the sea." Comp. Arabic *bahr*, "a lake" (?). Or may the root be מר, "bitter"? Comp. Lat. *mare*, *a-marus*.
Nahar, "a river." Comp. Heb. נהר, and Arabic *nahr*.
Yumu, "day." Comp. Heb. יום.

Ilamu, "the world." Comp. Heb. צולם.
'Ir, "a city." Comp. Heb. ציר.
Bit, "a house." Comp. Heb. בית.
Bab, "a gate." Comp. Chald. בבה, and Arabic *bab*.
Lisan, "a tongue," or "language." Comp. Heb. לשון; Chald. לשן.
Asar, "a place." Comp. Chald. אתר.
Mitu, "death." Comp. Heb. מות.
Susu, "a horse." Comp. Heb. סוס.

ADJECTIVES.

Rabu, "great." Comp. Heb. רב; whence the well-known Rabbi (רבא), "a great one, a doctor."
Tabu, "good." Comp. Chald. טב and Heb. טוב.
Bashu, "bad." Comp. Heb. מביש, "a base one," from בוש, "to be ashamed."
Madut, "many." Comp. Heb. מאד, "exceedingly."
Ruk, "far, wide." Comp. Heb. רחוק.

NUMERALS.

[The forms marked with an asterisk are conjectural.]

Ishtin, "one" (masc.) Comp. Heb. עשתי, in עשתי־עשר, "eleven."
Ikhit, "one" (fem.) Comp. Heb. אחת.
Shanai, "two" (masc.) Comp. Heb. שנים, שני.
Shalshat, "three" (masc.) Comp. Heb. שלשת.
Shilash, "three" (fem.) Comp. Heb. שלש.
Arbat, "four" (masc.) Comp. Heb. ארבעת.
Arba, "four" (fem.) Comp. Heb. ארבע.
Khamshat, "five" (masc.) Comp. Heb. חמשת.
Khamish, "five" (fem.) Comp. Heb. חמש.
Shashat, "six" (masc.) Comp. Heb. ששת.
Shash, "six" (fem.) Comp. Heb. שש.
Shibit, "seven" (masc.) Comp. Heb. שבעת.
Shibi, "seven" (fem.) Comp. Heb. שבע.
Shamnat,* "eight" (masc.) Comp. Heb. שמנת.
Tishit,* "nine" (masc.) Comp. Heb. תשעת.
Tishi,* "nine" (fem.) Comp. Heb. תשע.
Isrit, "ten" (masc.) Comp. Heb. עשרת.
Isri, "ten" (fem.) Comp. Heb. עשר.
Israi, "twenty." Comp. Heb. עשרים.
Shilashai, "thirty." Comp. Heb. שלשים.

Irba'ai, "forty." Comp. Heb. אַרְבָּצִים.
Khamshai, "fifty." Comp. Heb. חֲמִשִּׁים.
Shishai, "sixty." Comp. Heb. שִׁשִּׁים.
Shibai, "seventy." Comp. Heb. שִׁבְצִים.
Shamnai,* "eighty." Comp. Heb. שְׁמֹנִים.
Tishai, "ninety." Comp. Heb. תִּשְׁצִים.
Mai, or *Mi*, "a hundred." Comp. Heb. מֵאָה.

PRONOUNS.

[The forms marked with an asterisk are conjectural.]

Anaku, "I." Heb. אָנֹכִי.
Atta, "thou" (masc.) Heb. אַתָּה.
Atti,* "thou" (fem.) Heb. אַתְּ.
Shu, "he." Heb. הוּא.
Shi, "she." Heb. הִיא.
Aanakhni (?), "we." Heb. אֲנַחְנוּ.
Attun,* "ye" (masc.) Heb. אַתֶּם.
Attin,* "ye" (fem.) Heb. אַתֶּן.
Shunut, or *Shun*, "they" (masc.) Heb. הֵם, הֵמָּה.
Shinat, or *Shin*, "they" (fem.) Heb. הֵנָּה, הֵי.
Ma, "who, which." Heb. מַה.
Ullu, "that." Heb. אֵלֶּה, "these."

VERBS.

Alak, "to go." Heb. חלך.
Bakhar, "to collect." Comp. Heb. בחר, "to select."
Bana, "to create, to build." Heb. בנה.
Dana, "to give," in Niphal, *nadan*. Heb. נתן.
Din, "to judge." Heb. דין.
Duk, "to kill." Comp. Heb. דקק, "to beat small;" דוך, "to pound or bruise." Chald. דנד.
'Ibir, "to pass, cross." Heb. צבר.
'Ibush, "to make." Comp. Chald. צבד.
'Irish, "to ask, pray." Comp. Heb. אֲרֶשֶׁת, "request, desire."
Natsar, "to guard." Heb. נצר.
Naza, "to leap." Heb. נזה.
Nazal, "to flow, sink, descend." Heb. נזל.
Pakad, "to entrust." Heb. פקד.
Saga, "to grow, become great." Heb. שׂגא.

Shakan, "to dwell." Heb. שׁכן.
Shatar, "to write." Comp. Chald. שׁטרא, "a written contract."
Tsabat, "to hold, possess." Comp. Heb. צבת, "a bundle;" Arab, *tsabat*, "to hold tight;" Chald. צבחת, "tongs."

ADVERBS, CONJUNCTIONS, ETC.

U, "and." Heb. ו or וּ.
La, or *ul*, "not." Heb. לֹ.
Lapani, "before the face of." Heb. אל־פני.
Tsilli, "by favor of." Heb. צללי.
'Ilat, "except." Chald. אלא.
Adi, "until." Heb. צד.
Ki, "if." Heb. כי.

It remains to notice briefly some of the chief grammatical laws and forms. There is one remarkable difference between the Assyrian language and the Hebrew, namely, that the former has no article. In this it resembles the Syriac, which is likewise deficient in this part of speech.

Assyrian nouns, like Hebrew ones, are all either masculine or feminine. Feminine nouns end ordinarily in *-at* or *-it*, as Hebrew ones in *-eth*, *-ith*, *-uth*, or *-ah*. There is a dual number, as in Hebrew, and it has the same limited use, being applied almost exclusively to those objects which form a pair. The plural masculine is commonly formed by adding *-i* or *-ani* to the singular—terminations which recall the Hebrew addition of ים־; but sometimes by adding *-ut* or *-uti*, to which there is no analogy in Hebrew.[21] The plural feminine is made by changing *-it* into *-et*, and *-ăt* into *-āt*, or (if the word does not end in *t*), by adding *-āt*. Here again there is resemblance to, though not identity with, the Hebrew, which forms the feminine plural in *-oth* (ות־).

Assyrian, like Hebrew, adjectives, agree in gender and number with their substantives. They form the feminine singular in *ăt*, the plural masculine in *-i* and *-ut*, the plural feminine in *-āt* and *-et*.

In Assyrian, as in all other Semitic languages, the possessive pronouns are expressed by suffixes. These suffixes are, for the first person singular, *-ya*, or *-iya* (Heb. י־); for the second person singular masculine, *-ka* (Heb. ךָ־); for the second person singular feminine, *-ki* (Heb. ךְ־); for the third person singular masculine, *-shu* (Heb. ו־); for the third person singular feminine, -*sha* (Heb. הׁ-); for the first person plural, -*n* (Heb. נוּ-); for the second person plural masculine, -*kun* (Heb. כֻם-); for the second person plural feminine, -*kin* (Heb. כֻן-); for the third person plural masculine, *shun* (Heb. ס-); for the third person plural feminine, *shin* (Heb. ן-). The resemblance, it will be seen, is in most cases close, though in only one is there complete identity.

Assyrian verbs have five principal and four secondary voices. Only two of these—the *kal* and the *niphal*—are exactly identical with the Hebrew. The *pael*, however, corresponds nearly to the Hebrew *piel*, and the *aphel* to the Hebrew *hiphil*. In addition to these we find enumerated the *shaphil*, the *iphteal*, the *iphta'al*, the *istaphal*, and the *itaphal*. Several of these are well-known forms in Chaldee.

It is peculiar to Assyrian to have no distinctions of tense. The same form of the verb serves for the present, the past, and the future. The only distinctions of mood are an imperative and an infinitive, besides the indicative. There is also, in each voice, one participle.

The verbs are conjugated by the help of pronominal suffixes and prefixes, chiefly the latter, like the future (present) tense in Hebrew. The suffixes and prefixes are nearly identical with those used in Hebrew.

For further particulars on this interesting subject the student is referred to the modest but excellent work of M. Oppert, entitled " Élémens de la Grammaire Assyrienne,"[22] from which the greater portions of the above remarks are taken.

CHAPTER VI

ARCHITECTURE AND OTHER ARTS

"Architecti multarum artium solertes."—Mos. CHOR. (De Assyriis) i. 15.

The luxury and magnificence of the Assyrians, and the advanced condition of the arts among them which such words imply, were matters familiar to the Greeks and Romans, who, however, had little ocular evidence of the fact, but accepted it upon the strength of a very clear and uniform tradition. More fortunate than the nations of classical antiquity, whose comparative proximity to the time proved no advantage to them, we possess in the exhumed remains of this interesting people a mass of evidence upon the point, which, although in many respects sadly incomplete, still enables us to form a judgment for ourselves upon the subject, and to believe—on better grounds than they possessed—the artistic genius and multiform ingenuity of the Assyrians. As architects, as designers, as sculptors, as metallurgists, as engravers, as upholsterers, as workers in ivory, as glass-blowers, as embroiderers of dresses, it is evident that they equalled, if they did not exceed, all other Oriental nations. It is the object of the present chapter to give some account of their skill in these various respects. Something is now known of them all; and though in every case there are points still involved in obscurity, and recourse must therefore be had upon occasion to conjecture, enough appears certainly made out to justify such an attempt as the present, and to supply a solid groundwork of fact valuable in itself, even if it be insufficient to sustain in addition any large amount of hypothetical superstructure.

The architecture of the Assyrians will naturally engage our attention at the outset. It is from an examination of their edifices that we have derived almost all the knowledge which we possess of their progress in every art; and it is further as architects that they always enjoyed a special repute among their neighbors. Hebrew and Armenian united with Greek tradition in representing the Assyrians as notable builders at a very early time. When Asshur "went forth out of the land of Shinar," it was to build cities, one of which is expressly called "a great city." When the Armenians had to give an account of the palaces and other vast structures in their country, they ascribed their erection to the Assyrians. Similarly. when the Greeks sought to trace the civilization of Asia to its source, they carried it back to Ninus and Semiramis, whom they made the founders, respectively, of Nineveh and Babylon, the two chief cities of the early world.

Among the architectural works of the Assyrians, the first place is challenged by their palaces. Less religious, or more servile, than the Egyptians and the Greeks, they make their temples insignificant in comparison with the dwellings of their kings, to which indeed the temple is most commonly a sort of appendage. In the palace their art culminates—there every effort is made, every ornament lavished. If the architecture of the Assyrian palaces be fully considered, very little need be said on the subject of their other buildings.

The Assyrian palace stood uniformly on an artificial platform. Commonly this platform was composed of sun-dried-bricks in regular layers; but occasionally the material used was merely earth or rubbish, excepting towards the exposed parts—the sides and the surface which were always either of brick or of stone. In most cases the sides were protected by massive stone masonry, carried perpendicularly from the natural ground to a height somewhat exceeding that of the plat-form, and either made plain at the top or else crowned with stone battlements cut into gradines. The pavement consisted in part of stone slabs, part of kiln-dried bricks of a large size, often as much as two feet square. The stone slabs were sometimes inscribed, sometimes ornamented with an elegant pattern. (See [PLATE XLI., Fig. 2.]) Occasionally the terrace was divided into portions at different elevations, which were connected by staircases or inclined planes. The terrace communicated in the same way with the level ground at its base, being (as is probable) sometimes ascended in a single place, sometimes in several. These ascents were always on the side where the palace adjoined upon the neighboring town, and were thus protected from hostile attack by the town walls. [PLATE XLI., Fig. 1] Where the palace abutted upon the walls or projected beyond them—and the palace was always placed at the edge of a town, for the double advantage, probably, of a clear view and of fresh air—the platform rose perpendicularly or nearly so; and generally a water protection, a river, a moat, or a broad lake, lay at its base, thus rendering attack, except on the city side, almost impossible.

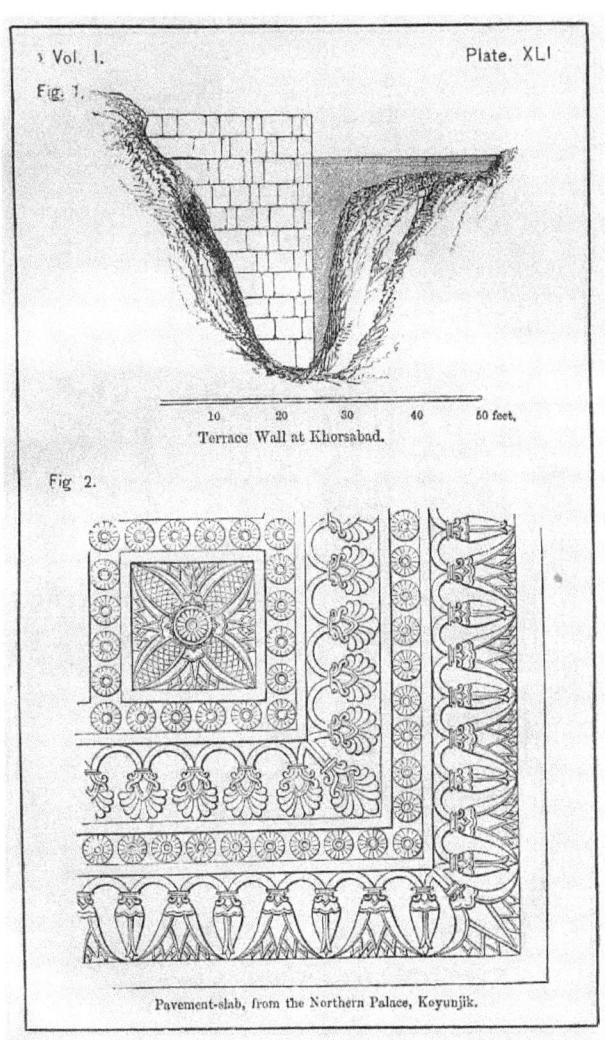

Terrace Wall at Khorsabad.

Pavement-slab, from the Northern Palace, Koyunjik.

PLATE XLI

The platform appears to have been, in general shape, a rectangle, or where it had different elevations, to have been composed of a rectangles. The mound of Khorsabad, which is of this latter character, resembles a gigantic T. [PLATE XLII., Fig. 1.]

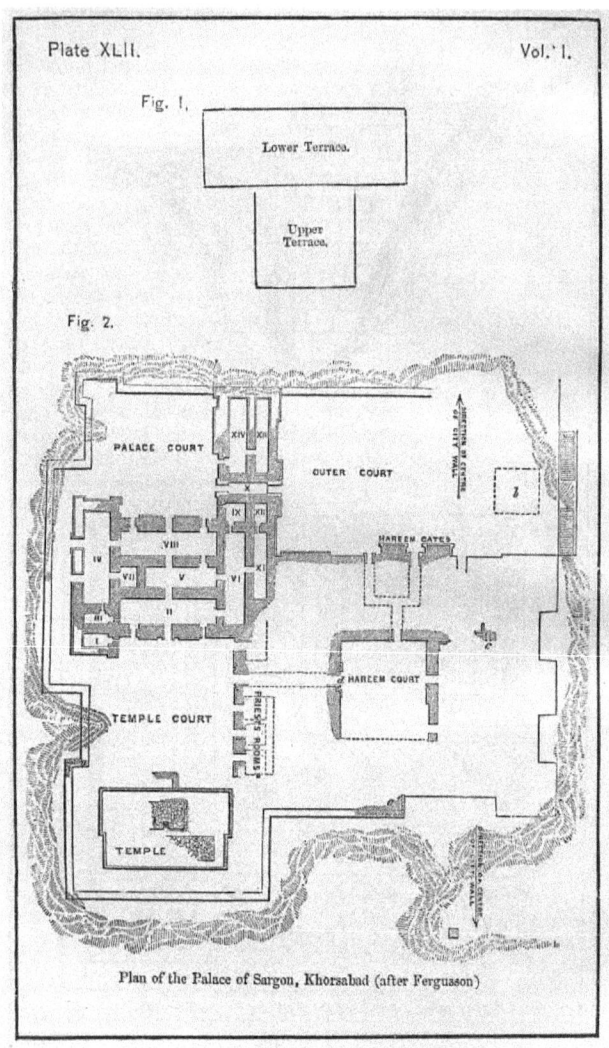

Plan of the Palace of Sargon, Khorsabad (after Fergusson)

PLATE XLII

It must not be supposed, however, that the rectangle was always exact. Sometimes its outline was broken by angular projections and indentations, as in the plan [PLATE XLII., Fig. 21.] where the shaded parts represent actual discoveries. Sometimes it grew to be irregular, by the addition of fresh portions, as new kings arose who determined on fresh erections. This is the ease at Nimrud, where the platform broadens towards its lower or southern end, and still more at Koyunjik and Nebbi Yunus, where the rectangular idea has been so overlaid as to have almost wholly disappeared. Palaces were commonly placed near one edge of the mound—more especially near the river edge probably for the better enjoyment of the prospect, and of the cool air over the water.

The palace itself was composed of three main elements, courts, grand halls, and small private apartments. A palace has usually from two to four courts, which are either square or oblong, and vary in size according to the general scale of the building. In the north-west palace at Nimrud, the most ancient of the edifices yet explored, one court only has been found, the dimensions of which are 120 feet by 90. At Khorsabad, the palace of Sargon has four courts. [PLATE XLII., Fig. 2.] Three of them are nearly square, the largest of these measuring 180 feet each Way, and the smallest about 120 feet; the fourth is oblong, and must have been at least 250 feet long and 150 feet wide. The palace of Sennacherib at Koyunjik, a much larger edifice than the palace of Sargon, has also three courts, which are respectively 93 feet by 84, 124 feet by 90, and 154 feet by 125. Esarhaddon's palace at Nimrud has a court 220 feet long and 100 wide. These courts were all paved either with baked bricks of large size, or with stone slabs, which were frequently patterned. Sometimes the courts were surrounded with buildings; sometimes they abutted upon the edge of the platform: in this latter case they were protected by a stone parapet, which (at least in places) was six feet high.

The grand halls of the Assyrian palaces constitute their most remarkable feature. Each palace has commonly several. They are apartments narrow for their length, measuring from three to five times their own width, and thus having always somewhat the appearance of galleries. The scale upon which they are built is, commonly, magnificent. In the palace of Asshur-izir-pal at Nimrud, the earliest of the discovered edifices, the great hall was 160 feet long by nearly 40 broad. In Sargon's palace at Khorsabad the size of no single room was so great; but the number of halls was remarkable, there being no fewer than five of nearly equal dimensions. The largest was 116 feet long, and 33 wide; the smallest 87 feet long, and 25 wide. The palace of Sennacherib at Koyuhjik contained the most spacious apartment yet exhumed. It was immediately inside the great portal, and extended in length 180 feet, with a uniform width of forty feet. In one instance only, so far as appears, was an attempt made to exceed this width. In the palace of Esarhaddon, the son of Sennacherib, a hall was designed intended to surpass all former ones. [PLATE XLIII., Fig. 2.] Its length was to be 165 feet, and its width 62; consequently it would have been nearly one-third larger than the great hall of Sennacherib, its area exceeding 10,000 square feet. But the builder who had designed this grand structure appears to have been unable to overcome the difficulty of carrying a roof over so vast an expanse. He was therefore obliged to divide his hall by a wall down the middle; which, though he broke it in an unusual way into portions, and kept it at some distance from both ends of the apartment, still had the actual effect of subdividing his grand room into four apartments of only moderate size. The halls were paved with sun-burnt brick. They were ornamented throughout by the elaborate sculptures, now so familiar to us, carried generally in a single, but sometimes in a double line, round the four walls of the apartment. The sculptured slabs rested on the ground, and clothed the walls to the height of 10 or 12 feet. Above, for a space which we cannot positively fix, but which was certainly not less than four or five feet, the crude brick wall was continued, faced here with burnt brick enamelled on the side towards the apartment, pleasingly and sometimes even brilliantly colored. 10 The whole height of the walls was probably from 15 to 20 feet.

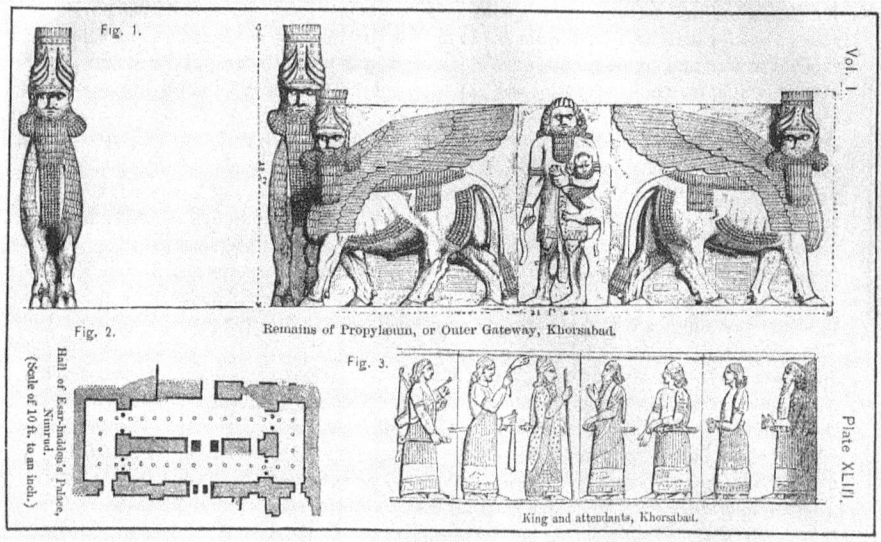

PLATE XLIII

By the side of the halls, or at their ends, and opening into them, or sometimes collected together into groups, with no hall near, are the smaller chambers of which mention has been already made. These chambers are in every case rectangular: in their proportions they vary from squares to narrow oblongs. 90 feet by 17, 85 by 16, 80 by 15, and the like. When they are square, the side is never more than about 25 feet. They are often as richly decorated as the halls, but sometimes are merely faced with plain slabs or plastered; while occasionally they have no facing at all, but exhibit throughout the crude brick. This, however, is unusual.

The number of chambers in a palace is very large. In Sennacherib's palace at Koyunjik, where great part of the building remains still unexplored, the excavated chambers amount to sixty-eight—all, be it remembered, upon the ground floor. The space covered by them and by their walls exceeds 40,000 square yards. As Mr. Fergusson observes, "the imperial palace of Sennacherib is, of all the buildings of antiquity, surpassed in magnitude only by the great palace-temple of Karnak; and when we consider the vastness of the mound on which it was raised, and the richness of the ornaments with which it was adorned, it is by no means clear that it was not as great, or at least as expensive, a work as the great palace-temple at Thebes." Elsewhere the excavated apartments are less numerous; but in no case is it probable that a palace contained on its ground floor fewer than forty or fifty chambers.

The most striking peculiarity which the ground-plans of the palaces disclose is the uniform adoption throughout of straight and parallel lines. No plan exhibits a curve of any kind, or any angle but a right angle. Courts, chambers, and halls are, in most cases, exact rectangles; and even where any variety occurs, it is only by the introduction of squared recesses or projections, which are moreover shallow and infrequent. When a palace has its own special platform, the lines of the building are further exactly parallel with those of the mound on which it is placed; and the parallelism extends to any other detached buildings that there may be anywhere upon the platform. When a mound is occupied by more palaces than one, sometimes this law still obtains, as at Nimrud, where it seems to embrace at any rate the greater number of the palaces; sometimes, as at Koyunjik, the rule ceases to be observed, and the ground-plan of each palace seems formed separately and independently, with no reference to any neighboring edifice.

Apart from this feature, the buildings do not affect much regularity. In courts and facades, to a certain extent, there is correspondence; but in the internal arrangements, regularity is decidedly the exception. The two sides of an edifice never correspond; room never answers to room; doorways are rarely in the middle of walls; where a rooms has several doorways, they are seldom opposite to one another, or in situations at all corresponding.

There is a great awkwardness in the communications. Very few corridors or passages exist in any of the buildings. Groups of rooms, often amounting to ten or twelve, open into one another; and we find comparatively few rooms to which there is any access except through some other room. Again, whole sets of apartments are sometimes found, between which and the rest of the palace all communication is cut off by thick walls. Another peculiarity in the internal arrangements is the number of doorways in the larger apartments, and their apparently needless multiplication. We constantly find two or even three doorways leading from a court into a hall, or from one hall into a second. It is difficult to see what could be gained by such an arrangement.

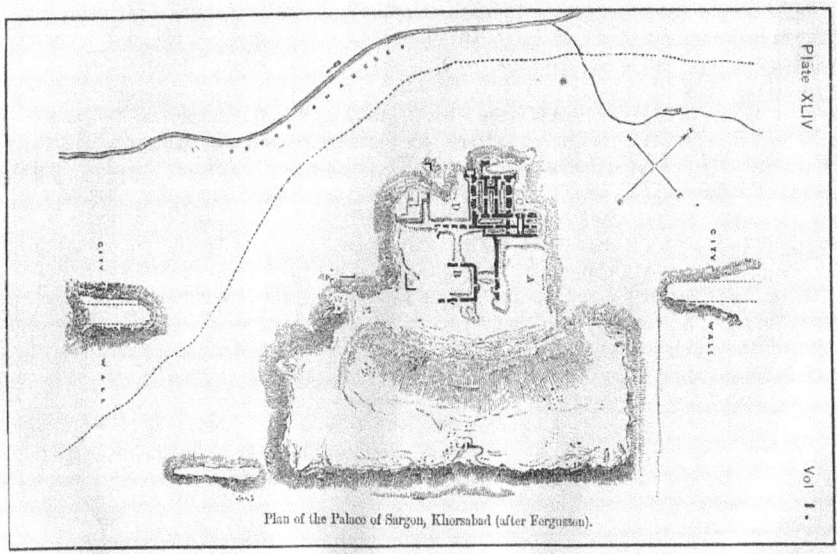

Plan of the Palace of Sargon, Khorsabad (after Fergusson).

PLATE XLIV

The disposition of the various parts of a palace will probably be better apprehended from an exact account of a single building than from any further general statements. For this purpose it is necessary to select a specimen from among the various edifices that have been disentombed by the labors of recent excavators. The specimen should be, if possible, complete; it should have been accurately surveyed, and the survey should have been scientifically recorded; it should further stand single and separate, that there may be no danger of confusion between its remains and those of adjacent edifices. These requirements, though nowhere exactly met, are very nearly met by the building at Khorsabad, which stands on a mound of its own, unmixed with other edifices, has been most carefully examined, and most excellently represented and described, and which, though not completely excavated, has been excavated with a nearer approach to completeness than any other edifice in Assyria. The Khorsabad building—which is believed to be a palace built by Sargon, the son of Sennacherib—will therefore be selected for minute description in this place, as the palace most favorably circumstanced, and the one of which we have, on the whole, the most complete and exact knowledge. [PLATE XLIV.]

The situation of the town, whereof the palace of Sargon formed a part, has been already described in a former part of this volume. The shape, it has been noted, was square, the angles facing the four cardinal points. Almost exactly in the centre of the north-west wall occurs the palace platform, a huge mass of crude brick, from 20 to 30 feet high, shaped like a T, the upper limb lying within the city walls, and the lower limb (which is at a higher elevation) projecting beyond the line of the walls to a distance of at least 500 feet. At present there is a considerable space between the ends of the wall and the palace mound; but anciently it is provable that they either abutted on the mound, or were separated from it merely by gateways. The mound, or at any rate the part of it which projected beyond the walls, was faced with hewn stone, carried perpendicularly from the plain to the top of the platform, and even beyond, so as to form a parapet protecting the edge of the platform. On the more elevated portion of the mound—that which projected beyond the walls stood the palace, consisting of three groups of buildings, the principal group lying towards the mound's northern angle. On the lower portion of the platform were several detached buildings, the most remarkable being a huge gateway or propylaeum, through which the entrance lay to the palace from the city. Beyond and below this, on the level of the city, the first or outer portals were placed, giving entrance to a court in front of the lower terrace.

A visitor approaching the palace had in the first place to pass through these portals. They were ornamented with colossal human-headed bulls on either side, and probably spanned by an arch above, the archivolte being covered with enamelled bricks disposed in a pattern. Received within the portals, the visitor found himself in front of a long wall of solid stone masonry, the revetement of the lower terrace, which rose from the outer court to a height of at least twenty feet. Either an inclined-way or a flight of steps—probably the latter—must have led up from the outer court to this terrace. Here the visitor found another portal or propylaeum of a magnificent character. [PLATE XLIII., Fig. 1.] Midway in the south-east side of the lower terrace, and about fifty feet from its edge, stood this grand portal, gateway ninety-feet in width, and at least twenty-five in depth, having on each side three winged bulls of gigantic size, two of them fifteen feet high, and the third nineteen feet. Between the two small bulls, which styled back to back, presenting their sides to the spectator, was a colossal figure, strangling a lion—the Assyria Hercules, according to most writers. The larger bulls stood at right angles to these figures, withdrawn within the portal, and facing the spectator. The space between the bulls, which is nearly twenty feet, was (it is probable) arched over. Perhaps the archway led into a chamber beyond which was a second archway and an inner portal, as marked in Mr. Fergusson's plan: but this is at present uncertain.

Besides the great portal, the only buildings as yet discovered on this lower platform, are a suite of not very extensive apartments. They are remarkable for their ornamentation. The walls are neither lined with slabs, nor yet (as is sometimes the case) painted, but the plaster of which they are composed is formed into sets of half pillars or reeding, separated from one another by pilasters with square sunk panels. The former kind of ornamentation is found also in Lower Chaldaea, and has been already represented; the latter is peculiar to this building. It is suggested that these apartments formed the quarters of the soldiers who kept watch over the royal residence.

About 300 feet from the outer edge of the lower terrace, the upper terrace seems to have commenced. It was raised probably about ten feet above the lower one. The mode of access has not been discovered, but is presumed to have been by a flight of steps, not directly opposite the propylaeum, but somewhat to the right, whereby entrance was given to the great court, into which opened the main gateways of the palace itself. The court was probably 250 feet long by 160 or 170 feet wide. The visitor, on mounting the steps, perhaps passed through another propylaeum (b in the plan); after which, if his business was with the monarch, he crossed the full length of the court, leaving a magnificent triple entrance, which is thought to have led to the king's hareem, on his left and making his way to the public gate of the palace, which fronted him when he mounted the steps. The hareem portal, which he passed, resembled in the main the great propylaeum of the lower platform; but, being triple, it was still more magnificent exhibiting two other entrances on either side of the main one, guarded each by a single pair of winged bulls of the smaller size. Along the hareem wall, from the gateway to the angle of the court, was a row of sculptured bas-reliefs, ten feet in height, representing the monarch with his attendant guards and officers. [PLATE XLIII., Fig. 3.] The facade occupying the end of the court was of inferior grandeur. [PLATE XLV., Fig.1.] Sculptures similar to those along the hareem wall adorned it; but its centre showed only a single gateway, guarded by one pair of the larger bulls, fronting the spectator, and standing each in a sort of recess, the character of which will be best understood by the ground-plan in the illustration. Just inside the bulls was the great door of the palace, a single door made of wood-apparently of mulberry,—opening inwards, and fastened on the inside by a bolt at bottom, and also by an enormous lock. This door gave entrance into a passage, 70 feet long and about 10 feet wide, paved with large slabs of stone, and adorned on either side with inscriptions, and with a double row of sculptures, representing the arrival of tribute and gifts for the monarch. All the figures here faced one way, towards the inner palace court into which the passage led. M. Botta believes that the passage was uncovered; while Mx. Fergusson imagines that it was vaulted throughout. It must in any case have been lighted from above; for it would have been impossible to read the inscriptions, or even to see the sculptures, merely by the light admitted at the two ends.

PLATE XLV

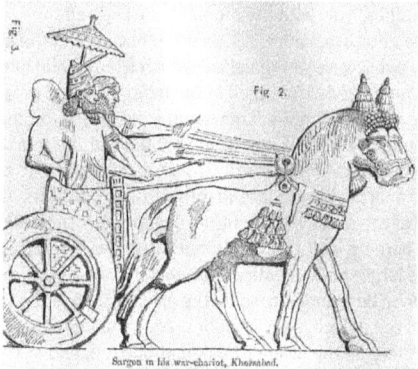

Sargon in his war-chariot, Khorsabad.

PLATE XLVA

From the passage in question—one of the few in the edifice—no doorway opened out either on the right hand or on the left. The visitor necessarily proceeded along its whole extent, as he saw the figures proceeding in sculptures, and, passing through a second portal, found himself in the great inner court of the palace, a square of about 100 or 160 feet, enclosed on two sides—the south-east and the south-west-by buildings, on the other two sides reaching to the edge of the terrace, which here gave upon, the open country. The buildings on the south-eastside, looking towards the north-west, and and joining the gateway by which the had entered, were of comparatively minor importance. They consisted of a few chambers suitable for officers of the court, and were approached from the court by two doorways, one on either side of the passage through which he had come. To his left, looking towards the north-east, were the great state apartments, the principal part of the palace, forming a facade, of which some idea may perhaps be formed from the representation. [PLATE XLVI.] The upper part of this representation is indeed purely conjectural; and when we come to consider the mode in which the Assyrian palaces were roofed and lighted, we shall perhaps find reason to regard it as not very near the truth; but the lower part, up to the top of the sculptures, the court itself, and the various accessories, are correctly given, and furnish the only perspective view of this part of the palace which has been as yet published.

North-West Court of Sargon's Palace at Khorsabad, restored. (After Fergusson.)

The great state apartments consisted of a suite of ten rooms. Five of these were halls of large dimensions; one was a long and somewhat narrow chamber, and the remaining four were square or slightly oblong apartments of minor consequence. All of them were lined throughout with sculpture. The most important seem to have been three halls en-suite (VIII., V., and II. in the plan), which are, both in their external and internal decorations, by far the most splendid of the whole palace. The first lay just within the north-east facade, and ran parallel to it. It was entered by three doorways, the central one ornamented externally. with two colossal bulls of the largest size, one on either side within the entrance, and with two pairs of smaller bulls, back to back, on the projecting pylons; the side ones guarded by winged genii, human or hawk-headed. The length of the chamber was 116 feet 6 inches, and its breadth 33 feet. Its sculptures represented the monarch receiving prisoners, and either personally or by deputy punishing them: [PLATE XLV., Fig. 3.] We may call it, for distinction's sake, "the Hall of Punishment."

The second hall (V. in the plan) ran parallel with the first, but did not extend along its whole length. It measured from end to end about 86 feet, and from side to side 21 feet 6 inches. Two doorways led into it from the first chamber, and two others led from it into two large apartments. One communicated with a lateral hall (marked VI. in the plan), the other with the third hall of the suite which is here the special object of our attention. This third hall (II. in the plan) was of the same length as the first, but was less wide by about three feet. It opened by three doorways upon a square, court, which has been called "the Temple Court," from a building on one side of it which will be described presently.

The sculptures of the second and third halls represented in a double row, separated by an inscribed space about two feet in width, chiefly the wars of the monarch, his battles, sieges, reception of captives and of spoil, etc. The monarch himself appeared at least four times standing in his chariot, thrice in calm procession, and once shooting his arrows against his enemies. [PLATE XLV., Fig. 2.] Besides these, the upper sculptures on one side exhibited sacred ceremonies.

Placed at right angles to this primary suite of three halls were two others, one (IV. in the plan) of dimensions little, if at all, inferior to those of the largest (No. VIII), the other (VI. in the plan) nearly of the same length, but as narrow as the narrowest of the three (No. V.). Of these two lateral halls the former communicated directly with No. VIII., and also by a narrow passage room (III. in the plan with No. II.) The other had direct communication both with No. II and No. V., but none with No. VIII. With this hall (No. VI.) three smaller chambers were connected (Nos. IX., XI., and XI.); with the other lateral hall, two only (Nos. III. and VII.). One chamber attached to this block of buildings (I. in the plan) opened only on the Temple Court. It has been suggested that it contained a staircase; but of this there is no evidence.

The Temple Court—a square of 150 feet—was occupied by buildings on three sides, and open on one only—that to the north-west. The state apartments closed it in on the north-east, the temple on the south-west: on the south-east it was bounded by the range of buildings called "Priests' Rooms" in the plan, chambers of less pretension than almost any that have been excavated. The principal facade here was that of the state apartments, on the north-east. On this, as on the opposite side of the palace, were three portals; but the two fronts were not of equal magnificence. On the side of the Temple Court a single pair of bulls, facing the spectator, guarded the middle portals; the side portals exhibited only figures of genii, while the spaces between the portals were occupied, not with bulls, but merely with a series of human figures, resembling those in the first or outer court, of which a representation has been already given. Two peculiarities marked the south-east facade. In the first place, it lay in a perfectly straight line, unbroken by any projection, which is very unusual in Assyrian architecture. In the second place, as if to compensate for this monotony in its facial line, it was pierced by no fewer than five doorways, all of considerable width, and two of them garnished with bulls, of namely, the second and the fourth. The bulls of the second gateway were of the larger, those of the fourth were of the smaller size; they stood in the usual manner, a little withdrawn within the gateways and looking towards the spectator.

Of the curious building which closed in the court on the third or south-west side, which is believed to have been a temple, the remains are unfortunately very slight. It stood so near the edge of the terrace that the greater part of it has fallen into the plain. Less than half of the ground-plan is left, and only a few feet of the elevation. The building may originally have been a square, or it may have been an oblong, as represented in the plan. It was approached from the court by a a flight of stone stops, probably six in number, of which four remain in place. This flight of steps was placed directly opposite to the central door of the south-west palace facade. From the level of the court, to that of the top of the steps, a height of about six feet, a solid platform of crude brick was raised as a basis for the temple; and this was faced, probably throughout its whole extent, with a solid wall of hard black basalt, ornamented with a cornice in gray limestone, of which the accompanying figures are representations. [PLATE. XLV., Fig. 4.] above this the external work has disappeared. Internally, two chambers may be traced, floored with a mixture of the stones and chalk; and round one of these are some fragments of bas-reliefs, representing sacred subjects, cut on the same black basalt as that by which the platform is cased, and sufficient to show that the same style of ornamentation prevailed here as in the palace.

The principal doorway on the north-west side of the Temple Court communicated by a passage, with another and similar doorway (d on the plan), which opened into a fourth court, the smallest and least ornamented of those on the upper platform.

The mass of building whereof this court occupied the centre, is believed to have constituted the hareem or private apartments of the monarch. It adjoined the state apartments at its northern angle, but had no direct communication with them. To enter it from them the visitor had either to cross the Temple Court and proceed by the passage above indicated, or else to go round by the great entrance (X in the plan) and obtain admission by the grand portals on the south-west side of the outer court. These latter portals, it is to be observed, are so placed as to command no view into the Hareem Court, though it is opposite to them. The passages by which they gave entrance into that court must have formed some such angles as those marked by the dotted lines in the plan, the result being that visitors, while passing through the outer court, would be unable to catch any sight of what was going on in the Hareem Court. even if the great doors happened to be open. Those admitted so far into the palace as the Temple Court were more favored or less feared. The doorway (d) on the south-east side of the Hareem Court is exactly opposite the chief doorway on the north-west side of the Temple Court, and there can be no reasonable doubt that a straight passage connected the two.

It is uncertain whether the Hareem Court was surrounded by buildings on every side, or open towards the south-west. M. Botta believed that it was open; and the analogy of the other courts would seem to make this probable. It is to be regretted, however, that this portion of the great Khorsabad ruin still remains so incompletely examined. Consisting of the private apartments, it is naturally less rich in sculptures than other parts; and hence it has been comparatively neglected. The labor would, nevertheless, be well employed which should be devoted to this part of the ruin, as it would give us (what we do not now possess) the complete ground-plan of an Assyrian palace. It is earnestly to be hoped that future excavators will direct their efforts to this easily attainable and interesting object.

The ground-pins of the palaces, and some sixteen feet of their elevations, are all that fire and time have left us of these remarkable monuments. The total destruction of the upper portion of every palatial building in Assyria, combined with the want of any representation of the royal residences upon the bas-reliefs, reduces us to mere conjecture with respect to their height, to the mode in which they were roofed and lighted, and even to the question whether they had or had not an upper story. On these subjects various views have been put forward by persons entitled to consideration; and to these it is proposed now to direct the reader's attention.

In the first place, then, had they an upper story? Mr. Layard and Mr. Fergusson decide this question in the affirmative. Mr. Layard even goes so far as to say that the fact is one which "can no longer be doubted." He rests this conclusion on two grounds first, on a belief that "upper chambers" are mentioned in the Inscriptions, and, secondly, on the discovery by himself, in Sennacherib's palace at Koyunjik, of what seemed to be an inclined way, by which he supposes that the ascent was made to an upper story. The former of these two arguments must be set aside as wholly uncertain. The interpretation of the architectural inscriptions of the Assyrians is a matter of far too much doubt at present to serve as a groundwork upon which theories can properly be raised as to the plan of their buildings. With regard to the inclined passage, it is to be observed that it did not appear to what it led. It may have conducted to a gallery looking into one of the great halls, or to an external balcony overhanging an outer court; or it may have been the ascent to the top of a tower, whence a look-out was kept up and down the river. Is it not more likely that this ascent should have been made for some exceptional purpose, than that it should be the only specimen left of the ordinary mode by which one half of a palace was rendered accessible? It is to be remembered that no remains of a staircase, whether of stone or of wood have been found in any of the palaces, and that there is no other instance in any of them even of an inclined passage. Those who think the palaces had second stories, believe these stories to have been reached by staircases of wood, placed in various parts of the buildings, which were totally destroyed by the conflagrations in which the palaces perished. But it is at least remarkable that no signs have been found in any existing walls of rests for the ends of beams, or of anything implying staircases. Hence M. Botta, the most careful and the most scientific of recent excavators, came to a very positive conclusion that the Khorsabad buildings had had no second story, a conclusion which it would not, perhaps, be very bold to extend to Assyrian edifices generally.

It has been urged by Mr. Fergusson that there must have been an upper story, because otherwise all the advantage of the commanding position of the palaces, perched on their lofty platforms, would have been lost. The platform at Khorsabad was protected, in the only places where its edge has been laid bare, by a stone wall or parapet six feet in height. Such a parapet continued along the whole of the platform would effectually have shut out all prospect of the open country, both from the platform itself and also from the gateways of the palace, which are on the same level. Nor could there well be any view at all from the ground chambers, which had no windows, at any rate within fifteen feet of the floor. To enjoy a view of anything but the dead wall skirting the mound, it was necessary (Mr. Fergusson thinks) to mount to a second story, which he ingeniously places, not over the ground rooms, but on the top of the outer and party walls, whose structure is so massive that their area falls (he observes) but little short of the area of the ground-rooms themselves.

This reasoning is sufficiently answered, in the first place, by observing that we know not whether the Assyrians appreciated the advantage of a view, or raised their palace platforms for any such object. They may have constructed them for security only, or for greater dignity and greater seclusion. They may have looked chiefly for comfort and have reared them in order to receive the benefit of every breeze, and at the same time to be above the elevation to which gnats and mosquitoes commonly rise. Or there may be a fallacy in concluding, from the very slight data furnished by the excavations of M. Botta, that a palace platform was, in any case, skirted along its whole length, by a six-foot parapet. Nothing is more probable than that in places the Khorsabad parapet may have been very much lower than this; and elsewhere it is not even ascertained that any parapet at all edged the platform. On the whole we seem to have no right to conclude, merely on account of the small portions of parapet wall uncovered by M. Botta, that an upper story was a necessity to the palaces. If the Assyrians valued a view, they may easily have made their parapets low in places: if they cared so little for it as to shut it out from all their halls and terraces, they may not improbably have dispensed with the advantage altogether.

The two questions of the roofing and lighting of the Assyrian palaces are so closely connected together that they will most conveniently be treated in combination. The first conjecture published on the subject of roofing was that of M. Flandin. who suggested that the chambers generally—the great halls at any rate—had been ceiled with a brick vault. He thought that the complete filling up of the apartments to the height of fifteen or twenty feet was thus best explained; and he believed that there were traces of the fallen vaulting in the debris with which the apartments were filled. His conjecture was combated, soon after he put it forth, by M. Botta, who gave it as his opinion—first, that the walls of the chambers, notwithstanding their great thickness, would have been unable, considering their material, to sustain the weight, and (still more to bear) the lateral thrust, of a vaulted roof; and, secondly, that such a roof, if it had existed at all, must have been made of baked brick or stone-crude brick being too weak for the purpose—and when it fell must have left ample traces of itself within the apartments, whereas, in none of them, though he searched, could he find any such traces. On this latter point M. Botta and M. Flandin—both eye witnesses—were at variance. M. Flandin believed that he had seen such traces, not only in numerous broken fragments of burnt brick strewn through all the chambers, but in occasional masses of brick-work contained in some of them actual portions, as he thought, of the original vaulting. M. Botta, however, observed—first, that the quantity of baked brick within the chambers was quite insufficient for a vaulted roof; and, secondly, that the position of the masses of brickwork noticed by M. Flandin was always towards the sides, never towards the centres of the apartments; a clear proof that they had fallen from the upper part of the walls above the sculptures, and not from a ceiling covering the whole room. He further observed that the quantity of charred wood and charcoal within the chambers, and the calcined appearance of all the slabs, were phenomena incompatible with any other theory than that of the destruction of the palace by the conflagration of a roof mainly of wood.

To these arguments of M. Botta may be added another from the improbability of the Assyrians being sufficiently advanced in architectural science to be able to construct an arch of the width necessary to cover some of the chambers. The principle of the arch was, indeed, as will be hereafter shown, well known to the Assyrians, but hitherto we possess no proof that they were capable of applying it on a large scale. The widest arch which has been found in any of the buildings is that of the Khorsabad town-gate uncovered by M. Place, which spans a space of (at most) fourteen or fifteen feet. But the great halls of the Assyrian palaces have a width of twenty-five, thirty, and even forty feet. It is at any rate uncertain whether the constructive skill of their architects could have grappled successfully with the difficulty of throwing a vault over so wide an interval as even the least of these.

M. Botta, after objecting, certainly with great force, to the theory of M. Flandin, proceeded to suggest a theory of his own. After carefully reviewing all the circumstances, he gave it as his opinion that the Khorsabad building had been roofed throughout with a flat, earth-covered roofing of wood. He observed that some of the buildings on the bas-reliefs had flat roofs, that flat roofs are still the fashion of the country, and that the debris within the chambers were exactly such as a roof of that kind would be likely, if destroyed by fire, to have produced. He further noticed that on the floors of the chambers, in various parts of the palace, there had been discovered stone rollers closely resembling those still in use at Mosul and Baghdad, for keeping close-pressed and hard the earthen surface of such roofs; which rollers had, in all probability, been applied to the same use by the Assyrians, and, being kept on the roofs, had fallen through during the conflagration.

The first difficulty which presented itself here was one of those regarded as most fatal to the vaulting theory, namely, the width of the chambers. Where flat timber roofs prevail in the East, their span seems never to exceed twenty-five feet. The ordinary chambers in the Assyrian palaces might, undoubtedly, therefore, have been roofed in this way, by a series of horizontal beans laid across them from side to side, with the ends resting upon the tops of the side walls. But the great halls seemed too wide to have borne such a roofing without supports. Accordingly, M. Botts suggested that in the greater apartments a single or a double row of pillars ran down the middle, reaching to the roof and sustaining it. His theory was afterwards warmly embraced by Mr. Fergusson, who endeavored to point out the exact position of the pillars in the three great halls of Sargon at Khorsabad. It seems, however, a strong and almost a fatal objection to this theory, that no bases of pillars have been found within the apartments, nor any marks on the brick floors of such bases or of the pressure of the pillars. M. Botta states that he made a careful search for bases, or for marks of pillars, on the pavement of the north-east hall (No. VIII.) at Khorsabad, but that he entirely failed to discover any. This negative evidence is the more noticeable as stone pillar-bases have been found in wide doorways, where they would have been less necessary than in the chambers, as pillars in doorways could have had but little weight to sustain.

M. Botta and Mr. Fergusson, who both suppose that in an Assyrian palace the entire edifice was roofed in, and only the courts left open to the sky, suggest two very different modes by which the buildings may have been lighted. M. Botta brings light in from the roof by means of wooden louvres, such as are still employed for the purpose in Armenia and parts of India, whereof he gives the representation which is reproduced. [PLATE XLVII., Fig. 7.] Mr. Fergusson introduces light from the sides, by supposing that the roof did not rest directly on the walls, but on rows of wooden pillars placed along the edge of the walls both internally towards the apartments and externally towards the outer air. The only ground for this supposition, which is of a very startling character, seems to be the occurrence in a single bas-relief, representing a city in Armenia, of what is regarded as a similar arrangement. But it must be noted that the lower portion of the building, represented opposite, bears no resemblance at all to the same part of an Assyrian palace, since in it perpendicular lines prevail, whereas, in the Assyrian palaces, the lower hues were almost wholly horizontal; and that it is not even Certain that the upper portion, where the pillars occur, is an arrangement for admitting light, since it may be merely an ornamentation.

The difficulties attaching to every theory of roofing and lighting which places the whole of an Assyrian palace under covert, has led some to suggest that the system actually adopted in the larger apartments was that hypoethral one which is generally believed to have prevailed in the Greek temples, and which was undoubtedly followed in the ordinary Roman house. Mr. Layard was the first to post forward the view that the larger halls, at any rate, were uncovered, a projecting ledge, sufficiently wide to afford shelter and shade, being carried round the four sides of the apartment while the centre remained open to the sky. The objections taken to this view are—first, that far too much heat and light would thereby have been admitted into the palace; secondly, that in the rainy season far too much rain would have come in for comfort; and, thirdly, that the pavement of the halls, being mere sun-dried brick, would, under such circumstances, have been turned into mud. If these objections are not removed, they would be, at any rate, greatly lessened by supposing the roofing to have extended to two-thirds or three-fourths of the apartment, and the opening to have been comparatively narrow. We may also suppose that on very bright and on very rainy days carpets or other awnings were stretched across the opening, which furnished a tolerable defence against the weather.

On the whole, our choice seems to lie—so far as the great halls are concerned—between this theory of the mode in which they were roofed and lighted, and a supposition from which archaeologists have hitherto shrunk, namely, that they were actually spanned from side to side by beams. If we remember that the Assyrians did not content themselves with the woods produced in their own country, but habitually cut timber in the forests of distant regions, as, for instance, of Amanus, Hermon, and Lebanon, which they conveyed to Nineveh, we shall perhaps not think it impassible that they may have been able to accomplish the feat of roofing in this simple fashion even chambers of thirteen or fourteen yards in width. Mr. Layard observes that rooms of almost equal width with the Assyrian halls are to this day covered in with beams laid horizontally from side to side in many parts of Mesopotamia, although the only timber used is that furnished by the indigenous palms and poplars. May not more have been accomplished in this way by the Assyrain architects, who had at their disposal the lofty firs and cedars of the above mentioned regions?

If the halls were roofed in this way, they may have been lighted by louvres; or the upper portion of the walls, which is now destroyed, may have been pierced by windows, which are of frequent occurrence, and seem generally to be some-what high placed, in the representations of buildings upon the sculptures. [PLATE XLVII Fig. 3.]

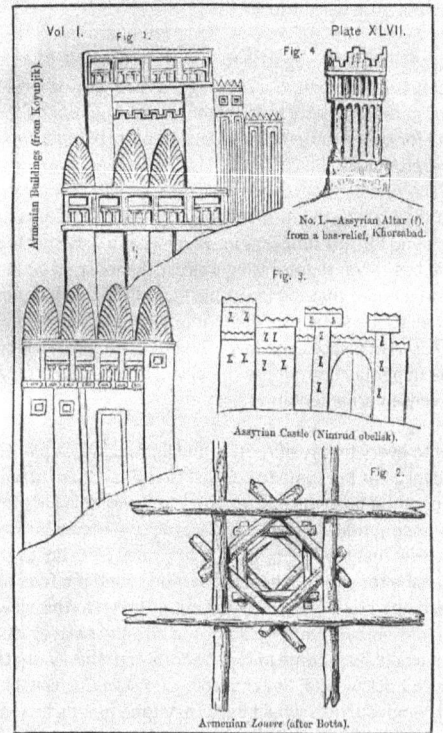

PLATE XLVII

It might have been expected that the difficulties with respect to Assyrian roofing and lighting which have necessitated this long discussion, would have received illustration, or even solution, from the forms of buildings which occur so frequently on the bas-reliefs. But this is not found to be the actual result. The forms are rarely Assyrian, since they occur commonly in the sculptures which represent the foreign campaigns of the kings; and they have the appearance of being to a great extent conventional, being nearly the same, whatever country is the object of attack. In the few cases where there is ground for regarding the building as native and not foreign, it is never palatial, but belongs either to sacred or to domestic architecture. Thus the monumental representations of Assyrian buildings which have come down to us, throw little or no light on the construction of their palaces. As, however, they have an interest of their own, and will serve to illustrate in some degree the domestic and sacred architecture of the people, some of the most remarkable of them will be here introduced.

PLATE XLVIII

The representation No. I. is from a slab at Khorsabad. [PLATE XLVII., Fig. 4.] It is placed on the summit of a hill, and is regarded by M. Botta as an altar. No. II. is from the same slab. [PLATE XLIX., Fig. 1.] It stands at the foot of the hill crowned by No. I. It has been called a "fishing pavilion;" but it is most probably a small temple, since it bears a good deal of resemblance to other representations which are undoubted temples, as (particularly) to No. V. No. III., which is from Lord Aberdeen's black stone, is certainly a temple, since it is accompanied by a priest, a sacred tree, and an ox for sacrifice. [PLATE XLIX., Fig. 2.] The representation No. IV. is also thought to be a temple. [PLATE XLIX., Fig. 3.] It is of earlier date than any of the others, being taken from a slab belonging to the North-west Palace at Nimrud, and is remarkable in many ways. First, the want of symmetry is curious, and unusual. Irregular as are the palaces of the Assyrian kings, there is for the most part no want of regularity in their sacred buildings. The two specimens here adduced (No. II. and No. III.) are proof of this; and such remains of actual temples as exist are in accordance with the sculptures in this particular. The right-hand aisle in No. IV., having nothing correspondent to it on the other side, is thus an anomaly in Assyrian architecture. The patterning of the pillars with chevrons is also remarkable; and their capitals are altogether unique. No. V. is a temple of a more elaborate character. [PLATE XLIX., Fig. 4.] It is from the sculptures of Asshur-banipal, the son of Esar-haddon, and possesses several features of great interest. The body of the temple is a columnar structure, exhibiting at either corner a broad pilaster surmounted by a capital composed of two sets of volutes placed one over the other. Between the two pilasters are two pillars resting upon very extraordinary rounded bases, and crowned by capitals not unlike the Corinthian. We might have supposed the bases mere figments of the sculptor, but for an independent evidence of the actual employment by the Assyrians of rounded pillar-bases. Mr. Layard discovered at Koyunjik a set of "circular pedestals," whereof he gives the representation which is figured. [PLATE LI., Fig. 1.] They appeared to form part of a double line of similar objects, extending from the edge of the platform to an entrance of the palace, and probably (as Mr. Layard suggests) supported the wooden pillars of a covered way by which the palace was approached on this side. Above the pillars the temple (No. V.) exhibits a heavy cornice or entablature projecting considerably, and finished at the top with a row of gradines. (Compare No. II.) At one side of this main building is a small chapel or oratory, also finished with gradines, against the wall of which is a representation of a king, standing in a species of frame arched at the top. A road leads straight up to this royal tablet, and in this road within a little distance of the king stands an altar. The temple occupies the top of a mound, which is covered with trees of two different kinds, and watered by rivulets. On the right is a "hanging garden," artificially elevated to the level of the temple by means of masonry supported on an arcade, the arch here used being not the round arch but a pointed one. No. VI. [PLATE L.] is unfortunately very imperfect, the entire upper portion having been lost. Even, however, in its present mutilated state it represents by far the most magnificent building that has yet been found upon the bas-reliefs. The facade, as it now stands, exhibits four broad pilasters and four pillars, alternating in pairs, excepting that, as in the smaller temples, pilasters occupy both corners. In two cases, the base of the pilaster is carved into the figure of a winged bull, closely resembling the bulls which commonly guarded the outer gates of palaces. In the other two the base is plain—a piece of negligence, probably, on the part of the artist. The four pillars all exhibit a rounded base, nearly though not quite similar to that of the pillars in No. V.; and this rounded base in every case rests upon the back of a walking lion.

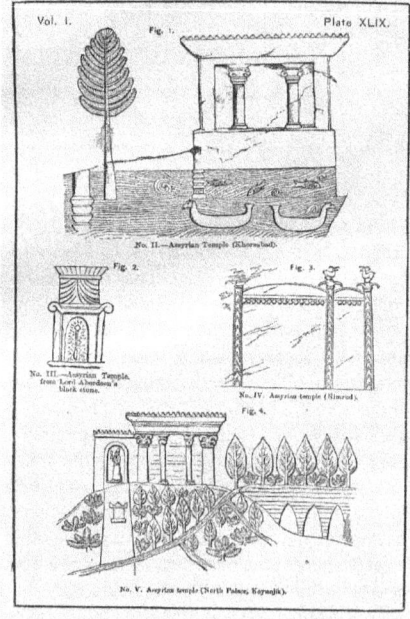

PLATE XLIX

We might perhaps have imagined that this was a mere fanciful or mythological device of the artist's, on a par with the representations at Bavian, where figures, supposed to be Assyrian deities, stand upon the backs of animals resembling dogs. But one of M. Place's architectural discoveries seems to make it possible, or even probable, that a real feature in Assyrian building is here represented M. Place found the arch of the town gateway which he exhumed at Khorsabad to spring from the backs of the two bulls which guarded it on either side. Thus the lions at the base of the pillars may be real architectural forms, as well as the winged bulls which support the pilasters. The lion was undoubtedly a sacred animal, emblematic of divine power, and especially assigned to Nergal, the Assyrian Mars, the god at once of war and of hunting. His introduction on the exteriors of buildings was common in Asia Minor but no other example occurs of his being made to support a pillar, excepting in the so-called Byzantine architecture of Northern Italy.

PLATE L

No. VII. a [PLATE LII., Fig. 1] introduces us to another kind of Assyrian temple, or perhaps it should rather be said to another feature of Assyrian temples—common to them with Babylonian—the tower or ziggurat. This appears to have been always built in stages, which probably varied in number—never, how-ever, so far as appears, exceeding seven. The sculptured example before us, which is from a bas-relief found at Koyunjik, distinctly exhibits four stages, of which the topmost, owing to the destruction of the upper portion of the tablet, is imperfect. It is not unlikely that in this instance there was above the fourth a fifth stage, consisting of a shrine like that which at Babylon crowned the great temple of Belus. The complete elevation would then have been nearly as in No. VII. b. [PLATE XLI., Fig. 3.]

The following features are worth of remark in this temple. The basement story is panelled with indented rectangular recesses, as was the ease at Nimrud [PLATE LIII.] and at the Birs the remainder are plain, as are most of the stages in the Birs temple. Up to the second of these squared recesses on either side there runs what seems to be a road or path, which sweeps away down the hill whereon the temple stands in a bold curve, each path closely matching the other. The whole building is perfectly symmetrical, except that the panelling is not quite uniform in width nor arranged quite regularly. On the second stage, exactly in the middle, there is evidently a doorway, and on either side of it a shallow buttress or pilaster. In the centre of the third story, exactly over the doorway of the second, is a squared niche. In front of the temple, but not exactly opposite its centre, may be seen the prophylaea, consisting of a squared doorway placed under a battlemented wall, between two towers also battlemented. It is curious that the paths do not lead to the propylaea, but seen to curve round the hill.

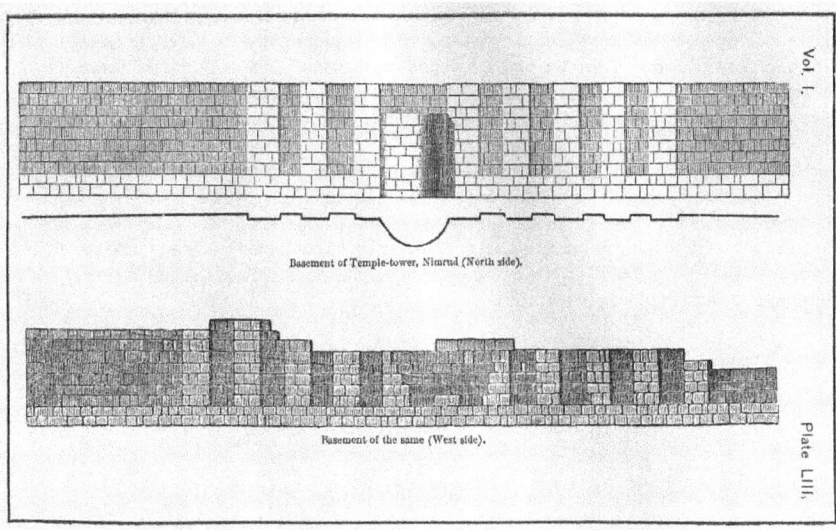

PLATE LIII

Remains of ziggurats similar to this have been discovered at Khorsabad, at Nimrud, and at Kileh-Sherghat. The conical mound at Khorsabad explored by M. Place was found to contain a tower in seven stages; that of Nimrud, which is so striking an object from the plain, and which was carefully examined by Mr. Layard, presented no positive proof of more than a single stage; but from its conical shape, and from the general analogy of such towers, it is believed to have had several stages. [PLATE LII., Fig. 2.] Mr. Layard makes their number five, and crowns the fifth with a circular tower terminating in a heavy cornice; but for this last there is no authority at all, and the actual number of the stages is wholly uncertain. The base of this ziggurat was a square, 167 feet 6 inches each way, composed of a solid mass of sun-dried brick, faced at bottom to the height of twenty feet with a wall of hewn stones, more than eight feet and a half in thickness. The outer stones were bevelled at the edges, and on the two most conspicuous sides the wall was ornamented with a series of shallow recesses arranged without very much attention to regularity. The other two sides, one of which abutted on and was concealed by the palace mound, while the other faced towards the city, were perfectly plain. At the top of the stone masonry was a row of gradines, such as are often represented in the sculptures as crowning an edifice. Above the stone masonry the tower was continued at nearly the same width, the casing of stone being simply replaced by one of burnt brick of inferior thickness. It is supposed that the upper stages were constructed in the same way. As the actual present height of the ruin is 140 feet, and the upper stages have so entirely crumbled away, it can scarcely be supposed that the original height fell much short of 200 feet.

The most curious of the discoveries made during the examination of this building, was the existence in its interior of a species of chamber or gallery, the true object of which still re-mains wholly unexplained. This gallery was 100 feet long, 12 feet high, and no more than 6 feet broad. It was arched or vaulted at top, both the side walls and the vaulting being of sun-dried brick. [PLATE LIV., Fig. 2.] Its position was exactly half-way between the tower's northern and southern faces, and with these it ran parallel, its height in the tower being such that its floor was exactly on a level with the top of the stone masonry, which again was level with the terrace or platform whereupon the Nimrud palaces stood. There was no trace of any way by which the gallery was intended to be entered; its walls showed no signs of inscription, sculpture, or other ornament; and absolutely nothing was found in it. Mr. Layard, prepossessed with an opinion derived from several confused notices in the classical writers, believed the tower to be a sepulchral monument, and the gallery to be the tomb in which was originally deposited "the embalmed body of the king." To account for the complete disappearance, not only of the body, but of all the ornaments and vessels found commonly in the Mesopotamian tombs, he suggested that the gallery had been rifled in times long anterior to his visit; and he thought that he found traces, both internally and externally, of the tunnel by which it had been entered. But certainly, if this long and narrow vault was intended to receive a body, it is most extraordinarily shaped for the purpose. What other sepulchral chamber is there anywhere of so enormous a, length? Without pretending to say what the real object of the gallery was, we may feel tolerably sure that it was not a tomb. The building which contained it was a temple tower, and it is not likely that the religious feelings of the Assyrians would have allowed the application of a religious edifice to so utilitarian a purpose.

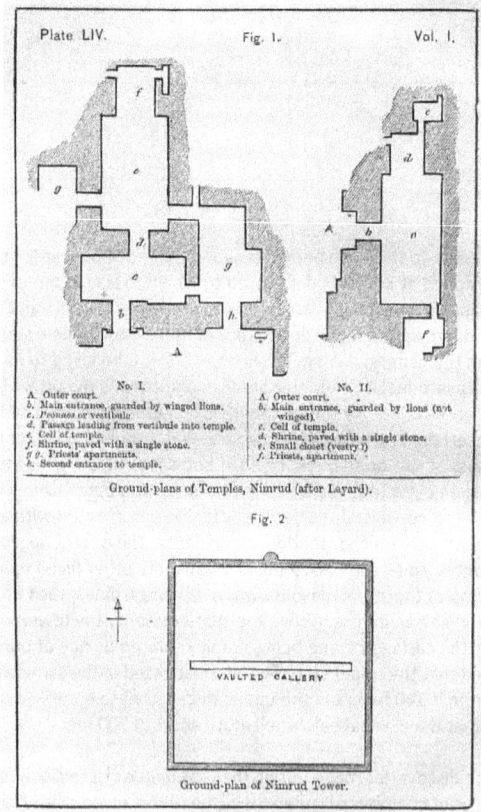

PLATE LIV

Besides the ziggerat or tower, which may commonly have been surmounted by a chapel or shrine, an Assyrian temple had always a number of basement chambers, in one of which was the principal shrine of the god. [PLATE LIV.,Fig. 1.] This was a square or slightly oblong recess at the end of an oblong apartment, raised somewhat above its level; it was paved (sometimes, if not always) with a single slab, the weight of which must occasionally have been as much as thirty tons. One or two small closets opened out from the shrine, in which it is likely that the priests kept the sacerdotal garments and the sacrificial utensils. Sometimes the cell of the temple or chamber into which the shrine opened was reached through another apartment, corresponding to the Greek pronaos. In such a case, care seems to have been taken so to arrange the outer and inner doorways of the vestibule that persons passing by the outer doorway should not be able to catch a sight of the shrine. Where there was no vestibule, the entrance into the cell or body of the temple seems to have been placed at the side, instead of at the end, probably with the same object. Besides these main parts of a temple, a certain number of chambers are always found, which appear to have been priests' apartments.

The ornamentation of temples, to judge by the few specimens which remain, was very similar to that of palaces. The great gateways were guarded by colossal bulls or lions see [PLATE LV.], accompanied by the usual sacred figures, and sometimes covered with inscriptions. The entrances and some portions of the chambers were ornamented with the customary sculptured slabs, representing here none but religious subjects. No great proportion of the interior, however, was covered in this way, the walls being in general only plastered and then painted with figures or patterns. Externally, enamelled bricks were used as a decoration wherever sculptured slabs did not hide the crude brick.

Entrance to smaller Temple, Nimrud (after Layard).

PLATE LV

Much the sane doubts and difficulties beset the subjects of the roofing and lighting of the temples as those which have been discussed already in connection with the palaces. Though the span of the temple-chambers is less than that of the great palace halls, still it is considerable, sometimes exceeding thirty feet. No effort seems made to keep the temple-chambers narrow, for their width is sometimes as much as two-thirds of their length. Perhaps, therefore, they were hypaethral, like the temples of the Greeks. All that seems to be certain is that what roofing they had was of wood, which at Nimrud was cedar, brought probably from the mountains of Syria.

Of the domestic architecture of the Assyrians we possess absolutely no specimen. Excavation has been hitherto confined to the most elevated portions of the mounds which mark the sites of cities, where it was likely that remains of the greatest interest would be found. Palaces, temples, and the great gates which gave entrance to towns, have in this way seen the light; but the humbler buildings, the ordinary dwellings of the people, remain buried beneath the soil, unexplored and even unsought for. In this entire default of any actual specimen of an ordinary Assyrian house, we naturally turn to the sculptured representations which are so abundant and represent so many different sorts of scenes. Even here, however, we obtain but little light. The bulk of the slabs exhibit the wars of the kings in foreign countries, and thus place before us foreign rather than Assyrian architecture. The processional slabs, which are another large class, contain rarely any building at all, and, where they furnish one, exhibit to us a temple rather than a house. The hunting scenes, representing wilds far from the dwellings of man, afford us, as might be expected, no help. Assyrian buildings, other than temples, are thus most rarely placed before us. In one case, indeed, we have an Assyrian city, which a foreign enemy is passing; but the only edifices represented are the walls and towers of the exterior, and the temple [No. VI., PLATE L.] whose columns rest upon lions. In one other we seem to have an unfortified Assyrian village; and from this single specimen we are forced to form our ideas of the ordinary character of Assyrian houses.

PLATE LVI

It is observable here, its the first place, that the houses have no windows, and are, therefore, probably lighted from the roof; next, that the roofs are very curious, since, although flat in some instances, they consist more often either of hemispherical domes, such as are still so common in the East, or of steep and high cones, such as are but seldom seen anywhere. Mr. Layard finds a parallel for these last in certain villages of Northern Syria, where all the houses have conical roofs, built of mud, which present a very singular appearance. [PLATE LVI., Fig. 2.] Both the domes and the cones of the Assyrian example have evidently an opening at the top, which may have admitted as much light into the houses as was thought necessary. The doors are of two kinds, square at the top, and arched; they are placed commonly towards the sides of the houses. The houses themselves seem to stand separate, though in close juxtaposition.

The only other buildings of the Assyrians which appear to require some notice are the fortified enceintes of their towns. The simplest of these consisted of a single battlemented wall, carried in lines nearly or quite straight along the four sides of the place, pierced with gates, and guarded at the angles, at the gates, and at intervals along the curtain with projecting towers, raised not very much higher than the walls, and (apparently) square in shape. [PLATE LVII., Fig 1.] In the sculptures we sometimes find the battlemented wall repeated twice or thrice in lines placed one above the other, the intention being to represent the defence of a city by two or three walls, such as we have seen existed on one side of Nineveh.

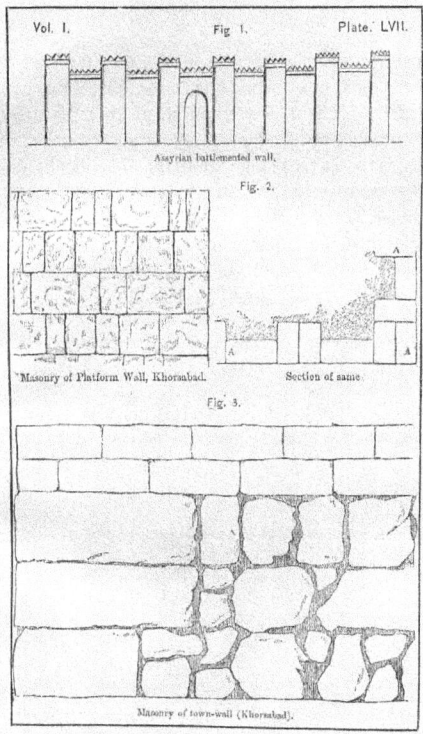

PLATE LVII

The walls were often, if not always, guarded by moats. Internally they were, in every case, constructed of crude brick; while externally it was common to face them with hewn stone, either from top to bottom, or at any rate to a certain height. At Khorsabad the stone revetement of one portion at least of the wall was complete; at Nimrud (Calah) and at Nineveh itself, it was partial, being carried at the former of those places only to the height of twenty feet. The masonry at Khorsabad was of three kinds. That of the palace mound, which formed a portion of the outer defence, was composed entirely of blocks of stone, square-hewn and of great size, the length of the blocks varying from two to three yards, while the width was one yard, and the height from five to six feet. [PLATE LVII., Fig.2.] The masonry was laid somewhat curiously. The blocks (A A) were placed alternately long-wise and end-wise against the crude brick (B), so as not merely to lie against it, but to penetrate it with their ends in many places. [PLATE LVII, Fig. 2.] Care was also taken to make the angles especially strong, as will be seen by the accompanying section.

The rest of the defences at Khorsabad were of an inferior character. The wall of the town had a width of about forty-five feet, and its basement, to the height of three feet, was constructed of stone; but the blocks were neither so large, nor were they hewn with the same care, as those of the palace platform. [PLATE LVII., Fig. 3.] The angles, indeed, were of squared stone; but even there the blocks measured no more than three feet in length and a foot in height: the rest of the masonry consisted of small polygonal stones, merely smoothed on their outer face, and roughly fitting together in a manner recalling the Cyclopian walls of Greece and Italy. They were not united by any cement. Above the stone basement was a massive structure of crude brick, without any facing either of burnt brick or of stone.

The third kind of masonry at Khorsabad was found outside the main wall, and may have formed either part of the lining of the moat or a portion of a tower, which may have projected in advance of the wall at this point. [PLATE LVIII., Fig. 1.] It was entirely of stone. The lowest course was formed of small and very irregular polygonal blocks roughly fitted together; above this came two courses of carefully squared stones more than a foot long, but less than six inches in width, which were placed end-wise, one over the other, care being taken that the joints of the upper tier should never coincide exactly with those of the lower. Above these was a third course of hewn stones, somewhat smaller than the others, which were laid in the ordinary manner. Here the construction, as discovered, terminated; but it was evident, from the debris of hewn stones at the foot of the wall, that originally the courses had been continued to a much greater height.

PLATE LVIII

In this description of the buildings raised by the Assyrians it has been noticed more than once that they were not ignorant of the use of the arch. The old notion that the round arch was a discovery of the Roman, and the pointed of the Gothic architecture, has gradually faded away with our ever-increasing knowledge of the actual state of the ancient world; and antiquarians were not, perhaps, very much surprised to learn, by the discoveries of Mr. Layard, that the Assyrians knew and used both kinds of arch in their constructions. Some interest, however, will probably be felt to attach to the two questions, how they formed their arches, and to what uses they applied them.

All the Assyrian arches hitherto discovered are of brick. The round arches are both of the crude and of the kiln-dried material, and are formed, in each case, of brick made expressly for vaulting, slightly convex at top and slightly concave at bottom, with one broader and one narrower end. The arches are of the simplest kind, being exactly semicircular, and rising from plain perpendicular jambs. The greatest width which any such arch has been hitherto found to span is about fifteen feet.

The only pointed arch actually discovered is of burnt brick. The bricks are of the ordinary shape, and not intended for vaulting. They are laid side by side up to a certain point, being bent into a slight arch by the interposition between them of thin wedges of mortar. The two sides of the arch having been in this way carried up to a point where the lower extremities of the two innermost bricks nearly touched, while a considerable space remained between their upper extremities instead of a key-stone, or a key-brick fitting the aperture, ordinary bricks were placed in it longitudinally, and so the space was filled in.

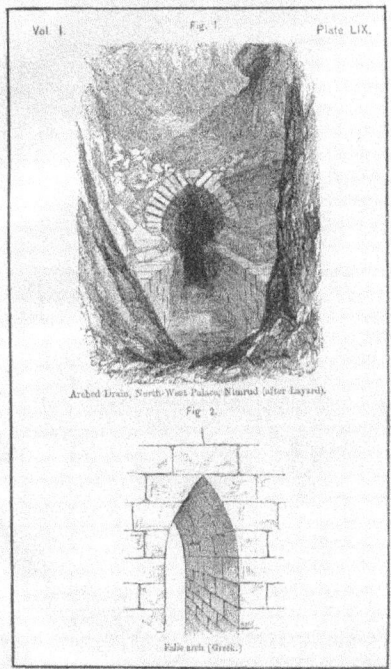

PLATE LIX

Another mode of constructing a pointed arch seems to be intended in a bas-relief, whereof a representation has been already given. The masonry of the arcade in No. V. [PLATE XLIX., Fig. 4] runs (it will be seen) in horizontal lines up to the very edge of the arch, thus suggesting a construction common in many of the early Greek arches, where the stones are so cut away that an arched opening is formed, though the real constructive principle of the arch has no place in such specimens.

With regard to the uses whereto the Assyrians applied the arch, it would certainly seem, from the evidence which we possess, that they neither employed it as a great decorative feature, nor yet as a main principle of construction. So far as appears, their chief use of it was for doorways and gateways. Not only are the town gates of Khorsabad found to have been arched over, but in the representations of edifices, whether native or foreign, upon the bas-reliefs, the arch for doors is commoner than the square top. It is most probable that the great palace gateways were thus covered in, while it is certain that some of the interior doorways in palaces had rounded tops. Besides this use of the arch for doors and gates, the Assyrians are known to have employed it for drains, aqueducts, and narrow chambers or galleries. [PLATE LVIII. Fig. 2.]; [PLATE LIX., Fig. 1.]

PLATE LX

It has been suggested that the Assyrians applied the two kinds of arches to different purposes, "thereby showing more science and discrimination than we do in our architectural works;" that "they used the pointed arch for underground work, where they feared great superincumbent pressure on the apex, and the round arch above ground, where that was not to be dreaded." [PLATE LIX., Fig. 2.] But this ingenious theory is scarcely borne out by the facts. The round arch is employed underground in two instances at Nimrud, besides occurring in the basement story of the great tower, where the superincumbent weight must have been enormous. And the pointed arch is used above ground for the aqueduct and hanging garden in the bas-relief (see [PLATE XLIX., Fig. 4]), where the pressure, though considerable, would not have been very extraordinary. It would seem, therefore, to be doubtful whether the Assyrians were really guided by any constructive principle in their preference of one form of the arch over the other.

In describing generally the construction of the palaces and other chief buildings of the Assyrians, it has been necessary occasionally to refer to their ornamentation; but the subject is far from exhausted, and will now claim, for a short space, our special attention. Beyond a doubt the chief adornment, both of palaces and temples, consisted of the colossal bulls and lions guarding the great gateways, together with the sculptured slabs wherewith the walls, both internal and external, were ordinarily covered to the height of twelve or sometimes even of fifteen feet. These slabs and carved figures will necessarily be considered in connection with Assyrian sculpture, of which they form the most important part. It will, therefore, only be noted at present that the extent of wall covered with the slabs was, in the Khorsabad palace, at least 4000 feet, or nearly four-fifths of a mile, while in each of the Koyunjik palaces the sculptures extended to considerably more than that distance.

The ornamentation of the walls above the slabs, both internally and externally, was by means of bricks painted on the exposed side and covered with an enamel. The colors are for the most part somewhat pale, but occasionally they possess some brilliancy. [PLATE LX., Fig 1.] Predominant among the tints are a pale blue, an olive green, and a dull yellow. White is also largely used; brown and black are not infrequent; red is comparatively rare. The subjects represented are either such scenes as occur upon the sculptured slabs, or else mere patterns—scrolls, honeysuckles, chevrons, gradines, guilloches, etc. In the scenes some attempt seems to be made at representing objects in their natural colors. The size of the figures is small; and it is difficult to imagine that any great effect could have been produced on the beholder by such minute drawings placed at such a height from the ground. Probably the most effective ornamentation of this kind was by means of patterns, which are often graceful and striking. [PLATE LX., 2.]

It has been observed that, so far as the evidence at present goes, the use of the column in Assyrian architecture would seem to have been very rare indeed. In palaces we have no grounds for thinking that they were employed at all excepting in certain of the interior doorways, which, being of unusual breadth, seem to have been divided into three distinct portals by means of two pillars placed towards the sides of the opening. The bases of these pillars were of stone, and have been found in situ; their shafts and capitals had disappeared, and can only be supplied by conjecture. In the temples, as we have seen, the use of the column was more frequent. Its dimensions greatly varied. Ordinarily it was too short and thick for beauty, while occasionally it had the opposite defect, being too tall and slender. Its base was sometimes quite plain, sometimes diversified by a few mouldings, sometimes curiously and rather clumsily rounded (as in No. II., [PLATE LXI., Fig. 1]). The shaft was occasionally patterned. The capital, in one instance (No. I., [PLATE LXI., Fig. 3]), approaches to the Corinthian; in another (No. II.) it reminds us of the Ionic; but the volutes are double, and the upper ones are surmounted by an awkward-looking abacus. A third (No. III., [PLATE. LXI., Fig. 2]) is very peculiar, and to some extent explains the origin of the second. It consists of two pairs of ibex horns, placed one over the other. With this maybe compared another (No. IV.). the most remarkable of all, where we have first a single pair of ibex horns, and then, at the summit, a complete figure of an ibex very graphically portrayed.

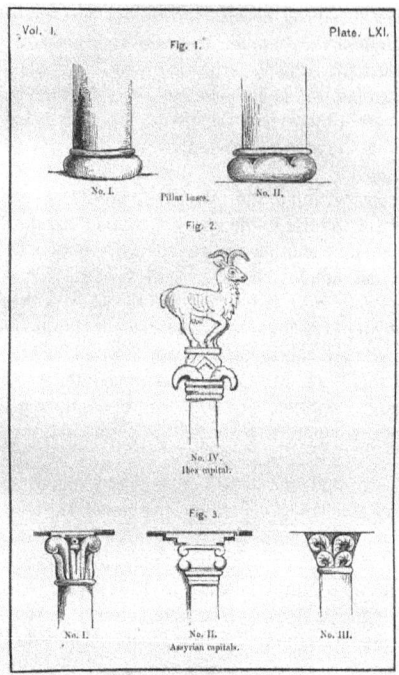

PLATE LXI

The beauty of Assyrian patterning has been already noticed. Patterned work is found not only on the enamelled bricks, but on stone pavement slabs, and around arched doorways leading from one chamber to another, where the patterns are carved with great care and delicacy upon the alabaster. The accompanying specimen of a doorway, which is taken from an unpublished drawing by Mr. Boutcher, is very rich and elegant, though it exhibits none but the very commonest of the Assyrian patterns. [PLATE LXII., Fig. 1.] A carving of a more elaborate type, and one presenting even greater delicacy of workmanship, has been given in an earlier portion of this chapter as an example of a patterned pavement slab. Slabs of this kind have been found in many of the palaces, and well deserve the attention of modern designers.

Ornamental doorway (North Palace, Kouyunjik).

Fig. 2.

Water-transport of stone for building (Kouyunjik).

PLATE LXII

When the architecture of the Assyrians is compared with that of other nations possessing about the same degree of civilization, the impression that it leaves is perhaps somewhat disappointing. Vast labor and skill, exquisite finish, the most extraordinary elaboration, were bestowed on edifices so essentially fragile and perishable that no care could have preserved them for manly centuries. Sun-dried brick, a material but little superior to the natural clay of which it was composed, constituted everywhere the actual fabric, which was then covered thinly and just screened from view by a facing, seldom more than a few inches in depth, of a more enduring and handsomer substance. The tendency of the platform mounds, as soon as formed, must have been to settle down, to bulge at the sides and become uneven at the top, to burst their stone or brick facings and precipitated them into the ditch below, at the same time disarranging and breaking up the brick pavements which covered their surface. The weight of the buildings raised upon the monads must have tended to hasten these catastrophes, while the unsteadiness of their foundations and the character of their composition must have soon had the effect of throwing the buildings themselves into disorder, of loosening the slabs from the walls, causing the enamelled bricks to start from their places, the colossal bulls and lions to lean over, and the roofs to become shattered and fall in. The fact that the earlier palaces were to a great extent dismantled by the later kings is perhaps to be attributed, not so much to a barbarous resolve that they would destroy the memorials of a former and a hostile dynasty, as to the circumstance that the more ancient buildings had fallen into decay and ceased to be habitable. The rapid succession of palaces, the fact that, at any rate from Sargon downwards, each monarch raises a residence, or residences, for himself, is yet more indicative of the rapid deterioration and dilapidation (so to speak) of the great edifices. Probably a palace began to show unmistakable symptoms of decay and to become an unpleasant residence at the end of some twenty-five or thirty years from the date of its completion; effective repairs were, by the very nature of the case, almost impossible; and it was at once easier and more to the credit of the monarch that he should raise a fresh platform and build himself a fresh dwelling than that he should devote his efforts to keeping in a comfortable condition the crumbling habitation of his predecessor.

It is surprising that, under these circumstances, a new style of architecture did not arise. The Assyrians were not, like the Babylonians, compelled by the nature of the country in which they lived to use brick as their chief building material. M. Botta expresses his astonishment at the preference of brick to stone exhibited by the builders of Khorsabad, when the neighborhood abounds in rocky hills capable of furnishing an inexhaustible supply of the better material. The limestone range of the Jebel Maklub is but a few miles distant, and many out-lying rocky elevations might have been worked with still greater facility. Even at Nineveh itself, and at Calah or Nimrud, though the hills were further removed, stone was, in reality, plentiful. The cliffs a little above Koyunjik are composed of a "hard sandstone," and a part of the moat of the town is carried through "compact silicious conglomerate." The town is, in fact, situated on "a spur of rock" thrown off from the Jebel Dlakiub, which, terminates at the edge of the ravine whereby Nineveh was protected on the south. Calah, too, was built on a number of "rocky undulations," and its western wall skirts the edge of "conglomerate" cliffs, which have been scarped by the hand of man. A very tolerable stone was thus procurable on the actual sites of these ancient cities; and if a better material had been wanted, it might have been obtained in any quantity, and of whatever quality was desired, from the Zagros range and its outlying rocky barriers. Transport could scarcely have caused much difficulty, as the blocks might have been brought from the quarries where they were hewn to the sites selected for the cities by water-carriage—a mode of transport well known to the Assyrians, as is made evident to us by the bas-reliefs. (See [PLATE LXII. Fig. 2.])

If the best possible building material was thus plentiful in Assyria, and its conveyance thus easy to manage, to what are we to ascribe the decided preference shown for so inferior a substance as brick? No considerable difficulty can have been experienced in quarrying the stone of the country, which is seldom very hard, and which was, in fact, cut by the Assyrians, whenever they had any sufficient motive for removing or making use of it. One answer only can be reasonably given to the question. The Assyrians had learnt a certain style of architecture in the alluvial Babylonia, and having brought it with them into A country far less fitted for it, maintained it from habit, not withstanding its unsuitableness. In some few respects, indeed, they made a slight change. The abundance of stone in the country induced them to substitute it in several places where in Babylonia it was necessary to use burnt brick, as in the facings of platforms and of temples, in dams across streams, in pavements sometimes, and universally in the ornamentation of the lover portions of palace and temple walls. But otherwise they remained faithful to their architectural traditions, and raised in the comparatively hilly Assyria the exact type of building which nature and necessity had led them to invent and use in the flat and stoneless alluvium where they had had their primitive abode. As platforms were required both for security and for comfort in the lower region, they retained them, instead of choosing natural elevations in the upper one. As clay was the only possible material in the one place, clay was still employed, notwithstanding the abundance of stone, in the other. Being devoid of any great inventive genius, the Assyrians found it easier to maintain and slightly modify a system with which they had been familiar in their original country than to devise a new one more adapted to the land of their adoption.

Next to the architecture of the Assyrians, their mimetic art seems to deserve attention. Though the representations in the works of Layard and Botta, combined with the presence of so many specimens in the great national museums of London and Paris, have produced a general familiarity with the subject, still, as a connected view of it in its several stages and branches is up to the present time a desideratum in our literature, it may not be superfluous here to attempt a brief account of the different classes into which their productions in this kind of art fall, and the different eras and styles under which they naturally range themselves.

Assyrian mimetic art consists of statues, bas-reliefs, metal-castings, carvings in ivory, statuettes in clay, enamellings on brick, and intaglios on stones and gems.

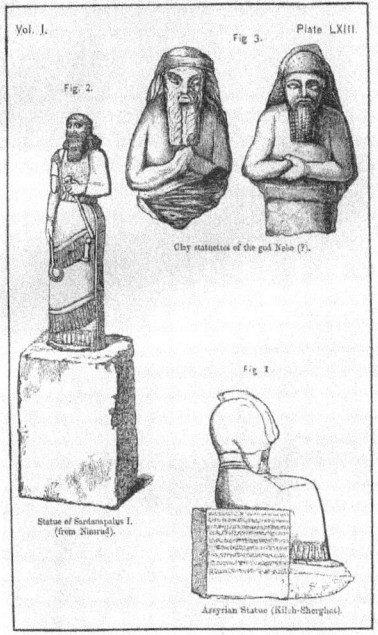

PLATE LXIII

Assyrian statues are comparatively rare, and, when they occur, are among the least satisfactory of this people's productions. They are coarse, clumsy, purely formal in their design, and generally characterized by an undue flatness, or want of breadth in the side view, as if they were only intended to be seen directly in front. Sometimes, however, this defect is not apparent. A sitting statue in black basalt, of the size of life, representing an early king, which Mr. Layard discovered at Kileh-Sherghat [PLATE LXIII, Fig. 1], and which is now in the British Museum, may be instanced as quite free from this disproportion. It is very observable, however, in another of the royal statues recently recovered [PLATE LXIII, Fig. 2], as it is also in the monolith bulls and lions universally. Otherwise, the proportions of the figures are commonly correct. They bear a resemblance to the archaic Greek, especially to that form of it which we find in the sculptures from Branchidae. They have just the same rudeness, heaviness, and stiff formality. It is difficult to judge of their execution, as they have mostly suffered great injury from the hand of man, or from the weather; but the royal statue here represented, which is in better preservation than any other Assyrian work "in the round" that has come down to us, exhibits a rather high finish. It is smaller than life, being about three and a half feet high: the features are majestic, and well marked; the hair and beard are elaborately curled; the arms and hands are well shaped, and finished with care. The dress is fringed elaborately, and descends to the ground, concealing all the lower part of the figure. The only statues recovered besides these are two of the god Nebo, brought from Nimrud, a mutilated one of Ishtar, or Astarte, found at Koyunjik [PLATE LXIII., Fig. 3], and a tolerably perfect one of Sargon, which was discovered at Idalium, in the island of Cyprus.

The clay statuettes of the Assyrians possess even less artistic merit than their statues. They are chiefly images of gods or genii, and have most commonly something grotesque in their appearance. Among the most usual are figures which represent either Mylitta (Bettis), or Ishtar. They are made in a fine terra cotta, which has turned of a pale red in baking, and are colored with a cretaceous coating, so as greatly to resemble Greek pottery. Another type is that of an old man, bearded, and with hands clasped, which we may perhaps identify with Nebo, the Assyrian Mercury, since his statues in the British Museum have a somewhat similar character. Other forms are the fish-god Nin, or Nin-ip [PLATE LXIV., Fig. 1]; and the deities, not yet identified, which were found by M. Botta under the pavement-bricks at Khorsahad. [PLATE LXIV., Fig. 2.] These specimens have the formal character of the statues, and are even more rudely shaped. Other examples, which carry the grotesque to an excess, appear to have been designed with greater spirit and freedom. Animal and human forms are sometimes intermixed in them; and while it cannot be denied that they are rude and coarse, it must be allowed, on the other hand, that they possess plenty of vigor. M. Botta has engraved several specimens, including two which have the hind legs and tail of a bull, with a human neck and arms, the head bearing the usual horned cap.

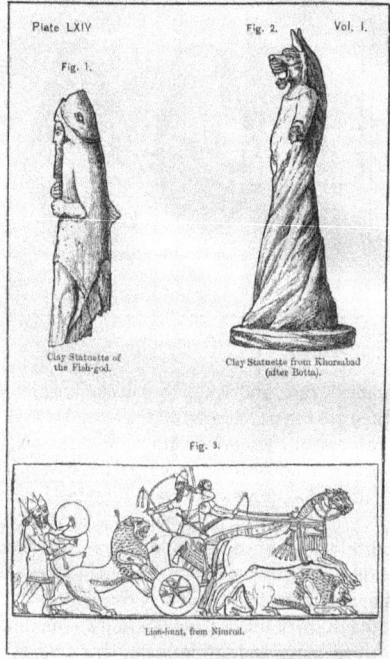

PLATE LXIV

Small figures of animals in terra cotta have also been found. They consist chiefly of dogs and ducks. A representation of each has been given in the chapter on the productions of Assyria. The dogs discovered are made of a coarse clay, and seem to have been originally painted. They are not wanting in spirit; but it detracts from their merit that the limbs are merely in relief, the whole space below the belly of the animal being filled up with a mass of clay for the sake of greater strength. The ducks are of a fine yellow material, and represent the bird asleep, with its head lying along its back.

Of all the Assyrian works of art which have come down to us, by far the most important are the bas-reliefs. It is here especially, if not solely, that we can trace progress in style; and it is here alone that we see the real artistic genius of the people. What sculpture in its full form, or in the slightly modified form of very high relief, was to the Greeks, what painting has been to modern European nations since the time of Cimabue, that low relief was to the Assyrians—the practical mode in which artistic power found vent among them. They used it for almost every purpose to which mimetic art is applicable; to express their religious feelings and ideas, to glorify their kings, to hand down to posterity the nation's history and its deeds of prowess, to depict home scenes and domestic occupations, to represent landscape and architecture, to imitate animal and vegetable forms, even to illustrate the mechanical methods which they employed in the construction of those vast architectural works of which the reliefs were the principal ornamentation. It is not too much to say that we know the Assyrians, not merely artistically, but historically and ethnologically, chiefly through their bas reliefs, which seem to represent to us almost the entire life of the people.

The reliefs may be divided under five principal heads:—1, War scenes, including battles, sieges, devastations of an enemy's country, naval expeditions, and triumphant returns from foreign war, with the trophies and fruits of victory; 2. Religious scenes, either mythical or real; 3. Processions generally of tribute-bearers, bringing the produce of their several countries to the Great King; 4. hunting and sporting scenes, including the chase of savage animals, and of animals sought for food, the spreading of nets, the shooting of birds, and the like; and 5. Scenes of ordinary life, as those representing the transport and erection of colossal bulls, landscapes, temples, interiors, gardens, etc.

The earliest art is that of the most ancient palaces at Nimrud. It belongs to the latter part of the tenth century before our era; the time of Asa in Judaea, of Omri and Ahab in Samaria, and of the Sheshonks in Egypt. It is characterized by much spirit and variety in the design, by strength and firmness, combined with a good deal of heaviness, in the execution, by an entire contempt for perspective, and by the rigid preservation in almost every case, both human and animal, of the exact profile both of figure and face. Of the illustrations already given in the present volume a considerable number belong to this period. The heads [PLATE XXXIII.], and the figures [PLATE XXXV.], represent the ordinary appearance of the men, while animal forms of the time will be found in the lion [PLATE XXV.], the ibex [PLATE XXV.], the gazelle [PLATE XXVII.], the horse [PLATE XXXI.], and the horse and wild bull [PLATE XXVIII.] It will be seen upon reference that the animal are very much superior to the human forms, a characteristic which is not, however, peculiar to the style of this period, but belongs to all Assyrian art, from its earliest to its latest stage. A favorable specimen of the style will be found in the lion-hunt which Mr. Layard has engraved in his "Monuments," and of which he himself observes, that it is "one of the finest specimens hitherto discovered of Assyrian sculpture." in [PLATE LXIV., Fig. 3.] The composition is at once simple and effective. The king forms the principal object, nearly in the centre of the picture, and by the superior height of his conical head-dress, and the position of the two arrows which he holds in the hand that draws the bow-string, dominates over the entire composition. As he turns round to shoot down at the lion which assails him from behind, his body is naturally and gracefully bent, while his charioteer, being engaged in urging his horses forward, leans naturally in the opposite direction, thus contrasting with the main figure and balancing it. The lion immediately behind the chariot is outlined with great spirit and freedom; his head is masterly; the fillings up of the body, however, have too much conventionality. As he rises to attack the monarch, he conducts the eye up to the main figure, while at the same time by this attitude his principal lines form a pleasing contrast to the predominant perpendicular and horizontal lines of the general composition. The dead lion in front of the chariot balances the living one behind it, and, with its crouching attitude, and drooping head and tail, contrasts admirably with the upreared form of its fellow. Two attendants, armed with sword and shield, following behind the living lion, serve to balance the horses drawing the chariot, without rendering the composition too symmetrical. The horses themselves are the weakest part of the picture; the forelegs are stiff and too slight, and the heads possess little spirit.

It is seldom that designs of this early period can boast nearly so much merit. The religious and processional pieces are stiff in the extreme; the battle scenes are overcrowded and confused; the hunting' scenes are superior to these, but in general they too fall far below the level of the above-described composition.

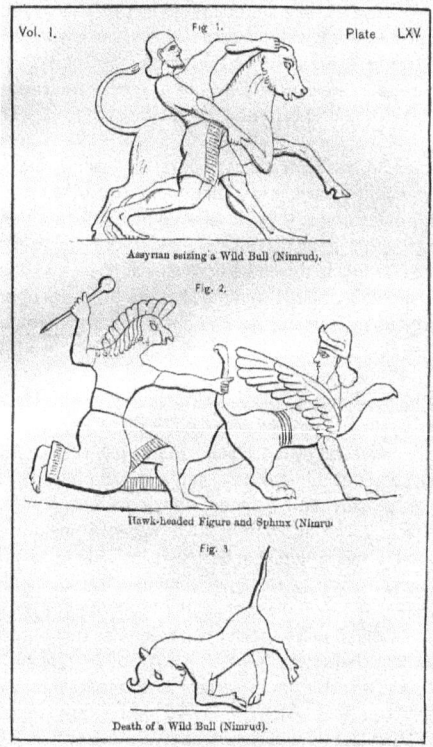

PLATE LXV

The best drawing of this period is found in the figures forming the patterns or embroidery of dresses. The gazelle, the ibex, the horse, and the horseman hunting the wild bull of which representations have been given, are from ornamental work of this kind. They are favorable specimens perhaps; but, still, they are representative of a considerable class. Some examples even exceed these in the freedom of their outline, and the vigorous action which they depict, as, for instance, the man seizing a wild bull by the horn and foreleg, which is figured. [PLATE LXV, Fig. 1.] In general, however, there is a tendency in these early drawings to the grotesque. Lions and bulls appear in absurd attitudes; hawk-headed figures in petticoats threaten human-headed lions with a mace or a strap, sometimes holding them by a paw, sometimes grasping then round the middle of the tail [PLATE LXV. Fig. 2]; priests hold up ibexes at arm's length by one of their hindlegs, so that their heads trail upon the ground; griffins claw after antelopes, or antelopes toy with winged lions; even in the hunting scenes, which are less simply ludicrous, there seems to be an occasional striving after strange and laughable attitudes, as when a stricken bull tumbles upon his head, with his tail tossed straight in the air [PLATE LXV., Fig. 31], or when a lion receives his death-wound with arms outstretched, and mouth wildly agape. [PLATE LXVI., Fig. 2.]

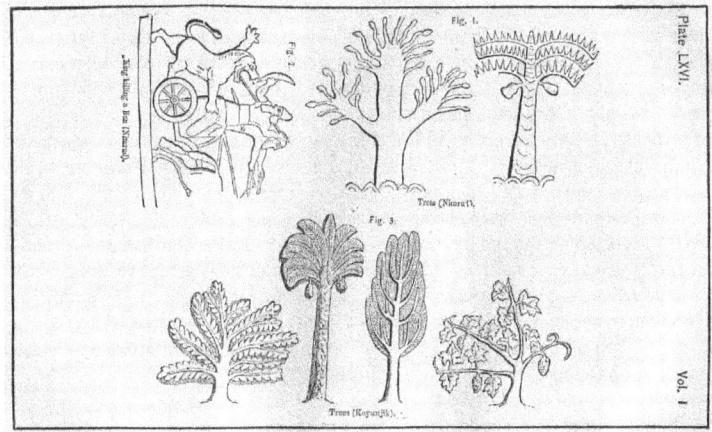

PLATE LXVI

King killing a lion (Nimrud).
PLATE LXVIA

The second period of Assyrian mimetic art extends from the latter part of the eighth to nearly the middle of the seventh century before our era; or, more exactly, from about B.C. 721 to B.C. 667. It belongs to the reigns of the three consecutive kings—Sargon, Sennacherib, and Esar-haddon, who were contemporary with Hezekiah and Manasseh in Judaea, and with the Sabacos (Shebeks) and Tirhakah (Tehiak) in Egypt. The sources which chiefly illustrate this period are the magnificent series of engravings published by MM. Flandin and Botta, together with the originals of a certain portion of them in the Louvre; the engravings in Mr. Layard's first folio work, from plate 68 to 83; those in his second folio work from plate 7 to 44, and from plate 50 to 56; the originals of many of these in the British Museum; several monuments procured for the British Museum by Mr. Loftus; and a series of unpublished drawings by Mr. Boutcher in the same great national collection.

The most obvious characteristic of this period, when we compare it with the preceding one, is the advance which the artists have made in their vegetable forms, and the pre-Raphaelite accuracy which they affect in all the accessories of their representations. In the bas-reliefs of the first period we have for the most part no backgrounds. Figures alone occupy the slabs, or figures and buildings. In some few instances water is represented in a very rude fashion; and once or twice only do we meet with trees, which, when they occur, are of the poorest and strangest character. (See [PLATE LXVI., Fig. 1.]) In the second period, on the contrary, backgrounds are the rule, and slabs without them form the exception. The vegetable forms are abundant and varied, though still somewhat too conventional. Date-palms, firs, and vines are delineated with skill and spirit; other varieties are more difficult to recognize. [PLATE LXVI., Fig. 3.] The character of the countries through which armies march is almost always given—their streams, lakes, and rivers, their hills and mountains, their trees, and in the case of marshy districts, their tall reeds. At the same time, animals in the wild state are freely introduced without their having any bearing on the general subject of the picture. The water teems with fish, and, where the sea is represented, with crabs, turtle, star-fish, sea-serpents, and other monsters. The woods are alive with birds; wild swine and stags people the marshes. Nature is evidently more and more studied; and the artist takes a delight in adorning the scenes of violence, which he is forced to depict, with quiet touches of a gentle character—rustics fishing or irrigating their grounds, fish disporting themselves, birds flying from tree to tree, or watching the callow young which look up to them from the nest for protection.

In regard to human forms, no great advance marks this period. A larger variety in their attitudes is indeed to be traced, and a greater energy and life appears in most of the figures; but there is still much the same heaviness of outline, the same over-muscularity, and the same general clumsiness and want of grace. Animal forms show a much more considerable improvement. Horses are excellently portrayed, the attitudes being varied, and the heads especially delineated with great spirit. Mules and camels are well expressed, but have scarcely the vigor of the horses. Horned cattle, as oxen, both with and without humps, goats, and sheep are very skilfully treated, being represented with much character, in natural yet varied attitudes, and often admirably grouped.

PLATE LXVII

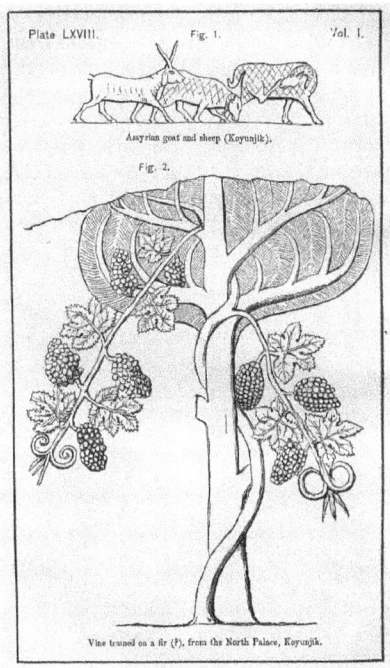

PLATE LXVIII

The composition during this period is more complicated and more ambitious than during the preceding one; but it may be questioned whether it is so effective. No single scene of the time can compare for grandeur with the lion-hunt above described. The battles and siege are spirited, but want unity; the hunting scenes are comparatively tame; the representations of the transport of colossal bulls possess more interest than artistic merit. On the other hand, the manipulation is decidedly superior; the relief is higher, the outline is more flowing, the finish of the features more delicate. What is lost in grandeur of composition is, on the whole, more than made up by variety, naturalness, improved handling, and higher finish.

The highest perfection of Assyrian art is in the third period, which extends from B.C. 667 to about B.C. 640. It synchronizes with the reign of Asshur-bani-pal, the son of Essarhaddon, who appears to have been contemporary with Gyges in Lydia, and with Psammetichus in Egypt. The characteristics of the time are a less conventional type in the vegetable forms, a wonderful freedom spirit, and variety in the forms of animals, extreme minuteness and finish in the human figures, and a delicacy in the handling considerably beyond that of even the second or middle period. The sources illustrative of this stage of the art consist of the plates in Mr. Layard's "Second Series of Monuments," from plate 45 to 49, the originals of these in the British Museum, the noble series of slabs obtained by Mr. Loftus from the northern palace of Koyunjik, and of the drawings made from them, and from other slabs, which were in a more damaged condition by Mr. Boutcher, who accompanied Mr. Loftus in the capacity of artist.

Vegetable forms are, on the whole, somewhat rare. The artists have relinquished the design of representing scenes with perfect truthfulness, and have recurred as a general rule to the plain backgrounds of the first period. This is particularly the case in the hunting scenes, which are seldom accompanied by any landscape whatsoever. In processional and military scenes landscape is introduced, but sparingly; the forms, for the most part, resembling those of the second period. Now and then, however, in such scenes the landscape has been made the object of special attention, becoming the prominent part, while the human figures are accessories. It is here that an advance in art is particularly discernible. In one set of slabs a garden seems to be represented. Vines are trained upon trees, which may be either firs or cypresses, winding elegantly around their stems, and on either side letting fall their pendent branches laden with fruit. [PLATE LXVIII.. Fig. 2.] Leaves. branches, and tendrils are delineated with equal truth and finish, a most pleasing and graceful effect being thereby produced. Irregularly among the trees occur groups of lilies, some in bud, some in full blow, all natural, graceful, and spirited. [PLATE LXIX., Fig. 1.]

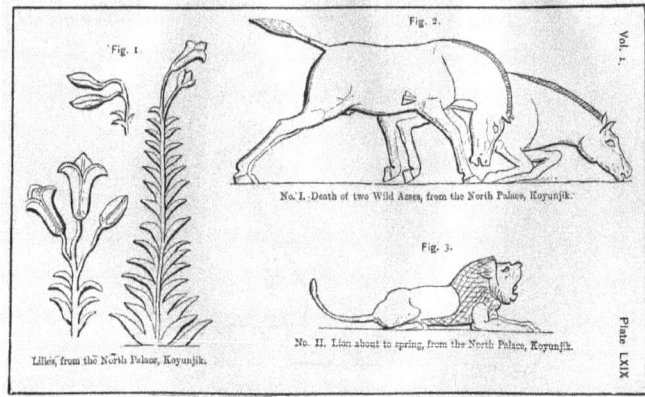

PLATE LXIX

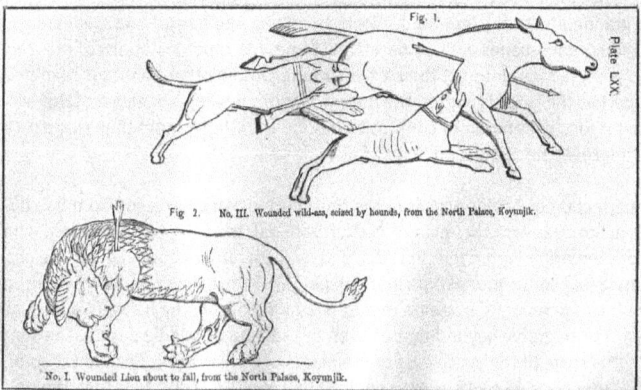

PLATE LXX

It is difficult to do justice to the animal delineation of this period. without reproducing before the eye of the reader the entire series of reliefs and drawings which belong to it. It is the infinite variety in the attitudes, even more than the truth and naturalness of any particular specimens, that impresses us as we contemplate the series. Lions, wild asses, dogs, deer, wild goats, horses, are represented in profusion: and we scarcely find a single form which is repeated. Some specimens have been already given, as the hunted stag and hind [PLATE XXVII.] and the startled wild ass [PLATE XXVI.] Others will occur among the illustrations of the next chapter. For the present it may suffice to draw attention to the spirit of the two falling asses in the illustration [PLATE LXIX., Fig. 3], and of the crouching lion in the illustration [PLATE LXIX., Fig. 2]; to the lifelike force of both ass and hounds in the representation [PLATE LXX., Fig. 1], and here particularly to the bold drawing of one of the dogs' heads in full, instead of in profile—a novelty now first occurring in the bas-reliefs. As instances of still bolder attempts at unusual attitudes, and at the same time of a certain amount of foreshortening, two further illustrations are appended. The sorely wounded lion in the first [PLATE LXX., Fig. 2] turns his head piteously towards the cruel shaft, while he totters to his fall, his limbs failing him, and his eyes beginning to close. The more slightly stricken king of beasts in the second [PLATE LXXI.], urged to fury by the smart of his wound, rushes at the chariot whence the shaft was sped, and in his mad agony springs upon a wheel, clutches it with his two fore-paws, and frantically grinds it between his teeth. Assyrian art, so far as is yet known, has no finer specimen of animal drawing than this head, which may challenge comparison with anything of the kind that either classic or modern art has produced.

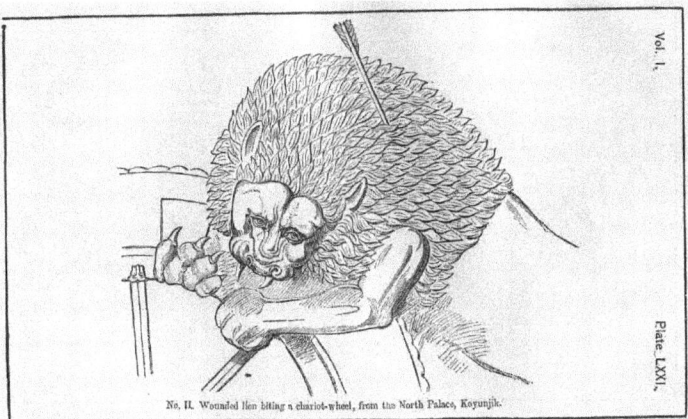

PLATE LXXI

PLATE LXXII

As a specimen at once of animal vigor and of the delicacy and finish of the workmanship in the human forms of the time, a bas-relief of the king receiving the spring of a lion, and shooting an arrow into his mouth, while a second lion advances at a rapid pace a little behind the first, may be adduced. (See [PLATE LXXII.]) The boldness of the composition, which represents the first lion actually in mid-air, is remarkable; the drawing of the brute's fore-paws, expanded to seize his intended prey, is lifelike and very spirited, while the head is massive and full of vigor. There is something noble in the calmness of the monarch contrasted with the comparative eagerness of the attendant, who stretches forward with shield and spear to protect has master from destruction, if the arrow fails. The head of the king is, unfortunately, injured; but the remainder of the figure is perfect and here, in the elaborate ornamentation of the whole dress, we have an example of the careful finish of the time—a finish, which is so light and delicate that it does not interfere with the general effect, being scarcely visible at a few yards' distance.

Lion-hunt in a river, from the North Palace, Koyunjik (ab. B. C. 660).

PLATE LXXIII

The faults which still remain in this best period of Assyrian art are heaviness and stiffness of outline in the human forms; a want of expression in the faces, and of variety and animation in the attitudes; and an almost complete disregard of perspective. If the worst of these faults are anywhere overcome, it would seem to be in the land lion-hunt, from which the noble head represented below is taken; and in the river-hunt of the same, beast, found on a slab too much injured to be re-moved, of which a representation is given. [PLATE LXXIII.] From what appears to have remained of the four figures towards the prow of the boat, we may conclude that there was a good deal of animation here. The drawing must certainly have been less stiff than usual; and if there is not much variety in the attitudes of the three spearmen in front, at any rate those attitudes contrast well, both with the stillness of the unengaged attendants in the rear, and with the animated but very different attitude of the king.

Before the subject of Assyrian sculpture is dismissed, it is necessary to touch the question whether the Assyrians applied color to statuary, and, if so, in what way and to what extent. Did they, like the Egyptians, cover the whole surface of the stone with a layer of stucco, and then paint the sculptured parts with strong colors—red, blue, yellow, white, and black? Or did they, like the Greeks, apply paint to certain portions of their sculptures only, as the hair, eyes, beard and draperies? Or finally, did they simply leave the stone in its natural condition, like the Italians and the modern sculptors generally?

The present appearance of the sculptures is most in accordance with the last of these three theories, or at any rate with that theory very slightly modified by the second. The slabs now offer only the faintest and most occasional traces of color. The evidence, however, of the original explorers is distinct, that at the time of discovery these traces were very much more abundant. Mr. Layard observed color at Nimrud on the hair, beard, and eyes of the figures, on the sandals and the bows, on the tongues of the eagle-headed mythological emblems, on a garland round the head of a winged priest(?), and on the representation of fire in the bas-relief of a siege. At Khorsabad, MM. Botta and Flandin found paint on the fringes of draperies, on fillets, on the mitre of the king, on the flowers carried by the winged figures, on bows and spearshafts, on the harness of the horses, on the chariots, on the sandals, on the birds, and sometimes on the trees. The torches used to fire cities, and the flames of the cities themselves, were invariably colored red. M. Flandin also believed that he could detect, in some instances, a faint trace of yellow ochre on the flesh and on the background of bas-reliefs, whence he concluded that this tint was spread over every part not otherwise colored.

It is evident, therefore, that the theory of an absence of color, or of a very rare use of it, must be set aside. Indeed, as it is certain that the upper portions of the palace walls, both inside and outside, were patterned with colored bricks, covering the whole space above the slabs, it must be allowed to be extremely improbable that at a particular line color would suddenly and totally cease. The laws of decorative harmony forbid such abrupt transitions; and to these laws all nations with any taste instinctively and unwittingly conform. The Assyrian reliefs were therefore, we may be sure, to some extent colored. The real question is, to what extent in the Egyptian or in the classical style?

In Mr. Layard's first series of "Monuments," a preference was expressed for what may be called the Egyptian theory. In the Frontispiece of that work, and in the second Plate, containing the restoration of a palace interior, the entire bas-reliefs were represented as strongly colored. A jet-black was assigned to the hair and beards of men and of all human-headed figures, to the manes and tails of horses, to vultures, eagle heads, and the like: a coarse red-brown to winged lions, to human flesh, to horses' bodies, and to various ornaments, a deep yellow to common lions, to chariot wheels, quivers, fringes, belts, sandals, and other portions of human apparel; white to robes, helmets, shields. tunic's, towns, trees, etc.; and a dull blue to some of the feathers of winged lions and genii, and to large portions of the ground from which the sculptures stood out. This conception of Assyrian coloring, framed confessedly on the assumption of a close analogy between the ornamentation of Assyria and that of Egypt, was at once accepted by the unlearned, and naturally enough was adopted by most of those who sought to popularize the new knowledge among their countrymen. Hence the strange travesties of Assyrian art which have been seen in so-called "Assyrian Courts," where all the delicacy of the real sculpture has disappeared, and the spectator has been revolted by grim figures of bulls and lions, from which a thick layer of coarse paint has taken away all dignity, and by reliefs which, from the same cause, have lost all spirit and refinement.

It is sufficient objection to the theory here treated of, that it has no solid basis of fact to rest upon. Color has only been found on portions of the bas-reliefs, as on the hair and beards of men, on head-ornaments, to a small extent on draperies, on the harness of horses, on sandals, weapons, birds, flowers, and the like. Neither the flesh of men, nor the bodies of animals, nor the draperies generally, nor the backgrounds (except perhaps at Khorsabad) present the slightest appearance of having been touched by paint. It is inconceivable that, if these portions of the sculptures were universally or even ordinarily colored, the color should have so entirely disappeared in every instance. It is moreover inconceivable that the sculptor, if he knew his work was about to be concealed beneath a coating of paint, should have cared to give it the delicate elaboration which is found at any rate in the later examples. All leads to the conclusion that in Assyrian as in classical sculpture, color was sparingly applied, being confined to such parts as the hair, eyes, and beards of men, to the fringes of dresses, to horse trappings, and other accessory parts of the representations. In this way the lower part of the wall was made to harmonize sufficiently with the upper portion, which was wholly colored, but chiefly with pale hues. At the same time a greater distinctness was given to the scenes represented upon the sculptured slabs, the color being judiciously applied to disentangle human from animal figures, dress from flesh, or human figures from one another.

The colors actually found upon the bas-reliefs are four only—red, blue, black, and white. The red is a good bright tint, far exceeding in brilliancy that of Egypt. On the sculptures of Khorsabad it approaches to vermilion, while on those of Nimrud it inclines to a crimson or a lake tint. It is found alternating with the natural stone on the royal parasol and mitre; with blue on the crests of helmets, the trappings of horses, on flowers, sandals, and on fillets; and besides, it occurs, unaccompanied by any other color, on the stems and branches of trees, on the claws of birds, the shafts of spears and arrows, bows, belts, fillets, quivers, maces, reins, sandals, flowers, and the fringe of dresses. It is uncertain whence the coloring matter was derived; perhaps the substance used was the suboxide of copper, with which the Assyrians are known to have colored their red glass.

The blue of the Assyrian monuments is an oxide of copper, sometimes containing also a trace of lead. Besides occurring in combination with red in the cases already mentioned, it was employed to color the foliage of trees, the plumage of birds, the heads of arrows, and sometimes quivers, and sandals.

PLATE LXXIV

White occurs very rarely indeed upon the sculptures. At Khorsabad it was not found of all; at Nimrud it was confined to the inner part of the eye on either side of the pupil, and in this position it occurred only on the colossal lions and bulls, and a very few other figures. On bricks and pottery it was frequent, and their (sp.) it is found to have been derived from tin; but it is uncertain whether the white of the sculptures was not derived from a commoner material.

Black is applied in the sculptures chiefly to the hair, beards, and eyebrows of men. It was also used to color the eyeballs not only of men, but also of the colossal lions and bulls. Sometimes, when the eyeball was thus marked, a line of black was further carried round the inner edge of both the upper and the lower eyelid. In one place black bars have been introduced to ornament an antelope's horns. On the older sculptures black was also the common color for sandals, which however were then edged with red. The composition of the black is uncertain. Browns upon the enamelled bricks are found to have been derived from, iron; but Mr. Layard believes the black upon the sculptures to have been, like the Egyptian, a bone black mixed with a little gum.

The ornamental metallurgy of the Assyrians deserves attention next to their sculpture. It is of three kinds, consisting, in the first place, of entire figures, or parts of figures, cast in a solid shape; secondly, of castings in a low relief; and thirdly, of embossed work wrought mainly with the hammer, but finished by a sparing use of the graving tool.

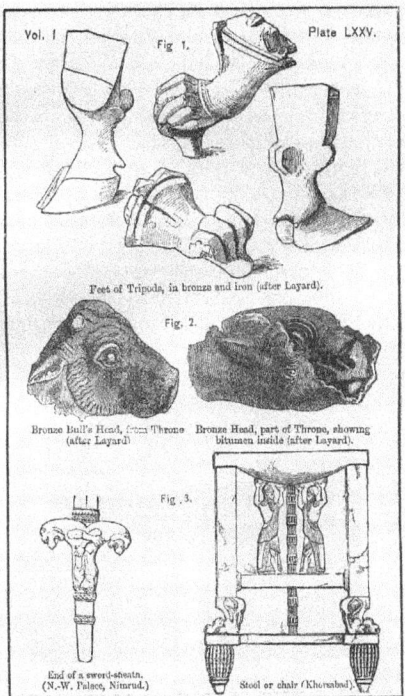

PLATE LXXV

The solid castings are comparatively rare, and represented none but animal forms. Lions, which seem to have been used as weights, occur most frequently, [PLATE LXXIV., Fig. 1.] None are of any great size; nor have we any evidence that the Assyrians could cast large masses of metal. They seem to have used castings, not (as the Greeks and the moderns) for the greater works of art, but only for the smaller. The forms of the few casts which have come down to us are good, and are free from the narrowness which characterizes the representations in stone.

Castings in a low relief formed the ornamentation of thrones [PLATE LXXIV., Figs. 2, 3], stools, and sometimes probably of chariots. They consisted of animal and human figures, winged deities, griffins, and the like. The castings were chiefly in open-work, and were attached to the furniture which they ornamented by means of small nails. They have no peculiar merit, being merely repetitions of the forms with which we are familiar from their occurrence on embroidered dresses and on the cylinders.

The embossed work of the Assyrians is the most curious and the most artistic portion of their metallurgy. Sometimes it consisted of mere heads and feet of animals, hammered into shape upon a model composed of clay mixed with bitumen. [PLATE LXXV., Figs. 1, 2.] Sometimes it extended to entire figures, as (probably) in the case of the lions clasping each other, so common at the ends of sword-sheaths (see [PLATE LXXV., Fig. 3]), the human figures which ornament the sides of chairs or stools, and the like. [PLATE. LXXV., Fig. 3.] Occasionally it was of a less solid but at the same time of a more elaborate character. In a palace inhabited by Sargon at Nimrud, and in close juxtaposition with a monument certainly of his time, were discovered by Mr. Layard a number of dishes, plates, and bowls, embossed with great taste and skill, which are among the most elegant specimens of Assyrian art discovered during the recent researches. Upon these were represented sometimes hunting scenes, sometimes combats between griffins and lions, or between men and lions, sometimes landscapes with trees and figures of animals, sometimes mere rows of animals following one another. One or two representations from these bowls have been already given. They usually contain a star or scarab in the centre, beyond which is a series of bands or borders, patterned most commonly with figures. [PLATE LXXVI., Fig 1.] It is impossible to give an adequate idea of the delicacy and spirit of the drawings, or of the variety and elegance of the other patterns, in a work of moderate dimensions like the present. Mr. Layard, in his Second Series of "Monuments," has done justice to the subject by pictorial representation, while in his "Nineveh and Babylon" he has described the more important of the vessels separately. The curious student will do well to consult these two works, after which he may examine with advantage the originals in the British Museum.

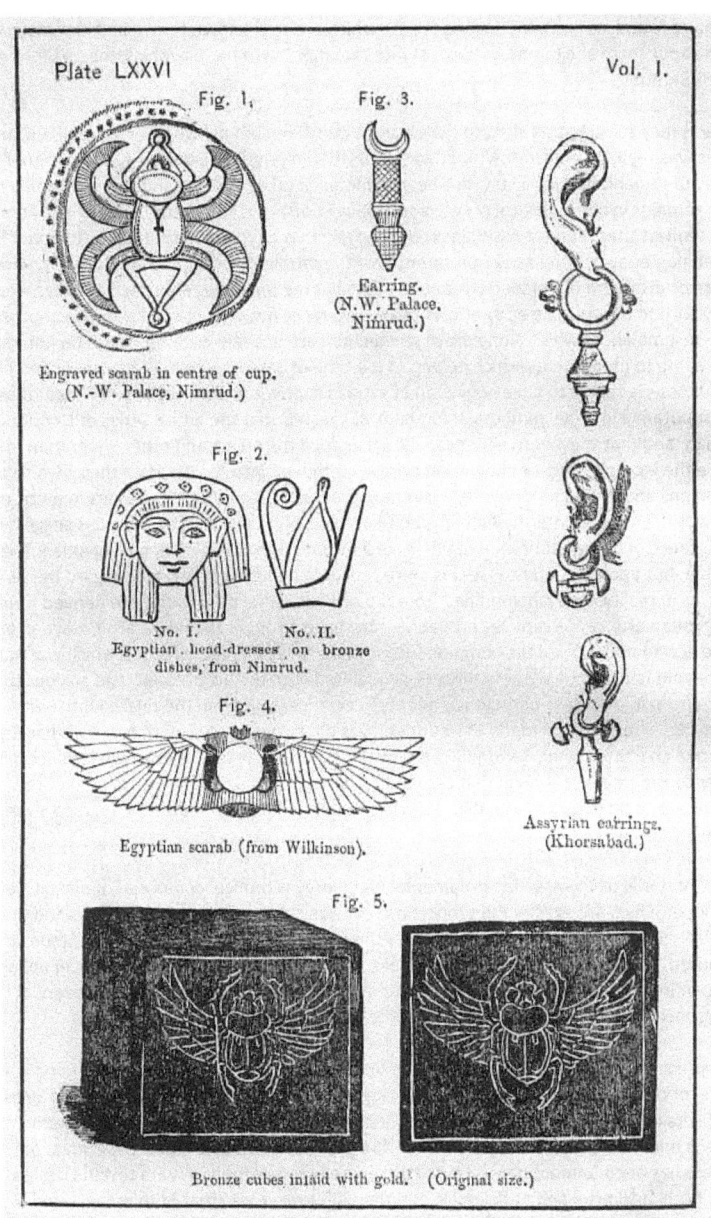

PLATE LXXVI

One of the most remarkable features observable in this whole series of monuments, is its semi-Egyptian character. The occurrence of the scarab has been just noticed. It appears on the bowls frequently, as do sphinxes of an Egyptian type; while sometimes heads and head-dresses purely

Egyptian are found, as in [PLATE LXXVI., Fig. 2], which are well-known forms, and have nothing Assyrian about them and in one or two instances we meet with hieroglyphics, the onk (or symbol of life), the ibis, etc.

These facts may seem at first sight to raise a great question namely, whether, afterall, the art of the Assyrians was really of home growth, or was not rather imported from the Egyptians, either directly or by way of Phoenicia. Such a view has been sometimes taken; but the most cursory study of the Assyrian remains in chronological order, is sufficient to disprove the theory, since it will at once show that the earliest specimens of Assyrian art are the most un-Egyptian in character. No doubt there are certain analogies even here, as the preference for the profile, the stiffness and formality, the ignorance or disregard of perspective, and the like; but the analogies are exactly such as would be tolerably sure to occur in the early efforts of any two races not very dissimilar to one another, while the little resemblances which alone prove connection, are entirely wanting. These do not appear until we come to monuments which belong to the time of Sargon, when direct connection between Egypt and Assyria seems to have begun, and Egyptian captives are known to have been transported into Mesopotamia in large numbers. It has been suggested that the entire series of Nimrud vessels is Phoenician, and that they were either carried off as spoil from Tyre and other Phoenician towns, or else were the workmanship of Phoenician captives removed into Assyria from their own country. The Sidonians and their kindred were, it is remarked, the most renowned workers in metal of the ancient world, and their intermediate position between Egypt and Assyria may, it is suggested, have been the cause of the existence among them of a mixed art, half Assyrian, half Egyptian. The theory is plausible; but upon the whole it seems mere consonant with all the facts to regard the series in question as in reality Assyrian, modified from the ordinary style by an influence derived from Egypt. Either Egyptian artificers—captives probably—may have wrought the bowls after Assyrian models, and have accidentally varied the common forms, more or less, in the direction which was natural to them from old habits; or Assyrian artificers, acquainted with the art of Egypt, and anxious to improve their own from it, may have consciously adopted certain details from the rival country. The workmanship, subjects, and mode of treatment, are all, it is granted, "more Assyrian than Egyptian," the Assyrian character being decidedly more marked than in the case of the ivories which will be presently considered; yet even in that case the legitimate conclusions seems to be that the specimens are to be regarded as native Assyrian, but as produced abnormally, under a strong foreign influence.

The usual material of the Assyrian ornamental metallurgy is bronze, composed of one part of tin to ten of copper which are exactly the proportions considered to be best by the Greeks and Romans, and still in ordinary use at the present day. In some instances, where more than common strength was required, as in the legs of tripods and tables, the bronze was ingeniously cast over an inner structure of iron. This practice was unknown to modern metallurgists until the discovery of the Assyrian specimens, from which it has been successfully imitated.

We may presume that, besides bronze, the Assyrians used, to a certain extent, silver and gold as materials for ornamental metal-work. The earrings, bracelets, and armlets worn by the kings and the great officers of state were probably of the more valuable metal, while the similar ornaments worn by those of minor may have been of silver. [PLATE LXXVI., Fig. 3.] One solitary specimen only of either class has been found; but Mr. Layard discovered several moulds, with tasteful designs for earrings, both at Nimrud and at Koyunjik; and the sculptures show that both in these and the other personal ornaments a good deal of artistic excellence was exhibited. The earrings are frequent in the form of a cross, and are sometimes delicately chased. The armlets and bracelets generally terminate in the heads of rams or bulls, which seem to have been rendered with spirit and taste.

PLATE LXXVII

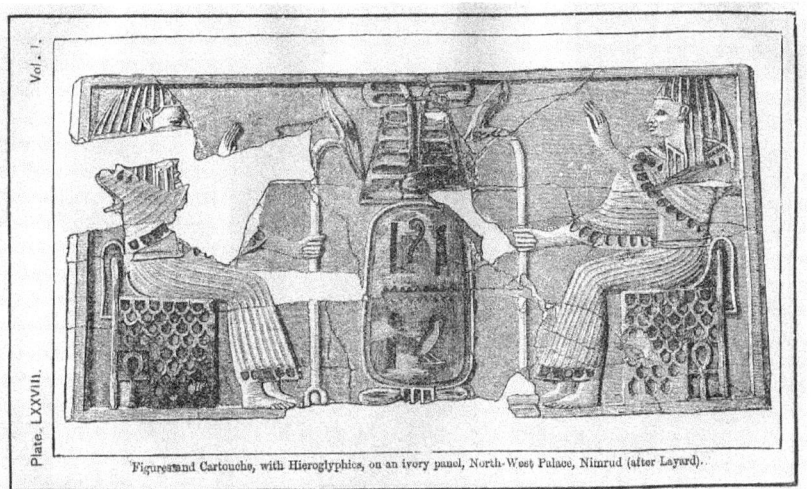

PLATE LXXVIII

By one or two instances it appears that the Assyrians knew how to inlay one metal with another. [PLATE LXXVI, Fig. 5.] The specimens discovered are scarcely of an artistic character, being merely winged scarabaei, outlined in gold on a bronze ground [PLATE LXXVI., Fig. 4.] The work, however, is delicate, and the form very much more true to nature than that which prevailed in Egypt.

The ivories of the Assyrians are inferior both to their metal castings and to their bas-reliefs. They consist almost entirely of a single series, discovered by Mr. Layard in a chamber of the North-West Palace at Nimrud, in the near vicinity of slabs on which was engraved the name of Sargon. The most remarkable point connected with them is the thoroughly Egyptian character of the greater number which at first sight have almost the appearance of being importations from the valley of the Nile. Egyptian profiles, head-dresses, fashions of dressing the hair, ornaments, attitudes, meet us at every turn; while sometimes we find the representations of Egyptian gods, and in two cases hieroglyphics within cartouches. (See [PLATE LXXVIII.]) A few specimens only are of a distinctly Assyrian type, as a fragment of a panel, figured by Mr. Layard [PLATE LXXVII., Fig. 1], and one or two others, in which the guilloche border appears. These carvings are usually mere low reliefs, occupying small panels or tablets, which were mortised or glued to the woodwork of furniture. They were sometimes inlaid in parts with blue grass, or with blue and green pastes let into the ivory, and at the same time decorated with gilding. Now and then the relief is tolerably high, and presents fragments of forms which seem to have had some artistic merit. The best of these is the fore part of a lion walking among reeds (p. 373), which presents analogies with the early art of Asia Minor. [PLATE LXXVII., Fig. 3.] One or two stags' heads have likewise been found, designed and wrought with much spirit and delicacy. [PLATE LXXVII., Fig. 3.] It is remarked that several of the specimens show not only a considerable acquaintance with art, but also an intimate knowledge of the method of working in ivory. One head of a lion was "of singular beauty," but unfortunately it fell to pieces at the very moment of discovery.

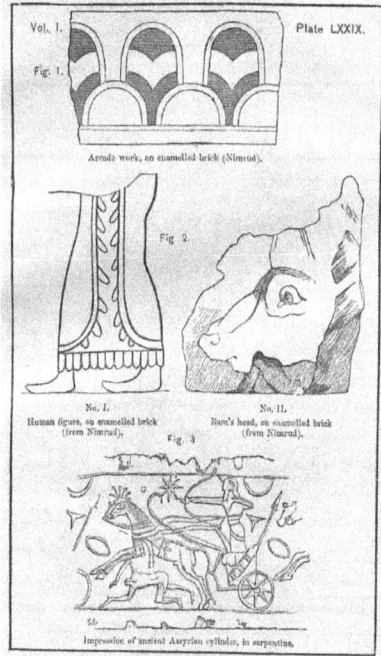

PLATE LXXIX

It is possible that some of the objects here described may be actual specimens of Egyptian art, sent to Sargon as tribute or presents, or else carried off as plunder in his Egyptian expedition. The appearance, however, which even the most Egyptian of them present, on a close examination, is rather that of Assyrian works imitated from Egyptian models than of genuine Egyptian productions. For instance, in the tablet figured on the page opposite, where we see hieroglyphics within a cartouche, the onk or symbol of life, the solar disk, the double ostrich-plume, the long hair-dress called namms, and the tam or kukupha sceptre, all unmistakable Egyptian features—we observe a style of drapery which is quite unknown in Egypt, while in several respects it is Assyrian, or at least Mesopotamian. It is scanty, like that of all Assyrian robed figures; striped, like the draperies of the Chaldaeans and Babylonians: fringed with a broad fringe elaborately colored, as Assyrian fringes are known to have been, and it has large hanging sleeves also fringed, a fashion which appears once or twice upon the Nimrud sculptures. [PLATE LXXVII, Fig. 4.] But if this specimen, notwithstanding its numerous and striking Egyptian features, is rightly regarded as Mesopotamian, it would seem to follow that the rest of the series must still more decidedly be assigned to native genius.

The enamelled bricks of the Assyrians are among the most interesting remains of their art. It is from these bricks alone that we are able to judge at all fully of their knowledge and ideas with respect to color; and it is from them also chiefly that an analysis has been made of the coloring materials employed by the Assyrian artists. The bricks may be divided into two classes—those which are merely patterned, and those which contain designs representing men and animals. The patterned bricks have nothing about them which is very remarkable. They present the usual guilloches, rosettes, bands, scrolls, etc., such as are found in the painted chambers and in the ornaments on dresses, varied with geometrical figures, as circles, hexagons, octagons, and the like; and sometimes with a sort of arcade-work, which is curious, if not very beautiful. [PLATE LXXIX., Fig. 1.] The colors chiefly used in the patterns are pale green, pale yellow, dark brown, and white. Now and then an intense blue and a bright red occur, generally together; but these positive hues are rare, and the taste of the Assyrians seems to have led them to prefer, for their patterned walls, pale and dull hues. The same preference appears, even more strikingly, in the bricks on which designs are represented. There the tints almost exclusively used are pale yellow, pale greenish blue, olive green, white, and a brownish black. It is suggested that the colors have faded, but of this there is no evidence. The Assyrians, when they used the primitive hues, seem, except in the case of red, to have employed subdued tints of them, and red they appear to have introduced very sparingly. Olive-green they affected for grounds, and they occasionally used other half-tints. A pale orange and a delicate lilac or pale purple were found at Khorsabad, while brown (as already observed) is far more common on the bricks than black. Thus the general tone of their coloring is quiet, not to say sombre. There is no striving after brilliant effects. The Assyrian artist seeks to please by the elegance of his forms and the harmony of his hues, not to startle by a display of bright and strongly-contrasted colors. The tints used in a single composition vary from three to five, which latter number they seem never to exceed. The following are the combinations of five hues which occur: brown, green, blue, dark yellow, and pale yellow; orange, lilac, white, yellow, and olive-green. Combinations of four hues are much more common: e.q., red, white, yellow, and black; deep yellow, brown lilac, white, and pale yellow; lilac, yellow, white, and green; yellow, blue, white, and brown, and yellow, blue, white, and olive-green. Sometimes the tints are as few as three, the ground in these cases being generally of a hue used also in the figures. Thus we have yellow, blue, and white on a blue ground and again the same colors on a yellow ground. We have also the simple combinations of white and yellow on a blue ground, and of white and yellow on an olive-green ground.

In every ease there is at harmony in the coloring. We find no harsh contrasts. Either the tones are all subdued, or if any are intense and positive, then all (or almost all) are so. Intense red occurs in two fragments of patterned bricks found by Mr. Layard. It is balanced by intense blue, and accompanied in each case by a full brown and a clear white, while in one case it is further accompanied by a pale green, which has a very good effect. A similar red appears on a design figured by M. Botta. Its accompaniments are white, black, and full yellow. Where lilac occurs, it is balanced by its complementary color, yellow, or by yellow and orange, and further accompanied by white. It is noticeable also that bright hues are not placed one against the other, but are separated by narrow bands of white, or brown and white. This use of white gives a great delicacy and refinement to the coloring, which is saved by it, even where the hues are the strongest, from being coarse or vulgar.

The drawing of the designs resembles that of the sculptures except that the figures are generally slimmer and less muscular. The chief peculiarity is the strength of the outline, which is almost always colored differently from the object drawn, either white, black, yellow, or brown. Generally it is of a uniform thickness (as in No. I., [PLATE LXXIX., Fig. 2]), sometimes, though rarely, it has that variety which characterizes good drawing (as in No. II., [PLATE LXXIX Fig. 2]). Occasionally there is a curious combination of the two styles, as in the specimen [PLATE LXXX., Fig. 1]—the most interesting yet discovered—where the dresses of the two main figures are coarsely outlined in yellow, while the remainder of the design is very lightly sketched in a brownish black.

PLATE LXXX

The size of the designs varies considerably. Ordinarily the figures are small, each brick containing several; but sometimes a scale has been adopted of such a size that portions of the same figure must have been on different bricks. A foot and leg brought by Mr. Layard from Nimrud must have belonged to a man a foot high; while part of a human face discovered in the same locality is said to indicate the form to which it belonged, a height of three feet. Such a size as this is, however, very unusual.

It is scarcely necessary to state that the designs on the bricks are entirely destitute of chiaroscuro. The browns and blacks, like the blues, yellows, and reds, are simply used to express local color. They are employed for hair, eyes, eye-brows, and sometimes for bows and sandals. The other colors are applied as follows: yellow is used for flesh, for shafts of weapons, for horse trappings, sometimes for horses, for chariots, cups, earrings bracelets, fringes, for wing-feathers, occasionally for helmets, and almost always for the hoofs of horses; blue is used for shields, for horses, for some parts of horse-trappings, armor, and dresses, for fish, and for feathers; white is employed for the inner part of the eye, for the linen shirts worn by men, for the marking on fish and feathers, for horses, for buildings, for patterns on dresses, for rams' heads, and for portions of the tiara of the king. Olive-green seems to occur only as a ground; red only in some parts of the royal tiara, orange and lilac only in the wings of winged monsters. It is doubtful how far we may trust the colors on the bricks as accurately or approximately resembling the real local hues. In some cases the intention evidently is to be true to nature, as in the eyes and hair of men, in the representations of flesh, fish, shields, bows, buildings, etc. The yellow of horses may represent cream-color, and the blue may stand for gray, as distinct from white, which seems to have been correctly rendered. The scarlet and white of the king's tiara is likely to be true. When, however, we find eyeballs and eyebrows white, while the inner part of the eye is yellow, the blade of swords yellow, and horses' hoofs blue we seem to have proof that, sometimes at any rate, local color was intentionally neglected, the artist limiting himself to certain hues, and being therefore obliged to render some objects untruly. Thus we must not conclude front the colors of dresses and horse trappings on the bricks which are three only, yellow, blue and white—that the Assyrians used no other hues than those, even for the robes of their kings. It is far more probable that they employed a variety of tints in their apparel, but did not attempt to render that variety on the ordinary painted bricks.

The pigments used by the Assyrians seem to have derived their tints entirely from minerals. The opaque white is found to be oxide of tin; the yellow is the antimoniate of lead, or Naples yellow, with a slight admixture of tin; the blue is oxide of copper, without any cobalt; the green is also from copper; the brown is from iron; and the red is a suboxide of copper. The bricks were slightly baked before being painted; they were then taken from the kiln, painted and enamelled on one side only, the flux and glazes used being composed of silicate of soda aided by oxide of lead; thus prepared, they were again submitted to the action of fire, care being taken to place the painted side upwards, and having been thoroughly baked were then ready for use.

The Assyrian intaglios on stones and gems are commonly of a rude description; but occasionally they exhibit a good deal of delicacy, and sometimes even of grace. They are cut upon serpentine, jasper, chalcedony, cornelian, agate, sienite, quartz, loadstone, amazon-stone, and lapis-lazuli. The usual form of the stone is cylindrical; the sides, however, being either slightly convex or slightly concave, most frequently the latter. [PLATE LXXIX., Fig. 3.] The cylinder is always perforated in the direction of its axis. Besides this ordinary form, a few gems shaped like the Greek—that is, either round or oval—have been found: and numerous impressions from such gems on sealing-clay show that they must have been a tolerably common. The subjects which occur are mostly the same as those on the sculptures—warriors pursuing their foes, hunters in full chase, the king slaying a lion, winged bulls before the sacred tree, acts of worship and other religious or mythological scenes. [PLATE LXXXI. Fig. 1.] There appears to have been a gradual improvement in the workmanship from the earliest period to the time of Sennacherib, when the art culminates. A cylinder found in the ruins of Sennacherib's palace at Koyunjik, which is believed with reason to have been his signet, is scarcely surpassed in delicacy of execution by any intaglio of the Greeks. [PLATE LXXXI., Fig. 1.] The design has a good deal of the usual stiffness, though even here something may be said for the ibex or wild-goat which stands upon the lotus flower to the left: but the special excellence of the gem is in the fineness and minuteness of its execution. The intaglio is not very deep but all the details are beautifully sharp and distinct, while they are on so small a scale that it requires a magnifying glass to distinguish them. The material of the cylinder is translucent green felspar, or amazon-stone, one of the hardest substances known to the lapidary.

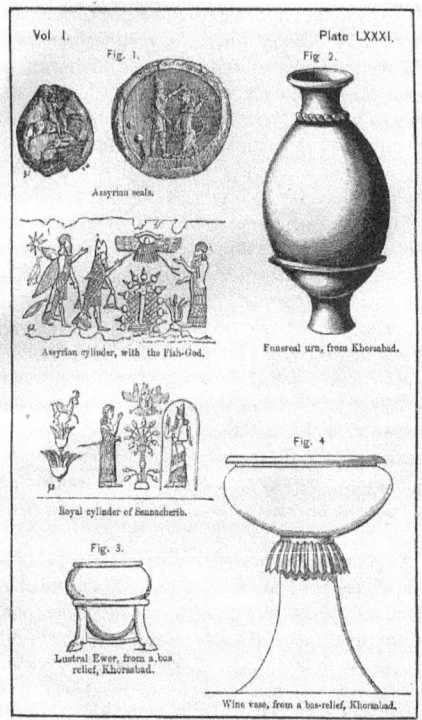

PLATE LXXXI

The fictile art of the Assyrians in its higher branches, as employed for directly artistic purposes, has been already considered; but a few pages may be now devoted to the humbler divisions of the subject, where the useful preponderates over the ornamental. The pottery of Assyria bears a general resemblance in shape, form, and use to that of Egypt; but still it has certain specific differences. According to Mr. Birch, it is, generally speaking, "finer in its paste, brighter in its color, employed in thinner masses, and for purposes not known in Egypt." Abundant and excellent clay is furnished by the valley of the Tigris, more especially by those parts of it which are subject to the annual inundation. The chief employment of this material by the Assyrians was for bricks, which were either simply dried in the sun, or exposed to the action of fire in a kiln. In this latter case they seem to have been uniformly slack-baked; they are light for their size, and are of a pale-red color. The clay of which the bricks were composed was mixed with stubble or vegetable fibre, for the purpose of holding it together—a practice common to the Assyrians with the Egyptians and the Babylonians. This fibre still appears in the sun-dried bricks, but has been destroyed by the heat of the kiln in the case of the baked bricks, leaving behind it, however, in the clay traces of the stalks or stems. The size and shape of the bricks vary. They are most commonly square, or nearly so; but occasionally the shape more resembles that of the ancient Egyptian and modern English brick, the width being about half the length, and the thickness half or two-thirds of the width. The greatest size to which the square bricks attain is a length and width of about two feet. From this maximum they descend by manifold gradations to a minimum of one foot. The oblong bricks are smaller; they seldom much exceed a foot in length, and in width vary from six to seven and a half inches. Whatever the shape and size of the bricks, their thickness is nearly uniform, the thinnest being as much as three inches in thickness, and the thickest not more than four inches or four and a half. Each brick was made in a wooden frame or mould. Most of the baked bricks were inscribed, not however like the Chaldaean, the Egyptian, and the Babylonian, with an inscription in a small square or oval depression near the centre of one of the broad faces, but with one which either covered the whole of one such face, or else ran along the edge. It is uncertain whether the inscription was stamped upon the bricks by a single impression, or whether it was inscribed by the potter with a triangular style. Mr. Birch thinks the former was the means used, "as the trouble of writing upon each brick would have been endless." Mr. Layard, however, is of a different opinion.

In speaking of the Assyrian writing, some mention has been made of the terra cotta cylinders and tablets, which in Assyria replaced the parchment and papyrus of other nations, being the most ordinary writing material in use through the country. The purity and fineness of the material thus employed is very remarkable, as well as its strength, of which advantage was taken to make the cylinders hollow, and thus at once to render them cheaper and more portable. The terra cotta of the cylinders and tablets is sometimes unglazed; sometimes the natural surface has been covered with a "vitreous silicious glaze or white coating." The color varies, being sometimes a bright polished brown, sometimes a pale yellow, sometimes pink, and sometimes a very dark tint, nearly black. The most usual color however for cylinders is pale yellow, and for tablets light red, or pink. There is no doubt that in both these cases the characters were impressed separately by the hand, a small metal style of rod being used for the purpose.

PLATE LXXXII

Terra cotta vessels, glazed and unglazed, were in common use among the Assyrians, for drinking and other domestic purposes. They comprised vases, lamps, jugs, amphorae, saucers, jars, etc. [PLATE LXXX., Fig. 2.] The material of the vessels is fine, though generally rather yellow in tone. The shapes present no great novelty, being for the most part such as are found both in the old Chaldaean tombs, and in ordinary Roman sepulchres. Among the most elegant are the funeral urns discovered by M. Botta at Khorsabad, which are with a small opening at top, a short and very scanty pedestal, and two raised rings, one rather delicately chased, by way of ornament. [PLATE LXXXI., Fig. 2.] Another graceful form is that of the large jars uncovered at Nimrud [PLATE LXXXII., Fig. 1], of which Mr. Layard gives a representation. Still more tasteful are some of the examples which occur upon the bas-reliefs, and seemingly represent earthen vases. Among these may be particularized a lustral ewer resting in a stand supported by bulls' feet, which appears in front of a temple at Khorsabad [PLATE LXXXI., Fig. 3], and a wine vase (see [PLATE LXXXI., Fig. 4]) of ample dimensions, which is found in a banquet scene at the same place. Some of the lamps are also graceful enough, and seem to be the prototypes out of which were developed the more elaborate productions of the Greeks. [PLATE LXXXII., Fig. 2.] Others are more simple, being without ornament of any kind, and nearly resembling a modern tea-pot (see No., IV. [PLATE LXXXII., Fig. 2.])

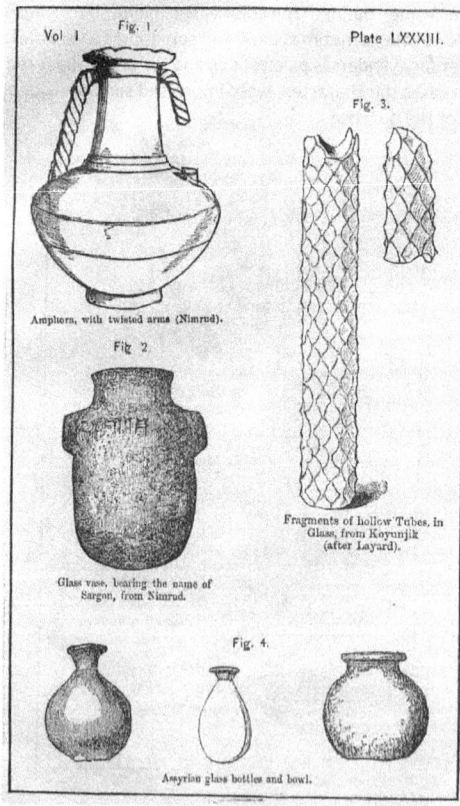

PLATE LXXXIII

The glazed pottery is, for the most part, tastefully colored. An amphora, with twisted arms, found at Nimrud (see [PLATE LXXXIII., Fig. 1]) is of two colors, a warm yellow, and a cold bluish green. The green predominates in the upper, the yellow in the under portion; but there is a certain amount of blending or mottling in the mid-region, which has a very pleasant effect. A similarly mottled character is presented by two other amphorae from the same place, where the general hue is a yellow which varies in intensity, and the mottling is with a violet blue. In some cases the colors are not blended, but sharply defined by lines, as in a curious spouted cup figured by Mr. Layard, and in several fragmentary specimens. Painted patterns are not uncommon upon the glazed pottery, though upon the unglazed they are scarcely ever found. The most usual colors are blue, yellow, and white; brown, purple, and lilac have been met with occasionally. These colors are thought to be derived chiefly from metallic oxides, over which was laid as a glazing a vitreous silicated substance. On the whole, porcelain of this fine kind is rare in the Assyrian remains, and must be regarded as a material that was precious and used by few.

Assyrian glass is among the most beautiful of the objects which have been exhumed. M. Botta compared it to certain fabrics of Venice and Bohemia, into which a number sit different colors are artificially introduced. But a careful analysis has shown that the lovely prismatic hues which delight us in the Assyrian specimens, varying under different lights with all the delicacy and brilliancy of the opal, are due, not to art, but to the wonder-working hand of time, which, as it destroys the fabric, compassionately invests it with additional grace and beauty. Assyrian glass was either transparent or stained with a single uniform color. It was composed, in the usual way, by a mixture of sand or silex with alkalis, and, like the Egyptian, appears to have been first rudely fashioned into shape by the blowpipe. It was then more carefully shaped, and, where necessary, hollowed out by a turning machine, the Marks of which are sometimes still visible. The principal specimens which have been discovered are small bottles and bowls, the former not more than three or four inches high, the latter from four to five inches in diameter, [PLATE LXXXIII., Fig. 4.] The vessels are occasionally inscribed with the name of a king, as is the case in the famous vase of Sargon, found by Mr. Layard at Nimrud, which is here figured. [PLATE LXXXIII., Fig. 2.] This is the earliest known specimen of transparent glass, which is not found in Egypt until the time of the Psammetichi. The Assyrians used also opaque glass, which they colored, sometimes red, with the suboxide of copper, sometimes white, sometimes of other hues. They seem not to have been able to form masses of glass of any considerable size; and thus the employment of the material must have been limited to a few ornamental, rather than useful, purposes. A curious specimen is that of a pipe or tube, honey-combed externally, which Mr. Layard exhumed at Koyunjik, and of which the cut [PLATE LXXXIII., Fig. 1] is a rough representation.

An object found at Nimrud, in close connection with several glass vessels, is of a character sufficiently similar to render its introduction in this place not inappropriate. This is a lens composed of rock crystal, about an inch and a half in diameter, and nearly an inch thick, having one plain and one convex surface, and somewhat rudely shaped and polished which, however gives a tolerably distinct focus at the distance of 4 1/2 inches from the plane side, and which may have been used either as a magnifying glass or to concentrate the rays of the sun. The form is slightly oval, the longest diameter being one and six-tenths inch, the shortest one and four-tenths inch. The thickness is not uniform, but greater on one side than on the other. The plane surface is ill-polished and scratched, the convex one, not polished on a concave spherical disk, but fashioned on a lapidary's wheel, or by some method equally rude. As a burn, glass the lens has no great power; but it magnifies fairly, and may have been of great use to those who inscribed, or to those who sought to decipher, the royal memoirs. It is the only object of the kind that has been found among the remains of antiquity, though it cannot he doubled that lenses were known and were used as burning glasses by the Greeks.

Some examples have been already given illustrating the tasteful ornamentation of Assyrian furniture. It consisted, so far as we know, of tables, chairs, couches, high stools, foot-stools, and stands with shelves to hold the articles needed for domestic purposes. As the objects themselves have in all cases ceased to exist, leaving behind them only a few fragments, it is necessary to have recourse to the bas-reliefs for such notices as may be thence derived of their construction and character. In these representations the most ordinary form of table is one in which the principal of our camp-stools seems to be adopted, the legs crossing each other as in the illustrations [PLATE LXXXIV.]. only two legs are represented, but we must undoubtedly regard these two as concealing two others of the same kind at the opposite end of the table. The legs ordinarily terminate in the feet of animals, sometimes of bulls, but more commonly of horses. Sometimes between the two legs we see a species of central pillar, which, however, is not traceable below the point where the legs cross one another. The pillar itself is either twisted or plain (see No. III., [PLATE LXXXIV.]). Another form of table, less often met with, but simpler, closely resembles the common table of the moderns. It has merely the necessary flat top, with perpendicular legs at the corners. The skill of the cabinet-makers enabled them to dispense in most instances with cross-bars (see No. I.), which are, however, sometimes seen (see No. II., No. III., and No. IV.), uniting the legs of this kind of tables. The corners are often ornamented with lions' or rams' heads, and the feet are frequently in imitation of some animal form (see No. III. and No. IV.). Occasionally we find a representation of a three-legged table, as the specimen [PLATE LXXXIV., Fig. 4], which is from a relief at Koyunjik. The height of tables appears to have been greater than with ourselves; the lowest reach easily to a man's middle; the highest are level with the upper part of the chest.

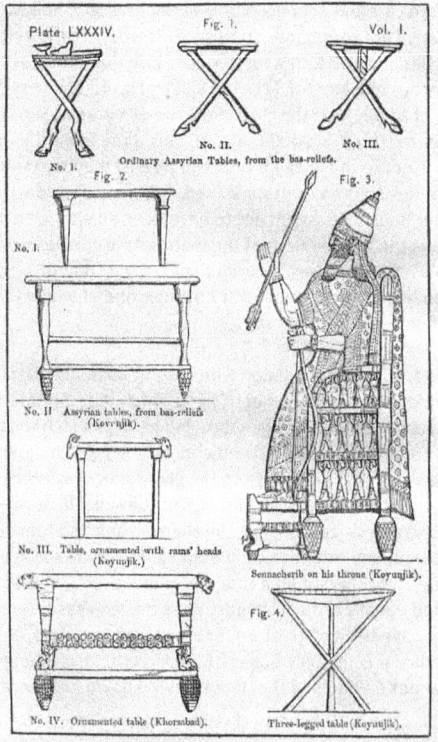

PLATE LXXXIV

Assyrian thrones and chairs were very elaborate. The throne of Sennacherib exhibited on its sides and arms three rows of carved figures, one above another (PLATE LXXXIV.,Fig. 3), supporting the bars with their hands. The bars, the arms, and the back were patterned. The legs ended in a pine-shaped ornament very common in Assyrian furniture. Over the back was thrown an embroidered cloth hinged at the end, which hung down nearly to the floor. A throne of Sargon's was adorned on its sides with three human figures, apparently representations of the king, below which was the war-horse of the monarch, caparisoned as for battle. [PLATE LXXXV., Fig. 1.] Another throne of the same monarch's had two large and four small figures of men at the side, while the back was supported on either side by a human figure of superior dimensions. The use of chairs with high backs, like these, was apparently confined to the monarchs. Persons of less exalted rank were content to sit on seats which were either stools, or chairs with a low back level with the arms.

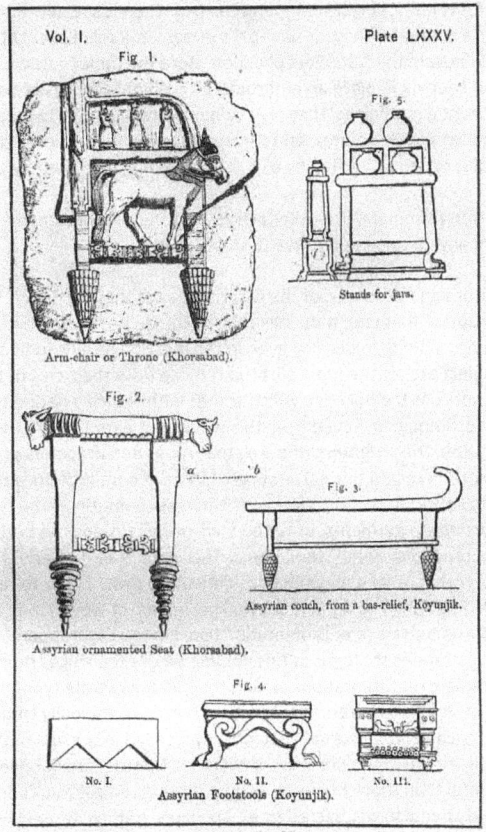

PLATE LXXXV

Seats of this kind, whether thrones or chairs, were no doubt constructed mainly of wood. The ornamental work may, however, have been of bronze, either cast into the necessary shape, or wrought into it by the hammer. The animal heads at the ends of arms seem to have fallen under the latter description [PLATE LXXXV., Fig. 2.] In some cases, ivory was among the materials used: it has been found in the legs of a throne at Koyunjik, and may not improbably have entered into the ornamentation of the best furniture very much more generally.

The couches which we find represented upon the sculptures are of a simple character. The body is flat, not curved; the legs are commonly plain, and fastened to each other by a cross-bar, sometimes terminating in the favorite pine-shaped ornament. One end only is raised, and this usually curves inward nearly in a semicircle. [PLATE LXXXV., Fig. 3.] The couches are decidedly lower than the Egyptian; and do not, like them, require a stool or steps in order to ascend them.

Stools, however, are used with the chairs or thrones of which mention was made above—lofty seats, where such a support for the sitter's feet was imperatively required. [PLATE LXXXV.. Fig. 4.] They are sometimes plain at the sides, and merely cut en chevron at the base; sometimes highly ornamented, terminating in lions' feet supported on cones, in the same (or in volutes), supported on balls, and otherwise adorned with volutes, lion castings, and the like. The most elaborate specimen is the stool (No. III.) which supports the feet of Asshur-bani-pal's queen on a relief brought from the North Palace at Koyunjik, and now in the National Collection. Here the upper corners exhibit the favorite gradines, guarding and keeping in place an embroidered cushion; the legs are ornamented with rosettes and with horizontal mouldings, they are connected together by two bars, the lower one adorned with a number of double volutes, and the upper one with two lions standing back to back; the stool stands on balls, surmounted first by a double moulding, and then by volutes.

Stands with shelves often terminate, like other articles of furniture, in animals' feet, most commonly lions', as in the accompanying specimens. [PLATE LXXXV., Fig. 5.]

Of the embroidered robes and draperies of the Assyrians, as of their furniture, we can judge only by the representations made of them upon the bas-reliefs. The delicate texture of such fabrics has prevented them from descending to our day even in the most tattered condition; and the ancient testimonies on the subject are for the most part too remote from the times of the Assyrians to be of much value. Ezekiel's notice is the only one which comes within such a period of Assyria's fall as to make it an important testimony, and even from this we cannot gather much that goes beyond the evidence of the sculptures. The sculptures show us that robes and draperies of all kinds were almost always more or less patterned; and this patterning, which is generally of an extremely elaborate kind, it is reasonable to conclude was the work of the needle. Sometimes the ornamentation is confined to certain portions of garments, as to the ends of sleeves and the bottoms of robes or tunics; at others it is extended over the whole dress. This is more particularly the case with the garments of the kings, which are of a magnificence difficult to describe, or to represent within a narrow compass. [PLATE LXXXVI, Fig. 1.] One or two specimens, however, may be given almost at random, indicating different styles of ornamentation usual in the royal apparel. Other examples will be seen in the many illustrations throughout this volume where the king is represented. It is remarkable that the earliest representations exhibit the most elaborate types of all, after which a reaction seems to set in simplicity is affected, which, however, is gradually trenched upon, until at last a magnificence is reached little short of that which prevailed in the age of the first monuments. The draperies of Asshur-izir-pal in the north-west palace at Nimrud, are at once more minutely labored and more tasteful than those of any later time. Besides elegant but unmeaning patterns, they exhibit human and animal forms, sacred trees, sphinxes, griffins, winged horses, and occasionally bull-hunts and lion-hunts. The upper part of this king's dress is in one instance almost covered with figures, which range themselves round a circular breast ornament, whereof the cut opposite is a representation. Elsewhere his apparel is less superb, and indeed it presents almost every degree of richness, from the wonderful embroidery of the robe just mentioned to absolute plainness. In the celebrated picture of the lion-hunt. [PLATE LXXXVI., Fig. 2.] With Sargon, the next king who has left many monuments, the case is remarkably different. Sargon is represented always in the same dress—a long fringed robe, embroidered simply with rosettes, which are spread somewhat scantily over its whole surface. Sennacherib's apparel is nearly of the same kind, or, if anything, richer, though sometimes the rosettes are omitted His grandson, Asshur-bani-pal, also affects the rosette ornament, but reverts alike to the taste and the elaboration of the early kings. He wears a breast ornament containing human figures, around which are ranged a number of minute and elaborate patterns. [PLATE LXXXVII.]

PLATE LXXXVII

To this account of the arts, mimetic and other, in which the Assyrians appear to have excelled, it might be expected that there should be added a sketch of their scientific knowledge. On this subject, however, so little is at present known, while so much may possibly become known within a short time, that it seems best to omit it, or to touch it only in the lightest and most cursory manner. When the numerous tablets now in the British Museum shall have been deciphered, studied, and translated, it will probably be found that they contain a tolerably full indication of what Assyrian science really was, and it will then be seen how far it was real and valuable, in what respects mistaken and illusory. At present this mine is almost unworked, nothing more having been ascertained than that the subjects whereof the tables treat are various, and their apparent value very different. Comparative philology seems to have been largely studied, and the works upon it exhibit great care and diligence. Chronology is evidently much valued, and very exact records are kept whereby the lapse of time can even now be accurately measured. Geography and history have each an important place in Assyrian learning; while astronomy and mythology occupy at least as great a share of attention. The astronomical observations recorded are thought to be frequently inaccurate, as might be expected when there were no instruments, or none of any great value. Mythology is a very favorite subject, and appears to be treated most fully; but hitherto cuneiform scholars have scarcely penetrated below the surface of the mythological tablets, baffled by the obscurity of the subject and the difficulty of the dialect (in) which they are written.

PLATE LXXXVIII

On one point alone, belonging to the domain of science, do the Assyrian representations of their life enable us to comprehend, at least to some extent, their attainments. The degree of knowledge which this people possessed on the subject of practical mechanics is illustrated with tolerable fulness in the bas-reliefs, more especially in the important series discovered at Koyunjik, where the transport of the colossal bulls from the quarry to the palace gateways is represented in the most elaborate detail. [PLATE LXXXVIII.] The very fact that they were able to transport masses of stone, many tons in weight, over a considerable space of ground, and to place then on the summit of artificial platforms from thirty to eighty (or ninety) feet high, would alone indicate considerable mechanical knowledge. The further fact, now made clear from the bas-reliefs, that they wrought all the elaborate carving of the colossi before they proceeded to raise them or put them in place, is an additional argument of their skill, since it shows that they had no fear of any accident happening in the transport. It appears from the representations that they placed their colossus in a standing posture, not on a truck or wagon of any kind, but on a huge wooden sledge, shaped nearly like a boat, casing it with an openwork of spars or beams, which crossed each other at right angles, and were made perfectly tight by means of wedges. To avert the great danger of the mass toppling over sideways, ropes were attached to the top of the casing, at the point where the beams crossed one another, and were held taut by two parties of laborers, one on either side of the statue. Besides these, wooden forks or props were applied on either side to the second set of horizontal cross-beams, held also by men whose business it would be to resist the least inclination of the huge stone to lean to one side more than to the other. The front of the sledge on which the colossus stood was curved gently upwards, to facilitate its sliding along the ground, and to enable it to rise with readiness upon the rollers, which were continually placed before it by laborers just in front, while others following behind gathered them up when the bulky mass had passed over there. The motive power was applied in front by four gangs of men who held on to four large cables, at which they pulled by means of small ropes or straps fastened to them, and passed under one shoulder and over the other—an arrangement which enabled them to pull by weight as much as by muscular strength, as the annexed figure will plainly show. [PLATE LXXXIX., Fig. 1.] The cables appear to have been of great strength, and are fastened carefully to four strong projecting pins—two near the front, two at the back part of the sledge, by a knot so tied that it would be sure not to slip. [PLATE LXXXIX., Fig. 4.] Finally, as in spite of the rollers, whose use in diminishing friction, and so facilitating progress, was evidently well understood, and in spite of the amount of force applied in front, it would have been difficult to give the first impetus to so great a mass, a lever was skilfully applied behind to raise the hind part of the sledge slightly, and so propel it forward, while to secure a sound and firm fulcrum, wedges of wood were inserted between the lever and the ground. The greater power of a lever at a distance from the fulcrum being known, ropes were attached to its upper end, which could not otherwise have been reached, and the lever was worked by means of them.

We have thus unimpeachable evidence as to the mode whereby the conveyance of huge blocks of stone along level ground was effected. But it may be further asked, how were the blocks raised up to the elevation at which we find them placed? Upon this point there is no direct evidence; but the probability is that they were drawn up inclined ways, sloping gently from the natural ground to the top of the platforms. The Assyrians were familiar with inclined ways, which they used almost always in their attacks on walled places, and which in many cases they constructed either of brick or stone. The Egyptians certainly employed them for the elevation of large blocks; and probably in the earlier times most nations who affected massive architecture had recourse to the same simple but uneconomical plan. The crane and pulley were applied to this purpose later. In the Assyrian sculptures we find no application of either to building, and no instance at all of the two in combination. Still each appears on the bas-reliefs separately—the crane employed for drawing water from the rivers, and spreading it over the lands, the pulley for lowering and raising the bucket in wells. [PLATE LXXXIX., Fig. 3.]

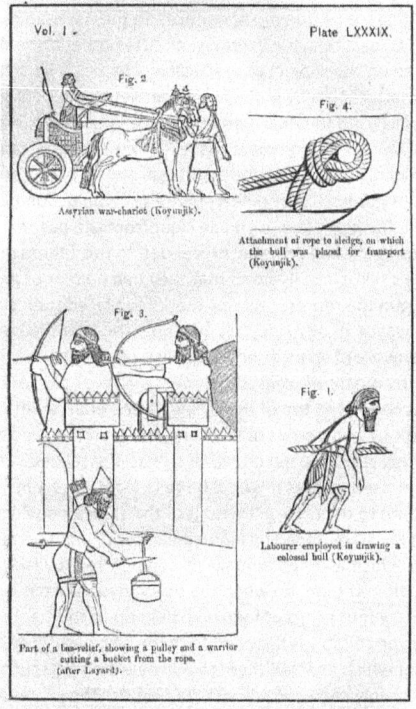

PLATE LXXXIX

We must conclude from these facts that the Assyrians had made considerable advances in mechanical knowledge, and were, in fact, acquainted, more or less, with most of the contrivances whereby heavy weights have commonly been moved and raised among the civilized nations of Europe. We have also evidence of their skill in the mechanical processes of shaping pottery and glass, of casting and embossing metals, and of cutting intaglios upon hard stones. Thus it was not merely in the ruder and coarser, but likewise in the more delicate processes, that they excelled. The secrets of metallurgy, of dyeing, enamelling, inlaying, glass-blowing, as well as most of the ordinary manufacturing processes, were known to them. In all the common arts and appliances of life, they must be pronounced at least on a par with the Egyptians, while in taste they greatly exceeded, not that nation only, but all the Orientals. Their "high art" is no doubt much inferior to that of Greece; but it has real merit, and is most remarkable considering the time when it was produced. It has grandeur, dignity, boldness, strength, and sometimes even freedom and delicacy; it is honest and painstaking, unsparing of labor, and always anxious for truth. Above all, it is not lifeless and stationary, like the art of the Egyptians and the Chinese, but progressive and aiming at improvement. To judge by the advance over previous works which we observe in the sculptures of the son of Esarhaddon, it would seem that if Assyria had not been assailed by barbaric enemies about his time, she might have anticipated by above a century the finished excellence of the Greeks.

CHAPTER VII

MANNERS AND CUSTOMS

"Whose arrows are sharp, and all their bows bent, their horses' hoofs shall be counted like flint, and their wheels like a whirlwind."—ISA. v. 28.

In reviewing, so far as our materials permit, the manners and customs of the Assyrians, it will be convenient to consider separately their warlike and their peaceful usages. The sculptures furnish very full illustration of the former, while on the latter they throw light far more sparingly.

The Assyrians fought in chariots, on horseback, and on foot. Like most ancient nations, as the Egyptians, the Greeks in the heroic times, the Canaanites, the Syrians, the Jews and Israelites, the Persians, the Gauls, the Britons, and many others, the Assyrians preferred the chariot as most honorable, and probably as most safe. The king invariably went out to war in a chariot, and always fought from it, excepting at the siege of a town, when he occasionally dismounted and shot his arrows on foot. The chief state-officers and other personages of high rank followed the same practice. Inferior persons served either as cavalry or as foot-soldiers.

The Assyrian war-chariot is thought to have been made of wood. Like the Greek and the Egyptian, it appears to have been mounted from behind where it was completely open, or closed only by means of a shield, which (as it seems) could be hung across the aperture. It was completely panelled at the sides, and often highly ornamented, as will be seen from the various illustrations given in this chapter. The wheels were two in number, and were placed far back, at or very near the extreme end of the body, so that the weight pressed considerably upon the pole, as was the case also in Egypt. They had remarkably broad felloes, thin and delicate spokes, and small or moderate sized axels. [PLATE LXXXIX. Fig. 2], and [PLATE XC., Figs. 1, 2.] The number of the spokes was either six or eight. The felloes appear to have been formed of three distinct circles of wood, the middle one being the thinnest, and the outer one far the thickest of the three. Sometimes these circles were fastened together externally by bands of mental, hatchet-shaped. In one or two instances we find the outermost circle divided by cross-bars, as if it had been composed of four different pieces.

Occasionally there is a fourth circle, which seems to represent a metal tire outside the felloe, whereby it was guarded from injury. This tire is either plain or ornamented.

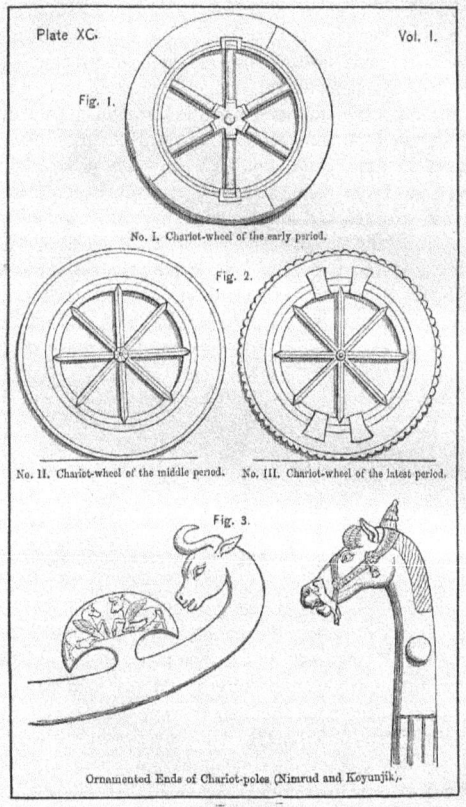

PLATE XC

The wheels were attached to an axletree, about which they revolved, in the usual manner. The body was placed directly upon the axletree and upon the pole, without the intervention of any springs. The pole started from the middle of the axle-tree, and, passing below the floor of the body in a horizontal direction, thence commonly curved upwards till it had risen to about half the height of the body, when it was again horizontal for awhile, once more curving upwards at the end. It usually terminated in an ornament, which was sometimes the head of an animal—a bull, a horse, or a duck—sometimes a more elaborate and complicated work of art. [PLATE XC., Fig. 3.] Now and then the pole continued level with the bottom of the body till it had reached its full projection, and then rose suddenly to the height of the top of the chariot. It was often strengthened by one or more thin bars, probably of metal; which united it to the upper part of the chariot-front.

Chariots were drawn either by two or three, never by four, horses. They seem to have had but a single pole. Where three horses were used, one must therefore have been attached merely by a rope or thong, like the side horses of the Greeks, and, can scarcely have been of much service for drawing the vehicle. He seems rightly regarded as a supernumerary, intended to take the place of one of the others, should either be disabled by a wound or accident. It is not easy to determine from the sculptures how the two draught horses were attached to the pole. Where chariots are represented without horses, we find indeed that they have always a cross-bar or yoke; but where horses are represented in the act of drawing a chariot, the cross-bar commonly disappears altogether. It would seem that the Assyrian artists, despairing of their ability to represent the yoke properly when it was presented to the eye end-wise, preferred, for the most part, suppressing it wholly to rendering it in an unsatisfactory manner. Probably a yoke did really in every case pass over the shoulders of the two draught horses, and was fastened by straps to the collar which is always seen round their necks.

These yokes, or cross-bars, were of various kinds. Sometimes they appear to have consisted of a mere slight circular bar, probably of metal, which passed through the pole; sometimes of a thicker spar, through which the pole itself passed. In this latter case the extremities were occasionally adorned with heads of animals. [PLATE XCI., Fig. 1.] The most common kind of yoke exhibits a double curve, so as to resemble a species of bow unstrung. [PLATE XCI., Fig. 2.] Now and then a specimen is found very curiously complicated, being formed of a bar curved strongly at either end, and exhibiting along its course four other distinct curvatures having opposite to there apertures resembling eyes, with an upper and a lower eyelid. [PLATE XCI., Fig. 3.] It has been suggested that this yoke belonged to a four-horse chariot, and that to each of the four eyes (a a a a) there was a steed attached; but, as no representation of a four-horse chariot has been found, this suggestion must be regarded as inadmissible. The probability seems to be that this yoke, like the others, was for two horses, on whose necks it rested at the points marked b b, the apertures (c c c c) lying thus on either side of the animals' necks, and furnishing the means whereby the he was fastened to the collar. It is just possible that we have in the sculptures of the later period a representation of the extremities (d d) of this kind of yoke, since in them a curious curve appears sometimes on the necks of chariot-horses, just above the upper end of the collar.

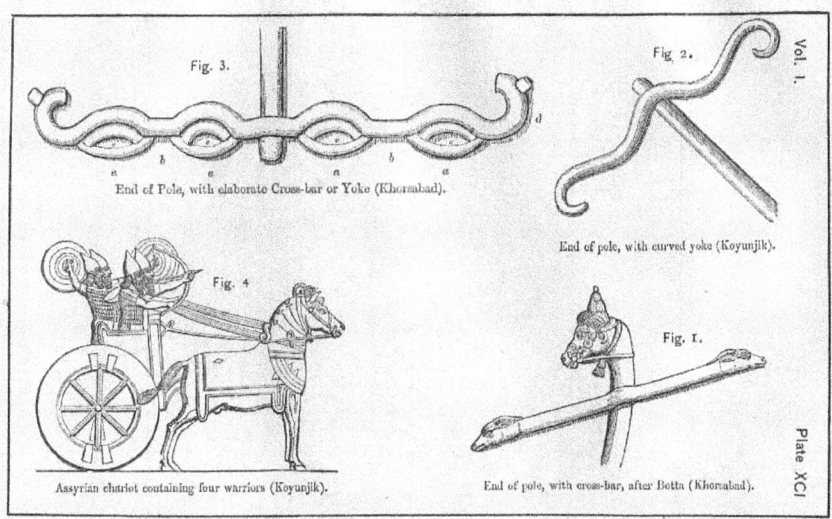

PLATE XCI

Assyrian chariots are exceedingly short: but, apparently, they must have been of a considerable width. They contain two persons at the least; and this number is often increased to three, and sometimes even to four. [PLATE XCI. Fig. 4.] The warrior who fights from a chariot is necessarily attended by his charioteer; and where he is a king, or a personage of high importance, he is accompanied by a second attendant, who in battle-scenes always bears a shield, with which he guards the person of his master. Sometimes, though rarely, four persons are seen in a chariot—the king or chief, the charioteer, and two guards, who protect the monarch on either side with circular shields or targes. The charioteer is always stationed by the side of the warrior, not as frequently with the Greeks, behind him. The guards stand behind, and, owing to the shortness of the chariot, must have experienced some difficulty in keeping their places. They are evidently forced to lean backwards from want of room, and would probably have often fallen out, had they not grasped with one hand a rope or strap firmly fixed to the front of the vehicle.

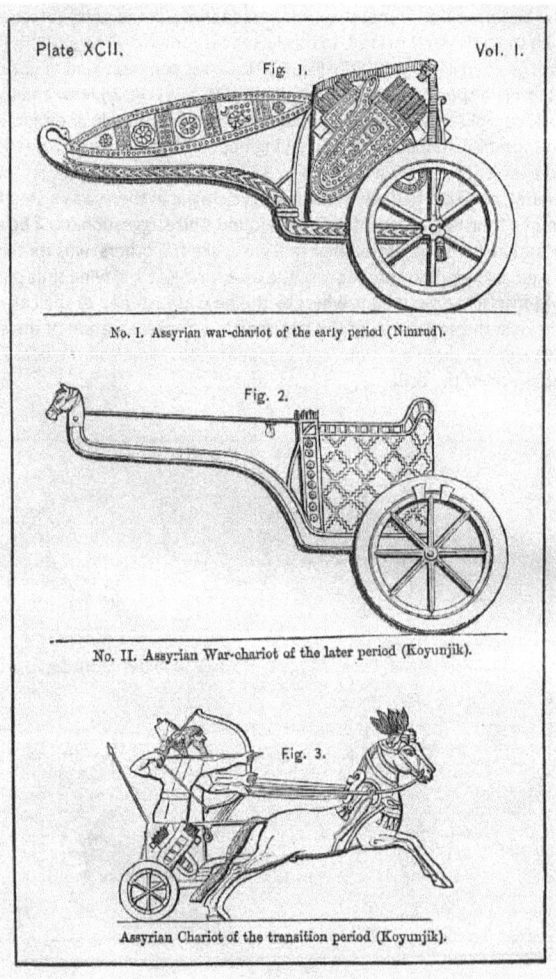

PLATE XCII

There are two principal types of chariots in the Assyrian sculptures, which may be distinguished as the earlier and the later. The earlier are comparatively low and short. The wheels are six-spoked, and of small diameter. The body is plain, or only ornamented by a border, and is rounded in front, like the Egyptian and the classical chariots. [PLATE XCII., Fig 1.] Two quivers are suspended diagonally at the side of the body, while a rest for a spear, commonly fashioned into the shape of a human head, occupies the upper corner at the back. From the front of the body to the further end of the pole, which is generally patterned and terminates in the head and neck of a ball or a duck, extends an ornamented structure, thought to have been of linen or silk stitched upon a framework of wood, which is very conspicuous in the representation. A shield commonly hangs behind these chariots, perhaps closing the entrance; and a standard is sometimes fixed in them towards the front, connected with the end of the pole by a rope or bar.

The later chariots are loftier and altogether larger than the earlier. The wheel is eight spoked, and reaches as high as the shoulders of the horses, which implies a diameter of about five feet. [PLATE XCII., Fig. 2.] The body rises a foot or rather more, above this; and the riders thus from their elevated position command the whole battle-field. The body is not rounded, but made square in front: it has no quivers attached to it externally, but has, instead, a projection at one or both of the corners which seems to have served as an arrow-case. This projection is commonly patterned, as is in many cases the entire body of the chariot, though sometimes the ornamentation is confined to an elegant but somewhat scanty border. The poles are plain, not patterned, sometimes, however, terminating in the head of a horse; there is no ornamental framework connecting them with the chariot, but in its stead we see a thin bar, attached to which, either above or below, there is in most instances a loop, whereto we may suppose that the reins were occasionally fastened. No shield is suspended behind these chariots; but we sometimes observe an embroidered drapery hanging over the back, in a way which would seem to imply that they were closed behind, at any rate by a cross-bar.

The trappings of the chariot-horses belonging to the two periods are not very different. They consist principally of a headstall, a collar, a breast-ornament, and a sort of huge tassel pendent at the horse's side. The headstall was formed commonly of three straps: one was attached to the bit at either end, and passed behind the ears over the neck; another, which was joined to this above, encircled the smallest part of the neck; while a third, crossing the first at right angles, was carried round the forehead and the cheek bones. At the point where the first and second joined, or a little in front of this, rose frequently a waving plume, or a crest composed of three huge tassels, one above another; while at the intersection of the second and third was placed a rosette or other suitable ornament. The first strap was divided where it approached the bit into two or three smaller straps, which were attached to the bit in different places. A fourth strap sometimes passed across the nose from the point where the first strap subdivided. All the straps were frequently patterned; the bit was sometimes shaped into an animal form and streamers occasional floated from the nodding plume or crest which crowned the heads of the war-steeds.

The collar is ordinarily represented as a mere broad band passing round the neck, not of the withers (as with ourselves). but considerably higher up, almost midway between the withers and the cheek-bone. Sometimes it is of uniform width while often it narrows greatly as it approaches the back of the neck. It is generally patterned, and appears to have been a mere flat leathern band. It is impossible to say in what exact way the pole was attached to it, though in the later sculptures we have elaborate representations of the fastening. The earlier sculptures seem to append to the collar one or more patterned straps, which, passing round the horse's belly immediately behind the fore legs, served to keep it in place, while at the same time they were probably regarded as ornamental; but under the later kings these belly Lands were either reduced to a single strap, or else dispensed with altogether.

The breast-ornament consists commonly of a fringe, more or less complicated. The simplest form, which is that of the most ancient times, exhibits a patterned strap with a single row of long tassels pendent from it, as in the annexed representation. At a later date we find a double and even a triple row of tassels.

The pendent side-ornament is a very conspicuous portion of the trappings. It is attached to the collar either by a long straight strap or by a circular band which falls on either side of the neck. The upper extremity is often shaped into the form of an animal's head, below which comes most commonly a circle or disk, ornamented with a rosette, a Maltese cross, a winged bull, or other sacred emblem, while below the circle hang huge tassels in a single row or smaller ones arranged in several rows. In the sculptures of Sargon at Khorsabad, the tassels of both the breast and side ornaments were colored, the tints being in most cases alternately red and blue.

Occasionally the chariot-horses were covered from the ears almost to the tail with rich cloths, magnificently embroidered over their whole surface.' [PLATE XCIII., Fig. 2.] These cloths encircled the neck, which they closely fitted, and, falling on either side of the body, were then kept in place by means of a broad strap round the rump and a girth under the belly.

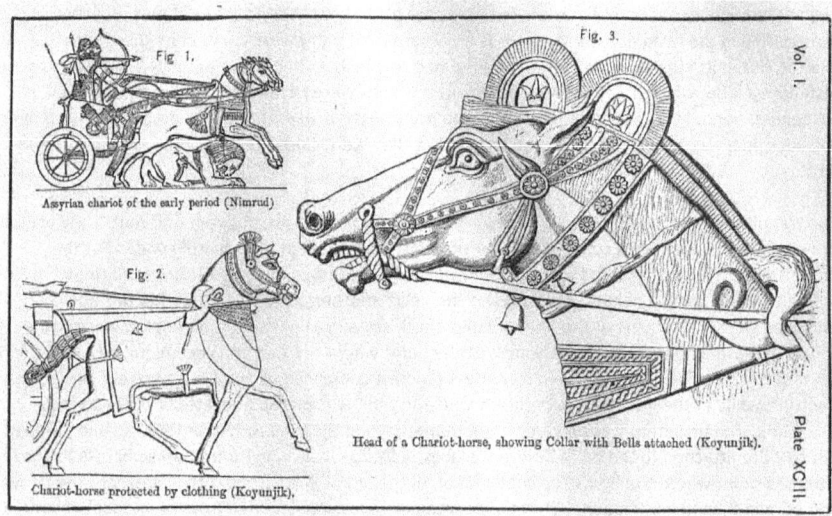

PLATE XCIII

A simpler style of clothing chariot-horses is found towards the close of the later period, where we observe, below the collar, a sort of triple breastplate, and over the rest of the body a plain cloth, square cut, with flaps descending at the arms and quarters, which is secured in its place by three narrow straps fastened on externally. The earlier kind of clothing has the appearance of being for ornament but this looks as if it was meant solely for protection.

Besides the trappings already noticed, the Assyrian chariot-horses had frequently strings of beads suspended round their necks, between the ears and the collar; they had also, not unfrequently, tassels or bells attached to different parts of the headstall [PLATE XCIII., Fig. 3], and finally they had, in the later period most commonly, a curious ornament upon the forehead, which covered almost the whole space between the ears and the eyes, and was composed of a number of minute bosses, colored, like the tassels of the breast ornament, alternately red and blue.

Each horse appears to have been driven by two reins—one attached to either end of the bit in the ordinary manner, and each passed through a ring or loop in the harness, whereby the rein was kept down and a stronger purchase secured to the driver. The shape of the bit within the mouth, if we may judge by the single instance of an actual bit which remains to us, bore a near resemblance to the modern snaffle. [PLATE XCIV., Fig. 1.] Externally the bit was large, and in most cases clumsy—a sort of cross-bar extending across the whole side of the horse's face, commonly resembling a double axe-head, or a hammer. Occasionally the shape was varied, the hatchet or hammer being replaced by forms similar to those annexed, or by the figure of a horse at full gallop. The rein seems, in the early times, to have been attached about midway in the cross-bar, while afterwards it became usual to attach it near the lower end. This latter arrangement was probably found to increase the power of the driver.

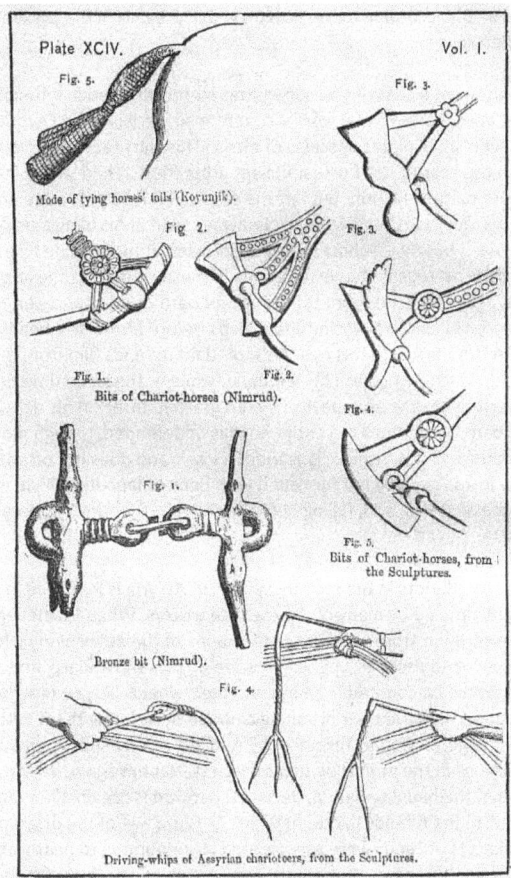

PLATE XCIV

The use of the bearing-rein, which prevailed in Egypt, was unknown to the Assyrians, or disapproved by them. The driving-reins were separate, not stitched or buckled together, and were held in the two hands separately. The right hand grasped the reins, whatever their number, which were attached at the horses' right cheeks, while the left hand performed the same office with the remaining reins. The charioteer urged his horses onward with a powerful whip, having a short handle, and a thick plaited or twisted lash, attached like the lash of a modern horsewhip, sometimes with, sometimes without, a loop, and often subdivided at the end into two or three tails. [PLATE XCIV., Fig. 4.]

Chariot-horses were trained to three paces, a walk, a trot, and a gallop. In battle-pieces they are commonly represented at full speed, in marches trotting, in processions walking in a stately manner. Their manes were frequently hogged, though more commonly they lay on the neck, falling (apparently) upon either side indifferently. Occasionally a portion only was hogged, while the greater part remained in its natural condition. The tail was uncut, and generally almost swept the ground, but was confined by a string or ribbon tied tightly around it about midway. Sometimes, more especially in the later sculptures, the lower half of the tail is plaited and tied up into a loop or bunch [PLATE XCIV., Fig. 5], according to the fashion which prevails in the present day through most parts of Turkey and Persia.

The warrior who fought from a chariot was sometimes merely dressed in a tunic, confined at the waist by a belt; sometimes, however, he wore a coat of mail, very like the Egyptian, consisting of a sort of shirt covered with small plates or scales of metal. This shirt reached at least as low as the knees, beneath which the chariot itself was sufficient protection. It had short sleeves, which covered the shoulder and upper part of the arm, but left the elbow and fore-arm quite undefended. The chief weapon of the warrior was the bow, which is always seen in his hands, usually with the arrow upon the string; he wears, besides, a short sword, suspended at his left side by a strap, and he has commonly a spear within his reach; but we never see him using either of these weapons. He either discharges his arrows against the foe from the standing-board of his chariot, or, commanding the charioteer to halt, descends, and, advancing a few steps before his horses' heads, takes a surer and more deadly aim from terra firma. In this case his attendant defends him from missiles by extending in front of him a shield, which he holds in his left hand, while at the same time he makes ready to repel any close assailant by means of a spear or sword grasped firmly in his right. The warrior's face and arms are always bare; sometimes the entire head is undefended, though more commonly it has the protection of a helmet. This, however, is without a visor, and does not often so much as cover the ears. In some few instances only is it furnished with flaps or lappets, which, where they exist, seem to be made of metal scales, and, falling over the shoulders, entirely conceal the ears, the back of the head, the neck, and even the chin.

The position occupied by chariots in the military system of Assyria is indicated in several passages of Scripture, and distinctly noticed by many of the classical writers. When Isaiah began to warn his countrymen of the 'miseries in store for them at the hands of the new enemy which first attacked Judea in his day, he described them as a people "whose arrows were sharp, and all their bows bent, whose horses' hoofs should be counted like flint, and their wheels like a whirlwind." When in after days he was commissioned to raise their drooping courage by assuring them that they would escape Sennacherib, who had angered God by his pride, he noticed, as one special provocation of Jehovah, that monarch's confidence in the multitude of his chariots. Nahum again, having to denounce the approaching downfall of the haughty nation, declares that God is "against her, and will burn her chariots in the smoke." In the fabulous account which Ctesias gave of the origin of Assyrian greatness, the war-chariots of Ninus were represented as amounting to nearly eleven thousand, while those of his wife and successor, Semiramis, were estimated at the extravagant number of a hundred thousand. Ctesias further stated that the Assyrian chariots, even at this early period, were armed with scythes, a statement contradicted by Xenophon, who ascribes this invention to the

Persians, and one which receives no confirmation from the monuments. Amid all this exaggeration and inventiveness, one may still trace a knowledge of the fact that war-chariots were highly esteemed by the Assyrians from a very ancient date, while from other notices we may gather that they continued to be reckoned an important arm of the military service to the very end of the empire.

Next to the war-chariots of the Assyrians we must place their cavalry, which seems to have been of scarcely less importance in their wars. Ctesias, who amid all his exaggerations shows glimpses of some real knowledge of the ancient condition of the Assyrian people, makes the number of the horsemen in their armies always greatly exceed that of the chariots. The writer of the book of Judith gives Holofernes 12,000 horse-archers, and Ezekiel seems to speak of all the "desirable young men" as "horsemen riding upon horses." The sculptures show on the whole a considerable excess of cavalry over chariots, though the preponderance is not uniformly exhibited throughout the different periods.

During the time of the Upper dynasty, cavalry appears to have been but little used. Tiglath-Pileser I. in the whole of his long Inscription has not a single mention of them, though he speaks of his chariots continually. In the sculptures of Asshur-izir-pal, the father of the Black-Obelisk king, while chariots abound, horsemen occur only in rare instances. Afterwards, under Sargon and Sennacherib, we notice a great change in this respect. The chariot comes to be almost confined to the king, while horsemen are frequent in the battle scenes.

In the first period the horses' trappings consisted of a head-stall, a collar, and one or more strings of beads. The head-stall was somewhat heavy, closely resembling that of the chariot-horses of the time, representations of which have been already given. It had the same heavy axe-shaped bit, the same arrangement of straps, and nearly the same ornamentation. The only marked difference was the omission of the crest or plume, with its occasional accompaniment of streamers. The collar was very peculiar. It consisted of a broad flap, probably of leather, shaped almost like a half-moon, which was placed on the neck about half way between the ears and the withers, and thence depended over the breast, where it was broadened out and ornamented by large drooping tassels. Occasionally the collar was plain, but more often it was elaborately patterned. Sometimes pomegranates hung from it, alternating with the tassels.

The cavalry soldiers of this period ride without any saddle. Their legs and feet are bare, and their seat is very remarkable. Instead of allowing their legs to hang naturally down the horses' sides, they draw them up till their knees are on a level with their chargers' backs, the object (apparently) being to obtain a firm seat by pressing the base of the horse's neck between the two knees. The naked legs seem to indicate that it was found necessary to obtain the fullest and freest play of the muscles to escape the inconveniences of a fall.

The chief weapon of the cavalry at this time is the bow. Sword and shield indeed are worn, but in no instance do we see them used. Cavalry soldiers are either archers or mere attendants who are without weapons of offence. One of these latter accompanies each horse-archer in battle, for the purpose of holding and guiding his steed while he discharges his arrows. The attendant wears a skull cap and a plain tunic, the archer has an embroidered tunic, a belt to which his sword is attached, and one of the ordinary pointed helmets.

In the second period the cavalry consists in part of archers, in part of spearmen. Unarmed attendants are no longer found, both spearmen and archers appearing to be able to manage their own horses. Saddles have now come into common use: they consist of a simple cloth, or flap of leather, which is either cut square, or shaped somewhat like the saddle-cloths of our own cavalry. A single girth beneath the belly is their ordinary fastening; but sometimes they are further secured by means of a strap or band passed round the breast, and a few instances occur of a second strap passed round the quarters. The breast-strap is generally of a highly ornamented character. The headstall of this period is not unlike the earlier one, from which it differs chiefly in having a crest, and also a forehead ornament composed of a number of small bosses. It has likewise commonly a strap across the nose, but none under the cheek-bones. It is often richly ornamented, particularly with rosettes, bells, and tassels.

The old pendent collar is replaced by one encircling the neck about halfway up, or is sometimes dispensed with altogether. Where it occurs, it is generally of uniform width, and is ornamented with rosettes or tassels. No conjecture has been formed of any use which either form of collar could serve; and the probability is that they were intended solely for ornament.

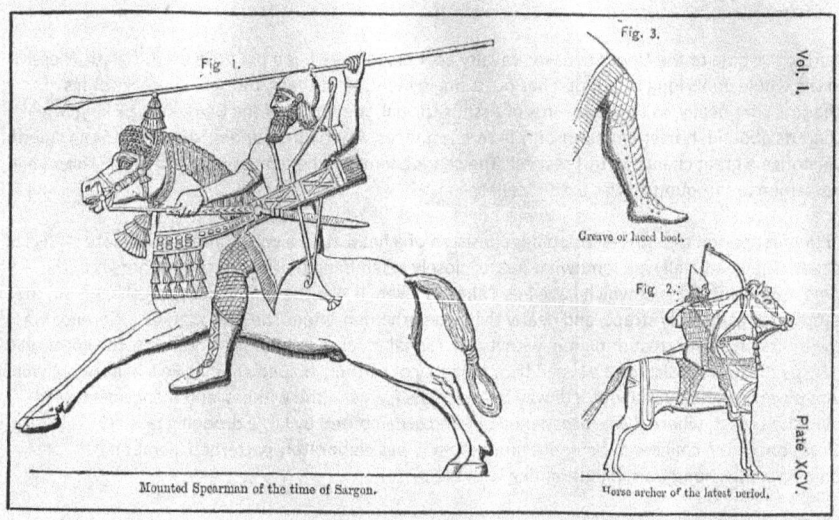

PLATE XCV

A great change is observable in the sculptures of the second period with respect to the dress of the riders. [PLATE XCV., Fig. 1.] The cavalry soldier is now completely clothed, with the exception of his two arms, which are bare from a little below the shoulder. He wears most commonly a tunic which fits him closely about the body, but below the waist expands into a loose kilt or petticoat, very much longer behind than in front, which is sometimes patterned, and always terminates in a fringe. Round his waist he has a broad belt; and another, of inferior width, from which a sword hangs, passes over his left shoulder. His legs are encased in a close-fitting pantaloon or trouser, over which he wears a laced boot or greave, which generally reaches nearly to the knee, though sometimes it only covers about half the calf. [PLATE XCV., Fig. 2.] This costume, which is first found in the time of Sargon, and continues to the reign of Asshur-bani-pal, Esarhaddon's son, may probably be regarded as the regular cavalry uniform under the monarchs of the Lower Empire. In Sennacherib's reign there is found in conjunction with it another costume, which is unknown to the earlier sculptures. This consists of a dress closely fitting the whole body, composed apparently of a coat of mail, leather or felt breeches, and a high greave or jack boot. [PLATE XCVI., Fig. 1.] The wearers of this costume are spearmen or archers indifferently. The former carry a long weapon, which has generally a rather small head, and is grasped low down the shaft. The bow of the latter is either round-arched or angular, and seems to be not more than four feet in length; the arrows measure less than three feet, and are slung in a quiver at the archer's back. Both spearmen and archers commonly carry swords, which are hung on the left side, in a diagonal, and sometimes nearly in a horizontal position. In some few cases the spearman is also an archer, and carries his bow on his right arm, apparently as a reserve in case he should break or lose his spear.

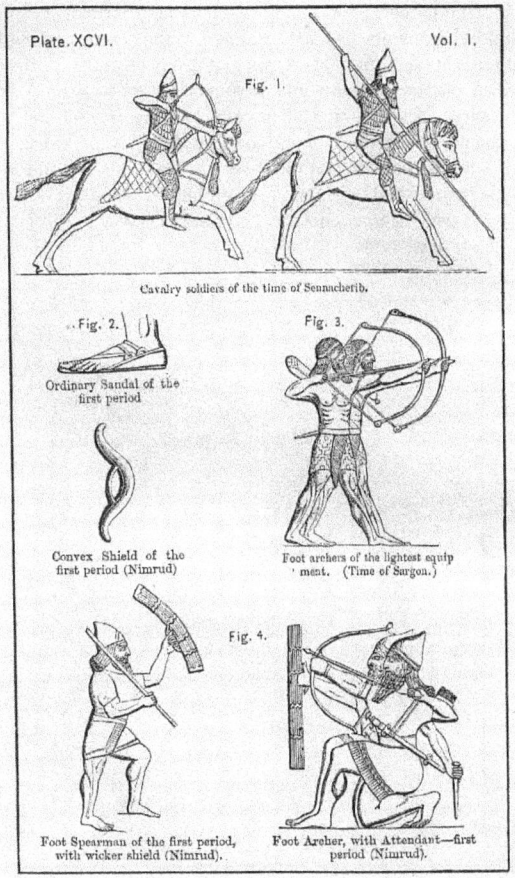

PLATE XCVI

The seat of the horseman is far more graceful in the second than in the first period his limbs appear to move freely, and his mastery over his horse is such that he needs no attendant. The spearman holds the bridle in his left hand; the archer boldly lays it upon the neck of his steed, who is trained either to continue his charge, or to stand firm while a steady aim is taken. [PLATE XCV., Fig. 3.]

In the sculptures of the son and successor of Esarhaddon, the horses of the cavalry carry not unfrequently, in addition to the ordinary saddle or pad, a large cloth nearly similar to that worn sometimes by chariot-horses, of which a representation has been already given. It is cut square with two drooping lappets, and covers the greater part of the body. Occasionally it is united to a sort of breastplate which protects the neck, descending about halfway clown the chest. The material may be supposed to have been thick felt or leather, either of which would have been a considerable protection against weapons.

While the cavalry and the chariots were regarded as the most important portions of the military force, and were the favorite services with the rich and powerful, there is still abundant reason to believe that Assyrian armies, like most others, consisted mainly of foot. Ctesias gives Minis 1,700,000 footmen to 210,000 horsemen, and 10,600 chariots. Xenophon contrasts the multitude of the Assyrian infantry with the comparatively scanty numbers of the other two services: Herodotus makes the Assyrians serve in the army of Xerxes on foot only. The author of the book of Judith assigns to Holofernes an infantry force ten times as numerous as his cavalry.—The Assyrian monuments entirely bear out the general truth involved in all these assertions, showing us, as they do, at least ten Assyrian warriors on foot for each one mounted on horseback, and at least a hundred for each one who rides in a chariot. However terrible to the foes of the Assyrians may have been the shock of their chariots and the impetuosity of their horsemen, it was probably to the solidity of the infantry, to their valor, equipment, and discipline, that the empire was mainly indebted for its long series of victories.

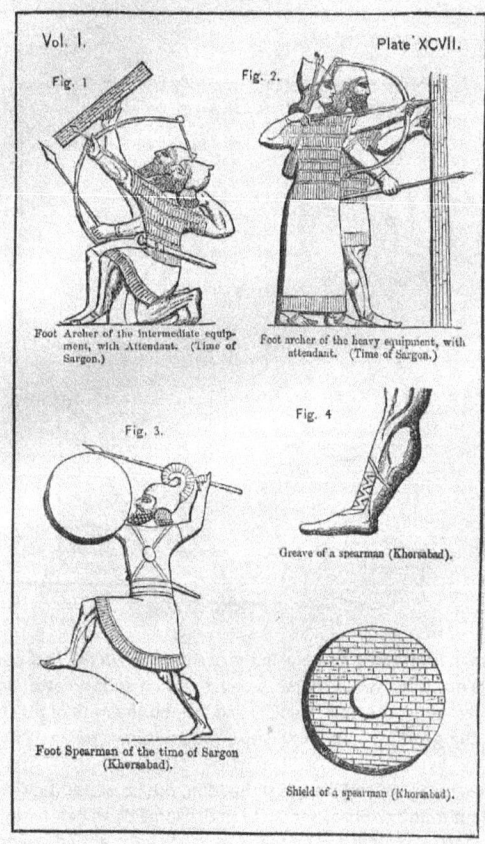

PLATE XCVII

In the time of the earliest sculptures, all the Assyrian foot-soldiers seem to have worn nearly the same costume. This consisted of a short tunic, not quite reaching to the knees, confined round the waist by a broad belt, fringed, and generally opening in front, together with a pointed helmet, probably of metal. The arms, legs, neck, and even the feet, were ordinarily bare, although these last had sometimes the protection of a very simple sandal. [PLATE XCVI., Fig. 2.] Swordsmen used a small straight sword or dagger which they wore at their left side in an ornamented sheath, and a shield which was either convex and probably of metal, or oblong-square and composed of wickerwork. [PLATE XCVI., Fig. 2.] Spearmen had shields of a similar shape and construction, and carried in their right hands a short pike or javelin, certainly not exceeding five feet in length. [PLATE XCVI., Fig. 4.] Sometimes, but not always, they carried, besides the pike, a short sword. Archers had rounded bows about four feet in length, and arrows a little more than three feet long. Their quivers, which were often highly ornamented, hung at their backs, either over the right or over the left shoulder. [PLATE XCVI., Fig. 4.] They had swords suspended at their left sides by a cross-belt, and often carried maces, probably of bronze or iron, which bore a rosette or other ornament at one end, and a ring or strap at the other. The tunics of archers were sometimes elaborately embroidered; and on the whole they seem to have been regarded as the flower of the foot-soldiery. Generally they are represented in pairs, the two being in most cases armed and equipped alike; but, occasionally, one of the pair acts as guard while the other takes his aim. In this case both kneel on one knee, and the guard, advancing his long wicker shield, protects both himself and his comrade from missiles, while he has at the same time his sword drawn to repel all hand-to-hand assailants. [PLATE XCVII., Fig. 1.]

In the early part of the second period, which synchronizes with the reign of Sargon, the difference in the costumes of the foot-soldiers becomes much more marked. The Assyrian infantry now consists of two great classes, archers and spear-men. The archers are either light-armed or heavy-armed, and of the latter there are two clearly distinct varieties. The light-armed have no helmet, but wear on their heads a mere fillet or band, which is either plain or patterned. [PLATE XCVI., Fig. 3.] Except for a cross-belt which supports the quiver, they are wholly naked to the middle. Their only garment is a tunic of the scantiest dimensions, beginning at the waist, round which it is fastened by a broad belt or girdle, and descending little more than half-way down the thigh. In its make it sometimes closely resembles the tunic of the first period, but more often it has the peculiar pendent ornament which has been compared to the scotch phillibeg, and which will be here given that name. It is often patterned with squares and gradines. The light-armed archer has usually bare feet; occasionally, however, he wears the slight sandal of this period, which is little more than a cap for the heel held in place by two or three strings passed across the instep. There is nothing remarkable in his arms, which resemble those of the preceding period: but it may be observed that, while shooting, he frequently holds two arrows in his right hand besides that which is upon the string. He shoots either kneeling or standing, generally the latter. His ordinary position is in the van of battle, though sometimes a portion of the heavy-armed troops precede him. He has no shield, and is not protected by an attendant, thus running more risk than any of the rest of the army.

The more simply equipped of the heavy archers are clothed in a coat of mail, which reaches from their neck to their middle, and partially covers the arms. Below this they wear a fringed tunic reaching to the knees, and confined at the waist by a broad belt of the ordinary character. Their feet have in most instances the protection of a sandal, and they wear on their heads the common or pointed helmet. They usually discharge their arrows kneeling on the left knee, with the right foot advanced before them. Daring this operation they are protected by an attendant, who is sometimes dressed like themselves, sometimes merely clad a tunic, without a coat of mail. Like them, he wears a pointed helmet; and while in one hand he carries a spear, with the other he holds forward a shield, which is either of a round form—apparently, of metal embossed with figures—or oblong-square in shape, and evidently made of wickerwork. Archers of this class are the least common, and scarcely ever occur unless in combination with some of the class which has the heaviest equipment.

The principal characteristic of the third or most heavily armed class of archers is the long robe, richly fringed, which descends nearly to their feet, thus completely protecting all the lower part of their person. [PLATE XCVII., Fig. 2.] Above this they wear a coat of mail exactly resembling that of archers of the intermediate class, which is sometimes crossed by a belt ornamented with crossbars. Their head is covered by the usual pointed helmet, and their feet are always, or nearly always, protected by sandals. They are occasionally represented without either sword or quiver, but more usually they have a short sword at their left side, which appears to have been passed through their coat of mail, between the armor plates, and in a few instances they have also quivers at their backs. Where these are lacking, they generally either carry two extra arrows in their right hand, or have the same number borne for them by an attendant. They are never seen unattended: sometimes they have one, sometimes two attendants, who accompany them, and guard them from attack. One of these almost always bears the long wicker shield, called by the Greeks [yeppov] which he rests firmly upon the ground in front of himself and comrade. The other, where there is a second, stands a little in the rear, and guards the archer's head with a round shield or targe. Both attendants are dressed in a short tunic, a phillibeg, a belt, and a pointed helmet. Generally they wear also a coat of mail and sandals, like those of the archer. They carry swords at their left sides, and the principal attendant, except when he bears the archer's arrows, guards him from attack by holding in advance a short spear. The archers of this class never kneel, but always discharge their arrows standing. They seem to be regarded as the most important of the foot-soldiers, their services being more particularly valuable in the siege of fortified places.

The spearmen of this period are scarcely better armed than the second or intermediate class of archers. Except in very rare instances they have no coat of mail, and their tunic, which is either plain or covered with small squares, barely reaches to the knee. The most noticeable point about them is their helmet, which is never the common pointed or conical one, but is always surmounted by a crest of one kind or another. [PLATE XCVII.. Fig. 3.] Another very frequent peculiarity is the arrangement of their cross-belts, which meet on the back and breast, and are ornamented at the points of junction with a circular disk, probably of metal. The shield of the spearman is also circular, and is formed generally, if not always—of wickerwork, with (occasionally) a central boss of wood or metal. [PLATE XCVII., Fig. 4.] In most cases their legs are wholly bare; but sometimes they have sandals, while in one or two instances they wear a low boot or greave laced in front, and resembling that of the cavalry. [PLATE XCVII.. Fig. 4.] The spear with which they are armed varies in length, from about four to six feet. [PLATE XCVIII.. Fig. 1.] It is grasped near the lower extremity, at which a weight was sometimes attached, in order the better to preserve the balance. Besides this weapon they have the ordinary short sword. The spear-men play an important part in the Assyrian wars, particularly at sieges, where they always form the strength of the storming party.

Some important changes seen to have been made under Sennacherib in the equipment and organization of the infantry force. These consisted chiefly in the establishment of a greater number of distinct corps differently armed, and in an improved equipment of the more important of them. Sennacherib appears to have been the first to institute a corps of slingers, who at any rate make their earliest appearance in his sculptures. They were kind of soldier well-known to the Egyptians and Sennacherib's acquaintance with the Egyptian warfare may have led to their introduction among the troops of Assyria. The slinger in most countries where his services were employed was lightly clad, and reckoned almost as a supernumerary. It is remarkable that in Assyria he is, at first, completely armed according to Assyrian ideas of completeness, having a helmet, a coat of mail to the waist, a tunic to the knees, a close-fitting trouser, and a short boot or greave. The weapon which distinguishes him appears to have consisted of two pieces of rope or string, attached to a short leathern strap which received the stone. [PLATE XCVIII., Fig. 4.] Previous to making his throw, the slinger seems to have whirled the weapon round his head two or three times, in order to obtain on increased impetus—a practice which was also known to the Egyptians and the Romans. With regard to ammunition, it does not clearly appear how the Assyrian slinger was supplied. He has no bag like the Hebrew slinger, no sinus like the Roman. Frequently we see him simply provided with a single extra stone, which he carries in his left hand. Sometimes, besides this reserve, he has a small heap of stones at his feet; but whether he has collected them from the field, or has brought them with him and deposited them where they lie, is not apparent.

Sennacherib's archers fall into four classes, two of which may be called heavy-armed and two light-armed. None of them exactly resemble the archers of Sargon. The most heavily equipped wears a tunic, a coat of mail reaching to the waist, a pointed helmet, a close-fitting trouser, and a short boot or greave. [PLATE XCVIII., Fig. 1.] He is accompanied by an attendant (or sometimes by two attendants) similarly attired, and fights behind a large wicker shield or gerrhon. A modification of this costume is worn by the second class, the archers of which have bare legs, a tunic which seems to open at the side, and a phillibeg. They fight without the protection of a shield, generally in pairs, who shoot together. [PLATE XCVIII., Fig. 3.]

The better equipped of the light-armed archers of this period have a costume which is very striking. Their head-dress consists of a broad fillet, elaborately patterned, from which there often depends on either side of the head a large lappet, also richly ornamented, generally of an oblong-square shape, and terminating in a fringe. [PLATE XCVIII., Fig. 2.] Below this they wear a closely fitting tunic, as short as that worn by the light-armed archers of Sargon, sometimes patterned, like that, with squares and gradines, sometimes absolutely plain. The upper part of this tunic is crossed by two belts of very unusual breadth, which pass respectively over the right and the left shoulder. There is also a third broad belt round the waist; and both this and the transverse belts are adorned with elegant patterns. The phillibeg depends from the girdle, and is seen in its full extent, hanging either in front or on the right side. The arms are naked from the shoulder, and the legs from considerably above the knee, the feet alone being protected by a scanty sandal. The ordinary short sword is worn at the side, and a quiver is carried at the back; the latter is sometimes kept in place by means of a horizontal strap which passes over it and round the body. [PLATE XCIX., Fig. 2.]

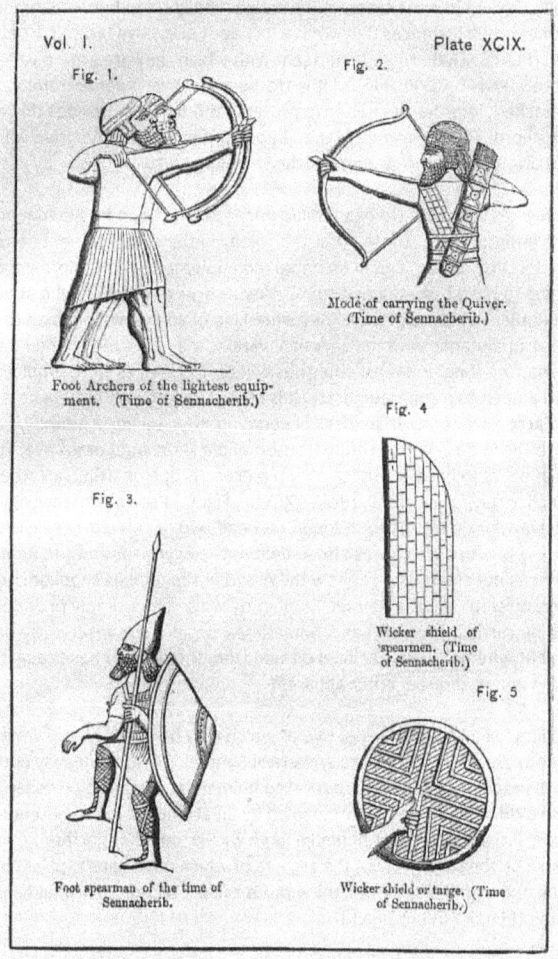

PLATE XCIX

The archers of the lightest equipment wear nothing but a fillet, with or without lappets, upon the head, and a striped tunic, longer behind than in front, which extends from the neck to the knees, and is confined at the waist by a girdle. [PLATE XCIX., Fig. 1.] Their arms, legs, and feet are bare, they have seldom any sword, and their quiver seems to be suspended only by a single horizontal strap, like that represented in [PLATE XCIX., Fig. 2.] They do not appear very often upon the monuments: when seen, they are interspersed among archers and soldiers of other classes.

Sennacherib's foot spearmen are of two classes only. The better armed have pointed helmets, with lappets protecting the ears, a coat of mail descending to the waist and also covering all the upper part of the arms, a tunic opening at the side, a phillibeg, close-fitting trousers, and greaves of the ordinary character. [PLATE XCIX., Fig. 3.] They carry a large convex shield, apparently of metal, which covers them almost from head to foot, and a spear somewhat less than their own height. Commonly they have a short sword at their right side. Their shield is often ornamented with rows of bosses towards the centre and around the edge. It is ordinarily carried in front; but when the warrior is merely upon the march, he often bears it slung at his back, as in the accompanying representation. There is reason to suspect that the spearmen of this description constituted the royal bodyguard. They are comparatively few in number, and are usually seen in close proximity to the monarch, or in positions which imply trust, as in the care of prisoners and of the spoil. They never make the attacks in sieges, and are rarely observed to be engaged in battle. Where several of them are seen together, it is almost always in attendance upon the king whom they constantly precede upon his journeys.

The inferior spearmen of Sennacherib are armed nearly like those of Sargon. They have crested helmets, plain tunics confined at the waist by a broad girdle, cross-belts ornamented with circular disks where they meet in the centre of the breast, and, most commonly, round wicker shields. The chief points wherein they differ from Sargon's spearmen is the following: they usually (though not universally) wear trousers and greaves; they have sleeves to their tunics, winch descend nearly to the elbow; and they carry sometimes, instead of the round shield, a long convex one arched at the top. [PLATE XCIX., fig. 4.] Where they have not this defence, but the far commoner targe, it is always of larger dimensions than the targe of Sargon, and is generally surrounded by a rim. [PLATE XCIX., Fig. 4.] Sometimes it appears to be of metal: but more often it is of wickerwork, either of the plain construction common in Sargon's time, or of one considerably more elaborate.

Among the foot soldiers of Sennacherib we seem to find a corps of pioneers. They wear the same dress as the better equipped of the spearmen, but carry in their hands, instead of a spear, a doubled-headed axe or hatchet, wherewith they clear the ground for the passage and movements of the army. They work in pairs, one pulling at the tree by its branches while the other attacks the stem with his weapon.

After Sennacherib's time we find but few alterations in the equipment of the foot soldiers. Esarhaddon has left us no sculptures, and in those of his son and successor, Asshur-bani pal, the costumes of Sennacherib are for the most part reproduced almost exactly. The chief difference is that there are not at this time quite so many varieties of equipment, both archers and spearmen being alike divided into two classes only, light armed and heavy-armed. The light-armed archers correspond to Sennacherib's bowmen of the third class. They have the fillet, the plain tunic, the cross-belts, the broad girdle, and the phillibeg. They differ only in having no lappets over the ears and no sandals. The heavy-armed archers resemble the first class of Sennacherib exactly, except that they are not seen shooting from behind the gerrhon.

In the case of the spearmen, the only novelty consists in the shields. The spearmen of the heavier equipment, though sometimes they carry the old convex oval shield, more often have one which is made straight at the bottom, and rounded only at top. [PLATE C., Fig. 1.] The spearmen of the lighter equipment have likewise commonly a shield of this shape, but it is of wicker work instead of metal, like that borne occasionally by the light-armed spearmen of Sennacherib.

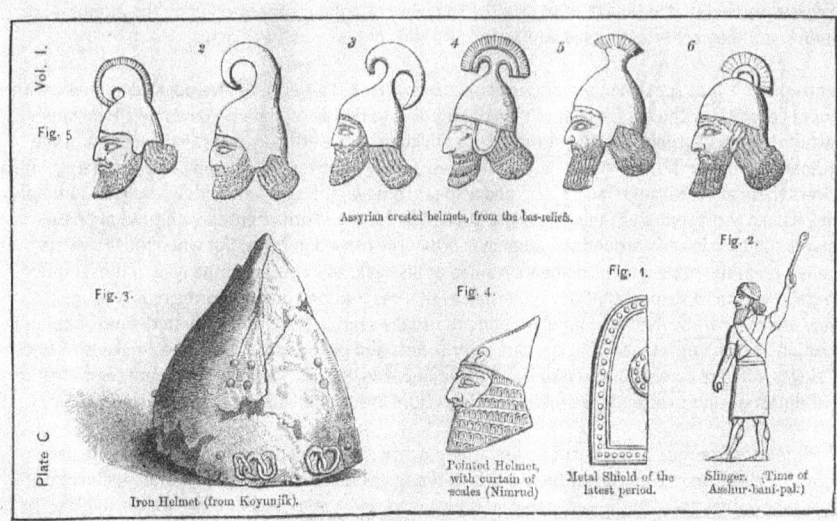

PLATE C

Besides spearmen and archers, we see among the foot soldiers of Asshur-bani-pal, slingers, mace-bearers, and men armed with battle axes. For the slingers Sennacherib's heavy equipment has been discarded; and they wear nothing but a plain tunic, with a girdle and cross-belts. [PLATE C., Fig. 2.] The mace-bearers and men with axes have the exact dress of Asshur-bani-pal's heavy-armed spearmen, and may possibly be spearmen who have broken or lost their weapons. It makes, however, against this view, that they have no shields, which spearmen always carry. Perhaps, therefore, we must conclude that towards the close of the empire, besides spearmen, slingers, and archers, there were distinct corps of mace-bearers and axe-bearers.

The arms used by the Assyrians have been mentioned, and to a certain extent described, in the foregoing remarks upon the various classes of their soldiers. Some further details may, however, be now added on their character and on the variety observable in them.

The common Assyrian pointed helmet has been sufficiently described already, and has received abundant illustration both in the present and in former chapters. It was at first regarded as Scythic in character; but Mr. Layard long ago observed that the resemblance which it bears to the Scythian cap is too slight to prove any connection. That cap appears, whether we follow the foreign, or the native representations of it, to have been of felt, whereas the Assyrian pointed helmet was made of metal: it was much taller than the Assyrian head-dress, and it was less upright. [PLATE C, Fig. 3.]

The pointed helmet admitted of but few varieties. In its simplest form it was a plain conical casque, with one or two rings round the base, and generally with a half-disk in front directly over the forehead. [PLATE C. Fig. 4.] Sometimes, however, there was appended to it a falling curtain covered with metal scales, whereby the chin, neck, ears, and back of the head were protected. More often it had, in lieu of this effectual but cumbrous guard, a mere lappet or cheek-piece, consisting of a plate of metal, attached to the rim, which descended over the ears in the form of a half-oval or semicircle. If we may judge by the remains actually found, the chief material of the helmet was iron; copper was used only for the rings and the half-disk in front, which were inlaid into the harder metal.

As if to compensate themselves for the uniformity to which they submitted in this instance, the Assyrians indulged in a variety of crested helmets. [PLATE. C., Fig. 5.] We cannot positively say that they invented the crest; but they certainly dealt with it in the free spirit which is usually seen where a custom is of home growth and not a foreign importation. They used either a plain metal crest, or one surmounted by tuffs of hair; and they either simply curved the crest forwards over the front of the helmet, or extended it and carried it back-wards also. In this latter case they generally made the curve a complete semicircle, while occasionally they were content with a small segment, less even than a quarter of a circle. They also varied considerably the shape of the lappet over the ear, and the depth of the helmet behind and before the lappet.

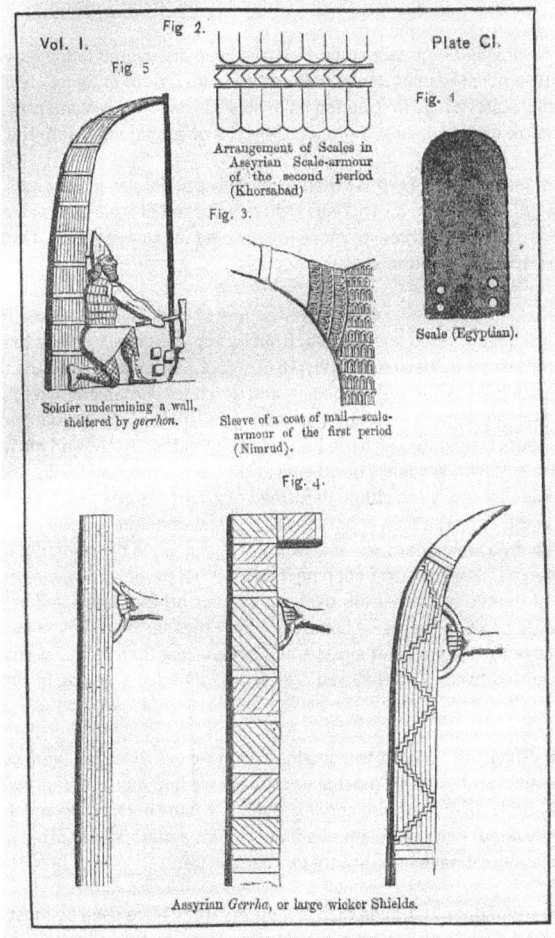

Assyrian coats of mail were of three sizes, and of two different constructions. In the earlier times they were worn long, descending either to the feet or to the knees; and at this period they seem to have been composed simply of successive rows of similar iron scales sewn on to a shirt of linen or felt. [PLATE CI., Fig. 1.] Under the later monarchs the coat of mail reached no lower than the waist, and it was composed of alternate bands of dissimilar arrangement and perhaps of different material. Mr. Layard suggests that at this time the scales, which were larger than before, were "fastened to bands of iron or copper." But it is perhaps more probable that scales of the old character alternated in rows with scales of a new shape and smaller dimensions. [PLATE CI., Fig. 2.] The old scales were oblong, squared at one end and rounded at the other, very much resembling the Egyptian. They were from two to three inches, or more, in length, and were placed side by side, so that their greater length corresponded with the height of the wearer. The new scales seem to have been not more than an inch long; they appear to have been pointed at one end, and to have been laid horizontally, each a little overlapping its fellow. It was probably found that this construction, while possessing quite as much strength as the other, was more favorable to facility of movement.

Remains of armor belonging to the second period have been discovered in the Assyrian ruins. The scales are frequently embossed over their whole surface with groups of figures and fanciful ornaments. The small scales of the first period have no such elaborate ornamentation, being simply embossed in the centre with a single straight line, which is of copper inlaid into the iron.

The Assyrian coat of mail, like the Egyptian, had commonly a short sleeve, extending about half way down to the elbow. [PLATE CI.. Fig. 1.] This was either composed of scales set similarly to those of the rest of the cuirass, or of two, three, or more rows placed at right angles to the others. The greater part of the arm was left without any protection.

A remarkable variety existed in the form and construction of the Assyrian shields. The most imposing kind is that which has been termed the gerrhon, from its apparent resemblance to the Persian shield mentioned under that name by Herodotus. [PLATE CI.. Fig. 1.] This was a structure in wickerwork, which equalled or exceeded the warrior in height, and which was broad enough to give shelter to two or even three men. In shape it was either an oblong square, or such a square with a projection at top, which stood out at right angles to the body of the shield; or, lastly, and most usually, it curved inwards from a certain height, gradually narrowing at the same time, and finally ending in a point. Of course a shield of this vast size, even although formed of a light material, was too heavy to be very readily carried upon the arm. The plan adopted was to rest it upon the ground, on which it was generally held steady by a warrior armed with sword or spear, while his comrade, whose weapon was the bow, discharged his arrows from behind its shelter. Its proper place was in sieges, where the roof-like structure at the top was especially useful in warding off the stones and other missiles which the besieged threw down upon their assailants. We sometimes see it employed by single soldiers, who lean the point against the wall of the place, and, ensconcing themselves beneath the penthouse thus improvised, proceed to carry on the most critical operations of the siege in almost complete security.

Modifications of this shield, reducing it to a smaller and more portable size, were common in the earlier times, when among the shields most usually borne we find one of wicker-work oblong-square in shape, and either perfectly flat, or else curving slightly inwards both at top and at bottom. This shield was commonly about half the height of a man, or a little more; it was often used as a protection for two, but must have been scanty for that purpose.

Round shields were commoner in Assyria than any others. They were used by most of those who fought in chariots, by the early monarchs' personal attendants, by the cross-belted spear-men, and by many of the spearmen who guarded archers. In the most ancient times they seem to have been universally made of solid metal, and consequently they were small, perhaps not often exceeding two feet, or two feet and a half, in diameter. They were managed by means of a very simple handle, placed in the middle of the shield at the back, and fastened to it by studs or nails, which was not passed over the arm but grasped by the hand. The rim was bent inwards, so as to form a deep groove all round the edge. The material of which these shields were composed was in some cases certainly bronze; in others it may have been iron: in a few silver, or even gold. Some metal shields were perfectly plain; others exhibited a number of concentric rings, others again were inlaid or embossed with tasteful and elaborate patterns.

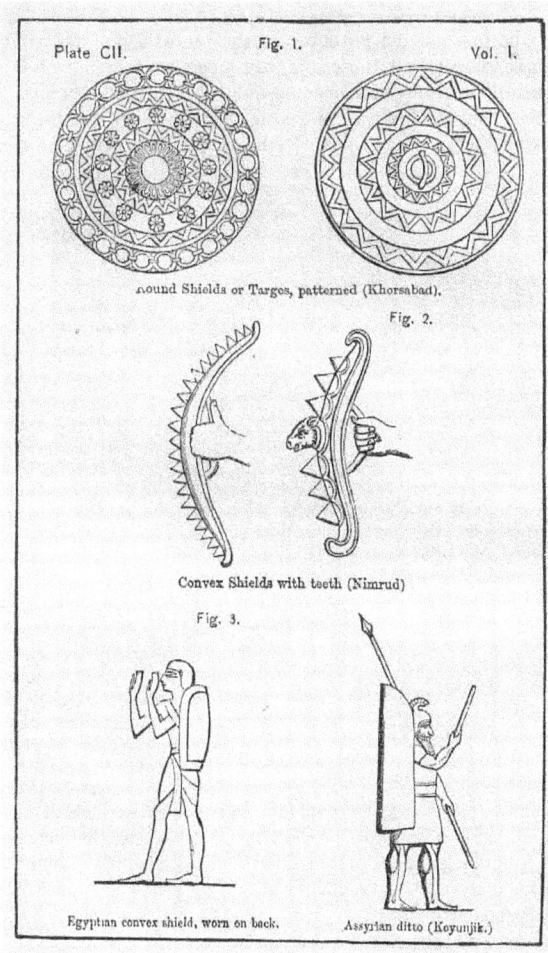

PLATE CII

Among the later Assyrians the round metal shield seems to have been almost entirely disused, its place being supplied by a wicker buckler of the same shape, with a rim round the edge made of solid wood or of metal, and sometimes with a boss in the centre. [PLATE CII., Fig. 1.] The weight of the metal shield must have been considerable; and this both limited their size and made it difficult to move them with rapidity. With the change of material we perceive a decided increase of magnitude, the diameter of the wicker buckler being often fully half the warrior's height, or not much short of three feet.

Convex shields, generally of an oblong form, were also in common use during the later period, and one kind is found in the very earliest sculptures. This is of small dimensions and of a clumsy make. Its curve is slight, and it is generally ornamented with a perpendicular row of spikes or teeth, in the centre of which we often see the head of a lion. [PLATE CII., Fig. 2.]

The convex shields of later date were very much larger than these. [PLATE CIII., Fig. 3.] They were sometimes square at bottom and rounded at top, in which case they were either made of wickerwork, or (apparently) of metal. These latter had generally a boss in the centre, and both this and the edge of the shield were often ornamented with a row of rosettes or rings. Shields of this shape were from four to five feet in height, and protected the warrior from the head to the knee. On a march they were often worn upon the back, like the convex shield of the Egyptians, which they greatly resembled.

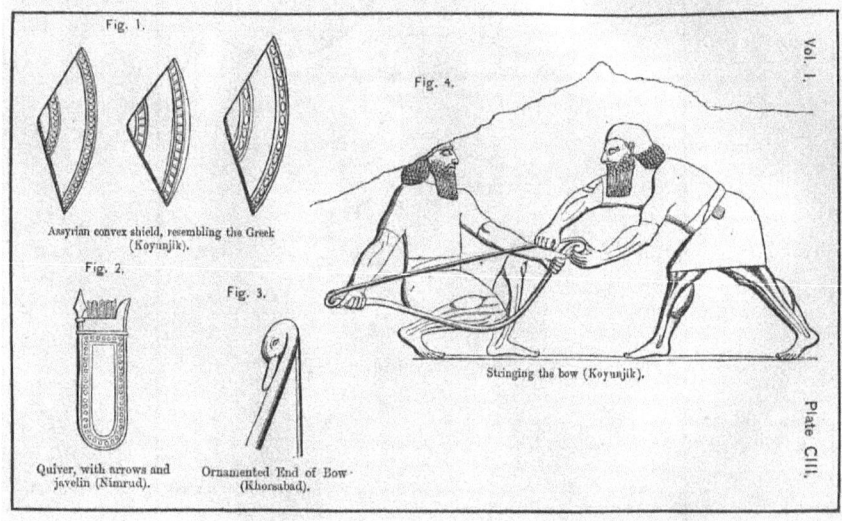

PLATE CIII

The more ordinary convex shield was of an oval form, like the convex shield of the Greeks, but larger, and with a more prominent centre. [PLATE CIII., Fig. 1.] In its greater diameter it must often have exceeded five feet, though no doubt sometimes it was smaller. It was generally ornamented with narrow bands round the edge and round the boss at the centre, the space between the bands being frequently patterned with ring; or otherwise. Like the other form of convex shield, it could be slung at the back, and was so carried on marches, on crossing rivers, and other similar occasions.

The offensive arms certainly used by the Assyrians were the bow, the spear, the sword, the mace, the sling, the axe or hatchet, and the dagger. They may also have occasionally made use of the javelin, which is sometimes seen among the arrows of a quiver. But the actual employment of this weapon in war has not yet been found upon the bas-reliefs. If faithfully represented, it must have been very short,—scarcely, if at all, exceeding three feet. [PLATE CIII., Fig. 2.]

Assyrian bows were of two kinds, curved and angular. Compared with the Egyptian, and with the bows used by the archers of the middle ages, they were short, the greatest length of the strung bow being about four feet. They seem to have been made of a single piece of wood, which in the angular bow was nearly of the same thickness throughout, but in the curved one tapered gradually towards the two extremities. At either end was a small knob or button, in the later times often carved into the representation of a duck's head. [PLATE CIII, Fig. 3.] Close above this was a notch or groove, whereby the string was held in place. The mode of stringing was one still frequently practised in the East. The bowman stooped, and placing his right knee against the middle of the bow on its inner side, pressed it downwards, at the same time drawing the two ends of the bow upwards with his two hands. [PLATE CIII, Fig. 4.] A comrade stood by, and, when the ends were brought sufficiently near, slipped the string over the knob into the groove, where it necessarily remained. The bend of the bow, thus strung, was slight. When full drawn, however, it took the shape of a half-moon, which shows that it must have possessed great elasticity. [PLATE CIV., Fig. 4.] The bow was known to be full drawn when the head of the arrow touched the archer's left hand.

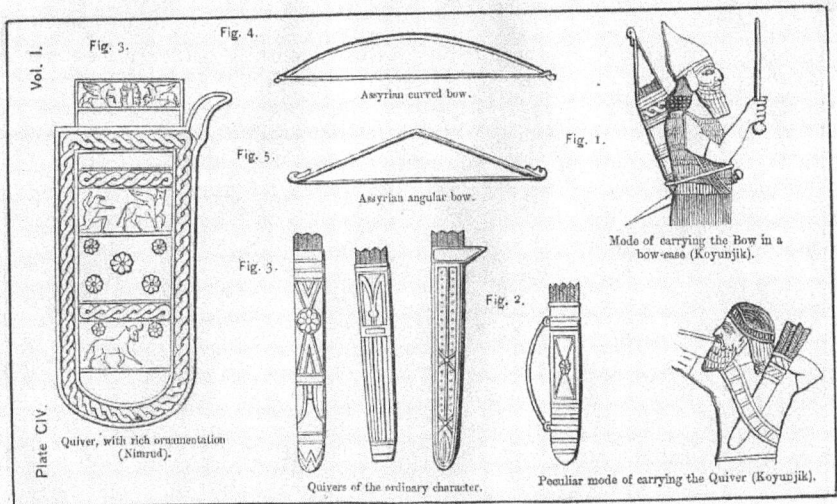

PLATE CIV

The Assyrian angular bow was of smaller size than the curved one. It was not often carried unless as a reserve by those who also possessed the larger and better weapon. [PLATE CIV., Fig. 5.]

Bows were but seldom unstrung. When not in use, they were carried strung, the archer either holding them by the middle with his left hand, or putting his arm through them, and letting them rest upon his shoulders, or finally carrying them at his back in a bow case. [PLATE CIV., Fig. I.] The bow-case was a portion of the quiver, as frequently with the Greeks, and held only the lower half of the bow, the upper portion projecting from it.

Quivers were carried by foot and horse archers at their backs, in a diagonal position, so that the arrows could readily be drawn from them over the right shoulder. They were commonly slung in this position by a strap of their own, attached to two rings, one near the top and the other near the bottom of the quiver, which the archer slipped over his left arm and his head. Sometimes, however, this strap seems to have been wanting, and the quiver was either thrust through one of the cross-belts, or attached by a strap which passed horizontally round the body a little above the girdle.

[PLATE CIV.,Fig. 2.] The archers who rode in chariots carried their quivers at the chariot's side, in the manner which has been already described and illustrated.

The ornamentation of quivers was generally elaborate. [PLATE CIV., Fig. 3.] Rosettes and bands constituted their most usual adornment; but sometimes these gave place to designs of a more artistic character, as wild bulls, griffins, and other mythic figures. Several examples of a rich type have been already given in the representations of chariots, but none exhibit this peculiarity. One further specimen of a chariot quiver is therefore appended, which is among the most tasteful hitherto discovered. [PLATE CIV., Fig. 3.]

The quivers of the foot and horse archers were less richly adorned than those of the bowmen who rode in chariots, but still they were in almost every case more or less patterned. The rosette and the band here too constituted the chief resource of the artist, who, however, often introduced with good effect other well-known ornaments, as the guilloche, the boss and cross, the zigzag, etc.

Sometimes the quiver had an ornamented rod attached to it, which projected beyond the arrows and terminated in a pomegranate blossom or other similar carving. [PLATE CV. Fig. 1]. To this rod was attached the rings which received the quiver strap, a triple tassel hanging from them at the point of attachment. The strap was probably of leather, and appears to have been twisted or plaited.

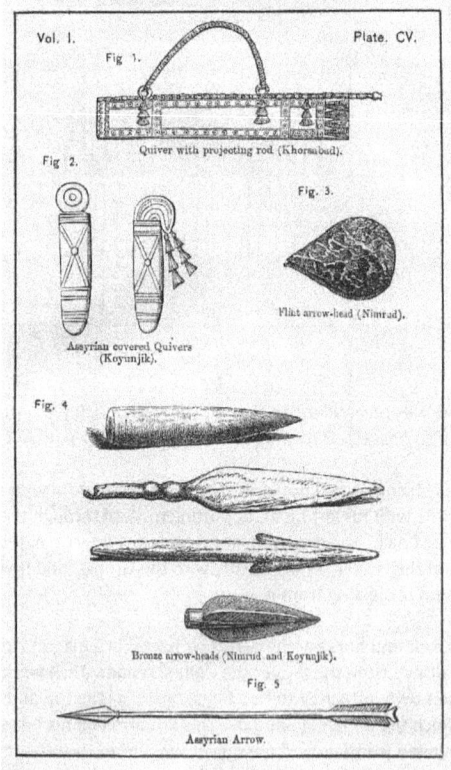

It is uncertain whether the material of the quivers was wood or metal. As, however, no remains of quivers have been discovered in any of the ruins, while helmets, shields, diggers, spear-heads, and arrow-heads have been found in tolerable abundance, we may perhaps assume that they were of the more fragile substance, which would account for their destruction. In this case their ornamentation may have been either by carving or painting, the bosses and rosettes being perhaps in some cases of metal, mother-of-pearl, or ivory. Ornaments of this kind were discovered by hundreds at Nimrud in a chamber which contained arms of many descriptions. Quivers have in some cases a curious rounded head, which seems to have been a lid or cap used for covering the arrows. They have also, occasionally, instead of this, a kind of bag at their top, which falls backwards, and is ornamented with tassels. [PLATE CV., Fig. 2.] Both these constructions, however, are exceptional, a very large majority of the quivers being open, and having the feathered ends of the arrows projecting from them.

There is nothing remarkable in the Assyrian arrows except their perfect finish and completeness in all that constitutes the excellence of such a weapon. The shaft was thin and straight, and was probably of reed, or of some light and tough wood. The head was of metal, either of bronze or iron, and was generally diamond-shaped, like a miniature spear-head. [PLATE CV., Fig. 4.] It was flattish, and for greater strength had commonly a strongly raised line down the centre. The lower end was hollowed, and the shaft was inserted into it. The notching and feathering of the shaft were carefully attended to. It is doubtful whether three feathers were used, as by ourselves and by the Egyptians, or two only as by many nations. The fact that we never see more than two feathers upon the monuments cannot be considered decisive, since the Assyrian artists, from their small knowledge of perspective, would have been unable to represent all three feathers. So far as we can judge from the representations, it would seem that the feathers were glued to the wood exactly as they are with ourselves. The notch was somewhat large, projecting beyond the line of the shaft—a construction rendered necessary by the thickness of the bowstring., which was seldom less than of the arrow itself. [PLATE CV., Fig. 5.]

The mode of drawing the bow was peculiar. It was drawn neither to the ear, nor to the breast, but to the shoulder. In the older sculptures the hand that draws it is represented in a curiously cramped and unnatural position, which can scarcely be supposed to be true to nature. But in the later bas-reliefs greater accuracy seems to have been attained, and there we probably see the exact mode in which the shooting was actually managed. The arrow was taken below the feathers by the thumb and forefinger of the right hand, the forefinger bent down upon it in the way represented in the accompanying illustration, and the notch being then placed upon the string, the arrow was drawn backwards by the thumb and forefinger only, the remaining three fingers taking no part in the operation. [PLATE CVI., Fig. 1.] The bow was grasped by the left hand between the fingers and the muscle of the thumb, the thumb itself being raised, and the arrow made to pass between it and the bow, by which it was kept in place and prevented from slipping. The arrow was then drawn till the cold metal head touched the forefinger of the left hand, upon which the right hand quitted its hold, and the shaft sped on its way. To save the left arm from being bruised or cut by the bowstring, a guard, often simply yet effectively ornamented, was placed upon it, at one end passing round the thumb and at the other round the arm a little above the elbow. [PLATE CVI., Fig. 2.]

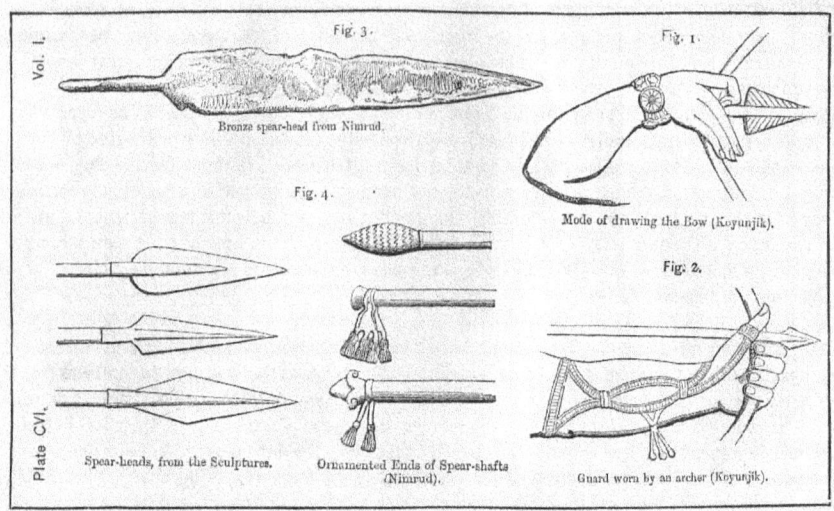

PLATE CVI

The Assyrians had two kinds of spears, one a comparatively short weapon, varying from five to six feet in length, with which they armed a portion of their foot soldiers, the other a weapon nine or ten feet long, which was carried by most of their cavalry. The shaft seems in both cases to have been of wood, and the head was certainly of metal, either bronze or iron. [PLATE CVI., Fig. 3.] It was most usually diamond-shaped, but sometimes the side angles were rounded off, and the contour became that of an elongated pear. [PLATE CVI., Fig. 4.] In other instances, the jambs of the spear-head were exceedingly short, and the point long and tapering. The upper end of the shaft was sometimes weighted, and it was often carved into some ornamental form, as a fir-cone or a pomegranate blossom, while in the earlier times it was further occasionally adorned with streamers. [PLATE CVI., Fig. 4.] The spear of the Assyrians seems never to have been thrown, like that of the Greeks, but was only used to thrust with, as a pike.

The common sword of the Assyrians was a short straight weapon, like the sword of the Egyptians, or the acinaces of the Persians. It was worn at the left side, generally slung by a belt of its own which was passed over the right shoulder, but sometimes thrust through the girdle or (apparently) through the armor. It had a short rounded handle, more or less ornamented [PLATE CVII.. Fig. 1], but without any cross-bar or guard, and a short blade which tapered gradually from the handle to the point. The swordsman commonly thrust with his weapon, but he could cut with it likewise, for it was with this arm that the Assyrian warrior was wont to decapitate his fallen enemy. The sheath of the sword was almost always tastefully designed, and sometimes possessed artistic excellence of a high order. [PLATE CVII., Fig. 3.] The favorite terminal ornament consisted of two lions clasping one another, with their heads averted and their mouths agape. Above this, patterns in excellent taste usually adorned the scabbard, which moreover exhibited occasionally groups of figures, sacred trees, and other mythological objects.

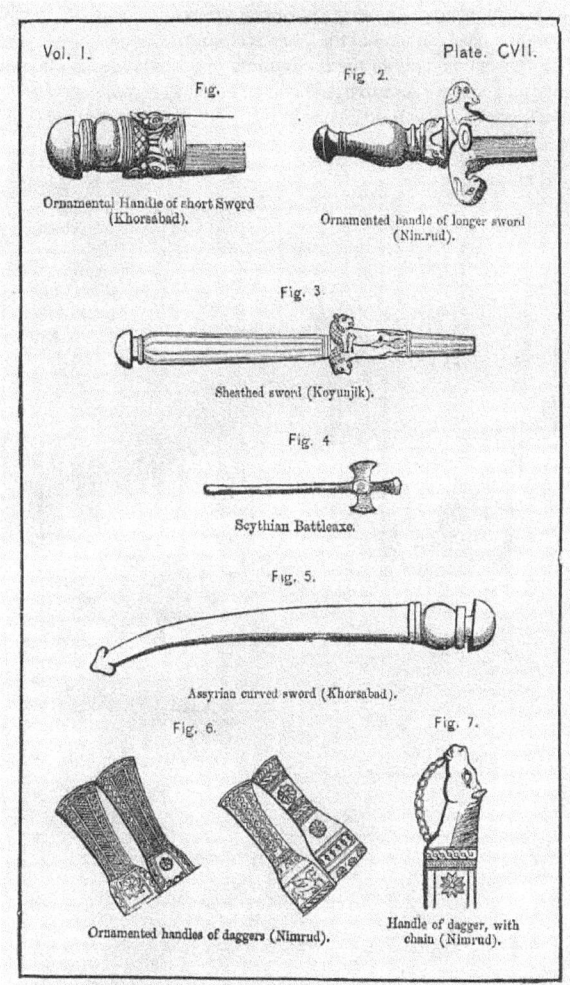

PLATE CVII

Instead of the short sword, the earlier warriors had a weapon of a considerable length. This was invariably slung at the side by a cross-belt passing over the shoulder. In its ornamentation it closely resembled the later short sword, but its hilt was longer and more tasteful.

One or two instances occur where the sword of an Assyrian warrior is represented as curved slightly. The sheath in these cases is plain, and terminates in a button. [PLATE CVII, Fig. 5.]

The Assyrian mace was a short thin weapon, and must either have been made of a very tough wood, or—and this is more probable of metal. [PLATE CVIII., Fig. 7.] It had an ornamented head, which was sometimes very beautifully modelled and generally a strap or string at the lower end, by which it could be grasped with greater firmness. Foot archers frequently carried it in battle, especially those who were in close attendance upon the king's person. It seems, however, not to have been often used as a warlike weapon until the time of the latest sculptures, when we see it wielded, generally with both hands, by a certain number of the combatants. In peace it was very commonly borne by the royal attendants, and it seems also to have been among the weapons used by the monarch himself, for whom it is constantly carried by one of those who wait most closely upon his person. [PLATE., CVIII., Fig. I.]

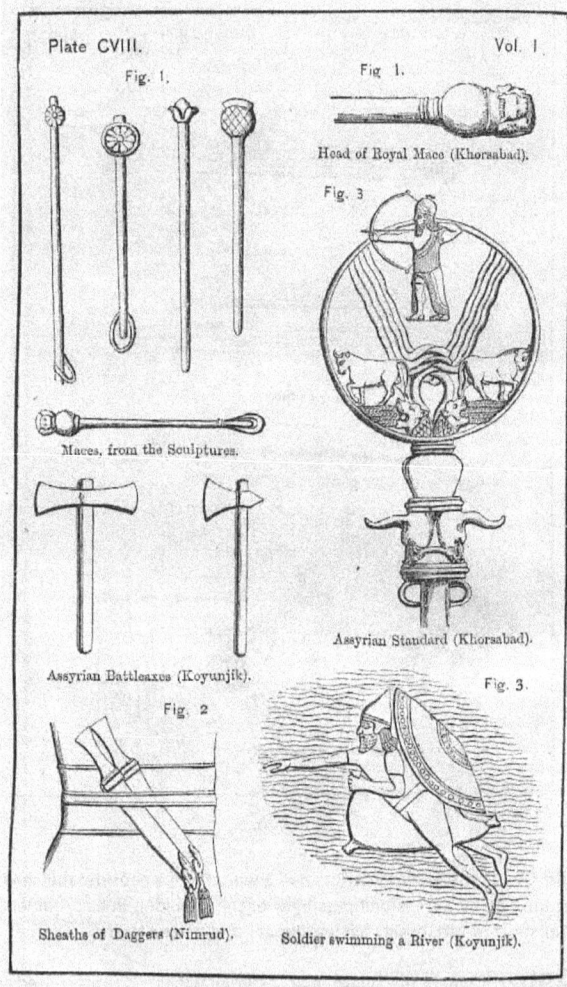

PLATE CVIII

The battle-axe was a weapon but rarely employed by the Assyrians. It is only in the very latest sculptures and in a very few instances that we find axes represented as used by the warriors for any other purpose besides the felling of trees. Where they are seen in use against the enemy, the handle is short, the head somewhat large, and the weapon wielded with one hand. Battle-axes had heads of two kinds. [PLATE CVIII., Fig. 1.] Some were made with two blades, like the bipennis of the Romans. and the labra of the Lydians and Carians; others more nearly resembled the weapons used by our own knights in the middle ages, having a single blade, and a mere ornamental point on the other side of the haft.

The dagger was worn by the Assyrian kings at almost all times in their girdles, and was further often assigned to the mythic winged beings, hawk headed or human-headed, which occur so frequently in the sculptures; but it seems to have been very seldom carried by subjects. It had commonly a straight handle, slightly concave, and very richly chased, exhibiting the usual Assyrian patterns, rosettes, chevrons, guilloches, pine-cones, and the like. [PLATE CVII., Fig. 6.] Sometimes, however, it was still more artistically shaped, being cast into the form of a horse's head and neck. In this case there was occasionally a chain attached at one end to the horse's chin, and at the other to the bottom of his neck, which, passing outside the hand, would give it a firmer hold on the weapon. The sheaths of daggers seem generally to have been plain, or nearly so, but occasionally they terminated in the head of an animal, from whose mouth depended a tassel. [PLATE CVIII., Fig. 2.]

Though the Assyrian troops were not marshalled by the aid of standards, like the Roman and the Egyptian, yet still a kind of standard is occasionally to be recognized in the bas-reliefs. This consists of a pole of no great height, fixed upright at the front of a chariot, between the charioteer and the warrior, and carrying at the top a circular frame, within which are artistic representations of gods or sacred animals. Two bulls, back to back, either trotting or running at speed, are a favorite device. Above there sometimes stands a figure in a horned cap, shooting his arrows against the enemy. Occasionally only one bull is represented, and the archer shoots standing upon the bull's back. Below the circular framework are minor ornaments, as lions' and bulls' heads, or streamers adorned with tassels. [PLATE CVIII., Fig. 2.]

We do not obtain much information from the monuments with respect to the military organization or the the tactics of the Assyrians. It is clear, however, that they had advanced beyond the first period in military matters, when men fight in a confused mass of mingled horse, foot, and chariots, heavy-armed and light-armed spear-men, archers, and stingers, each standing and moving as mere chance may determine. It is even certain that they had advanced beyond the second period, when the phalanx order of battle is adopted, the confused mass being replaced by a single serried body presenting its best armed troops to the enemy, and keeping in the rear, to add their weight to the charge, the weaker and more imperfectly protected. It was not really left for Cyaxares the Mede to be the first to organize an Asiatic army—to divide the troops into companies and form distinct bodies of the spearmen, the archers, and the cavalry. The Assyrian troops were organized in this way, at least from the time of Sennacherib, on whose sculptures we find, in the first place, bodies of cavalry on the march unaccompanied by infantry; secondly, engagements where cavalry only are acting against the enemy; thirdly, long lines of spearmen on foot marching in double file, and sometimes divided into companies; and, fourthly, archers drawn up together, but similarly divided into companies, each distinguished by its own uniform. We also meet with a corps of pioneers, wearing a uniform and armed only with a hatchet, and with bodies of slingers, who are all armed and clothed alike. If, in the battles and the sieges of this time, the troops seem to be to a great extent confused together, we may account for it partly by the inability of the Assyrian artists to represent bodies of troops in perspective, partly by their not aiming at an actual, but rather at a typical representation of events, and partly also by their fondness for representing, not the preparation for battle or its first shock, but the rout and flight of the enemy and their own hasty pursuit of them.

The wars of the Assyrians, like those of ancient Rome, consisted of annual inroads into the territories of their neighbors, repeated year after year, till the enemy was exhausted, sued for peace, and admitted the suzerainty of the more powerful nation. The king in person usually led forth his army, in spring or early summer, when the mountain passes were opened, and, crossing his own borders, invaded some one or other of the adjacent countries. The monarch himself invariably rode forth in his chariot, arrayed in his regal robes, and with the tiara upon his head: he was accompanied by numerous attendants, and generally preceded and followed by the spearmen of the Royal Guard, and a detachment of horse-archers. Conspicuous among the attendants were the charioteer who managed the reins, and the parasol-bearer, commonly a eunuch, who, standing in the chariot behind the monarch, held the emblem of sovereignty over his head. A bow-bearer, a quiver-bearer, and a mace-bearer were usually also in attendance, walking before or behind the chariot of the king, who, however, did not often depend for arms wholly upon them, but carried a bow in his left hand, and one or more arrows in his right, while he had a further store of the latter either in or outside his chariot. Two or three led horses were always at hand, to furnish a means of escape in any difficulty. The army, marshalled in its several corps, in part preceded the royal cortege, in part followed at a little distance behind it.

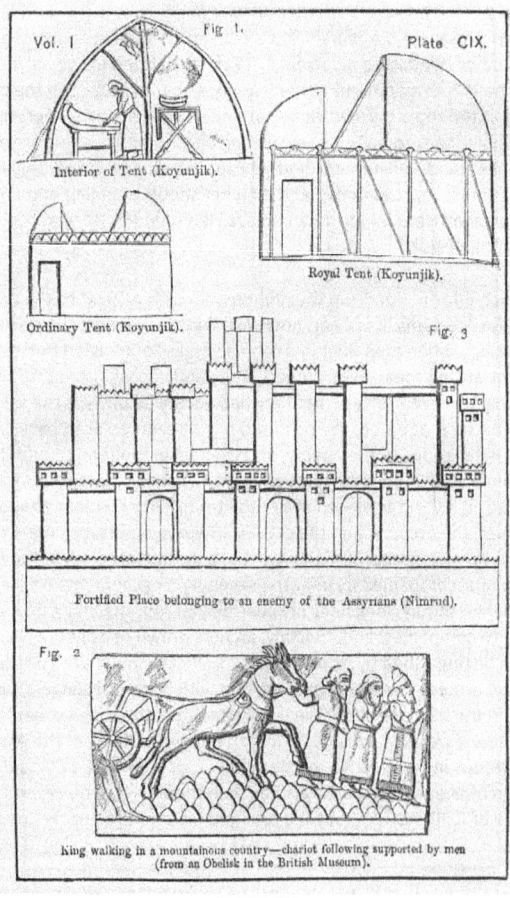

PLATE CIX

On entering the enemy's country, if a wooded tract presented itself, the corps of pioneers was thrown out in advance, and cleared away the obstructions. When a river was reached too deep to be forded, the horses were detached from the royal and other chariots by grooms and attendants; the chariots themselves were embarked upon boats and rowed across the stream; while the horses, attached by ropes to a post near the stern of the boat, swam after it. The horses of the cavalry were similarly drawn across by their riders. The troops, both cavalry and infantry, and the attendants, a very numerous body, swam the stream, generally upon inflated skins, which they placed under them, holding the neck in their left hand, and sometimes increasing the inflation as they went by applying the orifice at the top of the neck to their mouths. [PLATE CVIII., Fig. 3.] We have no direct evidence as to the mode in which the baggage of an army, which must have been very considerable, was conveyed, either along the general line of route, or when it was necessary to cross a river. We may conjecture that in the latter case it was probably placed upon rafts supported on inflated skins, such as those which conveyed stones from distant quarries to be used in the Assyrian buildings. In the former, we may perhaps assume that the conveyance was chiefly by beasts of burden, camels and asses, as the author of the book of Judith imagined. Carts may have been used to some extent; since they were certainly employed to convey back to Assyria the spoil of the conquered nations.

It does not appear whether the army generally was provided with tents or not. Possibly the bulk of the soldiers may have bivouacked in the open field, unless when they were able to obtain shelter in towns or villages taken from the enemy. Tents, however, were certainly provided for the monarch and his suite. [PLATE CIX., Fig. 1.] Like the tents of the Romans, these appear to have been commonly pitched within a fortified enclosure, which was of an oval shape. They were disposed in rows, and were all nearly similar in construction and form, the royal tent being perhaps distinguished from the others by a certain amount of ornamentation and by a slight superiority of size. The material used for the covering was probably felt. All the tents were made open to the sky in the centre, but closed in at either extremity with a curious semicircular top. [PLATE CIX., Fig. 1.] The two tops were unequal of size. Internally, either both of them, or at any rate the larger ones, were supported by a central pole, which threw out branches in different directions resembling the branches of a tree or the spokes of a parasol. Sometimes the walls of the tent had likewise the support of poles, which were kept in place by ropes passed obliquely from the top of each to the ground in front of them, and then firmly secured by pegs. Each tent had a door, square-headed, which was placed at the side, near the end which had the smaller covering. The furniture of tents consisted of tables, couches, footstools, and domestic utensils of various kinds. [PLATE CIX., Fig. 1.] Within the fortified enclosure, but outside the tents, were the chariot and horses of the monarch, an altar where sacrifice could be made, and a number of animals suitable for food, as oxen, sheep, and goats.

It appears that occasionally the advance of the troops was along a road. Ordinarily, however, they found no such convenience, but had to press forward through woods and over mountains as they best could. Whatever the obstructions, the chariot of the monarch was in some way or other conveyed across them, though it is difficult to suppose that he could have always remained, as he is represented, seated in it. Probably he occasionally dismounted, and made use of one of the led horses by which he was always accompanied, while sometimes he even condescended to proceed on foot. [PLATE CIX., Fig. 2.] Tile use of palanquins or litters seem not to have been known to the Assyrians, though it was undoubtedly very ancient in Asia; but the king was sometimes carried on men's shoulders, seated on his throne in the way that we see the enthroned gods borne in many of the sculptures.

The first object in entering a country was to fight, if possible, a pitched battle with the inhabitants. The Assyrians were always confident of victory in such an encounter, being better armed, better disciplined, and perhaps of stronger frames than any of their neighbors. There is no evidence to show how their armies were drawn up, or how the troops were handled in an engagement; but it would seem that in most cases, after a longer or a shorter resistance, the enemy broke and fled, sometimes throwing away his arms, at other tunes fighting as he retired, always vigorously pursued by horse and foot, and sometimes driven headlong into a river. Quarter was not very often given in a battle. The barbarous practice of rewarding those who carried back to camp the heads of foemen prevailed; and this led to the massacre in many cases even of the wounded, the disarmed, and the unresisting, though occasionally quarter was given, more especially to generals and other leading personages whom it was of importance to take alive. Even while the engagement continued, it would seem that soldiers might quit the ranks, decapitate a fallen foe, and carry off his head to the rear, without incurring any reproof; and it is certain that, so soon as the engagement was over, the whole army turned to beheading the fallen, using for this purpose the short sword which almost every warrior carried at his left side. A few unable to obtain heads, were forced to be content with gathering the spoils of the slain and of the fled, especially their arms, such as quivers, hews, helmets, and the like; while their more fortunate comrades, proceeding to an appointed spot in the rear, exhibited the tokens of their valor, or of their good luck, to the royal scribes, who took an exact account of the amount, of the spoil, and of the number of the enemy killed.

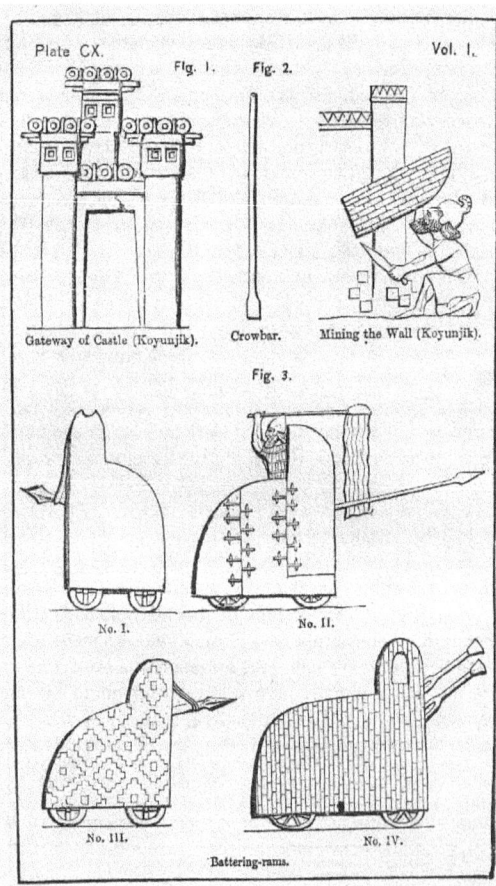

PLATE CX

When the enemy could no longer resist in the open field, he usually fled to his strongholds. Almost all the nations with whom the Assyrians waged their wars possessed fortified cities, or castles, which seem to have been places constructed with a good deal of skill, and possessed of no inconsiderable strength. According to the representations of the sculptures, they were all nearly similar in character, the defences consisting of high battlemented walls, pierced with loopholes or windows towards their upper part, and flanked at intervals along their whole course by towers. [PLATE CIX., Fig. 3.] Often they possessed two or more enceintes, which in the bas-reliefs are represented one above the other; and in these cases the outermost circuit was sometimes a mere plain continuous wall, as in the illustration. They were entered by large gateways, most commonly arched, and closed by two huge gates or doors, which completely filled up the aperture. Occasionally, however, the gateways were square-headed, as in the illustration, where there occurs, moreover, a very curious ornamentation of the battlements. [PLATE CX., Fig. 1.]

These fortified places the Assyrians attacked in three principal ways. Sometimes they endeavored to take them by escalade, advancing for this purpose a number of long ladders against different parts of the walls, thus distracting the enemy's attention and seeking to find a weak point. Up the ladders proceeded companies of spearmen and archers in combination, the spearmen invariably taking the lead, since their large shields afforded them a protection which archers advancing in file up a ladder could not have. Meanwhile from below a constant discharge was kept up by bowmen and slingers, the former of whom were generally protected by the gerrhon or high wicker shield, held in front of them by a comrade. The besieged endeavored to dislodge and break the ladders, which are often represented in fragments; or, failing in this attempt, sought by hurling down large stones, and by discharges from their bows and slings, to precipitate and destroy their assailants. If finally they were unable by these means to keep the Assyrians from reaching the topmost rounds of the ladders, they had recourse to their spears, and man to man, spear to spear, and shield to shield, they still struggled to defend themselves. The Assyrians always represent the sieges which they conduct as terminating successfully: but we may be tolerably sure that in many instances the invader was beaten back, and forced to relinquish his prey, or to try fresh methods of obtaining it.

If the escalade failed, or if it was thought unadvisable to attempt it, the plan most commonly adopted was to try the effect of the battering-ram. [PLATE CX., Fig. 3.] The Assyrian armies were abundantly supplied with these engines, of which we see as many as seven engaged in a single siege. They were variously designed and arranged. Some had a head shaped like the point of a spear; others, one more resembling the end of a blunderbuss. All of them were covered with a frame-work, which was of ozier, wood, felt, or skins, for the better protection of those who worked the implement; but some appear to have been stationary, having their framework resting on the ground itself, while others were moveable, being provided with wheels, which in the early times were six, but in the later times four only. Again, sometimes, combined with the ram and its framework was a moveable tower containing soldiers, who at once fought the enemy on a level, and protected the engine from their attacks. Fire was the weapon usually turned against the ram, torches, burning tow, or other inflammable substances being cast from the walls upon its framework, which, wherever it was of ozier or of wood, could be easily set alight and consumed. To prevent this result, the workers of the ram were sometimes provided with a supply of water, which they could direct through leathern or metal pipes against the combustibles. At other times they sought to protect themselves by suspending from a pole in front of their engine a curtain of cloth, leather, or some other non-inflammable substance.

Another mode of meeting the attacks of the battering-ram was by catching the point with a chain suspended by its two ends from the walls, and then, when the ram was worked, diverting the stroke by drawing the head upwards. To oppose this device, the besiegers provided some of their number with strong metal hooks, and stationed them below the ram, where they watched for the descent of the chain. As soon as ever it caught the head of the ram, they inserted their hooks into its links, and then hanging upon it with their whole weight, prevented its interference with the stroke.

Battering-rams were frequently used against the walls from the natural ground at their foot. Sometimes, however, the besiegers raised vast mounds against the ramparts, and advanced their engines up these, thus bringing theirs on a level with the upper and weaker portions of the defences. Of this nature probably were the mounds spoken of in Scripture as employed by the Babylonians and Egyptians, as well as the Assyrians, in their sieges of cities. The intention was not so much to pile up the mounds till they were on a level with the top of the walls as to work the battering-ram with greater advantage from them. A similar use was made of mounds by the Peloponnesian Greeks, who nearly succeeded in taking Plataea in this way. The mounds were not always composed entirely of earth; the upper portion was often made of several layers of stone or brick, arranged in regular order, so as to form a sort of paved road, up which the rams might be dragged with no great difficulty. Trees, too, were sometimes cut down and built into the mound.

Besides battering-rams, the Assyrians appear to have been acquainted with an engine resembling the catapult, or rather the balista of the Romans. [PLATE CXI., Fig. 1.] This engine, which was of great height, and threw stones of a large size, was protected, like the ram, by a framework, apparently of wood, covered with canvas, felt, or hides. The stones thrown from the engine were of irregular shape, and it was able to discharge several at the same time. The besiegers worked it from a mound or inclined plane, which enabled them to send their missiles to the top of the ramparts. It had to be' brought very close to the walls in order to be effective—a position which gave the besieged an opportunity of assailing it by fire. Perhaps it was this liability which caused the infrequent use of the engine in question, which is rare upon the earlier, and absent from the later, sculptures.

The third mode of attack employed by the Assyrians in their sieges of fortified places was the mine. While the engines were in full play, and the troops drawn up around the place assailed the defenders of the walls with their slings and bows, warriors, singly, or in twos and threes, advanced stealthily to the foot of the ramparts, and either with their swords and the points of their spears, or with implements better suited for the purpose, such as crowbars and pickaxes, attacked the foundations of the walls, endeavoring to remove the stones one by one, and so to force an entrance. While thus employed, the assailant commonly either held his shield above him as a protection or was guarded by the shield of a comrade; or, finally, if he carried the curved gerrhon, leant it against the wall, and then placed himself under its shelter. [PLATE CX., Fig. 2.] Sometimes, however, he dispensed with the protection of a shield altogether, and, trusting his helmet and coat of mail, which covered him at all vital points, pursued his labor without paying any attention to the weapons aimed at him by the enemy.

Occasionally the efforts of the besiegers were directed against the gates, which they endeavored to break open with axes, or to set on fire by an application of the torch. From this latter circumstance we may gather that the gates were ordinarily of wood, not, like those of Babylon and Veii, of brass. In the hot climate of Southern Asia wood becomes so dry by exposure to the sun that the most solid doors may readily be ignited and consumed.

PLATE CXI

When at last the city or castle was by some of these means reduced, and the garrison consented to surrender itself, the work of demolition, already begun, was completed. Generally the place was set on fire; sometimes workmen provided with pickaxes and other tools mounted upon the ramparts and towers, hurled down the battlements, broke breaches in the walls, or even levelled the whole building. [PLATE CXII., Fig. 1.] Vengeance was further taken by the destruction of the valuable trees in the vicinity, more especially the highly prized date-palms, which were cut with hatchets half through their stems at the distance of about two feet from the ground, and then pulled or pushed down. [PLATE CXI., Fig. 2.] Other trees were either treated similarly, or denuded of their branches. Occasionally the destruction was of a less wanton and vengeful character. Timber-trees were cut down for transport to Assyria, where they were used in the construction of the royal-palaces; and fruit-trees were occasionally taken up by the roots, removed carefully, and planted in the gardens and orchards of the conquerors. Meanwhile there was a general plundering of the captured place. The temples were entered, and the images of the gods, together, with the sacred vessels, which were often of gold and silver, were seized and carried off in triumph. [PLATE CXI., Fig. 4.] This was not mere cupidity. It was regarded as of the utmost importance to show that the gods of the

Assyrians were superior to those of other countries, who were powerless to protect either their votaries or even themselves from the irresistible might of the servants of Asshur. The ordinary practice was to convey the images of the foreign gods from the temples of the captured places to Assyria, and there to offer then at the shrines of the principal Assyrian deities. Hence the special force of the proud question, "Where are the gods of Hanath and of Arpad? Where are the gods of Sepharvaim, Hena, and Ivah? Where are they but carried captive to Assyria, prisoners and slaves in the temples of those deities whose power they ventured to resist?"

The houses of the city were also commonly plundered, and everything of value in them was carried off. Long files of men, each bearing some article of furniture out of the gate of a captured town, are frequent upon the bas-reliefs, where we likewise often observe in the train of a returning army carts laden with household stuff of every kind, alternating with long strings of captives. All the spoil seems to have been first brought by the individual plunderers to one place, where it was carefully sorted and counted in the presence and under the superintendence of royal scribes, who took an exact inventory of the whole before it was carried away by its captors. [PLATE CXI., Fig. 3.] Scales were used to determine the weight of articles made of the precious metals, which might otherwise have been subjected to clipping. We may conclude from these practices that a certain proportion of the value of all private spoil was either due to the royal treasury, or required to be paid to the gods in acknowledgment of their aid and protection. Besides the private spoil, there was a portion which was from the first set apart exclusively for the monarch. This consisted especially of the public treasure of the captured city, the gold and silver, whether in bullion, plate, or ornaments, from the palace of its prince, and the idols, and probably the other valuables from the temples.

The inhabitants of a captured place were usually treated with more or less of severity. Those regarded as most responsible for the resistance or the rebellion were seized; generally their hands were manacled either before them or behind their backs, while sometimes fetters were attached to their feet, and even rings passed through their lips, and in this abject guise they were brought into the presence of the Assyrian king. Seated on his throne in his fortified camp without the place, and surrounded by his attendants, he received them one by one, and instantly pronounced their doom. On some he proudly placed his foot, some he pardoned, a few he ordered for execution, many he sentenced to be torn from their homes and carried into slavery.

Various modes of execution seem to have been employed in the case of condemned captives. One of them was empalement. This has always been, and still remains, a common mode of punishment in the East; but the manner of empaling which the Assyrians adopted was peculiar. They pointed a stake at one end, and, having fixed the other end firmly into the ground, placed their criminal with the pit of his stomach upon the point, and made it enter his body just below the breastbone. This method of empaling must have destroyed life tolerably soon, and have thus been a far less cruel punishment than the crucifixion of the Romans. We do not observe it very often in the Assyrian sculptures, nor do we ever see it applied to more than a few individuals. It was probably reserved for those who were considered the worst criminals. Another very common mode of executing captives was by beating in their skulls with a mace. In this case the victim commonly knelt; his two hands were placed before him upon a block or cushion: behind him stood two executioners, one of whom held him by a cord round the neck, while the other, seizing his back hair in one hand, struck him a furious blow upon the head with a mace which he held in the other. [PLATE CXI., Fig. 5.] It must have been rarely, if ever, that a second blow was needed.

Decapitation was less frequently practised. The expression, indeed. "I cut off their heads," is common in the Inscriptions but in most instances it evidently refers to the practice, already noticed, of collecting the heads of those who had fallen in battle. Still there are instances, both in the Inscriptions and in the sculptures, of what appears to have been a formal execution of captives by beheading. In these cases the criminal, it would seem, stood upright, or bending a little forwards, and the executioner, taking him by a lock of hair with his left hand, struck his head from his shoulders with a short sword, which he held in his right. [PLATE CXII., Fig. 5.]

It is uncertain whether a punishment even more barbarous than these was not occasionally resorted to. In two or three bas-reliefs executioners are represented in the act of flaying prisoners with a knife. The bodies are extended upon the ground or against a wall, to which they are fastened by means of four pegs attached by strings or thongs to the two wrists and the two ankles. The executioner leans over the victim, and with his knife detaches the skin from the flesh. One would trust that this operation was not performed until life was extinct. We know that it was the practice of the Persians, and even of the barbarous Scythians, to flay the corpses, and not the living forms, of criminals and of enemies; we may hope, therefore, that the Assyrians removed the skin from the dead, to use it as a trophy or as a warning, and did not inflict so cruel a torture on the living.

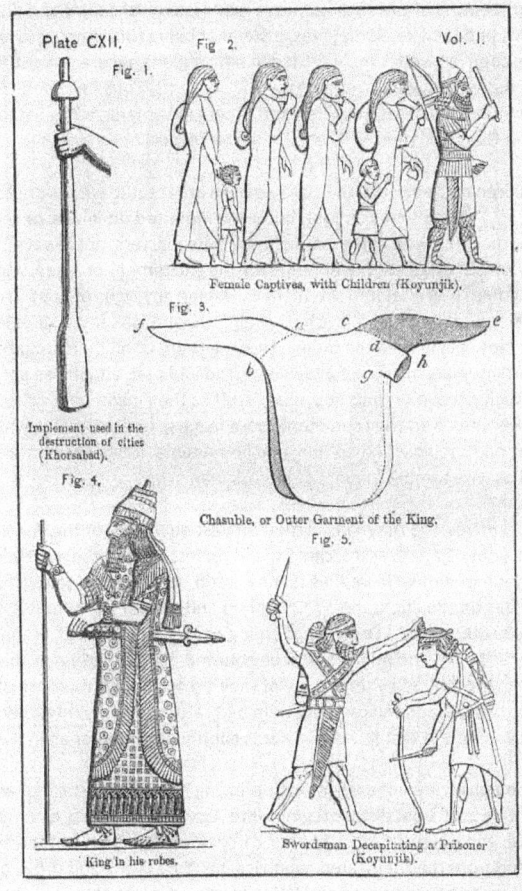

PLATE CXII

Sometimes the punishment awarded to a prisoner was mutilation instead of death. Cutting off the ears close to the head, blinding the eyes with burning-irons, cutting off the nose, and plucking out the tongue by the roots, have been in all ages favorite Oriental punishments. We have distinct evidence that some at least of these cruelties were practised by the Assyrians. Asshur-izir-pal tells us in his great Inscription that he often cut off the noses and the ears of prisoners; while a slab of Asshur-bani-pal, the son of Esarhaddon, shows a captive in the hands of the torturers, one of whom holds his head firm and fast, while another thrusts his hand into his mouth for the purpose of tearing out the tongue.

The captives carried away by the conquerors consisted of men, women, and children. The men were formed into bands, under the conduct of officers, who urged theme forward on their way by blows, with small regard to their sufferings. Commonly they were conveyed to the capital, where they were employed by the monarchs in the lower or higher departments of labor, according to their capacities. The skilled workmen were in request to assist in the ornamentation of shrines and palaces, while the great mass of the unskilled were made use of to quarry and drag stone, to raise mounds, make bricks, and the like. Sometimes, instead of being thus employed in task-work in or near the capital, the captives were simply settled in new regions, where it was thought that they would maintain the Assyrian power against native malcontents. Thus Esarhaddon planted Babylonians, Susanchites, Dehavites, Elamites, and others in Samaria, while Sargon settled his Samaritan captives in Gauzanitis and in "the cities of the Medes."

The women and children carried off by the conquerors were treated with more tenderness than the men. [PLATE CXII., Fig. 2.] Sometimes on foot, but often mounted on mules, or seated in carts drawn by bullocks or asses, they followed in the train of their new masters, not always perhaps unwilling to exchange the monotony of domestic life at home for the excitement of a new and unknown condition in a fresh country. We seldom see them exhibiting any signs of grief. The women and children are together, and the mothers lavish on their little ones the usual caresses and kind offices, taking them in their laps, giving then the breast, carrying them upon their shoulders, or else leading them by the hand. At intervals they were allowed to stop and rest; and it was not even the practice to deprive them of such portion of their household stuff as they might have contrived to secure before quitting their homes. This they commonly bore in a bag or sack, which was either held in the hand or thrown over one shoulder, When they reached Assyria, it would seem that they were commonly assigned as wives to the soldiers of the Assyrian army.

Together with their captives, the Assyrians carried off vast quantities of the domesticated animals, such as oxen, sheep, goats, horses, asses, camels, and mules. The numbers mentioned in the Inscriptions are sometimes almost incredible. Sennacherib, for instance, says that in one foray he bore off from the tribes on the Euphrates "7200 horses and mares, 5230 camels, 11,000 mules, 120,000 oxen, and 800,000 sheep"! Other kings omit particulars, but speak of the captured animals which they led away as being "too numerous to be counted," or "countless as the stars of heaven." The Assyrian sculptors are limited by the nature of their art to comparatively small numbers, but they show us horses, camels, and mules in the train of a returning army, together with groups of the other animals, indicative of the vast flocks and herds continually mentioned in the Inscriptions.

Occasionally the monarchs were not content with bringing home domesticated animals only, but took the trouble to transport from distant regions into Assyria wild beasts of various kinds. Tiglath-Pileser I. informs us in general terms that, besides carrying off the droves of the horses, cattle, and asses that he obtained from the subjugated countries, he "took away and drove off the herds of the wild goats and the ibexes, the wild sheep and the wild cattle;" and another monarch mentions that in one expedition he carried off from the middle Euphrates a drove of forty wild cattle, and also a flock of twenty ostriches. The object seems to have been to stock Assyria with a variety and an abundance of animals of chase.

The foes of the Assyrians would sometimes, when hard pressed, desert the dry land, and betake themselves to the marshes, or cross the sea to islands where they trusted that they might be secure from attack. Not unfrequently they obtained their object by such a retreat, for the Assyrians were not a maritime people. Sometimes, however, they were pursued. The Assyrians would penetrate into the marshes by means of reed boats, probably not very different from the terradas at present in use among the Arabs of the Mesopotamian marsh districts. Such boats are represented upon the bas-reliefs as capable of holding from three to five armed men. On these the Assyrian foot-soldiers would embark, taking with them a single boatman to each boat, who propelled the vessel much as a Venetian gondolier propels his gondola, i.e., with a single long oar or paddle, which he pushed from him standing at the stern. They would then in these boats attack the vessels of the enemy, which are always represented as smaller than theirs, run them down or board them, kill their crews or force them into the water, or perhaps allow them to surrender. Meanwhile, the Assyrian cavalry was stationed round the marsh among the tall reeds which thickly clothed its edge, ready to seize or slay such of the fugitives as might escape from the foot.

When the refuge sought was an island, if it lay near the shore, the Assyrians would sometimes employ the natives of the adjacent coast to transport beams of wood and other materials by means of their boats, in order to form a sort of bridge or mole reaching from the mainland to the isle whereto their foes had fled. Such a design was entertained, or at least professed, by Xerxes after the destruction of his fleet in the battle of Salamis, and it was successfully executed by Alexander the Great, who took in this way the new or island of Tyre. From a series of reliefs discovered at Khorsabad wo may conclude that more than two hundred years before the earlier of these two occasions, the Assyrians had conceived the idea, and even succeeded in carrying out the plan, of reducing islands near the coast by moles.

Under the Chaldaeans, whose "cry was in their ships," the Assyrians seem very rarely to have adventured themselves upon the deep. If their enemies fled to islands which could not be reached by moles, or to lands across the sea, in almost every instance they escaped. Such escapes are represented upon the sculptures, where we see the Assyrians taking a maritime town at one end, while at the other the natives are embarking their women and children, and putting to sea, without any pursuit being made after them. In none of the bas-reliefs do we observe any sea-going vessels with Assyrians on board and history tells us of but two or three expeditions by sea in which they took part. One of these was an expedition by Sennacharib against the coast of the Persian Gulf, to which his Chaldaean enemies had fled. On this occasion he brought shipwrights from Phoenicia to Assyria, and made them build him ships there, which were then launched upon the Tigris, and conveyed down to the sea. With a fleet thus constructed, and probably manned, by Phoenicians, Sennacherib crossed to the opposite coast, defeated the refugees, and embarking his prisoners on board, returned in triumph to the mainland. Another expedition was that of Shalmaneser IV. against the island Tyre. Assyrians are said to have been personally engaged in it; but here again we are told that they embarked in ships furnished to then by the Phoenicians, and maimed chiefly by Phoenician sailors.

When a country was regarded as subjugated, the Assyrian monarch commonly marked the establishment of his sovereignty by erecting a memorial in some conspicuous or important situation within the territory conquered, as an enduring sign of his having taken possession. These memorials were either engraved on the natural rock or on solid blocks of stone cut into the form of a broad low stele. They contained a figure of the king, usually enclosed in an arched frame; and an inscription, of greater or less length, setting forth his name, his titles, and some of his exploits. More than thirty such memorials are mentioned in the extant Inscriptions, and the researches of recent times have recovered some ten or twelve of them. They uniformly represent the king in his sacerdotal robes, with the sacred collar round his neck, and the emblems of the gods above his head, raising the right hand in the act of adoration, as if he were giving thanks to Asshur and his guardian deities on account of his successes.

It is now time to pass from the military customs of the Assyrians to a consideration of their habits and usages in time of peace, so far as they are made known to us either by historical records or by the pictorial evidence of the bas reliefs. And here it may be convenient to treat separately of the public life of the king and court, and of the private life of the people.

In Assyria, as in most Oriental countries, the keystone of the social arch, the central point of the system, round which all else revolved, and on which all else depended, was the monarch. "L'etat, c'est moi" might have been said with more truth by an Assyrian prince than even by the "Grand Monarque," whose dictum it is reported to have been. Alike in the historical notices, and in the sculptures, we have the person of the king presented to us with consistent prominence, and it is consequently with him that we most naturally commence the present portion of our inquiry.

The ordinary dress of the monarch in time of peace was a long flowing robe, reaching to the ankles, elaborately patterned and fringed, over which was worn, first, a broad belt, and then a species of open mantle, or chasuble, very curiously contrived. [PLATE CXII., Fig. 3.] This consisted mainly of two large flaps, both of which were commonly rounded, though sometimes one of them was square at bottom. These fell over the robe in front and behind, leaving the sides open, and so exposing the under dress to view. The two flaps must have been sewn together at the places marked with the dotted lines a b and c d, the space from a to c being left open, and the mantle passed by that means over the head. At d g there was commonly a short sleeve (h), which covered the upper part of the left arm, but the right arm was left free, the mantle falling of either side of it. Sometimes, besides the flaps, the mantle seems to have had two pointed wings attached to the shoulders (a f b and c e h in the illustration), which were made to fall over in front. Occasionally there was worn above the chasuble a broad diagonal belt ornamented with a deep fringe and sometimes there depended at the back of the dress a species of large hood.

The special royal head-dress was a tall mitre or tiara, which at first took the shape of the head, but rose above it to a certain height in a gracefully curved line, when it was covered in with a top, flat, like that of a hat, but having a projection towards the centre, which rose up into a sort of apex, or peak, not however pointed, but either rounded or squared off. The tiara was generally ornamented with a succession of bands, between which were commonly patterns more or less elaborate. Ordinarily the lowest band, instead of running parallel with the others, rose with a gentle curve towards the front, allowing room for a large rosette over the forehead, and for other similar ornaments. If we may trust the representations on the enamelled bricks, supported as they are to some extent by the tinted reliefs, we may say that the tiara was of three colors, red, yellow, and white. The red and white alternated in broad bands; the ornaments upon them were yellow, being probably either embroidered on the material of the head-dress in threads of gold, or composed of thin gold plates which may have been sown on. The general material of the tiara is likely to have been cloth or felt; it can scarcely have been metal, if the deep crimson tint of the bricks and the reliefs is true. [PLATE CXII., Fig. 4.]

In the early sculptures the tiara is more depressed than in the later, and it is also less richly ornamented. It has seldom more than two bands, viz., a narrow one at top, and at bottom a broader curved one, rising towards the front. To this last are attached two long strings or lappets, which fall behind the monarch's back to a level with his elbow. [PLATE CXIII., Fig. 1.]

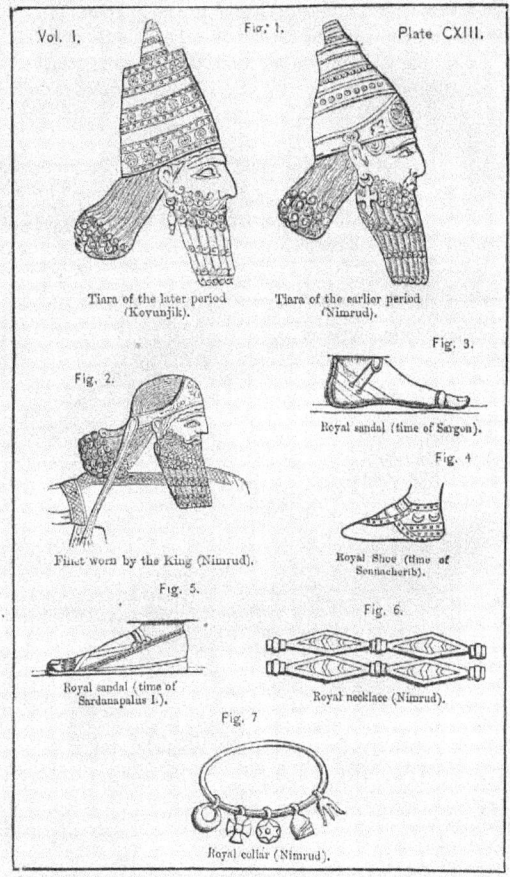

PLATE CXIII

Another head-dress which the monarch sometimes wore was a sort of band or fillet. This was either elevated in front and ornamented with a single rosette, like the lowest band of the tiara, or else of uniform width and patterned along its whole course. In either case there depended from it, on each side of the back hair, a long ribbon or streamer, fringed at the end and sometimes ornamented with a delicate pattern. [PLATE CXIII., Fig 2.]

The monarch's feet were protected by sandals or shoes. In the early sculptures sandals only appear in use, shoes being unknown (as it would seem) until the time of Sennacherib. The sandals worn were of two kinds. The simplest sort had a very thin sole and a small cap for the heel, made apparently of a number of strips of leather sewn together. It was held in place by a loop over the great-toe, attached to the fore part of the sole, and by a string which was laced backwards and forwards across the instep, and then tied in a bow. [PLATE CXIII., Fig. 4.]

The other kind of sandal had a very different sort of sole; it was of considerable thickness, especially at the heel, from which it gradually tapered to the toe. Attached to this was an upper leather which protected the heel and the whole of the side of the foot, but left the toes and the instep exposed. A loop fastened to the sole received the great-toe, and at the point where the loop was inserted two straps were also made fast, which were then carried on either side the great-toe to the top of the foot, where they crossed each other, and, passing twice through rings attached to the edge of the upper leather, were finally fastened, probably by a buckle, at the top of the instep. [PLATE CXIII., Fig. 6.]

The shoe worn by the later kings was of a coarse and clumsy make, very much rounded at the toe, patterned with rosettes, crescents, and the like, and (apparently) laced in front. In this respect it differed from the shoe of the queen, which will be represented presently, and also from the shoes worn by the tribute-bearers. [PLATE CXIII, Fig. 5.]

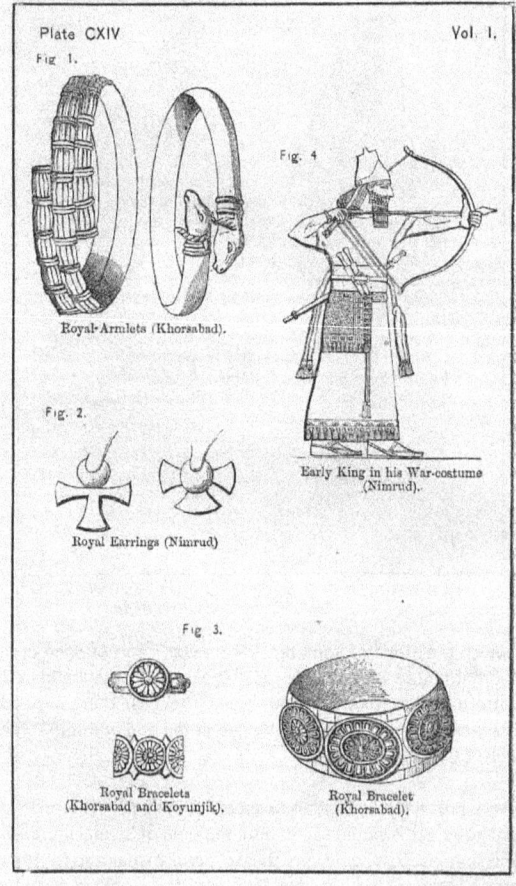

PLATE CXIV

The accessory portions of the royal costume were chiefly belts, necklaces, armlets, bracelets, and earrings. Besides the belt round the waist, in which two or three highly ornamented daggers were frequently thrust, and the broad fringed cross-belt, of which mention was made above, the Assyrian monarch wore a narrow cross-belt passing across his right shoulder, from which his sword hung at his left side. This belt was sometimes patterned with rosettes. It was worn over the front flap of the chasuble, but under the back flap, and was crossed at right angles by the broad fringed belt, which was passed over the right arm and head so as to fall across the left shoulder.

The royal necklaces were of two kinds. Some consisted merely of one or more strings of long lozenge-shaped beads slightly chased, and connected by small links, ribbed perpendicularly. [PLATE CXIII., Fig. 7.] The other kind was a band or collar, perhaps of gold, on which were hung a number of sacred emblems: as the crescent or emblem of the Moon-God, Sin; the four-rayed disk, the emblem of the Sun-God, Shamas; the six-rayed or eight-rayed disk, the emblem of Gula, the Sun-Goddess; the horned cap, perhaps the emblem of the king's guardian genius; and the double or triple bolt, which was the emblem of Vul, the god of the atmosphere. This sacred collar was a part of the king's civil and not merely of his sacerdotal dress; as appears from the fact that it was sometimes worn when the king was merely receiving prisoners. [PLATE CXIII., Fig. 8.]

The monarch wore a variety of armlets. The most common was a plain bar of a single twist, the ends of which slightly overlapped each other. A more elegant kind was similar to this, except that the bar terminated in animal heads carefully wrought, among which the heads of rams, horses, and ducks were the most common. A third sort has the appearance of being composed of a number of long strings or wires, confined at intervals of less than an inch by cross bands at right angles to the wires. This sort was carried round the arm twice, and even then its ends overlapped considerably. It is probable that all the armlets were of metal, and that the appearance of the last was given to it by the workman in imitation of an earlier and ruder armlet of worsted or leather. [PLATE CXIV., Fig. 1.] The bracelets of the king, like his armlets, were sometimes mere bars of metal, quite plain and without ornament. More often, however, they were ribbed and adorned with a large rosette at the centre. Sometimes, instead of one simple rosette, we see three double rosettes, between which project small points, shaped like the head of a spear. Occasionally these double rosettes appear to be set on the surface of a broad bar, which is chased so as to represent brickwork. In no case can we see how the bracelets were fastened; perhaps they were elastic, and were slipped over the hand. [PLATE CXIV., Fig. 3.]

Specimens of royal earrings have been already given in an earlier chapter of this volume. The most ordinary form in the more ancient times was a long drop, which was sometimes delicately chased Another common kind was an incomplete Maltese cross, one arm of the four being left out because it would have interfered with the ear. [PLATE CXIV., Fig. 2.] In later times there was a good deal of variety in the details; but the drop and the cross were always favorite features.

When the monarch went out to the hunt or to the battle, he laid aside such ornaments as encumbered him, reserving however his earrings, bracelets, and armlets, and then, stripping off his upper dress or chasuble, appeared in the under robe which has been already described. This robe was confined at the waist by a broad cincture or girdle, outside of which was worn a narrowish belt wherein daggers were often thrust. In early times this cincture seems to have been fastened by a ribbon with long streaming ends, which are very conspicuous in the Nimrud sculptures. At the same period the monarch often wore, when he hunted or went out to battle, a garment which might have been called an apron, if it had not been worn behind instead of in front. This was generally patterned and fringed very richly, besides being ornamented with one or more long pendent tassels. [PLATE CXIV., Fig. 4.]

The sacerdotal dress of the king, or that which he commonly wore when engaged in the rites of his religion, differed considerably from his ordinary costume. His inner garment, indeed, seems to have been the usual long gown with a fringe descending to the ankles; but this was almost entirely concealed under an ample outer robe, which was closely wrapped round the form and kept in place by a girdle. A deep fringe, arranged in two rows, one above the other, and carried round the robe in curved sweeps at an angle with the horizontal line, is the most striking feature of this dress, which is also remarkable for the manner in which it confines and conceals the left arm, while the right is left free and exposed to view. A representation of a king thus apparelled will be found in an earlier part of this work, taken from a statue now in the British Museum. It is peculiar in having the head uncovered, and in the form of the implement borne in the right hand. It is also incomplete as a representation, from the fact that all the front of the breast is occupied by an inscription. Other examples show that the tiara was commonly worn as a part of the sacerdotal costume; that the sacred collar adorned the breast, necklaces the neck, and bracelets the two arms; while in the belt, which was generally to some extent knotted, were borne two or three daggers. The mace seems to have been a necessary appendage to the costume, and was always grasped just below its head by the left hand.

We have but one representation of an Assyrian queen. Despite the well-known stories of Semiramis and her manifold exploits, it would seem that the Assyrians secluded their females with as rigid and watchful a jealousy as modern Turks or Persians. The care taken with respect to the direction of the passages in the royal hareem has been noticed already. It is quite in accordance with the spirit thus indicated, and with the general tenor of Oriental habits, that neither in inscriptions nor in sculptured representations do the Assyrians allow their women to make more than a most rare and occasional appearance. Fortunately for us, their jealousy was sometimes relaxed to a certain extent; and in one scene, recovered from the debris of an Assyrian palace we are enabled to contemplate at once the domestic life of the monarch and the attire and even the features of his consort.

It appears that in the private apartments, while the king, like the Romans and the modern Orientals, reclined upon a couch leaning his weight partly upon his left elbow, and having his right arm free and disposable, her majesty the queen sat in a chair of state by the couch's side, near its foot, and facing her lord. [PLATE CXV., Fig. 1.] Two eunuchs provided with large fans were in attendance upon the monarch, and the same number waited upon the queen, standing behind her chair. Her majesty, whose hair was arranged nearly like that of her royal consort, wore upon her head a band or fillet having something of the appearance of a crown of towers, such as encircles the brow of Cybele on Greek coins and statues. Her dress was a long-sleeved gown reaching from the neck to the feet, flounced and trimmed at the bottom in an elaborate way, and elsewhere patterned with rosettes, over which she wore a fringed tunic or frock descending half-way between the knees and the feet. [PLATE CXV., Fig. 3.] In addition to these two garments, she wore upon her back and shoulders a light cloak or cape, patterned (like the rest of her dress) with rosettes and edged with a deep fringe. Her feet were encased in shoes of a clumsy make, also patterned. Her ornaments, besides the crown upon her head, were earrings, a necklace, and bracelets. Her hair was cushioned, and adorned with a drapery which hung over the back. Her feet rested on a handsome footstool, also cushioned.

On the slab from which this description is taken the royal pair seem to be refreshing themselves with wine. Each supports on the thumb and fingers of the right hand a saucer or shallow drinking-cup, probably of some precious metal, which they raise to their lips simultaneously, as if they were pledging one another. The scene of the entertainment is the palace garden; for trees grow on either side of the main figures, while over their heads, a vine hangs its festoons and its rich clusters. By the side of the royal couch, and in front of the queen, is a table covered with a table-cloth, on which are a small box or casket, a species of shallow bowl which may have held incense or perfume of some kind, and a third article frequently seen in close proximity to the king, but of whose use it is impossible to form a conjecture. At the couch's head stands another curious article, a sort of tall vase surmounted by a sugarloaf, which probably represents an altar. The king bears in his left hand the lotus or sacred flower, while the queen holds in hers what looks like a modern fan. All the lower part of the monarch's person is concealed beneath a coverlet, which is plain, except that it has tassels at the corners and an embroidered border.

The officers in close attendance upon the monarch varied according to his employment. In war he was accompanied by his charioteer, his shield-bearer or shield-bearers, his groom, his quiver-bearer, his mace-bearer, and sometimes by his parasol-bearer. In peace the parasol-bearer is always represented as in attendance, except in hunting expeditions, or where he is replaced by a fan-bearer. The parasol, which exactly resembled that still in use throughout the East, was reserved exclusively for the monarch. [PLATE CXVI., Fig. 1.] It had a tall and thick pole, which the bearer grasped with both his hands, and in the early times a somewhat small circular top. Under the later kings the size of the head was considerably enlarged; and, at the same time, a curtain or flap was attached, which, falling from the edge of the parasol, more effectually protected the monarch from the sun's rays. The head of the parasol was fringed with tassels, and the upper extremity of the pole commonly terminated in a flower or other ornament. In the later time both the head and the curtain which depended from it were richly patterned. If we may trust the remains of color upon the Khorsabad sculptures, the tints preferred were red and white, which alternated in bands upon the parasol as upon the royal tiara.

King, Queen, and Attendants (Koyunjik). Fig. 1.

PLATE CXV

There was nothing very remarkable in the dress or quality of the royal attendants. Except the groom, the charioteer, and the shield-bearers, they were in the early times almost invariably eunuchs; but the later kings seem to have preferred eunuchs for the offices of parasol-bearer and fan-bearer only. The dress of the eunuchs is most commonly a long fringed gown, reaching from the neck to the feet, with very short sleeves, and a broad belt or girdle confining the gown at the waist. Sometimes they have a cross-belt also; and occasionally both this and the girdle round the waist are richly fringed. The eunuchs commonly wear earrings, and sometimes armlets and bracelets; in a few instances they have their necks adorned with necklaces, and their long dresses elaborately patterned. Their heads are either bare, or at most encircled with a fillet.

PLATE CXVI

A peculiar physiognomy is assigned to this class of persons—the forehead low, the nose small and rounded, the lips full, the chin large and double, the cheeks bloated. [PLATE CXV., Fig. 2.] They are generally represented as shorter and stouter than the other Assyrians. Though placed in confidential situations about the person of the monarch, they seem not to have held very high or important offices. The royal Vizier is never a eunuch, and eunuchs are rarely seen among the soldiers; they are scribes, cooks, musicians, perhaps priests; as they are grooms-in-waiting, huntsmen, parasol-bearers, and fan-bearers; but it cannot be said with truth that they had the same power in Assyria which they have commonly possessed in the more degraded of the Oriental monarchies. It is perhaps a sound interpretation of the name Rabsaris in Scripture to understand it as titular, not appellative, and to translate it "the Chief Eunuch" or "the Master of the Eunuchs;" and if so, we have an instance of the employment by one Assyrian king of a person of this class on an embassy to a petty sovereign: but the sculptures are far from bearing out the notion that eunuchs held the same high position in the Assyrian court as they have since held generally in the East, where they have not only continually filled the highest offices of state, but have even attained to sovereign power. On the contrary, their special charge seems rather to have been the menial offices about the person of the monarch, which imply confidence in the fidelity of those to whom they are entrusted, but not submission to their influence in the conduct of state affairs. And it is worthy of notice that, instead of becoming more influential as time went on, they appear to have become less so; in the later sculptures the royal attendants are far less generally eunuchs than in the earlier ones; and the difference is most marked in the more important offices.

It is not quite certain that the Chief Eunuch is represented upon the sculptures. Perhaps we may recognize him in an attendant, who commonly bears a fan, but whose special badge of office is a long fringed scarf or band, which hangs down below his middle both before him and behind him, being passed over the left shoulder. [PLATE CXVI., Fig. 2.] This officer appears, in one bas-relief, alone in front of the king; in another, he stands on the right hand of the Vizier, level with him, facing the king as he drinks; in a third, he receives prisoners after a battle; while in another part of the same sculpture he is in the king's camp preparing the table for his master's supper. There is always a good deal of ornamentation about his dress, which otherwise nearly resembles that of the inferior royal attendants, consisting of a long fringed gown or robe, a girdle fringed or plain, a cross-belt generally fringed, and the scarf already described. His head and feet are generally bare, though sometimes the latter are protected by sandals. He is found only upon the sculptures of the early period.

Among the officers who have free access to the royal person, there is one who stands out with such marked prominence from the rest that he has been properly recognized as the Grand Vizier or prime minister at once the chief counsellor of the monarch, and the man whose special business it was to signify and execute his will. The dress of the Grand Vizier is more rich than that of any other person except the monarch; and there are certain portions of his apparel which he and the king have alone the privilege of wearing. These are, principally, the tasselled apron and the fringed band depending from the fillet, the former of which is found in the early period only, while the latter belongs to no particular time, but throughout the whole series of sculptures is the distinctive mark of royal or quasi-royal authority. To these two may be added the long ribbon or scarf, with double streamers at the ends, which depended from, and perhaps fastened, the belt—a royal ornament worn also by the Vizier in at least one representation. [PLATE CXVI., Fig. 3.]

The chief garment of the Vizier is always a long fringed robe, reaching from the neck to the feet. This is generally trimmed with embroidery at the top, round the sleeves, and round the bottom. It is either seen to be confined by a broad belt round the waist, or else is covered from the waist to the knees by two falls of a heavy and deep fringe. In this latter case, a broad cross-belt is worn over the left shoulder, and the upper fall of fringe hangs from the cross-belt. A fillet is worn upon the head, which is often highly ornamented. The feet are sometimes bare, but more often are protected by sandals, or (as in the accompanying representation) by embroidered shoes. Earrings adorn the ears; bracelets, sometimes accompanied by armlets, the arms. A sword is generally worn at the left side.

The Vizier is ordinarily represented in one of two attitudes. Either he stands with his two hands joined in front of him, the right hand in the left, and the fingers not clasped, but left loose—the ordinary attitude of passive and respectful attention, in which officers who carry nothing await the orders of the king,—or he has the right arm raised, the elbow bent, and the right hand brought to a level with his month, while the left hand rests upon the hilt of the sword worn at his left side. [PLATE CXVII., Fig. 1.] In this latter case it may be presumed that we have the attitude of conversation, as in the former we have that of attentive listening. When the Vizier assumes this energetic posture he is commonly either introducing prisoners or bringing in spoil to the king. When he is quiescent, he stands before the throne to receive the king's orders, or witnesses the ceremony with which it was usual to conclude a successful hunting expedition.

PLATE CXVII

The pre-eminent rank and dignity of this officer is shown, not only by his participation in the insignia of royal authority, but also and very clearly by the fact that, when he is present, no one ever intervenes between him and the king. He has the undisputed right of precedence, so that he is evidently the first subject of the crown, and he alone, is seen addressing the monarch. He does not always accompany the king on his military expeditions but when he attends them, he still maintains his position, having a dignity greater than that of any general, and so taking the entire direction of the prisoners and of the spoil.

The royal fan-bearers were two in number. They were invariably eunuchs. Their ordinary position was behind the monarch, on whom they attended alike in the retirement of private life and in religious and civil ceremonies. On some occasions, however, one of the two was privileged to leave his station behind the king's chair or throne, and, advancing in front, to perform certain functions before the face of his master. He handed his master the sacred cup, and waited to receive it back, at the same time diligently discharging the ordinary duties of his office by keeping up a current of air and chasing away those plagues of the East—the flies. The fan-bearer thus privileged wears always the long tasselled scarf, which seems to have been a badge of office, and may not improbably mark him for the chief Eunuch. In the absence of the Vizier, or sometimes in subordination to him, he introduced the tribute-bearers to the king, reading out their names and titles from a scroll or tablet which he held in his left hand. [PLATE CXVII., Fig. 2.]

PLATE CXVIII

The fan carried by these attendants seems in most instances to have been made of feathers. It had a shortish handle, which was generally mere or less ornamented, and frequently terminated in the head of a ram or other animal. [PLATE CXVIII., Fig. 1.] The feathers were sometimes of great length, and bent gracefully by their own weight, as they were pointed slantingly towards the monarch. Occasionally a comparatively short fan was used, and the feathers were replaced by a sort of brush, which may have been made of horse-hair, or possibly of some vegetable fibre.

The other attendants on the monarch require no special notice. With regard to their number, however, it may be observed that, although the sculptures generally do not represent them as very numerous, there is reason to believe that they amounted to several hundreds. The enormous size of the palaces can scarcely be otherwise accounted for: and in one sculpture of an exceptional character, where the artist seems to have aimed at representing his subject in full, we can count above seventy attendants present with the monarch at one time. Of these less than one-half are eunuch; and these wear the long robe with the fringed belt and cross-belt. The other attendants wear in many cases the same costume; sometimes, however, they are dressed in a tunic and greaves, like the soldiers.

There can be no doubt that the court ceremonial of the Assyrians was stately and imposing. The monarch seems indeed not to have affected that privacy and seclusion which forms a predominant feature of the ceremonial observed in most Oriental monarchies. He showed himself very freely to his subjects on many occasions. He superintended in person the accomplishment of his great works. In war and in the chase he rode in an open chariot, never using a litter, though litters were not unknown to the Assyrians. In his expeditions he would often descend from his chariot, and march or fight on foot like the meanest of his subjects. But though thus familiarizing the multitude with his features and appearance, he was far from allowing familiarity of address. Both in peace and war he was attended by various officers of state, and no one had speech of him except through them. It would even seem as if two persons only were entitled to open a conversation with him—the Vizier and the Chief Eunuch. When he received them, he generally placed himself upon his throne, sitting, while they stood to address him. It is strongly indicative of the haughty pride of these sovereigns that they carried with them in their distant expeditions the cumbrous thrones whereon they were wont to sit when they dispensed justice or received homage. On these thrones they sat, in or near their fortified camps, when the battle or the siege was ended, and thus sitting they received in state the spoil and the prisoners. Behind them on such occasions were the two fan-bearers, while near at hand were guards, scribes, grooms, and other attendants. In their palace halls undoubtedly the ceremonial used was stricter, grander, and more imposing. The sculptures, however, furnish no direct evidence on this point, for there is nothing to mark the scene of the great processional pieces.

In the pseudo-history of Ctesias, the Assyrian kings were represented as voluptuaries of the extremest kind, who passed their whole lives within the palace, in the company of their concubines and their eunuchs, indulging themselves in perpetual ease, pleasure, and luxury. We have already seen how the warlike character of so many monarchs gives the lie to these statements, so far as they tax the Assyrian kings with sloth and idleness. It remains to examine the charge of over-addiction to sensual delights, especially to those of the lowest and grossest description. Now it is at least remarkable that, so far as we have any real evidence, the Assyrian kings appear as monogamists. In the inscription on the god Nebo, the artist dedicates his statue to his "lord Vol-lush (?) and his lady, Sammuramit." In the solitary sculptured representation of the private life of the king, he is seen in the company of one female only. Even in the very narrative of Ctesias, Ninus has but one wife, Semiramis; and Sardanapalus, notwithstanding his many concubines, has but five children, three sons and two daughters. It is not intended to press these arguments to an extreme, or to assume, on the strength of them, that the Assyrian monarchs were really faithful to one woman. They may have had—nay, it is probable that they had—a certain number of concubines; but there is really not the least ground for believing that they carried concubinage to an excess, or over-stepped in this respect the practice of the best Eastern sovereigns. At any rate they were not the voluptuaries which Ctesias represented them. A considerable portion of their lives was passed in the toils and dangers of war; and their peaceful hours, instead of being devoted to sloth and luxury in the retirement of the palace, were chiefly employed, as we shall presently see, in active and manly exercises in the field, which involved much exertion and no small personal peril.

PLATE CXIX

The favorite occupation of the king in peace was the chase of the lion. In the early times he usually started on a hunting expedition in his chariot, dressed as when he went out to war, and attended by his charioteer, some swordsmen, and a groom holding a led horse. He carried a bow and arrows, a sword, one or two daggers, and a spear, which last stood in a rest made for it at the back of the chariot. Two quivers, each containing an axe and an abundant supply of arrows, hung from the chariot transversely across its right side, while a shield armed with teeth was suspended behind. When a lion was found, the king pursued it in his chariot, letting fly his arrows as he went, and especially seeking to pierce the animal about the heart and head. Sometimes he transfixed the beast with three or four shafts before it succumbed. Occasionally the lion attacked him in his chariot, and was met with spear and shield, or with a fresh arrow, according to the exigencies of the moment, or the monarch's preference for one or the other weapon. On rare occasions the monarch descended to the ground, and fought on foot. He would then engage the lion in close combat with no other weapon but a short sword, which he strove to plunge, and often plunged, into his heart. [PLATE CXVIII., Fig. 2.]

In the later time, though the chariot was still employed to some extent in the lion-hunts, it appears to have been far more usual for the king to enjoy the sport on foot. He carried a straight sword, which seems to have been a formidable weapon; it was strong, very broad, and two feet or a little more in length. Two attendants waited closely upon the monarch, one of whom carried a bow and arrows, while the other was commonly provided with one or two spears. From these attendants the king took the bow or spear at pleasure, usually commencing the attack with his arrows, and finally despatching the spent animal with sword or spear, as he deemed best. Sometimes, but not very often, the spearman in attendance carried also a shield, and held both spear and shield in advance of his master to protect him from the animal's spring. Generally the monarch faced the danger with no such protection, and received the brute on his sword, or thrust him through with his pike. [PLATE CXVIII., Fig. 3;] [PLATE CXIX., Fig. 1.] Perhaps the sculptures exaggerate the danger which he affronted at such moments; but we can hardly suppose that there was not a good deal of peril incurred in these hand-to-hand contests.

Two modes of hunting the king of beasts were followed at this time. Either he was sought in his native haunts, which were then, as now, the reedy coverts by the side of the canals and great streams; or he was procured beforehand, conveyed to the hunting-ground, and there turned out before the hunters. In the former case the monarch took the field accompanied by his huntsmen and beaters on horse and foot, these last often holding dogs in leash, which, apparently, were used only to discover and arouse the game, but were not slipped at it when started. No doubt the hunt was sometimes entirely on the land, the monarch accompanying his beaters along one or other of the two banks of a canal or stream. But a different plan is known to have been adopted on some occasions. Disposing his beaters to the right and left upon both banks, the monarch with a small band of attendants would take ship, and, while his huntsmen sought to start the game on either side, he would have himself rowed along so as just to keep pace with them, and would find his sport in attacking such lions as took the water. The monarch's place on these occasions was the middle of the boat. Before him and behind him were guards armed with spears, who were thus ready to protect their master, whether the beast attacked him in front or rear. The monarch used a round bow, like that commonly carried in war, and aimed either at the heart or at the head. The spearmen presented their weapons at the same time, while the sides of the boat were also sufficiently high above the water to afford a considerable protection against the animal's spring. An attendant immediately behind the monarch held additional arrows ready for him; and after piercing the noble brute with three or four of these weapons, the monarch had commonly the satisfaction of seeing him sink down and expire. The carcass was then taken from the water, the fore and hind legs were lashed together with string, and the beast was suspended from the hinder part of the boat, where he hung over the water just out of the sweep of the oars.

At other times, when it was felt that the natural chase of the animal might afford little or no sport, the Assyrians (as above stated) called art to their assistance, and, having obtained a supply of lions from a distance, brought them in traps or cages to the hunting-ground, and there turned them out before the monarch. The walls of the cage was made of thick spars of wood, with interstices between them, through which the lion could both see and be seen: probably the top was entirely covered with boards, and upon these was raised a sort of low hut or sentry-box, just large enough to contain a man, who, when the proper moment arrived, peeped forth from his concealment and cautiously raised the front of the trap, which was a kind of drop-door working in a groove. [PLATE

CXIX., Fig. 2.] The trap being thus opened, the lion stole out, looking somewhat ashamed of his confinement, but doubtless anxious to vent his spleen on the first convenient object. The king, prepared for his attack, saluted him, as he left his cage, with an arrow, and, as he advanced, with others, which sometimes stretched him dead upon the plain, sometimes merely disabled him, while now and then they only goaded him to fury. In this case he would spring at the royal chariot, clutch some part of it, and in his agony grind it between his teeth, or endeavor to reach the inmates of the car from behind. If the king had descended from the car to the plain, the infuriated beast might make his spring at the royal person, in which case it must have required a stout heart to stand unmoved, and aim a fresh arrow at a vital part while the creature was in mid-air, especially if (as we sometimes see represented) a second lion was following close upon the first, and would have to be received within a few seconds. It would seem that the lions on some occasions were not to be goaded into making an attack, but simply endeavored to escape by flight. To prevent this, troops were drawn up in a double line of spearmen and archers round the space within which the lions were let loose, the large shields of the front or spearmen line forming a sort of wall, and the spears a chevaux de frise, through which it was almost impossible for the beasts to break. In front of the soldiers, attendants held hounds in leashes, which either by their baying and struggling frightened the animals back, or perhaps assisted to despatch them. [PLATE CXIX., Fig. 3.] The king meanwhile plied his bow, and covered the plain with carcasses, often striking a single beast with five or six shafts.

The number of lions destroyed at these royal battues is very surprising. In one representation no fewer than eighteen are seen upon the field, of which eleven are dead and five seriously wounded. The introduction of trapped beasts would seem to imply that the game, which under the earlier monarchs had been exceedingly abundant,—failed comparatively under the later ones, who therefore imported it from a distance. It is evident, however, that this scarcity was not allowed to curtail the royal amusement. To gratify the monarch, hunters sought remote and savage districts, where the beast was still plentiful, and, trapping their prey, conveyed it many hundreds of miles to yield a momentary pleasure to the royal sportsman.

It is instructive to contrast with the boldness shown in the lion-hunts of this remote period the feelings and conduct of the present inhabitants of the region. The Arabs, by whom it is in the main possessed, are a warlike race, accustomed from infancy to arms and inured to combat. "Their hand is against every man, and every man's hand is against them." Yet they tremble if a lion is but known to be near, and can only with the utmost difficulty be persuaded by an European to take any part in the chase of so dangerous an animal.

The lioness, no less than the lion, appears as a beast of chase upon the sculptures. It seems that in modern times she is quite as much feared as her consort. Indeed, when she has laid up cubs, she is even thought to be actually the more dangerous of the two. [PLATE CXX., Fig. 1.]

PLATE CXX

Next to the chase of the lion and lioness, the early Assyrian monarchs delighted in that of the wild bull. It is not quite certain what exact species of animal is sought to be expressed by the representations upon the sculptures; but on the whole it is perhaps most probable that the Aurochs or European bison (Bos urus of naturalists) is the beast intended. At any rate it was an animal of such strength and courage that, according to the Assyrian belief, it ventured to contend with the lion. [PLATE CXX., Fig. 2.] The Assyrian monarchs chased the wild bull in their chariots without dogs, but with the assistance of horsemen, who turned the animals when they fled, and brought them within the monarch's reach. [PLATE CXX., Fig. 3.] The king then aimed his arrows at them, and the attendant horsemen, who were provided with bows, seem to have been permitted to do the same. The bull seldom fell until he had received a number of wounds; and we sometimes see as many as five arrows still fixed in the body of one that has succumbed. It would seem that the bull, when pushed, would, like the lion, make a rush at the king's chariot, in which case the monarch seized him by one of the horns and gave him the coup de grace with his sword.

The special zest with which this animal was pursued may have arisen in part from its scarcity. The Aurochs is wild and shy; it dislikes the neighborhood of man, and has retired before him till it is now found only in the forests of Lithuania, Carpathia, and the Caucasus. It seems nearly certain that, in the time of the later kings, the species of wild cattle previously limited, whatever it was, had disappeared from Assyria altogether; at least this is the only probable account that can be given of its non-occurrence in the later sculptures, more especially in those of Asshur-bani-pal, the son of Esarhaddon, which seem intended to represent the chase under every aspect known at the time. We might therefore presume it to have been, even in the early period, already a somewhat rare animal. And so we find in the Inscriptions that the animal, or animals, which appear to represent wild cattle, were only met with in outlying districts of the empire—on the borders of Syria and in the country about Harrah; and then in such small numbers as to imply that even there they were not very abundant.

When the chase of the nobler animals—the lion and the wild bull—had been conducted to a successful issue, the hunters returned in a grand procession to the capital, carrying with then as trophies of their prowess the bodies of the slain. These were borne aloft on the shoulders of men, three or four being required to carry each beast. Having been brought to an appointed spot, they were arranged side by side upon the ground, the heads of all pointing the same way; and the monarch, attended by several of his principal officers, as the Vizier, the Chief Eunuch, the fan-bearers, the bow and mace bearers, and also by a number of musicians, came to the place, and solemnly poured a libation over the prostrate forms, first how-ever (as it would seem) raising the cup to his own lips. It is probable that this ceremony had to some extent a religious character. The Assyrian monarchs commonly ascribe the success of their hunting expeditions to the gods Nin (or Ninip) and Nergal; and we may well understand that a triumphant return would be accompanied by a thank-offering to the great protectors under whose auspices success had been achieved. [PLATE CXX., Fig. 4.]

Besides the wild bull and the lion, the Assyrians are known to have hunted the following animals: the onager or wild ass, the stag, the ibex or wild goat, the gazelle, and the hare.

The chase of the wild ass was conducted in various ways. The animal was most commonly pursued with dogs. The large and powerful hounds of the Assyrians, of which a certain use was made even in the chase of the lion, have been already noticed; but it may be desirable in this place to give a fuller account of them. They were of a type approaching to that of our mastiff, being smooth haired, strong limbed, with a somewhat heavy head and neck, small pointed but drooping ears, and a long tail, which was bushy and a little inclined to curl. They seem to have been very broad across the chest, and altogether better developed as to their fore than as to their hind parts, though even their hind legs were tolerably strong and sinewy. They must have been exceedingly bold, if they really faced the hunted lion; and their pace must have been considerable, if they were found of service in chasing the wild ass.

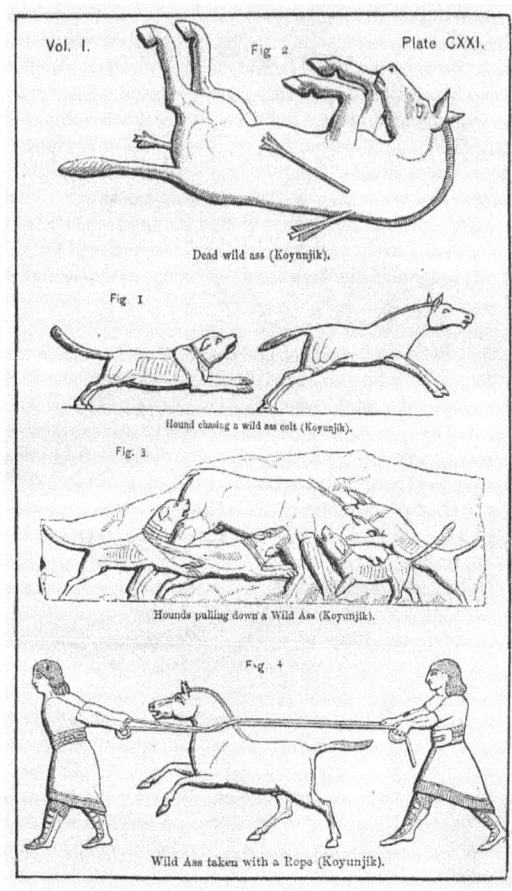

PLATE CXXI

The hunters are represented as finding the wild asses in herds, among which are seen a certain number of foals. The King and his chief attendants pursue the game on horseback, armed with bows and arrows, and discharging their arrows as they go. Hounds also—not now held in leash, but free—join in the hunt, pressing on the game, and generally singling out some one individual from the herd, either a young colt or sometimes a full-grown animal. [PLATE CXXI., Fig. 1.] The horsemen occasionally brought down the asses with their shafts. [PLATE CXXI.. Fig. 2.] When their archery failed of success, the chase depended on the hounds, which are represented as running even the full-grown animal to a stand, and then worrying him till the hunters came up to give the last blow. Considering the speed of the full-grown wild ass, which is now regarded as almost impossible to take, we may perhaps conclude that the animals thus run down by the hounds were such as the hunters had previously wounded; for it can scarcely be supposed that such heavily-made dogs as the Assyrian could really have caught an unwounded and full-grown wild ass. [PLATE CXXI., Fig. 3.]

Instead of shooting the wild ass, or hunting him to the death with hounds, an endeavor was sometimes made to take him alive. [PLATE CXXI., Fig. 4] A species of noose seems to have been made by means of two ropes interlaced, which were passed—how, we cannot say—round the neck of the animal, and held him in such a way that all his struggles to release himself were vain. This mode of capture recalls the use of the lasso by the South Americans and the employment of nooses by various nations, not merely in hunting, but in warfare. It is doubtful, however, if the Assyrian practice approached at all closely to any of these. The noose, if it may be so called, was of a very peculiar kind. It was not formed by means of a slip-knot at the end of a single cord, but resulted from the interlacing of two ropes one with the other. There is great difficulty in understanding how the ropes were got into their position. Certainly no single throw could have placed then, round the neck of the animal in the manner represented, nor could the capture have been effected, according to all appearance, by a single hunter. Two persons, at least, must have been required to combine their efforts—one before and one behind the creature which it was designed to capture.

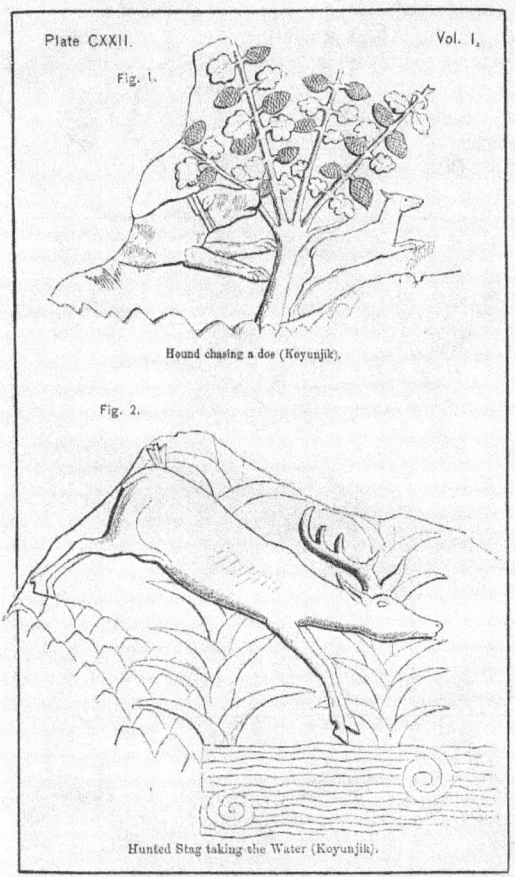

PLATE CXXII

Deer, which have always abounded in Assyria were either hunted with dogs, or driven by beaters into nets, or sometimes shot with arrows by sportsmen. The illustration (PLATE CXXII., Fig. 1) represents a dog in chase of a hind, and shows that the hounds which the Assyrians used for this purpose were of the same breed as those employed in the hunt of the lion and of the wild ass. In [PLATE CXXII., Fig. 2.] we have a stricken stag, which may, perhaps, have been also hard pressed by hounds, in the act of leaping from rocky ground into water. It is interesting to find this habit of the stag, with which the modern English sportsman is so familiar, not merely existing in Assyria, but noticed by Assyrian sculptors, at the distance of more than twenty-five centuries from our own time.

When deer were to be taken by nets, the sportsman began by setting in an upright position, with the help of numerous poles and pegs, a long, low net, like the [dikrvov] of the Greeks. [PLATE CXXII., Fig. 1.] This was carried round in a curved line of considerable length, so as to enclose an ample space on every side excepting one, which was left open for the deer to enter. The meshes of the net were large and not very regular. They were carefully secured by knots at all the angles. The net was bordered both at top and at bottom by a rope of much greater strength and thickness than that which formed the network; and this was fastened to the ground at the two extremities by pegs of superior size. [PLATE CXXIII., Fig. 2.] The general height of the net was about that of a man, but the two ends were sloped gently to the ground. Beaters, probably accompanied by dogs, roused the game in the coverts, which was then driven by shouts and barkings towards the place where the net was set. If it once entered within the two extremities of the net (a b, [PLATE CXXIII., Fig. 1]), its destruction was certain; for the beaters, following on its traces, occupied the space by which it had entered, and the net itself was not sufficiently visible for the deer to rise at it and clear it by a leap.

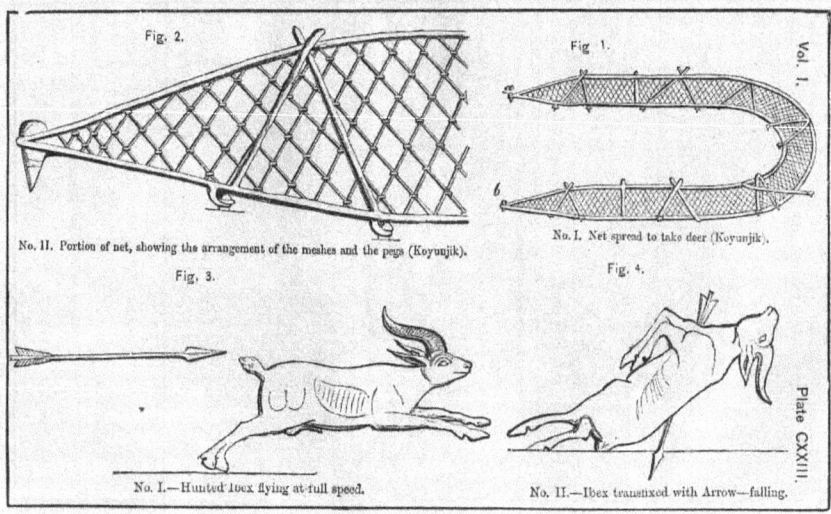

PLATE CXXIII

In the chase of the ibex or wild goat, horsemen were employed to discover the animals, which are generally found in herds, and to drive them towards the sportsman, who waited in ambush until the game appeared within bowshot. [PLATE CXXIII., Fig. 3.] An arrow was then let fly at the nearest or the choicest animal, which often fell at the first discharge. [PLATE CXXIII., Fig. 4.] The sport was tame compared with many other kinds, and was probably not much affected by the higher orders.

The chase of the gazelle is not shown on the sculptures. In modern times they are taken by the grayhound and the falcon, separately or in conjunction, the two being often trained to hunt together. They are somewhat difficult to run down with dogs only, except immediately after they have drunk water in hot weather. That the Assyrians sometimes captured them, appears by a hunting scene which Mr. Layard discovered at Khorsabad, where an attendant is represented carrying a gazelle on his shoulders, and holding a hare in his right hand. [PLATE CXXIV., Fig. 1.] As gazelles are very abundant both in the Sinjar country and in the district between the Tigris and the Zagros range, we may suppose that the Assyrians sometimes came upon them unawares, and transfixed them with their arrows before they could make their escape. They may also have taken them in nets, as they were accustomed to take deer; but we have no evidence that they did so.

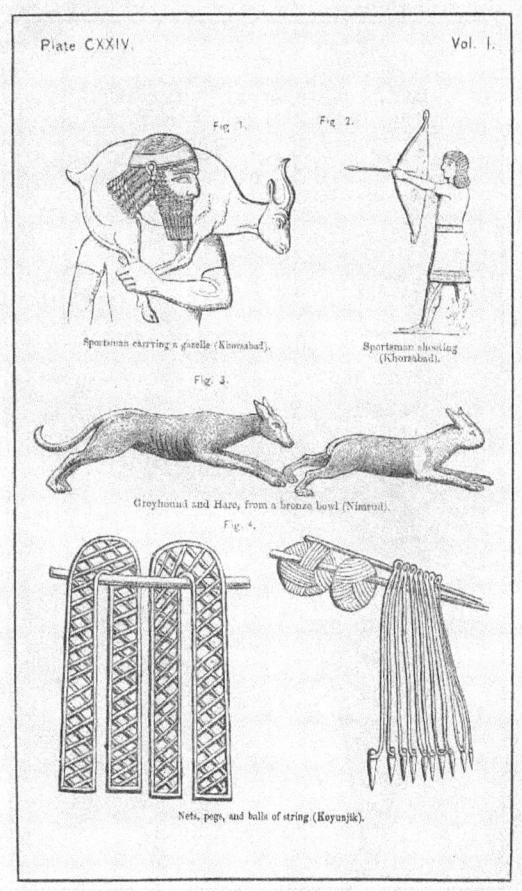

PLATE CXXIV

The hare is seen very commonly in the hands of those who attend upon the huntsmen. It is always represented as very small in proportion to the size of the men, whence we may perhaps conclude that the full-grown animal was less esteemed than the leveret. As the huntsmen in these representations have neither nets nor dogs, but seem to obtain their game solely by the bow, we must presume that they were expert enough to strike the hare as it ran.

There is no difficulty in making such a supposition as this, since the Assyrians have left us an evidence of their skill as marksmen which implies even greater dexterity. The game which they principally sought in the districts where they occasionally killed the hare and the gazelle seems to have been the partridge; and this game they had to bring down when upon the wing. We see the sportsmen in the sculptures aiming their arrows at the birds as they mount into the air [PLATE CXXIV., Fig. 21,] and in one instance we observe one of the birds in the act of falling to the ground, transfixed by a well aimed shaft. Such skill is not uncommon among savage hunting tribes, whose existence depends on the dexterity with which they employ their weapons; but it is rarely that a people which has passed out of this stage, and hunts for sport rather than subsistence, retains its old expertness.

PLATE CXXV

Hunting the hare with dogs was probably not very common, as it is only in a single instance that the Assyrian remains exhibit a trace of it. On one of the bronze dishes discovered by Mr. Layard at

Nimrud may be seen a series of alternate dogs and hares, which shows that coursing was not unknown to the Assyrians. [PLATE CXXIV., Fig. 3.] The dog is of a kind not seen elsewhere in the remains of Assyrian art. The head bears a resemblance to that of the wolf; but the form generally is that of a coarse greyhound, the legs and neck long, the body slim, and the tail curved at the end; offering thus a strong contrast to the ordinary Assyrian hound, which has been already represented more than once.

Nets may sometimes have been employed for the capture of small game, such as hares and rabbits, since we occasionally see beaters or other attendants carrying upon poles, which they hold over their shoulders, nets of dimensions far too small for them to have been used in the deer-hunts, with balls of string and pegs wherewith to extend them. [PLATE CXXIV., Fig. 4.] The nets in this case are squared at the ends, and seem to have been about eight or nine feet long, and less than a foot in height. They have large meshes, and, like the deer nets, are bordered both at top and bottom with a strong cord, to which the net-work is attached. Like the classical [evodia], they were probably placed across the runs of the animals, which, being baffled by then and turned from their accustomed tracks, would grow bewildered, and fall an easy prey to the hunters. Or, possibly, several of them may have been joined together, and a considerable space may then have been enclosed, within which the game may have been driven by the beaters. The ease of these three weak and tinnier animals, the gazelle, the hare, and the partridge, was not regarded as worthy of the monarch. When the king is represented as present, he takes no part in it, but merely drives in his chariot through the woods where the sportsmen are amusing themselves. Persons, however, of a good position, as appears from their dress and the number of their attendants, indulged in the sport, more especially eunuchs, who were probably those of the royal household. It is not unlikely that the special object was to supply the royal table with game.

The Assyrians do not seem to have had much skill as fishermen. They were unacquainted with the rod, and fished by means of a simple line thrown into the water, one end of which was held in the hand. [PLATE CXXV., Figs. 1, 2.] No float was used, and the bait must consequently have sunk to the bottom, unless prevented from so doing by the force of the stream. This method of fishing was likewise known and practised in Egypt, where, however, it was far more common to angle with a rod. Though Assyrian fish-hooks have not been found, there can be no doubt that that invention was one with which they were acquainted, as were both the Egyptians and the early Chaldaeans.

Fishing was carried on both in rivers and in stews or ponds. The angler sometimes stood or squatted upon the bank; at other times, not content with commanding the mere edge of the water, he plunged in, and is seen mid-stream, astride upon an inflated skin, quietly pursuing his avocation. [PLATE CXXVI., Fig. 1.] Occasionally he improved his position by amounting upon a raft, and, seated at the stern, with his back to the rower, threw out his line and drew the fish from the water. Now and then the fisherman was provided with a plaited basket, made of rushes or flags, which was fastened round his neck with a string, and hung at his back, ready to receive the produce of his exertions.

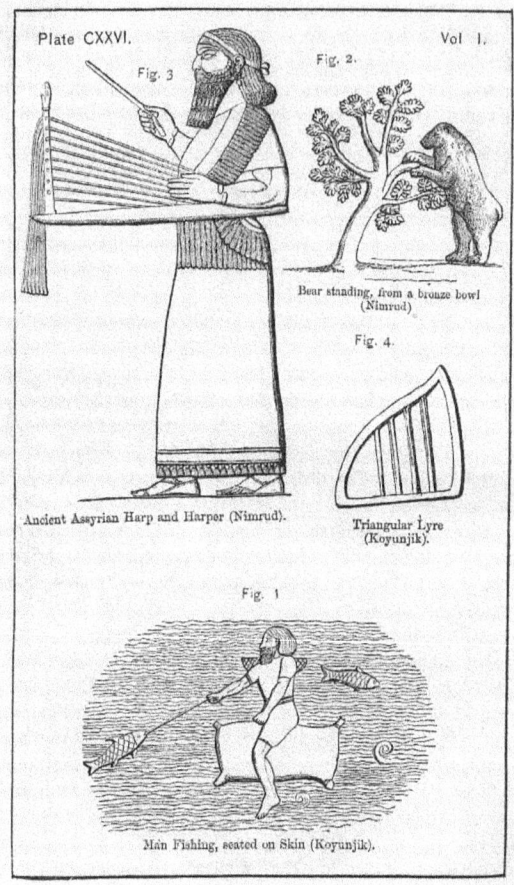

PLATE CXXVI

It does not appear that angling was practised by the Assyrians the way that the monuments show it to have been practised in Egypt, as an amusement of the rich. The fishermen are always poorly clothed, and seem to have belonged to the class which worked for its living. It is remarkable that do not anywhere in the sculptures see nets used for fishing; but perhaps we ought not to conclude from this that they were never so employed in Assyria. The Assyrian sculptors represented only occasionally the scenes of common everyday life; and we are seldom justified in drawing a negative conclusion as to the peaceful habits of the people on any point from the mere fact that the bas-reliefs contain no positive evidence on the subject.

A few other animals were probably, but not certainly, chased by the Assyrians, as especially the ostrich and the bear. The gigantic bird, which remained in Mesopotamia as late as the time of Xenophon, was well known to the Assyrian artists, who could scarcely have represented it with so much success, unless its habits had been described by hunters. The bear is much less frequent upon the remains than the ostrich; but its occurrence and the truthfulness of its delineation where it occurs, indicate a familiarity which may no doubt be due to other causes, but is probably traceable to the intimate knowledge acquired by those who hunted it. [PLATE CXXVI., Fig. 2.]

Of the other amusements and occupations of the Assyrians our knowledge is comparatively scanty; but some pages may be here devoted to their music, their navigation, their commerce, and their agriculture. On the first and second of these a good deal of light is thrown by the monuments, while some interesting facts with respect to the third and fourth may be gathered both from this source and also from ancient writers.

That the Babylonians, the neighbors of the Assyrians, and, in a certain sense, the inheritors of their empire, had a passion for music, and delighted in a great variety of musical instruments, has long been known and admitted. The repeated mention by Daniel, in his third chapter, of the cornet, flute, harp sackbut, psaltery, dulcimer, and all kinds of music—or, at any rate, of a number of instruments for which those terms were once thought the best English equivalents—has familiarized us with the fact that in Babylonia, as early as the sixth century B.C., musical instruments of many different kinds were in use. It is also apparent from the book of Psalms, that a variety of instruments were employed by the Jews. And we know that in Egypt as many as thirteen or fourteen different kinds were common. In Assyria, if there was not so much variety as this, there were at any rate eight or nine quite different sorts, some stringed, some wind, some merely instruments of percussion. In the early sculptures, indeed, only two or three musical instruments are represented. One is a kind of harp, held between the left arm and the side, and played with one hand by means of a quill or plectrum. [PLATE CXXVI., Fig. 3.] Another is a lyre, played by the hand; while a third is apparently cymbal. But in the later times we see besides these instruments—a harp of a different make played with both hands, two or three kinds of lyre, the double pipe, the guitar or cithern, the tambourine, a nameless instrument, and more than one kind of drum.

The harp of the early ages was a triangular instrument, consisting of a horizontal board which seems to have been about three feet in length, an upright bar inserted into one end of the board, commonly surmounted by an imitation of the human hand, and a number of strings which crossed diagonally from the board to the bar, and, passing through the latter, hung down some way, terminating in tassels of no great size. The strings were eight, nine, or ten in number, and (apparently) were made fast to the board, but could be tightened or relaxed by means of a row of pegs inserted into the upright bar, round which the strings were probably wound. No difference is apparent in the thickness of the strings; and it would seem therefore that variety of tone was produced solely by difference of length. It is thought that this instrument must have been suspended round the player's neck. It was carried at the left side, and was played (as already observed) with a quill or electrum held in the right hand, while the left hand seems to have been employed in pressing the strings so as to modify the tone, or stop the vibrations, of the notes. The performers on this kind of harp, and indeed all other Assyrian musicians, are universally represented as standing while they play.

The harp of later times was constructed, held, and played differently. It was still triangular, or nearly so; but the frame now consisted of a rounded and evidently hollow, sounding-board, to which the strings were attached with the help of pegs, and a plain bar whereto they were made fast below, and from which their ends depended like a fringe. The number of strings was greater than in the earlier harp, being sometimes as many as seventeen. The instrument was carried in such a way that the strings were perpendicular and the bar horizontal, while the sounding-board projected forwards at an angle above the player's head. It was played by the naked hand, without a plectrum; and both hands seem to have found their employment in pulling the strings. [PLATE CXXVII., Fig. 1.]

PLATE CXXVII

Three varieties of the lyre are seen in the Assyrian sculptures. One of them is triangular, or nearly so, and has only four strings, which, being carried from one side of the triangle to the other, parallel to the base, are necessarily of very unequal length. Its frame is apparently of wood, very simple, and entirely devoid of ornament. This sort of lyre has been found only in the latest sculptures. [PLATE CXXVI., Fig. 4.]

Another variety nearly resembles in its general shape the lyre of the Egyptians. It has a large square bottom or sounding-board, which is held, like the Egyptian, under the left elbow, two straight arms only slightly diverging, and a plain cross-bar at top. The number of strings visible in the least imperfect representation is eight; but judging by the width of the instrument, we may fairly assume that the full complement was nine or ten. The strings run from the cross-bar to the sounding-board, and must have been of a uniform length. This lyre was played by both hands, and for greater security was attached by a band passing round the player's neck. [PLATE CXXVII., Fig. 2.]

The third sort of lyre was larger than either of the others, and considerably more elaborate. It had probably a sounding-board at bottom, like the lyre just described, though this, being carried under the left elbow, is concealed in the representations. Hence there branched out two curved arms, more or less ornamented, which were of very unequal length; and these were joined together by a cross-bar, also curved, and projecting considerably beyond the end of the longer of the two arms. Owing to the inequality of the arms, the cross-bar sloped at an angle to the base, and the strings, which passed from the one to the other, consequently differed in length. The number of the strings in this lyre seems to have been either five or seven. [PLATE CXXVIII., Figs. 2, 3.]

PLATE CXXVIII

The Assyrian guitar is remarkable for the small size of the hollow body or sounding-board, and the great proportionate length of the neck or handle. There is nothing to show what was the number of the strings, nor whether they were stretched by pegs and elevated by means of a bridge. Both hands seen to be employed in playing the instrument, which is held across the chest in a sloping direction, and was probably kept in place by a ribbon or strap passed round the neck. [PLATE CXXVIII., Fig. 1.]

It is curious that in the Assyrian remains, while the double pipe is common, we find no instance at all either of the flute or of the single pipe. All three were employed in Egypt, and occur on the monuments of that country frequently; and though among the Greeks and Romans the double pipe was more common than the single one, yet the single pipe was well known, and its employment was not unusual. The Greeks regarded the pipe as altogether Asiatic, and ascribed its invention to Marsyas the Phrygian, or to Olympus, his disciple. We may conclude from this that they at any rate learnt the invention from Asia; and in their decided preference of the double over the single pipe we may not improbably have a trace of the influence which Assyria exercised over Asiatic, and thus even over Greek, music. [PLATE CXXVIII., Fig. 1.]

The Assyrian double pipe was short, probably not exceeding ten or twelve inches in length. It is uncertain whether it was really a single instrument consisting of two tubes united by a common mouthpiece, or whether it was not composed of two quite separate pipes, as was the case with the double pipes of the Greeks and Romans.

The two pipes constituting a pair seem in Assyria to have been always of the same length, not, like the Roman "right" and "left pipes," of unequal length, and so of different pitches. They were held and played, like the classical one, with either hand of the performer. There can be little doubt that they were in reality quite straight, though sometimes they have been awkwardly represented as crooked by the artist.

The tambourine of the Assyrian was round, like that in common use at the present day; not square, like the ordinary Egyptian. It seems to have consisted simply of a skin stretched on a circular frame, and to have been destitute altogether of the metal rings or balls which produce the jingling sound of the modern instrument. It was held at bottom by the left hand in a perpendicular position, and was struck at the side with the fingers of the right. [PLATE CXXIX., Fig. 1.]

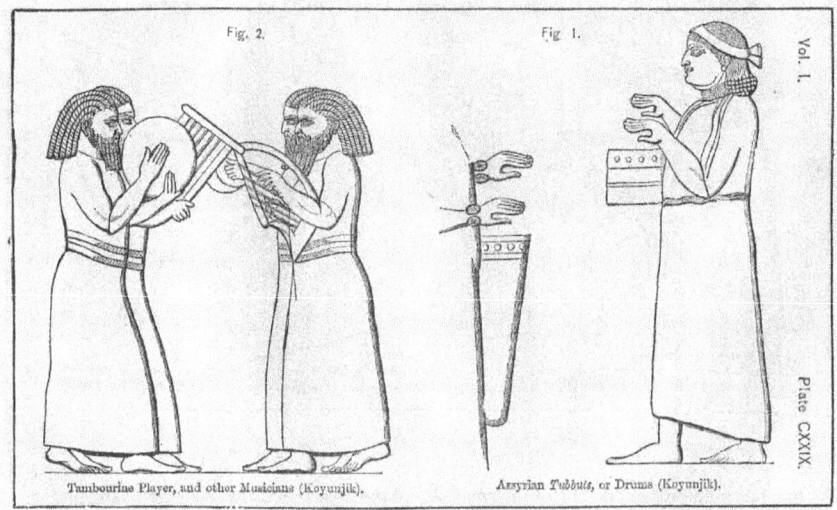

PLATE CXXIX

Assyrian cymbals closely resembled those in common use throughout the East at the present day. They consisted of two hemispheres of metal, probably of bronze, running off to a point, which was elongated into a bar or handle. The player grasped a cymbal in each hand, and either clashed theme together horizontally, or else, holding one cupwise in his left, brought the other down upon it perpendicularly with his right. [PLATE CXXX., Fig. 1.]

Two drums are represented on the Assyrian sculptures.

One is a small instrument resembling the tubbul, now frequently used by Eastern dancing girls. The other is of larger size, like the tubbul at top, but descending gradually in the shape of an inverted cone, and terminating almost in a point at bottom. Both were carried in front, against the stomach of the player—attached, apparently, to his girdle; and both were played in the same way, namely, with the fingers of the open hands on the top. [PLATE CXXX., Fig. 2.]

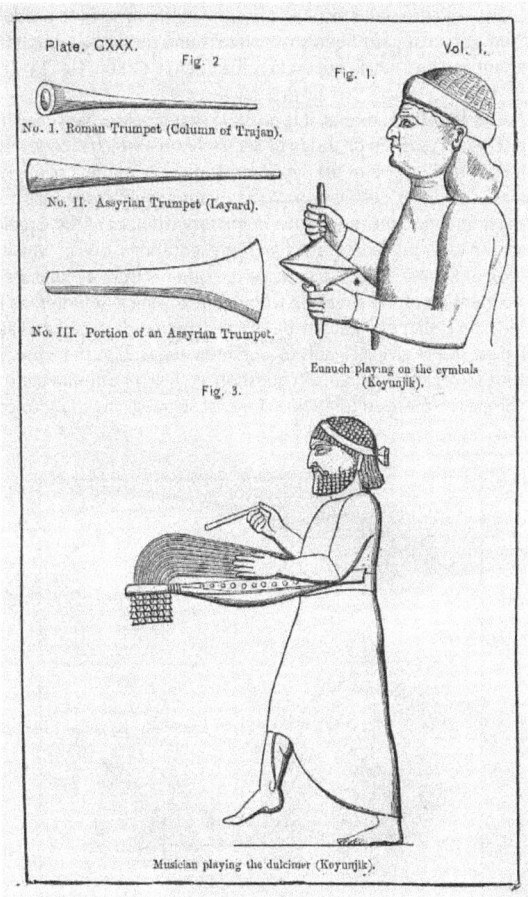

PLATE CXXX

A few instruments carried by musicians are of an anomalous appearance, and do not admit of identification with any known species. One, which is borne by a musician in a processional scene belonging to the time of Sennacherib, resembles in shape a bag turned upside-down. By the manner in which it is held, we may conjecture that it was a sort of rattle—a hollow square box of wood or metal, containing stones or other hard substances which produced a jingling noise when shaken. But the purpose of the semicircular bow which hangs from the box is difficult to explain, unless we suppose that it was merely a handle by which to carry the instrument when not in use. Rattles of different kinds are found among the musical instruments of Egypt; and one of them consists of a box with a long handle attached to it. The jingling noise produced by such instruments may have corresponded to the sound now emitted by the side-rings of the tambourine.

Another curious-looking instrument occurs in a processional scene of the time of Asshur-bani-pal, which has been compared to the modern santour, a sort of dulcimer. It consisted (apparently) of a number of strings, certainly not fewer than ten stretched over a hollow case or sounding-board. The musician seems to have struck the strings with a small bar or hammer held in his right hand, while at the same time he made some use of his left hand in pressing them so as to produce the right note. It is clear that this instrument must have been suspended round the neck, though the Assyrian artist has omitted to represent the belt which kept it in place. [PLATE CXXIX., Fig. 2.]

In addition to all these various instruments, it is possible that the Assyrians may have made use of a sort of horn. An object is represented on a slab of Sennacherib's which is certainly either a horn or a speaking-trumpet. It is carried by one of the supervisors of the works in a scene representing the conveyance of a colossal bull to its destination. In shape it no doubt resembles the modern speaking-trumpet, but it is almost equally near to the tuba or military trumpet of the Greeks and Romans. This will appear sufficiently on a comparison of the two representations, one of which is taken from Mr. Layard's representation of Sennacherib's slab, while the other is from a sculpture on the column of Trajan. As we have no mention of the speaking-trumpet in any ancient writer, as the shape of the object under consideration is that of a known ancient instrument of music, and as an ordinary horn would have been of great use in giving signals to workmen engaged as the laborers are upon the sculpture, it seems best to regard the object in question as such a horn—an instrument of great power, but of little compass—more suitable therefore for signal-giving than for concerts. [PLATE CXXX., Fig. 3.]

PLATE CXXXI

Passing now from the instruments of the Assyrians to the general features and character of their music, we may observe, in the first place, that while it is fair to suppose them acquainted with each form of the triple symphony, there is only evidence that they knew of two forms out of the three— viz, the harmony of instruments, and that of instruments and voices in combination. Of these two they seem greatly to have preferred the concert of instruments without voices; indeed, one instance alone shows that they were not wholly ignorant of the more complex harmony. Even this leaves it doubtful whether they themselves practised it: for the singers and musicians represented as uniting their efforts are not Assyrians, but Susianians, who come out to greet their conquerors, and do honor to the new sovereign who has been imposed on them, with singing, playing, and dancing.

Assyrian bands were variously composed. The simplest consisted of two harpers. A band of this limited number seems to have been an established part of the religious ceremonial on the return of the monarch from the chase, when a libation was poured over the dead game. The instrument in use on these occasions was the antique harp, which was played, not with the hand, but with the plectrum. A similar band appears on one occasion in a triumphal return from a military expedition belonging to the time of Sennacherib. [PLATE CXXI.]

In several instances we find bands of three musicians. In one case all three play the lyre. The musicians here are certainly captives, whom the Assyrians have borne off front their own country. It has been thought that their physiognomy is Jewish, and that the lyre which they bear in their hands may represent that "kind of harp" which the children of the later captivity hung up upon the willows when they wept by the rivers of Babylon. There are no sufficient grounds, however, for this identification. The lyre may be pronounced foreign, since it is unlike any other specimen; but its ornamentation with an animal head is sufficient to show that it is not Jewish. And the Jewish kinnor was rather a harp than a lyre, and had certainly more than four strings. Still, the employment of captives as musicians is interesting, though we cannot say that the captives are Jews. It shows us that the Assyrians, like the later Babylonians, were in the habit of "requiring" music from their prisoners, who, when transported into a "strange land," had to entertain their masters with their native melodies.

Another band of three exhibits to us a harper, a player on the lyre, and a player on the double pipe. A third shows a harper, a player on the lyre, and a musician whose instrument is uncertain. In this latter case it is quite possible that there may originally have been more musicians than three, for the sculpture is imperfect, terminating in the middle of a figure.

Bands of four performers are about as common as bands of three. On an obelisk belonging to the time of Asshur-izir-pal we see a band composed of two cymbal-players and two performers on the lyre. A slab of Sennacherib's exhibits four harpers arranged in two pairs, all playing with the plectrum on the antique harp. Another of the same date, which is incomplete, shows us a tambourine-player, a cymbal-player, a player on the nondescript instrument which has been called a sort of rattle, and another whose instrument cannot be distinguished. In a sculpture of a later period, which is represented above, we see a band of four, composed of a tambourine-player, two players on two different sorts of lyres, and a cymbal-player.

It is not often that we find representations of bands containing more than four performers. On the sculptures hitherto discovered there seem to be only three instances where this number was exceeded. A bas-relief of Sennacherib's showed five players, of whom two had tambourines; two, harps of the antique pattern; and one, cymbals. Another, belonging to the time of his grandson, exhibited a band of seven, three of whom played upon harps of the later fashion, two on the double pipe, one on the guitar, and one on the long drum with the conical bottom. Finally, we have the remarkable scene represented in the illustration, a work of the sane date, where no fewer than twenty-six performers are seen uniting their efforts. Of these, eleven are players on instruments, while the remaining fifteen are vocalists. The instruments consist of seven harps, two double pipes, a small drum or tubbel, and the curious instrument which has been compared to the modern santour. The players are all men, six out of the eleven being eunuchs. The singers consist of six women and nine children of various ages, the latter of whom seem to accompany their singing, as the Hebrews and Egyptians sometimes did, with clapping of the hands. Three out of the first four musicians are represented with one leg raised, as if dancing to the measure. [PLATE CXXXII., Fig. I.]

Band of musicians.

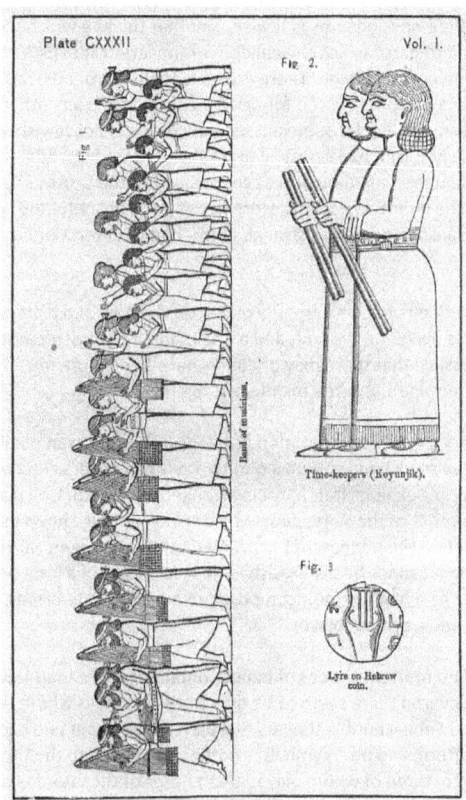

PLATE CXXXII

Bands in Assyria had sometimes, though not always, time-keepers or leaders, who took the direction of the performance. These were commonly eunuchs, as indeed were the greater number of the musicians. They held in one hand a double rod or wand, with which most probably they made their signals, and stood side by side facing the performers. [PLATE CXXXII., Fig. 2.]

The Assyrians seem to have employed music chiefly for festive and religious purposes. The favorite instrument in the religious ceremonies was the antique harp, which continued in use as a sacred instrument from the earliest to the latest times. On festive occasions the lyre was preferred, or a mixed band with a variety of instruments. In the quiet of domestic life the monarch and his sultana were entertained with concerted music played by a large number of performers: while in processions and pageants, whether of a civil or of a military character, bands were also very generally employed, consisting of two, three, four, five, or possibly more, musicians. Cymbals, the tambourine, and the instrument which has been above regarded as a sort of rattle, were peculiar to these processional occasions: the harp, the lyre, and the double pipe had likewise a place in them.

In actual war, it would appear that music was employed very sparingly, if at all, by the Assyrians. No musicians are ever represented in the battle-scenes: nor are the troops accompanied by any when upon the march. Musicians are only seen conjoined with troops in one or two marching processions, apparently of a triumphal character. It may consequently be doubted whether the Assyrian armies, when they went out on their expeditions, were attended, like the Egyptian and Roman armies, by military bands. Possibly, the musicians in the processional scenes alluded to belong to the court rather than to the camp, and merely take part as civilians in a pageant, wherein a share is also assigned to the soldiery.

In proceeding, as already proposed, to speak of the navigation of the Assyrians, it must be at once premised that it is not as mariners, but only as fresh-water sailors, that they come within the category of navigators at all. Originally an inland people, they had no power, in the earlier ages of their history, to engage in any but the secondary and inferior kind of navigation; and it would seem that, by the time when they succeeded in opening to themselves through their conquests a way to the Mediterranean and the Indian Ocean, their habits had become so fixed in this respect that they no longer admitted of change. There is satisfactory evidence which shows that they left the navigation of the two seas at the two extremities of their empire to the subject nations—the Phoenicians and the Babylonians contenting themselves with the profits without sharing the dangers of marine voyages, while their own attention was concentrated upon their two great rivers—the Tigris and the Euphrates, which formed the natural line of communication between the seas in question.

The navigation of these streams was important to the Assyrians in two ways. In the first place it was a military necessity that they should be able, readily and without delay, to effect the passage of both of them, and also of their tributaries, which were frequently too deep to be forded. Now from very early times it was probably found tolerably easy to pass an army over a great river by swimming, more especially with the aid of inflated skins, which would be soon employed for the purpose. But the materiel of the army—the provisions, the chariots, and the siege machines—was not so readily transported, and indeed could only be conveyed across deep rivers by means of bridges, rafts, or boats. On the great streams of the Tigris and Euphrates, with their enormous spring floods, no bridge, in the ordinary sense of the word, is possible. Bridges of boats are still the only ones that exist on either river below the point at which they issue from the gorges of the mountains. And these would be comparatively late inventions, long subsequent to the employment of single ferry boats. Probably the earliest contrivance for transporting the chariots, the stores, and the engines across a river was a raft, composed hastily of the trees and bushes growing in the neighborhood of the stream, and rendered capable of sustaining a considerable weight by the attachment to it of a number of inflated skins. A representation of such a raft, taken from a slab of Sennacherib, has been already given. Rafts of this kind are still largely employed in the navigation of the Mesopotamian streams, and, being extremely simple in their construction, may reasonably be supposed to have been employed by the Assyrians from the very foundation of their empire.

To these rafts would naturally have succeeded boats of one kind or another. As early as the time of Tiglath-Pileser I. (ab. B.C. 1120) we find a mention of boats as employed in the passage of the Euphrates. These would probably be of the kind described by Herodotus, and represented on one of the most ancient bas-reliefs—round structures like the Welsh coracles, made of wickerwork and covered with skins, smeared over with a coating of bitumen. Boats of this construction were made of a considerable size. The one represented contains a chariot, and is navigated by two men. [PLATE CXXXIII., Fig. 1.] In the later sculptures the number of navigators is raised to four, and the boats carry a heavy load of stone or other material. The mode of propulsion is curious and very unusual. The rowers sit at the stem and stern, facing each other, and while those at the stem pull, those at the stern must have pushed, as Herodotus tells us that they did. The make of the oars is also singular. In the earliest sculptures they are short poles, terminating in a head, shaped like a small axe or hammer; in the later, below this axe-like appendage, they have a sort of curved blade, which is, however, not solid, but perforated, so as to form a mere framework, which seems to require filling up. [PLATE CXXXIII., Fig. 3.]

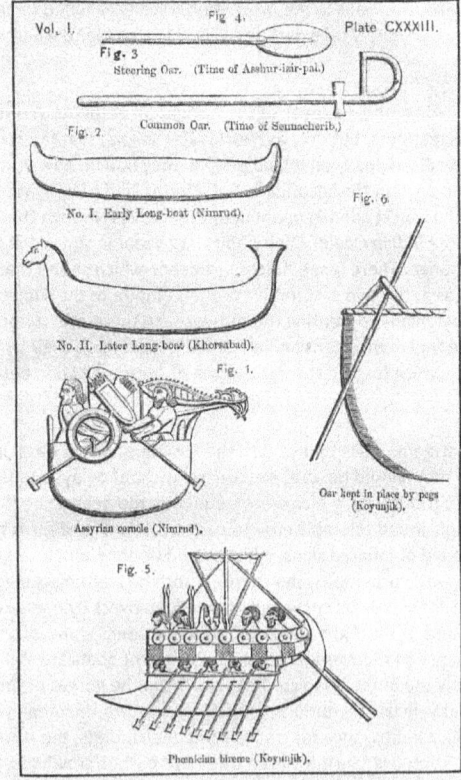

PLATE CXXXIII

Beside these round boats, which correspond closely with the kufas in use upon the Tigris and Euphrates at the present day, the Assyrians employed for the passage of rivers, even in very early times, a vessel of a more scientific construction. The early bas-reliefs exhibit to us, together with the kufas, a second and much larger vessel, manned with a crew of seven men—a helmsman and six rowers, three upon either side and capable of conveying across a broad stream two chariots at a time, or a chariot and two or three passengers. This vessel appears to have been made of planks. It was long, and comparatively narrow. It had a flattish bottom, and was rounded off towards the stem and stern, much as boats are rounded off towards the bows at the present day. It did not possess either mast or sail, but was propelled wholly by oars, which were of the same shape as those used anciently by the rowers in the round boats. In the steersman's hand is seen an oar of a different kind. It is much longer than the rowing oars, and terminates in an oval blade, which would have given it considerable power in the water. [PLATE CXXXIII., Fig. 4.] The helmsman steered with both hands; and it seems that his oar was lashed to an upright post near the stern of the vessel.

It is evident that before armies could look habitually to being transported across the Mesopotamian streams, wherever they might happen to strike them in their expeditions, by boats of these two kinds, either ferries must have been established at convenient intervals upon them, or traffic along their courses by means of boats must have been pretty regular. An Assyrian army did not carry its boats with it, as a modern army does its pontoons. Boats were commonly found in sufficient numbers on the streams themselves when an army needed them, and were impressed, or hired, to convey the troops across. And thus we see that the actual navigation of the streams had another object besides the military one of transport from bank to bank. Rivers are Nature's roads; and we may be sure that the country had not been long settled before a water communication began to be established between towns upon the river-courses, and commodities began to be transported by means of them. The very position of the chief towns upon time banks of the streams was probably connected with this sort of transport, the rivers furnishing the means by which large quantities of building material could be conveniently concentrated at a given spot, and by which supplies could afterwards be regularly received from a distance. We see in the Assyrian sculptures the conveyance of stones, planks, etc. along the rivers, as well as the passage of chariots, horses, and persons across them. Rafts and round boats were most commonly used for this purpose. When a mass of unusual size, as a huge paving-stone, or a colossal bull or lion, had to be moved, a long, flat-bottomed boat was employed, which the mass sometimes more than covered. In this case, as there was no room for rower's, trackers were engaged, who dragged the vessel along by means of ropes, which were fastened either to the boat itself or to its burden. [PLATE CXXXIII., Fig. 2.]

During the later period of the monarchy various improvements took place in Assyrian boat-building. The Phoenician and Cyprian expeditions of the later kings made the Assyrians well acquainted with the ships of first-rate nautical nations; and they seem to have immediately profited by this acquaintance, in order to improve the appearance and the quality of their own river boats. The clumsy and inelegant long-boat of the earlier times, as replaced, even for ordinary traffic, by a light and graceful fabric, which was evidently a copy from Phoenician models. Modifications, which would seem trifling if described, changed the whole character of the vessels, in which light and graceful curves took the place of straight lines and angles only just rounded off. The stem and stern were raised high above the body of the boat, and were shaped like fishes' tails or carved into the heads of animals. [PLATE CXXXIII., Fig. 2.] Oars, shaped nearly like modern ones, came into vogue, and the rowers were placed so as all to look one way, and to pull instead of pushing with their oars. Finally, the principle of the bireme was adopted, and river-galleys were constructed of such a size that they had to be manned by thirty rowers, who sat in two tiers one above the other at the sides of the galley, while the centre part, which seems to have been decked, was occupied by eight or ten other persons.

In galleys of this kind the naval architecture of the Assyrians seems to have culminated. They never, so far as appears, adopted for their boats the inventions with which their intercourse with Phoenicia had rendered them perfectly familiar, of masts, and sails. This is probably to be explained from the extreme rapidity of the Mesopotamian rivers, on which sailing boats are still uncommon. The unfailing strength of rowers was needed in order to meet and stem the force of the currents; and this strength being provided in abundance, it was not thought necessary to husband it or eke it out by the addition of a second motive power. Again, the boats, being intended only for peaceful purposes, were unprovided with beaks, another invention well known to the Assyrians, and frequently introduced into their sculptures in the representations of Phoenician vessels. [PLATE CXXXIII., Fig. 5.]

In the Assyrian biremes the oars of the lower tier were worked through holes in the vessel's sides. This arrangement would of course at once supply a fulcrum and keep the oars in their places. But it is not so easy to see how the oar of a common row-boat, or the uppermost tier of a bireme, obtained their purchase on the vessel, and were prevented from slipping along its side. Assyrian vessels had no rowlocks, and in general the oars are represented as simply rested without any support on the upper edge of the bulwark. But this can scarcely have been the real practice; and one or two representations, where a support is provided, may be fairly regarded as showing what the practice actually was. In the figure of a kufa, or round boat, already given, it will be seen that one oar is worked by means of a thong, like those of the Greeks, which is attached to a ring in the bulwark. In another bas-relief, several of the oars of similar boats are represented as kept in place by means of two pegs fixed into the top of the bulwark and inclined at an angle to one another. [PLATE CXXXIII., Fig. 6.] Probably one or other of these two methods of steadying the oar was in reality adopted in every instance.

With regard to Assyrian commerce, it must at the outset be remarked that direct notices in ancient writers of any real authority are scanty in the extreme. The prophet Nahum says indeed, in a broad and general way, of Nineveh, "Thou hast multiplied thy merchants above the stars of heaven;" and Ezekiel tells us, more particularly, that Assyrian merchants, along with others, traded with Tyre "in blue clothes, and broidered work, and in chests of rich apparel." But, except these two, there seem to be no notices of Assyrian trade in any contemporary or quasi-contemporary author. Herodotus, writing nearly two hundred years after the empire had come to an end, mentions casually that "Assyrian wares" had in very ancient times been conveyed by the Phoenicians to Greece, and there sold to the inhabitants. He speaks also of a river traffic in his own day between Armenia and Babylon along the course of the Euphrates, a fact which indirectly throws light upon the habits of earlier ages. Diodorus, following Ctesias, declares that a number of cities were established from very ancient times on the banks of both the Tigris and the Euphrates, to serve as marts of trade to the merchants who imported into Assyria the commodities of Media and Paraetacene. Among the most important of these marts, as we learn from Strabo, were Tiphsach or Thapsacus on the Euphrates, and Opis upon the Tigris.

It is from notices thus scanty, partial, and incidental, eked out by probability, and further helped by a certain number of important facts with respect to the commodities actually used in the country, whereof evidence has been furnished to us by the recent discoveries, that we have to form our estimate of the ancient commerce of the Assyrians. The Inscriptions throw little or no light upon the subject. They record the march of armies against foreign enemies, and their triumphant return laden with plunder and tribute, sometimes showing incidentally what products of a country were most in request among the Assyrians; but they contain no accounts of the journeys of merchants, or of the commodities which entered or quitted the country in the common course of trade.

The favorable situation of Assyria for trade has often attracted remark. Lying on the middle courses of two great navigable streams, it was readily approached by water both from the north-west and from the south-east. The communication between the Mediterranean and the Southern or Indian Ocean naturally—almost necessarily—followed this route. If Europe wanted the wares and products of India, or if India required the commodities of Europe, by far the shortest and easiest course was the line from the eastern Mediterranean across Northern Syria, and thence by one or other of the two great streams to the innermost recess of the Persian Gulf. The route by the Nile, the canal of Neco, and the Red Sea, was decidedly inferior, more especially on account of the dangerous navigation of that sea, but also because it was circuitous, and involved a voyage in the open ocean of at least twice the length of the other.

Again, Assyria lay almost necessarily on the line of land communication between the north-east and the south-west. The lofty Armenian mountain-chains—Niphates and the other parallel ranges—towards the north, and the great Arabian Desert towards the south, offered difficulties to companies of land-traders which they were unwilling to face, and naturally led them to select routes intermediate between these two obstacles, which could not fail to pass through some part or other of the Mesopotamian region.

The established lines of land trade between Assyria and her neighbors were probably very numerous, but the most important must have been some five or six. One almost certainly led from the Urumiyeh basin over the Keli-shin pass (lat. 37°, long. (45° nearly)), descending on Rowandiz, and thence following the course of the Greater Zab to Herir, whence it crossed the plain to Nineveh. At the summit of the Kell-shin pass is a pillar of dark blue stone, six feet in height, two in breadth, and one in depth, let into a basement block of the same material, and covered with a cuneiform inscription in the Scythic character. At a short distance to the westward on the same route is another similar pillar. The date of the inscriptions falls within the most flourishing time of the Assyrian empire, and their erection is a strong argument in favor of the use of this route (which is one of the very few possible modes of crossing the Zagros range) in the time when that empire was in full vigor.

Another line of land traffic probably passed over the same mountain-range considerably further to the south. It united Assyria with Media, leading from the Northern Ecbatana (Takht-i-Suleiman) by the Banneh pass to Suleimaniyeh, and thence by Kerkuk and Altura-Kiupri to Arbela and Nineveh.

There may have been also a route up the valley of the Lesser Zab, by Koi-Sinjah and over the great Kandil range into Lajihan. There are said to be Assyrian remains near Koi-Sinjah, at a place called the Bihisht and Jehennen ("the Heaven and Hell") of Nimrud, but no account has been given of them by any European traveller.

Westward there were probably two chief lines of trade with Syria and the adjacent countries. One passed along the foot of the Sinjar range by Sidikan (Arban) on the Khabour to Tiphsach (or Thapsacus) on the Euphrates, where it crossed the Great River. Thence it bent southwards, and, passing through Tadmor, was directed upon Phoenicia most likely by way of Damascus. Another took a more northern line by the Mons Masius to Harran and Seruj, crossing the Euphrates at Bir, and thence communicating both with Upper Syria and with Asia Minor. The former of these two routes is marked as a line of traffic by the foreign objects discovered in such abundance at Arban, by the name Tiphsach, which means "passage," and by the admitted object of Solomon in building Tadmor. The other rests on less direct evidence; but there are indications of it in the trade of Harran with Tyre which is mentioned by Ezekiel, and in the Assyrian remains near Seruj, which is on the route from Harran to the Bir fordway.

Towards the north, probably, the route most used was that which is thought by many to be the line followed by Xenophon, first up the valley of the Tigris to Til or Tilleh, and then along the Bitlis Chai to the lake of Van and the adjacent country. Another route may have led from Nineveh to Nisibis, thence through the Jebel Tur to Diarbekr, and from Diarbekr up the Western Tigris to Arghana, Kharput, Malatiyeh, and Asia Minor. Assyrian remains have been found at various points along this latter line, while the former is almost certain to have connected the Assyrian with the Armenian capital.

Armenian productions would, however, reach Nineveh and the other great central cities mainly by the Tigris, down which they could easily have been floated from Tilleh. or even from Diarbekr. Similarly, Babylonian and Susianian productions, together with the commodities which either or both of those countries imported by sea, would find their way into Assyria up the courses of the two streams, which were navigated by vessels capable of stemming the force of the current, at least as high as Opis and Thapsacus.

We may now proceed to inquire what were the commodities which Assyria, either certainly or probably, imported by these various lines of land and water communication. Those of which we seem to have some indication in the existing remains are gold, tin, ivory, lead, stones of various kinds, cedar-wood, pearls, and engraved seals.

Many articles in gold have been recovered at the various Assyrian sites where excavations have been made; and indications have been found of the employment of this precious metal in the ornamentation of palaces and of furniture. The actual quantity discovered has, indeed, been small; but this may be accounted for without calling in question the reality of that extraordinary wealth in the precious metals which is ascribed by all antiquity to Assyria. This wealth no doubt flowed in, to a considerable extent, from the plunder of conquered nations and the tribute paid by dependent monarchs. But the quantity obtained in this way would hardly have sufficed to maintain the luxury of the court and at the same time to accumulate, so that when Nineveh was taken there was "none end" of the store. It has been suggested that "mines of gold were probably once worked within the Assyrian dominions," although no gold is now known to be produced anywhere within her limits. But perhaps it is more probable that, like Judaea and Phoenicia, she obtained her gold in a great measure from commerce, taking it either from the Phoenicians, who derived it both from Arabia and from the West African coast, or else from the Babylonians, who may have imported it by sea from India.

Tin, which has not been found in a pure state in the remains of the Assyrians, but which enters regularly as an element into their bronze, where it forms from one-tenth to one-seventh of the mass, was also, probably, an importation. Tin is a comparatively rare metal. Abundant enough in certain places, it is not diffused at all widely over the earth's surface. Neither Assyria itself nor any of the neighboring countries are known to have ever produced this mineral. Phoenicia certainly imported it, directly or indirectly, from Cornwall and the Scilly Isles, which therefore became first known in ancient geography as the Cassiterides or "Tin Islands." It is a reasonable supposition that the tin wherewith the Assyrians hardened their bronze was obtained by their merchants from the Phoenicians in exchange for textile fabrics and (it may be) other commodities. If so, we may believe that in many instances the produce of our own tin mines which left our shores more than twenty-five centuries ago, has, after twice travelling a distance of many thousand miles, returned to seek a final rest in its native country.

Ivory was used by the Assyrians extensively in their furniture, and was probably supplied by them to the Phoenicians and the Greeks. It was no doubt sometimes brought to them by subject nations as tribute; but this source of supply is not sufficient to account, at once, for the consumption in Assyria itself, and for the exports from Assyria to foreign countries. A regular trade for ivory seems to have been carried on from very early times between India and Dedan (Bahrein,?) in the Persian Gulf. The travelling companies of the Dedanim, who conveyed this precious merchandise from their own country to Phoenicia, passed probably along the course of the Euphrates, and left a portion of their wares in the marts upon that stream, which may have been thence conveyed to the great Assyrian cities. Or the same people may have traded directly with Assyria by the route of the Tigris. Again, it is quite conceivable—indeed, it is probable—that there was a land traffic between Assyria and Western India by the way of Cabal, Herat, the Caspian Gates, and Media. Of this route we have a trace in the land animals engraved upon the well-known Black Obelisk, where the combination of the small-eared or Indian elephant and the rhinoceros with the two-humped Bactrian camel, sufficiently marks the line by which the productions of India, occasionally at, any rate, reached Assyria. The animals themselves were, we may be sure, very rarely transported. Indeed, it is not till the very close of the Persian empire that we find elephants possessed—and even then in scanty numbers—by the western Asiatic monarchs. But the more portable products of the Indus region, elephants' tusks, gold, and perhaps shawls and muslins, are likely to have passed to the west by this route with far greater frequency.

The Assyrians were connoisseurs in hard stones and gems, which they seem to have imported from all quarters. The lapis lazuli, which is found frequently among the remains as the material of seals, combs, rings, jars, and other small objects, probably came from Bactria or the adjacent regions, whence alone it is procurable at the present day. The cornelian used for cylinders may have come from Babylonia, which, according to Pliny furnished it of the best quality in the more ancient times. The agates or onyxes may have been imported from Susiana, where they were found in the bed of the Choaspes (Kerkhah), or they may possibly have been brought from India. Other varieties are likely to have been furnished by Armenia, which is rich in stones; and hence too was probably obtained the shamir, or emery-stone, by means of which the Assyrians were enabled to engrave all the other hard substances known to them.

That cedar-wood was imported into Assyria is sufficiently indicated by the fact that, although no cedars grew in the country, the beams in the palaces were frequently of this material. It may not, however, have been exactly an article of commerce, since the kings appear to have cut it after their successful expeditions into Syria, and to have carried it off from Lebanon and Amanus as part of the plunder of the country.

Pearls, which have been found in Assyrian ear rings, must have been procured from the Persian Gulf, one of the few places frequented by the shell-fish which produces then. The pearl fisheries in these parts were pointed out to Nearchus, the admiral of Alexander, and had no doubt been made to yield their treasures to the natives of the coasts and islands from a remote antiquity. The familiarity of the author of the book of Job with pearls is to be ascribed to the ancient trade in them throughout the regions adjoining the Gulf, which could not fail to bring them at an early date to the knowledge of the Hebrews.

Engraved stones, generally in the shape of scarabs, seem to have been largely imported from Egypt into Assyria, where they were probably used either as amulets or as seals. They have been found in the greatest plenty at Arban on the lower Khabour, the ancient Sidikan or Shadikanni, which lies nearly at the extreme west of the Assyrian territory; but many specimens have likewise been obtained from Nineveh and other of the central Assyrian cities.

If we were to indulge in conjecture, we might add to this list of Assyrian importations at least an equal number of commodities which, though they have not been found in the ancient remains, may be fairly regarded, on grounds of probability, as objects of trade between Assyria and her neighbors.

Frankincense, which was burnt in such lavish profusion in the great temple at Babylon, was probably offered in considerable quantities upon Assyrian altars, and could only have been obtained from Arabia. Cinnamon, which was used by the Jews from the time of the Exodus, and which was early imported into Greece by the Phoenicians, who received it from the Arabians can scarcely have been unknown in Assyria when the Hebrews were familiar with it. This precious spice must have reached the Arabians from Ceylon or Malabar, the most accessible of the countries producing it. Mullins, shawls, and other tissues are likely to have come by the same route as the cinnamon; and these may possibly have been among the "blue clothes and broidered work and rich apparel" which the merchants of Asshur carried to Tyre in "chests, bound with cords and made of cedar-wood." Dyes, such as the Indian lacca, raw cotton, ebony and other woods, may have come by the same line of trade; while horses and mules are likely to have been imported from Armenia, and slaves from the country between Armenia and the Halys River.

If from the imports of Assyria we pass to her exports, we leave a region of uncertain light to enter upon one of almost total darkness. That the "wares of Assyria" were among the commodities which the Phoenicians imported into Greece at a very early period, we have the testimony of Herodotus; but he leaves us wholly without information as to the nature of the wares themselves. No other classical writer of real authority touches the subject; and any conclusions that we may form upon it must be derived from one of two sources, either general probability, or the single passage in a sacred author which gives us a certain amount of authentic information. From the passage in question, which has been already quoted at length, we learn that the chief of the Assyrian exports to Phoenicia were textile fabrics, apparently of great value, since they were most carefully packed in chests of cedar-wood secured by cords. These fabrics may have been "blue cloaks," or "embroidery," or "rich dresses" of any kind, for all these are mentioned by Ezekiel; but we cannot say definitely which Assyria traded in, since the merchants of various other countries are joined in the passage with hers. Judging by the monuments, we should conclude that at least a portion of the embroidered work was from her looms and workshops; for, as has been already shown, the embroidery of the Assyrians was of the most delicate and elaborate description. She is also likely to have traded in rich apparel of all kinds, both such as she manufactured at home, and such as she imported from the far East by the lines of traffic which have been pointed out. Some of her own fabrics may possibly have been of silk, which in Roman times was a principal Assyrian export. Whether she exported her other peculiar productions, her transparent and colored glass, her exquisite metal bowls, plates, and dishes, her beautifully carved ivories, we cannot say. They have not hitherto been found in any place beyond her dominion, so that it would rather seem that she produced them only for home consumption. Some ancient notices appear to imply a belief on the part of the Greeks and Romans that she produced and exported various spices. Horace speaks of Assyrian nard Virgil of Assyrian amomuum, Tibullus of Assyrian odors generally. AEschylus has an allusion of the same kind in his Agamemnon. Euripide, and Theocritus, who mention respectively Syrian myrrh and Syrian frankincense, probably use the word "Syrian" for "Assyrian." The belief thus implied is not, however, borne out by inquiry. Neither the spikenard nor the amonmum, nor the myrrh tree, nor the frankincense tree, nor any other actual spice, is produced within the limits of Assyria, which must always have imported its own spices from abroad, and can only have supplied them to other countries as a carrier. In this capacity she may very probably, even in the time of her early greatness, have conveyed on to the coast of Syria the spicy products of Arabia and India, and thus have created an impression, which afterwards remained as a tradition, that she was a great spice-producer as well as a spice-seller.

In the same way, as a carrier, Assyria may have exported many other commodities. She may have traded with the Phoenicians, not only in her own products, but in the goods which she received from the south and east, from Bactria, India, and the Persian Gulf,—such as lapis lazuli, pearls, cinnamon, muslins, shawls, ivory, ebony, cotton. On the other hand, she may have conveyed to India, or at least to Babylon, the productions which the Phoenicians brought to Tyre and Sidon from the various countries bordering upon the Mediterranean Sea and even the Atlantic Ocean, as tin, hides, pottery, oil, wine, linen. On this point, however, we have at present no evidence at all; and as it is not the proper office of a historian to indulge at any length in mere conjecture, the consideration of the commercial dealings of the Assyrians may be here brought to a close.

On the agriculture of the Assyrians a very few remarks will be offered. It has been already explained that the extent of cultivation depended entirely on the conveyance of water. There is good reason to believe that the Assyrians found a way to spread water over almost the whole of their territory. Either by the system of kanats or subterranean aqueducts, which has prevailed in the East from very early times, or by an elaborate network of canals, the fertilizing fluid was conveyed to nearly every part of Mesopotamia, which shows by its innumerable mounds, in regions which are now deserts, how large a population it was made to sustain under the wise management of the great Assyrians monarchs. Huge dams seem to have been thrown across the Tigris in various places, one of which (the Afrui) still remains, seriously impeding the navigation. It is formed of large masses of squared stones, united together by cramps of iron. Such artificial barriers were intended, not (as Strabo believed) for the protection of the towns upon the river from a hostile fleet, but to raise the level of the stream, in order that its water might flow off into canals on one bank or the other, whence they could be spread by means of minor channels over large tracts of territory. The canals themselves have in most cases been gradually filled up. In one instance, however, owing either to the peculiar nature of the soil or to some unexplained cause, we are still able to trace the course of an Assyrian work of this class and to observe the manner and principles of its construction.

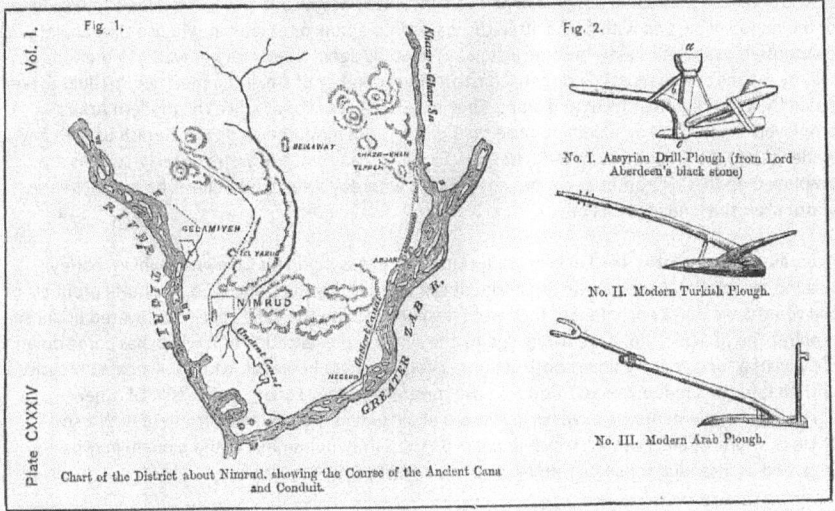

PLATE CXXXIV

In the tract of land lying between the lower course of the Great Zab River and the Tigris, in which was situated the important town of Calah (now Nimrud), a tract which is partly alluvial, but more generally of secondary formation, hard gravel, sandstone, or conglomerate, are the remains of a canal undoubtedly Assyrian, which was carried for a distance of more than five-and-twenty miles from a point on the Khazr or Ghazr Su, a tributary of the Zab, to the south-eastern corner of the Nimrud ruins. [PLATE CXXXIV., Fig. 1.] Originally the canal seems to have been derived from the Zab itself, the water of which was drawn off, on its northern bank, through a short tunnel—the modern Negoub—and then conducted along a cutting, first by the side of the Zab, and afterwards in a tortuous course across the undulating plain, into the ravine formed by the Shor-Derreh torrent. The Zab, when this part of the work was constructed, ran deep along its northern bank, and, sending a portion of its waters into the tunnel, maintained a constant stream in the canal. But after awhile the river abandoned its north bank for the opposite shore; and, water ceasing to flow through the Negoub tunnel, it became necessary to obtain it in some other way. Accordingly the canal was extended northwards, partly by cutting and partly by tunnelling to the Ghazr Su at about two miles above its mouth, and a permanent supply was thenceforth obtained from that stream. The work may have been intended in part to supply Calah with mountain water; but the remains of dams and sluices along its course sufficiently show that it was a canal for irrigation also. From it water was probably derived to fertilize the whole triangle lying south of Nimrud between the two streams, a tract containing nearly thirty square miles of territory, mostly very fertile, and with careful cultivation well capable of supporting the almost metropolitan city on which it abutted.

In Assyria it must have been seldom that the Babylonian system of irrigation could have been found applicable, and the water simply derived from the rivers by side-cuts, leading it off from the natural channel. There is but little of Assyria which is flat and alluvial; the land generally undulates, and most of it stands at a considerable height above the various streams. The water therefore requires to be raised from the level of the rivers to that of the lands before it can be spread over them, and for this purpose hydraulic machinery of one kind or another is requisite. In cases where the subterranean conduit was employed, the Assyrians probably (like the ancient and the modern Persians) sank wells at intervals, and raised the water from them by means of a bucket and rope, the latter working over a pulley. Where they could obtain a bank of a convenient height overhanging a river, they made use of the hand-swipe, and with its aid lifted the water into a tank or reservoir, whence they could distribute it over their fields. In some instances, it would seem, they brought water to the tops of hills by means of aqueducts, and then, constructing a number of small channels, let the fluid trickle down them among their trees and crops. They may have occasionally, like the modern Arabs, employed the labor of an animal to raise the fluid; but the monuments do not furnish us with any evidence of their use of this method. Neither do we find any trace of water-wheels, such as are employed upon the Orontes and other swift rivers, whereby a stream can itself be made to raise water from the land along its bunks.

According to Herodotus, the kinds of grain cultivated in Assyria in his time were wheat, barley, sesame, and millet. As these still constitute at the present day the principal agricultural products of the county, we may conclude that they were in all probability the chief species cultivated under the Empire. The plough used, if we may judge by the single representation of it which has come down to us, was of a rude and primitive construction—a construction, however, which will bear comparison with that of the implements to this day in use through modern Turkey and Persia. Of other agricultural implements we have no specimens at all, unless the square instrument with a small circle or wheel at each corner, which appears on the same monument as the plough, may be regarded as intended for some farming purpose. [PLATE CXXXIV., Fig. 2.]

Besides grain, it seems certain that the Assyrians cultivated the vine. The vine will grow well in many parts of Assyria; and the monuments represent vines, with a great deal of truth, not merely as growing in the countries to which the Assyrians made their expeditions, but as cultivated along the sides of the rivers near Nineveh, and in the gardens belonging to the palaces of the kings. In the former case they appear to grow without any support, and are seen in orchards intermixed with other fruit-trees, as pomegranates and figs. In the latter they are trained upon tall trees resembling firs, round whose stems they twine themselves, and from which their rich clusters droop. Sometimes the long lithe boughs pass across from tree to tree, forming a canopy under which the monarch and his consort sip their wine.

Before concluding this chapter, a few remarks will be added upon the ordinary private life of the Assyrians, so far as the monuments reveal it to us. Under this head will be included their dress, their food, their houses, furniture, utensils, carriages, etc., their various kinds of labor, and the implements of labor which were known to them.

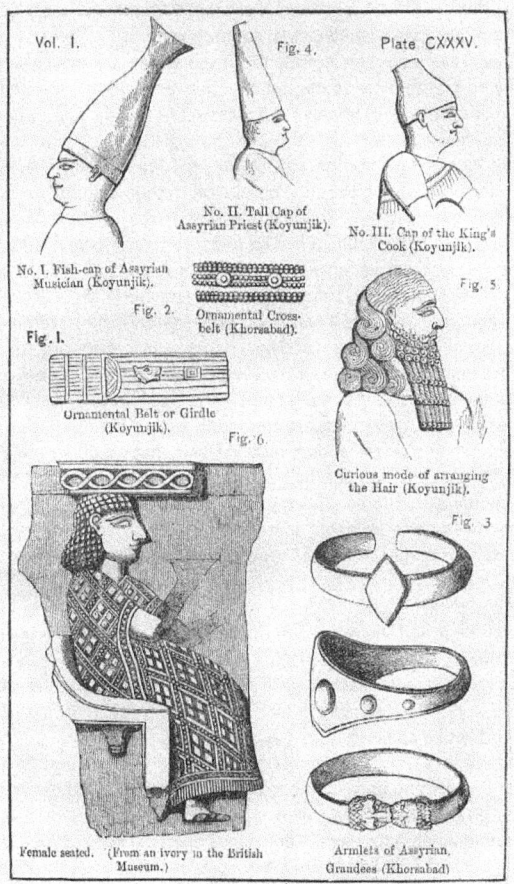

PLATE CXXXV

The ordinary dress of the common people in Assyria was a mere plain tunic, or skirt, reaching from the neck to a little above the knee, with very short sleeves, and confined round the waist by a broad belt or girdle. Nothing was worn either upon the head or upon the feet. The thick hair, carried in large waves from the forehead to the back of the head, and then carefully arranged in three, four, or five rows of stiff curls, was regarded as a sufficient protection both from sun and rain. No head-covering was ever worn, except by soldiers, and by certain officials, as the king, priests, and musicians. Sometimes, if the hair was very luxuriant, it was confined by a band or fillet, which was generally tied behind the back of the head. The beard was worn long, and arranged with great care, the elaboration being pretty nearly the same in the case of the king and of the common laborer. Laborers of a rank a little above the lowest wore sandals, indulged in a fringed tunic, and occasionally in a phillibeg, while a still higher class had a fringed tunic and phillibeg, together with the close-fitting trouser and boot worn by soldiers. These last are frequently eunuchs, who probably belonged to a corps of eunuch laborers in the employ of the king.

Persons of the humbler laboring class wear no ornament, neither armlet, bracelet, nor earrings. Armlets and bracelets mark high rank, and indeed are rarely found unless the wearer is either an officer of the court, or at any rate a personage of some consideration. Earrings seem to have descended lower. They are worn by the attendants on sportsmen, by musicians, by cavalry soldiers, and even occasionally by foot soldiers. In this last case they are seldom more than a simple ring, which may have been of bronze or of bone. In other cases the ring mostly supports a long pendant.

Men of rank appear to have worn commonly a long fringed robe reaching nearly to the feet. The sleeves were short, only just covering the shoulder. Down to the waist, the dress closely fitted the form, resembling, so far, a modern jersey; below this there was a slight expansion, but still the scantiness of the robe is very remarkable. It had no folds, and must have greatly interfered with the free play of the limbs, rendering rapid movements almost impossible. A belt or girdle confined it at the waist, which was always patterned, sometimes elaborately. [PLATE CXXXV., Fig. 1.] If a sword was carried, as was frequently the case, it was suspended, nearly in a horizontal position, by a belt over the left shoulder, to which it was attached by a ring, or rings, in the sheath. There is often great elegance in these cross-belts, which look as if they were embroidered with pearls or beads. [PLATE CXXXV., Fig. 2.] Fillets, earrings, armlets, and (in most instances) bracelets were also worn by Assyrians of the upper classes. The armlets are commonly simple bands, twisted round the arm once or twice, and often overlapping' at the ends, which are plain, not ornamented. [PLATE CXXXV., Fig.] The bracelets are of slighter construction; their ends do not meet; they would seem to have been of thin metal, and sufficiently elastic to be slipped over the hand on to the wrist, which they then fitted closely. Generally they were quite plain; but sometimes, like the royal bracelets, they bore in their centre a rosette. Sandals, or in the later times shoes, completed the ordinary costume of the Assyrian "gentleman."

Sometimes both the girdle round the waist, and the cross-belt, which was often worn without a sword, were deeply fringed, the two fringes falling one over the other, and covering the whole body from the chest to the knee. Sometimes, but more rarely, the long robe was discarded, and the Assyrian of some rank wore the short tunic, which was then, however, always fringed, and commonly ornamented with a phillibeg.

Certain peculiar head-dresses and peculiar modes of arranging the hair deserve special attention from their singularity. [PLATE CXXXV., Fig. 4.] They belong in general to musicians, priests, and other official personages, and may perhaps have been badges of office. For instance, musicians sometimes wear on their heads a tall stiff cap shaped like a fish's tail; at other times their head-dress is a sort of tiara of feathers.

Their hair is generally arranged in the ordinary Assyrian fashion; but sometimes it is worn comparatively short, and terminates in a double row of crisp curls. Priests have head-dresses shaped like truncated cones. A cook in one instance, wears a cap not unlike the tiara of the monarch, except that it is plain, and is not surmounted by an apex or peak. A harper has the head covered with a close-fitting cap, encircled with a row of large beads or pearl; from which a lappet depends behind, similarly ornamented. A colossal figure in a doorway, apparently a man, though possibly representing a god, has the hair arranged in six monstrous curls, the lowest three resting upon the shoulder. [PLATE CXXXV., Fig. 6.]

Women of the better sort seem to have been dressed in sleeved gowns, less scanty than those of the men, and either striped or else patterned and fringed. Outside this they sometimes wore a short cloak of the same pattern as the gown, open in front and falling over the arms, which it covered nearly to the elbows. Their hair was either arranged over the whole of the head in short crisp curls, or carried back in waves to the ears, and then in part twisted into long pendent ringlets, in part curled, like that of the men, in three or four rows at the back of the neck. [PLATE CXXXV., Fig. 5.] A girdle was probably worn round the waist, such as we see in the representations of goddesses, while a fringed cross-belt passed diagonally across the breast, being carried under the right arm and over the left shoulder. The feet seem to have been naked, or at best protected by a sandal. The head was sometimes encircled with a fillet.

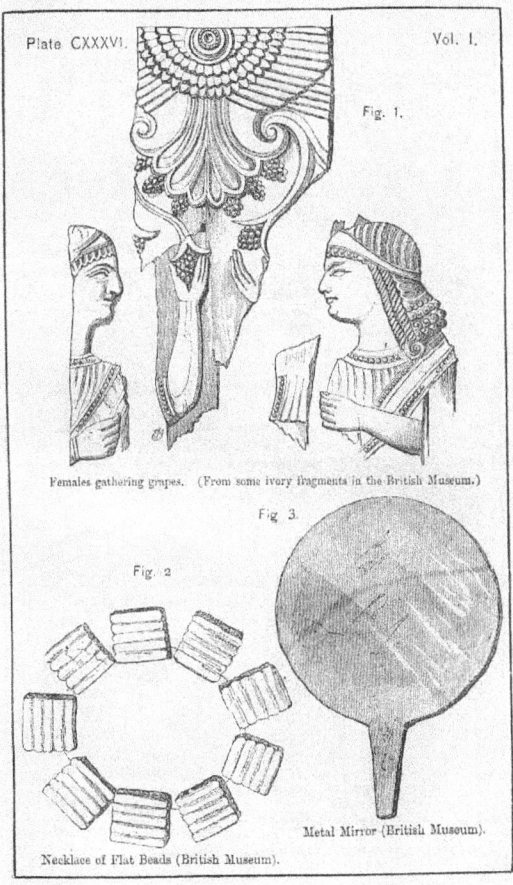

PLATE CXXXVI

Women thus apparelled are either represented as sitting in chairs and drinking from a shallow cup, or else as gathering grapes, which, instead of growing naturally, hang up on branches that issue from a winged circle. The circle would seem to be emblematic of the divine power which bestows the fruits of the earth upon man. [PLATE CXXXVI., Fig. 1.]

The lower class of Assyrian women are not represented upon the sculptures. We may perhaps presume that they did not dress very differently from the female captives so frequent on the bas-reliefs, whose ordinary costume is a short gown not covering the ankles, and an outer garment somewhat resembling the chasuble of the king. The head of these women is often covered with a hood where the hair appears, it usually descends in a single long curl. The feet are in every case naked.

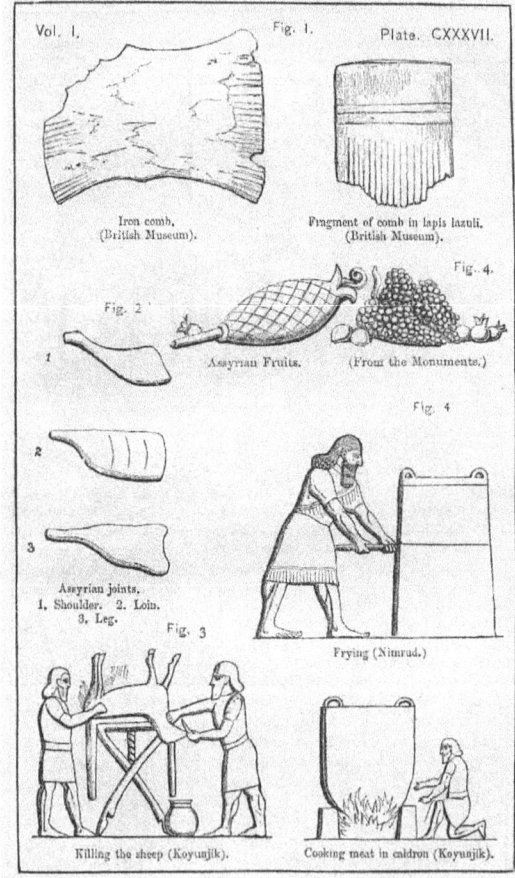

PLATE CXXXVII

The ornaments worn by women appear to have been nearly the same as those assumed by men. They consisted principally of earrings, necklaces, and bracelets. Earrings have been found in gold laid in bronze, some with and some without places for jewels. One gold earring still held its adornment of petals. Bracelets were sometimes of glass, and were slipped over the hand. Necklaces seem commonly to have been of beads, strung together. A necklace in the British Museum is composed of glass beads of a light blue color, square in shape and flat, with horizontal flutings. [PLATE CXXXVI., Fig. 2.] Glass finger-rings have also been found, which were probably worn by women.

We have a few remains of Assyrian toilet articles. A bronze disk, about nine inches in diameter, with a long handle attached, is thought to have been a mirror. In its general shape it resembles both the Egyptian and the classical mirrors; but, unlike them, it is perfectly plain, even the handle being a mere flat bar. [PLATE CXXXVI., Fig. 3.] We have also a few combs. One of these is of iron, about three and a half inches long, by two inches broad in the middle. It is double, like a modern small-tooth comb, but does not present the feature, common in Egypt, of a difference in the size of the teeth on the two sides. The very ancient use of this toilet article in Mesopotamia is evidenced by the fact, already noticed, that it was one of the original hieroglyphs whence the later letters were derived. Another comb is of lapis lazuli, and has only a single row of teeth. [PLATE CXXXVII., Fig. 1.] The small vases of alabaster or fine clay, and the small glass bottles which have been discovered in tolerable abundance, were also in all probability intended chiefly for the toilet. They would hold the perfumed unguents which the Assyrians, like other Orientals, were doubtless in the habit of using, and the dyes wherewith they sought to increase the beauty of the countenance.

No doubt the luxury of the Assyrian women in these and other respects was great and excessive. They are not likely to have fallen short of their Jewish sisters either in the refinements or in the corruptions of civilization. When then we hear of the "tinkling ornaments" of the Jewish women in Isaiah's time, "their combs, and round tires like the moon," their "chains and bracelets and mufflers," their "bonnets, and ornaments of the legs, and head-bands, and tablets and ear-rings," their "rings and nose-jewels," their "changeable suits of apparel, and mantles, and wimples, and crisping-pins," their "glasses, and fine linen, and hoods, and veils," their "sweet smells, and girdles, and well-set hair, and stomachers," we may be sure that in Assyria too these various refinements, or others similar to them, were in use, and consequently that the art of the toilet was tolerably well advanced under the second great Asiatic Empire. That the monuments contain little evidence on the point need not cause any surprise; since it is the natural consequence of the spirit of jealous reserve common to the Oriental nations, which makes them rarely either represent women in their mimetic art or speak of them in their public documents.

If various kinds of grain were cultivated in Assyria, such as wheat, barley, sesame, and millet, we may assume that the food of the inhabitants, like that of other agricultural nations, consisted in part of bread. Sesame was no doubt used, as it is at the present day, principally for making oil; while wheat, barley, and millet were employed for food, and were made into cakes or loaves. The grain used, whatever it was, would be ground between two stones, according to the universal Oriental practice even at the present day. It would then he moistened with water, kneaded in a dish or bowl, and either rolled into thin cakes, or pressed by the hand into smalls balls or loaves. Bread and cakes made in this way still form the chief food of the Arabs of these parts, who retain the habits of antiquity. Wheaten bread is generally eaten by preference; but the poorer sort are compelled to be content with the coarse millet or durra flour, which is made into cakes, and then eaten with milk, butter, oil, or the fat of animals.

Dates, the principal support of the inhabitants of Chaldaea, or Babylonia, both in ancient and in modern times, were no doubt also an article of food in Assyria, though scarcely to any great extent. The date-palm does not bear well above the alluvium, and such fruit as it produces in the upper country is very little esteemed. Olives were certainly cultivated under the Empire, and the oil extracted from them was in great request. Honey was abundant, and wine plentiful. Sennacherib called his land "a land of corn and wine, a land of bread and vineyards, a land of oil olive and of honey;" and the products here enumerated were probably those which formed the chief sustenance of the bulk of the people.

Meat, which is never eaten to any great extent in the East was probably beyond the means of most persons. Soldiers, however, upon an expedition were able to obtain this dainty at the expense of others; and accordingly we find that on such occasions they freely indulged in it. We see them, after their victories, killing and cutting up sheep and. oxen, and then roasting the joints, which are not unlike our own, on the embers of a wood-fires [PLATE CXXXVII., Fig. 2.] In the representations of entrenched camps we are shown the mode in which animals were prepared for the royal dinner. They were placed upon their backs on a high table, with their heads hanging over its edge; one man held them steady in this position, while another, taking hold of the neck, cut the throat a little below the chin. The blood dripped into a bowl or basin placed beneath the head on the ground. [PLATE CXXXVII., Fig. 3.] The animal was then no doubt, paunched, after which it was placed either whole, or in joints—in a huge pot or caldron, and, a fire being lighted underneath, it was boiled to such a point as suited the taste of the king. [PLATE CXXXVII., Fig. 5.] While the boiling progressed, some portions were perhaps fried on the fire below. [PLATE CXXXVII., Fig. 5.] Mutton appears to have been the favorite meat in the camp. At the court there would be a supply of venison, antelope's flesh, hares, partridges, and other game, varied perhaps occasionally with such delicacies as the flesh of the wild ox and the onager.

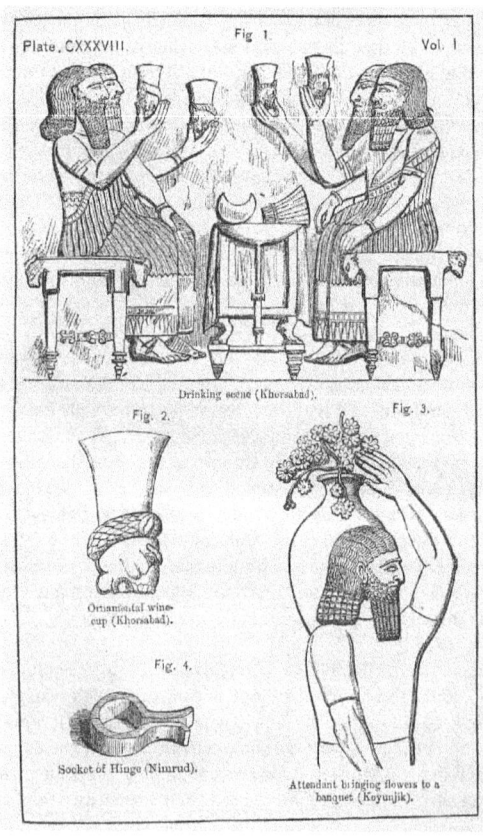

PLATE CXXXVIII

Fish must have been an article of food in Assyria, or the monuments would not have presented us; with so many instances of fishermen. Locusts were also eaten, and were accounted a delicacy, as is proved by their occurrence among the choice dainties of a banquet, which the royal attendants are represented in one bas-relief as bringing into the palace of the king. Fruits, as was natural in so hot a climate, were highly prized; among those of most repute were pomegranates, grapes, citrons, and, apparently, pineapples. [PLATE CXXXVII., Fig. 4.]

There is reason to believe that the Assyrians drank wine very freely. The vine was cultivated extensively, in the neighborhood of Nimrud and elsewhere; and though there is no doubt that, grapes were eaten, both raw and dried, still the main purpose of the vineyards was unquestionably the production of wine. Assyria was "a land of corn and wine," emphatically and before all else. Great banquets seem to have been frequent at the court, as at the courts of Babylon and Persia, in which drinking was practised on a large scale. The Ninevites generally are reproached as drunkards by Nahum. In the banquet-scenes of the sculptures, it is drinking and not eating that is represented. Attendants dip the wine-cups into a huge bowl or vase, which stands on the ground and reaches as high as a man's chest and carry them full of liquor to the guests, who straightway fall to a carouse. [PLATE CXXXVIII., Fig. 1.]

The arrangement of the banquets is curious. The guests, who are in one instance some forty or fifty in number, instead of being received at a common table, are divided into messes of four, who sit together, two and two, facing each other, each mess having its own table and its own attendant. The guests are all clothed in the long tasselled gown, over which they wear the deeply fringed belt and cross-belt. They have sandals on their feet, and on their arias armlets and bracelets. They sit on high stools, from which their legs dangle; but in no case have they footstools, which would apparently have been a great convenience. Most of the guests are bearded men, but intermixed with them we see a few eunuchs. Every guest holds in his right hand a wine-cup of a most elegant shape, the lower part modelled into the form of a lion's head, from which the cup itself rises in a graceful curve. [PLATE CXXXVIII., Fig. 2.] They all raise their cups to a level with their heads, and look as if they were either pledging each other, or else one and all drinking the same toast. Both the stools and the tables are handsome, and tastefully, though not very richly, ornamented. Each table is overspread with a table-cloth, which hangs down on either side opposite the guests, but does not cover the ends of the table, which are thus fully exposed to view. In their general make the tables exactly resemble that used in a banquet scene by a king of a later date, but their ornamentation is much less elaborate. On each of them appears to have been placed the enigmatical article of which mention has been already made as a strange object generally accompanying the king. Alongside of it we see in most instances a sort of rude crescent. These objects have probably, both of them, a sacred import, the crescent being the emblem of Sin, the Moon-God, while the nameless article had some unknown religious use or meaning.

In the great banqueting scene at Khorsabad, from which the above description is chiefly taken, it is shown that the Assyrians, like the Egyptians and the Greeks in the heroic times, had the entertainment of music at their grand feasts and drinking bouts. At one end of the long series of figures representing guests and attendants was a band of performers, at least three in number, two of whom certainly played upon the lyre. The lyres were ten-stringed, of a square shape, and hung round the player's neck by a string or ribbon.

The Assyrians also resembled the Greeks and Romans in introducing flowers into their feasts. We have no evidence that they wore garlands, or crowned themselves with chaplets of flowers, or scattered roses over their rooms; but still they appreciated the delightful adornment which flowers furnish. In the long train of attendance represented at Koyunjik as bringing the materials of a banquet into the palace of the king, a considerable number bear vases of flowers. [PLATE CXXXVIII., Fig. 3.] These were probably placed on stands, like those which are often seen supporting jars, and dispersed about the apartment in which the feast was held, but not put upon the tables.

We have no knowledge of the ordinary houses of the Assyrians other than that which we derive from the single representation which the sculptures furnish of a village certainly Assyrian. It appears from this specimen that the houses were small, isolated from one another, and either flat-roofed, or else covered in with a dome or a high cone. They had no windows, but must have been lighted from the top, where, in some of the roofs, an aperture is discernible. The doorway was generally placed towards one end of the house; it was sometimes arched, but more often square-headed.

The doors in Assyrian houses were either single, as commonly with ourselves, or folding (fores or valvoe), as with the Greeks and Romans, and with the modern French and Italians. Folding-doors were the most common in palaces. They were not hung upon hinges, like modern doors, but, like those of the classical nations, turned upon pivots. At Khorsabad the pavement slabs in the doorways showed everywhere the holes in which these pivots had worked, while in no instance did the wall at the side present any trace of the insertion of a hinge. Hinges, however, in the proper sense of the term, were not unknown to the Assyrians; for two massive bronze sockets found at Nimrud, which weighed more than six pounds each, and had a diameter of about five inches, must have been designed to receive the hinges of a door or gate, hung exactly as gates are now hung among ourselves. [PLATE CXXXVIII., Fig. 4.] The folding-doors were fastened by bolts, which were shot into the pavement at the point where the two doors met; but in the case of single doors a lock seems to have been used, which was placed about four feet from the ground, and projected from the door itself, so that a recess had to be made in the wall behind the door to receive the lock when the door stood open. The bolt of the lock was of an oblong square shape and was shot into the wall against which the door closed.

The ordinary character of Assyrian furniture did not greatly differ from the furniture of modern times. That of the poorer classes was for the most part extremely plain, consisting probably of such tables, couches, and low stools as we see in the representations which are so frequent, of the interiors of soldier's tents. In these the tables are generally of the cross-legged kind; the couches follow the pattern given in a previous page of this volume, except that the legs do not end in pine-shaped ornaments; and the stools are either square blocks, or merely cut en chevron. There are no chairs. The low stools evidently form the ordinary seats of the people, on which they sit to converse or to rest themselves. [PLATE CXXXIX., Fig. 1.] The couches seem to have been the beds whereon the soldiers slept, and it may be doubted if the Assyrians knew of any other. [PLATE CXXXIX., Fig. 2.] In the case of the monarch we have seen that the bedding consisted of a mattress, a large round pillow or cushion, and a coverlet; but in these simple couches of the poor we observe only a mattress, the upper part of which is slightly raised and fitted into the curvature of the arm, so as to make a substitute for a pillow. [PLATE CXXXIX., Fig. 2.] Perhaps, however, the day-laborer may have enjoyed on a couch of this simple character slumbers sounder and more refreshing than Sardanapalus amid his comparative luxury.

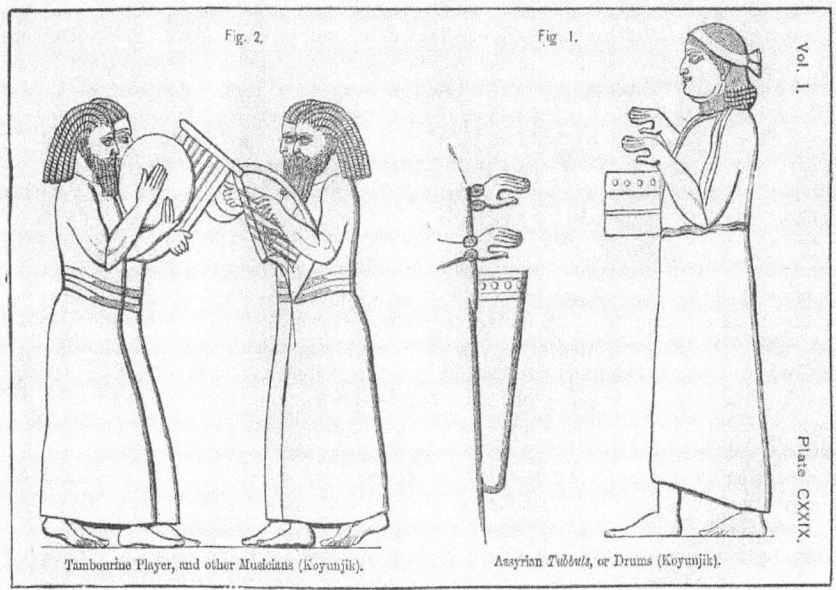

PLATE CXXXIX

The household utensils seen in combination with these simple articles of furniture are few and somewhat rudely shaped. A jug with a long neck, an angular handle, and a pointed bottom, is common: it usually hangs from a nail or hook inserted into the tent-pole. Vases and bowls of a simple form occur, but are less frequent. The men are seen with knives in their hands, and appear sometimes to be preparing food for their meals; but the form of the knife is marked very indistinctly. Some of the household articles represented have a strange and unusual appearance. One is a sort of short ladder, but with semicircular projections at the bottom, the use of which is not apparent; another may be a board at which some game was played; while a third is quite inexplicable. [PLATE CXXXIX., Fig. 8.] From actual discoveries of the utensils themselves, we know that the Assyrians used dishes of stone, alabaster, and bronze. They had also bronze cups, bowls, and plates, often elaborately patterned. The dishes had commonly a handle at the side, either fixed or movable, by which, when not in use, they could be carried or hung on pegs. [PLATE CXXXIX., Fig. 6.] Chaldrons of bronze were also common: they varied from five feet to eighteen inches in height, and from two feet and a half to six feet in diameter. Jugs, funnels, ladles, and jars have been found in the same metal; one of the funnels is shaped nearly like a modern wine strainer. [PLATE CXXXIX., Fig. 4.]

The Assyrians made use of bronze bells with iron tongues, and, to render the sound of these more pleasing, they increased the proportion of the tin to the copper, raising it front ten to fourteen per cent. The bells were always of small size, never (so far as appears) exceeding three inches and a quarter in height and two inches and a quarter in diameter. It is uncertain whether they were used, as modern bells, to summon attendants, or only attached, as we see them on the sculptures, to the collars and headstalls of horses.

Some houses, but probably not very many, had gardens attached to them. The Assyrian taste in gardening was like that of the French. Trees of a similar character, or tall trees alternating with short ones, were planted in straight rows at an equal distance from one another, while straight paths and walks, meeting each other at right angles, traversed the grounds. Water was abundantly supplied by means of canals drawn off from a neighboring river, or was brought by an aqueduct from a distance. A national taste of a peculiar kind, artificial and extravagant to a degree, caused the Assyrians to add to the cultivation of the natural ground the monstrous invention of "Hanging Gardens:" an invention introduced into Babylonia at a comparatively late date, but known in Assyria as early as the time of Sennacherib. A "hanging garden" was sometimes combined with an aqueduct, the banks of the stream which the aqueduct bore being planted with trees of different kinds. At other times it occupied the roof of a building, probably raised for the purpose, and was supported upon a number of pillars. [PLATE CXXXIX., Fig. 5.]

The employments of the Assyrians, which receive some illustration from the monuments, are, besides war and hunting—subjects already discussed at length—chiefly building, boating, and agriculture. Of agricultural laborers, there occur two or three only, introduced by the artists into a slab of Sennacherib's which represents the transport of a winged bull. They are dressed in the ordinary short tunic and belt, and are employed in drawing water from a river by the help of hand-swipes for the purpose of irrigating their lands. Boatmen are far more common. They are seen employed in the conveyance of masses of stone, and of other materials for building, ferrying men and horses across a river, guiding their boat while a fisherman plies his craft from it, assisting soldiers to pursue the enemy, and the like. They wear the short tunic and belt, and sometimes have their hair encircled with a fillet. Of laborers, employed in work connected with building, the examples are numerous. In the long series of slabs representing the construction of some of Sennacherib's great works, although the bulk of those employed as laborers appear to be foreign captives, there are a certain number of the duties—duties less purely mechanical than the others which are devolved on Assyrians. Assyrians load the hand-carts, and sometimes even draw them [PLATE CXXXIX., Fig. 7], convey the implements—pickaxes, saws, shovels, hatchets, beams, forks, coils of rope—place the rollers, arrange the lever and work it, keep the carved masses of stone steady as they are moved along to their proper places, urge on the gangs of forced laborers with sticks, and finally direct the whole of the proceedings by signals, which they give with their voice or with a long horn. Thus, however ample the command of naked human strength enjoyed by the Assyrian king, who had always at his absolute disposal the labor of many thousand captives, still there was in every great work much which could only be intrusted to Assyrians, who appear to have been employed largely in the grand constructions of their monarchs.

The implements of labor have a considerable resemblance to those in present use among ourselves. The saws were two-handed; but as the handle was in the same line with the blade, instead of being set at right angles to it, they must have been somewhat awkward to use. The shovels were heart-shaped, like those which Sir C. Fellows noticed in Asia Minor. The pickaxes had a single instead of a double head, while the hatchets were double-headed, though here probably the second head was a mere knob intended to increase the force of the blow. The hand-carts were small and of very simple construction: they were made open in front and behind, but had a slight framework at the sides. They had a pole rising a little in front, and were generally drawn by two men. The wheels were commonly four-spoked. When the load had been placed on the cart, it seems to have been in general secured by two bands or ropes, which were passed over it diagonally, so as to cross each other at the top.

Carts drawn by animals were no doubt used in the country; but they are not found except in the scenes representing the triumphant returns of armies, where it is more probable that the vehicles are foreign than Assyrian. They have poles—not shafts—and are drawn by two animals, either oxen, mules, or asses. The wheels have generally a large number of spokes—sometimes as many as eleven. Representations of these carts will be found in early pages.

The Assyrians appear to have made occasional use of covered carriages. Several vehicles of this kind are represented on an obelisk in the British Museum. They have a high and clumsy body, which shows no window, and is placed on four disproportionately low wheels, which raise it only about a foot from the ground. In front of this body is a small driving-place, enclosed in trelliswork, inside which the coachman stands to drive. Each of these vehicles is drawn by two horses. It is probable that they were used to convey the ladies of the court; and they were therefore carefully closed, in order that no curious glance of passers-by might rest upon the charming inmates. The carpentum, in which the Roman matrons rode at the great public festivals, was similarly closed, both in front and behind, as is evident from the representations which we have of it on medals and tombs.

Except in the case of these covered vehicles, and of the chariots used in war and hunting, horses (as already observed) were not employed for draught. The Assyrians appear to have regarded them as too noble for this purpose, unless where the monarch and those near to him were concerned, for whose needs nothing was too precious. On the military expeditions the horses were carefully fed and tended. Portable mangers were taken with the army for their convenience; and their food, which was probably barley, was brought to them by grooms in sieves or shallow boxes, whence no doubt it was transferred to the mangers. They appear to have been allowed to go loose in the camp, without being either hobbled or picketed. Care was taken to keep their coats clean and glossy by the use of the curry-comb, which was probably of iron.

Halters of two kinds were employed. Sometimes they consisted of a mere simple noose, which was placed in the horse's mouth, and then drawn tight round the chin. More often (as in the illustration) the rope was attached to a headstall, not unlike that of an ordinary bridle, but simpler, and probably of a cheaper material. Leading reins, fastened to the bit of an ordinary bridle, were also common.

Such are the principal points connected with the peaceful customs of the Assyrians, on which the monuments recently discovered throw a tolerable amount of light. Much still remains in obscurity. It is not possible as yet, without drawing largely on the imagination, to portray in any completeness the private life even of the Assyrian nobles, much less that of the common people. All that can be done is to gather up the fragments which time has spared; to arrange them in something like order, and present them faithfully to the general reader, who, it is hoped, will feel a certain degree of interest in them severally, as matters of archeology, and who will probably further find that he obtains from them in combination a fair notion of the general character and condition of the race, of its mingled barbarism and civilization, knowledge and ignorance, art and rudeness, luxury and simplicity of habits. The novelist and even the essayist may commendably eke out the scantiness of facts by a free indulgence in the wide field of supposition and conjecture: but the historian is not entitled to stray into this enchanted ground. He must be content to remain within the tame and narrow circle of established fact. Where his materials are abundant. he is entitled to draw graphic sketches of the general condition of the people; but where they are scanty, as in the present instance, he must be content to forego such pleasant pictures, in which the coloring and the filling-up would necessarily be derived, not from authentic data, but from his own fancy.

CHAPTER VIII

RELIGION

"The graven image, and the molten image."—NAHUM i. 14

The religion of the Assyrians so nearly resembled—at least in its external aspect, in which alone we can contemplate it—the religion of the primitive Chaldaeans, that it will be unnecessary, after the full treatment which that subject received in an earlier portion of this work, to do much more than notice in the present place certain peculiarities by which it would appear that the cult of Assyria was distinguished from that of the neighboring and closely connected country. With the exception that the first god in the Babylonian Pantheon was replaced by a distinct and thoroughly national deity in the Pantheon of Assyria, and that certain deities whose position was prominent in the one occupied a subordinate position in the other, the two religious systems may be pronounced, not similar merely but identical. Each of them, without any real monotheism, commences with the same preeminence of a single deity, which is followed by the same groupings of identically the same divinities; and after that, by a multitudinous polytheism, which is chiefly of a local character. Each country, so far as we can see, has nearly the same worship-temples, altars, and ceremonies of the same type—the same religious emblems—the same ideas. The only difference here is, that in Assyria ampler evidence exists of what was material in the religious system, more abundant representations of the objects and modes of worship; so that it will be possible to give, by means of illustrations, a more graphic portraiture of the externals of the religion of the Assyrians than the scantiness of the remains permitted in the case of the primitive Chaldaeans.

At the head of the Assyrian Pantheon stood the "great god." Asshur. His usual titles are "the great Lord," "the King of all the Gods," "he who rules supreme over the Gods." Sometimes he is called "the Father of the Gods," though that is a title which is more properly assigned to Belus. His place is always first in invocations. He is regarded throughout all the Assyrian inscriptions as the especial tutelary deity both of the kings and of the country. He places the monarchs upon their throne, firmly establishes then in the government, lengthens the years of their reigns, preserves their power, protects their forts and armies, makes their name celebrated, and the like. To him they look to give them victory over their enemies, to grant them all the wishes of their heart, and to allow them to be succeeded on their thrones by their sons and their sons' sons, to a remote posterity. Their usual phrase when speaking of him is "Asshur, my lord." They represent themselves as passing their lives in his service. It is to spread his worship that they carry on their wars. They fight, ravage, destroy in his name. Finally, when they subdue a country, they are careful to "set up the emblems of Asshur," and teach the people his laws and his worship.

The tutelage of Asshur over Assyria is strongly marked by the identity of his name with that of the country, which in the original is complete. It is also indicated by the curious fact that, unlike the other gods, Asshur had no notorious temple or shrine in any particular city of Assyria, a sign that his worship was spread equally throughout the whole land, and not to any extent localized. As the national deity, he had given name to the original capital; but even at Asshur (Kileh-Sherghat) it may be doubted whether there was any building which was specially his. Therefore it is a reasonable conjectures that all the shrines throughout Assyria were open to his worship, to whatever minor god they might happen to be dedicated.

In the inscriptions the Assyrians are constantly described as "the servants of Asshur," and their enemies as "the enemies of Asshur." The Assyrian religion is "the worship of Asshur." No similar phrases are used with respect to any of the other gods of the Pantheon.

We can scarcely doubt that originally the god Asshur was the great progenitor of the race, Asshur, the son of Shen, deified. It was not long, however, before this notion was lost, and Asshur came to be viewed simply as a celestial being—the first and highest of all the divine agents who ruled over heaven and earth. It is indicative of the (comparatively speaking) elevated character of Assyrian polytheism that this exalted and awful deity continued from first to last the main object of worship, and was not superseded in the thoughts of men by the lower and more intelligible divinities, such as

Shamas and Sin, the Sun and Moon, Nergal the God of War, Nin the God of Hunting, or Vul the wielder of the thunderbolt.

The favorite emblem under which the Assyrians appear to have represented Asshur in their works of art was the winged circle or globe, from which a figure in a horned cap is frequently seen to issue, sometimes simply holding a bow (Fig. I.), sometimes shooting his arrows against the Assyrians' enemies (Fig II.). This emblem has been variously explained; but the most probable conjecture would seem to be that the circle typifies eternity, while the wings express omnipresence, and the human figure symbolizes wisdom or intelligence. The emblem appears under many varieties. Sometimes the figure which issues from it has no bow, and is represented as simply extending the right hand (Fig. III.); occasionally both hands are extended, and the left holds a ring or chaplet (Fig. IV.). [PLATE CXLI., Fig. 1.] In one instance we see a very remarkable variation: for the complete human figure is substituted a mere pair of hands, which seem to come from behind the winged disk, the right open and exhibiting the palm, the left closed and holding a bow. [PLATE CXLI., Fig. 2.] In a large number of cases all sign of a person is dispensed with, the winged circle appearing alone, with the disk either plain or ornamented. On the other hand, there are one or two instances where the emblem exhibits three human heads instead of one—the central figure having on either side of it, a head, which seems to rest upon the feathers of the wing. [PLATE CXLI., Fig. 3.]

It is the opinion of some critics, based upon this form of the emblem, that the supreme deity of the Assyrians, whom the winged circle seems always to represent, was in reality a triune god. Now certainly the triple human form is very remarkable, and lends a color to this conjecture; but, as there is absolutely nothing, either in the statements of ancient writers, or in the Assyrian inscriptions, so far as they have been deciphered, to confirm the supposition, it can hardly be accepted as the true explanation of the phenomenon. The doctrine of the Trinity, scarcely apprehended with any distinctness even by the ancient Jews, does not appear to have been one of those which primeval revelation made known throughout the heathen world. It is a fanciful mysticism which finds a Trinity in the Eicton, Cneph, and Phtha of the Egyptians, the Oromasdes, Mithras, and Arhimanius of the Persians, and the Monas, Logos and Psyche of Pythagoras and Plato. There are abundant Triads in ancient mythology, but no real Trinity. The case of Asshur is, however, one of simple unity, He is not even regularly included in any Triad. It is possible, however, that the triple figure shows him to us in temporary combination with two other gods, who may be exceptionally represented in this way rather than by their usual emblems. Or the three heads may be merely an exaggeration of that principle of repetition which gives rise so often to a double representation of a king or a god, and which is seen at Bavian in the threefold repetition of another sacred emblem, the horned cap.

It is observable that in the sculptures the winged circle is seldom found except in immediate connection with the monarch. The great King wears it embroidered upon his robes, carries it engraved upon his cylinder, represents it above his head in the rock-tablets on which he carves his image a stands or kneels in adoration before it, fights under its shadow, under its protection returns victorious, places it conspicuously in the scenes where he himself is represented on his obelisks. And in these various representations he makes the emblem in a great measure conform to the circumstances in which he himself is engaged at the time. Where he is fighting, Asshur too has his arrow on the string, and points it against the king's adversaries. Where he is returning from victory, with the disused bow in the left hand and the right hand outstretched and elevated, Asshur takes the same attitude. In peaceful scenes the bow disappears altogether. If the king worships, the god holds out his hand to aid; if he is engaged in secular arts, the divine presence is thought to be sufficiently marked by the circle and wings without the human figure.

An emblem found in such frequent connection with the symbol of Asshur as to warrant the belief that it was attached in a special way to his worship, is the sacred or symbolical tree. Like the winged circle, this emblem has various forms. The simplest consists of a short pillar springing from a single pair of rams' horns, and surmounted by a capital composed of two pairs of rams' horns separated by one, two, or three horizontal bands; above which there is, first, a scroll resembling that which commonly surmounts the winged circle, and then a flower, very much like the "honeysuckle ornament" of the Greeks. More advanced specimens show the pillar elongated with a capital in the middle in addition to the capital at the top, while the blossom above the upper capital, and generally the stem likewise, throw out a number of similar smaller blossoms, which are sometimes replaced by fir-cones or pomegranates. [PLATE CXLI., Fig. 4.] Where the tree is most elaborately portrayed, we see, besides the stem and the blossoms, a complicated network of branches, which after interlacing with one another form a sort of arch surrounding the tree itself as with a frame. [PLATE CXLII., Fig.1.]

It is a subject of curious speculation, whether this sacred tree does not stand connected with the Asherah of the Phoenicians, which was certainly not a "grove," in the sense in which we commonly understand that word. The Asherah which the Jews adopted from the idolatrous nations with whom they came in contact, was an artificial structure, originally of wood, but in the later times probably of metal, capable of being "set" in the temple at Jerusalem by one king, and "brought out" by another. It was a structure for which "hangings" could be made, to cover and protect it, while at the same time it was so far like a tree that it could be properly said to be "cut down," rather than "broken" or otherwise demolished. The name itself seems to imply something which stood, straight up; and the conjecture is reasonable that its essential element was "the straight stem of a tree," though whether the idea connected with the emblem was of the same nature with that which underlay the phallic rites of the Greeks is (to say the least) extremely uncertain. We have no distinct evidence that the Assyrian sacred tree was a real tangible object: it may have been, as Mr. Layard supposes, a mere type. But it is perhaps on the whole more likely to have been an actual object; in which case we can not but suspect that it stood in the Assyrian system in much the same position as the Asherah in the Phoenician, being closely connected with the worship of the supreme god, and having certainly a symbolic character, though of what exact kind it may not be easy to determine.

An analogy has been suggested between this Assyrian emblem and the Scriptural "tree of life," which is thought to be variously reflected in the multiform mythology of the East. Are not such speculations somewhat over-fanciful There is perhaps, in the emblem itself, which combines the horns of the ram—an animal noted for procreative power—with the image of a fruit or flower-producing tree, ground for supposing that some allusion is intended to the prolific or generative energy in nature; but more than this can scarcely be said without venturing upon mere speculation. The time perhaps ere long arrive when, by the interpretation of the mythological tablets of the Assyrians, their real notions on this and other kindred subjects may become known to us. Till then, it is best to remain content with such facts as are ascertainable, without seeking to penetrate mysteries at which we can but guess, and where, even if we guess aright, we cannot know that we do so.

The gods worshipped in Assyria in the next degree to Asshur appear to have been, in the early times, Anu and Vul; in the later, Bel, Sin, Shamas, Vul, Nin or Ninip, and Nergal. Gula, Ishtar, and Beltis were favorite goddesses. Hoa, Nebo, and Merodach, though occasional objects of worship, more especially under the later empire, were in far less repute in Assyria than in Babylonia; and the two last-named may almost be said to have been introduced into the former country from the latter during the historical period.

For the special characteristics of these various gods—common objects of worship to the Assyrians and the Babylonians from a very remote epoch—the reader is referred to the first part of this volume, where their several attributes and their position in the Chaldaean Pantheon have been noted. The general resemblance of the two religious systems is such, that almost everything which has been stated with respect to the gods of the First Empire may be taken us applying equally to those of the Second; and the reader is requested to make this application in all cases, except where some shade of difference, more or less strongly marked, shall be pointed out. In the following pages, without repeating what has been said in the first part of this volume, some account will be given of the worship of the principal gods in Assyria and of the chief temples dedicated to their service.

ANU.

The worship of Anu seems to have been introduced into Assyria from Babylonia during the times of Chaldaean supremacy which preceded the establishment of the independent Assyrian kingdom. Shamas-Vul, the son of Ishii-Dagon, king of Chaldaea, built a temple to Anu and Vul at Asshur, which was then the Assyrian capital, about B.C. 1820. An inscription of Tiglath-Pileser I., states that this temple lasted for 621 years, when, having fallen into decay, it was taken down by Asshurdayan, his own great-grandfather. Its site remained vacant for sixty years. Then Tiglath-Pileser I., in the beginning of his reign, rebuilt the temple more magnificently than before; and from that time it seems to have remained among the principal shrines in Assyria. It was from a tradition connected with this ancient temple of Shamas-Vul, that Asshur in later times acquired the name of Telane, or "the Mound of Anu," which it bears in Stephen.

Anu's place among the "Great Gods" of Assyria is not so well marked as that of many other divinities. His name does not occur as an element in the names of kings or of other important personages. He is omitted altogether from many solemn invocations. It is doubtful whether he is one of the gods whose emblems were worn by the king and inscribed upon the rock-tablets. But, on the other hand, where he occurs in lists, he is invariably placed directly after Asshur; and he is often coupled with that deity in a way which is strongly indicative of his exalted character. Tiglath-Pileser I., though omitting him from his opening invocation, speaks of him in the latter part of his great Inscription, as his lord and protector in the next place to Asshur. Asshur-izir-pal uses expressions as if he were Anu's special votary, calling himself "him who honors Anu," or "him who honors Anu and Dugan." His son, the Black-Obelisk king, assigns him the second place in the invocation of thirteen gods with which he begins his record. The kings of the Lower Dynasty do not generally hold him in much repute; Sargon, however, is an exception, perhaps because his own name closely resembled that of a god mentioned as one of Anu's sons. Sargon not infrequently glorifies Anu, coupling him with Bel or Bil, the second god of the first Triad. He even made Anu the tutelary god of one of the gates of his new city, Bit-Sargina (Khorsabad), joining him in this capacity with the goddess Ishtar.

Anu had but few temples in Assyria. He seems to have had none at either Nineveh or Calah, and none of any importance in all Assyria, except that at Asshur. There is, however, reason, to believe that he was occasionally honored with a shrine in a temple dedicated to another deity.

BIL, or BEL.

The classical writers represent Bel as especially a Babylonian god, and scarcely mention his worship by the Assyrians; but the monuments show that the true Bel (called in the first part of this volume Bel-Nimrod) was worshipped at least as much in the northern as in the southern country. Indeed, as early as the time of Tiglath-Pileser I., the Assyrians, as a nation, were especially entitled by their monarchs "the, people of Belus;" and the same periphrasis was in use during the period of the Lower Empire. According to some authorities, a particular quarter of the city of Nineveh was denominated "the city of Belus" which would imply that it was in a peculiar way under his protection. The word Bel does not occur very frequently as an element in royal names: it was borne, however, by at least three early Assyrian kings: and there is evidence that in later times it entered as an element into the names of leading personages with almost as much frequency as Asshur.

The high rank of Bel in Assyria is very strongly marked. In the invocations his place is either the third or the second. The former is his proper position, but occasionally Anu is omitted, and the name of Bel follows immediately on that of Asshur. In one or two places he is made third, notwithstanding that Anu is omitted, Shamas, the Sun-god, being advanced over his head; but this is very unusual.

The worship of Bel in the earliest Assyrian times is marked by the royal names of Bel-snmili-kapi and Bel-lush, borne by two of the most ancient kings. He had a temple at Asshur in conjunction with Il or Ra, which must have been of great antiquity, for by the time of Tiglath-Pileser I. (B.C. 1130) it had fallen to decay and required a complete restoration, which it received from that monarch. He had another temple at Calah; besides which he had four "arks" or "tabernacles," the emplacement of which is uncertain. Among the latter kings, Sargon especially paid him honor. Besides coupling him with Anu in his royal titles, he dedicated to him—in conjunction with Beltis, his wife—one of the gates of his city, and in many passages he ascribes his royal authority to the favor of Bel and Merodach. He also calls Bel, in the dedication of the eastern gate at Khorsabad, "the establisher of the foundations of his city."

It may be suspected that the horned cap, which was no doubt a general emblem of divinity, was also in an especial way the symbol of this god. Esarhaddon states that he setup over "the image of his majesty the emblems of Asshur, the Sun, Bel, Nin, and Ishtar." The other kings always include Bel among the chief objects of their worship. We should thus expect to find his emblem among those which the kings specially affected; and as all the other common emblems are assigned to distinct gods with tolerable certainty, the horned cap alone remaining doubtful, the most reasonable conjecture seems to be that it was Bel's symbol.

It has been assumed in some quarters that the Bel of the Assyrians was identical with the Phoenician Dagon. A word which reads Da-gan is found in the native lists of divinities, and in one place the explanation attached seems to show that the term was among the titles of Bel. But this verbal resemblance between the name Dagon and one of Bel's titles is probably a mere accident, and affords no ground for assuming any connection between the two gods, who have nothing in common one with the other. The Bel of the Assyrians was certainly not their Fish-god; nor had his epithet Da-gaga any real connection with the word dag, "a fish." To speak of "Bel-Dagon" is thus to mislead the ordinary reader, who naturally supposes from the term that he is to identify the great god Belus, the second deity of the first Triad, with the fish forms upon the sculptures.

HEA, or HOA.

Hen, or Hoa, the third god of the first Triad, was not a prominent object of worship in Assyria. Asshur-izir-pal mentions him as having allotted to the four thousand deities of heaven and earth the senses of hearing, seeing, and understanding; and then, stating that the four thousand deities had transferred all these senses to himself, proceeds to take Hoa's titles, and, as it were, to identify himself with the god. His son, Shalmaneser II., the Black-Obelisk king gives Hoa his proper place in his opening invocation, mentioning him between Bel and Sin. Sargon puts one of the gates of his new city under Hoa's care, joining him with Bilat Ili—"the mistress of the gods"—who is, perhaps, the Sun-goddess, Gula. Sennacherib, after a successful expedition across a portion of the Persian Gulf, offers sacrifice to Hoa on the seashore, presenting him with a golden boat, a golden fish, and a golden coffer. But these are exceptional instances; and on the whole it is evident that in Assyria Hoa was not a favorite god. The serpent, which is his emblem, though found on the black stones recording benefactions, and frequent on the Babylonian cylinder-seals, is not adopted by the

Assyrian kings among the divine symbols which they wear, or among those which they inscribe above their effigies. The word Hoa does not enter as an element into Assyrian names. The kings rarely invoke him. So far as we can tell, he had but two temples in Assyria, one at Asshur (Kileh-Sherghat) and the other at Calah (Nimrud). Perhaps the devotion of the Assyrians to Nin—the tutelary god of their kings and of their capital—who in so many respects resembled Hoa, caused the worship of Hoa to decline and that of Nin gradually to supersede it.

MYLITTA, or BELTIS.

Beltis, the "Great Mother," the feminine counterpart of Bel, ranked in Assyria next to the Triad consisting of Anu, Bel, and Hoa. She is generally mentioned in close connection with Bel, her husband, in the Assyrian records. She appears to have been regarded in Assyria as especially "the queen of fertility," or "fecundity," and so as "the queen of the lands," thus resembling the Greek Demeter, who, like Beltis, was known as: "the Great Mother." Sargon placed one of his gates under the protection of Beltis in conjunction with her husband, Bel: and Asshur-bani-pal, his great-grandson, repaired and rededicated to her a temple at Nineveh, which stood on the great mound of Koyunjik. She had another temple at Asshur, and probably a third at Calah. She seems to have been really known as Beltis in Assyria, and as Mylitta (Mulita) in Babylonia, though we should naturally have gathered the reverse from the extant classical notices.

SIN, or THE MOON.

Sin, the Moon-god, ranked next to Beltis in Assyrian mythology, and his place is thus either fifth or sixth in the full lists, according as Beltis is, or is not, inserted. His worship in the time of the early empire appears from the invocation of Tiglath-Pileser I., where he occurs in the third place, between Bel and Shamas. [PLATE CXLII., Fig. 2.] His emblem, the crescent, was worn by Asshur-izir-pal, and is found wherever divine symbols are inscribed over their effigies by the Assyrian kings. There is no sign which is more frequent on the cylinder-seals, whether Babylonian or Assyrian, and it would thus seem that Sin was among the most popular of Assyria's deities. His name occurs sometimes, though not so frequently as some others, in the appellations of important personages, as e, g. in that of Sennacherib, which is explained to mean "Sin multiplies brethren." Sargon, who thus named one of his sons, appears to have been specially attached to the worship of Sin, to whom, in conjunction with Shamas, he built a temple at Khorsabad, and to whom he assigned the second place among the tutelary deities of his city.

The Assyrian monarchs appear to have had a curious belief in the special antiquity of the Moon-god. When they wished to mark a very remote period, they used the expression "from the origin of the god Sin." This is perhaps a trace of the ancient connection of Assyria with Babylonia, where the earliest capital, Ur, was under the Moon-god's protection, and the most primeval temple was dedicated to his honor.

Only two temples are known to have been erected to Sin in Assyria. One is that already mentioned as dedicated by Sargon at Bit-Sargina (Khorsabad) to the Sun and Moon in conjunction. The other was at Calah, and in that Sin had no associate.

SHAMAS.

Shamas, the Sun-god, though in rank inferior to Sin, seems to have been a still more favorite and more universal object of worship. From many passages we should have gathered that he was second only to Asshur in the estimation of the Assyrian monarchs, who sometimes actually place him above Bel in their lists. His emblem, the four-rayed orb, is worn by the king upon his neck, and seen more commonly than almost any other upon the cylinder-seals. It is even in some instances united with that of Asshur, the central circle of Asshur's emblem being marked by the fourfold rays of Shamas.

The worship of Shamas was ancient in Assyria. Tiglath-Pileser I., not only names him in his invocation, but represents himself as ruling especially under his auspices. Asshur-izir-pal mentions Asshur and Shamas as the tutelary deities under whose influence he carried on his various wars. His son, the Black-Obelisk king, assigns to Shamas his proper place among the gods whose favor he invokes at the commencement of his long Inscription. The kings of the Lower Empire were even more devoted to him than their predecessors. Sargon dedicated to him the north gate of his city, in conjunction with Vul, the god of the air, built a temple to him at Khorsabad in conjunction with Sin, and assigned him the third place among the tutelary deities of his new town. Sennacherib and Esarhaddon mention his name next to Asshur's in passages where they enumerate the gods whom they regard as their chief protectors.

Excepting at Khorsabad, where he had a temple (as above mentioned) in conjunction with Sin, Shamas does not appear to have had any special buildings dedicated to his honor. His images are, however, often noticed in the lists of idols, and it is probable therefore that he received worship in temples dedicated to other deities. His emblem is generally found conjoined with that of the moon, the two being placed side by side, or the one directly under the other. [PLATE CXLII., Fig. 3.]

VUL, or IVA.

This god, whose name is still so uncertain, was known in Assyria from times anterior to the independence, a temple having been raised in his sole honor at Asshur, the original Assyrian capital, by Shamas-Vul, the son of the Chaldaean king Ismi-Dagon, besides the temple (already mentioned) which the same monarch dedicated to him in conjunction with Anu. These buildings having fallen to ruin by the time of Tiglath-Pileser I., were by him rebuilt from their base; and Vul, who was worshipped in both, appears to have been regarded by that monarch as one of his special "guardian deities." In the Black-Obelisk invocation Vul holds the place intermediate between Sin and Shamas, and on the same monument is recorded the fact that the king who erected it held, on one occasion, a festival to Vul in conjunction with Asshur. Sargon names Vul in the fourth place among the tutelary deities of his city, and dedicates to him the north gate in conjunction with the Sun-god, Shamas. Sennacherib speaks of hurling thunder on his enemies like Vul, and other kings use similar expressions. The term Vul was frequently employed as an element in royal and other names; and the emblem which seems to have symbolized him—the double or triple bolt—appears constantly among those worn by the kings, and engraved above their heads on the rock-tablets. [PLATE CXLII., Fig. 4.]

Vul had a temple at Calah besides the two temples in which he received worship at Asshur. It was dedicated to him in conjunction with the goddess Shala, who appears to have been regarded as his wife.

It is not quite certain whether we can recognize any representations of Vul in the Assyrian remains. Perhaps the figure with four wings and a horned cap, who wields a thunderbolt in either hand, and attacks therewith the monster, half lion, half eagle, which is known to us from the Nimrod sculptures, may be intended for this deity. If so, it will be reasonable also to recognize him in the figure with uplifted foot, sometimes perched upon an ox, and bearing, like the other, one or two thunderbolts, which occasionally occurs upon the cylinders. It is uncertain, however, whether the former of these figures is not one of the many different representations of Nin, the Assyrian Hercules; and, should that prove the true explanation in the one case, no very great confidence could be felt in the suggested identification in the other.

GULA.

Gula, the Sum-goddess, does not occupy a very high position among the deities of Assyria. Her emblem, indeed, the eight-rayed disk, is borne, together with her husband's, by the Assyrian monarchs, and is inscribed on the rock-tablets, on the stones recording benefactions, and on the cylinder-seals, with remarkable frequency. But her name occurs rarely in the inscriptions, and, where it is found, appears low down in the lists. In the Black-Obelisk invocation, out of thirteen deities named, she is the twelfth. Elsewhere she scarcely appears, unless in inscriptions of a purely religious character. Perhaps she was commonly regarded as so much one with her husband that a separate and distinct mention of her seemed not to be requisite.

Gula is known to have had at least two temples in Assyria. One of these was at Asshur, where she was worshipped in combination with ten other deities, of whom one only, Ishtar, was of high rank. The other was at Calah, where her husband had also a temple. She is perhaps to be identified with Bilat-Ili, "the mistress of the gods," to whom Sargon dedicated one of his gates in conjunction with Hoa.

NINIP, or NIN.

Among the gods of the second order, there is none whom the Assyrians worshipped with more devotion than Nin, or Ninip. In traditions which are probably ancient, the race of their kings was derived from him, and after him was called the mighty city which ultimately became their capital. As early as the thirteenth century B.C. the name of Nin was used as an element in royal appellations; and the first king who has; left us an historical inscription regarded himself as being in an especial way under Nin's guardianship. Tiglath-Pileser I., is "the illustrious prince whom Asshur and Nin have exalted to the utmost wishes of his heart." He speaks of Nin sometimes singly, sometimes in conjunction with Asshur, as his "guardian deity." Nin and Nergal make his weapons sharp for him, and under Nin's auspices the fiercest beasts of the field fall beneath them. Asshur-izir-pal built him a magnificent temple at Nimrud (Calah). Shamas-Vul, the grandson of this king, dedicated to him the obelisk which he set up at that place in commemoration of his victories. Sargon placed his newly-built city in part under his protection, and specially invoked him to guard his magnificent palace. The ornamentation of that edifice indicated in a very striking way the reverence of the builder for this god, whose symbol, the winged bull, guarded all its main gateways, and who seems to have been actually represented by the figure strangling a lion, so conspicuous on the Hareem portal facing the great court. Nor did Sargon regard Nin as his protector only in peace. He ascribed to his influence the successful issue of his wars; and it is probably to indicate the belief which he entertained on this point that he occasionally placed Nin's emblems on the sculptures representing his expeditions. Sennacherib, the son and successor of Sargon, appears to have had much the same feelings towards Nin, as his father, since in his buildings he gave the same prominence to the winged bull and to the figure strangling the lion; placing the former at almost all his doorways, and giving the latter a conspicuous position on the grand facade of his chief palace. Esarhaddon relates that he continued in the worship of Nin, setting up his emblem over his own royal effigy, together with those of Asshur, Shamas, Bel, and Ishtar.

It appears at first sight as if, notwithstanding the general prominency of Nin in the Assyrian religious system, there was one respect in which he stood below a considerable number of the gods. We seldom find his name used openly as an element in the royal appellations. In the list of kings three only will be found with names into which the terms Nin enters. But there is reason to believe that, in the case of this god, it was usual to speak of him under a periphrasis; and this periphrasis entered into names in lieu of the god's proper designation. Five kings (if this be admitted) may be regarded as named after him, which is as large a number as we find named after any god but Vul and Asshur.

The principal temples known to have been dedicated to Nin in Assyria were at Calah, the modern Nimrud. There the vast structure at the north-western angle of the great mound, including the pyramidical eminence which is the most striking feature of the ruins, was a temple dedicated to the honor of Nin by Asshur-izir-pal, the builder of the North-West Palace. We can have little doubt that this building represents the "busta Nini" of the clasical writers, the place where Ninus (Nin or Nin-ip), who was regarded by the Greeks as the hero-founder of the nation, was interred and specially worshipped. Nin had also a second temple in this town, which bore the name of Bit-kura (or Beth-kura), as the other one did of Bit-zira (or Beth-zira). It seems to have been from the fame of Beth-zira that Nin had the title Pal-zira, which forms a substitute for Nin, as already noticed, in one of the royal names.

MERODACH.

Most of the early kings of Assyria mention Merodach in their opening invocations, and we sometimes find an allusion in their inscriptions, which seems to imply that he was viewed as a god of great power. But he is decidedly not a favorite object of worship in Assyria until a comparatively recent period. Vul-lush III., indeed claims to have been the first to give him a prominent place in the Assyrian Pantheon; and it may be conjectured that the Babylonian expeditions of this monarch furnished the impulse which led to a modification in this respect of the Assyrian religious system. The later kings, Sargon and his successors, maintain the worship introduced by Vul-lush. Sargon habitually regards his power as conferred upon him by the combined favor of Merodach and Asshur, while Esarhaddon sculptures Merodach's emblem, together with that of Asshur, over the images of foreign gods brought to him by a suppliant prince. No temple to Merodach, is, however, known to have existed in Assyria, even under the later kings. His name, however, was not infrequently used as an element in the appellations of Assyrians.

NERGAL.

Among the Minor gods, Nergal is one whom the Assyrians seem to have regarded with extraordinary reverence. He was the divine ancestor from whom the monarchs loved to boast that they derived their descent—the line being traceable, according to Sargon, through three hundred and fifty generations. They symbolized him by the winged lion with a human head, or possibly sometimes by the mere natural lion; and it was to mark their confident dependence on his protection that they made his emblems so conspicuous in their palaces. Nin and Nergal—the gods of war and hunting, the occupations in which the Assyrian monarchs passed their lives—were tutelary divinities of the race, the life, and the homes of the kings, who associate the two equally in their inscriptions and their sculptures.

Nergal, though thus honored by the frequent mention of his name and erection of his emblem, did not (so far as appears) often receive the tribute of a temple. Sennacherib dedicated one to him at Tarbisi (now Sherif-khan), near Khorsabad; and he may have had another at Calah (Nimrud), of which he is said to have been one of the "resident gods." But generally it would seem that the Assyrians were content to pay him honor in other ways without constructing special buildings devoted exclusively to his worship.

ISHTAR.

Ishtar was very generally worshipped by the Assyrian monarchs, who called her "their lady," and sometimes in their invocations coupled her with the supreme god Asshur. She had a very ancient temple at Asshur, the primeval capital, which Tiglath-Pileser I., repaired and beautified. Asshur-izir-pal built her a second temple at Nineveh, and she had a third at Arbela, which Asshur-bani-pal states that he restored. Sargon placed under her protection, conjointly with Anu, the western gate of his city; and his son, Sennacherib, seems to have viewed Asshur and Ishtar as the special guardians of his progeny. Asshur-bani-pal, the great hunting king was a devotee of the goddess, whom he regarded as presiding over his special diversion, the chase.

What is most remarkable in the Assyrian worship of Ishtar is the local character assigned to her. The Ishtar of Nineveh is distinguished from the Ishtar of Arbela, and both from the Ishtar of Babylon, separate addresses being made to them in one and the same invocation. It would appear that in this case there was, more decidedly than in any other, an identification of the divinity with her idols, from which resulted the multiplication of one goddess into many.

The name of Ishtar appears to have been rarely used in Assyria in royal or other appellations. It is difficult to account for this fact, which is the more remarkable, since in Phoenicia Astarte, which corresponds closely to Ishtar, is found repeatedly as an element in the royal titles.

NEBO.

Nebo must have been acknowledged as a god by the Assyrians from very ancient times, for his name occurs as an element in a royal appellation as early as the twelfth century B.C. He seems, however, to have been very little worshipped till the time of Vud-lush III., who first brought him prominently forward in the Pantheon of Assyria after an expedition which he conducted into Babylonia, where Nebo had always been in high favor. Vul-lush set up two statues to Nebo at Calah and probably built him the temple there which was known as Bit-Siggil, or Beth-Saggil, from whence the god derived one of his appellations. He did not receive much honor from Sargon; but both Sennacherib and Esarhaddon held him in considerable reverence, the latter even placing him above Merodach in an important invocation. Asshur-bani-pal also paid him considerable respect, mentioning him and his wife Warmita, as the deities under whose auspices he undertook certain literary labors.

It is curious that Nebo, though he may thus almost be called a late importation into Assyria, became under the Later Dynasty (apparently) one of most popular of the gods. In the latter portion of the list of Eponyms obtained from the celebrated "Canon," we find Nebo an element in the names as frequently as any other god excepting Asshur. Regarding this as a test of popularity we should say that Asshur held the first place; but that his supremacy was closely contested by Bel and Nebo, who were held in nearly equal repute, both being far in advance of any other deity.

Besides these principal gods, the Assyrians acknowledged and worshipped a vast number of minor divinities, of whom, however, some few only appear to deserve special mention. It may be noticed in the first place, as a remarkable feature of this people's mythological system, that each important god was closely associated with a goddess, who is commonly called his wife, but who yet does not take rank in the Pantheon at all in accordance with the dignity of her husband. Some of these goddesses have been already mentioned, as Beltis, the feminine counterpart of Bel; Gala, the Sun-goddess, the wife of Shamas; and Ishtar, who is sometimes represented as the wife of Nebo. To the same class belong Sheruha, the wife of Asshur; Anata or Anuta, the wife of Anu; Dav-Kina, the wife of Hea or Hoa; Shales, the wife of Vul or Iva; Zir-banit, the wife of Merodach; and Laz, the wife of Nergal. Nin, the Assyrian Hercules, and Sin, the Moon-god, have also wives, whose proper names are unknown, but who are entitled respectively "the Queen of the Land" and "the great Lady." Nebo's wife, according to most of the Inscriptions, is Warmita; but occasionally, as above remarked, this name is replaced by that of Ishtar. A tabular view of the gods and goddesses, thus far, will probably be found of use by the reader towards obtaining a clear conception of the Assyrian Pantheon:

TABLE of the Chief ASSYRIAN DEITIES, arranged in their proper order.

Gods.	Correspondent Goddesses.	Chief Seat of Worship (if any).
Asshur .	Sheruha.	
Anu . .	Anuta	Asshur (Kileh-Sherghat).
Bel . . .	Beltis	Asshur, Calah (Nimrud).
Noa. . .	Dav-Kina	Asshur, Calah.
Sin . . .	"The Great Lady" . .	Calah, Bit-Sargina (Khorsabad).
Shamas .	Gula.	Bit-Sargina.
Vul. . .	Shala	Asshur, Calah.
Nin. . . .	"The Queen of the Land,"	Calah, Nineveh.
Merodach	Zir-Banit.	
Nergal. .	Laz	Tarbisi (Sherif-Khan).
Nebo . .	Warmita (Ishtar?) . .	Calah.

It appears to have been the general Assyrian practice to unite together in the same worship, under the same roof, the female and the male principle. The female deities had in fact, for the most part, an unsubstantial character: they were ordinarily the mere reflex image of the male, and consequently could not stand alone, but required the support of the stronger sex to give then something of substance and reality. This was the general rule; but at the same time it was not without certain exceptions. Ishtar appears almost always as an independent and unattached divinity; while Beltis and Gula are presented to us in colors as strong and a form as distinct as their husbands, Bel and Shamas. Again, there are minor goddesses, such as Telita, the goddess of the great marshes near Babylon, who stand alone, unaccompanied by any male. The minor male divinities are also, it would seem, very generally without female counterparts.

Of these minor male divinities the most noticeable are Martu, a son of Anu, who is called "the minister of the deep," and seems to correspond to the Greek Erebus; Sargana, another son of Anu, from whom Sargon is thought by some to have derived his name Idak, god of the Tigris; Supulat, lord of the Euphrates; and Il or Ra, who seems to be the Babylonian chief god transferred to Assyria, and there placed in a humble position. Besides these, cuneiform scholars recognize in the Inscriptions some scores of divine names, of more or less doubtful etymology, some of which are thought to designate distinct gods, while others may be names of deities known familiarly to us under a different appellation. Into this branch of the subject it is not proposed to enter in the present work, which addresses itself to the general reader.

It is probable that, besides gods, the Assyrians acknowledged the existence of a number of genii, some of whom they regarded as powers of good, others as powers of evil. The winged figure wearing the horned cap, which is so constantly represented as attending upon the monarch when he is employed in any sacred function, would seem to be his tutelary genius—a benignant spirit who watches over him, and protects him from the spirits of darkness. This figure commonly bears in the right hand either a pomegranate or a pine-cone, while the left is either free or else supports a sort of plaited bag or basket. [PLATE CXLII., Fig. 6.] Where the pine-cone is carried, it is invariably pointed towards the monarch, as if it were the means of communication between the protector and the protected, the instrument by which grace and power passed from the genius to the mortal whom he had undertaken to guard. Why the pine-cone was chosen for this purpose it is difficult to form a conjecture. Perhaps it had originally become a sacred emblem merely as a symbol of productiveness after which it was made to subserve a further purpose, without much regard to its old symbolical meaning.

The sacred basket, held in the left hand, is of still more dubious interpretation. It is an object of great elegance, always elaborately and sometimes very tastefully ornamented. Possibly it may represent the receptacle in which the divine gifts are stored, and from which they can be taken by the genius at his discretion, to be bestowed upon the mortal under his care.

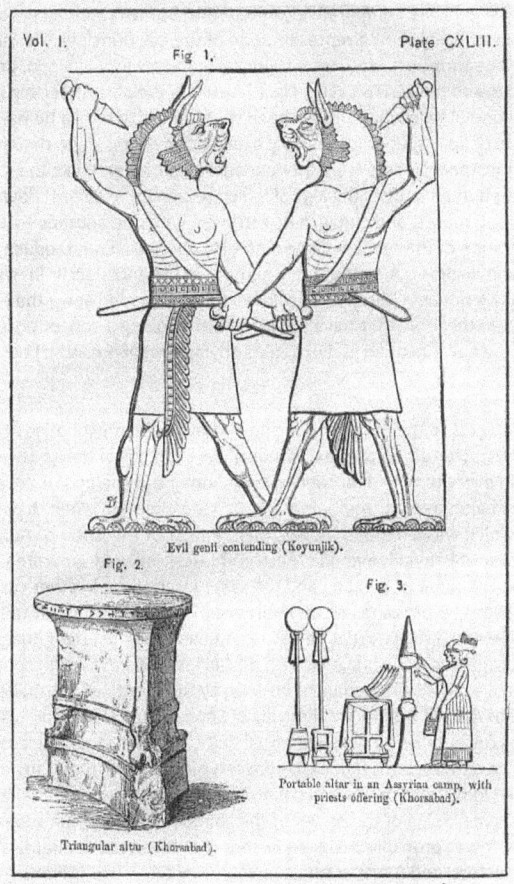

PLATE CXLIII

Another good genius would seem to be represented by the hawk-headed figure, which is likewise found in attendance upon the monarch, attentively watching his proceedings. This figure has been called that of a god, and has been supposed to represent the Nisroch of Holy Scripture; but the only ground for such an identification is the conjectural derivation of Nisroch from a root nisr, which in some Semitic languages signifies a "hawk" or "falcon." As nisr, however, has not been found with any such meaning in Assyrian, and as the word "Nisroch" nowhere appears in the Inscriptions, it must be regarded as in the highest degree doubtful whether there is any real connection between the hawk-headed figure and the god in whose temple Sennacherib was assassinated. [PLATE CXLII., Fig. 5.] The various readings of the Septuagint version make it extremely uncertain what was the name actually written in the original Hebrew text. Nisroch, which is utterly unlike any divine name hitherto found in the Assyrian records, is most probable a corruption. At any rate there are no sufficient grounds for identifying the god mentioned, whatever the true reading of his name may be, with the hawk-headed figure, which has the appearance of an attendant genius rather than that of a god, and which was certainly not included among the main deities of Assyria.

Representations of evil genii are comparatively infrequent; but we can scarcely be mistaken in regarding as either an evil genius, or a representation of the evil principle, the monster—half lion, half eagle—which in the Nimrud sculptures retreats from the attacks of a god, probably Vul, who assails him with thunderbolts. [PLATE CXLIII., Fig. I.] Again, in the case of certain grotesque statuettes found at Khorsabad, one of which has already been represented, where a human figure has the head of a lion with the ears of an ass, the most natural explanation seems to be that an evil genius is intended. In another instance, where we see two monsters with heads like the statuette just mentioned, placed on human bodies, the legs of which terminate in eagles' claws—both of them armed with daggers and maces, and engaged in a struggle with one another—we seem to have a symbolical representation of the tendency of evil to turn upon itself, and reduce itself to feebleness by internal quarrel and disorder. A considerable number of instances occur in which a human figure, with the head of a hawk or eagle, threatens a winged human-headed lion—the emblem of Nergal—with a strap or mace. In these we may have a spirit of evil assailing a god, or possibly one god opposing another—the hawk-headed god or genius driving Nergal (i.e., War) beyond the Assyrian borders.

If we pass from the objects to the mode of worship in Assyria, we must notice at the outset the strongly idolatrous character of the religion. Not only were images of the gods worshipped set up, as a matter of course, in every temple dedicated to their honor, but the gods were sometimes so identified with their images as to be multiplied in popular estimation when they had several famous temples, in each of which was a famous image. Thus we hear of the Ishtar of Arbela, the Ishtar of Nineveh, and the Ishtar of Babylon, and find these goddesses invoked separately, as distinct divinities, by one and the same king in one and the same Inscription. In other cases, without this multiplication, we observe expressions which imply a similar identification of the actual god with the mere image. Tiglath-Pileser I., boasts that he has set Anu and Vul (i.e., their images) up in their places. He identifies repeatedly the images which he carries off from foreign countries with the gods of those countries. In a similar spirit Sennacherib asks, by the mouth of Rabshakeh, "Where are the gods of Hamath and of Arpad? Where are the gods of Sepharvaim, Hena, and Ivah?"—and again unable to rise to the conception of a purely spiritual deity, supposes that, because Hezekiah has destroyed all the images throughout Judaea, he has left his people without any divine protection. The carrying off of the idols from conquered countries, which we find universally practised, was not perhaps intended as a mere sign of the power of the conqueror, and of the superiority of his gods to those of his enemies; it was probably designed further to weaken those enemies by depriving them of their celestial protectors; and it may even have been viewed as strengthening of the conqueror by multiplying his divine guardians. It was certainly usual to remove the images in a reverential manner; and it was the custom to deposit them in some of the principal temples of Assyria. We may presume that there lay at the root of this practice a real belief in the super-natural power of the in images themselves, and a notion that, with the possession of the images, this power likewise changed sides and passed over from the conquered to the conquerors.

Assyrian idols were in stone, baked clay, or metal. Some images of Nebo and of Ishtar have been obtained from the ruins. Those of Nebo are standing figures, of a larger size than the human, though not greatly exceeding it. They have been much injured by time, and it is difficult to pronounce decidedly on their original workmanship: but, judging by what appears, it would seem to have been of a ruder and coarser character than that of the slabs or of the royal statues. The Nebo images are heavy, formal, inexpressive, and not over well-proportioned; but they are not wanting in a certain quiet dignity which impresses the beholder. They are unfortunately disfigured, like so many of the lions and bulls, by several lines of cuneiform writing inscribed round their bodies; but this artistic defect is pardoned by the antiquarian, who learns from the inscribed lines the fact that the statues represent Nebo, and the time and circumstances of their dedication.

Clay idols are very frequent. They are generally in a good material, and are of various sizes, yet never approaching to the full stature of humanity. Generally they are mere statuettes, less than a foot in height. Specimens have been selected for representation in the preceding volume, from which a general idea of their character is obtainable. They are, like the stone idols, formal and inexpressive in style, while they are even ruder and coarser than those figures in workmanship. We must regard them as intended chiefly for private use among the mass of the population, while we must view the stone idols as the objects of public worship in the shrines and temples.

Idols in metal have not hitherto appeared among the objects recovered from the Assyrian cities. We may conclude, however, from the passage of Nahum prefixed to this chapter, as well as from general probability, that they were known and used by the Assyrians, who seem to have even admitted them—no less than stone statues—into their temples. The ordinary metal used was no doubt bronze; but in Assyria, as in Babylonia, silver, and perhaps in some few instances gold, may have been employed for idols, in cases where they were intended as proofs to the world at large of the wealth and magnificence of a monarch.

The Assyrians worshipped their gods chiefly with sacrifices and offerings, Tiglath-Pileser I., relates that he offered sacrifice to Anu and Vul on completing the repairs of their temple. Asshur-izir-pal says that he sacrificed to the gods after embarking on the Mediterranean. Vul-lush IV, sacrificed to Bel-Merodach, Nebo, and Nergal, in their respective high seats at Babylon, Borsippa, and Cutha. Sennacherib offered sacrifices to Hoa on the sea-shore after an expedition in the Persian Gulf. Esarhaddon "slew great and costly sacrifices" at Nineveh upon completing his great palace in that capital. Sacrifice was clearly regarded as a duty by the kings generally, and was the ordinary mode by which they propitiated the favor of the national deities.

Sacrificial scene (from an obelisk found at Nimrud).

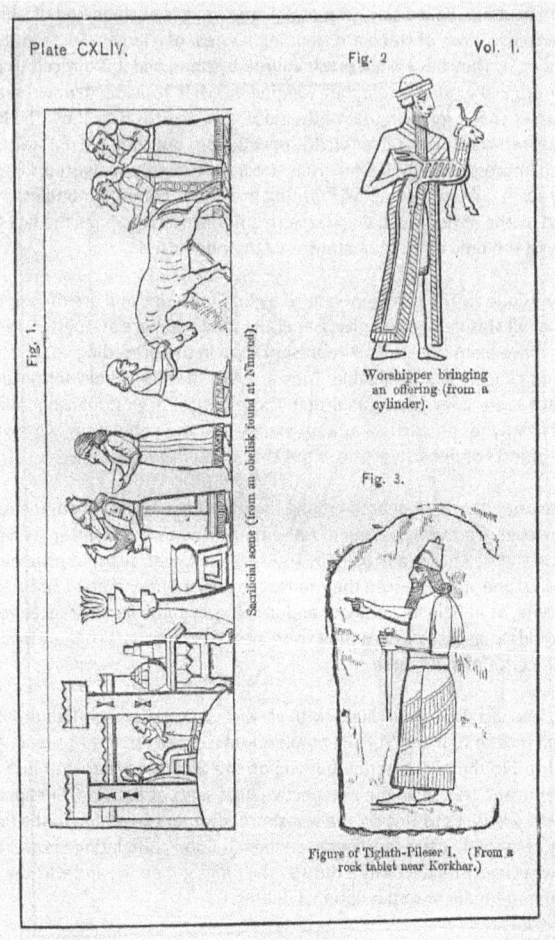

PLATE CXLIV

With respect to the mode of sacrifice we have only a small amount of information, derived from a very few bas-reliefs. These unite in representing the bull as the special sacrificial animal. In one we simply see a bull brought up to a temple by the king; but in another, which is more elaborate, we seem to have the whole of a sacrificial scene fairly, if not exactly, brought before us. [PLATE CXLIV., Fig. 1.] Towards the front of the temple, where the god, recognizable by his horned cap, appears seated upon a throne, with an attendant priest, who is beardless, paying adoration to him, advances a procession consisting of the king and six priests, one of whom carries a cup, while the other five are employed about the animal. The king pours a libation over a large bowl, fixed in a stand, immediately in front of a tall fire-altar, from which flames are rising. Close behind this stands the priest with a cup, from which we may suppose that the monarch will pour a second libation. Next we observe a bearded priest directly in front of the bull, checking the advance of the animal, which is not to be offered till the libation is over. The bull is also held by a pair of priests, who walk behind him and restrain him with a rope attached to one of his fore-legs a little above the hoof. Another pair of priests, following closely on the footsteps of the first pair, completes the procession: the four seem, from the position of their heads and arms, to be engaged in a solemn chant. It is probable, from the flame upon the altar, that there is to be some burning of the sacrifice; while it is evident, from the altar being of such a small size, that only certain parts of the animal can be consumed upon it. We may conclude therefore that the Assyrian sacrifices resembled those of the classical nations, consisting not of whole burnt offerings, but of a selection of choice parts, regarded as specially pleasing to the gods, which were placed upon the altar and burnt, while the remainder of the victim was consumed by priest or people.

Assyrian altars were of various shapes and sizes. One type was square, and of no great height; it had its top ornamented with gradines, below which the sides were either plain or fluted. Another which was also of moderate height, was triangular, but with a circular top, consisting of a single flat stone, perfectly plain, except that it was sometimes inscribed round the edge. [PLATE CXLIII. Fig. 2.] A third type is that represented in the sacrificial scene. [PLATE CXLIV.] This is a sort of portable stand— narrow, but of considerable height, reaching nearly to a man's chin. Altars of this kind seem to have been carried about by the Assyrians in their expeditions: we see them occasionally in the entrenched camps, and observe priests officiating at them in their dress of office. [PLATE CXLIII., Fig. 3.]

Besides their sacrifices of animals, the Assyrian kings were accustomed to deposit in the temples of their gods, as thank-offerings, many precious products from the countries which they overran in their expeditions. Stones and marbles of various kinds, rare metals, and images of foreign deities, are particularly mentioned; but it would seem to be most probable that some portion of all the more valuable articles was thus dedicated. Silver and gold were certainly used largely in the adornment of the temples, which are sometimes said to have been made "as splendid as the sun," by reason of the profuse employment upon them of these precious metals.

It is difficult to determine how the ordinary worship of the gods was conducted. The sculptures are for the most part monuments erected by kings; and when these have a religious character, they represent the performance by the kings of their own religious duties, from which little can be concluded as to the religious observances of the people. The kings seem to have united the priestly with the regal character; and in the religious scenes representing their acts of worship, no priest ever intervenes between them and the god, or appears to assume any but a very subordinate position. The king himself stands and worships in close proximity to the holy tree; with his own hand he pours libations; and it is not unlikely that he was entitled with his own arm to sacrifice victims.

But we can scarcely suppose that the people had these privileges. Sacerdotal ideas have prevailed in almost all Oriental monarchies, and it is notorious that they had a strong hold upon the neighboring and nearly connected kingdom of Babylon. The Assyrians generally, it is probable, approached the gods through their priests; and it would seem to be these priests who are represented upon the cylinders as introducing worshippers to the gods, dressed themselves in long robes, and with a curious mitre upon their heads. The worshipper seldom comes empty-handed. He carries commonly in his arms an antelope or young goat, which we may presume to be an offering intended to propitiate the deity. [PLATE CXLIV., Fig. 2.]

It is remarkable that the priests in the sculptures are generally, if not invariably, beardless. It is scarcely probable that they were eunuchs, since mutilation is in the East always regarded as a species of degradation. Perhaps they merely shaved the beard for greater cleanliness, like the priests of the Egyptians and possibly it was a custom only obligatory on the upper grades of the priesthood.

We have no evidence of the establishment of set festivals in Assyria. Apparently the monarchs decided, of their own will, when a feast should be held to any god; and, proclamation being made, the feast was held accordingly. Vast numbers, especially of the chief men, were assembled on such occasions; numerous sacrifices were offered, and the festivities lasted for several days. A considerable proportion of the worshippers were accommodated in the royal palace, to which the temple was ordinarily a mere adjunct, being fed at the king's cost, and lodged in the halls and other apartments.

The Assyrians made occasionally a religious use of fasting. The evidence on this point is confined to the Book of Jonah, which, however, distinctly shows both the fact and the nature of the usage. When a fast was proclaimed, the king, the nobles, and the people exchanged their ordinary apparel for sackcloth, sprinkled ashes upon their heads, and abstained alike from food and drink until the fast was over. The animals also that were within the walls of the city where the fast was commanded, had sackcloth placed upon them; and the same abstinence was enforced upon them as was enjoined on the inhabitants. Ordinary business was suspended, and the whole population united in prayer to Asshur, the supreme god, whose pardon they entreated, and whose favor they sought to propitiate. These proceedings were not merely formal. On the occasion mentioned in the book of Jonah, the repentance of the Ninevites seems to have been sincere. "God saw their works, that they turned from their evil way; and God repented of the evil that he had said that he would do unto them: and he did it not."

The religious sentiment appears, on the whole, to have been strong and deep-seated among the Assyrians. Although religion had not the prominence in Assyria which it possessed in Egypt, or even in Greece—although the temple was subordinated to the palace, and the most imposing of the representations of the gods were degraded to mere architectural ornaments—yet the Assyrians appear to have been really, nay, even earnestly, religious. Their religion, it must be admitted, was of a sensuous character. They not only practised image-worship, but believed in the actual power of the idols to give protection or work mischief; nor could they rise to the conception of a purely spiritual and immaterial deity. Their ordinary worship was less one of prayer than one by means of sacrifices and offerings. They could, however, we know, in the time of trouble, utter sincere prayers; and we are bound therefore to credit them with an honest purpose in respect of the many solemn addresses and invocations which occur both in their public and their private documents. The numerous mythological tablets testify to the large amount of attention which was paid to religious subjects by the learned; while the general character of their names, and the practice of inscribing sacred figures and emblems upon their signets, which was almost universal, seem to indicate a spirit of piety on the part of the mass of the people.

The sensuous cast of the religion naturally led to a pompous ceremonial, a fondness for processional display, and the use of magnificent vestments. These last are represented with great minuteness in the Nimrud sculptures. The dresses of those engaged in sacred functions seem to have been elaborately embroidered, for the most part with religious figures and emblems, such as the winged circle, the pine-cone, the pomegranate, the sacred tree, the human-headed lion, and the like. Armlets, bracelets, necklaces, and earrings were worn by the officiating priests, whose heads were either encircled with a richly-ornamented fillet, or covered with a mitre or high cap of imposing appearance. Musicians had a place in the processions, and accompanied the religious ceremonies with playing or chanting, or, in some instances, possibly with both.

It is remarkable that the religious emblems of the Assyrian are almost always free from that character of grossness which in the classical works of art, so often offends modern delicacy. The sculptured remains present us with no representations at all parallel to the phallic emblems of the Greeks. Still we are perhaps not entitled to conclude, from this comparative purity, that the Assyrian religion was really exempt from that worst feature of idolatrous systems—a licensed religious sensualism. According to Herodotus the Babylonian worship of Beltis was disgraced by a practice which even he, heathen as he was, regarded as "most shameful." Women were required once in their lives to repair to the temple of this goddess, and there offer themselves to the embrace of the first man who desired their company. In the Apocryphal Book of Baruch we find a clear allusion to the same custom, so that there can be little doubt of its having really obtained in Babylonia; but if so, it would seem to follow, almost as a matter of course, that the worship of the same identical goddess in the an joining country included a similar usage. It may be to this practice that the prophet Nahum alludes, where he denounces Nineveh as a "well-favored harlot," the multitude of whose harlotries was notorious.

Such then was the general character of the Assyrian religion. We have no means of determining whether the cosmogony of the Chaldaeans formed any part of the Assyrian system, or was confined to the lower country. No ancient writer tells us anything of the Assyrian notions on this subject, nor has the decipherment of the monuments thrown as yet any light upon it. It would be idle therefore to prolong the present chapter by speculating upon a matter concerning which we have at present no authentic data.

CHAPTER IX

CHRONOLOGY AND HISTORY

The chronology of the Assyrian kingdom has long exercised, and divided, the judgments of the learned. On the one hand, Ctesias and his numerous followers—including, among the ancients, Cephalion, Castor, Diodorus Siculus, Nicolas of Damascus, Trogus Pompeius, Velleius Paterculus, Josephus, Eusebius, and Moses of Chorene; among the moderns, Freret, Rollin, and Clinton have given the kingdom a duration of between thirteen and fourteen hundred years, and carried hack its antiquity to a time almost coeval with the founding of Babylon; on the other, Herodotus, Volney, lleeren, B. G. Niebuhr, Brandis, and many others, have preferred a chronology which limits the duration of the kingdom to about six centuries and a half, and places the commencement in the thirteenth century B.C. when a flourishing empire had already existed in Chaldaea, or Babylonia, for a thousand years, or more. The questions thus mooted remain still, despite of the volumes which have been written upon them, so far undecided, that it will be necessary to entertain and discuss theirs at some length in this place, before entering on the historical sketch which is needed to complete our account of the Second Monarchy.

The duration of a single unbroken empire continuously for 1306 (or 1360) years, which is the time assigned to the Assyrian Monarchy by Ctesias, must be admitted to be a thing hard of belief, if not actually incredible. The Roman State, with all its elements of strength, had (we are told), as kingdom, commonwealth, and empire, a duration of no more than twelve centuries. The Chaldaean Monarchy lasted, as we have seen, about a thousand years, from the time of the Elamite conquest. The duration of the Parthian was about five centuries of the first Persian, less than two and a half; of the Median, at the utmost, one and a half; of the later Babylonian, less than one. The only monarchy existing under conditions at all similar to Assyria, whereto an equally long—or rather a still longer—duration has been assigned with some show of reason, is Egypt. But there it is admitted that the continuity was interrupted by the long foreign domination of the Hyksos, and by at least one other foreign conquest—that of the Ethiopian Sabacos or Shebeks. According to Ctesias, one and the same dynasty occupied the Assyrian throne during the whole period, of thirteen hundred years. Sardanapalus, the last king in his list, being the descendant and legitimate successor of Ninus.

There can be no doubt that a monarchy lasting about six centuries and a half, and ruled by at least two or three different dynasties, is per se a thing far more probable than one ruled by one and the same dynasty for more than thirteen centuries. And therefore, if the historical evidence in the two cases is at all equal—or rather, if that which supports the more improbable account does not greatly preponderate—we ought to give credence to the more moderate and probable of the two statements.

Now, putting aside authors who merely re-echo the statements of others, there seem to be, in the present case, two and two only distinct original authorities—Herodotus and Ctesias. Of these two, Herodotus is the earlier. He writes within two centuries of the termination of the Assyrian rule, whereas Ctesias writes at least thirty years later. He is of unimpeachable honesty, and may be thoroughly trusted to have reported only what he had heard. He had travelled in the East, and had done his best to obtain accurate information upon Oriental matters, consulting on the subject, among others, the Chaldaeans of Babylon. He had, moreover, taken special pains to inform himself upon all that related to Assyria, which he designed to make the subject of an elaborate work distinct from his general history.

Ctesias, like Herodotus, had had the advantage of visiting the East. It may be argued that he possessed even better opportunities than the earlier writer for becoming acquainted with the views which the Orientals entertained of their own past. Herodotus probably devoted but a few months, or at most a year or two, to his Oriental travels; Ctesias passed seventeen years at the Court of Persia. Herodotus was merely an ordinary traveller, and had no peculiar facilities for acquiring information in the East; Ctesias was court-physician to Artaxerxes Mnemon, and was thus likely to gain access to any archives which the Persian kings might have in their keeping. But these advantages seem to have been more than neutralized by the temper and spirit of the man. He commenced his work with the broad assertion that Herodotus was "a liar," and was therefore bound to differ from him when he treated of the same periods or nations. He does differ from him, and also from Thucydides, whenever they handle the same transactions; but in scarcely a single instance where he differs from either writer does his narrative seem to be worthy of credit. The cuneiform monuments, while they generally confirm Herodotus, contradict Ctesias perpetually. He is at variance with Manetho on Egyptian, with Ptolemy on Babylonian, chronology. No independent writer confirms him on any important point. His Oriental history is quite incompatible with the narrative of Scripture. On every ground, the judgment of Aristotle, of Plutarch, of Arrian, of Scaliger, and of almost all the best critics of modern times, with respect to the credibility of Ctesias, is to be maintained, and his authority is to be regarded as of the very slightest value in determining any controverted matter.

The chronology of Herodotus, which is on all accounts to be preferred, assigns the commencement of the Assyrian Empire to about B.C. 1250, or a little earlier, and gives the monarchy a duration of nearly 650 years from that time. The Assyrians, according to him, held the undisputed supremacy of Western Asia for 520 years, or from about B.C. 1250 to about B.C. 730—after which they maintained themselves in an independent but less exalted position for about 130 years longer, till nearly the close of the seventh century before our era. These dates are not indeed to be accepted without reserve; but they are approximate to the truth, and are, at any rate, greatly preferable to those of Ctesias.

The chronology of Berosus was, apparently, not very different from that of Herodotus. There can be no reasonable doubt that his sixth Babylonian dynasty represents the line of kings which ruled in Babylon during the period known as that of the Old Empire in Assyria. Now this line, which was Semitic, appears to have been placed upon the throne by the Assyrians, and to have been among the first results of that conquering energy which the Assyrians at this time began to develop. Its commencement should therefore synchronize with the foundation of an Assyrian Empire. The views of Berosus on this latter subject may be gathered from what he says of the former. Now the scheme of Berosus gave as the date of the establishment of this dynasty about the year B.C. 1300; and as Berosus undoubtedly placed the fall of the Assyrian Empire in B.C. 625, it may be concluded, and with a near approach to certainty, that he would have assigned the Empire a duration of about 675 years, making it commence with the beginning of the thirteenth century before our era, and terminate midway in the latter half of the seventh.

If this be a true account of the ideas of Berosus, his scheme of Assyrian chronology would have differed only slightly from that of Herodotus; as will be seen if we place the two schemes side by side.

ASSYRIAN CHRONOLOGY.

ACCORDING TO HERODOTUS.		ACCORDING TO BEROSUS.	
	ab. B.C. ab. B.C.		ab. B.C. ab. B.C.
Great Empire, lasting 520 yrs.	1250 to 730	Assyrian Dynasty of 45 kings in Babylon (526 years)	1301 to 775
Revolt of Medes	730	Reign of Pul (about 28 years)	775 to 747
Curtailed Kingdom, lasting 130 years.	730 to 600	Assyrian kings from Pul to Saracus (122 years)	747 to 625
Destruction of Nineveh	600	Destruction of Nineveh	625

In the case of a history so ancient as that of Assyria, we might well be content if our chronology were vague merely to the extent of the variations here indicated. The parade of exact dates with reference to very early times is generally fallacious, unless it be understood as adopted simply for the sake of convenience. In the history of Assyria, however, we may make a nearer approach to exactness than in most others of the same antiquity, owing to the existence of two chronological documents of first-rate importance. One of these is the famous Canon of Ptolemy, which, though it is directly a Babylonian record, has important bearings on the chronology of Assyria. The other is an Assyrian Canon, discovered and edited by Sir H. Rawlinson in 1862, which gives the succession of the kings for 251 years, commencing (as is thought) B.C. 911 and terminating B. C. 660, eight years after the accession of the son and successor of Esarhaddon. These two documents, which harmonize admirably, carry up an exact Assyrian chronology almost from the close of the Empire to the tenth century before our era. For the period anterior to this we have, in the Assyrian records, one or two isolated dates, dates fixed in later times with more or less of exactness; and of these we might have been inclined to think little, but that they harmonize remarkably with the statements of Berosus and Herodotus, which place the commencement of the Empire about B.C. 1300, or a little later. We have, further, certain lists of kings, forming continuous lines of descent from father to son, by means of which we may fill up the blanks that would otherwise remain in our chronological scheme with approximate dates calculated from an estimate of generations. From these various sources the subjoined scheme has been composed, the sources being indicated at the side, and the fixed dates being carefully distinguished from those which are uncertain or approximate.

KINGS OF ASSYRIA.

B.C.	B.C.			
—	—	Bel-sumili-kapi * * * *	Called the founder of the kingdom on a genealogical tablet.	
—	—	Irba-vul. * * * *	Mentioned by Tiglath-Pileser I. as a former king. A very archaic tablet in the British Museum is dated in his reign.	
—	—	Asshur-iddin-akhi * * *	Mentioned by Tiglath-Pileser as a former king.	
Ab. 1440 to 1420		Asshur-bil-nisi-su	Mentioned on a synchronistic tablet, which connects them with the time of Purna-puriyas, the Chaldæan king. Asshur-upallit mentioned on Kileh-Sherghat bricks.	Early Kingdom.
— 1420 to 1400		Buzur-Asshur (successor)		
— 1400 to 1380		Asshur-upallit (successor)		
— 1380 to 1360		Bel-lush (his son)	Names and succession found on Kileh-Sherghat bricks, vases, etc. Shalmaneser mentioned also on a genealogical slab and in the standard inscription of Nimrud.	
— 1360 to 1340		Pud-il (his son)		
— 1340 to 1320		Vul-lush I. (his son)		
— 1320 to 1300		Shalmaneser I. (his son)		
— 1300 to 1280		Tiglathi-Nin (his son) * * * *	Mentioned on a genealogical tablet. Called "the conqueror of Babylon," and placed by Sennacherib 600 yrs. before his own capture of Babylon in B.C. 703.	
— 1230 to 1210		Bel-kudur-uzur	Mentioned on the synchronistic tablet as the predecessor of Nin-pala-zira.	
— 1210 to 1190		Nin-pala-zira (successor)	Names and relationship given in cylinder of Tiglath-Pileser I. Mentioned on the synchronistic tablet above spoken of. Date of Tiglath-Pileser I. fixed by the Bavian inscription. Dates of the other kings calculated from his at 20 years to a generation.	Great Empire of Herodotus. 526 years of Berosus.
— 1190 to 1170		Asshur-dayan I. (his son)		
— 1170 to 1150		Mutaggil-Nebo (his son)		
— 1150 to 1130		Asshur-ris-ilim (his son)		
— 1130 to 1110		Tiglath-Pileser I (his son)		
— 1110 to 1090		Asshur-bil-kala (his son)		
— 1090 to 1070		Shamas-Vul I (his brother) * * * *		
		Asshur-mazur * * * *	Mentioned in an inscription of Shalmaneser II.	
— 930 to 911		Asshur-dayan II.	The kings from Asshur-dayan II. to Vul-lush III. are proved to have been in direct succession by the Kileh-Sherghat and Nimrud monuments. The last nine reigns are given in the Assyrian Canon. The Canon is the sole authority for the last three. The dates of the whole series are determined from the Canon of Ptolemy by calculating back from B.C. 680, his date for the accession of Esar-haddon (Asaridanus). They might also be fixed from the year of the great eclipse.	
911 to 889		Vul-lush II. (his son)		
889 to 883		Tiglathi-Nin II. (his son)		
883 to 858		Asshur-izir-pal (his son)		
858 to 823		Shalmaneser II. (his son)		
823 to 810		Shamas-Vul II. (his son)		
810 to 781		Vul-lush III. (his son)		
781 to 771		Shalmaneser III.		
771 to 753		Asshur-dayan III.		
753 to 745		Asshur-lush		
745 to 727		Tiglath-Pileser II.	The years of these kings, from Esar-haddon upwards, are taken from the Assyrian Canon. The dates accord strictly with the Canon of Ptolemy. The last year of Asshur-bani-pal is to some extent conjectural.	Later Kingdom of Herodotus and Berosus.
727 to 722		Shalmaneser IV.		
722 to 705		Sargon		
705 to 681		Sennacherib (his son)		
681 to 668		Esar-haddon (his son)		
668 to 626(?)		Asshur-bani-pal (his son)		
626(?) to 625		Asshur-emid-ilin		

It will be observed that in this list the chronology of Assyria is carried back to a period nearly a century and a half anterior to B.C. 1300, the approximate date, according to Herodotus and Berosus, of the establishment of the "Empire." It might have been concluded, from the mere statement of Herodotus, that Assyria existed before the time of which he spoke, since an empire can only be formed by a people already flourishing. Assyria as an independent kingdom is the natural antecedent of Assyria as an Imperial power: and this earlier phase of her existence might reasonably have been presumed from the later. The monuments furnish distinct evidence of the time in question in the fourth, fifth, and sixth kings of the above list, who reigned while the Chaldaean empire was still flourishing in Lower Mesopotamia. Chronological and other considerations induce a belief that the four kings who follow like-wise belonged to it; and that, the "Empire" commenced with Tiglathi-Nin I., who is the first great conqueror.

The date assigned to the accession of this king, B.C. 1300, which accords so nearly with Berosus's date for the commencement of his 526 years, is obtained from the monuments in the following manner. First, Sennacherib, in an inscription set up in or about his tenth year (which was B.C. 694), states that he recovered from Babylon certain images of gods, which had been carried thither by Meroclach-idbin-akhi, king of Babylon, who had obtained them in his war with Tiglath-Pileser, king of Assyria, 418 years previously. This gives for the date of the war with Tiglath-Pileser the year B.C. 1112. As that monarch does not mention the Babylonian war in the annals which relate the events of his early years, we must suppose his defeat to have taken place towards the close of his reign, and assign him the space from B.C. 1130 to B.C. 1110, as, approximately, that during which he is likely to have held the throne. Allowing then to the six monumental kings who preceded Tiglath-Pileser average reigns of twenty years each, which is the actual average furnished by the lines of direct descent in Assyria, where the length of each reign is known, and allowing fifty years for the break between Tiglathi-Nin and Bel-kudur-uzur, we are brought to (1130 + 120 + 50) B.C. 1300 for the accession of the first Tiglathi-Nin, who took Babylon, and is the first king of whom extensive conquests are recorded. Secondly. Sennacherib in another inscription reckons 600 years from his first conquest of Babylon (B.C. 703) to a year in the reign of this monarch. This "six hundred" may be used as a round number; but as Sennacherib considered that he had the means of calculating exactly, he would probably not have used a round number, unless it was tolerably near to the truth. Six hundred years before B.C. 703 brings us to B.C. 1303.

The chief uncertainty which attaches to the numbers in this part of the list arises from the fact that the nine kings from Tiglathi-Nin downwards do not form a single direct line. The inscriptions fail to connect Bel-kudur-uzur with Tiglathi-Nin, and there is thus a probable interval between the two reigns, the length of which can only be conjectured.

The dates assigned to the later kings, from Vul-lush II., to Esarhaddon inclusive, are derived from the Assyrian Canon taken in combination with the famous Canon of Ptolemy. The agreement between these documents, and between the latter and the Assyrian records generally, is exact; and a conformation is thus afforded to Ptolemy which is of no small importance. The dates from the accession of Vul-lush II. (B.C. 911) to the death of Esarhaddon (B.C. 668) would seem to have the same degree of accuracy and certainty which has been generally admitted to attach to the numbers of Ptolemy. They have been confirmed by the notice of a great eclipse in the eighth year of Asshur-dayan III., which is undoubtedly that of June 15, B.C. 763.

The reign of Asshur-bani-pal (Sardanapalus), the son and successor of Esarhaddon, which commenced B.C. 668, is carried down to B.C. 626 on the combined authority of Berosus, Ptolemy, and the monuments. The monuments show that Asshur-bani-pal proclaimed himself king of Babylon after the death of Saul-mugina whose last year was (according to Ptolemy) B.C. 647: and that from the date of this proclamation he reigned over Babylon at least twenty years. Polyhistor, who reports Berosus, has left us statements which are in close accordance, and from which we gather that the exact length of the reign of Asshur-bani-pal over Babylon was twenty-one years. Hence, B.C. 626 is obtained as the year of his death. As Nineveh appears to have been destroyed B.C. 625 or 624, two years only are left for Asshur-bani-pal's son and successor, Asshur-emid-illin, the Saracus of Abydenus.

The framework of Assyrian chronology being thus approximately, and, to some extent, provisionally settled, we may proceed to arrange upon it the facts so far as they have come down to us, of Assyrian history.

In the first place, then, if we ask ourselves where the Assyrians came from, and at what time they settled in the country which thenceforth bore their name, we seem to have an answer, at any rate to the former of these two questions, in Scripture. "Out of that land"—the land of Shinar—"went forth Asshur, and builded Nineveh." The Assyrians, previously to their settlement on the middle Tigris, had dwelt in the lower part of the great valley—the flat alluvial plain towards the mouths of the two streams. It was here, in this productive region, where nature does so much for man, and so little needs to be supplied by himself, that they had grown from a family into a people; that they had learnt or developed a religion, and that they had acquired a knowledge of the most useful and necessary of the arts. It has been observed in a former chapter that the whole character of the Assyrian architecture is such as to indicate that their style was formed in the low flat alluvium, where there were no natural elevations, and stone was not to be had. It has also been remarked that their writing is manifestly derived from the Chaldaean; and that their religion is almost identical with that which prevailed in the lower country from a very early time. The evidence of the monuments accords thus, in the most striking way, with the statement of the Bible, exhibiting to us the Assyrians as a people who had once dwelt to the south, in close contact with the Chaldaeans, and had removed after awhile to a more northern position.

With regard to the date of their removal, we can only say that it was certainly anterior to the time of the Chaldaean kings, Purna-puriyas and Kurri-galzu, who seem to have reigned in the fifteenth century before our era. If we could be sure that the city called in later times Asshur bore that name when Shamas-Vul, the son of Ismi-Dagon, erected a temple there to Anu and Vul, we might assign to the movement a still higher antiquity for Shamas-Vul belongs to the nineteenth century B.C. As, however, we have no direct evidence that either the city or the country was known as Asshur until four centuries later, we must be content to lay it down that the Assyrians had moved to the north certainly as early as B.C. 1440, and that their removal may not improbably have taken place several centuries earlier.

The motive of the removal is shrouded in complete obscurity. It may have been a forced colonization, commanded and carried out by the Chaldaean kings, who may have originated a system of transplanting to distant regions subject tribes of doubtful fidelity; or it may have been the voluntary self-expatriation of an increasing race, pressed for room and discontented with its condition. Again, it may have taken place by a single great movement, like that of the Tartar tribes, who transferred their allegiance from Russia to China in the reign of the Empress Catherine, and emigrated in a body from the banks of the Dun to the eastern limits of Mongolia or it may have been a gradual and protracted change, covering a long term of years, like most of the migrations whereof we read in history. On the whole, there is perhaps some reason to believe that a spirit of enterprise about this time possessed the Semitic inhabitants of Lower Mesopotamia, who voluntarily proceeded northwards in the hope of bettering their condition. Terah conducted one body from Ur to Harran: another removed itself from the shores of the Persian Gulf to those of the Mediterranean; while probably a third, larger than either of these two, ascended the course of the

Tigris, occupied Adiabene, with the adjacent regions, and, giving its own tribal name of Asshur to its chief city and territory, became known to its neighbors first as a distinct, and then as an independent and powerful people.

The Assyrians for some time after their change of abode were probably governed by Babylonian rulers, who held their office under the Chaldaean Emperor. Bricks of a Babylonian character have been found at Kileh-Sherghat, the original Assyrian capital, which are thought to be of greater antiquity than any of the purely Assyrian remains, and which may have been stamped by these provincial governors. Ere long, however, the yoke was thrown off, and the Assyrians established a separate monarchy of their own in the upper country, while the Chaldaean Empire was still flourishing under native monarchs of the old ethnic type in the regions nearer to the sea. The special evidence which we possess of the co-existence side by side of these two kingdoms is furnished by a broken tablet of a considerably later date, which seems to have contained, when complete, a brief but continuous sketch of the synchronous history of Babylonia and Assyria, and of the various transactions in which the monarchs of the two countries had been engaged one with another, from the most ancient times. This tablet has preserved to its the names of three very early Assyrian kings—Asshur-bil-nisi-su, Buzur Asshur, and Asshur-upallit, of whom the two former are recorded to have made treaties of peace with the contemporary kings of Babylon; while the last-named intervened in the domestic affair's of the country, depriving an usurping monarch of the throne, and restoring it to the legitimate claimant, who was his own relation. Intermarriages, it appears, took place at this early date between the royal families of Assyria and Chaldaea; and Asshur-upallit, the third of the three kings, had united one of his daughters to Purna-puriyas, a Chaldaean monarch who has received notice in the preceding volume. On the death of Purna-puriyas, Kara-khar-das, the issue of this marriage, ascended the throne; but he had not reigned long before his subjects rebelled against his authority. A struggle ensued, in which he was slain, whereupon a certain Nazi-bugas, an usurper, became king, the line of Purna-puriyas being set aside. Asshur-upallit, upon this, interposed. Marching an army into Babylonia, he defeated and slew the usurper, after which he placed on the throne another son of Purna-puriyas, the Kurri-galzu already mentioned in the account of the king's of Chaldaea.

What is most remarkable in the glimpse of history which this tablet opens to us is the power of Assyria, and the apparent terms of equality on which she stands with her neighbor. Not only does she treat as an equal with the great Southern Empire—not only is her royal house deemed worthy of furnishing wives to its princes but when dynastic troubles arise there, she exercises a predominant influence over the fortunes of the contending parties, and secures victory to the side whose cause she espouses. Jealous as all nations are of foreign inter-position in their affairs, we may be sure that Babylonia would not have succumbed on this occasion to Assyria's influence, had not her weight been such that, added to one side in a civil struggle, it produced a preponderance which defied resistance.

After this one short lift, the curtain again drops over the history of Assyria for a space of about sixty years, during which our records tell us nothing but the mere names of the king's. It appears from the bricks of Kileh-Sherghat that Asshur-upallit was succeeded upon the throne by his son, Bel-lush, or Behiklhus (Belochush), who was in his turn followed by his son, Pudil, his grandson. Vul-lush, and his great-grandson, Shahmaneser, the first of the name. Of Bel-lush, Pudil, and Vul-lush I., we know only that they raised or repaired important buildings in their city of Asshur (now Kileh-Sherghat), which in their time, and for some centuries later, was the capital of the monarchy.

This place was not very favorably situated, being on the right bank of the Tigris, which is a far less fertile region than the left, and not being naturally a place of any great strength. The Assyrian territory did not at this time, it is probable, extend very far to the north: at any rate, no need was as yet felt for a second city higher up the Tigris valley, much less for a transfer of the seat of government in that direction. Calah was certainly, and Nineveh probably, not yet built; but still the kingdom had obtained a name among the nations; the term Assyria was applied geographically to the whole valley of the middle Tigris; and a prophetic eye could see in the hitherto quiescent power the nation fated to send expeditions into Palestine, and to bear off its inhabitants into captivity.

Shahnaneser I. (ab. B.C. 1320) is chiefly known in Assyrian history as the founder of Calah (Nimrud), the second, apparently, of those great cities which the Assyrian monarchs delighted to build and embellish. This foundation would of itself be sufficient to imply the growth of Assyria in his time towards the north, and would also mark its full establishment as the dominant power on the left as well as the right bank of the Tigris. Calah was very advantageously situated in a region of great fertility and of much natural strength, being protected on one side by the Tigris, and on the other by the Shor-Derreh torrent, while the Greater Zab further defended it at the distance of a few miles on the south and south-east, and the Khazr or Ghazr-Su on the north east. Its settlement must have secured to the Assyrians the undisturbed possession of the fruitful and important district between the Tigris and the mountains, the Aturia or Assyria Proper of later times, which ultimately became the great metropolitan region in which almost all the chief towns were situated.

It is quite in accordance with this erection of a sort of second capital, further to the north than the old one, to find, as we do, by the inscriptions of Asshur-izir-pal, that Shalmaneser undertook expeditions against the tribes on the upper Tigris, and even founded cities in those parts, which he colonized with settlers brought from a distance. We do not know what the exact bounds of Assyria towards the north were before his time, but there can be no doubt that he advanced them; and he is thus entitled to the distinction of being the first known Assyrian conqueror.

With Tiglathi-Nin, the son and successor of Shalmaneser I., the spirit of conquest displayed itself in a more signal and striking manner. The probable date of this monarch has already been shown to synchronize closely with the time assigned by Berosus to the connnencement of his sixth Babylonian dynasty, and by Herodotus to the beginning of his Assyrian Empire. Now Tiglathi-Nin appears in the Inscriptions as the prince who first aspired to transfer to Assyria the supremacy hitherto exercised, or at any rate claimed, by Babylon. He made war upon the southern kingdom, and with such success that he felt himself entitled to claim its conquuest, and to inscribe upon his signet-seal the proud title of "Conqueror of Babylonia." This signet-seal, left by him (as is probable) at Babylon, and recovered about six hundred years later by Sennacherib, shows to us that he reigned for some time in person at the southern capital, where it would seem that he afterwards established an Assyrian dynasty—a branch perhaps of his own family. This is probably the exact event of which Berosus spoke as occurring 526 years before Phul or Pul, and which Herodotus regarded as marking the commencement of the Assyrian "Empire." We must not, however, suppose that Babylonia was from this time really subject continuously to the Court of Nineveh. The subjection may have been maintained for a little less than a century; but about that time we find evidence that the yoke of Assyria had been shaken off, and that the Babylonian monarchs, who have Semitic names, and are probably Assyrians by descent, had become hostile to the Ninevite kings, and were engaged in frequent wars with them. No real permanent subjection of the Lower country to the Upper was effected till the time of Sargon; and even under the Sargonid dynasty revolts were frequent; nor were the Babylonians reconciled to the Assyrian sway till Esarhaddon united the two Crowns in his own person, and reigned alternately at the two capitals. Still, it is probable that, from the time of Tiglathi-Nin, the Upper country was recognized as the superior of the two: it had shown its might by a conquest and the imposition of a dynasty—proofs of power which were far from counterbalanced by a few retaliatory raids adventured upon under favorable circumstances by the Babylonian princes. Its influence was therefore felt, even while its yoke was refused; and the Semitizing of the Chaldaeans, commenced under Tiglathi-Nin, continued during the whole time of Assyrian preponderance; no effectual Turanian reaction ever set in; the Babylonian rulers, whether submissive to Assyria or engaged in hostilities against her, have equally Semitic names; and it does not appear that any effort was at any time made to recover to the Turanian element of the population its early supremacy.

The line of direct descent, which has been traced in uninterrupted succession through eight monarchs, beginning with Asshur-bel-nisi-su, here terminates; and an interval occurs which can only be roughly estimated as probably not exceeding fifty years. Another consecutive series of eight kings follows, known to us chiefly through the famous Tiglath-Pileser cylinder (which gives the succession of five of them), but completed from the combined evidence of several other documents. These monarchs, it is probable, reigned from about B.C. 1230 to B C. 1070.

Bel-kudur-uzur, the first monarch of this second series, is known to us wholly through his unfortunate war with the contemporary king of Babylon. It seems that the Semitic line of kings, which the Assyrians had established in Babylon, was not content to remain very long in a subject position. In the time of Bel-kudur-uzur, Vul-baladan, the Babylonian vassal monarch, revolted; and a war followed between him and his Assyrian suzerain, which terminated in the defeat and death of the latter, who fell in a great battle, about B.C. 1210.

Nin-pala-zira succeeded. It is uncertain whether he was any relation to his predecessor, but clear that he avenged him. He is called "the king who organized the country of Assyria, and established the troops of Assyria in authority." It appears that shortly after his accession, Vul-baladan of Babylon, elated by his previous successes, made an expedition against the Assyrian capital, and a battle was fought under the walls of Asshur in which Nin-pala-zira was completely successful. The Babylonians fled, and left Assyria in peace during the remainder of the reign of this monarch.

Asshur-dayan, the third king of the series, had a long and prosperous reign. He made a successful inroad into Babylonia, and returned into his own land with a rich and valuable booty. He likewise took down the temple which Shamas-Vul, the son of Ismi-Dagon, had erected to the gods Asshur and Vul at Asshur, the Assyrian capital, because it was in a ruinous condition, and required to be destroyed or rebuilt. Asshur-dayan seems to have shrunk from the task of restoring so great a work, and therefore demolished the structure which was not rebuilt for the space of sixty years from its demolition. He was succeeded upon the throne by his son Mutaggil-Nebo.

Mutaggil-Nebo reigned probably from about B.C. 1170 to B.C. 1150. We are informed that "Asshur, the great Lord, aided him according to the wishes of his heart, and established him in strength in the government of Assyria." Perhaps these expressions allude to internal troubles at the commencement of his reign, over which he was so fortunate as to triumph. We have no further particulars of this monarch.

Asshur-ris-ilim, the fourth king of the series, the son and successor of Mutaggil-Nebo, whose reign may be placed between B.C. 1150 and B.C. 1130, is a monarch of greater pretensions than most of his predecessors. In his son's Inscription he is called "the powerful king, the subduer of rebellious countries, he who has reduced all the accursed." These expressions are so broad, that we must conclude from them, not merely that Asshur-ris-ilim, unlike the previous kings of the line, engaged in foreign wars, but that his expeditions had a great success, and paved the way for the extensive conquests of his son and successor, Tiglath-Pileser. Probably he turned his arms in various directions, like that monarch. Certainly he carried them south-wards into Babylonia, where, as we learn from the synchronistic tablet of Babylonian and Assyrian history, he was engaged for some time in a war with Nebuchadnezzar (Nabuk-udor-uzur), the first known king of that name. It has been conjectured that he likewise carried them into Southern Syria and Palestine, and that, in fact, he is the monarch designated in the book of Judges by the name of Chushan-ris-athaim, who is called "the king of Mesopotamia (Aram-Naharaim)," and is said to have exercised dominion over the Israelites for eight years. This identification, however, is too uncertain to be assumed without further proof. The probable date of Chushan-ris-athaim is some two (or three) centuries earlier; and his title, "king of Mesopotamia," is one which is not elsewhere applied to Assyrians monarchs.

A few details have come clown to us with respect to the Babylonian war of Asshur-ris-ilim. It appears that Nebuchadnezzar was the assailant. He began the war by a march up the Diyalch and an advance on Assyria along the outlying Zegros hills, the route afterwards taken by the great Persian road described by Herodotus. Asshur-ris-ilim went out to meet him in person, engaged him in the mountain region, and repulsed his attack. Upon this the Babylonian monarch retired, and after an interval; the duration of which is unknown, advanced a second time against Assyria, but took now the direct line across the plain. Asshur-ris-ilim on this occasion was content to employ a general against the invader. He "sent" his chariots and his soldiers towards his southern border, and was again successful, gaining a second victory over his antagonist, who fled away, leaving in his hands forty chariots and a banner.

Tiglath-Pileser I., who succeeded Asshur-ris-ilim about B.C. 1130, is the first Assyrian monarch of whose history we possess copious details which can be set forth at some length. This is owing to the preservation and recovery of a lengthy document belonging to his reign in which are recorded the events of his first five years. As this document is the chief evidence we possess of the condition of Assyria, the character and tone of thought of the king, and indeed of the general state of the Eastern world, at the period in question—which synchronizes certainly with some portion of the dominion of the Judges over Israel, and probably with the early conquests of the Dorians in Greece—it is thought advisable to give in this place such an account of it, and such a number of extracts as shall enable the reader to form his own judgment on these several points.

The document opens with an enumeration and glorification of the "great gods" who "rule over heaven and earth," and are "the guardians of the kingdom of Tiglath-Pileser." These are "Asshur, the great Lord, ruling supreme over the gods; Bel, the lord, father of the gods, lord of the world; Sin, the leader(?) the lord of empire(?); Shamus, the establisher of heaven and earth; Vul, he who causes the tempest to rage over hostile lands; Nin, the champion who subdues evil spirits and enemies; and Ishtar, the source of the gods, the queen of victory, she who arranges battles." These deities, who (it is declared) have placed Tiglath-Pileser upon the throne, have "made him firm, have confided to him the supreme crown, have appointed him in might to the sovereignty of the people of Bel, and have granted him preeminence, exaltation, and warlike power," are invoked to make the "duration of his empire continue forever to his royal posterity, lasting as the great temple of Kharris-Matira."

In the next section the king glorifies himself, enumerating his royal titles as follows: "Tiglath-Pileser, the powerful king, king of the people of various tongues; king of the four regions; king of all kings; lord of lords; the supreme (?); monarch of monarchs; the illustrious chief, who, under the auspices of the Sun-god, being armed with the sceptre and girt with the girdle of power over mankind, rules over all the people of Bel; the mighty prince, whose praise is blazoned forth among the kings; the exalted sovereign, whose servants Asshur has appointed to the government of the four regions, and whose name he has made celebrated to posterity; the conqueror of many plains and mountains of the Upper and Lower country; the victorious hero, the terror of whose mane has overwhelmed all regions; the bright constellation who, as he wished, has warred against foreign countries, and under the auspices of Bel—there being no equal to him—has subdued the enemies of Asshur."

The royal historian, after this introduction, proceeds to narrate his actions first in general terms declaring that he has subdued all the lands and the peoples round about, and then proceeding to particularize the various campaigns which he had conducted during the first five years of his reign. The earliest of these was against the Muskai, or Moschians, who are probably identical with the Meshech of Holy Scripture—a people governed (it is said) by five kings, and inhabiting the countries of Alzi and Purukhuz, parts (apparently) of Taurus or Niphates. These Moschians are said to have neglected for fifty years to pay the tribute due from them to the Assyrians, from which it would appear that they had revolted during the reign of Asshur-dayan, having previously been subject to Assyria. At this time, with a force amounting to 20,000 men, they had invaded the neighboring district of Qummukh (Commagene), an Assyrian dependency, and had made themselves masters of it. Tiglath-Pileser attacked them in this newly-conquered country, and completely defeated their army. He then reduced Commagene, despite the assistance which the inhabitants received from some of their neighbors. He burnt the cities, plundered the temples, ravaged the open country, and carried off, either in the shape of plunder or of tribute, vast quantities of cattle and treasure.

The character of the warfare is indicated by such a passage as the following:

"The country of Kasiyara, a difficult region, I passed through. With their 20,000 men and their five kings, in the country of Qummukh I engaged. I defeated them. The ranks of their warriors in fighting the battle were beaten down as if by the tempest. Their carcasses covered the valleys and the tops of the mountains, I cut off their heads. Of the battlements of their cities I made heaps, like mounds of earth (?). Their moveables, their wealth, and their valuables I plundered to a countless amount. Six thousand of their common soldiers, who fled before my servants, and accepted my yoke, I took and gave over to the men of my own territory as slaves."

The second campaign was partly in the same region and with the same people. The Moschians, who were still loth to pay tribute, were again attacked and reduced. Commagene was completely overrun, and the territory was attached to the Assyrian empire. The neighboring tribes were assailed in their fastnesses, their cities burnt, and their territories ravaged. At the same time war was made upon several other peoples or nations. Among these the most remarkable are the Khatti (Hittites), two of whose tribes, the Kaskiaits and Urumians, had committed an aggression on the Assyrian territory: for this they were chastised by an invasion which they did not venture to resist, by the plundering of their valuables, and the carrying off of 120 of their chariots. In another direction the Lower Zab was crossed, and the Assyrian arms were carried into the mountain region of Zagros, where certain strongholds were reduced and a good deal of treasure taken.

The third campaign was against the numerous tribes of the Nairi, who seem to have dwelt at this time partly to the east of the Euphrates, but partly also in the mountain country west of the stream from Smmeisat to the Gulf of Iskenderun. These tribes, it is said, had never previously made their submission to the Assyrians. They were governed by a number of petty chiefs or "kings," of whom no fewer than twenty-three are particularized. The tribes east of the Euphrates seem to have been reduced with little resistance, while those who dwelt west of the river, on the contrary, collected their troops together, gave battle to the invaders, and made a prolonged and desperate defence. All, however, was in vain. The Assyrian monarch gained a great victory, taking 120 chariots, and then pursued the vanquished Nairi and their allies as far as "the Upper Sea,"—i.e., the Mediterranean. The usual ravage and destruction followed, with the peculiarity that the lives of the "kings" were spared, and that the country was put to a moderate tribute, viz., 1200 horses and 200 head of cattle.

In the fourth campaign the Aramaeans or Syrians were attacked by the ambitious monarch. They occupied at this time the valley of the Euphrates, from the borders of the Tsukhi, or Shuhites, who held the river from about Anah to Hit, as high up as Carchemish, the frontier town and chief stronghold of the Khatti or Hittites. Carchemish was not, as has commonly been supposed, Circesium, at the junction of the Khabour with the Euphrates, but was considerably higher up the stream, certainly near to, perhaps on the very site of, the later city of Mabog or Hierapolis. Thus the Aramaeans had a territory of no great width, but 230 miles long between its north-western and its south-eastern extremities. Tiglath-Pileser smote this region, as he tells us, "at one blow." First attacking and plundering the eastern or left bank of the river, he then crossed the stream in boats covered with skins, took and burned six cities on the right bank, and returned in safety with an immense plunder.

The fifth and last campaign was against the country of Musr or Muzr, by which some Orientalists have understood Lower Egypt. This, however, appears to be a mistake. The Assyrian Inscriptions designate two countries by the name of Musr or Muzr, one of them being Egypt, and the other a portion of Upper Kurdistan. The expedition of Tiglath-Pileser I., was against the eastern Musr, a highly mountainous country, consisting (apparently) of the outlying ranges of Zagros between the greater Zab and the Eastern Khabour. Notwithstanding its natural strength and the resistance of the inhabitants, this country was completely overrun in an incredibly short space. The armies which defended it were defeated, the cities burnt, the strongholds taken. Arin, the capital, submitted, and was spared, after which a set tribute was imposed on the entire region, the amount of which is not mentioned. The Assyrian arms were then turned against a neighboring district, the country of the Comani. The Comani, though Assyrian subjects, had lent assistance to the people of Musr, and it was to punish this insolence that Tiglath-Pileser resolved to invade their territory. Having defeated their main army, consisting of 20,000 men, he proceeded to the attack of the various castles and towns, some of which were stormed, while others surrendered at discretion. In both eases alike the fortifications were broken down and destroyed, the cities which surrendered being spared, while those taken by storm were burnt with fire. Ere long the whole of the "far-spreading country of the Comani" was reduced to subjection, and a tribute was imposed exceeding that which had previously been required from the people.

After this account of the fifth campaign, the whole result of the wars is thus briefly summed up:— "There fell into my hands altogether, between the commencement of my reign and my fifth year, forty-two countries with their kings, from the banks of the river Zab to the banks of the river Euphrates, the country of the Rhatti, and the upper ocean of the setting sun. I brought them under one government; I took hostages from them; and I imposed on them tribute and offerings."

From describing his military achievements, the monarch turns to an account of his exploits in the chase. In the country of the Hittites he boasts that he had slain "four wild bulls, strong and fierce," with his arrows; while in the neighborhood of Harran, on the banks of the river Khabour, he had killed ten large wild buffaloes (?), and taken four alive. These captured animals he had carried with him on his return to Asshur, his capital city, together with the horns and skins of the slain beasts. The lions which he had destroyed in his various journeys he estimates at 920. All these successes he ascribes to the powerful protection of Nin and Nergal.

The royal historiographer proceeds, after this, to give an account of his domestic administration, of the buildings which he had erected, and the various improvements which he had introduced. Among the former he mentions temples to Ishtar. Martu, Bel, Il or Ra, and the presiding deities of the city of Asshur, palaces for his own use, and castles for the protection of his territory. Among the latter he enumerates the construction of works of irrigation, the introduction into Assyria of foreign cattle and of numerous beasts of chase, the naturalization of foreign vegetable products, the multiplication of chariots, the extension of the territory, and the augmentation of the population of the country.

A more particular account is then given of the restoration by the monarch of two very ancient and venerable temples in the great city of Asshur. This account is preceded by a formal statement of the particulars of the monarch's descent from Ninpala-zira, the king who seems to be regarded as the founder of the dynasty—which breaks the thread of the narrative somewhat strangely and awkwardly. Perhaps the occasion of its introduction was, in the mind of the writer, the necessary mention, in connection with one of the two temples, of Asshur-dayan, the great-grandfather of the monarch. It appears that in the reign of Asshur-dayan, this temple, which, having stood for 641 years, was in a very ruinous condition, had been taken down, while no fresh building had been raised in its room. The site remained vacant for sixty years, till Tiglath-Pileser, having lately ascended the throne, determined to erect on the spot a new temple to the old gods, who were Anu and Vul, probably the tutelary deities of the city. His own account of the circumstances of the building and dedication is as follows:—

"In the beginning of my reign, Anu and Vul, the great gods, my lords, guardians of my steps, gave me a command to repair this their shrine. So I made bricks; I levelled the earth; I took its dimensions (?); I laid down its foundations upon a mass of strong rock. This place, throughout its whole extent, I paved with bricks in set order (?); fifty feet deep I prepared the ground; and upon this substructure I laid the lower foundations of the temple of Anu and Vul. From its foundations to its roof I built it up better than it was before. I also built two lofty towers (?) in honor of their noble godships, and the holy place, a spacious hall, I consecrated for the convenience of their worshippers, and to accommodate their votaries, who were numerous as the stars of heaven. I repaired, and built, and completed my work. Outside the temple I fashioned everything with the same care as inside. The mound of earth on which it was built I enlarged like the firmament of the rising stars (?), and I beautified the entire building. Its towers I raised up to heaven, and its roofs I built entirely of brick. An inviolable shrine(?) for their noble godships I laid down near at hand. Anu and Vul, the great gods, I glorified inside the shrine. I set them up in their honored purity, and the hearts of their noble godships I delighted."

The other restoration mentioned is that of a temple to Vul only, which, like that to Anu and Vul conjointly, had been originally built by Shamas-Vul, the son of Ismi-Dagon. This building had likewise fallen into decay, but had not been taken down like the other. Tiglath-Pileser states that he "levelled its site," and then rebuilt it "from its foundations to its roofs." enlarging it beyond its former limits, and adorning it. Inside of it he "sacrificed precious victims to his lord, Vul." He also deposited in the temple a number of rare stones or marbles, which he had obtained in the country of the Nairi in the course of his expeditions.

The inscription then terminates with the following long invocation:—

"Since a holy place, a noble hall, I have thus consecrated for the use of the Great Gods, my lords Anu and Vul, and have laid down an adytum for their special worship, and have finished it successfully, and have delighted the hearts of their noble godships, may Anu and Vul preserve me in power! May they support the men of my government! May they establish the authority of my officers! May they bring the rain, the joy of the year, on the cultivated land and the desert, during my time! In war and in battle may they preserve me victorious! Many foreign countries, turbulent nations, and hostile kings I have reduced under my yoke! to my children and my descendants, may they keep them in firm allegiance! I will lead my steps" (or, "may they establish my feet"), "firm as the mountains, to the last days, before Asshur and their noble godships!

"The list of my victories and the catalogue of my triumphs over foreigners hostile to Asshur, which Anu and Vul have granted to my arms, I have inscribed on my tablets and cylinders, and I have placed, [to remain] to the last days, in the temple of my lords, Ann and Vul. And I have made clean (?) the tablets of Shamas-Vul, my ancestor; I have made sacrifices, and sacrificed victims before them, and have set them up in their places. In after times, and in the latter days..., if the temple of the Great Gods, my lords Anu and Vul, and these shrines should become old and fall into decay, may the Prince who comes after me repair the ruins! May he raise altars and sacrifice victims before my tablets and cylinders, and may he set them up again in their places, and may he inscribe his name on them together with my name! As Anu and Vul, the Great Gods, have ordained, may he worship honestly with a good heart and full trust!

"Whoever shall abrade or injure my tablets and cylinders, or shall moisten them with water, or scorch them with fire, or expose them to the air, or in the holy place of God shall assign them a place where they cannot be seen or understood, or shall erase the writing and inscribe his own name, or shall divide the sculptures (?) and break them off from my tablets, may Anu and Vul, the Great Gods, my lords, consign his name to perdition! May they curse him with an irrevocable curse! May they cause his sovereignty to perish! May they pluck out the stability of the throne of his empire! Let not his offspring survive him in the kingdom! Let his servants be broken! Let his troops be defeated! Let him fly vanquished before his enemies! May Vul in his fury tear up the produce of his land! May a scarcity of food and of the necessaries of life afflict his country! For one day may he not be called happy! May his name and his race perish!"

The document is then dated—"In the month Kuzalla (Chisleu), on the 29th day, in the year presided over by Inailiya-pallik, the Rabbi-Turi."

Perhaps the most striking feature of this inscription, when it is compared with other historical documents of the same kind belonging to other ages and nations, is its intensely religious character. The long and solemn invocation of the Great Gods with which it opens, the distinct ascription to their assistance and guardianship of the whole series of royal successes, whether in war or in the chase; the pervading idea that the wars were undertaken for the chastisement of the enemies of Asshur, and that their result was the establishment in an ever-widening circle of the worship of Asshur; the careful account which is given of the erection and renovation of temples, and the dedication of offerings; and the striking final prayer—all these are so many proofs of the prominent place which religion held in the thoughts of the king who set up the inscription, and may fairly be accepted as indications of the general tone and temper of his people. It is evident that we have here displayed to us, not a decent lip-service, not a conventional piety, but a real, hearty earnest religious faith—a faith bordering on fanaticism—a spirit akin to that with which the Jews were possessed in their warfare with the nations of Canaan, or which the soldiers of Mahomet breathed forth when they fleshed their maiden swords upon the infidels. The king glorifies himself much; but he glorifies the gods more. He fights, in part, for his own credit, and for the extension of his territory; but he fights also for the honor of the gods, whom the surrounding nations reject, and for the diffusion of their worship far and wide throughout all known regions. His wars are religious wars, at least as much as wars of conquest; his buildings, or, at any rate, those on whose construction he dwells with most complacency, are religious buildings; the whole tone of his mind is deeply and sincerely religious; besides formal acknowledgments, he is continually letting drop little expressions which show that his gods are "in all his thoughts," and represent to him real powers governing and directing all the various circumstances of human life. The religious spirit displayed is, as might have been expected, in the highest degree exclusive and intolerant; but it is earnest, constant, and all-pervading.

In the next place, we cannot fail to be struck with the energetic character of the monarch, so different from the temper which Ctesias ascribes, in the broadest and most sweeping terms, to all the successors of Ninus. Within the first five years of his reign the indefatigable prince conducts in person expeditions into almost every country upon his borders; attacks and reduces six important nations, besides numerous petty tribes; receiving the submission of forty-two kings; traversing the most difficult mountain regions; defeating armies, besieging towns, destroying forts and strongholds, ravaging territories; never allowing himself a moment of repose; when he is not engaged in military operations, devoting himself to the chase, contending with the wild bull and the lion, proving himself (like the first Mesopotamian king) in very deed "a mighty hunter," since he counts his victims by hundreds; and all the while having regard also to the material welfare of his country, adorning it with buildings, enriching it with the products of other lands, both animal and vegetable, fertilizing it by means of works of irrigation, and in every way "improving the condition of the people, and obtaining for them abundance and security."

With respect to the general condition of Assyria, it may be noted, in the first place, that the capital is still Asshur, and that no mention is made of any other native city. The king calls himself "king of the four regions," which would seem to imply a division of the territory into districts, like that which certainly obtained in later times. The mention of "four" districts is curious, since the same number was from the first affected by the Chaldaeans, while we have also evidence that, at least after the time of Sargon, there was a pre-eminence of four great cities in Assyria. The limits of the territory at the time of the Inscription are not very dearly marked; but they do not seem to extend beyond the outer ranges of Zagros on the east, Niphates on the north, and the Euphrates upon the west. The southern boundary at the time was probably the commencement of the alluvium; but this cannot be gathered from the Inscription, which contains no notice of any expedition in the direction of Babylonia. The internal condition of Assyria is evidently flourishing. Wealth flows in from the plunder of the neighboring countries; labor is cheapened by the introduction of enslaved captives; irrigation is cared for; new fruits and animals are introduced; fortifications are repaired, palaces renovated, and temples beautified or rebuilt.

The countries adjoining upon Assyria at the west, the north, and the east, in which are carried on the wars of the period, present indications of great political weakness. They are divided up among a vast number of peoples, nations, and tribes, whereof the most powerful is only able to bring into the field a force of 20,000 men. The peoples and nations possess but little unity. Each consists of various separate communities, ruled by their own kings, who in war unite their troops against the common enemy; but are so jealous of each other, that they do not seem even to appoint a generalissimo. On the Euphrates, between Hit and Carchemish, are, first, the Tsukhi or Shuhites, of whom no particulars are given; and, next, the Aramaeans or Syrians, who occupy both banks of the river, and possess a number of cities, no one of which is of much strength. Above the Aramaeans are the Khatti or Hittites, whose chief city, Carchemish, is an important place; they are divided into tribes, and, like the Aramaeans, occupy both banks of the great stream. North and north-west of their country, probably beyond the mountain-range of Amanus, are the Muskai (Moschi), an aggressive people, who were seeking to extend their territory eastward into the land of the Qummukh or people of Commagene. These Qummukh hold the mountain country on both sides of the Upper Tigris, and have a number of strongholds, chiefly on the right bank. To the east they adjoin on the Kirkhi, who must have inhabited the skirts of Niphates, while to the south they touch the Nairi, who stretch from Lake Van, along the line of the Tigris, to the tract known as Commagene to the Romans. The Nairi have, at the least, twenty-three kings, each of whom governs his own tribe or city. South of the more eastern Nairi is the country of Muzra mountain tract well peopled and full of castles, probably the region about Amadiyeh and Rowandiz. Adjoining Muzr to the east or north-east, are the Quwanu or Comani, who are among the most powerful of Assyria's neighbors, being able, like the Moschi, to bring into the field an army of 20,000 men. At this time they are close allies of the people of Muzr—finally, across the lower Zab, on the skirts of Zagros, are various petty tribes of small account, who offer but little resistance to the arms of the invader.

Such was the position of Assyria among her neighbors in the latter part of the twelfth century before Christ. She was a compact and powerful kingdom, centralized under a single monarch, and with a single great capital, in the midst of wild tribes which clung to a separate independence, each in its own valley or village. At the approach of a great danger, these tribes might consent to coalesce and to form alliances, or even confederations; but the federal tie, never one of much tenacity, and rarely capable of holding its ground in the presence of monarchic vigor, was here especially weak. After one defeat of their joint forces by the Assyrian troops, the confederates commonly dispersed, each flying to the defence of his own city or territory, with a short-sighted selfishness which deserved and ensured defeat. In one direction only was Assyria confronted by a rival state pomsessing a power and organization in character not unlike her own, though scarcely of equal strength. On her southern frontier, in the broad flat plain intervening between the Mesopotamian upland and the sea—the kingdom of Babylon was still existing; its Semitic kings, though originally established upon the throne by Assyrian influence, had dissolved all connection with their old protectors, and asserted their thorough independence. Here, then, was a considerable state, as much centralized as Assyria herself, and not greatly inferior either in extent of territory or in population, existing side by side with her, and constituting a species of check, whereby something like a balance of power was still maintained in Western Asia, and Assyria: was prevented from feeling herself the absolute mistress of the East, and the uncontrolled arbitress of the world's destinies.

Besides the great cylinder inscription of Tiglath-Pileser there exist five more years of his annals in fragments, from which we learn that he continued his aggressive expeditious during this space, chiefly towards the north west, subduing the Lulumi in Northern Syria, attacking and taking Carchemish, and pursuing the inhabitants across the Euphrates in boats.

No mention is made during this time of any collision between Assyria and her great rival. Babylon. The result of the wars waged by Asshur-ris-ilim against Nebuchadnezzar I., had, apparently, been to produce in the belligerents a feeling of mutual respect; and Tiglath-Pileser, in his earlier years, neither trespassed on the Babylonian territory in his aggressive raids, nor found himself called upon to meet and repel any invasion of his own dominions by his southern neighbors. Before the close of his reign, however, active hostilities broke out between the two powers. Either provoked by some border ravage or actuated simply by lust of conquest, Tiglath-Pileser marched his troops into Babylonia. For two consecutive years he wasted with fire and sword the "upper" or northern provinces, taking the cities of Kurri-Galzu—now Akkerkuf—Sippara of the Sun, and Sippara of Anunit (the Sepharvaim or "two Sipparas" of the Hebrews), and Hupa or Opis, on the Tigris; and finally capturing Babylon itself, which, strong as it was, proved unable to resist the invader. On his return be passed up the valley of the Euphrates, and took several cities from the Tsukhi. But here, it would seem that he suffered a reverse. Merodach-iddiu-akhi, his opponent, if he did not actually defeat his army, must, at any rate, have greatly harassed it on its retreat; for he captured an important part of its baggage. Indulging a superstition common in ancient times, Tiglath-Pileser had carried with him in his expedition certain images of gods, whose presence would, it was thought, secure victory to his arms. Merodach-iddiu akhi obtained possession of these idols, and succeeded in carrying them off to Babylon, where they were preserved for more than 400 years, and considered as mementoes of victory.

The latter days of this great Assyrian prince were thus, unhappily, clouded by disaster. Neither he, nor his descendants, nor any Assyrian monarch for four centuries succeeded in recovering the lost idols, and replacing them in the shrines from which they were taken. A hostile and jealous spirit appears henceforth in the relations between Assyria and Babylon; we find no more intermarriages of the one royal house with the other; wars are frequent—almost constant—nearly every Assyrian monarch, whose history is known to us in any detail, conducting at least one expedition into Babylonia.

A work still remains, belonging to the reign of this king, from which it appears that the peculiar character of Assyrian mimetic art was already fixed in his time, the style of representation being exactly such as prevailed at the most flourishing period, and the workmanship, apparently, not very inferior. In a cavern from which the Tsupnat river or eastern branch of the Tigris rises, close to a village called Korkhar, and about fifty or sixty miles north of Drarbekr, is a bas-relief sculptured on the natural rock, which has been smoothed for the purpose, consisting of a figure of the king in his sacerdotal dress with the right arm extended and the left hand grasping the sacrificial mace, accompanied by an inscription which is read as follows:—"By the grace of Asshur, Shamas, and Vul, the Great Gods, I., Tiglath-Pileser, king of Assyria, son of Asshurris-ilim, king of Assyria, who was the son of Mutaggil-Nebo, king of Assyria, marching from the great sea of Akhiri' (the Mediterranean) to the sea of Nairi" (Lake of Van) "for the third time have invaded the country of Nairi." [PLATE CXLIV Fig. 3.]

The fact of his having warred in Lower Mesopotamia is almost the whole that is known of Tiglath-Pileser's son and successor, Asshur-bil-kala. A contest in which he was engaged with the Babylonian prince, Merodach-shapik-ziri (who seems to have been the successor of Merodach-iddin-akhi), is recorded on the famous synchronistic tablet, in conjunction with the Babylonian wars of his father and grandfather; but the tablet is so injured in this place that no particulars can be gathered from it. From a monument of Asshur-bil-kala's own time—one of the earliest Assyrian sculptures that has cone down to us—we may perhaps further conclude that he inherited something of the religious spirit of his father, and gave a portion of his attention to the adornment of temples, and the setting up of images.

The probable date of the reign of Asshur-bil-kala is about B.C. 1110-1090. He appears to have been succeeded on the throne by his younger brother, Shamas-Vul, of whom nothing is known, but that he built, or repaired, a temple at Nineveh. His reign probably occupied the interval between B.. 1090 and 1070. He would thus seem to have been contemporary with Smendes in Egypt and with Samuel or Saul in Israel. So apparently insignificant an event as the establishment of a kingdom in Palestine was not likely to disturb the thoughts, even if it came to the knowledge, of an Assyrian monarch. Shamas-Vul would no doubt have regarded with utter contempt the petty sovereign of so small a territory as Palestine, and would have looked upon the new kingdom as scarcely more worthy of his notice than any other of the ten thousand little principalities which lay on or near his borders. Could he, however, have possessed for a few moments the prophetic foresight vouchsafed some centuries earlier to one who may almost be called his countryman, he would have been astonished to recognize in the humble kingdom just lifting its head in the far West, and struggling to hold its own against Philistine cruelty and oppression, a power which in little more than fifty years would stand forth before the world as the equal, if not the superior, of his own state. The imperial splendor of the kingdom of David and Solomon did, in fact, eclipse for awhile the more ancient glories of Assyria. It is a notable circumstance that, exactly at the time when a great and powerful monarchy grew up in the tract between Egypt and the Euphrates, Assyria passed under a cloud. The history of the country is almost a blank for two centuries between the reigns of Shamas-Vul and the second Tiglathi-Nin, whose accession is fixed by the Assyrian Canon to B.C. 889. During more than three-fourths of this time, from about B.C. 1070 to B.C. 930, the very names of the monarchs are almost wholly unknown to us. It seems as if there was not room in Western Asia for two first-class monarchies to exist and flourish at the same time; and so, although there was no contention, or even contact, between the two empires of Judaea and Assyria, yet the rise of the one to greatness could only take place under the condition of a coincident weakness of the other.

It is very remarkable that exactly in this interval of darkness, when Assyria would seem, from the failure both of buildings and records, to have been especially and exceptionally weak, occurs the first appearance of her having extended her influence beyond Syria into the great and ancient monarchy of Egypt. In the twenty-second Egyptian dynasty, which began with Sheshonk I., or Shishak, the contemporary of Solomon, about B.C. 900, Assyrian names appear for the first time in the Egyptian dynastic lists. It has been supposed from this circumstance that the entire twenty-second dynasty, together with that which succeeded it, was Assyrian; but the condition of Assyria at the time renders such a hypothesis most improbable. The true explanation would seem to be that the Egyptian kings of this period sometimes married. Assyrian wives, who naturally gave Assyrian names to some of their children. These wives were perhaps members of the Assyrian royal family; or perhaps they were the daughters of the Assyrian nobles who from time to time were appointed as viceroys of the towns and small states which the Ninevite monarchs conquered on the skirts of their empire. Either of these suppositions is more probable than the establishment in Egypt of a dynasty really Assyrian at a time of extraordinary weakness and depression.

When at the close of this long period of obscurity, Assyria once more comes into sight, we have at first only a dim and indistinct view of her through the mists which still enfold and shroud her form. We observe that her capital is still fixed at Kileh-Sherghat, where a new series of kings, bearing names which, for the most part, resemble those of the earlier period, are found employing themselves in the repair and enlargement of public buildings, in connection with which they obtain honorable mention in an inscription of a later monarch. Asshur-dayan, the first monarch of this group, probably ascended the throne about B.C. 930, shortly after the separation of the two kingdoms of Israel and Judah. He appears to have reigned from about B.C. 930 to B.C. 911. He was succeeded in B.C. 911 by his son Vul-lush II., who held the throne from B.C. 911 to B.C. 889. Nothing is known at present of the history of these two monarchs. No historical inscriptions belonging to their reigns have been recovered; no exploits are recorded of them in the inscriptions of later sovereigns. They stand up before us the mere "shadows of mighty names"—proofs of the, uncertainty of posthumous fame, which is almost as often the award of chance as the deserved recompense of superior merit.

Of Tiglathi-Nin, the second monarch of the name, and the third king of the group which we are considering, one important historical notice, contained in an inscription of his son, has come down to us. In the annals of the great Asshur-izirpal inscribed on the Nimrud monolith, that prince, while commemorating his war-like exploits, informs us that he set up his sculptures at the sources of the Tsupnat river alongside of sculptures previously set up by his ancestors Tiglath-Pileser and Tiglathi-Nin. That Tiglathi-Nin should have made so distant an expedition is the more remarkable from the brevity of his reign, which only lasted for six years. According to the Canon, he ascended the throne in the year B.C. 889; he was succeeded in B.C. 883 by his son Asshur-izir-pal.

With Asshur-izir-pal commences one of the most flourishing periods of the Empire. During the twenty-five years of his active and laborious reign. Assyria enlarged her bounds and increased her influence in almost every direction, while, at the same time, she advanced rapidly in wealth and in the arts; in the latter respect leaping suddenly to an eminence which (so far as we know) had not previously been reached by human genius. The size and magnificence of Asshur-izir-pal's buildings, the artistic excellence of their ornamentation, the pomp and splendor which they set before us as familiar to the king who raised them, the skill in various useful arts which they display or imply, have excited the admiration of Europe, which has seen with astonishment that many of its inventions were anticipated, and that its luxury was almost equalled, by an Asiatic people nine centuries before the Christian era. It will be our pleasing task at this point of the history, after briefly sketching Asshur-izir-pal's wars, to give such an account of the great works which he constructed as will convey to the reader at least a general idea of the civilization and refinement of the Assyrians at the period to which we are now come.

Asshur-izir-pal's first campaign was in north-western Kurdistan and in the adjoining parts of Armenia. It does not present any very remarkable features, though he claims to have penetrated to a region "never approached by the kings his fathers." His enemies are the Numi or Elami (i.e., the mountaineers) and the Kirkhi, who seem to have left their name in the modern Kurkh. Neither people appears to have been able to make much head against him: no battle was fought: the natives merely sought to defend their fortified places; but these were mostly taken and destroyed by the invader. One chief, who was made prisoner, received very barbarous treatment; he was carried to Arbela, and there flayed and hung up upon the town wall.

The second expedition of Asshur-izir-pal, which took place in the same year as his first, was directed against the regions to the west and north-west of Assyria. Traversing the country of Qummukh, and receiving its tribute, as well as that of Serki and Sidikan (Arban), he advanced against the Laki, who seem to have been at this time the chief people of Central Mesopotamia, extending from the vicinity of Hatra as far as, or even beyond, the middle Euphrates. Here the people of a city called Assura had rebelled, murdered their governor, and called in a foreigner to rule over them. Asshur-izir-pal marched hastily against the rebels, who submitted at his approach, delivering up to his mercy both their city and their new king. The latter he bound with fetters and carried with him to Nineveh; the former he treated with almost unexampled severity. Having first plundered the whole place, he gave up the houses of the chief men to his own officers, established an Assyrian governor in the palace, and then, selecting from the inhabitants the most guilty, he crucified some, burnt others, and punished the remainder by cutting off their ears or their noses. We can feel no surprise when we are informed that, while he was thus "arranging" these matters, the remaining kings of the Laki submissively sent in their tribute to the conqueror, paying it with apparent cheerfulness, though it was "a heavy and much increased burden."

In his third expedition, which was in his second year, Asshur-izir-pal turned his arms to the north, and marched towards the Upper Tigris, where he forced the kings of the Nairi, who had, it appears, regained their independence, to give in their submission, and appointed them an annual tribute in gold, silver, horses, cattle, and other commodities. It was in the course of this expedition that, having ascended to the sources of the Tsupnat river, or Eastern Tigris, Asshur-izir-pal set up his memorial side by side with monuments previously erected on the same site by Tiglath-Pileser and by the first or second Tiglathi-Nin.

Asshur-izir-pal's fourth campaign was towards the south-east. He crossed the Lesser Zab, and, entering the Zagros range, carried fire and sword through its fruitful valleys—pushing his arms further than any of his ancestors, capturing some scores of towns, and accepting or extorting tribute from a dozen petty kings. The furthest extent of his march was probably the district of Zohab across the Shirwan branch of the Diyaleh, to which he gives the name of Edisa. On his return he built, or rather rebuilt, a city, which a Babylonian king called Tsibir had destroyed at a remote period, and gave to his new foundation the name of Dur-Asshur, in grateful acknowledgment of the protection vouchsafed him by "the chief of the gods."

In his fifth campaign the warlike monarch once more directed his steps towards the north. Passing through the country of the Qummukh, and receiving their tribute, he proceeded to war in the eastern portion of the Mons Masius, where he took the cities of Matyat (now Mediyat) and Kapranisa. He then appears to have crossed the Tigris and warred on the flanks of Niphates, where his chief enemy was the people of Kasiyara. Returning thence, he entered the territory of the Nairi, where he declares that he overthrew and destroyed 250 strong walled cities, and put to death a considerable number of the princes.

The sixth campaign of Asshur-izir-pal was in a westerly direction. Starting from Calah or Nimrud, he crossed the Tigris, and, marching through the middle of Mesopotamia a little to the north of the Sinjar range, took tribute from a number of subject towns along the courses of the rivers Jerujer, Khabour, and Euphrates, among which the most important were Sidikan (now Arban), Sirki, and Anat (now Anah). From Anat, apparently his frontier-town in this direction, he invaded the country of the

Tsukhi (Shuhites), captured their city Tsur, and forced them, notwithstanding the assistance which they received from their neighbors the Babylonians, to surrender the themselves. He then entered Chaldaea, and chastised the Chaldaeans, after which he returned in triumph to his own country.

His seventh campaign was also against the Shuhites. Released from the immediate pressure of his arms, they had rebelled, and had even ventured to invade the Assyrian Empire. The Laki, whose territory adjoined that of the Shuhites towards the north and east, assisted them. The combined army, which the allies were able to bring into the field amounted probably to 20,000 men, including a large number of warriors who fought in chariots. Asshur-izir-pal first attacked the cities on the left bank of the Euphrates, which had felt his might on the former occasion; and, having reduced these and punished their rebellion with great severity, he crossed the river on rafts, and fought a battle with the main army of the enemy. In this engagement he was completely victorious, defeating the Tsukhi and their allies with great slaughter, and driving their routed forces headlong into the Euphrates, where great numbers perished by drowning. Six thousand five hundred of the rebels fell in the battle; and the entire country on the right bank of the river, which had escaped invasion in the former campaign, was ravaged furiously with fire and sword by the incensed monarch. The cities and castles were burnt, the males put to the sword, the women, children, and cattle carried off. Two kings of the Laki are mentioned, of whom one escaped, while the other was made prisoner, and conveyed to Assyria by the conqueror. A rate of tribute was then imposed on the land considerably in advance of that to which it had previously been liable. Besides this, to strengthen his hold on the country, the conqueror built two new cities, one on either bank of the Euphrates, naming the city on the left bank after himself, and that on the right bank after the god Asshur. Both of these places were no doubt left well garrisoned with Assyrian soldiers, on whom the conqueror could place entire reliance.

Asshur-izir-pal's eighth campaign was nearly in the same quarter; but its exact scene lay, apparently, somewhat higher up the Euphrates. Hazilu, the king of the Laki, who escaped capture in the preceding expedition, had owed his safety to the refuge given him by the people of Beth-Adina. Asshur-izir-pal, who seems to have regarded their conduct on this occasion as an insult to himself, and was resolved to punish their presumption, made his eighth expedition solely against this bold but weak people. Unable to meet his forces in the field, they shut themselves up in their chief city, Kabrabi (?), which was immediately besieged, and soon taken and burnt by the Assyrians. The country of Beth-Adina, which lay on the left or east bank of the Euphrates, in the vicinity of the modern Balis, was overrun and added to the empire. Two thousand five hundred prisoners were carried off and settled at Calah.

The most interesting of Asshur-izir-pal's campaigns is the ninth, which was against Syria. Marching across Upper-Mesopotamia, and receiving various tributes upon his way, the Assyrian monarch passed the Euphrates on rafts, and, entering the city of Carchemish, received the submission of Sangara, the Hittite prince, who ruled in that town, and of various other chiefs, "who came reverently and kissed his sceptre." He then "gave command" to advance towards Lebanon. Entering the territory of the Patena, who adjoined upon the northern Hittites, and held the country about Antioch and Aleppo, he occupied the capital, Kinalua, which was between the Abri (or Afrin) and the Orontes; alarmed the rebel king, Lubarna, so that he submitted, and consented to pay a tribute; and then, crossing the Orontes and destroying certain cities of the Patena, passed along the northern flank of Lebanon, and reached the Mediterranean. Here he erected altars and offered sacrifices to the gods, after which he received the submission of the principal Phoenician states, among which Tyre, Sidon, Byblus, and Aradus may be distinctly recognized. He then proceeded inland, and visited the mountain range of Amanus, where he cut timber, set up a sculptured memorial, and offered sacrifice. After this he returned to Assyria, carrying with him, besides other plunder, a quantity of wooden beams, probably cedar, which he carefully conveyed to Nineveh, to be used in his public buildings.

The tenth campaign of Asshur-izir-pai, and the last which is recorded, was in the region of the Upper Tigris. The geographical details here are difficult to follow. We can only say that, as usual, the Assyrian monarch claims to have over-powered all resistance, to have defeated armies, burnt cities, and carried off vast numbers of prisoners. The "royal city" of the monarch chiefly attacked was Amidi, now Diarbekr, which sufficiently marks the main locality of the expedition.

While engaged in these important wars, which were all included within his first six years, Asshur-izir-pal, like his great predecessor, Tiglath-Pileser, occasionally so far unbent as to indulge in the recreation of hunting. He interrupts the account of his military achievements to record, for the benefit of posterity, that on one occasion he slew fifty large wild bulls on the left bank of the Euphrates, and captured eight of the same animals; while, on another, he killed twenty ostriches (?), and took captive the same number. We may conclude, from the example of Tiglath-Pileser, and from other inscriptions of Asshur-izir-pal himself, that the captured animals were convoyed to Assyria either as curiosities, or, more probably, as objects of chase. Asshur-izir-pal's sculptures show that the pursuit of the wild bull was one of his favorite occupations; and as the animals were scarce in Assyria, he may have found it expedient to import them.

Asshur-izir-pal appears, however, to have possessed a menagerie park in the neighborhood of Nineveh, in which were maintained a variety of strange and curious animals. Animals called paguts or pagats—perhaps elephants—were received as tribute from the Phoenicians during his reign, on at least one occasion, and placed in this enclosure, where (he tells us) they throve and bred. So well was his taste for such curiosities known, that even neighboring sovereigns sought to gratify it; and the king of Egypt, a Pharaoh probably of the twenty-second dynasty, sent him a present of strange animals when he was in Southern Syria, as a compliment likely to be appreciated. This love of the chase, which he no doubt indulged to some extent at home, found in Syria, and in the country on the Upper Tigris, its amplest and most varied exercise. In an obelisk inscription, designed especially to commemorate a great hunting expedition into these regions, he tells us that, besides antelopes of all sorts, which he took and sent to Asshur, he captured and destroyed the following animals:—lions, wild sheep, red deer, fallow-deer, wild goats or ibexes, leopards large and small, bears, wolves, jackals, wild boars, ostriches, foxes, hyaenas, wild asses, and a few kinds which have not been identified. From another inscription we learn that, in the course of another expedition, which seems to have been in the Mesopotamian desert, he destroyed 360 large lions, 257 large wild cattle, and thirty buffaloes, while he took and sent to Calah fifteen full-grown lions, fifty young lions, some leopards, several pairs of wild buffaloes and wild cattle, together with ostriches, wolves, red deer, bears, cheetas, and hyeenas. Thus in his peaceful hours he was still actively employed, and in the chase of many dangerous beasts was able to exercise the same qualities of courage, coolness, and skill in the use of weapons which procured him in his wars such frequent and such great successes.

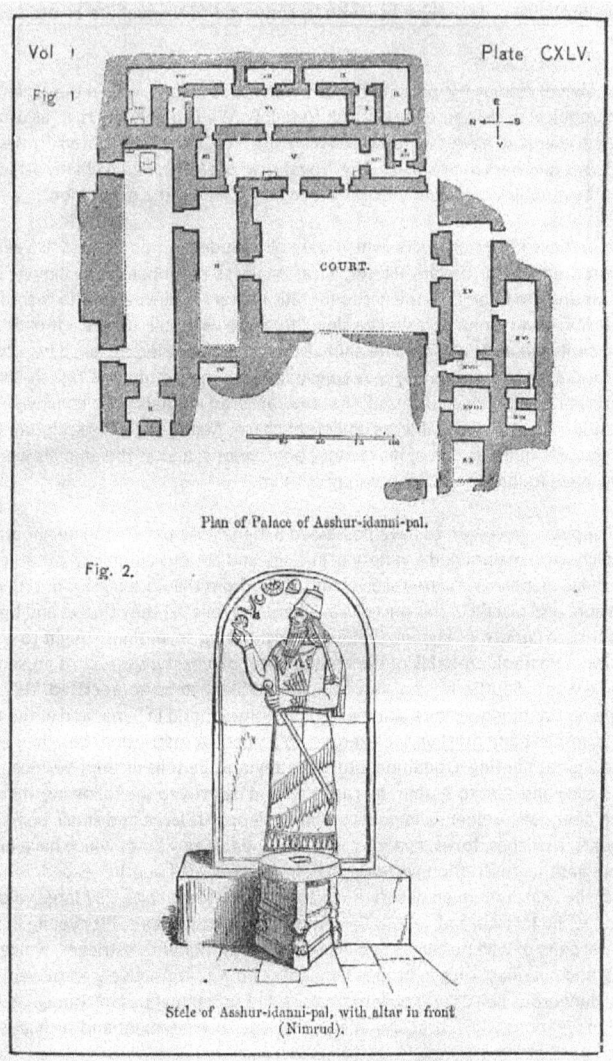

PLATE CXLV

Thus distinguished, both as a hunter and as a warrior, Asshur-izir-pal, nevertheless, excelled his predecessors most remarkably in the grandeur of his public buildings and the free use which he made of the mimetic and other arts in their ornamentation. The constructions of the earlier kings at Asshur (or Kileh-Sherghat), whatever merit they may have had, were beyond a doubt far inferior to those which, from the time of Asshur-izir-pal, were raised in rapid succession at Calah, Nineveh, and Beth-Sargina by that monarch and his successors upon the throne. The mounds of Kileh-Sherghat have yielded no bas-reliefs, nor do they show any traces of buildings on the scale of those which, at Nimrud, Koyunjik, and Khorsabad, provoke the admiration of the traveller. The great palace of

Asshur-izir-pal was at Calah, which he first raised from a provincial town to be the metropolis of the empire. [PLATE CXLV., Fig. 1.] It was a building 360 feet long by 300 broad, consisting of seven or eight large halls, and a far greater number of small chambers, grouped round a central court 130 feet long and nearly 100 wide. The longest of the halls, which faced towards the north, and was the first room entered by one who approached from the town, was in length 154 and in breadth 33 feet. The others varied between a size little short of this, and a length of 65 with a breadth of less than 20 feet. The chambers were generally square, or nearly so, and in their greatest dimensions rarely exceeded ten yards. The whole palace was raised upon a lofty platform, made of sun-burnt brick, but externally cased on every side with hewn stone. There were two grand facades, one facing the north, on which side there was an ascent to the platform from the town: and the other facing the Tigris, which anciently flowed at the foot of the platform towards the west. On the northern front two or three gateways, flanked with andro-sphinxes, gave direct access to the principal hall or audience chamber, a noble apartment, but too narrow for its length, lined throughout with sculptured slabs representing the various actions of the king, and containing at the upper or eastern end a raised stone platform cut into steps, which, it is probable, was intended to support at a proper elevation the carved throne of the monarch. A grand portal in the southern wall of the chamber, guarded on either side by winged human-headed bulls in yellow limestone, conducted into a second hall considerably smaller than the first, and having less variety of ornament, which communicated with the central court by a handsome gateway towards the south; and, towards the east, was connected with a third hall, one of the most remarkable in the palace. This chamber was a better-proportioned room than most, being about ninety feet long by twenty-six wide; it ran along the eastern side of the great court, with which it communicated by two gateways, and, internally, it was adorned with sculptures of a more finished and elaborate character than any other room in the building. Behind this eastern hall was another opening into it, of somewhat greater length, but only twenty feet wide; and this led to five small chambers, which here bounded the palace. South of the Great Court were, again, two halls communicating with each other; but they were of inferior size to those on the north and west, and were far less richly ornamented. It is conjectured that there were also two or three halls on the west side of the court between it and the river; but of this there was no very clear evidence, and it may be doubted whether the court towards the west was not, at least partially, open to the river. Almost every hall had one or two small chambers attached to it, which were most usually at the ends of the halls, and connected with them by large doorways.

Such was the general plan of the palace of Asshur-izir-pal. Its great halls, so narrow for their length, were probably roofed with beams stretching across them from side to side, and lighted by small louvres in their roofs after the manner already described elsewhere. Its square chambers may have been domed, and perhaps were not lighted at all, or only by lamps and torches. They were generally without ornamentation. The grand halls, on the contrary, and some of the narrower chambers, were decorated on every side, first with sculptures to the height of nine or ten feet, and then with enamelled bricks, or patterns painted in fresco, to the height, probably, of seven or eight feet more. The entire height of the rooms was thus from sixteen to seventeen or eighteen feet.

The character of Asshur-izir-pal's sculptures has been sufficiently described in an earlier chapter. They have great spirit, boldness, and force; occasionally they show real merit in the design; but they are clumsy in the drawing and somewhat coarse in the execution. What chiefly surprises us in regard to them is the suddenness with which the art they manifest appears to have sprung up, without going through the usual stages of rudeness and imperfection. Setting aside one mutilated statue, of very poor execution, and a single rock tablet, we have no specimens remaining of Assyrian mimetic art more ancient than this monarch. That art almost seems to start in Assyria, like Minerva from the head of Jove, full-grown. Asshur-izir-pal had undoubtedly some constructions of former monarchs to copy from, both in his palatial and in his sacred edifices; the old palaces and temples at Kileh-Sherghat must have had a certain grandeur; and in his architecture this monarch may have merely amplified and improved upon the models left him by his predecessors; but his ornamentation, so far as appears, was his own. The mounds of Kileh-Sherghat have yielded bricks in abundance, but not a single fragment of a sculptured slab. We cannot prove that ornamental bas-reliefs did not exist before the time of Asshur-izir-pal; indeed the rock tablets which earlier monarchs set up were sculptures of this character; but to Asshur-izir-pal seems at any rate to belong the merit of having first adopted bas-reliefs on an extensive scale as an architectural ornament, and of having employed them so as to represent by their means all the public life of the monarch.

The other arts employed by this king in the adornment of his buildings were those of enamelling bricks and painting in fresco upon a plaster. Both involve considerable skill in the preparation of colors, and the former especially implies much dexterity in the management of several very delicate processes.

The sculptures of Asshur-izir-pal, besides proving directly the high condition of mimetic art in Assyria at this time, furnish indirect evidence of the wonderful progress which had been made in various important manufactures. The metallurgy which produced the swords, sword-sheaths, daggers, earrings, necklaces, armlets, and bracelets of this period, must have been of a very advanced description. The coach-building which constructed the chariots, the saddlery which made the harness of the horses, the embroidery which ornamented the robes, must, similarly, have been of a superior character. The evidence of the sculptures alone is quite sufficient to show that, in the time of Asshur-izir-pal, the Assyrians were already a great and luxurious people, that most of the useful arts not only existed among them, but were cultivated to a high pitch, and that in dress, furniture, jewelry, etc., they were not very much behind the moderns.

Besides the magnificent palace which he built at Calah, Asshur-izir-pal is known also to have erected a certain number of temples. The most important of these have been already described. They stood at the north-western corner of the Nimrud platform, and consisted of two edifices, one exactly at the angle, comprising the higher tower or ziggurat, which stood out as a sort of corner buttress from the great mound, and a shrine with chambers at the tower's base; the other, a little further to the east, consisting of a shrine and chambers without a tower. These temples were richly ornamented both within and without; and in front of the larger one was an erection which seems to show that the Assyrian monarchs, either during their lifetime, or at any rate after their decease, received divine honors from their subjects. On a plain square pedestal about two feet in height was raised a solid block of limestone cut into the shape of an arched frame, and within this frame was carved the monarch in his sacerdotal dress, and with the sacred collar round his neck, while the five principal divine emblems were represented above his head. In front of this figure, marking (apparently) the object of its erection, was a triangular altar with a circular top, very much resembling the tripod of the Greeks. Here we may presume were laid the offerings with which the credulous and the servile propitiated the new god,—many a gift, not improbably, being intercepted on its way to the deity of the temple. [PLATE CXLV., Fig. 2.]

Another temple built by this monarch was one dedicated to Beltis at Nineveh. It was perhaps for the ornamentation of this edifice that he cut "great trees" in Amanus and elsewhere during his Syrian expedition, and had them conveyed across Mesopotamia to Assyria. It is expressly stated that these beams were carried, not to Calah, where Asshur-izir-pal usually resided, but to Nineveh.

A remarkable work, probably erected by this monarch, and set up as a memorial of his reign at the same city, is an obelisk in white stone, now in the British Museum. On this monument, which was covered on all its four sides with sculptures and inscriptions, now nearly obliterated, Asshur-izir-pal commemorated his wars and hunting exploits in various countries. The obelisk is a monolith, about twelve or thirteen feet high, and two feet broad at the base. It tapers slightly, and, like the Black

Obelisk erected by this monarch's son, is crowned at the summit by three steps or gradines. This thoroughly Assyrian ornamentation seems to show that the idea of the obelisk was not derived from Egypt, where the pyramidical apex was universally used, being regarded as essential to this class of ornaments. If we must seek a foreign origin for the invention, we may perhaps find it in the pillars which the Phoenicians employed, as ornaments or memorials, from a remote antiquity, objects possibly seen by the monarch who took tribute from Tyre, Sidon, Aradus, Byblus, and most of the maritime Syrian cities.

Another most important work of this great monarch was the tunnel and canal already described at length, by which at a vast expenditure of money and labor he brought the water of the Greater Zab to Calah. Asshur-izir-pal mentions this great work as his in his annals; and he was likewise commemorated as its author in the tablet set up in the tunnel by Sennacherib, when, two centuries later, he repaired it and brought it once more into use.

It is evident that Asshur-izir-pal, though he adorned and beautified both the old capital, Asshur, and the now rising city of Nineveh, regarded the town of Calah with more favor than any other, making it the ordinary residence of his court, and bestowing on it his chief care and attention. It would seem that the Assyrian dominion had by this time spread so far to the north that the situation of Asshur (or Kileh-Sherghat) was no longer sufficiently central for the capital. The seat of government was consequently moved forty miles further up the river. At the same time it was transferred from the west bank to the east, and placed in the fertile region of Adiabene, near the junction of the Greater Zab with the Tigris. Here, in a strong and healthy position, on a low spur from the Jebel Maklub, protected on either side by a deep river, the new capital grew to greatness. Palace after palace rose on its lofty platform, rich with carved woodwork, gilding, painting, sculpture, and enamel, each aiming to outshine its predecessors; while stone lions, sphinxes, obelisks, shrines, and temple-towers embellished the scene, breaking its monotonous sameness by variety. The lofty ziggurat attached to the temple of Nin or Hercules, dominating over the whole, gave unity to the vast mass of palatial and sacred edifices. The Tigris, skirting the entire western base of the mound, glassed the whole in its waves, and, doubling the apparent height, rendered less observable the chief weakness of the architecture. When the setting sun lighted up the view with the gorgeous hues seen only under an eastern sky, Calah must have seemed to the traveller who beheld it for the first time like a vision from fairy-land.

After reigning gloriously for twenty-five years, from B.C. 883 to B.C. 858, this great prince—"the conqueror" (as he styles himself), "from the upper passage of the Tigris to Lebanon and the Great Sea, who has reduced under his authority all countries from the rising of the sun to the going down of the same"—died, probably at no very advanced age, and left his throne to his son, who bore the name of Shalmaneser.

Shalmaneser II., the son of Asshur-izir-pal, who may probably have been trained to arms under his father, seems to have inherited to the full his military spirit, and to have warred with at least as much success against his neighbors. His reign was extended to the unusual length of thirty-five years, during which time he conducted in person no fewer than twenty-three military expeditions, besides entrusting three or four others to a favorite general. It would be a wearisome task to follow out in detail these numerous and generally uninteresting campaigns, where invasion, battle, flight, siege, submission, and triumphant return succeeded one another with monotonous uniformity. The style of the court historians of Assyria does not improve as time goes on. Nothing can well be more dry and commonplace than the historical literature of this period, which recalls the early efforts of the Greeks in this department, and exhibits a decided inferiority to the compositions of Stowe and Holinshed. The historiographer of Tiglath-Pileser I., between two and three centuries earlier, is much superior, as a writer, to those of the period to which we are come, who eschew all graces of style, contenting themselves with the curtest and dryest of phrases, and with sentences modelled on a single unvarying type.

Instead, therefore, of following in the direct track of the annalist whom Shalmaneser employed to record his exploits, and proceeding to analyze his account of the twenty-seven campaigns belonging to this reign, I shall simply present the reader with the general result in a few words, and then draw his special attention to a few of the expeditions which are of more than common importance.

It appears, then, that Shalmaneser, during the first twenty-seven years of his reign, led in person twenty-three expeditions into the territories of his neighbors, attacking in the course of these inroads, besides petty tribes, the following nations and countries:—Babylonia, Chaldaea, Media, the Zimri, Armenia, Upper Mesopotamia, the country about the head-streams of the Tigris, the Hittites, the Patena, the Tibareni, the Hamathites, and the Syrians of Damascus. He took tribute during the same time from the Phoenieian cities of Tyre, Sidon, and Byblus, from the Tsukhi or Shuhites, from the people of Muzr, from the Bartsu or Partsu, who are almost certainly the Persians, and from the Israelites. He thus traversed in person the entire country between the Persian Gulf on the south and Mount Niphates upon the north, and between the Zagros range (or perhaps the Persian desert) eastward, and, westward, the shores of the Mediterranean. Over the whole of this region he made his power felt, and even beyond it the nations feared him and gladly placed themselves under his protection. During the later years of his reign, when he was becoming less fit for warlike toils, he seems in general to have deputed the command of his armies to a subject in whom he had great confidence, a noble named Dayan-Asshur. This chief, who held an important office as early as Shahnaneser's fifth year, was in his twenty-seventh, twenty-eighth, thirtieth, and thirty-first employed as commander-in-chief, and sent out, at the head of the main army of Assyria, to conduct campaigns against the Armenians, against the revolted Patena, and against the inhabitants of the modern Kurdistan. It is uncertain whether the king himself took any part in the campaigns of these years, the native record the first and third persons are continually interchanged, some of the actions related being ascribed to the monarch and others to the general; but on the whole the impression left by the narrative is that the king, in the spirit of a well-known legal maxim assumes as his own the acts which he has accomplished through his representative. In his twenty-ninth year, however, Shalmaneser seems to have led an expedition in person into Khirki (the Niphates country), where he "overturned, beat to pieces, and consumed with fire the towns, swept the country with his troops, and impressed on the inhabitants the fear of his presence."

The campaigns of Shalmaneser which have the greatest interest are those of his sixth, eighth, ninth, eleventh, fourteenth, eighteenth, and twenty-first years. Two of these were directed against Babylonia, three against Ben-hadad of Damascus, and two against Khazail (Hazael) of Damascus.

In his eighth year Shalmaneser took advantage of a civil war in Babylonia between King Merodach-sum-adin and a younger brother, Merodach-bel-usati (?), whose power was about evenly balanced, to interfere in the affairs of that country, and under pretence of helping the legitimate monarch, to make himself master of several towns. In the following year he was still more fortunate. Having engaged, defeated, and slain the pretender to the Babylonian crown, he marched on to Babylon itself, where he was probably welcomed as a deliverer, and from thence proceeded into Chaldaea, or the tract upon the coast, which was at this time independent of Babylon, and forced its kings to become his tributaries. "The power of his army," he tells us, "struck terror as far as the sea."

The wars of Shalmaneser in Southern Syria commenced as early as his ninth year. He had succeeded to a dominion in Northern Syria which extended over the Patena, and probably over most of the northern Hittites; and this made his territories conterminous with those of the Phoenicians, the Hamathites, the southern Hittites, and perhaps the Syrians of Damascus. At any rate the last named people felt themselves threatened by the growing power on or near their borders, and, convinced that they would soon be attacked, prepared for resistance by entering into a close league with their neighbors. The king of Damascus, who was the great Ben-hadad, Tsakhulena, king of Hamath, Ahab, king of Israel, the kings of the southern Hittites, those of the Phoenician cities on the coast, and others, formed an alliance, and, uniting their forces, went out boldly to meet Shalnaneser, offering him battle. Despite, however, of this confidence, or perhaps in consequence of it, the allies suffered a defeat. Twenty thousand men fell in the battle. Many chariots and much of the material of war were captured by the Assyrians. But still no conquest was effected. Shalmaneser does not assert that he either received submission or imposed a tribute; and the fact that he did not venture to renew the war for five years seems to show that the resistance which he had encountered made him hesitate about continuing the struggle.

Five years, however, having elapsed, and the power of Assyria being increased by her successes in Lower Mesopotamia, Shalmaneser, in the eleventh year of his reign, advanced a second time against Hamath and the southern Hittites. Entering their territories unexpectedly, he was at first unopposed, and succeeded in taking a large number of their towns. But the troops of Ben-hadad soon appeared in the field. Phoenicia, apparently, stood aloof, and Hamath was occupied with her own difficulties; but Ben-hadad, having joined the Hittites, again gave Shalmaneser battle; and though that monarch, as usual, claims the victory, it is evident that he gained no important advantage by his success. He had once more to return to his own land without having extended his sway, and this time (as it would seem) without even any trophies of conquest.

Three years later, he made another desperate effort. Collecting his people "in multitudes that were not to be counted," he crossed the Euphrates with above a hundred thousand men. Marching southwards, he soon encountered a large army of the allies, Damascenes, Hamathites, Hittites, and perhaps Phoenicians, the first-named still commanded by the undaunted Ben-hadad. This time the success of the Assyrians is beyond dispute. Not only were the allies put to flight, not only did they lose most of their chariots and implements of war, but they appear to have lost hope, and, formally or tacitly, to have forthwith dissolved their confederacy. The Hittites and Hamathites probably submitted to the conqueror; the Phoenicians withdrew to their own towns, and Damascus was left without allies, to defend herself as she best might, when the tide of conquest should once more flow in this direction.

In the fourth year the flow of the tide came. Shalmaneser, once more advancing southward, found the Syrians of Damascus strongly posted in the fastnesses of the Anti-Lebanon. Since his last invasion they had changed their ruler. The brave and experienced Ben-hadad had perished by the treachery of an ambitious subject, and his assassin, the infamous Hazael, held the throne. Left to his own resources by the dissolution of the old league, this monarch had exerted himself to the utmost in order to repel the attack which he knew was impending. He had collected a very large army, including above eleven hundred chariots, and, determined to leave nothing to chance, had carefully taken up a very strong position in the mountain range which separated his territory from the neighboring kingdom of Hamath, or valley of Coele-Syria. Here he was attacked by Shalmaneser, and completely defeated, with the loss of 16,000 of his troops, 1121 of his chariots, a quantity of his war material, and his camp. This blow apparently prostrated him; and when, three years later, Shalmaneser invaded his territory, Hazael brought no army into the field, but let his towns, one after another, be taken and plundered by the Assyrians.

It was probably upon this last occasion, when the spirit of Damascus was cowed, and the Phoenician cities, trembling at the thought of their own rashness in having assisted Hazael and Ben-hadad, hastened to make their submission and to resume the rank of Assyrian tributaries, that the sovereign of another Syrian country, taking warning from the fate of his neighbors, determined to anticipate the subjection which he could not avoid, and, making a virtue of necessity, to place himself under the Assyrian yoke. Jehu, "son of Omri," as he is termed in the Inscription—i.e., successor and supposed descendant of the great Omri who built Samaria, sent as tribute to Shalmaneser a quantity of gold and silver in bullion, together with a number of manufactured articles in the more precious of the two metals. In the sculptures which represent the Israelitish ambassadors presenting this tribute to the great king, these articles appear carried in the hands, or on the shoulders, of the envoys, but they are in general too indistinctly traced for us to pronounce with any confidence upon their character. [PLATE CXLVI., Fig. 1]

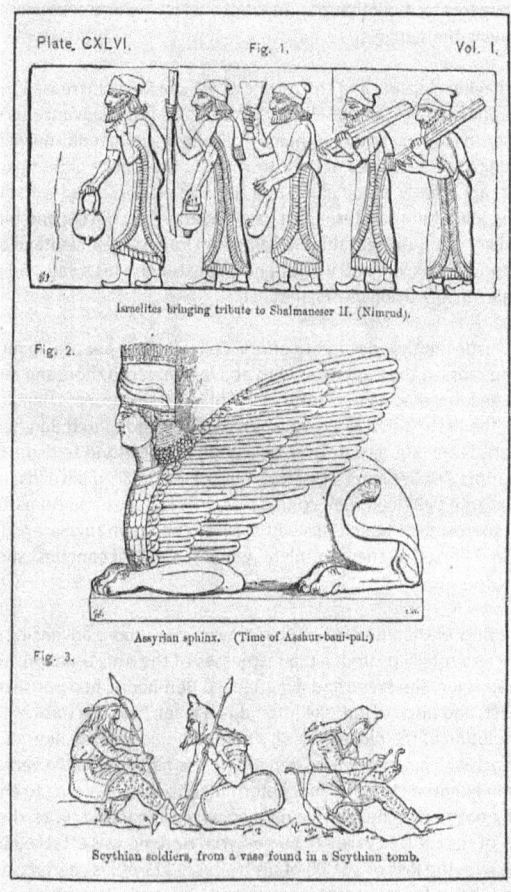

PLATE CXLVI

Shalmaneser had the same taste as his father for architecture and the other arts. He completed the ziggurat of the Great Temple of Nin at Calah, which his father had left unfinished, and not content with the palace of that monarch, built for himself a new and (probably) more magnificent residence on the same lofty platform, at the distance of about 150 yards. This edifice was found by Mr. Layard in so ruined a condition, through the violence which it had suffered, apparently at the hands of Esarhaddon, that it was impossible either to trace its plan or to form a clear notion of its ornamentation. Two gigantic winged bulls, partly destroyed, served to show that the grand portals of the chambers were similar in character and design to those of the earlier monarch, while from a number of sculptured fragments it was sufficiently plain that the walls had been adorned with bas-reliefs of the style used in Asshur-izir-pal's edifice. The only difference observable was in the size and subjects of the sculptures, which seemed to have been on a grander scale and more generally mythological than those of the North-West palace.

The monument of Shalmaneser which has attracted most attention in this country is an obelisk in black marble, similar in shape and general arrangement to that of Asshur-izir-pal, already described, but of a handsomer and better material. This work of art was discovered in a prostrate position under the debris which covered up Shalmaneser's palace. It contained bas-reliefs in twenty compartments, five on each of its four sides; the space above, between, and below then being covered with cuneiform writing, sharply inscribed in a minute character. The whole was in most excellent preservation.

The bas-reliefs represent the monarch, accompanied by his vizier and other chief officers, receiving the tribute of five nations, whose envoys are ushered into the royal presence by officers of the court, and prostrate themselves at the Great King's feet ere they present their offerings. The gifts brought are, in part, objects carried in the hand—gold, silver, copper in bars and cubes, goblets, elephants' tusks, tissues, and the like—in part, animals such as horses, camels, monkeys and baboons of different kinds, stags, lions, wild bulls, antelopes, and—strangest of all—the rhinoceros and the elephant. One of the nations, as already mentioned, is that of the Israelites. The others are, first, the people of Kirzan, a country bordering on Armenia, who present gold, silver, copper, horses, and camels, and fill the four highest compartments with a train of nine envoys: secondly, the Muzri, or people of Muzr, a country nearly in the same quarter, who are represented in the four central compartments, with six envoys conducting various wild animals; thirdly, the Tsukhi, or Shuhites, from the Euphrates, to whom belong the four compartments below the Muzri, which are filled by a train of thirteen envoys, bringing two lions, a stag, and various precious articles, among which bars of metal, elephants' tusks, and shawls or tissues are conspicuous; and lastly, the Patera, from the Orontes, who fill three of the lowest compartments with a train of twelve envoys bearing gifts like those of the Israelites.

Besides this interesting monument, there are very few remains of art which can be ascribed to Shalmaneser's time with any confidence. The sculptures found on the site of his palace belonged to a later monarch, who restored and embellished it. His own bas-reliefs were torn from their places by Esarhaddon, and by him defaced and used as materials in the construction of a new palace. We are thus left almost without materials for judging of the progress made by art during Shalmaneser's reign. Architecture, it may be conjectured, was modified to a certain extent, precious woods being employed more frequently and more largely than before; a fact of which we seem to have an indication in the frequent expeditions made by Shalmaneser into Syria, for the single purpose of cutting timber in its forests. Sculpture, to judge from the obelisk, made no advance. The same formality, the same heaviness of outline, the same rigid adherence to the profile in all representations both of man and beast, characterize the reliefs of both reigns equally, so far as we have any means of judging.

Shalmaneser seems to have held his court ordinarily at Calah, where he built his palace and set up his obelisk; but sometimes he would reside for a time at Nineveh or at Asshur. He does not appear to have built any important edifice at either of these two cities, but at the latter he left a monument which possesses some interest. This is the stone statue, now in a mutilated condition, representing a king seated, which was found by Mr. Layard at Kileh-Sherghat, and of which some notice has already been taken. Its proportions are better than those of the small statue of the monarch's father, standing in his sacrificial dress, which was found at Nimrud; and it is superior to that work of art, in being of the size of life; but either its execution was originally very rude, or it must have suffered grievously by exposure, for it is now wholly rough and unpolished.

The later years of Shahuaneser appear to have been troubled by a dangerous rebellion. The infirmities of age were probably creeping upon him. He had ceased to go out with his armies; and had handed over a portion of his authority to the favorite general who was entrusted with the command of his forces year after year. The favor thus shown may have provoked jealousy and even alarm. It may have been thought that the legitimate successor was imperilled by the exaltation of a subject whose position would enable him to in gratiate himself with the troops, and who might be expected, on the death of his patron, to make an effort to place the crown on his own head. Fears of this kind may very probably have so worked on the mind of the heir apparent as to determine him not to await his father's demise, but rather to raise the standard of revolt during his lifetime, and to endeavor, by an unexpected coup-de-main, to anticipate and ruin his rival. Or, possibly, Asshur-danin-pal, the eldest son of Shalmaneser, like too many royal youths, may have been impatient of the long life of his father, and have conceived the guilty desire, with which our fourth Henry is said to have taxed his first-born, a "hunger for the empty chair" of which the aged monarch, still held possession. At any rate, whatever may have been the motive that urged him on, it is certain that Asshur-danin-pal rebelled against his sire's authority, and, raising the standard of revolt, succeeded in carrying with him a great part of the kingdom. At Asshur, the old metropolis, which may have hoped to lure back the Court by its subservience, at Arbela in the Zab region, at Amidi on the Upper Tigris, at Tel-Apni near the site of Orfa, and at more than twenty other fortified places, Asshur-danin-pal was pro-claimed king, and accepted by the inhabitants for their sovereign. Shalmaneser must have felt himself in imminent peril of losing his crown. Under these circumstances he called to his assistance his second son Shamas-Vul, and placing him at the head of such of his troops as remained firm to their allegiance, invested him with full power to act as he thought best in the existing emergency. Shamas-Vul at once took the field, attacked and reduced the rebellious cities one after another, and in a little time completely crushed the revolt and reestablished peace throughout the empire. Asshur-danin-pal, the arch conspirator, was probably put to death; his life was justly forfeit; and neither Shamas-Vul nor his father is likely to have been withheld by any inconvenient tenderness from punishing treason in a near relative, as they would have punished it in any other person. The suppressor of the revolt became the heir of the kingdom; and when, shortly afterwards, Shalmaneser died, the piety or prudence if his faithful son was rewarded by the rich inheritance of the Assyrian Empire.

Shalmaneser reigned, in all, thirty-five years, from B.C. 858 to B.C. 823. His successor, Shamas-Vul, held the throne for thirteen years, from B.C. 823 to B.C. 810. Before entering upon the consideration of this latter monarch's reign, it will be well to cast your eyes once more over the Assyrian Empire, such as it has now become, and over the nations with which its growth had brought it into contact. Considerable changes had occurred since the time of Tiglath-Pileser I., the Assyrian boundaries having been advanced in several directions, while either this progress, or the movements of races beyond the frontier, had brought into view many new and some very important nations.

The chief advance which the "Terminus" of the Assyrians had made was towards the west and the north-west. Instead of their dominion in this quarter being bounded by the Euphrates, they had established their authority over the whole of Upper Syria, over Phoenicia, Hamath, and Samaria, or the kingdom of the Israelites. These countries were not indeed reduced to the form of provinces; on the contrary, they still retained their own laws, administration, and native princes; but they were henceforth really subject to Assyria, acknowledging her suzerainty, paying her an annual tribute, and giving a free passage to her armies through their territories. The limit of the Assyrian Empire towards the west was consequently at this time the Mediterranean, from the Gulf of Iskanderun to Cape

Carmel, or perhaps we should say to Joppa. Their north-western boundary was the range of Taurus next beyond Amanus, the tract between the two belonging to the Tibareni (Tubal), who had submitted to become tributaries. Northwards, little if any progress had been made. The chain of Niphates—"the high grounds over the effluents of the Tigris and Euphrates"—where Shalmaneser set up "an image of his majesty," seems still to be the furthest limit. In other words, Armenia is unconquered, the strength of the region and the valor of its inhabitants still protecting it from the Assyrian arms. Towards the east some territory seems to have been gained, more especially in the central Zagros region, the district between the Lower Zab and Holwan, which at this period bore the name of Hupuska; but the tribes north and south of this tract were still for the most part unsubdued. The southern frontier may be regarded as wholly unchanged: for although Shalmaneser warred in Babylonia, and even took tribute on one occasion from the petty kings of the Chaldaean towns, he seems to have made no permanent impression in this quarter. The Tsukhi or Shuhites are still the most southern of his subjects.

The principal changes which time and conquest had made among the neighbors of Assyria were the following. Towards the west she was brought into contact with the kingdom of Damascus, and, through her tributary Samaria with Judea. On the north-west she had new enemies in the Quins (Coans?) who dwelt on the further side of Amanus, near the Tibareni, in a part of the country afterwards called Cilicia, and the Cilicians themselves, who are now first mentioned. The Moschi seem to have withdrawn a little from this neighborhood, since they no longer appear either among Assyria's enemies or her tributaries. On the north all minor powers had disappeared; and the Armenians (Urarda) were now Assyria's sole neighbors. Towards the east she had come into contact with the Mannai, or Minni, about Lake Urumiyeh, with the Harkhar in the Van region and in north-western Kurdistan, with the Bartsu or Persians and the Mada or Medes in the country east of Zagros, the modern province of Ardelan, and with the Tsimri, or Zimri, in Upper Luristan. Among all her fresh enemies, she had not, however, as yet found one calculated to inspire any serious fear. No new organized monarchy presented itself. The tribes and nations upon her borders were still either weak in numbers or powerless from their intestine divisions; and there was thus every reason to expect a long continuance of the success which had naturally attended a large centralized state in her contests with small kingdoms or loosely-united confederacies. Names celebrated in the after history of the world, as those of the Medes and Persians, are now indeed for the first time emerging into light from the complete obscurity which has shrouded there hitherto; and tinged as they are with the radiance of their later glories, they show brightly among the many insignificant tribes and nations with which Assyria has been warring for centuries; but it would be a mistake to suppose that these names have any present importance in the narrative or represent powers capable as yet of contending on equal terms with the Assyrian Empire, or even of seriously checking the progress of her successes. The Medes and Persians are at this period no more powerful than the Zimri, the Minni, the Urarda, or than half a dozen others of the border nations, whose appellations sound strange in the ears even of the advanced student. Neither of the two great Arian peoples had as yet a capital city, neither was united under a king: separated into numerous tribes, each under its chief, dispersed in scattered towns and villages, poorly fortified or not fortified at, all, they were in the same condition as the Nairi, the Qummukh, the Patena, the Hittites, and the other border races whose relative weakness Assyria had abundantly proved in a long course of wars wherein she had uniformly been the victor.

The short reign of Shamas-Vul II., presents but little that calls for remark. Like Shalmaneser II., he resided chiefly at Calah, where, following the example of his father and grandfather, he set up an obelisk (or rather a stele) in commemoration of his various exploits. This monument, which is covered on three sides with an inscription in the hieratic or cursive character, contains an opening invocation to Nin or Hercules, conceived in the ordinary terms, the genealogy and titles of the king, an account of the rebellion of Asshur-bani-pal, together with its suppression, and Shamas-Vul's own annals for the first four years of his reign. From these we learn that he displayed the same active spirit as his two predecessors, carrying his arms against the Nairi on the north, against Media and Arazias on the east, and against Babylonia on the south. The people of Hupuska, the Minni, and the Persians (Bartsu) paid him tribute. His principal success was that of his fourth campaign, which was against Babylon. He entered the country by a route often used, which skirted the Zagros mountain range for some distance, and then crossed the flat, probably along the course of the Diyaleh, to the southern capital. The Babylonians, alarmed at his advance, occupied a strongly fortified place on his line of route, which he besieged and took after a vigorous resistance, wherein the blood of the garrison was shed like water. Eighteen thousand were slain; three thousand were made prisoners; the city itself was plundered and burnt, and Shamas-Vul pressed forward against the flying enemy. Hereupon the Babylonian monarch, Merodach-belatzu-ikbi, collecting his own troops and those of his allies, the Chaldaeans, the Aramaeans or Syrians, and the Zimri—a vast host—met the invader on the river Daban—perhaps a branch of the Euphrates—and fought a great battle in defence of his city. He was, however, defeated by the Assyrians, with the loss of 5000 killed, 2000 prisoners, 100 chariots, 200 tents, and the royal standard and pavilion. What further military or political results the victory may have had is uncertain. Shamas-Vul's annals terminate abruptly at this point, and we are left to conjecture the consequences of the campaign and battle. It is possible that they were in the highest degree important; for we find, in the next reign, that Babylonia, which has so long been a separate and independent kingdom, is reduced to the condition of a tributary, while we have no account of its reduction by the succeeding monarch, whose relations with the Babylonians, so far as we know, were of a purely peaceful character.

The stele of Shamas-Vul contains one allusion to a hunting exploit, by which we learn that this monarch inherited his grandfather's partiality for the chase. He found wild bulls at the foot of Zagros when he was marching to invade Babylonia, and delaying his advance to hunt them, was so fortunate as to kill several.

We know nothing of Shamas-Vul as a builder, and but little of him as a patron of art. He seems to have been content with the palaces of his father and grandfather, and to have been devoid of any wish to outshine them by raising edifices which should throw theirs into the shade. In his stele he shows no originality; for it is the mere reproduction of a monument well known to his predecessors, and of which we have several specimens from the time of Asshur-izir-pal downwards. It consists of a single figure in relief—a figure representing the king dressed in his priestly robes, and wearing the sacred emblems round his neck, standing with the right arm upraised, and enclosed in the customary arched frame. This figure, which is somewhat larger than life, is cut on a single solid block of stone, and then placed on another broader block, which serves as a pedestal. It closely resembles the figure of Asshur-izir-pal, whereof a representation has been already given.

The successor of Shamas-Vul was his son Vul-lush, the third monarch of that name, who ascended the throne B.C. 810, and held it for twenty-nine years, from B.C. 810 to B.C. 781. The memorials which we possess of this king's reign are but scanty. They consist of one or two slabs found at Nimrod, of a short dedicatory inscription on duplicate statues of the god Nebo brought from the same place, of some brick inscriptions from the mound of Nebbi Vunus, and of the briefest possible notices of the quarters in which he carried on war, contained in one copy of the Canon. As none of these records are in the shape of annals except the last, and as only these and the slab notices are historical, it is impossible to give any detailed account of this long and apparently important reign. We can only say that Vul-lush III., was as warlike a monarch as any of his predecessors, and that his efforts seem to have extended the Assyrian dominion in almost every quarter. He made seven expeditions across the Zagros range into Media, two into the Van country, and three into Syria. He tells us that in one of these expeditions he succeeded in making himself master of the great city of Damascus, whose kings had defied (as we have seen) the repeated attacks of Shalmaneser. He reckons as his tributaries in these parts, besides Damascus, the cities of Tyre and Sidon, and the countries of Khumri or Samaria, of Palestine or Philistia, and of Hudum (Idumaea or Edom). On the north and east he received tokens of submission from the Nairi, the Minni, the Medes, and the Partsu, or Persians. On the south, he exercised a power, which seems like that of a sovereign, in Babylonia; where homage was paid him by the Chaldaeans, and where, in the great cities of Babylon, Borsippa, and Cutha (or Tiggaba), he was allowed to offer sacrifice to the gods Bel, Nebo, and Nergal. There is, further, some reason to suspect that, before quitting Babylonia, he established one of his sons as viceroy over the country; since he seems to style himself in one place "the king to whose son Asshur, the chief of the gods, has granted the kingdom of Babylon."

It thus appears that by the time of Vul-lush III., or early in the eighth century u.e., Assyria had with one hand grasped Babylonia, while with the other she had laid hold of Philistia and Edom. She thus touched the Persian Gulf on the one side, while on the other she was brought into contact with Egypt. At the same time she had received the submission of at least some portion of the great nation of the Medes, who were now probably moving southwards from Azerbijan and gradually occupying the territory which was regarded as Media Proper by the Greeks and Romans. She held Southern Armenia, from Lake Van to the sources of the Tigris; she possessed all Upper Syria, including Commagene and Amanus she had tributaries even on the further side of that mountain range; she bore sway over the whole Syrian coast from Issus to Gaza; her authority was acknowledged, probably, by all the tribes and kingdoms between the coast and the desert, certainly by the Phoenicians, the Hamathites, the Patena, the Hittites, the Syrians of Damascus, the people of Israel, and the Idumaeans, or people of Edom. On the east she had reduced almost all the valleys of Zagros, and had tributaries in the great upland on the eastern side of the range. On the south, if she had not absorbed Babylonia, she had at least made her influence paramount there. The full height of her greatness was not indeed attained till a century later; but already the "tall cedar" was "exalted above all the trees of the field; his boughs were multiplied; his branches had become long; and under his shadow dwelt great nations."

Not much is known of Vul-lush III., as a builder, or as a patron of art. He calls himself the "restorer of noble buildings which had gone to decay," an expression which would seem to imply that he aimed rather at maintaining former edifices in repair than at constructing new ones. He seems, however, to have built some chambers on the mound of Nimrod, between the north-western and the south-western palaces, and also to have had a palace at Nineveh on the mound now called Nebbi Ynnus. The Nimrud chambers were of small size and poorly ornamented; they contained no sculptures; the walls were plastered and then painted in fresco with a variety of patterns. They may have been merely guard-rooms, since they appear to have formed a portion of a high tower. The palace at Nebbi Ynnus was probably a more important work; but the superstitious regard of the natives for the supposed tomb of Jonah has hitherto frustrated all attempts made by Europeans to explore that mass of ruins.

Among all the monuments recovered by recent researches, the only works of art assignable to the reign of Vul-lush are two rude statues of the god Nebo, almost exactly resembling one another. From the representation of one of them, given on a former page of this volume, the reader will see that the figures in question have scarcely any artistic merit. The head is disproportionately large, the features, so far as they can be traced, are coarse and heavy, the arms and hands are poorly modelled, and the lower part is more like a pillar than the figure of a man. We cannot suppose that Assyrian art was incapable, under the third Vul-lush, of a higher flight than these statues indicate; we must therefore regard them as conventional forms, reproduced from old models, which the artist was bound to follow. It would seem, indeed, that while in the representation of animals and of men of inferior rank, Assyrian artists were untrammelled by precedent, and might aim at the highest possible perfection, in religious subjects, and in the representation of kings and nobles, they were limited, by law or custom, to certain ancient forms and modes of expression, which we find repeated from the earliest to the latest times with monotonous uniformity.

If these statues, however, are valueless as works of art, they have yet a peculiar interest for the historian, as containing the only mention which the disentombed remains have furnished of one of the most celebrated names of antiquity—a name which for many ages vindicated to itself a leading place, not only in the history of Assyria, but in that of the world. To the Greeks and Romans Semiramis was the foremost of women, the greatest queen who had ever held a sceptre, the most extraordinary conqueror that the East had ever produced. Beautiful as Helen or Cleopatra, brave as Tomyris, lustful as Messalina, she had the virtues and vices of a man rather than a woman, and performed deeds scarcely inferior to those of Cyrus or Alexander the Great. It is an ungrateful task to dispel illusions, more especially such as are at once harmless and venerable for their antiquity; but truth requires the historian to obliterate from the pages of the past this well-known image, and to substitute in its place a very dull and prosaic figure—a Semiramis no longer decked with the prismatic hues of fancy, but clothed instead in the sober garments of fact. The Nebo idols are dedicated, by the Assyrian officer who had them executed, "to his lord Vul-lush and his lady Sammuramit" from whence it would appear to be certain, in the first place, that that monarch was married to a princess who bore this world-renowned name, and, secondly, that she held a position superior to that which is usually allowed in the East to a queen-consort. An inveterate Oriental prejudice requires the rigid seclusion of women; and the Assyrian monuments, thoroughly in accord with the predominant tone of Eastern manners, throw a veil in general over all that concerns the weaker sex, neither representing to us the forms of the Assyrian women in the sculptures, nor so much as mentioning their existence in the inscriptions. Very rarely is there an exception to this all but universal reticence. In the present instance, and in about two others, the silence usually kept is broken; and a native woman comes upon the scene to tantalize us by her momentary apparition. The glimpse that we here obtain does not reveal much. Beyond the fact that the principal queen of Vul-lush III., was named Semiramis, and the further fact, implied in her being mentioned at all, that she had a recognized position of authority in the country, we can only conclude, conjecturally, from the exact parallelism of the phrases used, that she bore sway conjointly with her husband, either over the whole or over a part of his dominions. Such a view explains, to some extent, the wonderful tale of the Ninian Semiramis, which was foisted into history by Ctesias; for it shows that he had a slight basis of fact to go upon. It also harmonizes, or may be made to harmonize, with the story of Semiramis as told by Herodotus, who says that she was a Babylonian queen, and reigned five generations before Nitocris, or about B.C. 755. For it is quite possible that the Sammuramit married to Vul-lush III., was a Babylonian princess, the last descendant of a long line of kings, whom the Assyrian monarch wedded to confirm through her his title to the southern provinces; in which case a portion of his subjects would regard her as their legitimate sovereign, and only recognize his authority as secondary and dependent upon hers. The exaggeration in which Orientals indulge, with a freedom that astonishes the sober nations of the West, would seize upon the unusual circumstance of a female having possessed a conjoint sovereignty, and would gradually group round the name a host of mythic details, which at last accumulated to such an extent that, to prevent the fiction from becoming glaring, the queen had to be thrown back into mythic times, with which such details were in harmony. The Babylonian wife of Vul-lush III., who gave him his title to the regions of the south, and reigned conjointly with him both in Babylonia and Assyria, became first a queen of Babylon, ruling independently and alone, and then an Assyrian empress, the conqueror of Egypt and Ethiopia, the invader of the distant India, the builder of Babylon, and the constructor of all the great works which were anywhere to be found in Western Asia. The grand figure thus produced imposed upon the uncritical ancients, and was accepted even by the moderns for many centuries. At length the school of Heeren and Niebuhr, calling common sense to their aid, pronounced the figure a myth. It remained for the patient explorers of the field of Assyrian antiquity in our own day to discover the slight basis of fact on which the myth was founded, and to substitute for the shadowy marvel of

Ctesias a very prosaic and commonplace princess, who, like Atossa or Elizabeth of York, strengthened her husband's title to his crown, but who never really made herself conspicuous by either great works or by exploits.

With Vul-lush III., the glories of the Nimrud line of monarchs come to a close, and Assyrian history is once more shrouded in a partial darkness for a space of nearly forty years, from B.C. 781 to B.C. 745. The Assyrian Canon shows us that three monarchs bore sway during this interval—Shalmaneser III., who reigned from B.C. 78l to B.C. 771, Asshur-dayan III., who reigned from B. C. 771 to B.C. 753, and Asshur-lush, who held the throne from the last-mentioned date to B.C.. 745, when he was succeeded by the second Tiglatli-Pileser. The brevity of these reigns, which average only twelve years apiece, is indicative of troublous times, and of a disputed, or, at any rate, a disturbed succession. The fact that none of the three monarchs left buildings of any importance, or, so far as appears, memorials of any kind, marks a period of comparative decline, during which there was a pause in the magnificent course of Assyrian conquests, which had scarcely known a check for above a century. The causes of the temporary inaction and apparent decline of a power which had so long been steadily advancing, would form an interesting subject of speculation to the political philosopher; but they are too obscure to be investigated here, where our space only allows us to touch rapidly on the chief known facts of the Assyrian history.

One important difficulty presents itself at this point of the narrative, in an apparent contradiction between the native records of the Assyrians and the casual notices of their history contained in the Second Book of Kings. The Biblical Pul—"the king of Assyria" who came up against the land of Israel and received from Menahem a thousand talents of silver, "that his hand might be with him to confirm the kingdom in his hand," is unnoticed in the native inscriptions, and even seems to be excluded from the royal lists by the absence of any name at all resembling his in the proper place in the famous Canon. Pul appears in Scripture to be the immediate predecessor of Tiglath Pileser. At any rate, as his expedition against Menahem is followed within (at the utmost) thirty-two years by an expedition of Tiglath Pileser against Pekah, his last year (if he was indeed a king of Assyria) cannot have fallen earlier than thirty-two years before Tiglath-Pileser's first. In other words, if the Hebrew numbers are historical some portion of Pul's reign must necessarily fill into the interval assigned by the Canon to the kings for which it is the sole authority—Shalmaneser III., Asshur-dayan III., and Asshur-lush. But these names are so wholly unlike the name of Pul that no one of them can possibly be regarded as its equivalent, or even as the original from which it was corrupted. Thus the Assyrian records do not merely omit Pul, but exclude him: and we have to inquire how this can be accounted for, and who the Biblical Pul is, if he is not a regular and recognized Assyrian monarch.

Various explanations of the difficulty have been suggested. Some would regard Pul as a general of Tiglath-Pileser (or of some earlier Assyrian king), mistaken by the Jews for the actual monarch. Others would identify him with Tiglath-Pileser himself. But perhaps the most probable supposition is, that he was a pretender to the Assyrian crown, never acknowledged at Nineveh, but established in the western (and southern) provinces so firmly, that he could venture to conduct an expedition into Lower Syria, and to claim there the fealty of Assyrians vassals. Or possibly he may have been a Babylonian monarch, who in the troublous times that had now evidently come upon the northern empire, possessed himself of the Euphrates valley, and thence descended upon Syria and Palestine. Berosus, it must be remembered, represented Pul as a Chaldaean king; and the name itself, which is wholly alien to the ordinary Assyrian type, has at least one counterpart among known Babylonian namies.

The time of Pul's invasion may be fixed by combining the Assyrian and the Hebrew chronologies within very narrow limits. Tiglath-Pileser relates that he took tribute from Menahem in a war which lasted from his fourth to his eighth year, or from B.C. 742 to B.C. 738. As Menahem only reigned ten years, the earliest date that can be assigned to Puls expedition will be B.C. 752, while the latest possible date will be B.C. 746, the year before the accession of Tiglath-Pileser. In any case the expedition fells within the eight years assigned by the Assyrian Canon to the reign of Asshur-lush, Tiglath-Pileser's immediate predecessor.

It is remarkable that into this interval falls also the famous era of Nabonassar, which must have marked some important change, dynastic or other, at Babylon. The nature of the change will be considered at length in the Babylonia a section. At present it is sufficient to observe that, in the declining condition of Assyria under the kings who followed Vul-lush III., there was naturally a growth of power and independence among the border countries. Babylon, repenting of the submission which she had made either to Vul-lush III., or to his father, Shamas-Vul II., once more vindicated her right to freedom, and resumed the position of a separate and hostile monarchy. Samaria, Damascus, Judaea, ceased to pay tribute. Enterprising kings, like Jeroboam II., and Menahem, taking advantage of Assyria's weakness, did not content themselves with merely throwing off her yoke, but proceeded to enlarge their dominions at the expense of her feudatories. Judging of the unknown from the known, we may assume that on the north and east there were similar defections to those on the west and south—that the tribes of Armenia and of the Zagros range rose in revolt, and that the Assyrian boundaries were thus contracted in every quarter.

At the same time, within the limits of what was regarded as the settled Empire, revolts began to occur. In the reign of Asshur-dayan III. (B.C. 771-753), no fewer than three important insurrections are recorded—one at a city called Libzu, another at Arapkha, the chief town of Arrapachitis, and a third at Gozan, the chief city of Gauzanitis or Mygdonia. Attempts were made to suppress these revolts; but it may be doubted whether they were successful. The military spirit had declined; the monarchs had ceased to lead out their armies regularly year by year, preferring to pass their time in inglorious ease at their rich and luxurious capitals. Asshur-dayan III., during nine years of his eighteen, remained at home, under-taking no warlike enterprise. Asshur-lush, his successor, displayed even less of military vigor. During the eight years of his reign he took the field twice only, passing six years in complete inaction. At the end of this time, Calah, the second city in the kingdom, revolted; and the revolution was brought about which ushered in the splendid period of the Lower Empire.

It was probably during the continuance of the time of depression, when an unwarlike monarch was living in inglorious ease amid the luxuries and refinements of Nineveh, and the people, sunk in repose, gave the themselves up to vicious indulgences more hateful in the eye of God than even the pride and cruelty which they were want to exhibit in war, that the great capital was suddenly startled by a voice of warning in the streets—a voice which sounded everywhere, through corridor, and lane, and square, bazaar and caravanserai, one shrill monotonous cry—"Yet forty days, and Nineveh shall be overthrown." A strange wild man, clothed in a rough garment of skin, moving from place to place, announced to the inhabitants their doom. None knew who he was or whence he had come; none had ever beheld him before; pale, haggard, travel-stained, he moved before then like a visitant from another sphere; and his lips still framed the fearful words—"Yet forty days, and Nineveh shall be overthrown." Had the cry fallen on them in the prosperous time, when each year brought its tale of victories, and every nation upon their borders trembled at the approach of their arms, it would probably have been heard with apathy or ridicule, and would have failed to move the heart of the nation. But coming, as it did, when their glory had declined; when their enemies, having been allowed a breathing space, had taken courage and were acting on the offensive in many quarters; when it was thus perhaps quite within the range of probability that some one of their numerous foes might shortly appear in arms before the place, it struck them with fear and consternation. The alarm communicated itself from the city to the palace; and his trembling attendants "came and told the king of Nineveh," who was seated on his royal throne in the great audience-chamber, surrounded by all the pomp and magnificence of his court. No sooner did he hear, than the heart of the king was touched, like that of his people; and he "arose from his throne, and laid aside his robe from him, and covered himself with sackcloth and sat in ashes." Hastily summoning his nobles, he had a decree framed, and "caused it to be proclaimed and published through Nineveh, by the decree of the king and his nobles, saying, Let neither man nor beast, herd nor flock, taste anything; let them not feed, nor drink water: but let man and beast be covered with sackcloth, and cry mightily unto God: yea, let them turn every one from his evil way, and from the violence that is in their hands." Then the fast was proclaimed, and the people of Nineveh, fearful of God's wrath, put on sackcloth "from the greatest of them even to the least of them." The joy and merriment, the revelry and feasting of that great city were changed into mourning and lamentation; the sins that had provoked the anger of the Most High ceased; the people humbled themselves; they "turned from their evil way," and by a repentance, which, if not deep and enduring, was still real and unfeigned, they appeased for the present the Divine wrath. Vainly the prophet sat without the city, on its eastern side, under his booth woven of boughs, watching, waiting, hoping (apparently) that the doom which he had announced would come, in spite of the people's repentance. God was more merciful than man. He had pity on the "great city," with its "six score thousand persons that could not discern between their right hand and their left," and, sparing the penitents, left their town to stand unharmed for more than another century.

The circumstances under which Tiglath-Pileser II., ascended the throne in the year B.C. 745 are unknown to us. No confidence can be placed in the statement of Bion and Polyhistor which seems to have been intended to refer to this monarch, whom they called Beletaras—a corruption perhaps of the latter half of the name—that he was, previously to his elevation to the royal dignity, a mere vine-dresser, whose occupation was to keep in order the gardens of the king. Similar tales of the low origin of self-raised and usurping monarchs are too common in the East, and are too often contradicted by the facts, when they come known to us, for much credit to attach to the story told by these late writers, the earlier of whom, must have written five or six hundred years after Tiglath-Pileser's time. We aught, however, conclude, without much chance of mistake, from such a story being told, that the king-intended acquired the throne irregularly; that either he was not of the blood royal, or that, being so, he was at any rate not the legitimate heir. And the conclusion at which we should thus arrive is confirmed by the monarch's inscriptions; for though he speaks repeatedly of "the kings his fathers." and even calls the royal buildings at Galati. "the palaces of his fathers," yet he never mentions his actual father's name in any record that has come down to us. Such a silence is so contrary to the ordinary practice of Assyrian monarchs, who glory in their descent and parade it on every possible occasion, that, where it occurs, we are justified in concluding the monarch to have been an usurper, deriving his title to the crown, not from his ancestry or from any law of succession, but from a successful revolution, in which he played the principal part. It matters little that such a monarch, when he is settled upon the throne, claims, in a vague and general way, connection with the kings of former times. The claim may often have a basis of truth; for in monarchies where polygamy prevails, and the kings have numerous daughters to dispose of, almost all the nobility can boast that they are of the blood royal. Where the claim is in no sense true, it will still be made; for it flatters the vanity of the monarch, and there is no one to gainsay it.

Only in such cases we are sure to find a prudent vagueness—an assertion of the fact of the connection, expressed in general terms, without any specification of the particulars on which the supposed fact rests.

On obtaining the crown whatever the circumstances under which he obtained it—Tiglath-Pileser immediately proceeded to attempt the restoration of the Empire by engaging in a series of wars, now upon one, now upon another frontier, seeking by his unwearied activity and energy to recover the losses suffered through the weakness of his predecessors, and to compensate for their laches by a vigorous discharge of all the duties of the kingly office. The order of these wars, which formerly it was impossible to determine, is now fixed by means of the Assyrian Canon, and we may follow the course of the expeditions conducted by Tiglath-Pileser II., with as much confidence and certainty as those of Tiglath-Pileser I., Asshur-izir-pal, or the second Shalmaneser. It is scarcely necessary, however, to detain the reader by going through the entire series. The interest of Tiglath-Pileser's military operations attaches especially to his campaigns in Babylonia and in Syria, where he is brought into contact with persons otherwise known to us. His other wars are comparatively unimportant. Under these circumstances it is proposed to consider in detail only the Babylonian and Syrian expeditions, and to dismiss the others with a few general remarks on the results which were accomplished by them.

Tiglath-Pileser's expeditions against Babylon were in his first and in his fifteenth years, B.C. 745 and 731. No sooner did he find himself settled upon the throne, than he levied an army, and marched against Southern Mesopotamia, which appears to have been in a divided and unsettled condition. According to the Canon of Ptolemy, Nabonassar then ruled in Babylon. Tiglath-Pileser's annals confuse the accounts of his two campaigns; but the general impression we gather from them is that, even in B.C. 745, the country was divided up into a number of small principalities, the sea-coast being under the dominion of Merodach-Baladan, who held his court in his father's city of Bit-Yakin; while in the upper region there were a number of petty princes, apparently independent, among whom may be recognized names which seem to occur later in Ptolemy's list, among the kings of Babylon to whom he assigns short reigns in the interval between Nabonassar and Mardocempalus (Merodach-Baladan). Tiglath-Pileser attacked and defeated several of these princes, taking the towns of Kur-Galzu (now Akkerkuf), and Sippara or Sepharvaim, together with many other places of less consequence in the lower portion of the country, after which he received the submission of Merodach-Baladan, who acknowledged him for suzerain, and consented to pay an annual tribute. Tiglath-Pileser upon this assumed the title of "King of Babylon" (B.C. 729), and offered sacrifice to the Babylonian gods in all the principal cities.

The first Syrian war of Tiglath-Pileser was undertaken in his third year (B.C. 743), and lasted from that year to his eighth. In the course of it he reduced to subjection Damascus, which had regained its independence, and was under the government of Rezin; Samaria, where Menahem, the adversary of Pul, was still reigning; Tyre, which was under a monarch bearing the familiar name of Hiram; Hamath, Gebal, and the Arabs bordering upon Egypt, who were ruled by a queen called Khabiba. He likewise met and defeated a vast army under Azariah (or Uzziah), king of Judah, but did not succeed in inducing him to make his submission. It would appear by this that Tiglath-Pileser at this time penetrated deep into Palestine, probably to a point which no Assyrian king but Vul-lush III., had reached previously. But it would seem, at the same time, that his conquests were very incomplete; they did not include Judaea or Philistia, Idumaea, or the tribes of the Hauran; and they left untouched the greater number of the Phoenician cities. It causes us, therefore, no surprise to find that in a short time, B.C. 734, he renewed his efforts in this quarter, commencing by an attack on Samaria, where Pekah was now king, and taking Ijon, and Abel-beth-maachah, and Jamoah, and Kedesh, and Hazor, and Gilead, and Galilee, and all the land of Naphtali, and carrying them captive to Assyria, thus "lightly afflicting, the land of Zebulun and the land of Naphtali," or the more northern portion of the Holy Land, about Lake Merom, and from that to the Sea of Gennesareth.

This attack was-followed, shortly (B.C. 733) by the most important of Tiglath-Pileser's Syrian wars. It appears that the common danger, which had formerly united the Hittites, Hamathites, and Damascenes in a close alliance, now caused a league to be formed between Damascus and Samaria, the sovereigns of which—Pekah and Rezin—made an attempt to add Judaea to their confederation, by declaring war against Ahaz, attacking his territory, and threatening to substitute in his place as king of Jerusalem a creature of their own, "the son of Tabeal." Hard pressed by his enemies, Ahaz applied to Assyria, offering to become Tiglath-Pileser's "servant"—i.e, his vassal and tributary—if he would send troops to his assistance, and save him from the impending danger. Tiglath-Pileser was not slow to obey this call. Entering Syria at the head of an army, he fell first upon Rezin, who was defeated, and fled to Damascus, where Tiglath-Pileser besieged him for two years, at the end of which time he was taken and slain. Next he attacked Pekah, entering his country on the north-east, where it bordered upon the Damascene territory, and overrunning the whole of the Trans-Jordanic provinces, together (apparently) with some portion of the Cis-Jordanic region. The tribes of Reuben and Gad, and the half-tribe of Manasseh, who had possessed the country between the Jordan and the desert from the time of Moses, were seized and carried away captive by the conqueror, who placed them in Upper Mesopotamia, on the affluents of the Bilikh and the Khabour, from about Harran to Nisibis. Some cities situated on the right bank of the Jordan, in the territory of Issachar, but belonging to Manasseh, were at the same time seized and occupied. Among these, Megiddo in the great plain of Esdraelon, and Dur or Dor upon the coast, some way below Tyre, were the most important. Dur was even thought of sufficient consequence to receive an Assyrian governor at the same time with the other principal cities of Southern Syria.

After thus chastising Samaria, Tiglath-Pileser appears to have passed on to the south, where he reduced the Philistines and the Arab tribes, who inhabited the Sinaitic desert as far as the borders of Egypt. Over these last he set, in lieu of their native queen, an Assyrian governor. He then returned towards Damascus, where he held a court, and invited the neighboring states and tribes to send in their submission. The states and tribes responded to his invitation. Tiglath-Pileser, before quitting Syria, received submission and tribute not only from Ahaz, king of Judah, but also from Mit'enna, king of Tyre; Pekah, king of Samaria; Khanun, king of Gaza; and Mitinti, king of Ascalon: from the Moabites, the Ammonites, the people of Arvad or Aradus, and the Idumaeans. He thus completely re-established the power of Assyria in this quarter, once more recovering to the Empire the entire tract between the coast and the desert from Mount Amanus on the north to the Red Sea and the confines of Egypt.

One further expedition was led or sent by Tiglath-Pileser into Syria, probably in his last year. Disturbances having occurred from the revolt of Mit'enna of Tyre and the murder of Pekah of Israel by Hoshea, an Assyrian army marched westward, in B.C. 725, to put them down. The Tyrian monarch at once submitted; and Hoshea, having entered into negotiations, agreed to receive investiture into his kingdom at the hands of the Assyrians, and to hold it as an Assyrian territory. On these terns peace was re-established, and the army of Tiglath-Pileser retired and recrossed the Euphrates.

Besides conducting these various campaigns, Tiglath-Pileser employed himself in the construction of some important works at Calah, which was his usual and favorite residence. He repaired and adorned the palace of Shalmaneser II., in the centre of the Nimrud mound; and he built a new edifice at the south-eastern corner of the platform, which seems to have been the most magnificent of his erections. Unfortunately, in neither case were his works allowed to remain as he left them. The sculptures with which he adorned Shalmaneser's palace were violently torn from their places by Esar-haddon, and, after barbarous ill-usage, were applied to the embellishment of his own residence by that monarch. The palace which he built at the south-eastern corner of the Nimrud mound was first ruined by some invader, and then built upon by the last Assyrian king. Thus the monuments of Tiglath-Pileser II., come to us in a defaced and unsatisfactory condition, rendering it difficult for us to do full justice either to his architectural conceptions or to his taste in ornamentation. We can see, however, by the ground plan of the building which Mr. Loftus uncovered beneath the ruins of Mr. Layard's south-east palaces that the great edifice of Tiglath-Pileser was on a scale of grandeur little inferior to that of the ancient palaces, and on a plan very nearly similar. The same arrangement of courts and halls and chambers, the same absence of curved lines or angles other than right angles, the same narrowness of rooms in comparison with their length, which have been noted in the earlier buildings, prevailed also in those of this king. With regard to the sculptures with which, after the example of the former monarchs, he ornamented their walls, we can only say they seem to have been characterized by simplicity of treatment—the absence of all ornamentation, except fringes, from the dresses, the total omission of backgrounds, and (with few exceptions) the limitation of the markings to the mere outlines of forms. The drawing is rather freer and more spirited than that of the sculptures of Asshur-izir-pal; animal forms, as camels, oxen, sheep, and goats, are more largely introduced, and there is somewhat less formality in the handling. But the change is in no respect very decided, or such as to indicate an era in the progress of art.

Tiglath-Pileser appears, by the Assyrian Canon, to have had a reign of eighteen years. He ascended the throne in B.C. 747, and was succeeded in B.C. 727 by Shalmaneser, the fourth monarch who had borne that appellation.

It is uncertain whether Shalmaneser IV, was related to Tiglath-Pileser or not. As, however, there is no trace of the succession having been irregular or disputed, it is most probable that he was his son. He ascended the throne in B.C. 727, and ceased to reign in B.C. 722, thus holding the royal power for less than six years. It was probably very soon after his accession, that, suspecting the fidelity of Samaria, he "came up" against Hoshea, king of Israel, and, threatening him with condign punishment, so terrified him that he made immediate submission. The arrears of tribute were rendered, and the homage due from a vassal to his lord was paid; and Shalmaneser either returned into his own country or turned his attention to other enterprises. But shortly afterwards he learnt that Hoshea, in spite of his submission and engagements, was again contemplating defection; and, conscious of his own weakness, was endeavoring to obtain a promise of support from an enterprising monarch who ruled in the neighboring country of Egypt. The Assyrian conquests in this quarter had long been tending to bring them into collision with the great power of Eastern Africa, which had once held, and always coveted, the dominion of Syria. Hitherto such relations as they had had with the Egyptians appear to have been friendly. The weak and unwarlike Pharaohs who about this time bore sway in Egypt had sought the favor of the neighboring Asiatic power by demanding Assyrian princesses in marriage and affecting Assyrian names for their offspring. But recently an important change had occurred. A brave Ethiopian prince had descended the valley of the Nile at the head of a swarthy host, had defeated the Egyptian levies, had driven the reigning monarch into the marshes of the Delta, or put him to a cruel death, and had established his own dominion firmly, at any rate over the upper country. Shebek the First bore sway in Memphis in lieu of the blind Bocchoris; and Hoshea, seeing in this bold and enterprising king the natural foe of the Assyrians, and therefore his own natural ally and friend, "sent messengers" with proposals, which appear to have been accepted; for on their return Hoshea revolted openly, withheld his tribute, and declared himself independent. Shalmaneser, upon this, came up against Samaria for the second time, determined now to punish his vassal's perfidy with due severity. Apparently, he was unresisted; at any rate, Hoshea fell into his power, and was seized, bound, and shut up in prison. A year or two later Shalmaneser made his third and last expedition into Syria. What was the provocation given him, we are not told; but this time, he came up throughout all the land and being met with resistance, he laid formal siege to the capital. The siege commenced in Shahnaneser's fourth year, B.C. 724, and was protracted to his sixth, either by the efforts of the Egyptians, or by the stubborn resistance of the inhabitants. At last, in B.C. 722, the town surrendered, or was taken by storm; but before this consummation had been reached, Shalmaneser's reign would seem to have come to an end in consequence of a successful revolution.

While he was conducting these operations against Samaria, either in person or by means of his generals, Shalmaneser appears to have been also engaged in hostilities with the Phoenician towns. Like Samaria, they had revolted at the death of Tiglath-Pileser; and Shalmaneser, consequently, marched into Phoenecia at the beginning of his reign, probably in his first year, overran the entire country, and forced all the cities to resume their position of dependence. The island Tyre, however, shortly afterwards shook off the yoke. Hereupon Shalmaneser "returned" into these parts, and collecting a fleet from Sidon, Paleo-Tyrus, and Akko, the three most important of the Phoenician towns after Tyre, proceeded to the attack of the revolted place. His vessels were sixty in number, and were manned by eight hundred Phoenician rowers, co-operating with probably, a smaller number of unskilled Assyrians. Against this fleet the Tyrians, confiding in their maritime skill, sent out a force of twelve vessels only, which proved, however, quite equal to the occasion; for the assailants were dispersed and driven off, with the loss of 500 prisoners.

Shalmaneser, upon this defeat, retired, and gave up all active operations, contenting himself with leaving a body of troops on the mainland, over against the city, to cut off the Tyrians from the supplies of water which they were in the habit of drawing from the river Litany, and from certain aqueducts which conducted the precious fluid from springs in the mountains. The Tyrians, it is said, held out against this pressure for five years, satisfying their thirst with rain water, which they collected in reservoirs. Whether they then submitted, or whether the attempt to subdue them was given up, is uncertain, since the quotation from Menander, which is our sole authority for this passage of history, here breaks off abruptly.

The short reign of Shalmaneser IV, was, it is evident, sufficiently occupied by the two enterprises of which accounts have now been given—the complete subjugation of Samaria, and the attempt to reduce the island Tyre. Indeed, it is probable that neither enterprise had been conducted when a dynastic revolution, caused by the ambition of a subject, brought the unhappy monarch's reign to an untimely end. The conquest of Samaria is claimed by Sargon as an event of his first year; and the resistance of the Tyrians, if it really continued during the full space assigned to it by Menander, must have extended beyond the terns of Shalmaneser's reign, into the first or second year of his successor. It was probably the prolonged absence of the Assyrian monarch from his capital, caused by the obstinacy of the two cities which he was attacking, that encouraged a rival to come forward and seize the throne; just as in the Persian history we shall find the prolonged absence of Canbyses in Egypt produce a revolution and change of dynasty at Susa. In the East, where the monarch is not merely the chief but the sole power in the state, the moving spring whose action must be continually exerted to prevent the machinery of government from standing still, it is always dangerous for the reigning prince to be long away from his metropolis. The Orientals do not use the language of mere unmeaning compliment when they compare their sovereigns with the sun, and speak of them as imparting light and life to the country and people over which they rule. In the king's absence all languishes; the course of justice is suspended; public works are stopped; the expenditure of the Court, on which the prosperity of the capital mainly depends, being withdrawn, trade stagnates, the highest branches suffering most; artists are left without employment; work-men are discharged; wages fall; every industry is more or less deranged, and those engaged in it suffer accordingly; nor is there any hope of a return of prosperity until the king comes home. Under these circumstances a general discontent prevails; and the people, anxious for better times, are ready to welcome any pretender who will come forward, and, on any pretext whatever, declare the throne vacant, and claim to be its proper occupant. If Shalmaneser continued to direct in person the siege of Samaria during the three years of its continuance, we cannot be surprised that the patience of the Ninevites was exhausted, and that in the third year they accepted the rule of the usurper who boldly proclaimed himself king.

What right the new monarch put forward, what position he had previously held, what special circumstances, beyond the mere absence of the rightful king, facilitated his attempts, are matters on which the monuments throw no light, and on which we must therefore be content to be ignorant. All that we can see is, that either personal merit or official rank and position must have enabled him to establish himself; for he certainly did not derive any assistance from his birth, which must have been mediocre, if not actually obscure. It is the custom of the Babylonian and Assyrian kings to glory in their ancestry, and when the father has occupied a decently high position, the son declares his sire's name and rank at the commencement of each inscription, but Sargon never, in any record, names his father, nor makes the slightest allusion to his birth and descent, unless it be in vague phrases, wherein he calls the former kings of Assyria, and even those of Babylonia, his ancestors. Such expressions seem to be mere words of course, having no historical value: and it would be a mistake even to conclude from them that the new king intended seriously to claim the connection of kindred with the monarchs of former times.

It has been thought indeed, that Sargon, instead of cloaking his usurpation under some decent plea of right, took a pride in boldly avowing it. The name Sargon has been supposed to be one which he adopted as his royal title at the time of his establishment upon the throne, intending by the adoption to make it generally known that he had acquired the crown, not by birth or just claim, but by his own will and the consent of the people. Sargon, or Sar-gina, as the native name is read, means "the firm" or "well-established king," and (it has been argued) "shows the usurper." The name is certainly unlike the general run of Assyria royal titles; but still, as it is one which is found to have been previously borne by at least one private person in Assyria, it is perhaps best to suppose that it was the monarch's real original appellation, and not assumed when he came to the throne; in which case no argument can be founded upon it.

Military success is the best means of confirming a doubtful title to the leadership of a warlike nation. No sooner, therefore, was Sargon accepted by the Ninevites as king than he commenced a series of expeditions, which at once furnished employment to unquiet spirits, and gave the prestige of military glory to his own name. He warred successively in Susiana, in Syria, on the borders of Egypt, in the tract beyond Amanus, in Melitene and southern Armenia, in Kurdistan, in Media, and in Babylonia. During the first fifteen years of his reign, the space which his annals cover, he kept his subjects employed in a continual series of important expeditions, never giving himself, nor allowing them, a single year of repose. Immediately upon his accession he marched into Susiana, where he defeated Hum-banigas, the Elamitie king, and Merodach-Baladan, the old adversary of Tiglath-Pileser, who had revolted and established himself as king over Babylonia. Neither monarch was, however, reduced to subjection, though an important victory was gained, and many captives taken, who were transported into the country of the Hittites, In the same year, B.C. 722, he received the submission of Samaria, which surrendered, probably, to his generals, after it had been besieged two full years. He punished the city by depriving it of the qualified independence which it had enjoyed hitherto, appointing instead of a native king an Assyrian officer to be its governor, and further carrying off as slaves 27,280 of the inhabitants. On the remainder, however, he contented himself with re-imposing the rate of tribute to which the town had been liable before its revolt.—The next year, B.C. 721, he was forced to march in person into Syria in order to meet and quell a dangerous revolt. Yahu-bid (or Ilu-bid), king of Hamath—a usurper like Sargon himself—had rebelled, and had persuaded the cities of Arpad Zimira, Damascus, and Samaria to cast in their lot with his, and to form a confederacy, by which it was imagined that effectual resistance might be offered to the Assyrian arms. Not content merely to stand on the defensive in their several towns, the allies took to the field; and a battle was fought at Kar-kar or Garrrar (perhaps one of the many Aroers), where the superiority of the Assyrian troops was once more proved, and Sargon gained a complete victory over his enemies. Yahu-bid himself was taken and beheaded; and the chiefs of the revolt in the other towns were also put to death.

Having thus crushed the rebellion and re-established tranquillity throughout Syria, Sargon turned his arms towards the extreme south, and attacked Gaza, which was a dependency of Egypt. The exact condition of Egypt at this time is open to some doubt. According to Manetho's numbers, the twenty-fifth or Ethiopian dynasty had not yet begun to reign. Bocchoris the Saite occupied the throne, a humane but weak prince, of a contemptible presence, and perhaps afflicted with blindness. No doubt such a prince would tempt the attack of a powerful neighbor; and, so for, probability might seem to be in favor of the Manethonian dates. But, on the other hand, it must be remembered that Egypt had lately taken an aggressive attitude, incompatible with a time of weakness: she had intermeddled between the Assyrian crown and its vassals, by entering into a league with Hoshea: and she had extended her dominion over a portion of Philistia, thereby provoking a collision with the Great Power of the East. Again, it is worthy of note that the name of the Pharaoh who had dealings with Hoshea, if it does not seen at first sight very closely to resemble the Egyptian Shebek, is, at any rate, a possible representative of that word, while no etymological skill can force it into agreement with any other name in this portion of the Egyptian lists. Further, it is to be remarked that at this point of the Assyrian annals, a Shebek appears in them, holding a position of great authority in Egypt, though not dignified with the title of king. These facts furnish strong grounds for believing that the Manethonian chronology, which can be proved to be in many points incorrect, has placed the accession of the Ethiopians somewhat too late, and that that event occurred really as early as B.C. 725 or B.C. 730.

At the same time, it must be allowed that all difficulty is not removed by this supposition. The Shebek Sibahe (or Sibaki) of the Assyrian record bears an inferior title, and not that of king. He is also, apparently, contemporary with another authority in Egypt, who is recognized by Sargon as the true "Pharaoh," or native ruler. Further, it is not till eight or nine years later that any mention is made of Ethiopia as having an authority over Egypt or as in any way brought into contact with Sargon. The proper conclusion from these facts seems to be that the Ethiopians established themselves gradually; that in B.C. 720, Shebek or Sabaco, though master of a portion of Egypt, had not assumed the royal title, which was still borne by a native prince of little power—Bocchoris, or Scthos—who held his court somewhere in the Delta; and that it was not till about the year B.C. 712 that this shadowy kingdom passed away, that the Ethiopian rule was extended over the whole of Egypt, and that Sabaco assumed the full rank of an independent monarch.

If this be the true solution of the difficulty which has here presented itself, we must conclude that the first actual collision between the powers of Egypt and Assyria took place at a time very unfavorable to the former. Egypt was, in fact, divided against itself, the fertile tract of the Delta being under one king, the long valley of the Nile under another. If war was not actually going on, jealousy and suspicion, at any rate, must have held the two sovereigns apart; and the Assyrian monarch, coming at such a time of intestine feud, must have found it comparatively easy to gain a triumph in this quarter.

The armies of the two great powers met at the city of Rapikh, which seems to be the Raphia of the Greeks and Romans, and consequently the modern Refah a position upon the coast of the Mediterranean Sea, about half-way between Gaza and the Wady-el-Arish, or "River of Egypt." Here the forces of the Philistines, under Khanun, king of Gaza, and those of Shebek, the Tar-dan (or perhaps the Sultan) of Egypt, had effected a junction, and awaited the approach of the invader. Sargon, having arrived, immediately engaged the allied army, and succeeded in defeating it completely, capturing Khanun, and forcing Shebek to seek safety in flight. Khanun was deprived of his crown and carried off to Assyria by the conqueror.

Such was the result of the first combat between the two great powers of Asia and Africa. It was an omen of the future, though it was scarcely a fair trial of strength. The battle of Raphia foreshadowed truly enough the position which Egypt would hold among the nations from the time that she ceased to be isolated, and was forced to enter into the struggle for preeminence, and even for existence, with the great kingdoms of the neighboring continent. With rare and brief exceptions, Egypt has from the time of Sargon succumbed to the superior might of whatever power has been dominant in

Western Asia, owning it for lord, and submitting, with a good or bad grace, to a position involving a greater or less degree of dependence. Tributary to the later Assyrian princes, and again, probably, to Nebuchadnezzar, she had scarcely recovered her independence when she fell under the dominion of Persia. Never successful, notwithstanding all her struggles, in thoroughly shaking off this hated yoke, she did but exchange her Persian for Greek masters, when the empire of Cyrus perished. Since then, Greeks, Romans, Saracens, and Turks have, each in their turn, been masters of the Egyptian race, which has paid the usual penalty of precocity in the early exhaustion of its powers.

After the victories of Aroer and Raphia, the Assyrian monarch appears to have been engaged for some years in wars of comparatively slight interest towards the north and the north-east. It was not till B.C. 715, five years after his first fight with the Egyptians, that he again made an expedition towards the south-west, and so came once more into contact with nations to whose fortunes we are not wholly indifferent. His chief efforts on this occasion were directed against the peninsula of Arabia. The wandering tribes of the desert, tempted by the weak condition to which the Assyrian conquest had reduced Samaria, made raids, it appears, into the territory at their pleasure, and carried off plunder. Sargon determined to chastise these predatory bands, and made an expedition into the interior, where "he subdued the uncultivated plains of the remote Arabia, which had never before given tribute to Assyria," and brought under subjection the Thamudites, and several other Arab tribes, carrying off a certain number and settling them in Samaria itself, which thenceforth contained an Arab element in its population. Such an effect was produced on the surrounding nations by the success of this inroad, that their princes hastened to propitiate Sargon's favor by sending embassies, and excepting the position of Assyrian tributaries. The reigning Pharaoh, whoever he may have been, It-hamar, king of the Sabaeans, and Tsamsi, queen of the Arabs, thus humbled themselves, sending presents, and probably entering into engagements which bound them for the future.

Four years later (B.C. 711) Sargon led a third expedition into these parts, regarding it as important to punish the misconduct of the people of Ashdod. Ashdod had probably submitted after the battle of Raphia, and had been allowed to retain its native prince, Azuri. This prince, after awhile, revolted, withheld his tribute, and proceeded to foment rebellion against Assyria among the neighboring monarchs; whereupon Sargon deposed him, and made his brother Akhimit king in his place. The people of Ashdod, however, rejected the authority of Akhimit, and chose a certain Yaman, or Yavan, to rule over them, who strengthened himself by alliances with the other Philistine cities, with Judaea, and with Edom. Immediately upon learning this. Sargon assembled his army, and proceeded to Ashdod to punish the rebels; but, before his arrival, Yaman had fled away, and "escaped to the dependencies of Egypt, which" (it is said) "were under the rule of Ethiopia." Ashdod itself, trusting in the strength from which it derived its name, resisted; but Sargon laid siege to it and in a little time forced it to surrender. Yaman fled to Egypt, but his wife and children were captured and, together with the bulk of the inhabitants, were transported into Assyria, while their place was supplied by a number of persons who had been made prisoners in Sargon's eastern wars. An Assyrian governor was set over the town.

The submission of Ethiopia followed. Ashdod, like Samaria, had probably been encouraged to revolt by promises of foreign aid. Sargon's old antagonist, Shebek, had recently brought the whole of Egypt under his authority, and perhaps thought the time had come when he might venture once more to measure his strength against the Assyrians. But Sargon's rapid movements and easy capture of the strong Ashdod terrified him, and produced a change of his intentions. Instead of marching into Philistia and fighting a battle, he sent a suppliant embassy, surrendered Yaman, and deprecated Sargon's wrath. The Assyrian monarch boasts that the king of Meroe, who dwelt in the desert, and had never sent ambassadors to any of the kings his predecessors, was led by the fear of his majesty to direct his steps towards Assyria and humbly bow down before him.

At the opposite extremity of his empire, Sargon soon after-wards gained victories which were of equal or greater importance. Having completely reduced Syria, humiliated Egypt, and struck terror into the tribes of the north and east, he determined on a great expedition against Babylon. Merodach-Baladan had now been twelve years in quiet possession of the kingdom. He had established his court at Babylon, and, suspecting that the ambition of Sargon would lead him to attempt the conquest of the south he had made preparations for resistance by entering into close alliance with the Susianians under Sutruk-Nakhunta on the one hand, and with the Aramaean tribes above Babylonia on the other. Still, when Sargon advanced against him, instead of giving him battle, or even awaiting him behind the walls of the capital, he at once took to flight. Leaving garrisons in the more important of the inland towns, and committing their defence to his generals, he himself hastened down to his own city of Beth-lakin, which was on the Euphrates, near its mouth, and, summoning the Aramaeans to his assistance, prepared for a vigorous resistance in the immediate vicinity of his native place. Posting himself in the plain in front of the city, and protecting his front and left flank with a deep ditch, which he filled with water from the Euphrates, he awaited the advance of Sargon, who soon appeared at the head of his troops, and lost no time in beginning the attack. We cannot follow with any precision the exact operations of the battle, but it appears that Sargon fell upon the Babylonian troops, defeated them, and drove them into their own dyke, in which many of therm were drowned, at the same time separating them from their allies, who, on seeing the disaster, took to flight, and succeeded in making their escape. Merodach-Baladan, abandoning his camp, threw himself with the poor remains of his army into Beth-Yakin, which Saigon then besieged and took. The Babylonian monarch fell into the hands of his rival, who plundered his palace and burnt his city, but generously spared his life. He was not, however, allowed to retain his kingdom, the government of which was assumed by Sargon himself, who is the Arceanus of Ptolemy's Canon.

The submission of Babylonia was followed by the reduction of the Aramaeans, and the conquest of at least a portion of Susiana. To the Susianin territory Sargon transported the Comnumkha from the Upper Tigris, placing the mixed population under a governor, whom he made dependent on the viceroy of Babylon.

The Assyrian dominion was thus firmly established on the shores of the Persian Gulf. The power of Babylon was broken. Henceforth the Assyrian rule is maintained over the whole of Chaldaea and Babylonia, with few and brief interruptions, to the close of the Empire. The reluctant victim struggles in his captor's grasp, and now and then for a short space shakes it off; but only to be seized again with a fiercer gripe, until at length his struggles cease, and he resigns himself to a fate which he has come to regard as inevitable. During the last fifty years of the Empire, from B.C. 650 to B.C. 625, the province of Babylon was almost as tranquil as any other.

The pride of Sargon received at this time a gratification which he is not able to conceal, in the homage which was paid to him by sovereigns who had only heard of his fame, and who were safe from the attacks of his armies. While he held his court at Babylon, in the year B.C. 708 or 707, he gave audience to two embassies from two opposite quarters, both sent by islanders dwelling (as he expresses it) "in the middle of the seas" that washed the outer skirts of his dominions. Upir, king of Asmun, who ruled over an island in the Persian Gulf,—Khareg, perhaps, or Bahrein,—sent messengers, who bore to the Great King the tribute of the far East. Seven Cyprian monarchs, chiefs of a country which lay "at the distance of seven days from the coast, in the sea of the setting sun," offered him by their envoys the treasures of the West. The very act of bringing presents implied submission; and the Cypriots not only thus admitted his suzerainty, but consented to receive at his hands and to bear back to their country a more evident token of subjection. This was an effigy of the Great King carved in the usual form, and accompanied with an inscription recording his name and titles, which was set up at Idalium, nearly in the centre of the island, and made known to the Cypriots the form and appearance of the sovereign whom it was not likely that they would ever see.

The expeditions of Sargon to the north and north-east had results less splendid than those which he undertook to the south-west and the south; but it may be doubted whether they did not more severely try his military skill and the valor of his soldiers. The mountain tribes of Zagros, Taurus, and Niphates,—Medes, Armaenians, Tibarini, Moschi, etc.,—were probably far braver men and far better soldiers than the levies of Egypt, Susiana, and Babylon. Experience, moreover, had by this time taught the tribes the wisdom of uniting against the common foe, and we find Ambris the Tibareni in in alliance with Mita the Moschian, and Urza the Armenian, when he ventures to revolt against Sargon. The submission of the northern tribes was with difficulty obtained by a long and fierce struggle, which—so far as one belligerent was concerned —terminated in a compromise. Ambris was deposed, and his country placed under an Assyrian governor; Mita consented, after many years of resistance, to pay a tribute; Urza was defeated, and committed suicide, but the general pacification of the north was not effected until a treaty was made with the king of Van, and his good-will purchased by the cession to him of a considerable tract of country which the Assyrians had previously taken from Urza.

On the side of Media the resistance offered to the arms of Sargon seems to have been slighter, and he was consequently able to obtain a far more complete success. Having rapidly overrun the country, he seized a number of the towns and "annexed them to Assyria," or, in other words, reduced a great portion of Media into the form of a province. He also built in one part of the country a number of fortified posts. He then imposed a tribute on the natives, consisting entirely of horses, which were perhaps required to be of the famous Nisaean breed.

After his fourteenth year, B.C. 708, Sargon ceased to lead out his troops in person, employing instead the services of his generals. In the year B.C. 707 a disputed succession gave him an opportunity of interference in Illib, a small country bordering on Susiana. Nibi, one of the two pretenders to the throne, had applied for aid to Sutruk-Nakhunta, king of Elam, who held his court at Susa, and had received the promise of his favor and protection. Upon this, the other claimant, who was named Ispabara, made application to Sargon, and was readily received into alliance, Sargon sent to his assistance "seven captains with seven armies," who engaged the troops of Sutruk-Naklnurta, defeated them, and established Ispabara on the throne? In the following year, however, Sutruk-Nakhunta recovered his laurels, invading Assyria in his turn, and capturing cities which he added to the kingdom of Susiana.

In all his wars Sargon largely employed the system of whole-sale deportation. The Israelites were removed from Samaria, and planted partly in Gozan or Mygdonia, and partly in the cities recently taken from the Medes. Hamath and Damascus were peopled with captives from Armenia and other regions of the north. A portion of the Tibareni were carried captive to Assyria, and Assyrians were established in the Tibarenian country. Vast numbers of the inhabitants of the Zagros range were also transported to Assyria; Babylonians, Cuthaeans, Sepharvites, Arabians, and others, were placed in Samaria; men from the extreme east (perhaps Media) in Ashdod. The Commukha were removed from the extreme north to Susiana; and Chaldaeans were brought from the extreme south to supply their place. Everywhere Sargon changed the abodes of his subjects, his aim being, as it would seem, to weaken the stronger races by dispersion, and to destroy the spirit of the weaker ones by severing at a blow all the links which attach a patriotic people to the country it has long inhabited. The practice had not been unknown to previous monarchs, but it had never been employed by any so generally or on so grand a scale as it was by this king.

From this sketch of Sargon's wars, we may now proceed to a brief consideration of his great works. The magnificent palace which he erected at Khorsabad was by far the most important of his constructions. Compared with the later, and even with the earlier buildings of a similar kind erected by other kings, it was not remarkable for its size. But its ornamentation was unsurpassed by that of any Assyrian edifice, with the single exception of the great palace of Asshur-bani-pal at Koyunjik. Covered with sculptures, both internally and externally, generally in two lines, one over the other, and, above this, adorned with enamelled bricks, arranged in elegant and tasteful patterns; approached by noble flights of steps and through splendid propylaea; having the advantage, moreover, of standing by itself, and of not being interfered with by any other edifice, it had peculiar beauties of its own, and may be pronounced in many respects the most interesting of the Assyrian building's. United to this palace was a town enclosed by strong walls, which formed a square two thousand yards each way. Allowing fifty square yards to each individual, this space would have been capable of accommodating 80,000 persons. The town, like the palace, seems to have been entirely built by Sargon, who imposed on it his own name, an appellation which it retained beyond the time of the Arab conquest.

It is not easy to understand the exact object of Sargon in building himself this new residence. Dur-Sargina was not the Windsor or Versailles of Assyria—a place to which the sovereign could retire for country air and amusements from the bustle and heat of the metropolis. It was: as we have said, a town, and a town of considerable size, being very little lees than half as large as Nineveh itself. It is true that it possessed the advantage of a nearer vicinity to the mountains than Nineveh: and had Sargon been, like several of his predecessors, a mighty hunter, we might have supposed that the greater facility of obtaining sport in the woods and valleys of the Zagros chain formed the attraction which led him to prefer the region where he built his town to the banks of the Tigris. But all the evidence that we possess seems to show that this monarch was destitute of any love for the chase; and seemingly we must attribute his change of abode either to mere caprice, or to a desire to be near the mountains for the sake of cooler water, purer air, and more varied scenery. It is no doubt true, as M. Oppert observes, that the royal palace at Nineveh was at this time in a ruinous state; but it could not have been more difficult or more expensive to repair it than to construct a new palace, a new mound, and a new town, on a fresh site.

Previously to the construction of the Khorsabad palace, Sargon resided at Caleb. He there repaired and renovated the great palace of Asshur-izir-pal, which had been allowed to fall to decay. At Nineveh he repaired the walls of the town, which were ruined in many places, and built a temple to Nebo and Merodach; while in Babylonia he improved the condition of the embankments, by which the distribution of the waters was directed and controlled. He appears to have been to a certain extent a patron of science, since a large number of the Assyrian scientific tablets are proved by the dates upon then: to have been written in his day.

The progress of mimetic art under Sargon is not striking but there are indications of an advance in several branches of industry, and of an improved taste in design and in ornamentation. Transparent glass seems now to have been first brought into used and intaglios to have been first cut upon hard stones. The furniture of the period is greatly superior in design to any previously represented, and the modelling of sword-hilts, maces, armlets, and other ornaments is peculiarly good. The enamelling of bricks was carried under Sargon to its greatest perfection: and the shape of vases, goblets, and boats shows a marked improvement upon the works of former times. The advance in animal forms, traceable in the sculptures of Tiglath-Pileser II., continues: and the drawing of horses' heads, in particular, leaves little to desire.

After reigning gloriously over Assyria for seventeen years, and for the last five of them over Babylonia also, Sargon died, leaving his crown to the most celebrated of all the Assyrian Monarchs, his son Sennacherib, who began to reign B.C. 705. The long notices which we possess of this monarch in the books of the Old Testament, his intimate connection with the Jews, the fact that he was the object of a preternatural exhibition of the Divine displeasure, and the remarkable circumstance that this miraculous interposition appears under a thin disguise in the records of the Greeks, have always attached an interest to his name which the kings of this remote period and distant region very rarely awaken. It has also happened, curiously enough, that the recent Mesopotamian researches have tended to give to Sennacherib a special prominence over other Assyrian monarchs, more particularly in this country, our great excavator having devoted his chief efforts to the disinterment of a palace of this king's construction, which has supplied to our National Collection almost one-half of its treasures. The result is, that while the other sovereigns who bore sway in Assyria are generally either wholly unknown, or float before the mind's eye as dim and shadowy forms, Sennacherib stands out to our apprehension as a living and breathing man, the impersonation of all that pride and greatness which we assign to the Ninevite kings, the living embodiment of Assyrian haughtiness, Assyrian violence, and Assyrian power. The task of setting forth the life and actions of this prince, which the course of the history now imposes on its compiler, if increased in interest, is augmented also in difficulty, by the grandeur of the ideal figure which has possession of men's minds.

The reign of Sennacherib lasted twenty-four years, from B.C. 705 to B.C. 681. The materials which we possess for his history consist of a record written in his fifteenth year, describing his military expeditions and his buildings up to that time; of the Scriptural notices to which reference has already been made; of some fragments of Polyhistor preserved by Eusebius; and of the well-known passage of Herodotus which contains a mention of his name. From these documents we shall be able to make out in some detail the chief actions of the earlier portion of his reign, but they fail to supply any account of his later years, unless we may assign to that portion of his life some facts mentioned by Polyhistor, to which there is no allusion in the native records.

It seems probable that troubles both abroad and at home greeted the new reign. The Canon of Ptolemy shows a two years' interregnum at Babylon (from B.C. 704 to B.C. 702) exactly coinciding with the first two years of Sennacherib. This would imply a revolt of Babylon from Assyria soon after his accession, and either a period of anarchy or rapid succession of pretenders, none of whom held the throne for so long a time as a twelvemonth. Polyhistor gives us certain details, from which we gather that there were at least three monarchs in the interval left blank by the Canon—first, a brother of Sennacherib, whose name is not given; secondly, a certain Hagisa, who wore the crown only a month; and, thirdly, Merodach-Baladan, who had escaped from captivity, and, having murdered Hagisa, resumed the throne of which Sargon had deprived him six or seven years before. Sennacherib must apparently have been so much engaged with his domestic affairs that he could not devote his attention to these Babylonian matters till the second year after his accession. In B.C. 703 he descended on the lower country and engaged the troops of Merodach-Baladan, which consisted in part of native Babylonians, in part of Susianians, sent to his assistance by the king of Elam. Over this army Sennacherib gained a complete victory near the city of Ibis, after which he took Babylon, and overran the whole of Chaldaea, plundering (according to his own account) seventy-six large towns and 420 villages. Merodach-Baladan once more made his escape, flying probably to Susiana, where we afterwards find his sons living as refugees. Sennacherib, before quitting Babylon, appointed as tributary king an Assyrian named Belipni, who seems to be the Belibus of Ptolemy's Canon, and the Elibus of Polyhistor. On his return from Babylonia he invaded and ravaged the territory of the Aramaean tribes on the middle Euphrates—the Tumuna, Ruhua, Gambulu, Khindaru, and Pukudu (Pekod), the Nabatu or Nabathaeans, the Hagaranu or Hagarenes, and others, carrying into captivity more than 200,000 of the inhabitants, besides great numbers of horses, camels, asses, oxen, and sheep.

In the following year, B.C. 702, Sennacherib made war on the tribes in Zagros, forcing Ispabara, whom Sargon had established in power, to fly from his country, and conquering many cities and districts, which he attached to Assyria, and placed under the government of Assyrian officers.

The most important of all the expeditions contained in Sennacherib's records is that of his fourth year, B.C. 701, in which he attacked Luliya king of Sidon, and made his first expedition against Hezekiah king of Judah. Invading Syria with a great host, he made Phoenicia the first object of his attack. There Luliya—who seems to be the Mullins of Menander, though certainly not the Elulaeus of Ptolemy's Canon, had evidently raised the standard of revolt, probably during the early years of Sennacherib, when domestic troubles seem to have occupied his attention. Luliya had, apparently, established his dominion over the greater part of Phoenicia, being lord not only of Sidon, or, as it is expressed in the inscription, of Sidon the greater and Sidon the less, but also of Tyre, Ecdippa, Akko, Sarepta, and other cities. However, he did not venture to await Sennacherib's attack, but, as soon as he found the expedition was directed against himself, he took to flight, quitting the continent and retiring to an island in the middle of the sea—perhaps the island Tyre, or more probably Cyprus. Sennacherib did not attempt any pursuit, but was content to receive the submission of the various cities over which Luliya had ruled, and to establish in his place, as tributary monarch, a prince named Tubal. He then received the tributes of the other petty monarchs of these parts, among whom are mentioned Abdilihat king of Avrad. Hurus-milki king of Byblus. Mitinti king of Ashdod, Puduel king of Beth-Ammon, a king of Moab, a king of Edom, and (according to some writers) a "Menahem king of Samaria." After this Sennacherib marched southwards to Ascalon, where the king, Sidka, resisted him, but was captured, together with his city, his wife, his children, his brothers, and the other members of his family. Here again a fresh prince was established in power, while the rebel monarch was kept prisoner and transported into Assyria. Four towns dependent upon Ascalon, viz., Razor, Joppa, Beneberak, and Beth Dagon, were soon afterwards taken and plundered.

Sennacherib now pressed on against Egypt. The Philistine city of Ekron had not only revolted from Assyria, expelling its king, Path, who wwas opposed to the rebellion, but had entered into negotiations with Ethiopia and Egypt, and had obtained a promise of support from them. The king of Ethiopia was probably the second Shebek (or Sabaco) who is called Sevechus by Manetho, and is said to have reigned either twelve or fourteen yeats. The condition of Egypt at the time was peculiar. The Ethiopian monarch seems to have exercised the real sovereign power: but native princes were established under him who were allowed the title of king, and exercised a real though delegated authority over their several cities and districts. On the call of Ekron both princes and sovereign had hastened to its assistance, bringing with them an army consisting of chariots, horsemen, and archers, so numerous that Sennacherib calls it "a host that could not be numbered." The second great battle between the Assyrians and the Egyptians took place near a place called Altaku, which is no doubt the Eltekeh of the Jews, a small town in the vicinity of Ekron. Again the might of Africa yielded to that of Asia. The Egyptians and Ethiopians were defeated with great slaughter. Many chariots, with their drivers, both Egyptian and Ethiopian, fell into the hands of the conqueror, who also took alive several "sons" of the principal Egyptian monarch. The immediate fruit of the victory was the fall of Altaku, which was followed by the capture of Tamna, a neighboring town. Sennacherib then "went on" to Ekron, which made no resistance, but opened its gates to the victor. The princes and chiefs who had been concerned in the revolt he took alive and slew, exposing their bodies on stakes round the whole circuit of the city walls. Great numbers of inferior persons who were regarded as guilty of rebellion, were sold as slaves. Padi, the expelled king, the friend to Assyria, was brought back, reinstated in his sovereignty, and required to pay a small tribute as a token of dependence.

The restoration of Padi involved a war with Hezekiah, king of Judah. When the Ekronites determined to get rid of a king whose Assyrian proclivities were distasteful to them, instead of putting him to death, they arrested him, loaded him with chains, and sent him to Hezekiah for safe keeping. By accepting this charge the Jewish monarch made himself a partner in their revolt; and it was in part to punish this complicity, in part to compel him to give up Padi, that Sennacherib, when he had sufficiently chastised the Ekronite rebels, proceeded to invade Judaea, Then it was—in the fourteenth year of Hezekiah, according to the present Hebrew text—that "Sennacherib, king of Assyria, came up against all the fenced cities of Judah and took them. And Hezekiah, king of Judah, sent to the king of Assyria to Lshish, saying, I have offended; return from me; that which thou puttest on me will I bear. And the king of Assyria appointed unto Hezekiah, king of Judah, three hundred talents of silver and thirty talents of gold. And Hezekiah gave him all the silver that was found in the house of the Lord, and in the treasures of the king's house. At that time did Hezekiah cut off [the gold from] the doors of the house of the Lord, and [from] the pillars which Hezekiah, king of Judah, had overlaid, and gave it to the king of Assyria."

Such is the brief account of this expedition and its consequences which is given us by the author of the Second Book of Kings, who writes from a religious point of view, and is chiefly concerned at the desecration of holy things to which the imminent peril of his city and people forced the Jewish monarch to submit. It is interesting to compare with this account the narrative of Sennacherib himself, who records the features of the expedition most important in his eyes, the number of the towns taken and of the prisoners carried into captivity, the measures employed to compel submission, and the nature and amount of the spoil which he took with him to Nineveh.

"Because Hezekiah, king of Judah," says the Assyrian monarch, "would not submit to my yoke, I came up against him, and by force of arms and by the might of my power I took forty-six of his strong fenced cities; and of the smaller towns which were scattered about I took and plundered a countless number. And from these places I captured and carried off as spoil 200,150 people, old and young, male and female, together with horses and mares, asses and camels, oxen and sheep, a countless multitude. And Hezekiah himself I shut up in Jerusalem, his capital city, like a bird in a cage, building towers round the city to hem him in, and raising banks of earth against the gates, so as to prevent escape.... Then upon this Hezekiah there fell the fear of the power of my arms and he sent out to me the chiefs and the elders of Jerusalem with thirty talents of gold and eight hundred talents of silver, and divers treasures, a rich and immense booty.... All these things were brought to me at Nineveh, the seat of my government, Hezekiah having sent them by way of tribute, and as a token of his submission to my power."

It appears then that Sennacherib, after punishing the people of Ekron, broke up from before that city, and entering Judaea proceeded towards Jerusalem, spreading his army over a wide space, and capturing on his way a vast number of small towns and villages, whose inhabitants he enslaved and carried off to the number of 200,000. Having reached Jerusalem, he commenced the siege in the usual way, erecting towers around the city, from which stones and arrows were discharged against the defenders of the fortifications, and "casting banks" against the walls and gates. Jerusalem seems to have been at this time very imperfectly fortified. The "breaches of the city of David" had recently been "many;" and the inhabitants had hastily pulled down the houses in the vicinity of the wall to fortify it. It was felt that the holy place was in the greatest danger. We may learn from the conduct of the people, as described by one of themselves, what were the feelings generally of the cities threatened with destruction by the Assyrian armies. Jerusalem was at first "full of stirs and tumult;" the people rushed to the housetops to see if they were indeed invested, and beheld "the choicest valleys full of chariots, and the horsemen set in array at the gates." Then came "a day of trouble, and of treading down, and of perplexity"—a day of "breaking down the walls and of crying to the mountains." Amidst this general alarm and mourning there were, however, found some whom a wild despair made reckless, and drove to a ghastly and ill-timed merriment. When God by His judgments gave an evident "call to weeping, and to mourning, and to baldness, and to girding with sackcloth—behold joy and gladness, slaying oxen and killing sheep, eating flesh and drinking wine"— "Let us eat and drink, for to-morrow we shall die." Hezekiah after a time came to the conclusion that resistance would be vain, and offered to surrender upon terms, an offer which Sennacherib, seeing the great strength of the place, and perhaps distressed for water, readily granted. It was agreed that Hezekiah should undertake the payment of an annual tribute, to consist of thirty talents of gold and three hundred talents of silver, and that he should further yield up the chief treasures of the place as a "present" to the Great King. Hezekiah, in order to obtain at once a sufficient supply of gold, was forced to strip the walls and pillars of the Temple, which were overlaid in parts with this precious metal. He yielded up all the silver from the royal treasury and from the treasury of the Temple; and this amounted to five hundred talents more than the fixed rate of tribute. In addition to these sacrifices, the Jewish monarch was required to surrender Padi, his Ekronite prisoner, and was mulcted in certain portions of his dominions, which were attached by the conqueror to the territories of neighboring kings.

Sennacherib, after this triumph, returned to Nineveh, but did not remain long in repose. The course of events summoned him in the ensuing year B.C. 700—to Babylonia, where Merodach-Baladan, assisted by a certain Susub, a Chaldaean prince, was again in arms against his authority. Sennacherib first defeated Susub, and then, directing his march upon Beth-Yakin, forced Merodach-Baladan once more to quit the country and betake himself to one of the islands of the Persian Gulf, abandoning to Sennacherib's mercy his brothers and his other partisans. It would appear that the Babylonian viceroy Belibus, who three years previously had been set over the country by Sennacherib, was either actively implicated in this revolt, or was regarded as having contributed towards it by a neglect of proper precautions. Sennacherib, on his return from the sea-coast, superseded him, placing upon the throne his own eldest son, Asshur-inadi-su, who appears to be the Asordanes of Polyhistor, and the Aparanadius or Assaranadius of Ptolemy's Canon.

The remaining events of Sennacherib's reign may be arranged in chronological order without much difficulty, but few of them can be dated with exactness. We lose at this point the invaluable aid of Ptolemy's Canon, which contains no notice of any event recorded in Sennacherib's inscriptions of later date than the appointment of Assaranadius.

It is probable in that in the year B.C. 699 Sennacherib conducted his second expedition into Palestine. Hezekiah, after his enforced submission two years earlier, had entered into negotiations with the Egyptians, and looking to receive important succors from this quarter, had again thrown off his allegiance. Sennacherib, understanding that the real enemy whom he had to fear on his south-western frontier was not Judaea, but Egypt, marched his army through Palestine—probably by the coast route—and without stopping to chastise Jerusalem, pressed southwards to Libnah and Lachish, which were at the extreme verge of the Holy Land, and were probably at this tune subject to Egypt. He first commenced the siege of Lachish with all his power; and while engaged in this operation, finding that Hezekiah was not alarmed by his proximity, and did not send in his submission, he detached a body of troops from Ins main force, and sent it under a Tartan or general, supported by two high officers of the court—the Rabshakeh or Chief Cupbearer, and the Rob-saris or Chief Eunuch—to summon the rebellious city to surrender. Hezekiah was willing to treat, and sent out to the Assyrian camp, which was pitched just outside the walls, three high officials of his own to open negotiations. But the Assyrian envoys had not cone to debate or even to offer terms, but to require the unconditional submission of both king and people. The Rabshakeh or cupbearer, who was familiar with the Hebrew language, took the word and delivered his message in insulting phrase, laughing at the simplicity which could trust in Egypt, and the superstitious folly which could expect a divine deliverance, and defying Hezekiah to produce so many as two thousand trained soldiers capable of serving as cavalry. When requested to use a foreign rather than the native dialect, lest the people who were upon the walls should hear, the bold envoy, with an entire disregard of diplomatic forms, raised his voice and made a direct appeal to the popular fears and hopes thinking to produce a tumultuary surrender of the place, or at least an outbreak of which his troops might have taken advantage. His expectations, however, were disappointed; the people made no response to his appeal, but listened in profound silence; and the ambassadors, finding that they could obtain nothing from the fears of either king or people, and regarding the force that they had brought with them as insufficient for a siege, returned to their master with the intelligence of their ill-success. The Assyrian monarch had either taken Lachish or raised its siege, and was gone on to Libnah, where the envoys found him. On receiving their report, he determined to make still another effort to overcome Hezckiah's obstinacy and accordingly he despatched fresh messengers with a letter to the Jewish king, in which he was reminded of the fate of various other kingdoms and peoples which had resisted the Assyrians, and once more urged to submit himself. It was this letter perhaps a royal autograph—which Hezekiah took into the temple and there "spread it before the Lord," praying God to "bow down his ear and hear; to open his eyes and see, and hear the words of Sennacherib, which had sent to reproach the living God." Upon this Isaiah was commissioned to declare to his afflicted sovereign that the kings of Assyria were mere instruments in God's hands to destroy such, nations as He pleased, and that none of Sennacherib's threats against Jerusalem should be accomplished. God, Isaiah told him would "put his hook in Sennacherib's nose, and his bridle in his lips, and turn him back by the way by which he came." The Lord had said, concerning the king of Assyria, "He shall not come into this city, nor shoot an arrow there, nor come before it with shield, nor cast a bank against it. By the way that he came, by the same shall he return, and shall not come into this city. For I will defend this city, to save it, for my own sake, and for my servant David's sake."

Meanwhile it is probable that Sennacherib, having received the submission of Libnah, had advanced upon Egypt. It was important to crush an Egyptian army which had been collected against him by a certain Sethos, one of the many native princes who at this time ruled in the Lower country before the great Ethiopian monarch Tehrak or Tirhakah, who was known to be on his march, should effect a junction with the troops of this minor potentate. Sethos, with his army, was at Pelusium; and Sennacherib, advancing to attack him, had arrived within sight of the Egyptian host, and pitched his camp over against the camp of the enemy, just at the time to when Hezekiah received his letter and made the prayer to which Isaiah was instructed to respond. The two hosts lay down at night in their respective stations, the Egyptians and their king full of anxious alarm, Sennacherib and his Assyrians proudly confident, intending on the morrow to advance to the combat and repeat the lesson taught at Raphia and Altaku. But no morrow was to break on the great mass of those who took their rest in the tents of the Assyrians. The divine fiat had gone forth. In the night, as they slept, destruction fell upon them. "The angel of the Lord went out, and smote in the camp of the Assyrians an hundred fourscore and five thousand; and when they arose early in the morning, behold, they were all dead corpses." A miracle, like the destruction of the first-born, had been wrought, but this time on the enemies of the Egyptians, who naturally ascribed their deliverance to the interposition of their own gods; and seeing the enemy in confusion and retreat, pressed hastily after him, distressed his flying columns, and cut off his stragglers. The Assyrian king returned home to Nineveh, shorn of his glory, with the shattered remains of his great host, and cast that proud capital into a state of despair and grief, which the genius of an AEschylus might have rejoiced to depict, but which no less powerful pen could adequately portray.

It is difficult to say how soon Assyria recovered from this terrible blow. The annals of Sennacherib, as might have been expected, omit it altogether, and represent the Assyrian monarch as engaged in a continuous series of successful campaigns, which seem to extend uninterruptedly from his third to his tenth year. It is possible that while the Assyrian expedition was in progress, under the eye of Sennacherib himself, a successful war was being conducted by one of his generals in the mountains of Armenia, and that Sennacherib was thus enabled, without absolutely falsifying history, to parade as his own certain victories gained by this leader in the very year of his own reverse. It is even conceivable that the power of Assyria was not so injured by the loss of a single great army, as to make it necessary for her to stop even for one year in the course of her aggressive warfare; and thus the expeditions of Sennacherib may form an uninterrupted series, the eight campaigns which are assigned to him occupying eight consecutive years. But on the other hand it is quite as probable that there are gaps in the history, some years having been omitted altogether. The Taylor Cylinder records but eight campaigns, yet it was certainly written as late as Sennacherib's fifteenth year. It contains no notice of any events in Sennacherib's first or second year; and it may consequently make other omissions covering equal or larger intervals. Thus the destruction of the Assyrian army at Pelusium may have been followed by a pause of some years' duration in the usual aggressive expeditions; and it may very probably have encouraged the Babylonians in the attempt to shake off the Assyrian yoke, which they certainly made towards the middle of Sennacherib's reign.

But while it appears to be probable that consequences of some importance followed on the Pelusiac calamity, it is tolerably certain that no such tremendous results flowed from it as some writers have imagined. The murder of the disgraced Sennacherib "within fifty-five days" of his return to Nineveh, seems to be an invention of the Alexandrian Jew who wrote the Book of Tobit. The total destruction of the empire in consequence of the blow, is an exaggeration of Josephus, rashly credited by some moderns. Sennacherib did not die till B.C. 681, seventeen years after his misfortune; and the Empire suffered so little that we find Esar-haddon, a few years later, in full possession of all the territory that any king before him had over held, ruling from Babylonia to Egypt, or (as he himself expresses it) "from the rising up of the sun to the going down of the same." Even Sennacherib himself was not prevented by his calamity from undertaking important wars during the latter part of his reign. We shall see shortly that he recovered Babylon, chastised Susiana, and invaded Cilicia, in the course of the seventeen years which intervened between his flight from Pelusium and his decease. Moreover, there is evidence that he employed himself during this part of his reign in the consolidation of the Western provinces, which first appear about his twelfth year as integral portions of the Empire, furnishing eponyms in their turn, and thus taking equal rank with the ancient provinces of Assyria Proper, Adiabene, and Mesopotamia.

The fifth campaign of Sennacherib, according to his own annals, was partly in a mountainous country which he calls Nipur or Nibur—probably the most northern portion of the Zagros range where it abuts on Ararat. He there took a number of small towns, after which he proceeded westward and contended with a certain Maniya king of Dayan, which was a part of Taurus bordering on Cilicia. He boasts that he penetrated further into this region than any king before him; and the boast is confirmed by the fact that the geographical names which appear are almost entirely new to us. The expedition was a plundering raid, not an attempt at conquest. Sennacherib ravaged the country, burnt the towns, and carried away with him all the valuables, the flocks and herds, and the inhabitants.

After this it appears that for at least three years he was engaged in a fierce struggle with the combined Babylonians and Susianians. The troubles recommenced by an attempt of the Chaldaeans of Beth-Yakin to withdraw themselves from the Assyrian territory, and to transfer their allegiance to the Elymaean king. Carrying with them their gods and their treasures, they embarked in their ships, and crossing "the Great Sea of the Rising Sun"—i.e., the Persian Gulf—landed on the Elamitic coast, where they were kindly received and allowed to take up their abode. Such voluntary removals are not uncommon in the East; and they constantly give rise to complaints and reclamations, which not unfrequently terminate in an appeal to the arbitrament of the sword. Sennacherib does not inform us whether he made any attempt to recover his lost subjects by diplomatic representations at the court of Susa. If he did, they were unsuccessful; and in order to obtain redress, he was compelled to resort to force, and to undertake an expedition into the Elamitie territory. It is remarkable that he determined to make his invasion by sea. Their frequent wars on the Syrian coasts had by this time familiarized the Assyrians with the idea, if not with the practice, of navigation; and as their suzerainty over Phoenicia placed at their disposal a large body of skilled shipwrights, and a number of the best sailors in the world, it was natural that they should resolve to employ naval as well as military force to advance their dominion. We have seen that, as early as the time of Shalmaneser, the Assyrians ventured themselves in ships, and, in conjunction with the Phoenicians of the mainland, engaged the vessels of the Island Tyre. It is probable that the precedent thus set was followed by later kings, and that both Sargon and Sennacherib had had the permanent, or occasional services of a fleet on the Mediterranean. But there was a wide difference between such an employment of the navies belonging to their subjects on the sea, to which they were accustomed, and the transfer to the opposite extremity of the empire of the naval strength hitherto confined to the Mediterranean. This thought—certainly not an obvious one—seems to have first occurred to Sennacherib. He conceived the idea of having a navy on both the seas that washed his dominions; and, possessing on his western coast only an adequate supply of skilled shipwrights and sailors he resolved on transporting from his western to his eastern shores such a body of Phoenicians as would enable him to accomplish his purpose. The shipwrights of Tyre and Sidon were carried across Mesopotamia to the Tigris, where they constructed for the Assyrian monarch a fleet of ships like their own galleys, which descended the river to its mouth, and astonished the populations bordering on the Persian Gulf with spectacle never before seen in those waters. Though the Chaldaeans had for centuries navigated this inland sea, and may have occasionally ventured beyond its limits, yet neither as sailors nor as ship-builders was their skill to compare with that of the Phoenicians. The masts and sails, the double tiers of oars, the sharp beaks of the Phoenician ships, were (it is probable) novelties to the nations of these parts, who saw now, for the first time, a fleet debouche from the Tigris, with which their own vessels were quite incapable of contending.

When his fleet was ready Sennacherib put to sea, and crossed in his Phoenician ships from the mouth of the Tigris to the tract occupied by the emigrant Chaldaeans, where he landed and destroyed the newly-built city, captured the inhabitants, ravaged the neighborhood, and burnt a number of Susianian towns, finally reembarking with his captives. Chaldaean and Susianian whom he transported across the gulf to the Chaldaean coast, and then took with him into Assyria. This whole expedition seems to have taken the Susianians by surprise. They had probably expected an invasion by land, and had collected their forces towards the north-western frontier, so that when the troops of Sennacherib landed far in their rear, there were no forces in the neighborhood to resist them. However, the departure of the Assyrians on an expedition regarded as extremely perilous, was the signal for a general revolt of the Babylonians, who once more set up a native king in the person of Susub, and collected an army with which they made ready to give the Assyrians battle on their return. Perhaps they cherished the hope that the fleet which had tempted the dangers of an unknown sea would be seen no more, or expected that, at the best, it would bring back the shattered remnants of a defeated army. If so, they were disappointed. The Assyrian troops landed on their coast flushed with success, and finding the Babylonians in revolt, proceeded to chastise them; defeated their forces in a great battle; captured their king, Susub; and when the Susianians came, somewhat tardily, to their succor, attacked and routed their army. A vast number of prisoners, and among them Susub himself, were carried off by the victors and conveyed to Nineveh.

Shortly after this successful campaign, possibly in the very next year, Sennacherib resolved to break the power of Susiana by a great expedition directed solely against that country. The Susianians had, as already related, been strong enough in the reign of Sargon to deprive Assyria of a portion of her territory; and Kudur-Nakhunta, the Elymaean king, still held two cities, Beth-Kahiri and Raza, which were regarded by Sennacherib as a part of his paternal inheritance. The first object of the war was the recovery of these two towns, which were taken without any difficulty and reattached to the Assyrian Empire. Sennacherib then pressed on into the heart of Susiana, taking and destroying thirty-four large cities, whose names he mentions, together with a still greater number of villages, all of which he gave to the flames. Wasting and destroying in this way he drew near to Vadakat or Badaca, the second city of the kingdom, where Kudur-Nakhunta had for the time fixed his residence. The Elamitic king, hearing of his rapid approach, took fright, and, hastily quitting Badaca, fled away to a city called Khidala, at the foot of the mountains, where alone he could feel himself in safety. Sennacherib then advanced to Badaca, besieged it, and took it by assault; after which affairs seem to have required his presence at Nineveh, and, leaving his conquest incomplete, he returned home with a large booty.

A third campaign in these parts, the most important of all, followed. Susub, the Chaldaean prince whom Sennacherib had carried off to Assyria, in the year of his naval expedition escaped from his confinement, and, returning to Babylon, was once more hailed as king by the inhabitants. Aware of his inability to maintain himself on the throne against the will of the Assyrians, unless he were assisted by the arms of a powerful ally, he resolved to obtain, if possible, the immediate aid of the neighboring Elamitic monarch. Kolar-Nakhunta, the late antagonist of Sennacherib, was dead, having survived his disgraceful flight from Badaca only three months; and Ummanminan, his younger brother, held the throne. Susub, bent on contracting an alliance with this prince, did not scruple at an act of sacrilege to obtain his end. He broke open the treasury of the great temple of Bel at Babylon, and seizing the gold and silver belonging to the god, sent it as a present to Ummanminan, with an urgent entreaty that he would instantly collect his troops and march to his aid. The Elamitic monarch, yielding to a request thus powerfully backed, and perhaps sufficiently wise to see that the interests of Susiana required an independent Babylon, set his troops in motion without any delay, and advanced to the banks of the Tigris. At the same time a number of the Aramaean tribes on the middle Euphrates, which Sennacherib had reduced in his third year, revolted, and sent their forces to swell the army of Susub. A great battle was fought at Khaluli, a town on the lower Tigris, between the troops of Sennacherib and this allied host; the combat was long and bloody, but at last the Assyrians conquered. Susub and his Elamitic ally took to flight and made their escape. Nebosumiskun, a son of Merodach-Baladan, and many other chiefs of high rank, were captured. The army was completely routed and broken up. Babylon submitted, and was severely punished; the fortifications were destroyed, the temples plundered and burnt, and the images of the gods broken to pieces. Perhaps the rebel city now received for viceroy Regibelus or Mesesimordachus, whom the Canon of Ptolemy, which is silent about Susub, makes contemporary with the middle portion of Sennacherib's reign.

The only other expedition which can be assigned, on important evidence, to the reign of Sennacherib, is one against Cilicia, in which he is said to have been opposed by Greeks. According to Abydenus, a Greek fleet guarded the Cilician shore, which the vessels of Sennacherib engaged and defeated. Polyhistor seems to say that the Greeks also suffered a defeat by land in Cilicia itself, after which Sennacherib took possession of the country, and built Tarsus there on the model of Babylon. The prominence here given to Greeks by Greek writers is undoubtedly remarkable, and it throws a certain amount of suspicion over the whole story. Still, as the Greek element in Cyprus was certainly important at this time, and as the occupation of Cilicis, by the Assyrians may have appeared to the Cyprian Greeks to endanger their independence, it is conceivable that they lent some assistance to the natives of the country, who were a hardy race, fond of freedom, and never very easily brought into subjection. The admission af a double defeat makes it evident that the tale is not the invention of Greek national vanity. Abydenus and Polyhistor probably derive it from Berosus, who must also have made the statement that Tarsus was now founded by Sennacherib, and constructed, after the pattern of Babylon. The occupation of newly conquered countries, by the establishnient in them of large cities in which foreign colonists were placed by the conquerors, was practice commenced by Sargon, which his son is not unlikely to have followed. Tarsus was always regarded by the Greeks as an Assyrian town; and although they gave different accounts of the time of its foundation, their disagreement in this respect does not invalidate their evidence as to the main fact itself, which is intrinsically probable. The evidence of Polyhistor and Abydenus as to the date of the foundation, representing, as it must, the testimony of Berosus upon the point, is to be preferred; and we may accept it as a fact, beyond all reasonable doubt, that the native city of St. Paul derived, if not its origin, yet, at any rate, its later splendor and magnificence, from the antagonist of Hezekiah.

That this Cilician war occurred late in the reign of Sennacherib, appears to follow from the absence of any account of it from his general annals. These, it is probable, extend no further than his sixteenth year, B.C. 689, thus leaving blank his last eight years, from B.C. 689 to 681. The defeat of the Greeks, the occupation of Cilicia, and the founding of Tarsus, may well have fallen into this interval. To the same time may have belonged Sennacherib's conquest of Edom.

There is reason to suspect that these successes of Sennacherib on the western limits of his empire were more than counterbalanced by a contemporaneous loss at the extreme south-east. The Canon of Ptolemy marks the year B.C. 688 as the first of an interregnum at Babylon which continues from that date till the accession of Esar-haddon in B.C. 680. Interregna in this document—[—Greek—] as they are termed—indicate periods of extreme disturbance, when pretender succeeded to pretender, or when the country was split up into a number of petty kingdoms. The Assyrian yoke, in either case, must have been rejected; and Babylonia must have succeeded at this time in maintaining, for the space of eight years, a separate and independent existence, albeit troubled and precarious. The fact that she continued free so long, while she again succumbed at the very commencement of the reign of Esar-haddon, may lead us to suspect that she owed this spell of liberty to the increasing years of the Assyrian monarch, who, as the infirmities of age crept upon him, felt a disinclination towards distant expeditions.

The military glory of Sennacherib was thus in some degree tarnished; first, by the terrible disaster which befell his host on the borders of Egypt; and, secondly, by his failure to maintain the authority which, in the earlier part of his reign, he had estaldished over Babylon. Still, notwithstanding these misfortunes, he must be pronounced one of the most successful of Assyria's warrior kings, and altogether one of the greatest princes that ever sat on the Assyrian throne. His victories of Eltekeh and Khaluli seem to leave been among the most important battles that Assyria ever gained. By the one Egypt and Ethiopia, by the other Susiana and Babylon, were taught that, even united, they were no match for the Assyrian hosts. Sennacherib thus wholesomely impressed his most formidable enemies with the dread of his arms, while at the same time he enlarged, in various directions, the limits of his dominions. He warred in regions to which no earlier Assyrian monarch had ever penetrated; and he adopted modes of warfare on which none of them had previously ventured. His defeat of a Greek fleet in the Eastern Mediterranean, and his employment of Phoenicians in the Persian Gulf, show an enterprise and versatility which we observe in few Orientals. His selection of Tarsus for the site of a great city indicates a keen appreciation of the merits of a locality, if he was proud, haughty, and self-confident, beyond all former Assyrian kings, it would seem to have been because he felt that he had resources within himself—that he possessed a firm will, a bold heart, and a fertile invention. Most men would have laid aside the sword and given themselves wholly to peaceful pursuits, after such a disaster as that of Pelusium. Sennacherib accepted the judgment as a warning to attempt no further conquests in those parts, but did not allow the calamity to reduce him to inaction. He wisely turned his sword against other enemies, and was rewarded by important successes upon all his other frontiers.

But if, as a warrior, Sennacherib deserves to be placed in the foremost rank of the Assyrian kings, as a builder and a patron of art he is still more eminent. The great palace which he raised at Nineveh surpassed in size and splendor all earlier edifices, and was never excelled in any respect except by one later building. The palace of Asshur-bani-pal, built on the same platform by the grandson of Sennacherib, was, it must be allowed, more exquisite in its ornamentation; but even this edifice did not equal the great work of Sennacherib in the number of its apartments, or the grandeur of its dimensions. Sennacherib's palace covered an area of above eight acres. It consisted of a number of grand halls and smaller chambers, arranged round at least three courts or quadrangles. These courts were respectively 154 feet by 125, 124 feet by 90, and probably a square of about 90 feet. Round the smallest of the courts were grouped apartments of no great size, which, it may be suspected, belonged to the seraglio of the king. The seraglio seems to have been reached through a single narrow passage, leading out of a long gallery—218 feet by 25—which was approached only through two other passages, one leading from each of the two main courts. The principal halls were immediately within the two chief entrances one on the north-east, the other on the opposite or south-west front of the palace. Neither of these two rooms has been completely explored: but the one appears to have been more than 150 and the other was probably 180 feet in length, while the width of each was a little more than 40 feet. Besides these two great halls and the grand gallery already described, the palace contained about twenty rooms of a considerable size, and at least forty or fifty smaller chambers, mostly square, or nearly so, opening out of some hall or large apartment. The actual number of the rooms explored is about sixty; but as in many parts the examination of the building is still incomplete, we may fairly conjecture that the entire number was not less than seventy or eighty.

The palace of Sennacherib preserved all the main features of Assyrian architecture. It was elevated on a platform, eighty or ninety feet above the plain, artificially constructed, and covered with a pavement of bricks. It had probably three grand facades—one on the north-east, where it was ordinarily approached from the town, and the two others on the south-east and the south-west, where it was carried nearly to the edge of the platform, and overhung the two streams of the Khosr-su and the Tigris. Its principal apartment was that which was first entered by the visitor. All the walls ran in straight lines, and all the angles of the rooms and passages were right angles. There were more passages in the building than usual but still the apartments very frequently opened into one another; and almost one-half of the rooms were passage-rooms. The doorways were mostly placed without any regard to regularity, seldom opposite one another, and generally towards the corners of the apartments. There was the curious feature, common in Assyrian edifices, of a room being entered from a court, or from another room, by two or three doorways, which is best explained by supposing that the rank of the person determined the door by which he might enter. Squared recesses in the sides of the rooms were common. The thickness of the walls was great. The apartments, though wider than in other palaces, were still narrow for their length, never much exceeding forty feet; while the courts were much better proportioned.

It was in the size and the number of his rooms, in his use of passages, and in certain features of his ornamentation, that Sennacherib chiefly differed from former builders. He increased the width of the principal state apartments by one-third, which seems to imply the employment of some new mode or material for roofing. In their length he made less alteration, only advancing from 150 to 180 feet, evidently because he aimed, not merely at increasing the size of his rooms, but at improving their proportions. In one instance alone—that of a gallery or passage-room, leading (apparently) from the more public part of the palace to the hareem or private apartments—did he exceed this length, uniting the two portions of the palace by a noble corridor, 218 feet long by 25 feet wide. Into this corridor he brought passages from the two public courts, which he also united together by a third passage, thus greatly facilitating communication between the various blocks of buildings which composed his vast palatial edifice.

The most striking characteristic of Sennacherib's ornamentation is its strong and marked realism. It was under Sennacherib that the practice first obtained of completing each scene by a background, such as actually existed as the time and place of its occurrence. Mountains, rocks, trees, roads, rivers, lakes, were regularly portrayed, an attempt being made to represent the locality, whatever it might be, as truthfully as the artist's skill and the character of his material rendered possible. Nor was this endeavor limited to the broad and general features of the scene only. The wish evidently was to include all the little accessories which the observant eye of an artist might have noted if he had made his drawing with the scene before him. The species of trees is distinguished, in Sennacherib's bas-reliefs; gardens, fields, ponds, reeds, are carefully represented; wild animals are introduced, as stags, boars, and antelopes; birds fly from tree to tree, or stand over their nests feeding the young who stretch up to them; fish disport themselves in the waters; fishermen ply their craft; boatmen and agricultural laborers pursue their avocations; the scene is, as it were, photographed, with all its features—the least and the most important—equally marked, and without any attempt at selection, or any effort after artistic unity.

In the same spirit of realism Sennacherib chooses for artistic representation scenes of a commonplace and everyday character. The trains of attendants who daily enter his palace with game and locusts for his dinner, and cakes and fruit for his dessert, appear on the walls of his passages, exactly as they walked through his courts, bearing the delicacies in which he delighted. Elsewhere he puts before us the entire process of carving and transporting a colossal bull, from the first removal of the huge stone in its rough state from the quarry, to its final elevation on a palace mound as part of the great gateway of a royal residence. We see the trackers dragging the rough block, supported on a low flat-bottomed boat, along the course of a river, disposed in gangs, and working under taskmasters who use their rods upon the slightest provocation. The whole scene must be represented, and so the trackers are all there, to the number of three hundred, costumed according to their nations, and each delineated with as much care as it he were not the exact image of ninety-nine others. We then observe the block transferred to land, and carved into the rough semblance of a bull, in which form it is placed on a rude sledge and conveyed along level ground by gangs of laborers, arranged nearly as before, to the foot of the mound at whose top it has to be placed. The construction of the mound is most elaborately represented. Brickmakers are seen moulding the bricks at its base, while workmen, with baskets at their backs, full of earth, bricks, stones, or rubbish, toil up the ascent—for the mound is already half raised—and empty their burdens out upon the summit. The bull, still lying on its sledge, is then drawn up an inclined plane to the top by four gangs of laborers, in the presence of the monarch and his attendants. After this the carving is completed, and the colossus, having been raised into an upright position, is conveyed along the surface of the platform to the exact site which it is to occupy. This portion of the operation has been represented in one of the illustrations in an earlier part of this volume. From the representation there given the reader may form a notion of the minuteness and elaboration of this entire series of bas-reliefs.

Besides constructing this new palace at Nineveh, Sennacherib seems also to have restored the ancient residence of the kings at the sane place, a building which will probably be found whenever the mound of Nebbi-Yunus is submitted to careful examination. He confined the Tigris to its channel by an embankment of bricks. He constructed a number of canals or aqueducts for the purpose of bringing good water to the capital. He improved the defences of Nineveh, erecting towers of a vast size at some of the gates. And, finally, he built a temple to the god Nergal at Tarbisi (now Sherif khan), about three miles from Nineveh up the Tigris.

In the construction of these great works he made use chiefly, of the forced labor with which his triumphant expeditions into foreign countries had so abundantly supplied him. Chaldaeans, Aramaeans, Armenians, Cilicianns and probably also Egyptians, Ethiopians, Elamites, and Jews, were employed by thousands in the formation of the vast mounds, in the transport and elevation of the colossal bulls, in the moulding of the bricks, and the erection of the walls of the various edifices, in the excavation of the canals, and the construction of the embankments. They wrought in gangs, each gang having a costume peculiar to it, which probably marked its nation. Over each was placed a number of taskmasters, armed with staves, who urged on the work with blows, and severely punished any neglect or remissness. Assyrian foremen had the general direction of the works, and were entrusted with all such portions as required skill or judgment. The forced laborers often worked in fetters, which were sometimes supported by a bar fastened to the waist, while sometimes they consisted merely of shackles round the ankles. The king himself often witnessed the labors, standing in his chariot, which on these occasions was drawn by some of his attendants.

The Assyrian monuments throw but little light on the circumstances which led to the assassination of Sennacherib; and we are reduced to conjecture the causes of so strange an event. Our various sources of information make it clear that he had a large family of sons. The eldest of them, Asshurinadi-su, had been entrusted by Sennacherib with the government of Babylon and might reasonably have expected to succeed him on the throne of Assyria; but it is probable that he died before his father, either by a natural death, or by violence, during one of the many Babylonian revolts. It may be suspected that Sennacherib had a second son, of whose name Nergal was the first element; and it is certain that he had three others, Adrammelech (or Ardumuzanes), Sharezer, and Esar-haddon. Perhaps, upon the death of Asshur-inadi-su, disputes arose about the succession. Adrammelech and Sharezer, anxious to obtain the throne for themselves, plotted against the life of their father, and having slain him in a temple as he was worshipping, proceeded further to remove their brother Nergilus, who claimed the crown and wore it for a brief space after Sennacherib's death. Having murdered him, they expected to obtain the throne without further difficulty; but Esar-haddon, who at the time commanded the army which watched the Armenian frontier, now came forward, assumed the title of King, and prepared to march upon Nineveh. It was winter, and the inclemency of the weather precluded immediate movement. For some months probably the two assassins were recognized as monarchs at the capital, while the northern army regarded Esar-haddon as the rightful successor of his father. Thus died the great Sennacherib, a victim to the ambition of his sons.

It was a sad end to a reign which, on the whole, had been so glorious; and it was a sign that the empire was now verging on that decline which sooner or later overtakes all kingdoms, and indeed all things sublunary. Against plots without, arising from the ambition of subjects who see, or think they see, at any particular juncture an opportunity of seizing the great prize of supreme dominion, it is impossible, even in the most vigorous empire, to provide any complete security. But during the period of vigor, harmony within the palace, and confidence in each other inspires and unites all the members of the royal house. When discord has once entered inside the gates, when the family no longer holds together, when suspicion and jealousy have replaced the trust and affection of a happier time, the empire has passed into the declining stage, and has already begun the descent which conducts, by quick or slow degrees, to destruction. The murder of Sennacherib, if it was, as perhaps it was, a judgment on the individual, was, at least equally, a judgment on the nation. When, in an absolute monarchy, the palace becomes the scene of the worst crimes, the doom of the kingdom is sealed—it totters to its fall—and requires but a touch from without to collapse into a heap of ruins.

Esar-haddon, the son and successor of Sennacherib, is proved by the Assyrian Canon, to have ascended the throne of Assyria in B.C. 681—the year immediately previous to that which the Canon of Ptolemy makes his first year in Babylon, viz., B.C. 680. He was succeeded by his son Asshur-bani-pal, or Sardanapalus, in B.C. 668, and thus held the crown no more than thirteen years. Esar-haddon's inscriptions show that he was engaged for some time after his accession in a war with his half-brothers, who, at the head of a large body of troops, disputed his right to the crown. Esar-haddon marched from the Armenian frontier, where (as already observed) he was stationed at the time of his father's death, against this army, defeated it in the country of Khanirabbat (north-west of Nineveh), and proceeding to the capital, was universally acknowledged king. According to Abydenus,

Adrammelech fell in the battle; but better authorities state that both he and his brother, Sharezer, escaped into Armenia, where they were kindly treated by the reigning monarch, who gave them lands, which long continued in the possession of their posterity.

The chief record which we possess of Esar-haddon is a cylinder inscription, existing in duplicate, which describes about nine campaigns, and may probably have been composed in or about his tenth year. A memorial which he set up at the mouth of the Nahr-el-Kolb, and a cylinder of his son's, add some important information with respect to the latter part of his reign. One or two notices in the Old Testament connect him with the history of the Jews. And Abydenus, besides the passage already quoted, has an allusion to some of his foreign conquests. Such are the chief materials from which the modern inquirer has to reconstruct the history of this great king.

It appears that the first expedition of Esar-haddon was into Phoenicia. Abdi-Milkut king of Sidon, and Sandu-arra king of the adjoining part of Lebanon, had formed an alliance and revolted from the Assyrians, probably during the troubles which ensued on Sennacherib's death. Esar-haddon attacked Sidon first, and soon took the city; but Aladi-Milkut made his escape to an island—Aradus or Cyprus—where, perhaps, he thought himself secure. Esar-haddon, however, determined on pursuit. He traversed the sea "like a fish," and made Abdi-Milkut prisoner; after which he turned his arms against Sandu-arra, attacked him in the fastnesses of his mountains, defeated his troops, and possessed himself of his person. The rebellion of the two captive kings was punished by their execution; the walls of Sidon were destroyed; its inhabitants, and those of the whole tract of coast in the neighborhood, were carried off into Assyria, and thence scattered among the provinces; a new town was built, which was named after Esarhaddon, and was intended to take the place of Sidon as the chief city of these parts; and colonists were brought from Chaldaea and Susiana to occupy the new capital and the adjoining region. An Assyrian governor was appointed to administer the conquered province.

Esar-haddon's next campaign seems to have been in Armenia. He took a city called Arza**, which, he says, was in the neighborhood of Muzr, and carried off the inhabitants, together with a number of mountain animals, placing the former in a position "beyond the eastern gate of Nineveh." At the same time he received the submission of Tiuspa the Cimmerian.

His third campaign was in Cilicia and the adjoining regions. The Cilicians, whom Sennacherib had so recently subdued, reasserted their independence at his death, and allied themselves with the Tibareni, or people of Tubal, who possess at the high mountain tract about the junction of Amaans and Taurus. Esar-haddon inflicted a defeat on the Cilicians, and then invaded the mountain region, where he took twenty-one towns and a larger number of villages, all of which he plundered and burnt. The inhabitants he carried away captive, as usual but he made no attempt to hold the ravaged districts by means of new cities or fresh colonists.

This expedition was followed by one or two petty wars in the north-west and the north-east after which Esar-haddon, probably about his sixth year B.C. 675, made an expedition into Chaldaea. It appears that a son of Merodach-Baladan, Nebo-zirzi-sidi by name, had re-established himself on the Chaldaean coast, by the help of the Susianians; while his brother, Nahid-Marduk, had thought it more prudent to court the favor of the great Assyrian monarch, and had quitted his refuge in Susiana to present himself before Esar-haddon's foot-stool at Nineveh. This judicious step had all the success that he could have expected or desired. Esar-haddon, having conquered the ill-judging Nebo-zirzi-sidi, made over to the more clear-sighted Nahid-Marduk the whole of the maritime region that had been ruled by his brother. At the same time the Assyrian monarch deposed a Chaldaean prince who had established his authority over a small town in the neighborhood of Babylon, and set up another in his place, thus pursuing the same system of division in Babylonia which we shall hereafter find that he pursued in Egypt.

Esar-haddon after this was engaged in a war with Edom. He there took a city which bore the same name as the country—a city previously, he tells us, taken by his father—and transported the inhabitants into Assyria, at the same time carrying off certain images of the Edomite gods. Hereupon the king, who was named Hazael, sent an embassy to Nineveh, to make submission and offer presents, while at the same time he supplicated Isar-haddon to restore his gods and allow them to be conveyed back to their own proper country. Esarhaddon granted the request, and restored the images to the envoy; but as a compensation for this boon, he demanded an increase of the annual tribute, which was augmented in consequence by sixty-five camels. He also nominated to the Edomite throne, either in succession or in joint sovereignty, a female named Tabua, who had been born and brought up in his own palace.

The expedition next mentioned on Esar-haddon's principal cylinder is one presenting some difficulty. The scene of it is a country called Bazu, which is said to be "remote, on the extreme confines of the earth, on the other side of the desert." It was reached by traversing it hundred and forty farsakhs (490 miles) of sandy desert, then twenty farsakhs (70 miles) of fertile land, and beyond that a stony region. None of the kings of Assyria, down to the time of Esar-haddon, had ever penetrated so far. Bazu lay beyond Khazu, which was the name of the stony tract, and Bazu had for its chief town a city called Yedih, which was under the rule of a king named Laile. It is thought, from the combinaqon of these names, and from the general description of the region—of its remoteness and of the way in which it was reached—that it was probably the district of Arabia beyond Nedjif which lies along the Jebel Shammer, and corresponds closely with the modern Arab kingdom of Hira. Esar-haddon boasts that he marched into the middle of the territory, that he slew eight of its sovereigns, and carried into Assyria their gods, their treasures, and their subjects; and that, though Laile escaped him, he too lost his gods, which were seized and conveyed to Nineveh. Then Laile, like the Idumaean monarch above mentioned, felt it necessary to humble himself. He went in person to the Assyrian capital, prostrated himself before the royal footstool, and entreated for the restoration of his gods; which Esar-haddon consented to give back, but solely on the condition that Laile became thenceforth one of his tributaries.

If this expedition was really carried into the quarter here supposed, Esar-haddon performed a feat never paralleled in history, excepting by Augustus and Nushirvan. He led an army across the deserts which everywhere guard Arabia on the land side, and penetrated to the more fertile tracts beyond them, a region of settled inhabitants and of cities. He there took and spoiled several towns; and he returned to his own country without suffering disaster. Considering the physical perils of the desert itself, and the warlike character of its inhabitants, whom no conqueror has ever really subdued, this was a most remarkable success. The dangers of the simoom may have been exaggerated, and the total aridity of the northern region may have been overstated by many writers; but the difficulty of carrying water and provisions for a large army, and the peril of a plunge into the wilderness with a small one, can scarcely be stated in too strong terms, and have proved sufficient to deter most Eastern conquerors from even the thoughts of an Arabian expedition. Alexander would, perhaps, had he lived, have attempted an invasion from the side of the Persian Gulf; and Trajan actually succeeded in bringing under the Roman yoke an outlying portion of the country—the district between Damascus and the Red Sea; but Arabia has been deeply penetrated thrice only in the history of the world; and Esar-haddon is the sole monarch who ever ventured to conduct in person such an attack.

From the arid regions of the great peninsula Esar-haddon proceeded, probably in another year, to the invasion of the marsh-country on the Euphrates, where the Aramaean tribe of the Gambulu had their habitations, dwelling (he tells us) "like fish, in the midst of the waters"—doubtless much after the fashion of the modern Khuzeyl and Affej Arabs, the latter of whom inhabit nearly the same tract. The sheikh of this tribe had revolted; but on the approach of the Assyrians he submitted himself, bringing in person the arrears of his tribute and a present of buffaloes, whereby he sought to propitiate the wrath of his suzerain. Esar-haddon states that he forgave him; that he strengthened his capital with fresh works, placed a garrison in it, and made it a stronghold to protect the territory against the attacks of the Susianians.

The last expedition mentioned on the cylinder, which seems not to have been conducted by the king in person, was against the country of Bikni, or Bikan, one of the more remote regions of Media—perhaps Azerbijan. No Assyrian monarch before Esar-haddon had ever invaded this region. It was under the government of a number of chiefs—the Arian character of whose names is unmistakable—each of whom ruled over his own town and the adjacent district. Esar-haddon seized two of the chiefs and carried them off to Assyria, whereupon several others made their submission, consenting to pay a tribute and to divide their authority with Assyrian officers.

It is probable that these various expeditions occupied Esarhaddon from B.C. 681, the year of his accession, to B.C. 671, when it is likely that they were recorded on the existing cylinder. The expeditions are ten in number, directed against countries remote from one another; and each may well have occupied an entire year. There would thus remain only three more years of the king's reign, after the termination of the chief native record, during which his history has to be learnt from other sources. Into this space falls, almost certainly, the greatest of Esar-haddon's exploits the conquest of Egypt; and, probably, one of the most interesting episodes of his reign—the punishment and pardon of Manasseh. With the consideration of these two events the military history of his reign will terminate.

The conquest of Egypt by Esar-haddon, though concealed from Herodotus, and not known even to Diodorus, was no secret to the more learned Greeks, who probably found an account of the expedition in the great work of Berosus. All that we know of its circumstances is derived from an imperfect transcript of the Nahr-el-Kelb tablet, and a short notice in the annals of Esar-haddon's son and successor, Asshur-bani-pal, who finds it necessary to make an allusion to the former doings of his father in Egypt, in order to render intelligible the state of affairs when he himself invades the country. According to these notices, it would appear that Esar-haddon, having entered Egypt with a large army, probably in B.C. 670, gained a great battle over the forces of Tirhakah in the lower country, and took Memphis, the city where the Ethiopian held his court, after which he proceeded southwards, and conquered the whole of the Nile valley as far as the southern boundary of the Theban district. Thebes itself was taken and Tirhakah retreated into Ethiopia. Esar-haddon thus became master of all Egypt, at least as far as Thebes or Diospolis, the No or No-Amon of scripture. He then broke up the country into twenty governments, appointing in each town a ruler who bore the title of king, but placing all the others to a certain extent under the authority of the prince who reigned at Memphis. This was Neco, the father of Psammetichus (Psamatik I.)—a native Egyptian of whom we have some mention both in Herodotus and in the fragments of Manetho. The remaining rulers were likewise, for the most part, native Egyptians: though in two or three instances the governments appear to have been committed to Assyrian officers. Esar-haddon, having made these arrangements, and having set up his tablet at the mouth of the Nahr-el-Kelb side by side with that of Rameses II., returned to his own country, and proceeded to introduce sphinxes into the ornamentation of his palaces, while, at the same time, he attached to his former titles an additional clause, in which he declared himself to be "king of the kings of Egypt, and conqueror of Ethiopia."

The revolt of Manasseh king of Judah may have happened shortly before or shortly after the conquest of Egypt. It was not regarded as of sufficient importance to call for the personal intervention of the Assyrian monarch. The "captains of the host of the king of Assyria" were entrusted with the task of Manasseh's subjection; and, proceeding into Judaea, they "took him, and bound him with chains, and carried him to Babylon," where Esar-haddon had built himself a palace, and often held his court. The Great king at first treated his prisoner severely; and the "affliction" which he thus suffered is said to have broken his pride and caused him to humble himself before God, and to repent of all the cruelties and idolatries which had brought this judgment upon him. Then God "was entreated of him, and heard his supplication, and brought him back again to Jerusalem into his kingdom." The crime of defection was overlooked by the Assyrian monarch, Manasseh was pardoned, and sent back to Jerusalem: where he was allowed to resume the reins of government, but on the condition, if we may judge by the usual practice of the Assyrians in such cases, of paying an increased tribute.

It may have been in connection with this restoration of Manasseh to his throne—an act of doubtful policy from an Assyrian point of view—that Esar-haddon determined on a project by which the hold of Assyria upon Palestine was considerably strengthened. Sargon, as has been already observed when he removed the Israelites from Sumaria, supplied their place by colonists from Babylon, Cutha, Sippara, Ava, Hamath, and Arabia; this planting a foreign garrison in the region which would be likely to preserve its fidelity. Esar-haddon resolved to strengthen this element. He gathered men from Babylon, Orchoe, Susa, Elymais, Persia, and other neighboring regions, and entrusting them to an officer of high rank—"the great and noble Asnapper"—had them conveyed to Palestine and settled over the whole country, which until this time must have been somewhat thinly peopled. The restoration of Manasseh, and the augmentation of this foreign element in Palestine, are thus portions, but counterbalancing portions, of one scheme—a scheme, the sole object of which was the pacification of the empire by whatever means, gentle or severe, seemed best calculated to effect the purpose.

The last years of Esar-haddon were, to some extent, clouded with disaster. He appears to have fallen ill in B.C. 669: and the knowledge of this fact at once produced revolution in Egypt. Tirhakah issued from his Ethiopian fastnesses, descended the valley of the Nile, expelled the kings set up by Esar-haddon, and re-established his authority over the whole country. Esar-haddon, unable to take the field, resolved to resign the cares of the empire to his eldest son, Asshur-bani-pal, and to retire into a secondary position. Relinquishing the crown of Assyria, and retaining that of Babylon only, he had Asshur-bani-pal proclaimed king of Assyria, and retired to the southern capital. There he appears to have died in B.C. 668, or early in B.C. 667, leaving Asshur-bani-pal sole sovereign of the entire empire.

Of the architecture of Esar-haddon, and of the state of the arts generally in his time, it is difficult to speak positively. Though he appears to have been one of the most indefatigable constructors of great works that Assyria produced, having erected during the short period over which his reign extended no fewer than four palaces and above thirty temples, yet it happens unfortunately that we are not as yet in a condition to pronounce a decisive judgment either on the plan of his buildings or on the merits of their ornamentation of his three great palaces, which were situated at Babylon, Calah, and Nineveh, one only—that at Calah or Nimrud has been to any large extent explored. Even in this case the exploration was far from complete, and the ground plan of his palace is still very defective. But this is not the worst. The palace itself had never been finished; its ornamentation had scarcely been begun; and the little of this that was original had been so damaged by a furious conflagration, that it perished almost at the moment of discovery. We are thus reduced to judge of the sculptures of Esar-haddon by the reports of those who saw them ere they fell to pieces, and by one or two drawings, while we have to form our conception of his buildings from a half-explored fragment of a half-finished palace, which was moreover destroyed by fire before completion.

The palace of Esar-haddon at Calah was built at the south-western corner of the Nimrud mound, abutting towards the west on the Tigris, and towards the south on the valley formed by the Shor-Derreh torrent. It faced northwards, and was entered on this side from the open space of the platform, through a portal guarded by two winged bulls of the ordinary character. The visitor on entering found himself in a large court, 280 feet by 100, bounded on the north side by a mere wall, but on the other three sides surrounded by buildings. The main building was opposite to him, and was entered from the court by two portals, one directly facing the great northern gate of the court, and the other a little to the left hand, the former guarded by colossal bulls, the latter merely reveted with slabs. These portals both led into the same room—the room already described in an earlier page of this work—which was designed on the most magnificent scale of all the Assyrian apartments, but was so broken up through the inability of the architect to roof in a wide space without abundant support, that, practically, it formed rather a suite of four moderate-sized chambers than a single grand hall. The plan of this apartment will be seen by referring to [PLATE XLIII., Fig. 2.] Viewed as a single apartment, the room was 165 feet in length by 62 feet in width, and thus contained an area of 10,230 square feet, a space nearly half as large again as that covered by the greatest of the halls of Sennacherib, which was 7200 feet. Viewed as a suite of chambers, the rooms may be described as two long and narrow halls running parallel to one another, and communicating by a grand doorway in the middle, with two smaller chambers placed at the two ends, running at right angles to the principal ones. The small chambers were 62 feet long, and respectively 19 feet and 23 feet wide; the larger ones were 110 feet long, with a width respectively of 20 feet and 28 feet. The inner of the two long parallel chambers communicated by a grand doorway, guarded by sphinxes and colossal lions, either with a small court or with a large chamber extending to the southern edge of the mound; and the two end rooms communicated with smaller apartments in the same direction. The buildings to the right and left of the great court seem to have been entirely separate from those at its southern end: to the left they were wholly unexamined; on the right some explorations were conducted which gave the usual result of several long narrow apartments, with perhaps one or two passages. The extent of the palace westward, southward, and eastward is uncertain: eastward it was unexplored; southward and westward the mound had been eaten into by the Tigris and the Shor-Derreh torrent.

The walls of Esar-haddon's palace were composed, in the usual way, of sun-dried bricks, reveted with slabs of alabaster. Instead, however, of quarrying fresh alabaster slabs for the purpose, the king preferred to make use of those which were already on the summit of the mound, covering the walls of the north-western and central palaces, which, no doubt, had fallen into decay. His workmen tore down these sculptured monuments from their original position, and transferring them to the site of the new palace, arranged them so as to cover the freshly-raised walls, generally placing the carved side against the crude brick, and leaving the back exposed to receive fresh sculptures, but sometimes exposing the old sculpture, which, however, in such cases, it was probably intended to remove by the chisel. This process was still going on, when either Esarhaddon died and the works were stopped, or the palace was destroyed by fire. Scarcely any of the new sculptures had been executed. The only exceptions were the bulls and lions at the various portals, a few reliefs in close proximity to them, and some complete figures of crouching sphinxes, which had been placed as ornaments, and possibly also as the bases of supports, within the span of the two widest doorways. There was nothing very remarkable about the bulls; the lions were spirited, and more true to nature than usual; the sphinxes were curious, being Egyptian in idea, but thoroughly Assyrianized, having the horned cap common on bulls, the Assyrian arrangement of hair, Assyrian earrings, and wings nearly like those of the ordinary winged bull or lion. [PLATE CXLVI., Fig. 2.] The figures near the lions were mythic, and exhibited somewhat more than usual grotesqueness, as we learn from the representations of them given by Mr. Layard.

While the evidence of the actual monuments as to the character of Esar-haddon's buildings and their ornamentation is thus scanty, it happens, curiously, that the Inscriptions furnish a particularly elaborate and detailed account of them. It appears, from the principal record of the time, that the temples which Esar-haddon built in Assyria and Babylonia—thirty-six in number—were richly adorned with plates of silver and gold, which made then (in the words of the Inscription) "as splendid as the day." His palace at Nineveh, a building situated on the mound called Nebbi Yunus, was, we are told, erected upon the site of a former palace of the kings of Assyria. Preparations for its construction were made, as for the great buildings of Solomon by the collection of materials, iii wood, stone, and metal, beforehand: these were furnished by the Phoenician, Syrian, and Cyprian monarchs, who sent to Nineveh for the purpose great beams of cedar, cypress, and ebony, stone statues, and various works in metals of different kinds. The palace itself is said to have exceeded in size all buildings of former kings. It was roofed with carved beams of cedar-wood; it was in part supported by columns of cypress wood, ornamented and strengthened with rings of silver and of iron; the portals were guarded by stone bulls and lions; and the gates were made of ebony and cypress ornamented with iron, silver, and ivory. There was, of course, the usual adornment of the walls by means of sculptured slabs and enamelled bricks. If the prejudices of the Mahometans against the possible disturbance of their dead, and against the violation by infidel hands of the supposed tomb of Jonah, should hereafter be dispelled, and excavations be freely allowed in the Nebbi Yunus mound, we may look to obtain very precious relics of Assyrian art from the palace of Esar-haddon, now lying buried beneath the village or the tombs which share between them this most important site.

Of Esar-haddon's Babylonian palace nothing is at present known, beyond the mere fact of its existence; but if the mounds at Hillah should ever be thoroughly explored, we may expect to recover at least its ground-plan, if not its sculptures and other ornaments. The Sherif Khan palace has been examined pretty completely. It was very much inferior to the ordinary palatial edifices of the Assyrians, being in fact only a house which Esar-haddon built as a dwelling for his eldest son during his own lifetime. Like the more imposing buildings of this king, it was probably unfinished at his decease. At any rate its remains add nothing to our knowledge of the state of art in Esar-haddon's time, or to our estimate of that monarch's genius as a builder.

After a reign of thirteen years, Esar-haddon, "king of Assyria, Babylon, Egypt, Meroe, and Ethiopia," as he styles himself in his later inscriptions, died, leaving his crown to his eldest son, Asshur-bani-pal, whom he had already associated in the government. Asshur-bani-pal ascended the throne in B.C. 668, or very early in B.C. 667; and his first act seems to have been to appoint as viceroy of Babylon his younger brother Saul-Mugina, who appears as Sam-mughes in Polyhistor, and as Saosduchinus in the Canon of Ptolemy.

The first war in which Asshur-bani-pal engaged was most probably with Egypt. Late in the reign of Esar-haddon, Tirhakah (as already stated 619) had descended from the upper country, had recovered Thebes, Memphis, and most of the other Egyptian cities, and expelled from them the princes and governors appointed by Esar-haddon upon his conquest. Asshur-bani-pal, shortly after his accession, collected his forces, and marched through Syria into Egypt, where he defeated the army sent against him by Tirhakah in a great battle near the city of Kar-banit. Tirhakah, who was at Memphis, hearing of the disaster that had befallen his army, abandoned Lower Egypt, and sailed up the Nile to Thebes, whither the forces of Asshur-bani-pal followed him; but the nimble Ethiopian retreated still further up the Nile valley, leaving all Egypt from Thebes downwards to his adversary. Asshur-bani-pal, upon this, reinstated in their former governments the various princes and rulers whom his lather had originally appointed, and whom Tirhakah had expelled; and then, having rested and refreshed his army by a short stay in Thebes, returned victoriously by way of Syria to Nineveh.

Scarcely was he departed when intrigues began for the restoration of the Ethiopian power. Neco and some of the other Egyptian governors, whom Asshur-bani-pal had just reinstated in their posts, deserted the Assyrian side and went over to the Ethiopians. Attempts were made to suppress the incipient revolt by the governors who continued faithful; Neco and one or two of his copartners in guilt were seized and sent in chains to Assyria; and some of the cities chiefly implicated, as Sais, Mendes, and Tanis (Zoan), were punished. But the efforts at suppression failed. Tirliakah entered Upper Egypt, and having established himself at Thebes, threatened to extend his authority once more over the whole of the Nilotic valley. Thereupon Asshur-bani-pal, having forgiven Neco, sent him, accompanied by a strong force, into Egypt; and Tirhakah was again compelled to quit the lower country and retire to Upper Egypt, where he soon after died. His crown fell to his step-son, Urdamane, who is perhaps the Rud-Amun of the Hieroglyphics. This prince was at first very successful. He descended the Nile valley in force, defeated the Assyrians near Memphis, drove them to take refuge within its walls, besieged and took the city, and recovered Lower Egypt. Upon this Asshur-bani-pal, who was in the city of Asshur when he heard the news, went in person against his new adversary, who retreated as he advanced, flying from Memphis to Thebes, and from Thebes to a city called Kipkip, far up the course of the Nile. Asshur-bani-pal and his army now entered Thebes, and sacked it. The plunder which was taken, consisting of gold, silver, precious stones, dyed garments, captives male and female, ivory, ebony, tame animals (such as monkeys and elephants) brought up in the palace, obelisks, etc., was carried off and conveyed to Nineveh. Governors were once more set up in the several cities, Psammetichus being probably among them; and, hostages having been taken to secure their fidelity, the Assyrian monarch returned home with his booty.

Between his first and second expedition into Egypt, Asshur-bani-pal was engaged in warlike operations on the Syrian coast, and in transactions of a different character with Cilicia. Returning from Egypt, he made an attack on Tyre, whose king, Baal, had offended him, and having compelled him to submit, exacted from him a large tribute, which he sent away to Nineveh. About the same time Asshur-bani-pal entered into communication with the Cilician monarch, whose name is not given, and took to wife a daughter of that princely house, which was already connected with the royal race of the Sargonids.

Shortly after his second Egyptian expedition, Asshur-bani-pal seems to have invaded Asia Minor. Crossing the Taurus range, he penetrated to a region never before visited by any Assyrian monarch; and, having reduced various towns in these parts and returned to Nineveh, he received an embassy of a very unusual character. "Gyges, king of Lydia," he tells us, "a country on the sea-coast, a remote place, of which the kings his ancestors had never even heard the name, had formerly learnt in a dream the fame of his empire, and had sent officers to his presence to perform homage on his behalf." He now sent a second time to Asshur-bani-pal, and told him that since his submission he had been able to defeat the Cimmerians, who had formerly ravaged his land with impunity; and he begged his acceptance of two Cimmerian chiefs, whom he had taken in battle, together with other presents, which Asshur-bani-pal regarded as a "tribute." About the same time the Assyrian monarch repulsed the attack of the "king of Kharbat," on a district of Babylonia, and, having taken Kharbat, transported its inhabitants to Egypt.

After thus displaying his power and extending his dominions towards the south-west, the north-west, and the south-east, Asshur-bani-pal turned his arms towards the north-east, and invaded Minni, or Persarmenia—the mountain-country about Lakes Van and Urumiyeh. Akhsheri, the king, having lost his capital, Izirtu, and several other cities, was murdered by his subjects; and his son, Vahalli, found himself compelled to make submission, and sent an embassy to Nineveh to do homage, with tribute, presents, and hostages. Asshur-bani-pal received the envoys graciously, pardoned Vahalli, and maintained him upon the throne, but forced him to pay a heavy tribute. He also in this expedition conquered a tract called Paddiri, which former kings of Assyria had severed from Minni and made independent, but which Asshur-bani-pal now attached to his own empire, and placed under an Assyrian governor.

A war of some duration followed with Elam, or Susiana, the flames of which at one time extended over almost the whole empire. This war was caused by a transfer of allegiance. Certain tribes, pressed by a famine, had passed from Susiana into the territories of Asshur-bani-pal, and were allowed to settle there; but when, the famine being over, they wished to return to their former country, Asshur-bani-pal would not consent to their withdrawal. Urtaki, the Susianian king, took umbrage at this refusal, and, determining to revenge himself, commenced hostilities by an invasion of Babylonia. Belubager, king of the important Aramaean tribe of the Gambulu, assisted him and Saul-Mugina, in alarm, sent to his brother for protection. An Assyrian army was dispatched to his aid, before which Urtaki fled. He was, however, pursued, caught and defeated. With some difficulty he escaped and returned to Susa, where within a year he died, without having made any fresh effort to injure or annoy his antagonist.

His death was a signal for a domestic revolution which proved very advantageous to the Assyrians. Urtaki had driven his older brother, Umman-aldas, from the throne, and, passing over the rights of his sons, had assumed the supreme authority. At his death, his younger brother, Temin-Umman, seized the crown, disregarding not only the rights of the sons of Umman-aldas, but likewise those of the sons of Urtaki. As the pretensions of those princes were dangerous, Temin-Umman endeavored to seize their persons with the intention of putting them to death; but they, having timely warning of their danger, fled; and, escaping to Nineveh with their relations and adherents, put themselves under the protection of Asshur-bani-pal. It thus happened that in the expedition which now followed, Asshur-bani-pal had a party which favored him in Elam itself. Temin-Umman, however, aware of this internal weakness, made great efforts to compensate for it by the number of his foreign allies. Two descendants of Merodach-Baladan, who had principalities upon the coast of the Persian Gulf, two mountain chiefs, one of them a blood-connection of the Assyrian crown, two sons of Belu-bagar, sheikh of the Gambulu, and several other inferior chieftains, are mentioned as bringing their troops to his assistance, and fighting in his cause against the Assyrians. All, however, was in vain. Asshur-bani-pal defeated the allies in several engagements, and finally took Temin-Umman prisoner, executed him, and exposed his head over one of the gates of Nineveh. He then divided Elam between two of the sons of Urrtaki, Umman-ibi and Tammarit, establishing the former in Susa, and the latter at a town called Khidal in Eastern Susiana. Great severities were exercised upon the various princes and nobles who had been captured. A son of Temin-Umman was executed with his father. Several grand-sons of Merodach-Baladin suffered mutilation, A Chaldaean prince and one of the chieftains of the Clambulu had their tongues torn out by the roots. Another of the Gambulu chiefs was decapitated. Two of the Temin-Umman's principal officers were chained and flayed. Palaya, a grandson of Merodach-Baladan, was mutilated. Asshur-bani-pal evidently hoped to strike terror into his enemies by these cruel, and now unusual, punishments, which, being inflicted for the most part upon royal personages, must have made a profound impression on the king-reverencing Asiatics.

The impression made was, however, one of horror rather than of alarm. Scarcely had the Assyrians returned to Nineveh, when fresh troubles broke out. Saul-Mugina, discontented with his position, which was one of complete dependence upon his brother, rebelled, and, declaring himself king of Babylon in his own right, sought and obtained a number of important allies among his neighbors. Umman-ibi, though he had received his crown from Asshur-bani-pal, joined him, seduced by a gift of treasure from the various Babylonian temples. Vaiteha, a powerful Arabian prince, and Nebo-belsumi, a surviving grandson of Merodach-Baladan, came into the confederacy; and Saul-Mugina had fair grounds for expecting that he would be able to maintain his independence. But civil discord—the curse of Elam at this period—once more showed itself, and blighted all these fair prospects. Tammarit, the brother of Ummman-ibi, finding that the latter had sent the flower of his army into Babylonia, marched against him, defeated and slew him, and became king of all Elam. Maintaining, however, the policy of his brother, he entered into alliance with Saul-Mugina, and proceeded to put himself at the head of the Elamitic contingent, which was serving in Babylonia. Here a just Nemesis overtook him. Taking advantage of his absence, a certain Inda-bibi (or Inda-bigas), a mountain-chief from the fastnesses of Luristan, raised a revolt in Elam, and succeeded in seating himself upon the throne. The army in Babylonia declining to maintain the cause of Tammarit, he was forced to fly and conceal himself, while the Elamitic troops returned home. Saul-Mugina then lost the most important of his allies at the moment of his greatest danger for his brother had at length marched against him at the head of an immense army, and was overrunning his northern provinces. Without the Elamites it was impossible for Babylon to contend with Assyria in the Open field.

All that Saul-Mugina could do was to defend his towns, which Asshur-bani-pal besieged and took, one after another. The rebel fell into his brother's hands, and suffered a punishment more terrible than any that the relentless conqueror had as yet inflicted on his captured enemies. Others had been mutilated, or beheaded; Saul-Mugina was burnt. The tie of blood, which was held to have aggravated the guilt of his rebellion, was not allowed to be pleaded in mitigation of his sentence.

A pause of some years' duration now occurred. The relations between Assyria and Susiana were unfriendly, but not actually hostile. Inda-bibi had given refuge to Nebo-bel-sumi at the time of Saul Mugina's discomfiture, and Asshur-bani-pal repeatedly but vainly demanded the surrender of the refugee. He did not, however, attempt to enforce his demand by an appeal to arms; and Inda-bibi might have retained his kingdom in peace, had not domestic troubles arisen to disturb him. He was conspired against by the commander of his archers, a second Umman-aldas, who killed him and occupied his throne. Many pretenders, at the same time, arose in different parts of the country; and Asshur-bani-pal, learning how Elam was distracted, determined on a fresh effort to conquer it. He renewed his demand for the surrender of Nebo-bel-sumi, who would have been given up had he not committed suicide. Not content with this success, he (ab. B.C. 645) invaded Elam, besieged and took Bit-Inibi, which had been strongly fortified, and drove Umunan-aldas out of the plain country into the mountains. Susa and Badaca, together with twenty-four other cities, fell into his power; and Western Elam being thus at his disposal, he placed it under the government of Tammarit, who, after his flight from Babylonia, had become a refugee at the Assyrian court. Umman-aldas retained the sovereignty of Eastern Elam.

But it was not long before fresh changes occurred. Tammarit, finding himself little more than puppet-king in the hands of the Assyrians, formed a plot to massacre all the foreign troops left to garrison this country, and so to make himself an independent monarch. His intentions, however, were discovered, and the plot failed. The Assyrians seized him, put him in bonds, and sent him to Nineveh. Western Elam passed under purely military rule, and suffered, it is probable, extreme severities. Under these circumstances, Umman-aldas took heart, and made ready, in the fastnesses to which he had fled, for another and a final effort. Having levied a vast army, he, in the spring of the next year, made himself once more master of Bit-Imbi, and, establishing himself there, prepared to resist the Assyrians. Their forces shortly appeared; and, unable to hold the place against their assaults, Umman-aldas evacuated it with his troops, and fought a retreating fight all the way back to Susa, holding the various strong towns and rivers in succession. Gallant, however, as was his resistance it proved ineffectual. The lines of defence which he chose were forced, one after another; and finally both Susa and Badaca were taken, and the country once more lay at Asshur-bani-pal's mercy. All the towns made their submission. Asshur-bani-pal, burning with anger at their revolt, plundered the capital of its treasures, and gave the other cities up to be spoiled by his soldiers for the space of a month and twenty-three days. He then formally abolished Susianian independence, and attached the country as a province to the Assyrian empire. Thus ended the Susianian war, after it had lasted, with brief interruptions, for the space of (probably) twelve years.

The full occupation given to the Assyrian arms by this long struggle encouraged revolt in other quarters. It was probably about the time when Asshur-bani-pal was engaged in the thick of the contest with Umman-ibi and Saul-Mugina that Psammetichus declared himself independent in Egypt, and commenced a war against the princes who remained faithful to their Assyrian suzerain. Gyges, too, in the far north-west, took the opportunity to break with the formidable power with which he had recently thought it prudent to curry favor, and sent aid to the Egyptian rebel, which rendered him effective service. Egypt freed herself from the Assyrian yoke, and entered on the prosperous period which is known as that of the twenty-sixth (Saite) dynasty. Gyges was less fortunate. Assailed shortly by a terrible enemy, which swept with resistless force over his whole land, he lost his life in the struggle. Assyria was well and quickly avenged; and Ardys, the new monarch, hastened to resume the deferential attitude toward Asshur-bani-pal which his father had unwisely relinquished.

Asshur-bani-pal's next important war was against the Arabs. Some of the desert tribes had, as already mentioned, lent assistance to Saul-Mugina during his revolt against his suzerain, and it was to punish this audacity that Asshur-bani-pal undertook his expedition. His principal enemy was a certain Vaiteha, who had for allies Natun, or Nathan, king of the Nabathivans, and Ammu-ladin, king of Kedar. The fighting seems to have extended along the whole country bordering the Euphrates valley from the Persian Gulf to Syria, and thence southwards by Damascus to Petra. Petra itself, Muhab (or Moab), Hudumimtukrab (Edom), Zaharri (perhaps Zoar), and several other cities were taken by the Assyrians. The final battle was fought at a place called Kutkhuruna, in he mountains near Damascus, where the Arabians were defeated with great slaughter, and the two chief, who had led the Arab contingent to the assistance of Saul-Mugina were made prisoners by the Assyrians. Asshur-bani-pal had them conducted to Nineveh, and there publicly executed.

The annals of Asshur-bani-pal here terminate. They exhibit him to us as a warrior more enterprising and more powerful than any of his predecessors, and as one who enlarged in almost every direction the previous limits of the empire. In Egypt he completed the work which his father Esar-haddon had begun, and established the Assyrian dominion for some years, not only at Sais and at Memphis, but at Thebes. In Asia Minor he carried the Assyrian arms far beyond any former king, conquering large tracts which had never before been invaded, and extending the reputation of his greatness to the extreme western limits of the continent. Against his northern neighbors he contended with unusual success, and towards the close of his reign he reckoned, not only the Minni, but the Urarda, or true Armenians, among his tributaries. Towards the south, he added to the empire the great country of Susiana, never subdued until his reign: and on the west, he signally chastised if he did not actually conquer, the Arabs.

To his military ardor Asshur-bani-pal added a passionate addiction to the pleasure of the chase. Lion-hunting was his especial delight. Sometimes along the banks of reedy streams, sometimes borne mid-channel in his pleasure galley, he sought the king of beasts in his native haunts, roused him by means of hounds and beaters from his lair, and despatched him with his unerring arrows. Sometimes he enjoyed the sport in his own park of paradise. Large and fierce beasts, brought from a distance, were placed in traps about the grounds, and on his approach were set free from their confinement, while he drove among them in his chariot, letting fly his shafts at each with a strong and steady hand, which rarely failed to attain the mark it aimed at. Aided only by two or three attendants armed with spears, he would encounter the terrific spring of the bolder beasts, who rushed frantically at the royal marksman and endeavored to tear him from the chariot-board. Sometimes he would even voluntarily quit this vantage-ground, and, engaging with the brutes on the same level, without the protection of armor, in his everyday dress, with a mere fillet upon his head, he would dare a close combat, and smite them with sword or spear through the heart.

When the supply of lions fell short, or when he was satiated with this kind of sport. Asshur-bani-pal would vary his occupation, and content himself with game of an inferior description. Wild bulls were probably no longer found in Assyria or the adjacent countries, so that he was precluded from the sport which, next to the chase of the lion occupied and delighted the earlier monarchs. He could indulge, however, freely in the chase of the wild ass still to this day a habitant of the Mesopotamian region; and he would hunt the stag, the hind, and the ibex or wild goat. In these tamer kinds of sport he seems, however, to have indulged only occasionally—as a light relaxation scarcely worthy of a great king.

Asshur-bani-pal is the only one of the Assyrian monarchs to whom we can ascribe a real taste for learning and literature. The other kings were content to leave behind them some records of the events of their reigns, inscribed on cylinders, slabs, bulls, or lions, and a few dedicatory inscriptions, addresses to the gods whom they especially worshipped. Asshur-bani-pal's literary tastes were far more varied—indeed they were all-embracing. It seems to have been under his direction that the vast collection of clay tablets—a sort of Royal Library—was made at Nineveh, from which the British Museum has derived perhaps the most valuable of its treasures. Comparative vocabularies, lists of deities and their epithets, chronological lists of kings and eponyms, records of astronomical observations, grammars, histories, scientific works of various kinds, seems to have been composed in the reign, and probably at the bidding of this prince, who devoted to their preservation certain chambers in the palace of his grandfather, where they were found by Mr. Layard. The clay tablets on which they were inscribed lay here in such multitudes in some instances entire, but more commonly broken into fragments—that they filled the chambers to the height of a foot or more from the floor. Mr. Layard observes with justice that "the documents thus discovered at Nineveh probably exceed [in amount of writing] all that has yet been afforded by the monuments of Egypt." They have yielded of late years some most interesting results, and will probably long continue to be a mine of almost inexhaustible wealth to the cuneiform scholar.

As a builder, Asshur-bani-pal aspired to rival, if not even to excel, the greatest of the monarchs who had preceded him. His palace was built on the mound of Koyunjik, within a few hundred yards of the magnificent erection of his grandfather, with which he was evidently not afraid to challenge comparison. It was built on a plan unlike any adopted by former kings. The main building consisted of three arms branching from at common centre, and thus in its general shape resembled a gigantic T. The central point was reached by a long ascending gallery lined with sculptures, which led from a gateway, with rooms attached, at a corner of the great court, first a distance of 190 feet in a direction parallel to the top bar of the T, and then a distance of 80 feet in a direction at right angles to this, which brought it down exactly to the central point whence the arms branched. The entire building was thus a sort of cross, with one long arm projecting from the top towards the left or west. The principal apartments were in the lower limb of the cross. Here was a grand hall, running nearly the whole length of the limb, at least 145 feet long by 28 feet broad, opening towards the east on a great court, paved chiefly with the exquisite patterned slabs of which a specimen has already been given, and communicating towards the west with a number of smaller rooms, and through them with a second court, which looked towards the south-west and the south. The next largest apartment was in the right or eastern arm of the cross. It was a hall 108 feet long by 24 feet wide, divided by a broad doorway in which were two pillar-bases, into a square antechamber of 24 feet each way, and an inner apartment about 80 feet in length. Neither of the two arms of the cross was completely explored; and it is uncertain whether they extended to the extreme edge of the eastern and western courts, thus dividing each of there into two; or whether they only reached into the courts a certain distance. Assuming the latter view as the more probable, the two courts would have measured respectively 310 and 330 feet from the north-west to the south-east, while they must have been from 230 to 250 feet in the opposite direction. From the comparative privacy of the buildings, and from the character of the sculptures, it appears probable that the left or western arm of the cross formed the hareem of the monarch.

The most remarkable feature in the great palace of Asshur-bani-pal was the beauty and elaborate character of the ornamentation. The courts were paved with large slabs elegantly patterned. The doorways had sometimes arched tops beautifully adorned with rosettes, lotuses, etc. The chambers and passages were throughout lined with alabaster slabs, bearing reliefs designed with wonderful spirit, and executed with the most extraordinary minuteness and delicacy. It was here that were found all those exquisite hunting scenes which have furnished its most interesting illustrations to the present history. Here, too, were the representations of the private life of the monarch, of the trees and flowers of the palace garden, of the royal galley with its two banks of oars, of the libation over four dead lions, of the temple with pillars supported on lions, and of various bands of musicians, some of which have been already given. Combined with these peaceful scenes and others of a similar character, as particularly a long train, with game, nets, and dogs, returning from the chase, which formed the adornment of a portion of the ascending passage, were a number of views of sieges and battles, representing the wars of the monarch in Susiana and elsewhere. Reliefs of a character very similar to these last were found by Mr. Layard in certain chambers of the palace of Sennacherib, which had received their ornamentation from Asshur-bani-pal. They were remarkable for the unusual number and small size of the figures, for the variety and spirit of the attitudes, and for the careful finish of all the little details of the scenes represented upon them. Deficient in grouping, and altogether destitute of any artistic unity, they yet give probably the best representation that has come down to us of the confused melee of an Assyrian battle, showing us at one view, as they do, all the various phases of the flight and pursuit, the capture and treatment of the prisoners, the gathering of the spoil, and the cutting off the heads of the slain. These reliefs form now a portion of our National Collection. A good idea may be formed of them from Mr. Layard's Second Series of Monuments, where they form the subject of five elaborate engravings.

Besides his own great palace at Koyun-jik, and his additions to the palace of his grandfather at the same place, Asshur-bani-pal certainly constructed some building, or buildings, at Nebbi Yunus, where slabs inscribed with his name and an account of his wars have been found. If we may regard him as the real monarch whom the Greeks generally intended by their Sardanapalus, we may say that, according to some classical authors, he was the builder of the city of Tarsus in Cilicia, and likewise of the neighboring city of Anchialus; though writers of more authority tells us that Tarsus, at any rate, was built by Sennacherib. It seems further to have been very generally believed by the Greeks that the tomb of Sardanapalus was in this neighborhood. They describe it as a monument of some height, crowned by a statue of the monarch, who appeared to be in the act of snapping his fingers. On the stone base was an inscription in Assyrian characters, of which they believed the sense to run as follows:—"Sardanapalus, son of Anacyndaraxes, built Tarsus and Anchialus in one day. Do thou, O stranger, eat, and drink, and amuse thyself; for all the rest of human life is not worth so much as this"—"this" meaning the sound which the king was supposed to be making with his fingers. It appears probable that there was some figure of this kind, with an Assyrian inscription below it, near Anchialus; but, as we can scarcely suppose that the Greeks could read the cuneiform writing, the presumed translation of the inscription would seem to be valueless. Indeed, the very different versions of the legend which are given by different writers sufficiently indicate that they had no real knowledge of its purport. We may conjecture that the monument was in reality a stele containing the king in an arched frame, with the right hand raised above the left, which is the ordinary attitude, and an inscription below commemorating the occasion of its erection. Whether it was really set up by this king or by one of his predecessors, we cannot say. The Greeks, who seem to have known more of Asshur-bani-pal than of any other Assyrian monarch, in consequence of his war in Asia Minor and his relations with Gyges and Ardys, are not unlikely to have given his name to any Assyrian monument which they found in these parts, whether in the local tradition it was regarded as his work or no.

Such, then, are the traditions of the Greeks with respect to this monarch. The stories told by Ctesias of a king, to whom he gives the same name, and repeated from him by later writers, are probably not intended to have any reference to Asshur-bani-pal, the son of Esar-haddon, but rather refer to his successor, the last king. Even Ctesias could scarcely have ventured to depict to his countrymen the great Asshur-bani-pal, the vanquisher of Tirhakah, the subduer of the tribes beyond the Taurus, the powerful and warlike monarch whose friendship was courted by the rich and prosperous Gyges, king of Lydia, as a mere voluptuary, who never put his foot outside the palace gates, but dwelt in the seraglio, doing woman's work, and often dressed as a woman. The character of Asshur-bani-pal stands really in the strongest contrast to the description—be it a portrait, or be it a mere sketch from fancy—which Ctesias gives of his Sardanapalus. Asshur-bani-pal, was beyond a doubt one of Assyria's greatest kings. He subdued Egypt and Susiana; he held quiet possession of the kingdom of Babylon; he carried his arms deep into Armenia; he led his troops across the Taurus, and subdued the barbarous tribes of Asia Minor. When he was not engaged in important wars, he chiefly occupied himself in the chase of the lion, and in the construction and ornamentation of temples and palaces. His glory was well known to the Greeks. He was no doubt one of the "two kings called Sardanapalus," celebrated by Hellanicus; he must have been "the warlike Sardanapalus" of Cailisthenes; Herodotus spoke of his great wealth; and Aristophanes used his name as a by-word for magnificence. In his reign the Assyrian dominions reached their greatest extent, Assyrian art culminated, and the empire seemed likely to extend itself over the whole of the East. It was then, indeed, that Assyria most completely answered the description of the Prophet—"The Assyrian was a cedar in Lebanon, with fair branches, and with a shadowing shroud, and of high stature; and his top was among the thick boughs. The waters made him great; the deep set him up on high with her rivers running about his plants, and sent out her little rivers unto all the trees of the field. Therefore his height was exalted above all the trees of the field, and his boughs were multiplied, and his branches became long, because of the multitude of waters, when he shot forth. All the fowls of the heaven made their nests in his boughs, and under his branches did all the beasts of the field bring forth their young, and under his shadow dwelt all great nations. Thus was he fair in his greatness, in the length of his branches for his root was by great waters. The cedars in the garden of God could not hide him; the fir-trees were not like his boughs; and the chestnut-trees were not like his branches; nor any tree in the garden of God was like unto him in his beauty."

In one respect, however, Assyria, it is to be feared, had made but little advance beyond the spirit of a comparatively barbarous time. The "lion" still "tore in pieces for his whelps, and strangled for his lionesses, and filled his holes with prey, and his dens with ravin." Advancing civilization, more abundant literature, improved art, had not softened the tempers of the Assyrians, nor rendered them more tender and compassionate in their treatment of captured enemies. Sennacherib and Esar-haddon show, indeed, in this respect, some superiority to former kings. They frequently spared their prisoners, even when rebels, and seem seldom to have had recourse to extreme punishments. But Asshur-bani-pal reverted to the antique system of executions, mutilations, and tortures. We see on his bas-reliefs the unresisting enemy thrust through with the spear, the tongue torn from the mouth of the captive accused of blasphemy, the rebel king beheaded on the field of battle, and the prisoner brought to execution with the head of a friend or brother hung round his neck. We see the scourgers preceding the king as his regular attendants, with their whips passed through their girdles; we behold the operation of flaying performed either upon living or dead men; we observe those who are about to be executed first struck on the face by the executioner's fist. Altogether we seem to have evidence, not of mere severity, which may sometimes be a necessary or even a merciful policy, but of a barbarous cruelty, such as could not fail to harden and brutalize alike those who witnessed and those who inflicted it. Nineveh, it is plain, still deserved the epithet of "a bloody city," or "a city of bloods." Asshur-bani-pal was harsh, vindictive, unsparing, careless of human suffering—nay, glorying in his shame, he not merely practised cruelties, but handed the record of them down to posterity by representing them in all their horrors upon his palace walls.

It has been generally supposed that Asshur-bani-pal died about B.C. 648 or 647, in which case he would have continued to the end of his life a prosperous and mighty king. But recent discoveries render it probable that his reign was extended to a much greater length—that, in fact, he is to be identified with the Cinneladanus of Ptolemy's Canon, who held the throne of Babylon from B.C. 647 to 626. If this be so, we must place in the later years of the reign of Asshur-bani-pal the commencement of Assyria's decline—the change whereby she passed from the assailer to the assailed, from the undisputed primacy of Western Asia to a doubtful and precarious position.

This change was owing, in the first instance, to the rise upon her borders of an important military power in the centralized monarchy, established, about B.C. 640, in the neighboring territory of Media.

The Medes had, it is probable, been for some time growing in strength, owing to the recent arrival in their country of fresh immigrants from the far East. Discarding the old system of separate government and village autonomy, they had joined together and placed themselves under a single monarch; and about the year B.C. 634, when Asshur-bani-pal had been king for thirty-four years, they felt themselves sufficiently strong to undertake an expedition against Nineveh. Their first attack, however, failed utterly. Phraortes, or whoever may have been the real leader of the invading army, was completely defeated by the Assyrians; his forces were cut to pieces, and he himself was among the slain. Still, the very fact that the Medes could now take the offensive and attack Assyria was novel and alarming; it showed a new condition of things in these parts, and foreboded no good to the power which was evidently on the decline and in danger of losing its preponderance. An enterprising warrior would doubtless have followed up the defeat of the invader by attacking him in his own country before he could recover from the severe blow dealt him; but the aged Assyrian monarch appears to have been content with repelling his foe, and made no effort to retaliate. Cgaxares, the successor of the slain Median king, effected at his leisure such arrangements as he thought necessary before repeating his predecessor's attempt. When they were completed—perhaps in B.C. 632—he led his troops into Assyria, defeated the Assyrian forces in the field, and, following up his advantage, appeared before Nineveh and closely invested the town. Nineveh would perhaps have fallen in this year; but suddenly and unexpectedly a strange event recalled the Median monarch to his own country, where a danger threatened him previously unknown in Western Asia.

When at the present day we take a general survey of the world's past history, we see that, by a species of fatality—by a law, that is, whose workings we cannot trace—there issue from time to time out of the frozen bosons of the North vast hordes of uncouth savages—brave, hungry, countless—who swarm into the fairer southern regions determinedly, irresistibly; like locusts winging their flight into a green land. How such multitudes come to be propagated in countries where life is with difficulty sustained, we do not know; why the impulse suddenly seizes them to quit their old haunts and move steadily in a given direction, we cannot say: but we see that the phenomenon is one of constant recurrence, and we therefore now scarcely regard it as being curious or strange at all. In Asia. Cimmerians, Scythians, Parthians, Mongols, Turks; in Europe, Gauls, Goths, Huns, Avars, Vandals, Burgundians, Lombards, Bulgarians, have successively illustrated the law, and made us familiar with its operation. But there was a time in history before the law had come into force; and its very existence must have been then unsuspected. Even since it began to operate, it has so often undergone prolonged suspension, that the wisest may be excused if, under such circumstances, they cease to bear it in mind, and are as much startled when a fresh illustration of it occurs, as if the like had never happened before. Probably there is seldom an occasion of its coming into play which does not take men more or less by surprise, and rivet their attention by its seeming strangeness and real unexpectedness.

If Western Asia had ever, in the remote ages before the Assyrian monarchy was established, been subject to invasions of this character—which is not improbable—at any rate so long a period had elapsed since the latest of them, that in the reigns of Asshur-pani-pal and Cyaxares they were wholly forgotten and the South reposed in happy unconsciousness of a danger which might at any time have burst upon it, had the Providence which governs the world so willed. The Asiatic steppes had long teemed with a nomadic population, of a war-like temper, and but slightly attached to its homes, which ignorance of its own strength and of the weakness and wealth of its neighbors had alone prevented from troubling the great empires of the South. Geographic difficulties had at once prolonged the period of ignorance, and acted as obstructions, if ever the idea arose of pushing exploring parties into the southern regions; the Caucasus, the Caspian, the sandy deserts of Khiva and Kharesm, and the great central Asiatic mountain-chains, forming barriers which naturally restrained the northern hordes from progressing in this direction. But a time had now arrived when these causes were no longer to operate; the line of demarcation which had so long separated North and South was to be crossed; the flood-gates were to be opened, and the stream of northern emigration was to pour itself in a resistless torrent over the fair and fertile regions from which it had hitherto been barred out. Perhaps population had increased beyond all former precedent; perhaps a spirit of enterprise had arisen; possibly some slight accident—the exploration of a hunter hard pressed for food, the chattering tongue of a merchant, the invitation of a traitor—may have dispelled the ignorance of earlier times, and brought to the knowledge of the hardy North the fact that beyond the mountains and the seas, which they had always regarded as the extreme limit of the world, there lay a rich prey inviting the coming of the spoiler.

The condition of the northern barbarians, less than two hundred years after this time, has been graphically portrayed by two of the most observant of the Greeks, who themselves visited the Steppe country to learn the character and customs of the people. Where civilization is unknown, changes are so slow and slight, that we may reasonably regard the descriptions of Herodotus and Hippocrates, though drawn in the fifth century before our era, as applying, in all their main points, to the same race two hundred years earlier. These writers describe the Scythians as a people coarse and gross in their habits, with large fleshy bodies, loose joints, soft swollen bellies, and scanty hair. They never washed themselves; their nearest approach to ablution was a vapor-bath, or the application of a paste to their bodies which left them glossy on its removal. They lived either in wagons, or in felt tents of a simple and rude construction; and subsisted on mare's milk and cheese, to which the boiled flesh of horses and cattle was added, as a rare delicacy, occasionally. In war their customs were very barbarous. The Scythian who slew an enemy in battle immediately proceeded to drink his blood. He then cut off the head, which he exhibited to his king in order to obtain his share of the spoil; after which he stripped the scalp from the skull and hung it on his bridle-rein as a trophy. Sometimes he flayed his dead enemy's right arm and hand, and used the skin as a covering for his quiver. The upper portion of the skull he commonly made into a drinking-cup. The greater part of each day he spent on horseback, in attendance on the huge herds of cattle which he pastured. His favorite weapon was the bow, which he used as he rode, shooting his arrows with great precision. He generally carried, besides his bow and arrows, a short spear or javelin, and sometimes bore also a short sword or a battleaxe. [PLATE CXLVI., Fig. 3.]

The nation of the Scythians comprised within it a number of distinct tribes. At the head of all was a royal tribe, corresponding to the "Golden Horde" of the Mongols, which was braver and more numerous than any other, and regarded all the remaining tribes in the light of slaves. To this belonged the families of the kings, who ruled by hereditary right, and seem to have exercised a very considerable authority. We often hear of several kings as bearing rule at the same time; but there is generally some indication of disparity, from which we gather that—in times of danger at any rate—the supreme power was really always lodged in the hands of a single man.

The religion of the Scythians was remarkable, and partook of the barbarity which characterized most of their customs. They worshiped the Sun and Moon, Fire, Air, Earth, Water, and a god whom Herodotus calls Hercules. But their principal religious observance was the worship of the naked sword. The country was parcelled out into districts, and in every district was a huge pile of brushwood, serving as a temple to the neighborhood, at the top of which was planted an antique sword or scimitar. On a stated day in each year solemn sacrifices, human and animal, were offered at these shrines; and the warm blood of the victims was carried up from below and poured upon the weapon. The human victims—prisoners taken in war—were hewn to pieces at the foot of the mound, and their limbs wildly tossed on high by the votaries, who then retired, leaving the bloody fragments where they chanced to fall. The Scythians seem to have had no priest caste; but they believed in divination; and the diviners formed a distinct class which possessed important powers. They were sent for whenever the king was ill, to declare the cause of his illness, which they usually attributed to the fact that an individual, whom they named, had sworn falsely by the Royal Hearth. Those accused in this way, if found guilty by several bodies of diviners, were beheaded for the offence, and their original accusers received their property. It must have been important to keep on good terms with persons who wielded such a power as this.

Such were the most striking customs of the Scythian people, or at any rate of the Scythians of Herodotus, who were the dominant race over a large portion of the Steppe country. Coarse and repulsive in their appearance, fierce in their tempers, savage in their habits, not individually very brave, but powerful by their numbers, and by a mode of warfare which was difficult to meet, and in which long use had given them great expertness, they were an enemy who might well strike alarm even into a nation so strong and warlike as the Medes. Pouring through the passes of the Caucasus—whence coming or what intending none knew—horde after horde of Scythians blackened the rich plains of the South. On they came, as before observed, like a flight of locusts, countless, irresistible—swarming into Iberia and Upper Media—finding the land before them a garden, and leaving it behind them a howling wilderness. Neither age nor sex would be spared. The inhabitants of the open country and of the villages, if they did not make their escape to high mountain tops or other strongholds, would be ruthlessly massacred by the invaders, or at best, forced to become their slaves. The crops would be consumed, the herds swept off or destroyed, the villages and homesteads burnt, the whole country made a scene of desolation. Their ravages would resemble those of the Huns when they poured into Italy, or of the Bulgarians when they overran the fairest provinces of the Byzantine Empire. In most instances the strongly fortified towns would resist them, unless they had patience to sit down before their walls and by a prolonged blockade to starve them into submission. Sometimes, before things reached this point, they might consent to receive a tribute and to retire. At other times, convinced that by perseverance they would reap a rich reward, they may have remained till the besieged city fell, when there must have ensued an indescribable scene of havoc, rapine, and bloodshed. According to the broad expression of Herodotus, the Scythians were masters of the whole of Western Asia from the Caucasus to the borders of Egypt for the space of twenty-eight years. This statement is doubtless an exaggeration; but still it would seem to be certain that the great invasion of which he speaks was not confined to Media, but extended to the adjacent countries of Armenia and Assyria, whence it spread to Syria and Palestine. The hordes probably swarmed down from Media through the Zagros passes into the richest portion of Assyria, the flat country between the mountains and the Tigris. Many of the old cities, rich with the accumulated stores of ages, were besieged, and perhaps taken, and their palaces wantonly burnt, by the barbarous invaders. The tide then swept on. Wandering from district to district, plundering everywhere, settling nowhere, the clouds of horse passed over Mesopotamia, the force of the invasion becoming weaker as it spread itself, until in Syria it reached its term through the policy of the Egyptian king, Psammetichus. This monarch, who was engaged in the siege of Ashdod, no sooner heard of the approach of a great Scythian host, which threatened to overrun Egypt, and had advanced as far as Ascalon, than he sent ambassadors to their leader and prevailed on him by rich gifts to abstain from his enterprise. From this time the power of the invaders seems to have declined. Their strength could not but suffer by the long series of battles, sieges, and skirmishes in which they were engaged year after year against enemies in nowise contemptible; it would likewise deteriorate through their excesses; and it may even have received some injury from intestine quarrels. After awhile, the nations whom they had overrun, whose armies they had defeated, and whose cities they had given to the flames, began to recover themselves. Cyaxares, it is probable, commenced an aggressive war against such of the invaders as had remained within the limits of his dominions, and soon drove them beyond his borders. Other kings may have followed his example. In a little while long, probably, before the twenty-eight years of Herodotus had expired—the Scythian power was completely broken. Many bands may have returned across the Caucasus into the Steppe country. Others submitted, and took service under the native rulers of Asia. Great numbers were slain and except in a province of Armenia which henceforward became known as Sacasene, and perhaps in one Syrian town, which we find called Scythopolis, the invaders left no trace of their brief but terrible inroad.

If we have been right in supposing that the Scythian attack fell with as much severity on the Assyrians as on any other Asiatic people, we can scarcely be in error if we ascribe to this cause the rapid and sudden decline of the empire at this period. The country had been ravaged and depopulated, the provinces had been plundered, many of the great towns had been taken and sacked, the palaces of the old kings had been burnt, and all the gold and silver that was not hid away had been carried off. Assyria, when the Scythians quitted her, was but the shadow of her former self. Weak and exhausted, she seemed to invite a permanent conqueror. If her limits had not much shrunk, if the provinces still acknowledged her authority, it was from habit rather than from fear, or because they too had suffered greatly from the northern barbarians. We find Babylon subject to Assyria to the very last; and we seem to see that Judaea passed from the rule of the Assyrians under that of the Babylonians, without any interval of independence or any need of re-conquest. But if these two powers at the south-eastern and the south-western extremities of the empire continued faithful, the less distant nations could scarcely have thrown off the yoke.

Asshur-bani-pal, then, on the withdrawal of the barbarians, had still an empire to rule, and he may be supposed to have commenced some attempts at re-organizing and re-invigorating the governmental system to which the domination of the Scythe must have given a rude shock. But he had not time to effect much. In B.C. 626 he died, after a reign of forty-two years, and was succeeded by his son, Asshur-emid-ilin, whom the Greeks called Saracus. Of this prince we possess but few native records; and, unless it should be thought that the picture which Ctesias gave of the character and conduct of his last Assyrian king deserves to be regarded as authentic history, and to be attached to this monarch, we must confess to an almost equal dearth of classical notices of his life and actions. Scarcely anything has come down to us from his time but a few legends on bricks, from which it appears that he was the builder of the south-east edifice at Nimrud, a construction presenting some remarkable but no very interesting features. The classical notices, apart from the tales which Ctesias originated, are limited to a few sentences in Abydenus, and a word or two in Polyhistor. Thus nearly the same obscurity which enfolds the earlier portion of the history gathers about the monarch in whose person the empire terminated; and instead of the ample details which have crowded upon us now for many consecutive reigns, we shall be reduced to a meagre outline, partly resting upon conjecture, in our portraiture of this last king.

Saracus, as the monarch may be termed after Abydenus, ascended the throne at a most difficult and dangerous crisis in his country's history. Assyria was exhausted; and perhaps half depopulated by the Scythic ravages. The bands which united the provinces to the sovereign state, though not broken, had been weakened, and rebellion threatened to break out in various quarters. Ruin had overtaken many of the provincial towns; and it would require a vast outlay to restore their public buildings. But the treasury was wellnigh empty, and did not allow the new monarch to adopt in his buildings the grand and magnificent style of former kings. Still Saracus attempted something. At Calah he began the construction of a building which apparently was intended for a palace, but which contrasts most painfully with the palatial erections of former kings. The waning glory of the monarchy was made patent both to the nation and to strangers by an edifice where coarse slabs of common limestone, unsculptured and uninscribed, replaced the alabaster bas-reliefs of former times; and where a simple plaster above the slabs was the substitute for the richly-patterned enamelled bricks of Sargon, Sennacherib, and Asshur-bani-pal. A set of small chambers, of which no one exceeded forty-five feet in length and twenty-five feet in its greatest breadth, sufficed for the last Assyrian king, whose shrunken Court could no longer have filled the vast halls of his ancestors. The Nimrud palace of Saracus seems to have covered less than one-half of the space occupied by any former palace upon the mound; it had no grand facade, no magnificent gateway; the rooms, curiously misshapen, as if taste had declined with power and wealth, were mostly small and inconvenient, running in suites which opened into one another without any approaches from courts or passages, roughly paved with limestone flags, and composed of sun-dried bricks faced with limestone and plaster. That Saracus should have been reduced even to contemplate residing in this poor and mean dwelling is the strongest possible proof of Assyria's decline and decay at a period preceding the great war which led to her destruction.

It is possible that this edifice may not have been completed at the time of Saracus's death, and in that case we may suppose that its extreme rudeness would have received certain embellishments had he lived to finish the structure. While it was being erected, he must have resided elsewhere. Apparently, he held his court at Nineveh during this period; and was certainly there that he made his last arrangements for defence, and his final stand against the enemy, who took advantage of his weak condition to press forward the conquest of the empire.

The Medes, in their strong upland country, abounding in rocky hills, and running up in places into mountain-chains, had probably suffered much less from the ravages of the Scyths than the Assyrians in their comparatively defenceless plains. Of all the nations exposed to the scourge of the invasion they were evidently the first to recover themselves, partly from the local causes here noticed, partly perhaps from their inherent vigor and strength. If Herodotus's date for the original inroad of the Scythians is correct, not many years can have elapsed before the tide of war turned, and the Medes began to make head against their assailants, recovering possession of most parts of their country, and expelling or overpowering the hordes at whose insolent domination they had chafed from the first hour of the invasion. It was probably as early as B.C. 627, five years after the Scyths crossed the Caucasus, according to Herodotus, that Cyaxares, having sufficiently re-established his power in Media, began once more to aspire after foreign conquests. Casting his eyes around upon the neighboring countries, he became aware of the exhaustion of Assyria, and perceived that she was not likely to offer an effectual resistance to a sudden and vigorous attack. He therefore collected a large army and invaded Assyria from the east, while it would seem that the Susianians, with whom he had perhaps made an alliance, attacked her from the south.

To meet this double danger. Saracus, the Assyrian king, determined on dividing his forces: and, while he entrusted a portion of them to a general, Nabopolassar, who had orders to proceed to Babylon and engage the enemy advancing from the sea, he himself with the remainder made ready to receive the Medes. In idea this was probably a judicious disposition of the troops at his disposal; it was politic to prevent a junction of the two assailing powers, and, as the greater danger was that which threatened from the Medes, it was well for the king to reserve himself with the bulk of his forces to meet this enemy. But the most prudent arrangements may be disconcerted by the treachery of those who are entrusted with their execution; and so it was in the present instance. The faithless Nabopolassar saw in his sovereign's difficulty his own opportunity and, instead of marching against Assyria's enemies, as his duty required him, he secretly negotiated an arrangement with Cyaxares, agreed to become his ally against the Assyrians, and obtained the Median king's daughter as a bride for Nebuchadnezzar, his eldest son. Cyaxares and Nabopolassar then joined their efforts against Nineveh; and Saracus, unable to resist them, took counsel of his despair, and, after all means of resistance were exhausted, burned himself in his palace. It is uncertain whether we possess any further historical details of the siege. The narrative of Ctesias may embody a certain number of the facts, as it certainly represented with truth the strange yet not incredible termination. But on the other hand, we cannot feel sure, with regard to any statement made solely by that writer, that it has any other source than his imagination. Hence the description of the last siege of Nineveh, as given by Diodorus on the authority of Ctesias, seems undeserving of a place in history, though the attention of the curious may properly be directed to it.

The empire of the Assyrians thus fell, not so much from any inherent weakness, or from the effect of gradual decay, as by an unfortunate combination of circumstances—the occurrence of a terrible inroad of northern barbarians just at the time when a warlike nation, long settled on the borders of Assyria, and within a short distance of her capital, was increasing, partly by natural and regular causes, partly by accidental and abnormal ones, in greatness and strength. It will be proper, in treating of the history of Media, to trace out, as far as our materials allow, these various causes, and to examine the mode and extent of their operation. But such an inquiry is not suited for this place, since, if fully made, it would lead us too far away from our present subject, which is the history of Assyria; while, if made partially, it would be unsatisfactory. It is therefore deferred to another place. The sketch here attempted of Assyrian history will now be brought to a close by a few observations on the general nature of the monarchy, or its extent in the most flourishing period, and on the character of its civilization.

The independent kingdom of Assyria covered a space of at least a thousand years; but the empire can, at the utmost, be considered to have lasted a period short of seven centuries, from B.C. 1300 to B.C. 625 or 624—the date of the conquest of Cyaxares. In reality, the period of extensive domination seems to have commenced with Asshur-ris-ilim, about B.C. 1150, so that the duration of the true empire did not much exceed five centuries. The limits of the dominion varied considerably within this period, the empire expanding or contracting according to the circumstances of the time and the personal character of the prince by whom the throne was occupied. The extreme extent appears not to have been reached until almost immediately before the last rapid decline set in, the widest dominion belonging to the time of Asshur-bani-pal, the conqueror of Egypt, of Susiana, and of the Armenians. In the middle part of this prince's reign Assyria was paramount over the portion of Western Asia included between the Mediterranean and the Halys on the one hand, the Caspian Sea and the great Persian desert on the other. Southwards the boundary was formed by Arabia and the Persian Gulf; northwards it seems at no time to have advanced to the Euxine or to the Caucasus, but to have been formed by a fluctuating line, which did not in the most flourishing period extend so far as the northern frontier of Armenia. Besides her Asiatic dominions, Assyria possessed also at this time a portion of Africa, her authority being acknowledged by Egypt as far as the latitude of Thebes. The countries included within the limits thus indicated, and subject during the period in question to Assyrian influence, were chiefly the following: Susiana, Chaldaea, Babylonia, Media, Matiene or the Zagros range, Mesopotamia; parts of Armenia, Cappadocia, and Cilicia; Syria, Phoenicia, Palestine. Idummaea, a portion of Arabia, and almost the whole of Egypt. The island of Cyprus was also, it is probable, a dependency. On the other hand, Persia Proper, Bactria, and Sogdiana, even Hyrcania, were beyond the eastern limit of the Assyrian sway, which towards the north did not on this side reach further than about the neighborhood of Kasvin, and towards the south was confined within the barrier of Zagros. Similarly on the west, Phrygia, Lydia, Lycia, even Pamphylia, were independent, the Assyrian arms having never, so far as appears, penetrated westward beyond Cilicia or crossed the river Halys.

The nature of the dominion established by the great Mesopotamian monarchy over the countries included within the limits above indicated, will perhaps be best understood if we compare it with the empire of Solomon. Solomon reigned over all the kingdoms from the river (Euphrates) unto the land of the Philistines and unto the border of Egypt: they brought presents and served Solomon all the days of his life. The first and most striking feature of the earliest empires is that they are a mere congeries of kingdoms: the countries over which the dominant state acquires an influence, not only retain their distinct individuality, as is the case in some modern empires, but remain in all respects such as they were before, with the simple addition of certain obligations contracted towards the paramount authority. They keep their old laws, their old religion, their line of kings, their law of succession, their whole internal organization and machinery; they only acknowledge an external suzerainty which binds them to the performance of certain duties towards the Head of the Empire. These duties, as understood in the earliest times, may be summed up in the two words "homage" and "tribute;" the subject kings "serve" and "bring presents." They are bound to acts of submission; must attend the court of their suzerain when summoned, unless they have a reasonable excuse; must there salute him as a superior, and otherwise acknowledge his rank; above all, they must pay him regularly the fixed tribute which has been imposed upon them at the time of their submission or subjection, the unauthorized withholding of which is open and avowed rebellion. Finally, they must allow his troops free passage through their dominions, and must oppose any attempt at invasion by way of their country on the part of his enemies. Such are the earliest and most essential obligations on the part of the subject states in an empire of the primitive type like that of Assyria; and these obligations, with the corresponding one on the part of the dominant power of the protection of its dependants against foreign foes, appear to have constituted the sole links which joined together in one the heterogeneous materials of which that empire consisted.

It is evident that a government of the character here described contains within it elements of constant disunion and disorder. Under favorable circumstances, with an active and energetic prince upon the throne, there is an appearance of strength, and a realization of much magnificence and grandeur. The subject monarchs pay annually their due share of "the regulated tribute of the empire;" and the better to secure the favor of their common sovereign, add to it presents, consisting of the choicest productions of their respective kingdoms. The material resources of the different countries are placed at the disposal of the dominant power; and skilled workmen are readily lent for the service of the court, who adorn or build the temples and the royal residences, and transplant the luxuries and refinements of their several states to the imperial capital. But no sooner does any untoward event occur, as a disastrous expedition, a foreign attack, a domestic conspiracy, or even an untimely and unexpected death of the reigning prince, than the inherent weakness of this sort of government at once displays itself—the whole fabric of the empire falls asunder—each kingdom re-asserts its independence—tribute ceases to be paid—and the mistress of a hundred states suddenly finds herself thrust back into her primitive condition, stripped of the dominion which has been her strength, and thrown entirely upon her own resources. Then the whole task of reconstruction has to be commenced anew—one by one the rebel countries are overrun, and the rebel monarchs chastised—tribute is re-imposed, submission enforced, and in fifteen or twenty years the empire has perhaps recovered itself. Progress is of course slow and uncertain, where the empire has continually to be built up again from its foundations, and where at any time a day may undo the work which it has taken centuries to accomplish.

To discourage and check the chronic disease of rebellion, re-course is had to severe remedies, which diminish the danger to the central power, at the cost of extreme misery and often almost entire ruin to the subject kingdoms. Not only are the lands wasted, the flocks and herds carried off, the towns pillaged and burnt, or in some cases razed to the ground, the rebel king deposed and his crown transferred to another, the people punished by the execution of hundreds or thousands as well as by an augmentation of the tribute money; but sometimes wholesale deportation of the inhabitants is practised, tens or hundreds of thousands being carried away captive by the conquerors, and either employed in servile labor at the capital or settled as colonists in a distant province. With this practice the history of the Jews, in which it forms so prominent a feature, has made us familiar. It seems to have been known to the Assyrians from very early times, and to have become by degrees a sort of settled principle in their government. In the most flourishing period of their dominion—the reigns of Sargon, Sennacherib, and Esar-haddon—it prevailed most widely, and was carried to the greatest extent. Chaldaeans were transported into Armenia, Jews and Israelites into Assyria and Media, Arabians, Babylonians, Susianians, and Persians into Palestine—the most distant portions of the empire changed inhabitants, and no sooner did a people become troublesome from its patriotism and love of independence, than it was weakened by dispersion, and its spirit subdued by a severance of all its local associations. Thus rebellion was in some measure kept down, and the position of the central or sovereign state was rendered so far more secure; but this comparative security was gained by a great sacrifice of strength, and when foreign invasion came, the subject kingdoms, weakened at once and alienated by the treatment which they had received, were found to have neither the will nor the power to give any effectual aid to their enslaver.

Such, in its broad and general outlines, was the empire of the Assyrians. It embodied the earliest, simplest, and most crude conception which the human mind forms of a widely extended dominion. It was a "kingdom-empire," like the empires of Solomon, of Nebuchadnezzar, of Chedor-laomer, and probably of Cyaxares, and it the best specimen of its class, being the largest, the longest in duration, and the best known of all such governments that has existed. It exhibits in a marked way both the strength and weakness of this class of monarchies—their strength in the extraordinary magnificence, grandeur, wealth, and refinement of the capital; their weakness in the impoverishment, the exhaustion, and the consequent disaffection of the subject states. Ever falling to pieces, it was perpetually reconstructed by the genius and prowess of a long succession of warrior princes, seconded by the skill and bravery of the people. Fortunate in possessing for a longtime no very powerful neighbor, it found little difficulty in extending itself throughout regions divided and subdivided among hundreds of petty chiefs incapable of union, and singly quite unable to contend with the forces of a large and populous country. Frequently endangered by revolts, yet always triumphing over them, it maintained itself for five centuries gradually advancing its influence, and was only overthrown after a fierce struggle by a new kingdom formed upon its borders, which, taking advantage of a time of exhaustion, and leagued with the most powerful of the subject states, was enabled to accomplish the destruction of the long-dominant people.

In the curt and dry records of the Assyrian monarchs, while the broad outlines of the government are well marked, it is difficult to distinguish those nicer shades of system and treatment which no doubt existed, and in which the empire of the Assyrians differed probably from others of the same type. One or two such points, however, may perhaps be made out. In the first place, though religious uniformity is certainly not the law of the empire, yet a religious character appears in many of the wars, and attempts at any rate seem to be made to diffuse everywhere a knowledge and recognition of the gods of Assyria. Nothing is more universal than the practice of setting up in the subject countries the laws of Asshur or "altars to the Great Gods." In some instances not only altars but temples are erected, and priests are left to superintend the worship and secure its being properly conducted. The history of Judaea is, however, enough to show that the continuance of the national worship was at least tolerated, though some formal acknowledgment of the presiding deities of Assyria on the part of the subject nations may not improbably have been required in most cases.

Secondly, there is an indication that in certain countries immediately bordering on Assyria endeavors were made from time to time to centralize and consolidate the empire, by substituting, on fit occasions, for the native chiefs, Assyrian officers as governors. The persons appointed are of two classes—"collectors" and "treasurers." Their special business is, of course, as their names imply, to gather in the tribute due to the Great King, and secure its safe transmission to the capital; but they seem to have been, at least in some instances, entrusted with the civil government of their respective districts. It does not appear that this system was ever extended very far, Lebanon on the west, and Mount Zagros on the east, may be regarded as the extreme limits of the centralized Assyria. Armenia, Media, Babylonia, Susiana, most of Phoenicia, Palestine, Philistia, retained to the last their native monarchs; and thus Assyria, despite the feature here noticed, kept upon the whole her character of a "kingdom-empire."

The civilization of the Assyrians is a large subject, on which former chapters of this work have, it is hoped, thrown some light, and upon which only a very few remarks will be here offered by way of recapitulation. Deriving originally letters and the elements of learning from Babylonia, the Assyrians appear to have been content with the knowledge thus obtained, and neither in literature nor in science to have progressed much beyond their instructors. The heavy incubus of a dead language lay upon all those who desired to devote themselves to scientific pursuits; and, owing to this, knowledge tended to become the exclusive possession of a learned or perhaps a priest class, which did not aim at progress, but was satisfied to hand on the traditions of former ages. To understand the genius of the Assyrian people we must look to their art and their manufactures. These are in the main probably of native growth; and from them we may best gather an impression of the national character. They show us a patient, laborious, pains-taking people, with more appreciation of the useful than the ornamental, and of the actual than the ideal. Architecture, the only one of the fine arts which is essentially useful, forms their chief glory; sculpture, and still more painting, are subsidiary to it. Again, it is the most useful edifice—the palace or house—whereon attention is concentrated—the temple and the tomb, the interest attaching to which is ideal and spiritual, are secondary, and appear (so far as they appear at all) simply as appendages of the palace. In the sculpture it is the actual the historically true—which the artist strives to represent. Unless in the case of a few mythic figures connected with the religion of the country, there is nothing in the Assyrian bas-reliefs which is not imitated from nature. The imitation is always laborious, and often most accurate and exact. The laws of representation, as we understand them, are sometimes departed from, but it is always to impress the spectator with ideas in accordance with truth. Thus the colossal bulls and lions have five legs, but in order that they may be seen from every point of view with four; the ladders are placed edgewise against the walls of besieged towns, but it is to show that they are ladders, and not mere poles; walls of cities are made disproportionately small, but it is done, like Raphael's boat, to bring them within the picture, which would otherwise be a less complete representation of the actual fact. The careful finish, the minute detail, the elaboration of every hair in a beard, and every stitch in the embroidery of a dress, reminds us of the Dutch school of painting, and illustrates strongly the spirit of faithfulness and honesty which pervades the sculptures, and gives them so great a portion of their value. In conception, in grace, in freedom and correctness of outline, they fall undoubtedly far behind the inimitable productions of the Greeks; but they have a grandeur and a dignity, a boldness, a strength, and an appearance of life, which render them even intrinsically valuable as works of art, and, considering the time at which they were produced, must excite our surprise and admiration. Art, so far as we know, had existed previously only in the stiff and lifeless conventionalism of the Egyptians. It belonged to Assyria to confine the conventional to religion, and to apply art to the vivid representation of the highest scenes of human life. War in all its forms—the march, the battle, the pursuit, the siege of towns, the passage of rivers and marshes, the submission and treatment of captives, and the "mimic war" of hunting the chase of the lion, the stag, the antelope, the wild bull, and the wild ass, are the chief subjects treated by the Assyrian sculptors; and in these the conventional is discarded; fresh scenes, new groupings, bold and strange attitudes perpetually appear, and in the animal representations especially there is a continual advance, the latest being the most spirited, the most varied, and the most true to nature, though perhaps lacking somewhat of the majesty and grandeur of the earlier. With no attempt to idealize or go beyond nature, there is a growing power of depicting things as they are—an increased grace and delicacy of execution, showing that Assyrian art was progressive, not stationary, and giving a promise of still higher excellence, had circumstances permitted its development.

The art of Assyria has every appearance of thorough and entire nationality; but it is impossible to feel sure that her manufactures were in the same sense absolutely her own. The practice of borrowing skilled workmen from the conquered states would introduce into Nineveh and the other royal cities the fabrics of every region which acknowledged the Assyrian sway; and plunder, tribute, and commerce would unite to enrich them with the choicest products of all civilized countries. Still, judging by the analogy of modern times, it seems most reasonable to suppose that the bulk of the manufactured goods consumed in the country would be of home growth. Hence we may fairly assume that the vases, jars, bronzes, glass bottles, carved ornaments in ivory and mother-of-pearl, engraved gems, bells, dishes, earrings, arms, working implements, etc., which have been found at Nimrud, Khorsabad, and Koyunjik, are mainly the handiwork of the Assyrians. It has been conjectured that the rich garments represented as worn by the kings and others were the product of Babylon, always famous for its tissues; but even this is uncertain; and they are perhaps as likely to have been of home manufacture. At any rate the bulk of the ornaments, utensils, etc'., may be regarded as native products. They are almost invariably of elegant form, and indicate a considerable knowledge of metallurgy and other arts as well as a refined taste. Among them are some which anticipate inventions believed till lately to have been modern. Transparent glass (which, however, was known also in ancient Egypt) is one of these; but the most remarkable of all is the lens discovered at Nimrud, of the use of which as a magnifying agent there is abundant proof. If it be borne in mind, in addition to all this, that the buildings of the Assyrians show them to have been well acquainted with the principle of the arch, that they constructed tunnels, aqueducts, and drains, that they knew the use of the pulley, the lever, and the roller, that they understood the arts of inlaying, enamelling, and overlaying with metals, and that they cut gems with the greatest skill and finish, it will be apparent that their civilization equalled that of almost any ancient country, and that it did not fall immeasurably behind the boasted achievements of the moderns. With much that was barbaric still attaching to them, with a rude and inartificial government, savage passions, a debasing religion, and a general tendency to materialism, they were, towards the close of their empire, in all the ordinary arts and appliances of life, very nearly on a par with ourselves; and thus their history furnishes a warning—which the records of nations constantly repeat—that the greatest material prosperity may co-exist with the decline—and herald the downfall—of a kingdom.

APPENDIX

Due to the number of symbols anduses of original laanguages for reasons of clarity and ease of reading these particular bits we have included the original fascimile pages below.

APPENDIX.

A.

OF THE MEANINGS OF THE ASSYRIAN ROYAL NAMES.

THE names of the Assyrians, like those of the Hebrews, seem to have been invariably significant. Each name is a sentence, fully or elliptically expressed, and consists consequently of at least two elements. This number is frequently—indeed, commonly—increased to three, which are usually a noun in the nominative case, a verb active agreeing with it, and a noun in the objective or accusative case governed by the verb. The genius of the language requires that in names of this kind the nominative case should invariably be placed first; but there is no fixed rule as to the order of the two other words; the

An example of the simplest form of name is Sar-gon, or Sar-gina, "the established king," *i.e.* "(I am) the established king." The roots are *Sar*, or in the full nominative, *sarru*, the common word for "king" (compare Heb. שׂר, שרה, etc.,), and *kin* (or *gin*),³ "to establish," a root akin to the Hebrew כן.

A name equally simple is Buzur-Asshur, which means either "Asshur is a stronghold," or "Asshur is a treasure;" *buzur* being the Assyrian equivalent of the Hebrew בצר, which has this double signification. (See Gesen. "Lex." p. 155.) A third name of the same simple form is Saül-mugina (Sammughes), which probably means "Saül (is) the establisher," *mugina* being the participial form of the same verb which occurs in Sar-*gina* or Sargon.⁴

There is another common form of Assyrian name consisting of two elements, the latter of which is the name of a god, while the former is either *shamas* or *shamsi* (Heb. שמש), the common word for "servant," or else a term significative of worship, adoration, reverence, or the like. Of the former kind, there is but one royal name, viz., Shamas-Vul, "the servant of Vul," a name exactly resembling in its formation the Phœnician Abdistartus, the Hebrew Obadiah, Abdiel, etc., and the Arabic Abdallah.⁵ Of the latter kind are the two royal names, Tiglathi-Nin and Mutaggil-Nebo. Tiglathi-Nin is from *tiglat* or *tiklat*, "adoration, reverence" (comp. Chald. הכל, "to trust in"), and Nin or Ninip, the Assyrian Hercules. The meaning is "Adoratio (sit) Herculi"—"Let worship (be given to) Hercules." Mutaggil-Nebo is "confiding in" or "worshipping Nebo"—*mutaggil* being from the same root as *tiglat*, but the participle, instead of the abstract substantive. A name very similar in its construction is that of the Caliph Motawakkil Billah.⁶

Names of the common threefold type are Asshur-iddin-akhi, Asshur-izir-pal,[10] Sin-akhi-irib (Sennacherib), Asshur-akh-iddina (Esar-haddon), and Asshur-bani-pal. Asshur-idden-akhi is "Asshur has given brothers," *iddin* being the third person singular of *nadan*, "to give" (comp. Heb. נתן), and *akhi* being the plural of *akhu*, "a brother" (comp. Heb. אח). Asshur-izir-pal is "Asshur protects (my) son," *izir* (for *inzir*) being derived from a root corresponding to the Hebrew נצר, "to protect," and *pal* being (as already explained[11]) the Assyrian equivalent for the Hebrew בן and the Syriac *bar*, "a son." The meaning of Sin-akhi-irib (Sennacherib) is "Sin (the Moon) has multiplied brethren," *irib* being from *raba* (Heb. רבה), "to augment, multiply." Asshur-akh-iddina is "Asshur has given a brother," from roots already explained; and Asshur-bani-pal is "Asshur has formed a son," from *Asshur, bani,* and *pal; bani* being the participle of *bana,* "to form, make" (comp. Heb. בנה).

Other tri-elemental names are Asshur-ris-ilim, Bel-kudur uzur, Asshur-bil-kala, Nin-pala-zira, and Bel-sumili-kapi. Asshur-ris-ilim either signifies "Asshur (is) the head of the gods," from Asshur, *ris*, which is equivalent to Heb. ראש, "head," and *ilim*, the plural of *il* or *el,* "god;" or perhaps it may mean "Asshur (is) high-headed," from *Asshur, ris,* and *elam*, "high," *ris-elim* being equivalent to the *sir-buland* of the modern Persians.[12] Bel-kudur-uzur means "Bel protects my seed," or "Bel protects the youth," as will be explained in the next volume under Nebuchadnezzar. Asshur-bil-kala means probably "Asshur (is) lord altogether," from *Asshur, bil,* "a lord" (Heb. בצל), and *kala*, "wholly;" a form connected with the Hebrew כל or כל "all," Nin-pala-zira is of course "Nin (Hercules) is the son of Zira," as already explained under Tiglath-Pileser.[13] Bel-sumili-kapi is conjectured to be "Bel of the left hand,"[14] or "Bel (is) left handed," from *Bel, sumilu,* an equivalent of שמאל, "the left," and *kapu* (= כ), "a hand."

four elements.[15] These are the first and last of our list, Asshur-bil-nisi-su, and the king commonly called Asshur-emid-ilin, whose complete name was (it is thought) Asshur-emid-ili-kin, or possibly Asshur-kinat-ili-kain. The last king's name is thought to mean "Asshur is the establisher of the power of the gods"—the second element, which is sometimes written as *emid* (comp. צמר), sometimes as *nirik*, being translated in a vocabulary by *kinat*, "power," while the last element (which is omitted on the monarch's bricks) is of course from *kin* (the equivalent of כון), which has been explained under Sargon. The name of the other monarch presents no difficulty. Asshur-bil-nisi-su means "Asshur (is) the lord of his people," from *bil* or *bilu*, "lord," *nis*, "a man" (comp. Heb. אנוש), and *su*, "his" (= Heb. ו).

To these names of monarchs may be added one or two names of princes, which are mentioned in the records of the Assyrians, or elsewhere; as Asshur-danin-pal, the eldest son of the great Shalmaneser, and Adrammelech and Sharezer, sons of Sennacherib. Asshur-danin-pal seems to be "Asshur strengthens a son," from *Asshur*, *pal*, and *danin*, which has the force of "strengthening" in Assyrian.[16] Adrammelech has been explained as *decus regis*, "the king's glory;"[17] but it would be more consonant with the propositional character of the names generally to translate it "the king (is) glorious," from *adir* (אדר) or אדיר, "great, glorious," and *melek* (מלך), "a king." Or Adrammelech may be from *ediru* (comp. צדר), a common Assyrian word meaning "the arranger" and *melek*, and may signify "the king arranges," or "the king is the arranger."[18] Sharezer, if that be the true reading, would seem to be "the king protects," from *sar* or *sarru*, "a king" (as in Sargon), and a form, *izir*, from *nazar* or *natsar*,[19] "to guard, protect." The Armenian equivalent, however, for this name, San-asar, may be the proper form; and this would apparently be "The Moon (Sin) protects."

Nothing is more remarkable in this entire catalogue of names than their predominantly religious character. Of the thirty-nine kings and princes which the Assyrian lists furnish, the names of no fewer than thirty-one contain, as one element, either the name or the designation of a god. Of the remaining eight, five have doubtful names,[20] so that there remain three only whose names are known to be purely of a secular character.[21] Thirteen names, one of which was borne by two kings, contain the element Asshur; three, two of which occur twice, contain the element Nin;[22] two, one of which was in such favor as to occur four times,[23] contain the element Vul; three contain the element Bel; one the element Nebo; and one the element Sin.[24] The names occasionally express mere facts of the mythology, as Nin-pala-zira, "Nin (is) the son of Zira," Bel-sumili-kapi, "Bel (is) left-handed," and the like. More often the fact enunciated is one in which the glorification of the deity is involved; as, Asshur-bil-nisi-su, "Asshur (is) the lord of his people;" Buzur-Asshur, "a stronghold (is) Asshur;" Asshur-bil-kala, "Asshur (is) lord altogether." Frequently the name seems to imply some special thankfulness to a particular god for the particular child in question, who is viewed as having been his gift, in answer to a vow or to prayer. Of this kind are Asshur-akh-iddina (Esar-haddon), Sin-akhi-irib (Sennacherib), Asshur-bani-pal, etc.; where the god named seems to be thanked for the child whom he has caused to be born. Such names as Tiglathi-Nin, Tiglath-Pileser, express this feeling even more strongly, being actual ascriptions of praise by the grateful parent to the deity whom he regards as his benefactor. In a few of the names, as Mutaggil-Nebo and Shamas-Iva, the religious sentiment takes a different turn. Instead of the parent merely expressing his own feelings of gratitude towards this or that god, he dedicates in a way his son to him, assigning to him an appellation which he is to verify in his after-life by a special devotion to the deity of whom in his very name he professes himself the "servant" or the "worshipper."

B.

TABULAR VIEW OF THE NAMES ASSIGNED TO THE ASSYRIAN KINGS AT DIFFERENT TIMES AND BY DIFFERENT WRITERS.

Sir H. Rawlinson in 1860.	G. Smith in 1870.	Dr. Hincks.	M. Oppert in 1869.a
. . . . .	Bel-sumili-kapi ?	. . . .	Bel-kat-irassu.
. . . . .	Asshur-bilu-nisi-su	. . . .	Asur-bel-nisi-su.
. . . . .	Buzur-Asshur	. . . .	Busur-Asur
. . . . .	Asshur-upallit	. . . .	Asur-uballat.
Bel-lush	Bilu-nirari (?)	. . . .	Bel-likh-khis.
Pud-il	Pudi-el.	. . . .	Pudi-el.
Vul-lush I.b	Vul-nirari I. (?)	. . . .	Bin-likh-khis I.
Shalma-Bar c	Sallim-manu-uzur I.	Divanu-rish	Salman-asir II.
. . . . .	Tukulti-Ninip I.	. . . .	Tuklat-Ninip I.
. . . . .	Vul-nirari II. (?)	. . . .	Bin-likh-khis II.
Nin-pala-kura d	Nin-pala-zara	Ninip-pal-isri	Ninip-habal-asar.
Asshur-daha-il	Asshur-dayan I.	Assur-dayan	Asur-dayan.
Mutaggil-Nebo	Mutaggil-Nabu.	. . . .	Mutakkil-Nabu.
Asshur-ris-ilim	Asshur-ris-elim	. . . .	Asur-ris-isi.
Tiglath-Pileser I.	Tukulti-pal-zara I.	Tiklat-pal-isri I.	Tuklat-habal-asar I.
Asshur-bani-pal I.	Asshur-bil-kala	. . . .	Asur-iddanna-habal
. . . . .	Samsi-Vul I.	. . . .	. . . . .
. . . . .	Asshur-rabu-amar	. . . .	
. . . . .	Asshur-muzur	. . . .	
Asshur-adan-akhi	Asshur-iddin-akhi	. . . .	Asur-iddin-akhe.
Asshur-dan-il	Asshur-dayan II.	. . . .	Asur-edil-el I.
Vul-lush II.	Vul-nirari III. (?)	. . . .	Bin-likh-khis III.
Tiglathi-Ninip	Tukulti-Ninip II.	Shimish Bar	Tuklat-Ninip II.
Asshur-idanni-pal	Asshur-nazir-pal e	Asshur-yuzhur bal f	Asur-nazir-habal
Shalmanu-sar I.	Sallim-manu-uzur II.	Divanu-Bara	Salman-asir III.
Shamash-Vul	Samsi-Vul II.	Shamsi-Yav	Samas-Bin.
Vul-lush III.	Vul-nirari IV. (?)	. . . .	Bin-likh-khis IV.
. . . . .	Sallim-manu-uzur III.	. . . .	Salman-asir IV.
. . . . .	Asshur-dayan III.	. . . .	Asur-edil-el II.
. . . . .	Asshur-nirari (?)	. . . .	Asur-likh-khis.
Tiglath-Pileser II. g	Tukulti-pal-zara II.	Tiklat-pal-isri II.	Tuklat-habal-asa II.
Shalmanu-sar II.	Sallim-manu-uzur IV.	. . . .	Salman-asir V.
Sargina	Sar-gina h	Sar-gina	Saryu-kin.
Sennacherib	Sennacherib i	Tsin-akhi-irib	Sin-akhe-irib.
Esar-haddon	Esar-haddon i	Asshur-akh-idin	Asur-akh-iddin.
Asshur-bani-pal	Asshur-bani-pal	Asshur-idanna-bal	Asur-bani-habal.
Assur-emit-ili	Asshur-emit-ilin	. . . .	Asur-edil-el III.

a In this list I have taken the forms of the names either from M. Oppert's own article in the *Revue archéologique* for 1869, or from the "Manuel d'Histoire ancienne de l'Orient" of his disciple, M. François Lenormant (5th ed. 1869).

b This name is composed of three elements, all of which are doubtful. The first is the god of the atmosphere, who has been called Vul, Iva, Yav, Yam, Yem, Ao, Bin, and U or Hu. The second element has been read as *likh*, *zala*, and *erim*; the third as *gab*, *khus*, and *pathir*. Both of them are most uncertain.

c Or Shalma-ris. This name was originally thought to be different from that of the Black-Obelisk king, but is now regarded as a mere variant, and as equivalent to the Scriptural Shalmaneser. The last element is the same word as the name of the Assyrian Hercules, who has been called Bar, Nin or Ninip, and Ussur, and who possibly bore all these appellations. Sir H. Rawlinson originally called this king Temenbar. ("Commentary," p. 22.)

d Or Nin-pala-*zira*. (Rawlinson's "Herodotus," 1st edition.)

e The middle element of this name was thought to represent the root "to give," and to have the power of *iddin* or *idanni*; but a variant reading in the recently discovered Canon employs the phonetic complement of *ir*, thus showing that the root must be the one ordinarily represented by the character, namely נצר, "to protect," which will form *nazir* in the Benoni, and *izir* (for *inzir*) in the third person of the aorist.

f Originally Dr. Hincks called this monarch Asshur-*akh*-bal. (Layard's "Nin. and Bab." p. 615.) Mr. Fox Talbot still prefers this reading. ("Athenæum," No. 1839, p. 120.)

g This, of course, is following the Hebrew literation. The Assyrian is read as Tukulti-pal-zara.

h Or, more fully, Sarru-gina.

i The Assyrian names of Sennacherib and Esar-haddon, according to Mr. G. Smith, were Sin-akhi-irba and Asshur-akh-iddina.

www.ingramcontent.com/pod-product-compliance
Lightning Source LLC
Chambersburg PA
CBHW071244160426
43196CB00009B/1153